*Writing for the*

# FASHION
# BUSINESS

# Writing for the

# FASHION

# BUSINESS

KRISTEN K. SWANSON
*Northern Arizona University*

JUDITH C. EVERETT
*Northern Arizona University*

*Fairchild Books, Inc.*
*New York*

Director of Sales and Acquisitions: Dana Meltzer-Berkowitz
Executive Editor: Olga T. Kontzias
Senior Development Editor: Jennifer Crane
Development Editor: Cate DaPron
Art Director: Adam B. Bohannon
Production Manager: Ginger Hillman
Senior Production Editor: Elizabeth Marotta
Photo Researcher: Erin Fitzsimmons
Copy Editor: Cate DaPron
Cover Design: Adam B. Bohannon
Text Design: Nicola Ferguson

**Focus Strategic Communications, Inc.**
Project Managers: Adrianna Edwards, Ron Edwards
Formatter: Carol Magee
Proofreader: Linda Szostak
Indexer: Carol Roberts

Library of Congress Catalog Card Number: 2007934509
ISBN-13: 978-1-56367-439-6
ISBN-10: 1-56367-439-4

GST R 133004424
Printed in USA

# TABLE OF CONTENTS

# EXTENDED TABLE
# OF CONTENTS

# Introduction

*Writing for the Fashion Business* is an exciting, one-of-a-kind textbook focused on writing in the fashion industry. Writing is a threshold skill for hiring and promoting professionals in the fashion business. College recruiters continually stress that writing is a critical skill, and they lament the fact that many students leave college not fully prepared to do the kind of writing that will be required of them in the business world.

The National Commission on Writing surveyed 120 major American corporations and found that half of these companies take writing into consideration when hiring professional-level employees. Further, two thirds of salaried employees have writing responsibilities. The Commission's report (published in 2004 by the College Board) stated in very blunt language that people who cannot write proficiently do not get hired, and managers take writing ability into account when making promotion decisions. The report went on to advise that applicants who submit poorly written cover letters are not likely to get an interview. From the beginning, writing is a skill that students will need in order to be successful in the workplace.

Our experience of teaching writing to merchandising students spans the past two decades. To build *Writing for the Fashion Business*, we have pieced together course materials from writing guides, journalism and mass communication resources, business communication resources, other fashion textbooks, and professional examples.

*Writing for the Fashion Business* introduces students to the writing process. Then it systematically addresses the different writing situations that students may encounter in the professional fashion world—writing in the context of such disparate media as newspapers, magazines, broadcast media, advertising, public relations, and new media.

*Writing for the Fashion Business* details other forms of writing as well, including doing scholarly writing, writing fashion-oriented books, and writing business and employment communications. Along the way, this textbook gives students numerous opportunities to practice writing and to develop a writing portfolio that will give them confidence in their writing abilities.

In Part One, Chapter 1, "Effective Fashion Communications," introduces the myriad places where effective written communication is needed in the fashion industry. Chapter 2, "The Writing Process," describes and details the larger writing process, from identifying the audience to proofreading the final draft—skills that can then be applied to all the forms of writing examined throughout the remainder of the book.

Part Two focuses on fashion journalism. Through newspapers, magazines, and broadcast media, journalists spotlight the fashion industry. They bring consumer and trade audiences the latest information on new products, classic designers, fashion trends, and business analyses. Newspapers have been reporting fashion stories since the 19th century. Writers and editors work to bring out the latest news via daily, weekly, monthly, and less frequently published newspapers. Chapter 3, "Writing for Newspapers," covers the role of newspapers for a fashionable society.

Fashion magazines have been in existence for over 150 years. Consumer fashion magazines are directed toward end users, and they consist of fashion, general interest, men's, shelter, and business titles. Trade fashion magazines focus on information for industry insiders, publishing articles that pertain directly to the business of fashion. Chapter 4, "Writing for Magazines," looks at the magazine industry and the writing opportunities in this field.

Broadcast media came into the U.S. culture during the 20th century. Radio and, later, network and cable television became the primary resources for nearly instantaneous news, information, and entertainment. Chapter 5, "Writing for Broadcast Media," introduces the role of broadcast media in disseminating fashion information. Fashion journalism and communication is an excellent place for students to put their writing skills to work.

Part Three explores the three primary communication channels for making fashion promotion communication come to life: advertising, public relations, and new media. In fashion advertising, writing is used to analyze the client and the product, and to develop the creative message and media where the message will be presented. Writing also takes place as the advertising message is placed in print, broadcast, or any other medium for the audience to see or to hear. All this is examined closely in Chapter 6, "Writing for Advertising."

Public relations for fashion-related businesses starts with a critical analysis of the needs of the client. A variety of public relations tools assist the writer in conveying a message to the audience, as is shown in Chapter 7, "Writing for Public Relations." Among these tools are news releases, media kits, feature stories written for newspapers or magazines, pitch letters, annual reports, speeches, and fund-raising letters. Fashion public relations personnel are also involved with such activities as news conferences and fashion events, from fashion shows to product launch parties and more.

The Internet offers a wide range of fashion writing opportunities. Fashion Web sites promote and sell apparel, luxury fashion, and everything in between. Journalists, advertisers, and public relations personnel are among the writers offering exciting, up-to-the-minute information on the Web. Chapter 8, "Writing for New Media," explores the career opportunities related to fashion writing on the Web.

Part Four, the last section of *Writing for the Fashion Business*, examines some less obvious forms of fashion writing. Fashion research, for example, covers historic and cultural aspects of dress, anthropology, consumer behavior related to fashion, retailing, textiles, aesthetics and design, fiber arts, merchandising, advertising, social and psychological aspects of dress, and much more. Such writing is covered in Chapter 9, "Scholarly Writing."

Writing books on fashion is another avenue that may interest readers of this book. This is the topic of Chapter 10, "Writing Books." People inside and beyond the fashion industry read fashion-related books for information and entertainment. Among the many topics for fashion books are fiction, biographies and memoirs, fashion design, and fashion history.

As stated earlier, essential writing skills are necessary across the business environment, including the fashion industry. Good writers within the corporate environment express themselves clearly and professionally with powerful writing skills. Solid business writing includes proper presentation of letters, memos, reports, proposals, and the like. All these elements are covered in Chapter 11, "Writing Business Communications." To get a job in fashion, students need to prepare a strong résumé, write an effective application letter, and possess strong interviewing skills. This aspect of fashion writing is discussed in Chapter 12, "Writing Employment Messages."

*Writing for the Fashion Business* concludes with several appendixes that are intended to be quick guides for use in conjunction with the chapters. These appendixes are "Grammar Mechanics," "Documentation Format," "Effective Document Design," "Web Source Location and Evaluation," and "Oral Presentations."

*Writing for the Fashion Business* is written to give a logical and informative order to writing. As instructors and authors, we have developed this text to be used as curriculum needs dictate. Some writing courses may want to tackle every type of writing, while other courses may use individual chapters selectively. Therefore, the book is written with the understanding that each chapter may be used independently or collectively as part of the fashion business.

We have enjoyed writing this book as a collaborative project with each other and with our former and present students. We hope you will find writing as rewarding as we have.

# ACKNOWLEDGMENTS

This book began with a seemingly simple question from our friend Olga Kontzias, Executive Editor of Fairchild Books: "Do you know anyone interested in writing a book about writing for fashion?" The topic really interested us. We felt a strong desire to join the many authors who have written about writing from various points of view—from English composition, business communication, creative writing, journalism, and promotion communication to writing for academic and scholarly publications. No other book about writing for fashion was currently available. Thank you, Olga, for planting the seed. Also at Fairchild, we have had the privilege of working with Joseph Miranda, Acquisitions Editor; Jennifer Crane, Senior Development Editor; and Elizabeth Marotta, Senior Production Editor.

We have especially enjoyed working with our freelance editor, Cate DaPron. In a positive and humorous way, she has motivated us to become more consistent and technically correct writers. Proofreading, proofreading, proofreading is just as much a requirement for writing professionals as it is a necessary habit for writing students.

Special thanks go to Adrianna and Ron Edwards, Carol Magee, Carol Roberts, and Linda Szostak of Focus Strategic Communications for their tremendous effort in getting this book to print.

We want to thank Alexxis Avalon of the International Academy of Design and Technology, Tampa; Judi Dormaar of Lethbridge Community College; and Audria Green of the International Academy of Design and Technology, Chicago, for their review and constructive criticism of our first draft of the manuscript for this book.

We also want to recognize several of our colleagues at the School of Communication at Northern Arizona University. Mary Tolan offered suggestions to strengthen our chapters on journalism. Donna Henrichs provided insight into the practices of advertising and public relations. Laura Umphrey critiqued our chapter on scholarly writing. Martin Sommerness provided comments on effective communication and the writing process. Richard Rogers provided assistance with MLA documentation.

We have been thrilled to see the work of so many of our students improve during their academic careers. Several student projects were so impressive that their work has been included as examples in this publication. We extend a special thank-you to former and current students Amanda Hobbs, Tiffany Carlyon, Rachel Gray, Ryan Mandino, Lindsay Haldeman, and Michelle Marchi.

We were very pleased with the positive responses from busy professionals willing to share their writing experiences and wisdom with future fashion industry writers. Thanks to Marylou Luther, David Wolfe, Teri Agins, Jenny Fine, Penny Martin, Deby Green, Lisa Pagel, Amy Swift, Valerie Steele, Robyn Waters, and Melissa Turner for contributing the book's Industry Profiles.

A special appreciation goes to James Power and Christopher Everett, who supported our "writing time" and provided encouragement to get the project finished.

Kristen K. Swanson
Judith C. Everett

# Part One

# WRITING IN THE FASHION ENVIRONMENT

Writing is fundamental to the fashion industry. Professionals depend on written sources every day to help them be successful in their jobs. They read trade newspapers and magazines, Web sites, and consumer publications to keep up-to-date with fashion and industry trends. Fashion executives use written reports to analyze the overall health of their business and the economy. Consumers, too, depend on writing to inform them of fashion and industry trends, the health of the economy, and important and entertaining information about the fashion industry.

Fashion businesses generate advertising and public relations materials to inform journalists and editors, consumers, employees, government officials, stockholders, and other stakeholders of important industry news. A fashion business could not survive without strong writers on their staffs.

Fashion writing is currently in vogue as a popular or "pop" culture topic of film and television, as evidenced by the Golden Globe awards. Meryl Streep won the award for best performance by an actress in a motion picture for her portrayal of editor-in-chief Miranda Priestly in the movie *The Devil Wears Prada*. Additionally, the television show *Ugly Betty* won the award for best television series. Lead actress America Ferrera won for best performance by an actress in a television series for her portrayal of Betty Suarez, the hard-working assistant to the editor-in-chief of the fictional fashion magazine *Mode*. As a competitive task, contestants on the television show *America's Next Top Model* are routinely asked to speak on camera portraying both fashion journalists and celebrity spokespersons for fashion products.

We'll say it again: Writing is essential in the fashion business. We begin this book by introducing effective written communications in Chapter 1, "Effective Fashion Communications." In Chapter 2, "The Writing Process," we describe the writing process, which can then be applied to all of the forms of writing detailed throughout the remainder of the book.

# ONE

## *Effective Fashion Communication*

After you have read this chapter, you should be able to discuss the following:

• The communication process

• The role of writing in the communication process

• Writing for fashion at the primary, secondary, retail, and auxiliary levels

Today is Thursday, which means that on my way to the gym for morning exercise I must stop by the local convenience store and pick up the *New York Times* to read "ThursdayStyles." Stories in today's issue include the new fashion direction of a star designer, the fashion statement made by a newly elected South American leader, how jeans fit, seasonal makeup colors, and a recap of the latest men's wear shows: all that and more in ten pages. And, if I had talked myself out of the drive to the gym, I could have read all this online—for free! For this reader, both traditional, ink-on-your-fingertips newsprint and modern Internet technology are effective ways to communicate about fashion.

This chapter begins by discussing communication and the communication model. The next section focuses on fashion specifically. The fashion industry is divided into four levels, and writing occurs at each one. Each is discussed here, from the primary level to the secondary level to the retail level. The discussion finishes with the auxiliary level, which assists all levels of the fashion industry.

# COMMUNICATION

**Communication** is the transmission or exchange of information and/or messages (Swanson & Everett, 2007) and is illustrated using the communication process (Figure 1.1). The communication process involves a sender encoding a message and sending that message for decoding by a receiver who provides a response through feedback. Noise can interfere with the communication process throughout.

Communication begins with the sender (source of information). Fashion businesses transmit many messages every day to individuals and organizations. The sender selects a combination of words or symbols to be presented in written, oral, and/or visual form. This arrangement is termed **encoding**. Developing a fashion message that the intended audience, the receiver, can easily understand is a major challenge of communication. The encoded message is conveyed to the receiver through various **channels**, methods by which the message is translated. Word-of-mouth promotion, fashion advertising and journalism, publicity, special events, and fashion shows are among the many channels for conveying the fashion message.

The receiver's task is **decoding** the message, or transforming it back into thought. This step forces the receiver to interpret what he or she believes the sender intended; how a message is understood depends upon the receiver's **frame of reference**, or past experiences. Attitudes, values, perceptions of fashion, and cultural background are

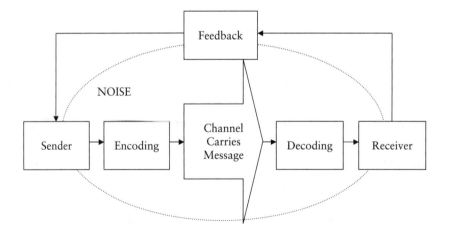

FIGURE 1.1. Communication model. Source: Swanson, K. K., & Everett, J. C. (2007). *Promotion in the merchandising environment* (2nd ed.). New York: Fairchild Books.

among the characteristics that help the receiver understand the message—or that sometimes cause the receiver to misinterpret the message.

**Noise** refers to outside factors that interfere with reception, or distort the fashion message. One example of noise is the numerous image and product advertisements placed before the table of contents in a fashion magazine. The advertisements are clustered together, more or less distorting the message that each advertisement would convey if it were viewed separately.

When the receiver sends back some type of response, or **feedback**, the sender will know whether the message has been understood. Feedback closes the loop of communication by letting the source know whether the message has been accurately sent, decoded, and acted upon. Fashion businesses ask for feedback by including requests for the receiver to call a toll-free number, visit a retail store, or click a Web site.

---

*Portfolio Exercise:* **Read an article of your choice from a current fashion magazine. After you have read the article, analyze it by writing your answers to the following questions about the communication model:**

- **Who is the sender?**
- **Who is the receiver?**
- **How was the message encoded?**
- **How was the message decoded?**
- **What other channels of communication could carry this message?**
- **Is a feedback mechanism in place?**
- **What noise is interfering with the message?**

---

Communication combines imagery, dialogue, and composition to shape messages that draw us in and provide meaning. Heller (1998) groups communication into five main types:

- **Written communication** is the exchange of information by forming symbols (words) on a surface (paper or computer monitor) with an instrument (pen or keyboard and word processing software). Used as an organizational tool to provide permanent and accessible communication, it is basic to most literate societies.

- **Spoken (and heard) communication** uses the voice to exchange information. Spoken exchanges are immediate and are the primary way most individuals and businesses operate on a day-to-day basis. Societies that do not have a written language rely on spoken language for communication. Spoken communication has a personal quality and is often more convenient than visual or written communication because it is done on the spot. Spoken communication also allows for immediate feedback. As part of popular culture, we speak about or hear about fashion on a daily basis. Conversations, interviews, speeches, debates, and commentary are among the types of spoken communication.
- **Nonverbal communication (symbolic gestures)** means exchanging information without speaking, instead relying on actions or gestures to convey meaning. This form of communication may be more influential than written or spoken communication because of the positive or negative cues it delivers to the receiver. Some examples of nonverbal communication are facial expressions, hand motions, posture, appearance, and dress.
- **Visual communication** uses sight to exchange information. A very powerful form of communication, it is often the dominant type when combined with other categories of communication. Visual communication is dynamic, using color, line, silhouette, and other elements of design to make fashion come alive in graphic illustrations, video, or live presentations. Some of the types of visual communication are photographs, logos, color stories, charts, graphs, and live presentations (such as fashion shows and visual displays).
- **Multimedia communication** uses several methods of communication simultaneously to exchange information, often using information technology to assist in transmitting the message. The message is more likely to create interest and be remembered when multiple forms of communication are used. Types of multimedia communication are abundant. Among them are print and broadcast editorial content, and advertising in magazines and newspapers and on television. Video clips, CD-ROMs, podcasts, DVDs, and the Internet are other important multimedia communication vehicles.

One focus of this textbook is written communication, a permanent type of communication that can be used to record the fashion message. Written communication takes on various forms—personal, scholarly, business, journalistic, and promotion—illustrated in Table 1.1.

**Table 1.1.** Types of written communication.

| TYPE | PURPOSE | AUDIENCE | EXAMPLES |
|---|---|---|---|
| Personal | Entertain, enlighten | Friends, family, yourself | Letters, diaries, journals |
| Journalistic | Inform, entertain | Readers, viewers | Magazine and newspaper articles: print and online |
| Promotion | Inform, entertain, persuade | Consumers, suppliers, producers | Advertisements, media releases, written promotional materials |
| Scholarly | Advance knowledge | Teachers, colleagues, industry professionals | Research papers, journal articles |
| Business (technical) writing | Accomplish tasks | Supervisors, subordinates, customers or clients | Reports, memos, letters, e-mail |

Adapted from Pfeiffer, W. (2004). *Pocket guide to technical writing (3rd ed.).* Upper Saddle River, NJ: Pearson Prentice Hall.

- Personal writing is the most relaxed type of writing and occurs between family and friends or is written to oneself ( journaling). All writing, including personal writing, begins with the writing process, which is the topic of Chapter 2.
- Journalistic writing is informational and can provide entertainment. Journalistic writing appears in newspapers, magazines, and broadcast media. Part Two of this textbook covers journalistic writing: for newspapers in Chapter 3, for magazines in Chapter 4, and for broadcast media in Chapter 5.
- Promotion writing also informs and entertains the audience. Part Three of this textbook focuses on promotion writing: for advertising in Chapter 6, for public relations in Chapter 7, and for new media delivery in Chapter 8.
- Scholarly writing is often the most formal type of writing and is used to advance knowledge among colleagues and industry professionals. Scholarly writing, which tends to produce lengthier publications than the other forms

of communication we've just identified, is the topic of Chapter 9. Written communication is also used to write books, another lengthier form of communication that is the topic of Chapter 10.

- Business writing, a very concise form of writing, is used in the work world to accomplish tasks. It is the topic of Chapter 11, and is a logical partner with employment messages, the topic of Chapter 12.

Fashion is expressed through each of these communication types. But what is fashion? We will explore this question in the next section.

# FASHION

**Fashion** is the prevailing style of expression popular at any given time (Swanson & Everett, 2007). Fashion products change rapidly and are often considered non-necessities. As a business, fashion is ever-changing! It affects nearly everyone, even those who don't think they're affected. Fashion reflects our society and culture and is a major influence in popular culture.

**Fashion businesses** are firms that design, manufacture, distribute, and/or promote fashion-related apparel and accessories for men, women, and children. The business also includes home fashions. Written communication is evident everywhere in the fashion industry.

The fashion industry is divided into four levels (Figure 1.2) that work independently and interdependently to serve the consumer. The **primary level** consists of raw material (textile) producers, who grow or develop fibers and spin them into fabric. The **secondary level** consists of manufacturers. These industry members purchase fabrics, materials, and findings from primary-level members, and make the apparel or accessory products. Manufacturers then sell the goods to retailer buyers, who make up the **retail level**. Businesses are abundant at the retail level, providing new fashions to consumers on a continuous basis. The **auxiliary level** supports the work of the other three levels simultaneously. Members of the auxiliary level include the fashion press, research and consulting services, trade associations, and other support services.

Writing is a necessity for most fashion professionals. It is used on a daily basis at all levels of the fashion industry to communicate the fashion story. Written exchanges are used to inform suppliers, vendors, retailers, consumers, employees, press representatives, government officials, stockholders, and the public at large.

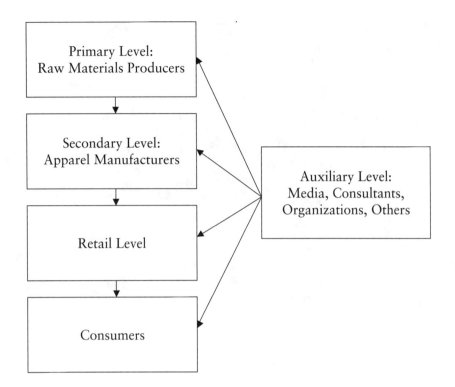

FIGURE 1.2. Fashion industry levels.

## WRITING AT THE PRIMARY LEVEL

Fashion starts at the primary level. The primary level consists of textiles—fibers, yarns, and finished fabrics. During the writing of this textbook, IBM ran a popular commercial titled "Farm" (Figure 1.3). The characters, surrounded by baahing sheep, are industry members—farmer, designer, weaver, buyer, shipper, seller—experiencing communication problems. The help desk associate solves their problem by offering an IBM product. The punch line comes at the end of the spot when the help desk associate asks, "Who are you?" and the character replies, "Shepherd." The spot implies that the shepherd, with his sheep, may be the only industry member not worried about communication. This advertisement does a good job of illustrating the importance of communication at the primary level.

Figure 1.4 illustrates the primary level. The four basic components of the primary level are fiber processing, yarn spinning, fabric production, and

FIGURE 1.3. IBM's "Farm" commercial.

fabric finishing. **Fibers** are the basic unit for making textile fabrics. Fibers are classified as **natural fibers,** supplied by a farmer or rancher, or **manufactured fibers,** supplied by chemical producers. Natural fiber suppliers recover fibers that have been grown on an animal or a plant. Such suppliers are constantly challenged by rising costs of labor, feed, pesticides, fertilizers, and transportation (Yeager & Teter-Justice, 2003). They must compete with foreign suppliers and manufactured fiber suppliers, who constantly work to capture larger shares of the fiber market. In additional, they must respond to concerns about the environment and animal rights.

Manufactured fiber producers use products from nature such as wood chips or petroleum products, but they chemically change these substances into fiber form. These producers are also challenged by rising costs of labor and petroleum, along with changing balances of trade and the negative effects of fiber production on the environment (Yeager & Teter-Justice, 2003). Both the natural fiber supplier and the manufactured fiber producer must be communication-savvy, articulating their needs in writing and using the written word to advance positive information about the industry.

Both natural fiber and manufactured fiber producers provide fibers to **yarn producers,** who combine fibers into usable yarn structures. **Spinners** make **spun yarns**

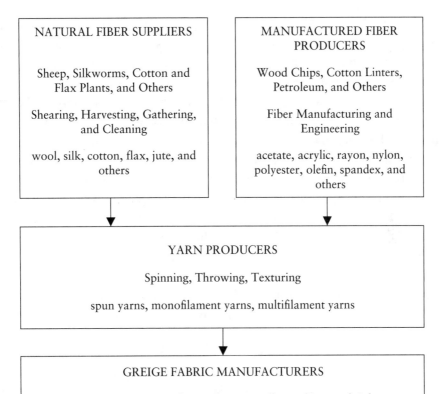

**NATURAL FIBER SUPPLIERS**

Sheep, Silkworms, Cotton and Flax Plants, and Others

Shearing, Harvesting, Gathering, and Cleaning

wool, silk, cotton, flax, jute, and others

**MANUFACTURED FIBER PRODUCERS**

Wood Chips, Cotton Linters, Petroleum, and Others

Fiber Manufacturing and Engineering

acetate, acrylic, rayon, nylon, polyester, olefin, spandex, and others

**YARN PRODUCERS**

Spinning, Throwing, Texturing

spun yarns, monofilament yarns, multifilament yarns

**GREIGE FABRIC MANUFACTURERS**

Weaving, Knitting, Braiding, Felting, Needlepunching, and Others

top and bottom weight fabrics; accessory fabrics; upholstery; window, wall and floor covering fabrics; and others

**CONVERTERS**

Mechanical and Chemical Finishing

finished fabric

FIGURE 1.4. Primary level.

from short, **staple length** fibers (measured in inches). **Throwsters** make **filament yarns** from long, **filament length** fibers (measured in yards or meters). Written communication is necessary to ensure that the multiple twisting and plying operations are accurate, and the proper assortment of yarns is available to fabric manufacturers.

Fabric manufacturers use many techniques to turn yarn into fabric. **Weavers** use two or more sets of yarns interlaced at right angles on a **loom** to make **woven fabrics**. **Knitters** use **knitting machines** to create **knit fabric** from one yarn interconnected through a series of loops. Fabric manufacturers also make fabric from solutions (for example, foam or film), from fibers (for example, felt or nonwovens), from yarns (for example, braided or knotted), or from other fabrics (for example, composite fabrics). The manufactured fabric is a **greige good** because it has not been finished (*greige* is a French word meaning "natural"; that is, it has not yet been washed, bleached, dyed, or subjected to other treatments).

Written communication is critical at this stage, as fabric manufacturers and textile engineers (1) develop equipment and devices that reduce time and energy consumption, and (2) make textile structures that perform well for the ultimate consumer (Yeager & Teter-Justice, 2003).

Greige goods are sent to **converters**, who transform cloth into finished fabric. Converters "finish" the fabric through mechanical or chemical means. The finish may be temporary or permanent, and may change the aesthetic, performance, or durability function of the fabric. Dyeing and printing of textiles are specialized finishes. Dyeing can be applied at the solution, fiber, yarn, or fabric stage, while printing typically is applied at the fabric stage of the primary level. Converters use written communication to make certain that fabrics meet the requirements and expectations of the apparel, accessory, or home fashion manufacturers who buy the finished fabric for use at the secondary level of the fashion industry.

---

*Portfolio Exercise:* **Shop at a local store to compare fabrics used in fashion items. Note your answers to the following questions:**

- **What store and department did you shop? Who is the identified target market?**
- **What fabrics caught your eye? Why? Because of their color, their design, their pattern, or something else?**
- **What kinds of fabrics (knit or woven, prints or solids) are the most popular?**

- What is the prominent color story?
- Examine several of the most popular styled items for fiber content. What are the most popular fibers? Are they natural fibers or manufactured ones? Why do you think these fibers are currently popular?
- Can you make predictions about the continued use of these fibers in the future?

Summarize your findings in a written report. 💼

## WRITING AT THE SECONDARY LEVEL

Fashion products are developed and produced at the secondary level (Figure 1.5). Stages one through four in Figure 1.5 represent the **merchandising function** of an apparel manufacturing firm, which consists of planning, development, and presentation of the product line. Additionally, this area decides on the product, approves the styling, establishes the pricing, and schedules the timing of deliveries. (Keiser & Garner, 2007). The **production function** for an apparel manufacturer is represented in stages five through eight. The production function includes approval of the technical design, development

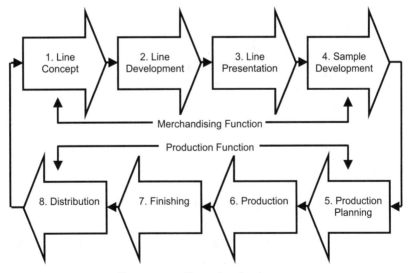

FIGURE 1.5. Secondary level.

of specifications, costing the product, development of production patterns, grading, marker making, cutting, sewing, finishing, and arranging for distribution of the sewn products (Keiser & Garner). Writing is critical at each of these stages.

1.  The design process begins with Line Concept. During this stage, trends are researched and themes are defined for presentation on **concept boards,** a collection of photos, sketches, and swatches that express the design direction for the group. While the concept boards are visual presentations, written notes or scripts are also developed to accompany the presentations to make sure the trends in color, silhouette, and fabric are accurately articulated.

2.  During the Line Development stage, the **line,** or overall collection of garments for a particular season, is developed. Critical to the line are written line plans that specify the number of garments needed for each category. The plans may provide a broad overview of the line based on sales goals, or they may provide very specific numbers based on color and style.

3.  The line is presented to technical staff and sourcing managers at the Line Presentation stage. Again, writing is critical at this stage. The technical staff is responsible for writing specifications for construction of each garment that will be part of the line, somewhere between 30 and 50 items. Additionally, sourcing managers secure materials, writing meticulous contracts between the company and its domestic or international contractors.

4.  The first pattern, first sample garment, and production pattern are made at the Sample Development stage. At this stage, styling, fit, and the overall feasibility of the design are evaluated. Pattern-makers develop the pattern using draping design, flat pattern design, or a computer-aided design system. While this stage focuses mainly on the pattern and the sample, a strong comprehension of writing is needed in order to understand directions and use a computer-aided design system.

5.  In the Production Planning stage in apparel product development, the showroom samples are made and distributed to sales representatives who show the line to retail buyers. Writing orders is a major responsibility for sales representatives. At this stage, fabrics and findings are purchased, and exact costing is developed. Every garment in production is tracked with a written **cost sheet.** The cost sheet provides a record of the style used and the cost of labor and materials. In addition, a written sequence of operations is developed at this stage, using standardized stitching and seams diagrams.

6.  The Production stage begins with grading the production pattern and making the marker. **Grading** is the increasing or decreasing of the production pattern to

reflect the firm's size range. The **marker** is the layout of pattern pieces on the fabric for cutting. The marker indicates how all pattern pieces in all sizes will be arranged for cutting. The marker is prepared for **spreading,** which is laying multiple layers of cloth on a table and cutting the pattern components from the spread. Commonly, pattern-making, grading, and marker-making, along with spreading and cutting, are computerized functions that require production workers to have specialized reading and writing abilities in order to monitor the computer controls. Next, production workers assemble and sew the fashion products. Employees must understand written instructions to assure that the assembly is done correctly so that items are not rejected by the quality assurance department.

7. The Finishing stage involves preparing garments for the selling floor. Written instructions help assembly workers know how to wet-process, dye, and wash the garments, and prepare the garments with hangtags.

8. In the Distribution stage, the sewn products are readied for distribution. Garments leave the manufacturing facility "floor ready," with written documents including carton labels and shipping documents. These goods are delivered to businesses at the retail level of the fashion industry.

*Portfolio Exercise:* **Select a garment from your wardrobe. Analyze the garment by trying to determine which steps were done first, second, third, and so on, in order to construct the garment. These steps are considered a sequence of operations for sewing the garment. Write these instructions as a sequence of steps, and then pass the sequence to a partner and have that person determine the clarity of your steps. If necessary, rewrite some steps to make your instructions more clear.**

# WRITING AT THE RETAIL LEVEL

According to Elaine Stone in *The Dynamics of Fashion*, "retailing is . . . the heart of the fashion industry" (2004, p. 387). The retail level consists of businesses that buy apparel, accessories, and home fashions from entities at the secondary level, and sell these fashion goods to the consumer.

There are many types of retailers in today's marketplace. **Department stores** carry general lines of merchandise, including apparel, home fashions, and housewares.

---

**BOX 1.1 QUALITY ASSURANCE—A CRITICAL COMPONENT**

**Quality assurance** is the commitment that a business makes to creating and delivering high-quality products and service. The business involves its workers from the start so that the focus is on preventing errors rather than detecting them. Every production step and every garment from the assembly line is subject to a quality assurance review. Quality assurance involves conformity to written standards and specifications that must be communicated to all personnel responsible for manufacturing a quality product.

---

**Specialty stores** offer limited lines of related merchandise targeted to a specific customer defined by age, size, or shared tastes (Stone, 2004). Any retail operation that sells goods for less than the suggested retail price is considered a **discount store**. Department, specialty, and discount stores are often part of a **chain organization**, a group of four or more centrally owned stores.

Other types of fashion retailers are expanding in the marketplace. **Off-price retailers** sell brand-name and designer merchandise at "lower-than-normal" retail prices (Stone, 2004, p. 399). **Factory outlet stores** are discount operations run by the designer or manufacturer. **Category killers** are also growing in the retail scene. These superstores carry one type of good that is offered at great depth at low prices because of volume buying. **Boutiques** are small, individually owned stores that often carry unique assortments that other types of stores consider too risky to try to sell.

Retailers use written communication every day to correspond with customers, vendors, and employees in a multitude of ways. Billing statements, merchandise orders, and personal correspondence are examples of written transactions between retailers and customers. Employees are provided with written policies and procedures so they can understand what is expected of them on the job. And no longer is a contract sealed with a handshake: Today, written communication is used to invoice, track, and finance transactions between retailers and vendors.

Nonstore retailing, one of the first types of retailing to appear in the 1800s, is seeing resurgence in the 21st century. Currently, **nonstore retailing** consists of four formats: direct selling, catalog retailing, TV home shopping, and Internet shopping (Stone, 2004). (Internet shopping is sometimes called "e-tailing.") **Direct selling** allows independent sales associates to buy inventory and sell it directly to customers in their territory. **Catalog retailing** uses the mail as a distribution vehicle, provides toll-free phone numbers for customers to call to place their order, and uses credit card payments to close the sale.

**TV home shopping** takes the catalog sales technique a step further by demonstrating the merchandise to television viewers. **Internet shopping** sites allow a virtual version of the department store, specialty store, or catalog retailer, complete with editorial content and visual effects to change the complete landscape of the shopping experience. Advertising copy, broadcast scripts, catalog copy, and Web design are just a few forms of written communication vital to these nonstore retailers.

---

*Portfolio Exercise:* **Select a specific retailer in your community and write a report about that business. In your report, include the name and location of the business, what type of retailer the business is, what merchandise is carried, comparative prices, and assortments. Where is the merchandise positioned on the fashion cycle? Does the retailer carry private label merchandise? What is the perception of quality for the retailer?**

---

# WRITING AT THE AUXILIARY LEVEL

The auxiliary level provides assistance to all other levels of the fashion industry. And, not surprisingly, much of this assistance is in the form of writing. The auxiliary level consists of fashion media, promotion agencies, information resources, and professional or trade organizations that assist fashion businesses in delivering fashion messages to other levels of the industry and the consumer. The focus of this textbook is writing, and much of that writing takes place at the auxiliary level.

## *Fashion Journalism*

Fashion journalists play an important role in disseminating fashion information. Fashion products are very visual and tactile; fashion press writers are responsible for conveying what they see and feel so the reader can get a sense of the fashion importance of the product.

The fashion industry depends on a variety of trade and consumer magazines and newspapers for assistance in interpreting fashion information. People working in the fashion industry are the intended audience for **trade publications**. Newspapers such as *Women's Wear Daily* (*WWD*) and *Daily News Record* (*DNR*), and magazines such as *Stores* are essential reading for retail executives. Consumers are the intended audience for **consumer publications**. Walk into any Barnes and Noble bookstore and you will be amazed at the variety of fashion interest magazines available for sale. *Ebony, Essence, W, Vogue, InStyle, Details, Lucky*—the list goes on, providing fashion information for all demographic groups.

Broadcast media provide valuable information for the fashion industry. The Style® Network, part of E! Entertainment Television, Inc., has brought fashion information into the home through cable television. Network television morning news and entertainment programs regularly feature fashion segments, and celebrity shows such as *Entertainment Tonight* always cover fashion as part of celebrity culture.

## Fashion Promotion

The auxiliary level includes many promotion agencies responsible for developing advertising, publicity, public relations, or other promotional services for their clients. *Advertising* is any nonpersonal information paid for and controlled by a sponsoring organization (Swanson & Everett, 2007). Advertising agencies create fashion campaigns and buy media space or time for their clients at all levels of the fashion industry.

*Publicity* is nonpaid, unsponsored information delivered through the media, initiated by a party seeking to tell the public about a product, service, or idea. Publicity is a major tool used by public relations agencies to project a positive image about an organization to the public.

**Market research** agencies provide services for the auxiliary level. They focus on providing retailers and manufacturers with information on the buying habits and preferences of their clients' target markets (Frings, 2005). These agencies use various tools, including surveys and point-of-sale data, to collect demographic and psychographic information. For example, many consumer products have a survey included with a warranty request. The survey asks demographic questions such as gender and age of the receiver. In addition, the survey asks receivers what magazines they read and what hobbies they participate in (psychographic questions), in order to try to determine the lifestyle of the consumer. Once the information has been gathered, the agencies develop strategies to assist in product development, production, distribution, or promotion of the fashion product at the textile, manufacturing, or retail levels of the industry.

## Fashion Services

The auxiliary level is made up of many businesses that help members of the fashion industry organize and keep track of important fashion information. Called **fashion services**, these organizations are resources for fashion reporting, forecasting, and consulting, and are available as a fee service or through subscription (Frings, 2005). One well-known information source is the Doneger Group. This company provides forecasting and other analyses for its clients.

The Fashion Group International (FGI) is a global nonprofit professional organization that serves as an important information source for professional members in the industry. Twice yearly, it provides a DVD presentation of the latest trends from the New York, Paris, London, and Milan ready-to-wear shows. It also publishes newsletters, maintains a Web site, and hosts events for its membership at the chapter, national, and international levels.

**Trade associations** support particular segments of the fashion industry and are part of the auxiliary level. The National Retail Federation (NRF) is the largest retail trade association in the United States. Every January, it hosts a national trade show in New York City to allow retailers to view the latest retail services and technology. It also publishes *Stores* magazine, in which it disseminates valuable information to industry members. Cotton Incorporated® is another well-known organization that specifically promotes research and use of cotton fibers and fabrics. Among other publications, Cotton Incorporated® publishes *Lifestyle Monitor*, which is a weekly update on consumer attitudes and behavior regularly featured in *Women's Wear Daily*.

Writing is a common skill among all auxiliary level members. Whether it's a fashion report, a trend forecast, a media release, advertising copy, or one of many other forms, writing is critical in spreading the fashion message to industry members and consumers.

---

*Portfolio Exercise:* **Read several consecutive issues of WWD or DNR. After reading the issues, write a report on the following:**

- **What is a trade publication?**
- **What specific industry group is this type of publication directed at?**
- **What regular features and special features did you notice in the issues you read?**
- **In several paragraphs, explain how the information contained in the article could help a fashion producer or merchant.**

**Repeat the exercise for a consumer publication such as the *New York Times* or the *Wall Street Journal*, focusing specifically on fashion-related articles.**

- **What makes this publication different from a trade publication?**
- **In several paragraphs, explain how the information contained in the article could help a fashion consumer.**

**Repeat the exercise with a consumer fashion magazine such as *Vogue* or *Glamour*.**

- **What publication did you read?**
- **To what specific consumer group is this publication directed? What other groups do you think the publication would be of interest to?**
- **In several paragraphs, explain how the information contained in the articles could help a fashion consumer.**

---

As we'll explore in Chapter 2, effective written communication requires that we develop techniques for determining the fashion audience, building a vocabulary appropriate for the fashion environment, and using correct grammar and format to present the fashion message at all levels of the fashion industry.

## SUMMARY

Communication is multifaceted. We communicate visually and through speech and writing. Communication takes place when a sender and a receiver accept and agree on the message, as illustrated in the communication model. Noise can interfere with that communication.

The fashion industry is divided into four levels, and writing occurs at each level. The primary level produces greige goods from raw materials and sells those goods to the secondary level. Written communication makes certain that all requirements and expectations of raw materials (fibers, yarns, and fabric) are acceptable to the manufacturers who buy the finished fabric for use at the secondary level of the fashion industry.

Manufacturers make up the secondary level, producing apparel and accessories. Explicit written standards and specifications provide communication to all personnel responsible for manufacturing quality product at the secondary level.

The goods produced at the secondary level are distributed to the ultimate consumer at the retail level. The retail level is diverse, consisting of everything from small "mom and pop" entrepreneurs to large fashion conglomerates. Retailers use written communication every day to correspond with customers, vendors, and employees in a multitude of ways.

The fourth, auxiliary, level of the fashion industry assists all the other levels in promoting the fashion message. Auxiliary members include fashion media, promotion agencies, and fashion services. Writing is a critical skill for all members involved in the auxiliary level.

## KEY TERMS

Auxiliary level
Boutique
Catalog retailing
Category killer
Chain organization
Channel
Communication
Concept board
Consumer publication
Converter
Cost sheet
Decoding
Department store
Direct selling
Discount store

Encoding
Factory outlet store
Fashion
Fashion business
Fashion service
Feedback
Fiber
Filament length
Filament yarn
Frame of reference
Grading
Greige good
Internet shopping
Knit fabric
Knitter

Knitting machine

Line

Loom

Manufactured fiber

Marker

Market research

Merchandising function

Multimedia communication

Natural fiber

Noise

Nonstore retailing

Nonverbal communication

Off-price retailer

Primary level

Production function

Quality assurance

Retail level

Secondary level

Specialty store

Spinner

Spoken communication

Spreading

Spun yarn

Staple length

Throwster

Trade association

Trade publication

TV home shopping

Visual communication

Weaver

Woven fabric

Written communication

Yarn producer

## CASE STUDY

### *Tucson Rodeo Fashion Fiasco*

Tucson, Arizona, is one of the fastest growing cities in one of the fastest growing states in the United States. With a population of approximately 530,000 people and a median age of 36, Tucson boasts a diverse population of 61% white and 29% Hispanic citizens. Among the other groups represented in Tucson's population are Native Americans, making Tucson the 8th largest city in Native American citizens and the 23rd largest in Hispanic citizens.

Tourism is the second-largest industry in the Tucson region, contributing more than $2 billion annually to the local economy. Tourism supports 1 out of every 10 jobs in Tucson, and is one of the most rapidly growing job sectors. The peak of the tourism season is late fall, winter, and early spring, when Tucson attracts visitors from colder climates to enjoy the southwestern city with its warm temperatures and diverse cultural and geographic landscapes. Many wealthy Mexican citizens travel across the U.S. border to shop in Tucson. La Encantada, one of the newest shopping centers in Tucson, is perfectly situated within five miles of six luxury resorts and spas.

In 2003, the real estate developer Westcor opened Phase I of an upscale shopping center in Tucson. La Encantada is an intimate, open-air lifestyle center with extensive landscaping, upscale shops, walkways, patios, and courtyards that invite pedestrian interaction. The design concept blends La Encantada into the area's natural surroundings, and is designed to accentuate scenic views and protect local neighborhoods.

The center has 258,000 square feet of space, built on 37 acres. There are 55-plus chic retail shops and restaurants. Amenities include courtyards designed for entertainment, community, and school events. La Encantada has 1,300 parking spaces, including 176 covered parking spaces, and an auto court with valet parking.

One of Tucson's premier winter events is La Fiesta de los Vaqueros (Celebration of the Cowboys). The event has grown to a nine-day celebration centered on the Tucson Rodeo, one of the top 20 professional rodeos in North America.

La Fiesta de los Vaqueros takes place each year at the end of February at the Tucson Rodeo Grounds, at the peak of the tourist season. The centerpiece of the Rodeo is the Tucson Rodeo Parade. Each year, tens of thousands of people enjoy western-themed floats and buggies, historic horse-drawn coaches, festive Mexican folk dancers, marching bands, and elaborately outfitted riders. It is the world's longest non-motorized parade.

In cooperation with the rodeo planning committee, the Marketing Department at La Encantada Mall was asked to create a fashion event to tie into the festivities taking place during the Tucson Rodeo Week. The marketing department came up with the theme *La Moda de los Vaqueros*, which was used to promote La Encantada in print and broadcast advertising, a cowboy art show to be on display for nine days, and a festival fashion show, featuring merchandise from mall tenants, to be presented during the opening weekend of Tucson Rodeo Week.

Mall tenants, including Parachute, Cache, Ann Taylor, Lucy, Coldwater Creek, J. Jill, and White House/Black Market, agreed to supply garments for the show. Professional models were hired from the local Ford Modeling Agency. Makeup services were donated by MAC, which operates a store at La Encantada, and hair styling was contributed by the stylists at nearby Canyon Ranch Spa.

The ad campaign created by La Encantada Mall Marketing was featured in *Tucson* magazine and in the *Arizona Daily Star* and *Tucson Citizen* newspapers, as well as in the local broadcast media. Tucson Rodeo posters listed the event as a sponsored activity.

The weather was unusually warm on the morning of the fashion show, but it was a clear and sunny morning. It was just the kind of day that the Tucson Visitor's Bureau promotes in its promotional materials. The parking lots started to fill with shoppers, and the mall management was thrilled. They anticipated a great turnout for the show.

The fashion show was scheduled for 3 p.m., and excitement started to build. The models, merchants, hair stylists, and makeup artists were ready to show the best of what the mall had to offer. Live music by a local mariachi band was playing, and mall interns were distributing flyers about the show, as well as free water bottles with the La Encantada logo. But, at the time the show was scheduled to begin, only 25 people were sitting in the audience. The mall marketing director, the store managers, and the representatives from the Tucson Rodeo were extremely disappointed. They could not figure out why the audience was so small.

## CASE STUDY QUESTIONS

1.  What do you think went wrong?
2.  How could the mall management and the participating stores have improved their promotional efforts to attract a large crowd for the event?
3.  Should the event have been held at another time?
4.  What other types of supporting fashion events would be most successful to tie in to the annual rodeo?
5.  Suggest additional methods for the mall and rodeo planners to promote such special events.

## INDUSTRY PROFILE

*Marylou Luther*

**What is your current job and title? Can you describe the main responsibilities for your job?**

My current job and title is Editor, International Fashion Syndicate. I write a weekly question-and-answer column that is syndicated to newspapers throughout the country. For some of those papers, I cover the seasonal runway collections in Milan and Paris. When the rtw [ready-to-wear] collections are happening, I attend those.

**What is a typical day at work like?**

In between, I spend, on average, 25% of my day on the computer, setting up interviews, answering e-mails, opening mail; 25% visiting designers in Manhattan's garment district; 25% writing; and 25% working in my role as creative director of The Fashion Group International, a non-profit organization dedicated to the dissemination of information about fashion and related industries.

**At what point did you decide to pursue a career in writing for a fashion-related business?**

One year out of college (I was graduated from the University of Nebraska), I was offered a job at the *Des Moines Register*. The managing editor told me I would be the new fashion editor. I told him I didn't know a thing about fashion. He said, "You'll learn."

**Describe your first writing job. What was the most important or interesting thing you wrote for that job/publication?**

My first writing job I began the day after graduation at the *Lincoln Journal*. I wrote wedding stories, engagements, and a rare feature story. My main asset was moving my boss' car every two hours so she would not get a ticket.

*What are you currently reading (books, magazines, Web sites, newspapers, other media)? Do you have a favorite author or publication?*

I just finished *The Beautiful Fall* (a book about Karl Lagerfeld and Yves Saint Laurent, set mainly in the 1970s). I have just started Gene Pressman's *Chasing Cool* and Barack Obama's *The Audacity of Hope.* I read *Vogue, Bazaar, W, WWD, The New Yorker,* and *Vanity Fair* regularly. My favorite writers are Thomas Friedman and Paul Krugman of the *New York Times.* They're both op ed writers.

*What advice do you have for students interested in a writing career? Do you have any recommendations for students?*

My advice is to read two books: *The Careful Writer* by Theodore Bernstein and *Watch Your Language* by Theodore Bernstein and Jacques Barzun.

## REFERENCES

Frings, G. S. (2005). *Fashion from concept to consumer.* Upper Saddle River, NJ: Prentice Hall.

Heller, R. (1998). *Communicate clearly.* London: Dorling Kindersley Limited.

Keiser, S. J., & Garner, M. B. (2007). *Beyond design.* New York: Fairchild Books.

Stone, E. (2004). *The dynamics of fashion* (2nd ed.). New York: Fairchild Books.

Swanson, K. K., & Everett, J. C. (2007). *Promotion in the merchandising environment* (2nd ed.). New York: Fairchild Books.

Yeager, J. I., & Teter-Justice, L. K. (2003). *Textiles for residential and commercial interiors* (2nd ed.). New York: Fairchild Books.

# TWO

## *The Writing Process*

After you have read this chapter, you should be able to discuss the following:
- The six stages of the writing process: planning, shaping, drafting, revising, editing, and proofreading
- Communicating in an ethical manner to avoid plagiarism and libel

So, you have been assigned to write a paper on your favorite fashion designer. Have others always told you "You write well!" and you're looking forward to the assignment? Or, have you always struggled with writing, avoiding it when possible and wishing this assignment could be replaced by something more up your alley?

You are truly no different from a news reporter assigned to cover the retail holiday sales forecast or a feature writer assigned to write about Nancy Pelosi as the first female Speaker of the House, and about her influence on Capitol Hill. Writers are nervous about filling a blank page with something readers or viewers will find interesting and enjoyable. The most important rule every good writer has learned is *Don't be afraid of it!*

Whether you find writing easy or challenging, this chapter is intended to help you understand the writing process. Once you are familiar with the writing process in general, you can modify it for the other kinds of writing addressed in the following chapters. You, too, can take pride in writing fashion messages that readers will find interesting, informative, and enjoyable!

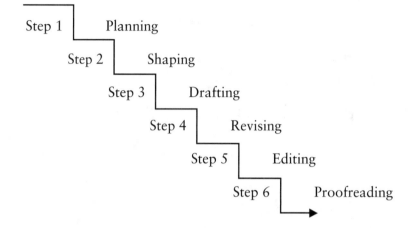

**FIGURE 2.1.** The writing process in six stages. Adapted from Kirszner, L. G., & Mandell, S. R. (2005). *The Wadsworth handbook* [Instructor's Edition]. Boston: Thomson Wadsworth.

This chapter discusses the writing process. That process begins with planning the fashion message. Next, we will discuss shaping the fashion message using an outline. Once these steps in the writing process have been completed, we will discuss drafting the fashion message, followed by revising and editing the fashion message. Proofreading cannot be stressed enough and is the focus of the final step in the writing process. This chapter concludes with a discussion of ethics in communication and how to avoid plagiarism.

## THE WRITING PROCESS

Writing fashion messages involves structure and creativity. Kirszner and Mandell (2005) structure the writing process into six stages, as illustrated in Figure 2.1:

1. **Planning**—Consider the purpose, audience, and tone; choose a topic; discover ideas to write about.
2. **Shaping**—Decide how to organize the material.
3. **Drafting**—Write the first draft.

4. **Revising**—"Re-see" what has been written; write additional drafts.
5. **Editing**—Check grammar, spelling, punctuation, and mechanics.
6. **Proofreading**—Check for typographical errors.

## PLANNING

Good writing is designed with a specific purpose, audience, and tone in mind. Read the following passage by Sara James (2007, p. 150):

> Perched halfway between the Blue Ridge Parkway and the Appalachian Trail, near North Carolina's northern border with Tennessee, Micaville isn't a town—it's a T in the road. There is a tiny post office with a narrow stream running by, a country store, a Presbyterian church, and the flagstone-faced Taylor Togs facility, which Marcus Wainwright and David Neville, the English collaborators behind the five-year-old American sportswear line Rag & Bone, visit each season to direct production of their denim and twill clothing.

This is the first paragraph from an article written for *Men's Vogue* about two British-born designers who are making made-in-America clothing and saving an Appalachian factory. Was your interest in American sportswear, or made-in-America clothing, or an Appalachian factory sparked as you read the copy? If so, then the writing fulfilled its purpose to get the reader's attention and highlight a new sportswear brand.

On the other hand, you might have been turned off by the passage because you are not interested in the place or the product. The author may have used a tone that did not grab your attention. Writers walk a fine line in turning their audience on or off to the fashion message.

This article makes an appeal to persuade the audience to consider buying from Rag & Bone. The article is supplemented with photographs that show the designers, storefront, and denim and twill products. The article is introduced with the headline "Mountain Rescue" and a sub-headline. The copy, visual images, font, and other elements of this piece all work together to achieve the intended purpose and appeal to the target audience. Like this article, every piece of fashion writing should consider the purpose, audience, and tone.

## *Purpose*

The best way to begin any piece of writing is to choose a topic and research it to decide how you might write about it. Later in this chapter, we will discuss brainstorming a topic. As you read and learn about your topic, you need to think about what you want to say about it. You, the writer, need to have a clear understanding of the topic before you can communicate it to others.

As you think logically about the topic, you begin to identify the **central idea** or **purpose statement**. The purpose statement answers two questions: (1) *Why am I writing this fashion message?* and (2) *What do I want to accomplish with this fashion message?* The purpose statement should be condensed into one or two sentences that will direct the remainder of your writing. Kirszner and Mandell (2005) offer these as possible purposes for a written piece:

- **Reflect**—To express private feelings
- **Inform**—To convey factual information
- **Persuade**—To convince readers
- **Evaluate**—To make a judgment about something
- **Discover**—To gather ideas or record observations
- **Affirm**—To express strongly held beliefs or values

Writing a purpose statement causes you to specifically determine why you are writing and what response you want from your audience. The purpose statement can become the lead-in sentence to an outline, or simply the first few words of the document. A purpose statement can be direct, beginning with the purpose, or it can be more indirect, drawing the reader into the topic with an attention-getting statement ahead of the purpose statement.

---

*Purpose Statement #1:* **The purpose of this magazine article is to report on the top ten *must have* looks for the fall season. (direct)**

*Purpose Statement #2:* **Fall takes us in new directions with fur collars, cigarette-legged pants, romantic blouses, and seven other *must have* looks for the fall season. (indirect)**

---

---

*Portfolio Exercise:* **Read three articles from various fashion publications. After you have read each article, determine what the purpose of the article was (to reflect, inform, persuade, evaluate, discover, or affirm). Next, write out the purpose statement for each article. You should be able to articulate the purpose statement in one or two sentences.**

---

## Audience

All writing is done with a specific audience in mind. The particular group of readers or viewer that the piece is targeted to is the **audience**.

Eakins (2005) suggests that a writer should answer four questions when profiling an audience:

1. Who will read the message?
2. What do the readers know about the subject?
3. What is the relationship between the readers and the writer?
4. What is the reading style of the audience?

*Who will read the message?* Be specific about *who* your actual readers are. Picture them in your head as you sit down to compose. While you may not be able to put a specific name to your readers, you can develop a general profile about them. The profile may include some or all of the following characteristics: age, education, occupational background, culture, needs of the reader, rapport you have with the reader, and reader's expectations. Messages should be tailored to meet the needs of the audience. For example, a magazine writer targeting the readers of *Seventeen* may write about the same vivid colors and vibrant prints that appear in *Glamour*. However, the tone and imagery presented in the *Seventeen* article would be age-appropriate for the teenage market.

*What do the readers know about the subject?* In order to connect with your audience, you need to be aware of their knowledge of the subject matter. Audiences range from having very little knowledge about the topic to having a very high level of understanding. Your goal is to determine where your audience fits, and then to write to their level. If your audience is familiar with terms such as "prestige brands" or "trademark infringement," it is enough to present the term and continue. If your audience is less familiar with fashion-specific vocabulary, you may need to define the term and explain the concept to provide a link for understanding.

---

*Example #1:* **China has developed awareness of prestige brands—exclusive brands for which high prices have created high demand.**

*Example #2:* **Increased trademark infringement suits have been reported as a result of increased online retail Web sites. Trademark infringement is the violation of use of a registered trademark, and it occurs when counterfeit goods are sold as the real item.**

---

Fashion dictionaries such as *Fairchild's Dictionary of Fashion* and *Fairchild's Dictionary of Textiles* are useful tools to assist writers in explaining fashion vocabulary. Develop a sense of your audience so that you can explain if necessary, but not include more information than necessary.

---

*Portfolio Exercise:* **Open any textbook you are using for a fashion-related class. Turn to the end of a chapter that you have already studied and find the keyword section. Select 10 keywords and use each one in a sentence. After you have written the sentences, trade with a partner and have that person read your sentences while you read your partner's sentences. While reading the sentences, both of you should circle each unfamiliar word. Return the sentences to the original author. For each circled word, rewrite the sentence. Use the textbook as a reference to further explain the concept.**

---

*What is the relationship between the readers and the writer?* Different fashion messages illustrate diverse relationships between the writer and the audience. Hosts on television shows illustrate this quite clearly when they speak to the audience as if they are speaking to long-time friends. They take a conversational approach to addressing the audience. However, a letter informing stockholders of the annual meeting portrays a much different relationship. Although stockholders have a vested interest in the company, they are often strangers to the writer.

*What is the reading style of the audience?* Not every piece of writing is read in the same manner. When reading a piece of fiction, a reader may read slowly, absorbing every word and getting immersed in the plot line. However, that same reader may read the headlines of an online newspaper quickly, just catching the highlights. Eakins (2005) identifies these common reading styles:

- **Skimming**—Reading lightly and quickly to get the main points
- **Scanning**—Reading quickly to find particular information
- **Searching**—Alternating between scanning and focusing
- **Receptive Reading**—Careful reading for thorough understanding
- **Critical Reading**—Reading with thoughtful consideration so as to evaluate

If the article you are writing is one that you expect your reader will be scanning, skimming, or searching, state the purpose of the message very directly as a heading or as the first sentence in a paragraph. Be concise in your writing so the reader can search for and find the information efficiently and effectively.

## Tone

**Tone** is the way a message sounds to the audience. It conveys the writer's attitude or mood about the subject. Messages can be serious or lighthearted, personal or detached, positive or negative. Tone tells the reader what you think about the topic, and it should remain consistent with the purpose and the selected audience (Kirszner & Mandell, 2005). Also, once the tone of a piece has been set, it should remain constant throughout the piece. Set the tone through word choice, sentence length, paragraph length, voice, and person.

Earlier, we used the example of a television host who uses a conversational tone with the audience. In writing, a conversational tone is often considered **informal writing**. Often, the purpose of informal writing is to cause reflection (Kirszner & Mandell, 2005). Commonly, informal writing uses the first person ("I"). Magazine articles, for example, are often written in an informal, first-person style to establish a sense of familiarity between the reader and the writer. In this textbook, we have used the second person ("you") when addressing the reader to give a sense of some familiarity between author and reader. In general, audiences appreciate having writers attempt to understand the audience's feelings. Using a first-person or second-person tone can help authors show that they are in touch with their audience.

While magazine articles are generally informal, scholarly journal articles tend to be formal in tone. **Formal writing** often requires summarizing, analyzing, or evaluating people, ideas, or situations. Much formal writing is intended to persuade an audience to accept a particular point of view or position (Kirszner & Mandell, 2005). The tone is more strict. Formal writing uses the third person (about the subject).

When you are writing to strangers, it is always better to write more formally. When the audience is not familiar with the writer, informal writing can make the audience perceive the writer as ill-prepared or lazy or lacking self-confidence.

## SHAPING

After you have determined the purpose, audience, and tone for your message, you need to decide how to organize your thoughts. The best way to do this is with an **outline**. An outline is a plan for structuring the fashion message. You can use it to distinguish major points from supporting ideas.

Many beginning writers consider outlining a waste of time. Perhaps they are experiencing a crisis in time management and just want to get the project done. They would rather start writing the document and worry about organization later. What these inexperienced writers do not understand is that writing an outline really *saves* time in the writing process. Writers who take the time to outline and organize the material before writing save valuable time in the long run. Writing a document without an outline has been compared to taking a road trip without a map. If you do not begin with a concrete plan, you have no idea where you will finish. This may be acceptable for a spring break trip, but not for a semester-long term paper.

Besides saving time, developing an outline before writing the first draft provides for a more accurate message. Outlining reduces the chance that you will leave out essential information or include nonessential information.

Additionally, outlining allows you to concentrate on one part of the message at a time. You can distinguish between major points and minor points, and you can sequence the ideas in the most appropriate manner.

## Outlines

An outline allows you to organize your thoughts before you worry about sentence structure, grammar, or other mechanics of writing. Outlines use a hierarchical structure. This means the items in the outline are arranged in a ranked order. More important ideas (first-level headings) are ranked higher than less important ideas (second-level headings, and so forth). Outlines can be developed as less formal or more formal documents, depending on the writer's needs. An informal outline is a simple list of points, with only one or two levels of headings. A formal outline is more complex and follows a structured format using multiple levels of subordination.

## Outline Content

One mistake that beginning writers make is to believe that once ideas are placed in the outline, they cannot be moved. In fact, the whole reason to construct an outline is to see the initial order of the manuscript, and then move and arrange content as necessary when writing the first draft. Woolever (1999) has suggested five steps of outlining:

1. List your ideas.
2. Categorize these ideas.
3. Prioritize the categories.
4. Write a complete sentence for each category heading.
5. Check the outline for balance and logic.

*List your ideas.* In this outlining step, you should brainstorm about your topic. Start with a blank sheet of paper or a blank computer screen, and generate a list of ideas you have about your topic. *Write down everything!* At this point in the process, it is too early to discard any idea. No idea is too silly, too far afield, or unimportant. Say, for example, that you are a contributing editor for a prominent fashion magazine and you've been assigned to write a retrospective piece on Charles Frederick Worth. Figure 2.2 shows some of the ideas you might jot down.

*Categorize these ideas.* Once you believe your list is complete, think about how the topics can be divided into broad categories. Try several categories until you find those categories that include as many of your ideas as possible. Finally, give each category father of haute couture

Marie Vernet, wife and muse

Empress Eugénie important client

first designer to use models

first designer to present in a runway style

first designer to use interchangeable parts

used many embellishments and decorations

Englishman in Paris

continues to be influential

FIGURE 2.2. Brainstorming ideas for an outline.

a relevant heading. Figure 2.3 illustrates how the brainstorming ideas might be categorized.

*Prioritize the categories.* Now that you have developed categories, you need to decide which category is most important. This category will appear first in your document. Which category should appear second? Which category should appear third? At the conclusion of this step, you should have all categories prioritized. A sensible way to prioritize the categories about Charles Frederick Worth might be as follows: introductory statement, training, opportunity at Maison Gageline, "firsts," clientele, innovations, and concluding statement.

The outline developed in Figures 2.2 and 2.3 used a topical/functional organizational structure that was also somewhat chronological. Both topical/functional and chronological are organizational patterns that may help you in prioritizing your categories. Guffey (2007) offers these organizational patterns:

- **Compare/contrast**—Present the idea and show alternative similarities and differences.
- **Chronological**—Arrange ideas in a time sequence to show history.
- **Geographical/spatial**—Organize ideas by regions or areas.
- **Topical/functional**—Arrange ideas by topics or functions.
- **Journalism pattern**—Arrange ideas in paragraphs devoted to Who, What, When, Where, Why, and How.

**Categorizing Brainstorming Ideas**

Important firsts—first designer to:

- present collection of dresses that could be ordered by his customers
- use mannequins, called "doubles" who deliberately resembled his principle customers
- sign his clothes as if they were a work of art
- convince customers to wear what he thought they should wear rather than the other way around
- realize aesthetic perfection must be built on technical excellence
- apply an artist's standards to the design and construction of a dress
- set up own maison de couture, Paris's first true haute couture house

Innovations

- styles designed in black so client could choose sleeve, flounce, other components and have designs custom made
- each part of his clothing fit interchangeable, each sleeve could fit several bodices
- sold  designs wholesale for adaptation for foreign dressmakers and stores

Clients

- Dressed Empress Eugénie, wife of Napoleon III
- Members of the international upper classes
- Princess Pauline Metternich, wife of Austrian ambassador
- Queen Victoria

Wife and sons

- Marie Vernet, wife and muse
- sons Gaston and Jean Philippe
- sons organized the Chambre Syndicale de la couture Parisienne

Training

- Maison Gageline, a silk mercer specializing in ready-made coats and shawls
- Apprenticeship at Swan and Edgar's
- Being English, knew tailoring methods

FIGURE 2.3. Categorizing brainstorming ideas.

- **Value/size**—Arrange ideas beginning with the most valuable, biggest, or most important item. Discuss remaining items in descending order.
- **Importance**—Build the outline from most to least or least to most important ideas.
- **Simple/complex**—Begin with simple ideas and move to more complex ideas.
- **Best case/worst case**—Describe the best and worst possible outcomes.

*Write a complete sentence for each category heading.* After you have prioritized your categories, develop each category heading into a complete sentence as in Figure 2.4. This helps you focus your thinking and helps ensure that you have clear points to make, not just a series of random ideas (Woolever, 1999). This sentence will become the topic sentence for the paragraph. Once you have written each heading as a complete sentence, arrange your ideas from the original list in logical order under the category headings. During this stage of outlining, you may decide to add additional points or remove points that have become unnecessary detail.

*Check the outline for balance and logic.* This is the last step in outlining. In this step, you want to make sure each category heading has a sufficient number of subpoints to stand alone as one or more paragraphs in the document. Each heading should have a minimum of two subpoints. If a particular heading is not strong enough to stand on its own, combine it with another category heading.

During this step, you also want to review the sequencing to ensure that the order of the categories is the best order possible. Refer back to your purpose statement and audience analysis. Does the outline you've developed address your original purpose statement and meet the needs of your intended audience? If it does, then you are ready to move to the drafting stage. If it does not, then you need to work through the outlining steps again—to ensure that your message is on target before you begin writing. As was stressed earlier, outlining is not a waste of time but rather a most valuable tool to save time in writing. You may not develop the best outline the first time you try, but with practice you will understand how outlining can make you a more proficient writer.

## Mind-Mapping

"A picture is worth a thousand words." This is frequently true for fashion students, who are often visual thinkers. You may find it easier to understand a picture, an

**Complete Outline**

**Thesis:** Modern fashion, as we know it in the 21st century, can be attributed to Charles Fredrick Worth, an innovative designer of the 19th century who is considered the father of haute couture.

1. Introductory statements
2. The training that Charles Frederick Worth gained in childhood and young adulthood set the foundation for ground-breaking firsts and innovations that would forever change fashion.
   - Born 1825
   - Cashiered at dress-goods store, in England
   - Learned tailoring methods in England
   - Apprenticed at Swan and Edgar's
3. Charles Frederick Worth moved to Paris at age 20, and found work at Maison Gageline, a silk merchant specializing in ready-made coats and shawls.
   - Created his own designs
   - Met his future wife and muse, Marie Vernet
   - Gained prominence to open his own couture house, the first true haute couture house
4. Opening the first haute couture house in Paris was only one of many firsts that Charles Frederick Worth introduced to the fashion world.
   - Presented collection of dresses that could be ordered by customers
   - Used mannequins, called "doubles," deliberately resembled principle customers
   - Signed clothes as works of art
   - Convinced customers to wear what he thought they should wear rather than the other way around
5. Many international members of the upper classes became Worth clients.
   - Empress Eugénie, wife of Napoleon III
   - Princess Pauline Metternich, wife of Austrian ambassador
   - Queen Victoria
6. In addition to being the first designer to introduce many contemporary practices, Charles Frederick Worth was also an innovative merchandiser.
   - Designed styles in black so client could have garments custom made
   - Designed clothing parts to fit interchangeably, each sleeve could fit several bodices
   - Sold designs wholesale for adaptation for foreign dressmakers and stores
7. Charles Frederick Worth has had a lasting influence of the fashion industry he began in the early 19th century.
   - House of Worth
   - Died 1895
   - Sons, Gaston and Jean Philippe, organized the Chambre Syndicale de la couture Parisienne
8. Summary—lasting influence

FIGURE 2.4. A completed outline in sentence form.

## BOX 2.1 FORMAL OUTLINES

Roman numeral outlines are a common rank-ordered form of formal outlining (see Figure 2.5). Capital letter roman numerals are used for first-level headings (I, II, III), capital letter arabic letters are used for second-level headings (A, B, C), arabic numerals are used for third-level headings (1, 2, 3), and lowercase arabic letters are used for fourth-level headings (a, b, c). A detailed outline may move to even a fifth level, using lowercase roman numerals (i, ii, iii).

When developing an outline, remember these two primary points:

**1.** Second-level headings are always subdivisions of first-level headings, third-level headings are always subdivisions of second-level headings, and so forth. Therefore, each level must have at least two subdivisions (I and II, A and B, 1 and 2, a and b, i and ii). If the topic cannot be divided into at least two subdivisions, it should be merged with another topic above or below it in the outline structure.

**2.** All headings of the same level must be grammatically consistent. If point A uses an action verb, then point B should also use an action verb. If point I is a complete sentence, then point II should also be a complete sentence. This is termed *parallelism*, and it will be discussed later in this chapter.

```
 I.  Main Idea
     A.  1st major point
         1.  Evidence
             a. Detail
             b. More detail
         2.  More evidence
     B.  2nd major point
         1.  Evidence
         2.  More evidence
     C.  3rd major point
         1.  Evidence
         2.  More evidence
II.  Second Main Idea
```

FIGURE 2.5. Basic outline format.

Guffey (2007) suggests these tips for making outlines:

- Define the main topic in the title.
- Divide the topic into three to five main points.
- Break the components into subpoints.
- Do not put a single item under a major component if you only have one subpoint. Instead, integrate it with the main point above or below the item, or reorganize.
- Make each component exclusive (no overlapping).
- Use details, illustrations, and evidence to support subpoints.

illustration, or a visual element than a written statement. **Mind-mapping** is a tool to help visual thinkers collect information and visually decide how to organize it before developing an outline. A mind-map does not replace an outline. Rather, it is a tool to help you, the writer, organize an outline. Figure 2.6 is an example of a mind-map using the Charles Frederick Worth example discussed previously.

Woolever (1999) presents these easy steps for developing a mind-map:

1. Write your main topic in the middle of a sheet of paper and draw a shape around it. Make sure your paper is large so you can branch out as necessary.

2. Think of subtopics that relate to the main topic. Write each subtopic on the sheet of paper and put different shapes around the subtopics to differentiate them from the main idea. To express your subtopics, use one or two key words rather than long phrases.

3. Connect the subtopics to the main topic with solid lines.

4. Repeat the process for each subtopic, brainstorming details, examples, illustrations, or evidence that supports each subtopic. Enclose each detail or piece of evidence in a new shape to further differentiate it from the subtopics.

5. Connect the shapes to the subtopics with solid lines.

When you have finished the mind-map, you will have a visual "map" of the relationships among the topics. You can then arrange this map into an outline following the outlining steps previously discussed.

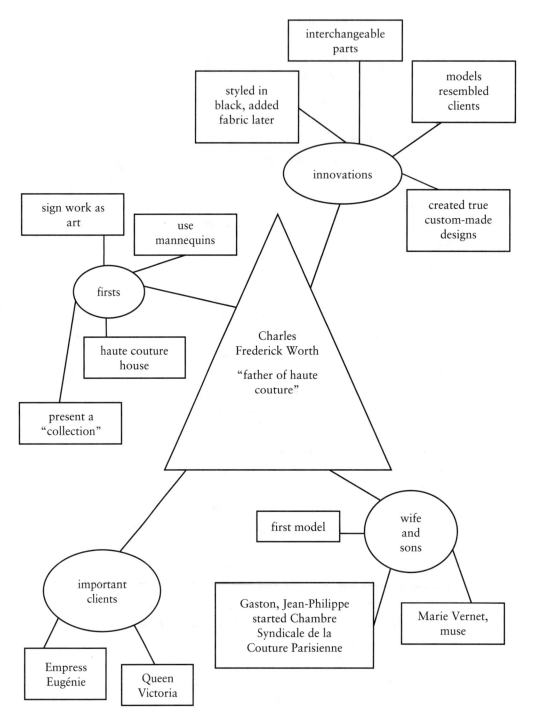

**FIGURE 2.6.** Example of a mind-map.

---

*Portfolio Exercise:* **Pick your favorite fashion designer and develop an outline and a mind-map for a report on that designer. Follow the instructions above, including brainstorming, categorizing, and prioritizing your ideas. Then develop a complete sentence for each main heading. Use the outline to determine if you have included relevant facts and eliminated unnecessary information. Also use the outline as a check to make sure you have not repeated yourself. Each fact should be included just once, in whatever section of the outline is most appropriate for it.**

---

# DRAFTING

You are now ready to begin writing your fashion message. Yes, it has taken some time and thought to get to this stage, but the preplanning work was worth it! Your ideas are well thought out in a logical sequence made easy by using an outline.

Always remember that at this point, you are preparing a *draft*, not the final fashion message. A **draft** is a preliminary version of the document. You will edit and rewrite your document several times before you present it to your editor, publisher, supervisor, or instructor—who will also edit and rewrite your fashion message, once or several times.

Of course, even though we call the first writing a draft, it should be as complete as possible. Do not think that a draft can be sketchy and full of holes to be filled in later. Good writers develop comprehensive drafts so they can use the revising stage of the writing process to polish their fashion message.

When the first draft of this textbook was written, the publisher's staff asked for a clean, consistently typed manuscript. They provided manuscript guidelines regarding paper size, margins, headings, numbering, and spacing requirements. For some specific guidance on manuscript preparation, see Appendix C, "Effective Document Design." A copy of a page from the manuscript draft is shown in Figure 2.7. The manuscript page looks very different from the page you are reading. Most publishers ask authors to submit work in an easy-to-read draft format with space for editing. Only after the manuscript has been revised for the final time do publishers put the fashion message into production. Production consists of printing or posting the fashion message in its final form, whether that is a newspaper or magazine article, Web site content, a scholarly article published in a journal, or some other form. This occurs in nearly all publishing. Newspapers, magazines, broadcast scripts, public relations pieces, books, and academic unnecessary information. Also use the outline as a check to make sure you have not repeated yourself, facts should be included once in the most appropriate section of the outline.

**Drafting**

You are now ready to begin writing your fashion message. Yes, it has taken some time and thought to get to this stage, but the preplanning work was well worth it! Your ideas are well thought through in a logical sequence made easy by using an outline.

Always remember that you are preparing a *draft* first, not the final fashion message. A *draft* is a preliminary version of the document which will be edited and rewritten. You will edit and rewrite your document several times before you present it to your editor, publisher, supervisor, or instructor who will also edit and rewrite your fashion message once or several times. Even though we call the first writing a draft, it should be as complete as possible. Do not be fooled into thinking a draft can be sketchy and full of holes to be filled in later. Good writers develop comprehensive drafts so they can use the revising stage of the writing process to polish their fashion message.

When we wrote the draft of this textbook for Fairchild Publications, the publisher's staff asked us to provide a clean, consistently typed manuscript. They asked us to follow manuscript guidelines including paper size, margin, heading, numbering,

and spacing requirements. A copy of a page from the manuscript draft is shown in Figure 2.7. The manuscript page looks very different from the page you are reading. Most publishers ask authors to submit work in an easy-to-read draft format that can be edited. Only after the manuscript has been revised for the final time do publishers put the fashion message into production. This occurs in nearly all publishing. Newspapers, magazines, broadcast scripts, public relations pieces, books, and academic journals request that writers submit their work in draft form using specified guidelines. These pieces are edited before the document is put into production. Most publications adhere to specific rules of style published in a stylebook. In later chapters specific stylebooks will be discussed. Appendix B, Documentation formats, introduces some specific stylebooks.

Refer to your outline or notes and start writing your draft. Generally it is best to start writing your ideas down write rapidly, not worrying about spelling, grammar or other mechanics at this point. If you spend time making corrections as you write, you often lose your train of thought. Once your ideas are down on paper, you can revise your message later. The following discussion identifies techniques for writing effective fashion messages, first at the sentence level and then at the paragraph level.

**Sentences**

Writing is a matter of personal style. However, there are fundamental guidelines that apply to all types of writing including sentence structure. One of these guidelines is *Subjects and Verbs* Always use complete sentences to express ideas. A complete sentence contains a subject and a verb (or a verb phrase). The subject is a noun or

FIGURE 2.7. Page from a manuscript draft.

journals request that writers submit their work in draft form using specified guidelines. These pieces are edited before the document is put into production. Most publications adhere to specific rules of style, published in a **stylebook**. Appendix B, "Documentation Format," introduces some specific stylebooks.

Refer to your outline or notes and start writing your draft. Generally, it is best to start writing your ideas down rapidly, not worrying about spelling, grammar, or other mechanics at this point. If you spend time making corrections as you write, you often lose your train of thought. Put your ideas down on paper first; you can revise your message later.

In the following discussion, we'll identify techniques for writing effective fashion messages, first at the sentence level, and then at the paragraph level.

## *Sentences*

Writing is a matter of personal style. However, there are fundamental guidelines that apply to all types of writing. One of these guidelines is sentence structure. Here, we'll discuss the primary components of a good sentence. The bottom line: A complete sentence makes sense (Clark & Clark, 2004).

*Subjects and Verbs* Always use complete sentences to express ideas. A complete sentence contains a subject and a verb (or a verb phrase). The **subject** is a noun or pronoun that interacts with the verb. The **verb** is a word that shows action or describes a condition. (In a **verb phrase,** the last verb in the phrase is considered the main verb.)

Subjects may be simple or compound. **Simple subjects** consist of a single noun or pronoun. **Compound subjects** contain two or more nouns or pronouns, and are linked by *and, but, or,* or *nor.*

---

*Sentence Example #1:* **Julie [simple subject]** *was* **[verb] promoted to Divisional Merchandise Manager. (makes sense)**

*Sentence Example #2:* **Barb and Sara [compound subject], as a result of their excellent customer service,** *were able to attract* **[verb phrase,** *attract* **is the final verb] several new clients. (makes sense)**

---

*Phrases and Clauses* Within sentences, words are grouped into three units: phrases, dependent clauses, and independent clauses. **Phrases** do not contain a subject or a verb and must always relate to or modify another part of the sentence.

---

*Sentence Example #3:* **She went *to the meeting*. [phrase]**

---

Both dependent clauses and independent clauses contain subjects and verbs. The difference is that an **independent clause** is a complete sentence and a complete thought that can stand by itself, while a **dependent clause** must rely on another part of the sentence for its meaning.

---

*Sentence Example #4:* ***He spoke with the committee.* [independent clause]**

*Sentence Example #5:* ***After he visited the branch store,* [dependent clause] he went home.**

---

*Sentence Type* There are four main sentence types: simple, compound, complex, and compound–complex. A **simple sentence** contains one independent clause that expresses only one complete thought. A **compound sentence** contains two or more independent clauses connected by conjunctions (*and, but, because, since, until,* and others). A sentence with two independent clauses must be joined by a conjunction or by a semicolon (;) or it becomes a **run-on sentence**. A comma alone cannot join two independent clauses. Joining the clauses with only a comma creates a comma splice, which careful writers avoid.

---

*Sentence Example #6:* **Most trend forecasts were presented using creative visual *boards one was* presented using PowerPoint software. [run-on sentence]**

*Sentence Example #7:* **Most trend forecasts were presented using creative visual *boards, but one* was presented using PowerPoint software. [revised sentence]**

*Sentence Example #8:* **Some customers responded by** *telephone, others* **visited the Web site. [comma splice sentence]**

*Sentence Example #9:* **Some customers responded by** *telephone; however, oth-* **ers visited the Web site. [revised sentence]**

---

A **complex sentence** includes one independent clause and one or more dependent clauses. A **compound–complex** sentence contains at least two independent clauses and at least one dependent clause.

---

*Sentence Example #10:* **She completed the window display. (simple sentence)**

*Sentence Example #11:* **Ryan completed the window display** *while* **[conjunction] Katie began working on the floor display. (compound sentence)**

*Sentence Example #12:* *After she finished the sale* **[dependent clause],** *Brittney went on her break* **[independent clause]. (complex sentence)**

*Sentence Example #13:* *After they studied for their exam* **[dependent clause],** *they went to bed* **[independent clause],** *but they were unable to sleep much that night* **[dependent clause]. (compound–complex sentence)**

---

Sentence types should vary within a piece of writing. Most sentences should be simple or complex with the focus on one independent clause in each sentence. Compound and complex sentences can add variety to a paragraph, adding interest for the reader. Be cautious, however; having too many clauses can weaken the meaning of your message.

A good sentence places the main point near the beginning of the sentence. This allows the reader to understand what is important immediately without having to read through long introductory phrases or clauses. This is the style you would use when writing for newspapers. When writing for magazines, however, you can modify the sentence structure and use vivid adjectives to draw the reader into the story before addressing the main point.

Sentence length should be varied within a message, but it should average no more than 15 to 20 words. The more important the point is, the shorter the sentence should be. Reserve long sentences to support your main idea. If your sentences are too long, look for conjunctions that you can remove; then, the two independent clauses can become two sentences. Another strategy: Read the sentence out loud—wherever you find you must pause or take a breath is usually the place where a longer sentence can be broken into two shorter sentences.

*Voice* Sentences are more interesting to a reader when they are written in the active voice rather than the passive voice. **Active voice** sentences emphasize the person or thing performing an action. **Passive voice** sentences emphasize the action itself. There is a place for each type of sentence in effective writing. Writers of fiction prefer to use many active-voice sentences in order to make readers feel as if they are actually in the story and participating in the action. The passive voice is used when a distant approach is more appropriate. Readers can become frustrated with passive-voice writing if they cannot determine who or what is doing something.

---

*Passive Voice Example #1:* **It is recommended [passive] that you use a ¼-inch seam allowance around the curved neckline.**

*Active Voice Example #1:* **The product developer *recommends* [active] that you use a ¼-inch seam allowance around the curved neckline.**

*Passive Voice Example #2:* **The fact that color is the most important aspect of a garment to get the customer's attention *was revealed* [passive] in the study.**

*Active Voice Example #2:* **The study *revealed* [active] that color is the most important aspect of a garment to get the customer's attention.**

*Passive Voice Example #3:* **Many sketches *were reviewed* [passive] in the initial phase of line development.**

*Active Voice Example #3:* **We reviewed [active] many sketches in the initial phase of line development.**

---

Review Passive-Voice Example #1. One hint that the sentence is written in the passive voice is the use of *it* as the first word of the sentence. In the corrected active-voice example, *it* has been replaced by a noun: *product developer*. When writing, try to avoid using *it* as the first word of a sentence.

Look again at Passive Voice Example #2 and notice that using the passive voice requires more words to present the idea. Passive-voice sentences are wordier than active-voice sentences because they leave out the person or thing performing the action.

Pfeiffer (2004) makes some sensible suggestions for when the active voice should be used:

- Use the active voice when you want to emphasize who is responsible for an action (*"We reviewed many sketches"* instead of *"Many sketches were reviewed"*).
- Rewrite a top-heavy sentence so the main idea that was the last part of the sentence is now at the beginning of the sentence (*"The study revealed"* instead of *"was revealed in the study"*).
- Use the proper name of a company, person, job title, or other noun (*"The Product Developer recommends"* instead of *"It is recommended"*).

*Parallelism* The term **parallelism** means that words or groups of words used similarly within a sentence should be expressed in the same format. Parallel structure applies to words appearing in a series, appearing in a list, or joined by conjunctions. If the first idea begins with a noun or pronoun, so must all the other ideas in the series. Similarly, if the first item ends with *-ed*, *-ing*, or *-ion*, each item in the series must use that same verb ending.

---

*Parallel Example #1:* **We are concerned with the *quality of fabric, where it is located,* and *how much it will cost to transport it.* (not parallel)**

*Parallel Example #2:* **We are concerned with the *quality, location*, and *transportation costs* of the fabric. (parallel nouns)**

*Parallel Example #3:* **You may obtain a free sample of Sally Hansen® Insta-dri™ anti-chip topcoat with *a call* to our toll-free number, *returning* the enclosed postcard, or *enter* promotional code 5555 when visiting our Web site. (not parallel)**

*Parallel Example #4:* **You may obtain a free sample of Sally Hansen®
Insta-dri™ anti-chip topcoat by calling our toll-free number,** *returning* **the
enclosed postcard, or** *entering* **promotional code 5555 when you visit our Web
site. (parallel verbs)**

In this section, we've identified how to write an effective sentence. In the next
section, we'll present guidelines for forming those sentences into paragraphs.

## Paragraphs

According to Pfeiffer (2004), paragraphs have two objectives: (1) to state and develop the
topic, and (2) to maintain reader interest in the main topic. Just as variety is pleasing in
sentence length, variety is pleasing in paragraph length. The rule of thumb for paragraph
length is six to eight lines of type (not six to eight sentences). The first and last paragraphs
of most manuscripts are shorter than the paragraphs in the body of the document.

Pfeiffer (2004) has some other tips for writing engaging paragraphs:

- Put the main topic of the paragraph in the first sentence. This sentence,
  commonly called the **topic sentence,** identifies the central idea of the
  paragraph. Readers who skim paragraphs read the first sentence to
  determine whether to read further.
- Keep paragraphs short. Readers need visual breaks, which allow them to
  rest or at least take a breath. If you cannot address the topic completely in
  one paragraph, divide the paragraph at a convenient place and continue
  your discussion of the topic in the next paragraph.
- If you have many related points, use bullets, numbers, or other list formats
  to group the items together. This makes the information easier to read.
- When possible, avoid extensive use of numbers. Use tables or figures to
  present numerical data.

Refer back to your outline as you are developing paragraphs. Each heading in
your outline should be covered with approximately the same number of paragraphs.
If one topic is covered in much more detail than other topics, the reader will consider
this part of the message to be the more important. Likewise, if you devote very few

paragraphs to a specific topic, the reader will think the information in that part of the message is less important.

*Direct or Indirect Paragraphs* Paragraphs can be written in a direct pattern or an indirect pattern. A **direct pattern** presents the main topic in the first sentence, and supporting detail is presented in later sentences. An **indirect pattern** presents supporting detail in the first sentences. These sentences lead up to the topic sentence, which appears near the conclusion of the paragraph.

You can also apply direct and indirect organization to the entire piece of writing. In direct writing, the piece opens by telling the audience the nature of the message, and then presenting supporting detail. In indirect writing, the piece presents all the supporting detail first and concludes the fashion message with the topic of the message.

*Coherent Paragraphs* Skilled writers use coherence techniques to keep readers interested in the message (Lehman & Dufrene, 2005). When writing is coherent, sentences stick together with each sentence linked in some way to the preceding and following sentences. Likewise, paragraphs flow from one to the next, with transition sentences or headings to tell readers what they will read next.

Fashion messages that do not have cohesion often leave the reader experiencing abrupt changes in thought with no transition to the next idea. Here are some ways that you can achieve cohesion in your writing:

- Repeat a word or idea that was in the previous sentence or paragraph.

---

*Cohesion Example #1:* **The design team took** *responsibility* **for the fall line. The** *responsibility* **was shared equally between the lead designer and the assistants.**

---

- Use a pronoun that represents a noun used in the preceding sentence or paragraph.

---

*Cohesion Example #2:* **The design team took** *responsibility* **for the fall line.** *It* **[the responsibility] was shared equally between the lead designer and the assistants.**

---

- Use connecting words, such as *however* or *therefore*.

---

*Cohesion Example #2:* **The design team was responsible for the fall line. However, the lead designer gave special recognition to the assistants who worked on the project.**

---

We are nearing the end of the writing process. Next, we edit and rewrite the fashion message. Yes, *we edit and rewrite the fashion message.*

# REVISING

No piece of writing should ever be considered finished until it has been edited and rewritten at least once if not several times. Up to this point in the writing process, we have concentrated on the instructions for writing; now we turn our attention to developing style in a written piece through revising. As Kirszner and Mandell have said, this is a time to "re-see" what you have written and write additional drafts (2005, p. 33).

Previously, we talked about tone, which is very similar to style. Style is defined as "the way something is written" (Woolever, 1999, p. 91). In their classic guide to writing, Strunk and White (2000) talk about style as being the sounds that words make on paper. People who read the same author regularly can easily recognize that author's style. With good writing, it is almost as if you can hear the writer speaking to you.

Style is developed in different ways for different types of writing. A writer of a magazine article may develop a more informal style by using descriptive words that pull the reader into the story. A writer for a trade publication may develop a more formal style, directing the reader immediately to the facts. Style is developed based on the intended audience and the medium in which the fashion message will appear.

---

*Portfolio Exercise:* **Read the following sentence from Brunel (2002, p. 11):**

**Just like jeans, T-shirts became one of the 20th century's most universal and mythical items of clothing—with more than two billion a year sold worldwide.**

**Notice how the style changes with the rearrangement of words in this example:**

**With more than two billion a year sold worldwide, the T-shirt, like jeans, became one of the 20th century's most universal—and mythical—items of clothing.**

**Now, read a paragraph from a fashion-related publication and select your favorite sentence. Write the sentence at the top of a blank piece of paper. Now rewrite the sentence as many times as you can, using the same words but different arrangements. After you have written the sentences, trade with a partner and take turns reading the original sentence out loud followed by the rewritten sentences. Can you hear a different style revealed in each sentence by the different arrangement of words?**

Style guides can assist you in achieving satisfactory style. Strunk and White (2000) make several suggestions:

- Place yourself in the background. Your writing should draw attention to the content of the writing, rather than the mood of the author.
- Write naturally, using words and phrases that are part of your vocabulary.
- Make sure the reader knows who is speaking.

Other guidelines for developing clarity through style include emphasizing important points, avoiding complications in the message, and avoiding biased language.

Using proper punctuation and creating effective document design—two more critical components of creating your fashion message—will be discussed in Appendixes A and C, respectively.

## Emphasize Important Points

When you talk to someone, how do you know what is most important in what they are saying to you? They may speak loudly or softly. They may blurt out the message in the first words they say to you, or they may build up the message with a story before they disclose the important news at the climax. What they are doing is controlling through inflection in their voice what is most important in their message.

The same is true in writing. Not every word in a sentence should have equal importance. The message should be controlled through word usage and placement in the sentence—either delivered immediately, at the beginning of the sentence, or disclosed selectively, providing a climax in the sentence. Likewise, not every sentence in a paragraph should have equal significance. The writer should strategically control delivery at the most appropriate place in the paragraph.

## Avoid Complicating the Message

When you are editing for style, closely related to emphasizing the important points is avoiding making the writing any more complicated than necessary.

- Avoid **wordiness**—using more words to make a point when fewer words would be adequate. Examples: *now* would be a better choice than *at the present time*, and *based on the fact that* can easily be replaced by *because*.
- Avoid **qualifiers**—those extra words that can creep in before you get to the point of the sentence. Qualifiers include words such as *very*, *pretty*, *really*, and other words that do not add to the topic.
- Avoid **redundancy**—phrases in which one word or idea is repeated unnecessarily (Lehman & Dufrene, 2005). Examples: *dollar amount* (*dollar* is already an amount—the idea does not have to be repeated); *basic fundamentals* (by definition, fundamentals are basic); and *very true* (something cannot be more true or less true). Use precise words rather than general words when appropriate.

## Avoid Biased Language

Good writing is **bias-free**. This means that word choice and expressions are free of prejudice toward gender, sexual orientation, racial or ethnic group, disability, or age. Most people do not intend to be insensitive, but they often are not aware of words or phrases that might offend others. Writing without bias recognizes that differences should be mentioned only when relevant (American Psychological Association, 2005). (See Box 2.2.)

The revising stage is the place for you to concentrate on rewriting the fashion message to make sure you say what you want to say in an effective manner.

## Box 2.2 Avoiding Offensive Language

Here, we'll take a look at some specific areas where biased language can creep in: gender; sexual orientation; race, ethnicity, or religion; age; and disability. Of course, any language that readers might consider distasteful or insulting, such as profane language, should not be used.

*Avoiding Gender Bias* We have all heard *hunk* or *chick* or other words used in a belittling manner. In writing, words such as these can be considered offensive to the reader—similar to an insult. Such language, termed **sexist language,** occurs when a writer does not apply the same terminology to both men and women (Kirszner & Mandell, 2005).

While the *hunk/chick* example is meant to be obvious, other examples of sexist language are not always so noticeable. Referring to men and women in stereotyped roles and occupations is sexist language. Outdated job titles such as *salesman* are sexist. Instead of *salesman*, use *sales associate*, which does not imply male or female.

If you know a person's gender, use it. If you do not know a person's gender, do not use the generic *he* or *him*. Instead, balance the use of *he or she* or *him or her* in the singular form, or use *they* in the plural form throughout the message (keep an eye on your subject–verb agreement). Another way to avoid sexist language is to use the person's job title in place of the pronoun. For example, use the job title *store manager* in place of *he or she*. Avoid using *he/she*, *him/her*, or the *s/he* construction.

In writing, adult females should always be referred to as women. Likewise, adult males are men. When writing about a woman whose marital status is irrelevant, use *Ms.* instead of *Miss* or *Mrs.* Conversely, if a woman refers to herself as *Miss* or *Mrs.*, use the form she prefers.

On that same note, always apply parallel construction when referring to people in writing. If you use the first name of one individual, use the first name of all the individuals in your message. If you refer to one individual with a title such as *Ms.*, refer to all the people in your message with their appropriate titles.

*Avoiding Sexual Orientation Bias* A person's sexual orientation should be used in writing only if it is relevant to the topic. If identifying sexual orientation is necessary in the written piece, use neutral terms such as *gay*, *lesbian*, or *bisexual*.

**Box 2.2** *(continued)*

*Avoiding Racial, Ethnic, or Religious Bias* When referring to any racial, ethnic, or religious group, use neutral words, or words that the group itself uses in formal writing when referring to itself (Kirszner & Mandell, 2005). Determining what's appropriate is not always easy. For example, people from East Asia once referred to themselves as *Orientals.* Now these individuals refer to themselves as *Asian* or *Asian Americans,* or by their country of origin, such as *Korean.*

Just as with sexual orientation, racial or ethnic identification should be used only if it is relevant to the topic. If one racial, ethnic, or religious group is identified, all groups should be identified. And, of course, no group should be referred to in a stereotypical way.

*Avoiding Age Bias* Potentially offensive labels related to age should be avoided in writing. We offer the term *old hag* as an obvious example. However, there are other terms that writers should be aware of and avoid. Some, but not all, older people prefer the terms *senior citizens, senior,* or *elderly,* while others prefer the term *older adult* (not *old adult*).

In some writing, it may be appropriate to use a term representing an age cohort, such as *Baby Boomer* or *Generation X*—as long as your audience understands what ages the label means. Referring to specific age ranges such as *ages 25 to 34* and omitting age-defined labels may be the best practice. Like racial or ethnic identity, age should be used only if it is relevant to the topic. Young writers should also avoid generalizing that any individual who is older than the writer is *old.*

*Avoiding Disability Bias* People who have disabilities should not be labeled as such in writing unless it is relevant to the topic. To avoid disability bias in writing, refer to the person first and the disability second. For example, instead of using the term *blind employees*, use *employees with visual impairments* to address the person first and the disability second. Additionally, avoid negatively connoted words or words that are judgmental in nature— such as *handicapped, afflicted,* and *victim*—when writing about persons with disabilities. Do not use the word *normal* to describe people who do not have disabilities. Instead, use the term *typical* to refer to the nondisabled community.

# EDITING

Every language has a system of rules to define the structure of the language. That system of rules is known as **grammar**. We've already discussed several rules of the English language in this chapter. For example, subject–verb agreement in sentence structure is a grammar rule. During the editing stage of the writing process, you will review your grammar thoroughly to check that the mechanics of the fashion message are accurate. Appendix A, "Grammar Mechanics," offers a review of grammar basics. Additionally, you should refer to a stylebook such as Strunk and White's *Elements of Style*, or other grammar and usage handbooks such as the *Harbrace College Handbook*, for help with the rules of the English language.

## *Take Advantage of Grammar Checkers and Spelling Checkers*

Every document composed on a computer should be automatically edited with the word processing application's spell-check and grammar-check functions before it is completed. These functions are excellent tools to use to begin the editing process. The spell-check function can identify strings of letters that have not been identified as real words programmed into the software dictionary. The grammar-check tool can check for common errors such as fragmented sentences.

Although these tools start the editing process, it is not complete until the *writer* has also edited the fashion message. For example, spell-checkers and grammar-checkers do not check for word sense. The software package cannot tell the difference between *they're*, *there*, and *their* or *to*, *too*, and *two*, and other homophones. The spell-checker also does not check for specialized words such as *Schiaparelli* or *microfiber*. The grammar-checker can point out constructions that it has been programmed to recognize as errors, but it cannot always provide a solution. So, while they're very helpful, these functions are not perfect. As the writer, after you've used these functions, you need to edit your work yourself to make sure that the correct words have been used and that the document reads well.

## *Use Proper Punctuation*

**Punctuation** is the standardized marks used in writing to clarify meaning and separate structural units. Lynne Truss, author of the best-selling book *Eats, Shoots & Leaves* (2004), talks of punctuation as "traffic signals of language . . . telling us to slow down, take notice, take a detour or stop" (p. 7). With the advent of e-mail and text-messaging, many people have become sloppy with punctuation, in some cases avoiding it altogether. Writers should concentrate on using punctuation correctly.

Specific punctuation marks, rules of capitalization, and other grammar mechanics are reviewed in Appendix A.

In our final section on revising a document, we will concentrate on the image of your document. What good is a well-written fashion message if the image is so poor that the reader ignores the message? Creative document design is the focus of Appendix C, "Effective Document Design." In fashion design, the image of a garment is essential to the success of the design. This is also true with written messages, which should have a polished image to encourage the reader to read and take action from the message.

## *Two Final Thoughts about Editing*

First, style does not come through immediately when you're writing the first draft of a fashion message. Style is developed over time once you are confident in what you have to say. Creating style takes experience.

And second, all good writers have someone they can turn to in order to edit their work for style. They trust that editor to give constructive criticism that will make the fashion message better. Good writers do not take editing suggestions personally; rather, they understand the value of a fresh set of eyes reading the document for content and structure.

## PROOFREADING

Once you are satisfied with your fashion message, you are ready to proofread—the final and arguably the most important stage of the writing process. Your credibility is on the line every time someone else reads your writing, so that writing should be as near to perfect as possible. **Proofreading** means rereading every word carefully to make sure the document is error free.

Proofreading for all kinds of errors at once is extremely difficult. Therefore, you should do your proofreading in a systematic manner. Read your document three or more times, each time concentrating on a different element:

1. Content, organization, and style
2. Mechanics, grammar, punctuation, capitalization
3. Format and layout

During the first proofreading of your document, look for errors in content, organization, and style. The following is a checklist of questions you should ask yourself during this phase of proofreading:

- Is the fashion message complete? Has important information been included and unnecessary information eliminated?
- Has information in the fashion message been checked for accuracy?
- Is the fashion message presented clearly and in a logical order?

During the second reading of your document, concentrate on grammar, punctuation, capitalization, and other mechanics of writing. Although most word processing packages have a grammar-check tool, mistakes can still be overlooked. As the writer, you have the final proofreading responsibility. Refer to Appendix A for assistance with grammar mechanics.

Proofread your document a third time, reviewing the format and layout. Review Appendix C for assistance with format and layout. Also, as a kind of shorthand for marking your manuscript as you proofread it, make use of the standard proofreading marks shown in Figure 2.8. You're likely to see these marks again when you submit manuscripts to your editor at any professional organization you are writing for.

Here are some tips to help you proofread better:

- Proofread with a fresh set of eyes. Allow some time to pass between revising and proofreading the document, preferably at least one day.
- Read your document out loud.
- Read your document sentence by sentence, starting at the end.

| | | | |
|---|---|---|---|
| ℓ | Delete | (ital) | Set in italic type |
| ○ | Close up; delete space | (rom) | Set in roman type |
| ℓ | Delete and close up (use only when deleting letters within a word) | (bf) | Set in boldface type |
| (stet) | Let it stand | (lc) | Set in lowercase |
| # | Insert space | (caps) | Set in capital letters |
| (eq #) | Make space between words equal; make space between lines equal | (sc) | Set in small capitals |
| (hr #) | Insert hair space | (wf) | Wrong font; set in correct type |
| (ls) | Letterspace | ⨯ | Check type image; remove blemish |
| ¶ | Begin new paragraph | ∨ | Insert here or make superscript |
| □ | Indent type one em from right or left | ∧ | Insert here or make subscript |
| ] | Move right | ⌄ | Insert comma |
| [ | Move left | ς ⌄ | Insert apostrophe or single quotation mark |
| ][ | Center | | Insert quotation marks |
| ⌐ | Move up | ⊙ | Insert period |
| ⌣ | Move down | (set)? | Insert question mark |
| (fl) | Flush left | ;\| | Insert semicolon |
| (fr) | Flush right | ⌃ or :\| | Insert colon |
| = | Straighten type; align horizontally | = | Insert hyphen |
| ‖ | Align vertically | M | Insert em dash |
| (tr) | Transpose | N | Insert en dash |
| (sp) | Spell out | {\|⨏ or (\|) | Insert parentheses |

FIGURE 2.8. Proofreading marks. Adapted from the University of Chicago Press. (2003). *Chicago manual of style: The essential guide for writers, editors, and publishers.* (15th ed.). Chicago: University of Chicago Press.

- Have someone proofread with you. Print two copies of the document and have the second person follow along on one copy while you read aloud from the other. Spell every proper noun, number, or other difficult word out loud so it can be double-checked.

# COMMUNICATE ETHICALLY

Whether you are writing a fashion editorial, a term paper, a script for broadcast, or a memo to your supervisor, it is important to state the information in a truthful, honest, and fair manner. Relevant information should be presented to the reader even if it is a viewpoint different from your own. The fashion message should not be embellished or the facts exaggerated beyond what is necessary to create interest in the story. The writing should be presented clearly so that the reader can easily understand the message. All writing should be presented in a manner that respects the self-worth of the reader.

Because they are serious ethical lapses and potentially legal offenses, plagiarism and libel are the final topics of this chapter.

## PLAGIARISM

**Plagiarism** is the act of using—or passing off as one's own—an idea, the writing, or the creative thought of another (Swanson & Everett, 2007). Plagiarism may further be defined as using a source in a written document without citing the original reference correctly in an in-text parenthetical citation, footnote, or endnote. Writers can avoid plagiarism by following guidelines established in style guides such as the *Chicago Manual of Style*, *MLA Handbook*, or *Publication Manual of the American Psychological Association*. Appendix B offers a guide to some of the most common styles used in the fashion business.

In the previous paragraph, an in-text citation—Swanson & Everett, 2007—was used to show the reader that this material was originally found in another source. An **in-text citation** is a reference within the body of the document that briefly tells the reader where the information originally came from. The in-text citation corresponds to an entry on the reference list that gives complete information about the resource. The **reference list**, found at the end of the document, is an alphabetical listing of all resources used in a written document. The reference list includes all the information the reader needs in order to retrieve the original source. This includes the author's last name and initials, the name of the publication, the title of the article or book, the date the material was originally published, page numbers, and a URL if the reference is a Web site.

You can look up "Swanson, K. K., & Everett, J. C. (2007)" on the reference page at the end of this chapter and find the complete source citation. It is unethical to use information that you have obtained from another print, broadcast, or Web source without identifying the original author and providing the publication information. It can lead to the loss of your job and to the loss of your reputation as a writer. Potentially, it could lead to a copyright infringement lawsuit.

# LIBEL

**Libel** is false written or spoken statements that damage a person's reputation; subject the person to hatred, contempt, or ridicule; or injure the person's business or occupational pursuits (Brooks, Kennedy, Moen, & Ranly, 2005). Libel is a serious issue for reporters, who must be extremely careful about what they write. Any reporter who regularly reports about arrests or other serious crimes should have a working knowledge of libel law. Early in a story, reporters should state clearly what crime is involved, and should then provide enough information so the reader recognizes the crime that was identified. In trial coverage, good note-taking is a must. Anything that is said in open court is fair game (Brooks et al., 2005).

## SUMMARY

This chapter has concentrated on the six stages of the writing process: planning, shaping, drafting, revising, editing, and proofreading. *Planning* involves determining the purpose of a piece of writing with a purpose statement, analyzing the audience, and developing a tone for the fashion message. *Shaping* is developed through the use of an outline and mind-map. During the *drafting* stage, sentences and paragraphs are constructed. *Revising* includes "re-seeing" the fashion message. During the revising stage, the writer should decide which parts of the sentence to emphasize, avoid writing complicated messages, and avoid using biased language. *Editing* requires making corrections to the grammar, spelling, and punctuation, and designing the document effectively. *Proofreading* is the final and most important stage in the writing process.

All written messages should be written in an ethical manner that is honest, fair, and truthful. Plagiarism and libel are serious ethical offenses.

## KEY TERMS

Active voice

Audience

Bias-free

Central idea

Complex sentence

Compound sentence

Compound subject

Compound–complex sentence

Dependent clause

Direct pattern

Draft

Formal writing

Grammar

Independent clause

Indirect pattern

Informal writing

In-text citation

Libel

Mind-mapping

Outline

Parallelism

Passive voice

Phrase

Plagiarism

Proofreading

Punctuation

Purpose statement

Qualifier

Redundancy

Reference list

Run-on sentence

Sexist language

Simple sentence

Simple subject

Stylebook

Subject

Tone

Topic sentence

Verb

Verb phrase

Wordiness

## CASE STUDY

### Calvin ~~Kline~~ Klein

Professor Lopez teaches an introduction to fashion class at a four-year university. This is often the first course fashion students take, so Professor Lopez wants to make sure students understand the importance of writing in the fashion industry. Students are required to write a research paper with the goal of learning writing skills in the class so that they can apply these skills in later fashion classes.

At the beginning of each semester, the professor hands out a syllabus with a description of and a warning about the unethical practice known as plagiarism. *Plagiarism*, as it is defined in the university's student code of conduct, is any attempt to knowingly or deliberately misrepresent another's work as your own. Students are also educated about other types of misconduct, including the following:

- Cheating, or attempting to gain unfair advantage over other student
- Fabrication, or attempting to present information as true when the author knows it is false
- Fraud, or attempting to deceive the instructor or other administrators of the university
- Facilitating academic dishonesty, or attempting to assist an act of academic dishonesty by another individual

As well, students are educated about the consequences of plagiarism and other forms of academic misconduct. As a faculty member, Professor Lopez may decide to assign the student extra work, require the student to repeat the assignment, reduce the grade, award no credit for the assignment, or reduce the final grade in the course. In severe cases of misconduct, the student may be expelled from the class and even asked to leave the university.

Professor Lopez spends time in class throughout the semester describing ways to present sources—such as paraphrasing, citing sources in the text, formatting a reference page—and discussing other ways to present research materials. To help students avoid plagiarism, she regularly provides examples and answers students' questions about citing sources. Additionally, the APA style guide is required for the class, and students are directed to various writing guides and Web sites that illustrate the correct way to cite sources.

Researching and writing a report on a contemporary or historic fashion designer is a routine assignment in this class. Fashion designers are exciting to learn about and are covered widely in the fashion press, so students can easily locate information using books, periodicals, and Web sites. Being able to readily locate resources is a positive aspect of the assignment. The down side of this assignment is that biographic information about fashion designers does not change very dramatically from semester to semester, so many of the reports are similar to one another and similar to reports from prior semesters.

Therefore, tone and style are very important when Professor Lopez reads and evaluates these papers. Sentences that don't seem to fit with the previous section, words that are not common in a student's vocabulary, passages containing information that is not common knowledge, and sections that do not have a reference citation are all clues that some part of the research paper was plagiarized.

Upon reading a paper submitted by Barbara Franklin, Professor Lopez is sure she read a paper with very similar content during the previous semester. The professor keeps duplicate copies of research papers so she can compare projects from one semester to another. She finds the paper from the previous semester, recognizing the work originally submitted by Josie Tanaka who is currently enrolled in one of the professor's other courses. Upon comparison of both papers, it is evident to Professor Lopez that Barbara just retyped Josie's paper, changing a few words here and there, and submitted it as original work. There is evidence of the same misspelled word, *Kline* instead of *Klein*, used in several instances.

## CASE STUDY QUESTIONS

1.  What should Professor Lopez do?
2.  Should Barbara be penalized? If so, how?
3.  Should Josie be penalized? If so, how?
4.  Should Professor Lopez change the topic of the research paper? If so, to what?
5.  What steps should Professor Lopez take in the future to prevent this from happening again?
6.  Do you think students in general take seriously the unethical practice of plagiarism? Or is it so commonplace that they don't think about it?
7.  What should universities do to curb plagiarism?
8.  Is it up to the university or the students to stop plagiarism?
9.  Suggest additional actions to consider in the case of plagiarism or other unethical practices.

## INDUSTRIAL PROFILE

### *David Wolfe*

***What is your current job and title? Can you describe the main responsibilities for your job?***

Creative Director, The Doneger Group. Among my many responsibilities, I formulate an "overview" eighteen months ahead of the selling season, predicting incoming trends in fashion design, lifestyle movements, color, fabric, merchandising, and all aspects of pop culture. I produce several PowerPoint presentations each year and present them in the Doneger offices and various other venues around the world to audiences of retailers, manufacturers, students, and social groups. I also write a regular "blog" column for the Doneger Web site. As the fashion spokesperson for the company, I talk to reporters and appear on TV and radio.

***What is a typical day at work like?***

I am happy to say that I have no such thing as a "typical" day. I travel a great deal, domestically and to Europe. Those trips are for research (shopping, museums, theaters, people-watching) and also to make presentations. When in New York City, I do go to the office three days each week and spend most of that time editing photos and writing.

***At what point did you decide to pursue a career in writing for a fashion-related business?***

I began my career writing newspaper advertising copy for a small chain of department stores in Ohio, where I was born. I moved into fashion illustration when I moved to London late in the 1960s and remained in Europe until returning to New York early in the 1980s. During that period, I combined writing and illustrating when I joined the then-emerging Trend Forecasting sector. I also wrote extensively for fashion magazines and journals, both consumer and trade.

***Describe your first writing job. What was the most important or interesting thing you wrote for that job/publication?***

My first writing job was boring! As an entry-level advertising copywriter, it was my job to write the "Sale Listings" (e.g., Cashmere Cardigan, was $125, now $68.) More interesting writing came later when I wrote the forecasts for I.M. International and TFS The Fashion Service, the Doneger Design Direction. My initial entry into consumer fashion writing was reviewing the European collections for a newspaper, *The Palm Beach Post* (Florida). I also have been a major editor/contributor for more than twenty years to two Asian high fashion glossy publications: *Couture* and *MenMode*.

**What are you currently reading (books, magazines, Web sites, newspapers, other media)? Do you have a favorite author or publication?**

I am constantly reading, both for my job and for recreation. I read *WWD* religiously, also *Vogue*, *Harper's Bazaar*, *Vanity Fair*, *More*, *Details*, and many other magazines. I read the *New York Times* and *Wall Street Journal* online. My favorite authors (for recreational rereading) are Jane Austen, Mark Helprin, Thomas Hardy, and Armistead Maupin.

**What advice do you have for students interested in a writing career? Do you have any recommendations for students?**

Read! Read! Read! Fiction as well as nonfiction. It is vital to have an in-depth background in fashion history and the personalities in the industry. Learn grammar and don't rely on spell-check (fashion terms are notoriously absent from spell-check).

## REFERENCES

American Psychological Association. (2005). *Concise rules of APA style*. Washington, DC: Author.

Brooks, B. S., Kennedy, G., Moen, D. R., & Ranly, D. (2005). *News reporting and writing* (8th ed.). Boston: Bedford/St. Martin's.

Brunel, C. (2002). *The T-shirt book*. New York: Assouline Publishing.

Clark, J. L., & Clark, L. R. (2004). *HOW 10: A handbook for office professionals* (10th ed.). Mason, OH: South-Western.

Eakins, P. (2005). *Writing for interior design*. New York: Fairchild Books.

Guffey, M. E. (2007). *Essentials of business communication* (7th ed.). Mason, OH: South-Western.

James, S. (2007, March/April). Mountain rescue. *Men's Vogue*, 150, 152.

Kirszner, L. G., & Mandell, S. R. (2005). *The Wadsworth handbook* [Instructor's Edition]. Boston: Thomson Wadsworth.

Lehman, C. M., & Dufrene, D. D. (2005). *Business communication* (14th ed.). Mason, OH: South-Western.

Pfeiffer, W. S. (2004). *Pocket guide to technical writing* (3rd ed.). Upper Saddle River, NJ: Pearson Prentice Hall.

Strunk, W., Jr., & White, E. B. (2000). *The elements of style* (4th ed.). Needham Heights, MA: Longman.

Swanson, K. K., & Everett, J. C. ( 2007). *Promotion in the merchandising environment* (2nd ed.). New York: Fairchild Books.

Truss, L. (2004). *Eats, shoots & leaves*. New York: Gotham Books.

Woolever, K. R. (1999). *Writing for the technical professions*. New York: Addison Wesley Longman.

# Part Two

# FASHION JOURNALISM

Many introduction to fashion books consider fashion journalism, which supports and enhances all levels of the fashion industry, to be an auxiliary service to the fashion industry. But for people involved in fashion journalism, providing information about the fashion industry—about new products, classic designers, fashion trends, and business analyses—to consumer and trade audiences is their primary responsibility.

Newspapers have been reporting fashion stories since the 19th century. Writers and editors work to bring the latest news via the daily, weekly, monthly, or less frequently published newspapers. Chapter 3, "Writing for Newspapers," covers the role of newspapers for a fashionable society.

In the United States, fashion magazines came into existence over 150 years ago with *Godey's Lady's Book,* edited by Sara Joseph Hale. This magazine helped women of the 19th century win acceptance in the world of work, in addition to presenting the latest styles of fashion to an eager audience. *Godey's Lady's Book,* which is no longer published, set the stage for the leaders of the fashion field today, including such magazines as *Vogue, Harper's Bazaar, Elle,* and *W.* Consumer magazines are directed toward end users and consist of fashion, general interest, men's, shelter, and business titles. Trade magazines focus on information for industry insiders; these magazines publish articles pertaining to the business world. Chapter 4, "Writing for Magazines," looks at the magazine industry and the writing opportunities in this field.

Broadcast media came into U.S. culture during the 20th century. Radio and, later, broadcast television and cable television became the primary resources for almost instantaneous news, information, and entertainment. Products and fashion news are regular features on broadcast news and entertainment programming. Although radio does not have the visual impact found on television or cable channels, it is still a place for updated information. Television influences what we wear, as we imitate and emulate the announcers, actors, and celebrities we see. Additionally, such special events as New York Fashion Week and Target's Fall Fashion Show, with acrobats climbing down the "vertical runway" in front of Rockefeller Plaza, are considered newsworthy broadcast stories. Chapter 5, "Writing for Broadcast Media," introduces us to the role of broadcast media in disseminating fashion information. Fashion journalism and communication is an excellent place to put your writing skills to work.

# THREE

## *Writing for Newspapers*

After you have read this chapter, you should be able to discuss the following:

• The role of newspapers and fashion journalism

• How to write a fashion story for a newspaper

• How the newspaper industry is changing

Fashion stories have been a regular feature in most newspapers for a very long time. A fashion article appeared on page 1 of the first issue of the *New York Times* on September 18, 1851, reporting on women who had worn Amelia Bloomer's controversial bifurcated garments at various New York locations during the previous day (Byrnes, 1951). Figure 3.1 is an artist's rendering of the "bloomer suit" that caused such a stir.

Many newspapers followed the original format of the *New York Times*, which placed most fashion news adjacent to the society pages. Newspaper articles generally follow two formats: news stories and feature articles. Historically, fashion feature stories in newspapers provided a service to female readers; they also stimulated interest in fashion, assisting local merchants in selling new products.

This chapter looks at the various types of newspapers, their characteristics, and the people who work for them. After introducing the categories of newspapers and explaining how newspapers are produced, we will look at how to write various types of stories—from starting the research to writing the news story or

FIGURE 3.1. Artist's rendering of the
"bloomer suit."

feature article. The piece of writing is not complete until the content is focused
and polished. This chapter ends with a discussion of the trends influencing newspapers today.

## NEWS AND THE ROLE OF FASHION JOURNALISM

Events, from the mundane to the exotic, are reported in newspapers. **Newspapers** are
publications whose main function is to report the news, as well as provide special
information to their readers. Newspaper content also includes such information as

weather reports, television schedules, stock reports, and commentary on politics, economics, arts, culture, and entertainment. Most newspapers are issued daily or weekly on **newsprint**, which is a grainy, lightweight paper. From local concerns to international issues, information provided by "the press" is about what's going on in the neighborhood or across the planet.

Newspapers trace their roots to the handwritten news sheets posted in the public marketplaces of ancient Rome and to the first printed newspapers that appeared in China during the Tang Dynasty during AD 618–907 ("Newspaper," 2005). The first newspaper published in the American colonies was *Public Occurrences Both Foreign and Domestick* in Boston in 1690 ("Newspaper"). What we know of as newspapers today—with editorial commentary, news reports, and social information supported through selling advertising space—emerged in Great Britain in the mid-18th century.

According to Cathy Horyn, fashion critic for the *New York Times,* most newspapers did not encourage specialization when she started her career in the 1980s. "It never occurred to me that you needed sartorial ambition to be a fashion writer, any more than you needed a background in crops and land prices to write about farming" (Horyn, 2005, p. G1). The nature of the newspaper business at that time was to avoid specialized niches. Anything could happen at a newspaper. In 1969, the *New York Times* sent Gloria Emerson, the reporter assigned to cover the haute couture collections in Paris, to cover the Vietnam War—at Emerson's request (Horyn 2005). Sports reporters nearly always covered sports, while most reporters covered news or features, fashion-related or not.

## NEWSPAPER FORMATS

Newspapers in the United States are generally available in one of two sizes: broadsheet or tabloid. The **broadsheet** format measures 13 inches by 21.5 inches, while the **tabloid** layout measures 10 inches by 14.5 inches. The term *tabloid* also refers to a type of newspaper that carries stories about celebrities, crimes, and scandals, with sensational or exaggerated headlines. However, any newspaper can be printed on tabloid-size pages. Broadsheets are associated with more traditional journalistic standards and may be perceived as more reliable resources than tabloids. Figures 3.2a and 3.2b illustrate a broadsheet format compared to a tabloid format.

# SPRING 2008 FASHION WEEK

### OSCAR DE LA RENTA | CAROLINA HERRERA

# Feathers, Tie-Dyes, Bows, and Sashes

**By PIA CATTON**

Victoria Beckham was there, and caused a stir. Roger Federer walked in, and the crowd broke into applause. The Polyphonic Spree played live on a stage above the runway. Yet even with all the distractions, Oscar de la Renta's spring collection was the star, and it commanded attention easily.

The looks were a mix of the requisite — short-sleeve suits, pretty day dresses, and the latest rendition of the designer's signature poofy cocktail dress — and the fashion forward.

Mr. de la Renta has been incorporating ikat and ethnic prints into his collections, but this spring, they seemed to increase in quantity and strength. Bold prints that looked inspired by Africa were shown in deep reds and browns, others that suggested Grecian motifs appeared in olive green. So when a beautiful tie-dyed cardigan in a cashmere-

silk blend showed up on the runway, it seemed perfectly in keeping with the global mood. Manipulated fabrics — a white lacquered knit sweater or a textured copper silk sweater — also made a strong showing.

As for evening, the collection proved once again that this house is tough to beat. The show's final look was by far its most exciting: a black-and-white gown with overlapping petals and a long black feather extending from the waist to the shoulder. It's the kind of dress that might restrict some activities — dancing, sitting — but who needs that? It's a dress from an era of high glamour. Other evening looks incorporated color vividly, especially a ballroom gown with a yellow bodice and a brown silk faille skirt.

At Carolina Herrera, the mood was equally colorful, which lent a merry, optimistic air to the collection. The first look down the runway was a white top embroidered with a giant blue cornflow-

er and black shorts. Who wouldn't be happy wearing that?

Several dresses and gowns contrasted florals with linear designs. Sometimes the lines were more prominent, as with a peachy gown decorated with vertical lines and topped with a red and black flowing ribbon; other times, the flowers won out, as with a white gown decorated at the chest with a bold flower and vertical stripe of color below. Either way, the mood was ebullient.

Bows and sashes were in no short order; their contrasting colors and angular shapes offered up just the right feminine dash. Pleats and embroidery, such as opaque stones on a white column gown, emphasized luxurious attention to detail. What's striking about Carolina Herrera is the consistency of the creativity that shows up on the runway. Ms. Herrera may be known for her white shirts, but the colorful prints in her collections are reliably pleasing to the eye.

*OSCAR DE LA RENTA*

### NANETTE LEPORE

## Picasso-Inspired Daywear

Nanette Lepore sent out a spring collection of figure-flattering fluttery dresses, wide-leg trousers, and tailored skirts, among other unmistakably feminine pieces. The women of Pablo Picasso's paintings provided the inspiration for the designer, whose palette this season included artistic prints in bold colors such as fuchsia, coral, and curry. A number of standout looks included a pale yellow mixed with a muted purple-gray hue. In one such ensemble, a warm gray blouse with lemon beading and embroidery was worn with belted, sand-color shorts; in another, a lustrous slate dress was cinched with a yellow-and-black snakeskin belt. Tangerine and beige worked well together in a plunging-neckline dress that mixed stripes and flowers, and trailed past the knee. That color combination was also featured in a wrap-style blouse, which was shown with a bow-adorned pencil skirt. Two shoe lines by Ms. Lepore — sling-backs and sandals for her eponymous footwear collection, and colorful, casual pairs she designs for Keds — complimented the whimsical looks of the runway presentation.

*Martha Mercer*

Carolina Herrera      Oscar de la Renta

---

### LUCA LUCA | MILLY | KATE SPADE | JACK SPADE

# Spring Bouquets Grace the Runway

A fresh bouquet of pastel hues played up the ladylike chiffon dresses, and crochet and wool gauze shorts at Luca Luca. Silk jackets featured unexpected, but not incongruous, accents in the form of petal-shaped panels where lapels would have been. Designer Luca Orlandi worked with the most delicate of fabrics, from silk shantung to silk organza and linen gauze, without sacrificing the sharp finish of good construction. Working primarily with spring ready hues, from seafoam to silvery mauve and pale blush, Mr. Orlandi drew inspiration from modern stained glass as well, according to his show notes. Among the most memorable looks in the collection was an embroidered silk minidress in ivory that turned down at the bodice, not unlike a gracefully wilted flower. A pink crinkled dress of rayon and silk featured eye-catching feather details that moved as they caught a breeze.

*Rebecca Thomas*

With an abundance of cable knit cardigans in navy and Kelly green combinations, and sleek pencil skirts in nautical or hibiscus prints, the spring 2008 collection at Milly was undeniably American and inspired by the classics. But the girlish Connecticut-born designer, Michelle Smith, is also a devoted Francophile who showed her eye for Riviera chic by adding sexy wrist-length driving gloves and black silk turbans to those lush looks. From a runway entrance framed by a teardrop archway, model Gome be spectacled, suggesting a

bookish it-girl getting her first taste of spring fashion) emerged in leafy, print-heavy ensembles fit for Palm Beach. Belted sheath dresses and sweaters with sailor stitches struck just the right chord beneath satin day coats. The collection didn't lack sultry looks either. A revealing maillot and a succession of bikini bottoms in navy and white were paired with gold accents and sweaters tied loosely at the neck.

*R.T.*

Kate Spade's women's collection and Jack Spade's men's line unveiled their spring bags and accessories yesterday while lifeguards served up bite-size hors d'oeuvres in a beach-like setting at a gallery in Chelsea. Neon and patent leather were prominent at Kate Spade, as was wicker in what appeared to be a Hamptons-meets-Studio 54-themed collection. A square wicker purse with a neon yellow handle was placed by ballerina flats made of cork with wood soles, which were lined in neon pink patent leather with a bow at the toes. Sandals with a seahorse design seemed more suited for the beach than a walk in the city. Animal prints and skins popped up sporadically, as did some more conventional boxy Kate Spade bags. The Jack Spade collection was more toned down and girly. Heavy leather briefcases, lined ties in colors such as crimson and gold, and large canvas overnight bags were perfect for transitioning from work to weekend.

*Laura Silsbery*

Milly      Luca Luca

**FIGURE 3.2a.** Broadsheet newspaper format.

FIGURE 3.2b. Tabloid newspaper format.

## NEWSPAPER CATEGORIES

Newspapers are categorized by how frequently they publish. They are published at intervals of once daily, to once a week, to once a month, to quarterly (four times each year), to even less frequently.

### *Daily Newspapers*

**Daily newspapers** print at least one edition each day. Morning editions feature news from the previous day. Evening editions, which have declined dramatically during the past 10 years, contain information about events occurring earlier in the day of publication. Most daily newspapers publish a bigger weekend edition, commonly on Sundays in the United States. A wide range of local news, sports, business, and arts and entertainment stories account for approximately one third of the pages in a daily newspaper. The other two thirds of the paper contain commercial advertising.

The largest daily newspaper in the United States is *USA Today*, with a national circulation of 2.3 million copies ("Newspaper," 2005). Other large-circulation daily newspapers include the *New York Times* and the *Los Angeles Times*. Many large daily newspapers publish regional editions, which feature information for varied geographic regions. For example, the *Wall Street Journal* publishes five different editions: three national U.S. regional editions, in addition to its European and Asian editions. These large daily newspapers are considered national newspapers, even though they target various regions. Stories printed in these resources are of general interest throughout the United States or the locations served by the international editions.

Some large regional newspapers focus on issues related to a particular state or region. For example, the *Arizona Republic* is considered to be more of a regional newspaper than other newspapers in the state, publishing news from all of Arizona. The *Arizona Daily Sun*, the *Tucson Daily Star*, and the *East Valley Tribune* are other Arizona daily newspapers that focus mainly on local and community features, but they do contain other matters relevant to the state, region, or nation.

## Weekly Newspapers

**Weekly newspapers** publish once a week with news of interest to people in smaller geographic regions, such as a small city, a town, or a neighborhood. Weekly newspapers spotlight local happenings; high school sports; traffic accidents; and local social, political, and governmental issues. Rarely do weekly newspapers feature national or international news, instead presenting more in-depth coverage of local and community activities. The *New Times*, a weekly newspaper in the tabloid format, is distributed for free in the Phoenix, Arizona area and nearby locations.

## Special Interest Newspapers

**Special interest newspapers** are targeted to particular audiences, such as ethnic communities, large universities, unions and trade organizations, and arts groups. Ethnic publications look at local, national, and international news, and examine it in terms of the impact on a particular ethnic population. Large universities often have daily or weekly newspapers, covering campus events and local news that influence the university environment. Publications for unions and trade organizations have a close relationship with the fashion industry. We'll discuss this category just a little later. Arts weeklies are devoted to theatrical, music, and fashion events, and provide critiques of current exhibits, music, books, or fashion shows; they also publish schedules of upcoming arts events in the community.

Some examples follow: *El Independiente* is a special interest paper directed toward Mexican Americans and Native Americans in south Tucson, Arizona. The three major educational institutions in Arizona have student newspapers. At the University of Arizona in Tucson, the paper called the *Daily Wildcat* is published five days a week; Arizona State University has the *State Press*, which also is published five days a week; the *Lumberjack* is published once a week at Northern Arizona University. The *New Times* is a weekly publication that covers music, entertainment, and restaurant reviews, as well as the regional art scene.

## *Trade Newspapers*

**Trade newspapers** provide information to specific businesses, industries, or occupations—but in newspaper format. Some trade newspapers are so important to the industry that they are published five days each week. For example, *Women's Wear Daily* is published Monday through Friday, and *Daily News Record* is published three times a week. The stories take on more immediacy than would be found in a consumer or trade magazine. During market weeks, daily reports and critiques of fashion shows are presented as quickly after a show as possible, usually the next day. New York Fashion Week is so significant that *Women's Wear Daily* publishes a Saturday edition tha 'week. See Figure 3.3. We will discuss trade magazines in Chapter 4.

Timely stories, such as the subway and bus bombings in London that took place in July 2005, are reported in trade newspapers. *Women's Wear Daily* gave an account of the event itself, in addition to stories about how the attacks impacted retailers, designers, the economy, and tourists traveling in London that week. The stories were directed toward the target audience of *Women's Wear Daily* readers, who were interested in the influence that the attacks may have on the fashion industry in general, as well as toward visitors, since many of its readers travel to London on a regular basis.

Women's Wear Daily • The Retailers' Daily Newspaper • February 3, 2007 • $2.00

# WWDWEEKEND

What's on Your iPod?/8
Designer Cheat Sheet/24
Retailers: Go for Glam/26

## Don't Worry, Be Happy

It's buuuuaack, New York Fashion Week is upon us, and while some may associate the event with blood, sweat and tears, others plow through the collections with nothing less than a smile. Take, for instance, Michael Kors, who couldn't be more thrilled as he unpacks a fresh shipment of his fall '07 handbags. For more behind-the-scenes looks, see pages 16 to 22.

**FIGURE 3.3.** Cover of *Women's Wear Daily* Saturday edition during New York Fashion Week.

## *Supermarket Tabloids*

**Supermarket tabloids** are national weekly publications, printed on newsprint in the dimensions of a tabloid newspaper. These publications specialize in celebrity news, celebrity fashion, gossip, astrology, and peculiar stories about ordinary people. The distribution procedure for supermarket tabloids is more like magazine and mass-market distribution than like typical newspaper delivery processes, which are described later in this chapter. Supermarket tabloids have been given that name due to the location where these publications are sold, alongside the checkout lines of supermarkets. Due to the often exaggerated nature of the stories in supermarket tabloids, critics do not consider these papers to be serious journalism.

## NEWSPAPER PRODUCTION

Most newspapers are produced in a standardized manner. First, news editors dispense assignments about newsworthy events to reporters. Each reporter does background research, gathers information, conducts interviews, and drafts the story on his or her computer. Then, a copy editor edits the reporter's story and writes a headline. The story is returned to the news editor, who reviews the story and headline before approving the story for inclusion in the paper. In the meantime, photographers are often assigned to shoot pictures to go along with the story; and graphic artists may be asked to create charts or diagrams that will accompany and help clarify the text.

**Fashion journalists** use their training in news-gathering and reporting to write about fashion trends, fashion shows, and fashion collections, and to cover newsmakers in the field. While large newspapers like the *Washington Post* and the *New York Times* have several reporters covering the industry, smaller newspapers might have only one fashion writer on the entire newspaper staff, or none at all.

Members of the advertising staff sell space in the newspaper to advertisers in order to generate revenue for operational costs. Artists lay out the pages on which space has been blocked out for advertising, articles, photographs, and illustrations. The finished computer-generated layouts are sent to the newspaper's printing facilities, where technicians convert the electronic files into actual newspapers. Individuals in the circulation department make sure the newspapers arrive on doorsteps, on newsstands, and in newspaper-dispensing machines as quickly as possible.

The three brief paragraphs in this "Newspaper Production" section should carry with them the message that the editorial decisions and the pace of operation that are required in order to produce daily or even weekly papers are accomplished under critical as well as stressful deadlines.

# WRITING TO BE READ

Writing a good story for a newspaper begins with finding an appropriate idea. Often, journalists bounce ideas off each other in brainstorming sessions. A news release for a new book or an event being held for a new store opening might trigger compelling ideas for newspaper stories.

Understanding the audience that reads your particular newspaper is also helpful in writing to be read. Talking with readers of the newspaper you work for can provide you with a number of ideas for articles. Say, for example, that you're interviewing someone who is an authority or expert for a current story. That interview, or the small talk before or after the interview, could generate another story idea. Another way to cultivate article ideas is to set aside 20 to 30 minutes each day to telephone readers of your newspaper. Call five people each day and ask questions about their interests and concerns.

Ask yourself what you are interested in. Have you purchased a new sofa, or visited a new retailer? There could be a story about shopping for a sofa. What are the color, style, or image trends? Where can a consumer find the best prices or the highest quality? There might be an article about a new business opening in the area. Who is the owner? What products are being sold? Are there any other new shops in that area, showing a business trend?

## TYPES OF STORIES

Newspapers present two types of articles: news and feature stories. **News stories** involve the day-to-day events and activities of people in the target audience. Reporters cover speeches, attend news conferences and meetings, and write other basic stories of interest to their readers. Robin Givhan, the fashion editor for the *Washington Post*, covers news stories related to the fashion industry. One day, she might cover the gala opening of the Chanel exhibit at the Metropolitan Museum of Art in New York, and the next day she might report on an event at the Hermès boutique at Tysons Corner.

News stories may be generated from a wide variety of sources. The reporter might do any of the following: cover a speech or keynote address at a trade show, attend a news conference where the results of sales are scheduled to be announced or where new executive personnel or products will be introduced, be present at meetings or special events to report who was there and what they were wearing, and participate in everyday activities that lead to other basic news stories. News stories are timely and generally are written quickly for immediate publication.

**Feature stories** are journalistic articles that are original and descriptive. Some feature stories have entertainment as a focus; other features have the primary purpose of providing information. While news articles usually are written in an inverted pyramid style, which will be described later in this chapter, feature stories generally are more fluid and resemble short stories. They have distinct beginnings, middles, and ends, and they must be read in their entirety to make sense. Very often, feature stories are human interest-oriented rather than being directed toward newsworthy happenings. Feature stories are written in a descriptive manner, with more creativity, and they are written in a style that evokes more imagery. For example, the feature writer might describe an individual's appearance in an imaginative manner, which might be edited out of a news story. The feature can be written about almost any topic, but typically it is written about an unusual person, place, or activity. A feature story written for the *Washington Post* could be an in-depth article about the inspiration for the latest Zac Posen fashion collection.

## REPORTING TOOLS

Whether the article is a news report or a feature story, the generally accepted practices of journalism are followed. The story must be written with accuracy. The writer must verify the facts, quote accurately, and be fair and precise with descriptions. The writer must also follow the style that the newspaper expects its writers to follow. In relation to writing, *style* refers to a uniform approach to punctuation, abbreviation, capitalization, spelling, and the use of titles. Today, most U.S. newspapers follow the style established by the Associated Press (AP), the major wire service. The AP publishes a stylebook, *The Associated Press Stylebook and Briefing on Media Law*.

Once the general topic is decided, the writer starts to do research and background development. The writer might start by observing and interviewing people who know something about the topic. For her story about the Chanel exhibit, Robin Givhan offered the following observation:

> One morning earlier this week, a particular Manhattan archetype climbed aboard a crosstown bus that was headed toward the Metropolitan Museum of Art. She was a discreet blonde dressed in a short black overcoat, crisp khaki trousers and a pair of taupe and black ballet flats. From some distance away, it was possible to make out the embossed interlocking C's on the cap of her shoes. She was a Chanel lady. One quickly assumed that her crocodile handbag was real. Could she be a fan heading to a sneak peak at the Met's Chanel exhibition? (2005, ¶ 1)

Opening a story with an observation, such as this one, allows the author to capture the reader's attention, emphasizing some of the iconic images associated with the House of Chanel.

---

*Portfolio Exercise:* **Write a description of a friend. Show it to the friend. Does she recognize herself? Next, describe a building or some other location on a street. Have a friend read the description. Can he figure out where the place is located? Is there anything you have overlooked? How sharp is your vision?**

---

## Interviewing

Another way to start your research is through the interview process. Interviews offer the best chance to pick up quotes, enlightening anecdotes, and bits of humanity that will help you bring the story to life. While facts and figures can come from a variety of resources, humanity is best transmitted from person to person. We'll discuss other types of journalistic research methods and provide additional information about interviewing in Chapter 4.

In order to get the most from interviewees, you must prepare before the interview. Here is where some homework comes in handy. Finding out some facts about the person or event will help you to know what to ask. Be sure to put together a list of possible questions before the interview.

During the first few minutes of the interview, you set the tone and establish a relationship with the subject. If you gain the individual's confidence, demonstrate your knowledge, and prepare for questions to come, your chance for a successful interview increases.

Once you've established a rapport with the person you're interviewing, you need to listen to what that person has to say. Even though you have a set of questions prepared in advance, you can learn much more from the "expert" you are interviewing. The interviewee knows more about the subject than you do. That is why you wanted the interview in the first place. You do not have to stick to your predetermined list of questions; the interviewee may have answers you did not prepare for.

How can you remember what went on during the conversation? Few of us are able to rely on memorization. You should keep a notebook and practice taking notes. Concentrate on key facts and phrases—you will not be able to write down everything. As soon as possible, write down as much as you can remember, including anecdotes, names, addresses, titles, numbers, and descriptions of the subject and the scene. When you have permission to use one, a tape recorder can take down exactly what the interviewee has told you.

As the interview comes to an end, take a few minutes to go over any tricky spellings, technical information, or any numbers. Reconfirm your understanding of key points. The interview should give you a variety of comments that can be quoted directly as dialogue. And, of course, information you obtain from interviews can lead you to other resources.

---

*Portfolio Exercise:* **Conduct an interview. Ask your mother, aunt, or grandmother what kinds of clothing she wore in high school or college. Were they purchased at a particular store or were they homemade? How did she feel about the style of the clothes or the store where they were purchased? Develop a few questions of your own. Write your version of her description. Check your accuracy by showing your writing to your subject. Did you get it right? Rewrite the story until you do.**

---

## Gathering Information by Traditional Methods

To support the information you gained by interviewing, you might enhance the story by looking into an array of public and private records. The data kept by various government agencies, businesses, and nonprofit organizations can offer facts not known to your interview subjects, or can back up what interviewees have already told you.

The resources that can provide background information on an individual are vast. You can start by checking the newspaper library. To get even more data, check educational records, organization membership files, family statistics (such as births, deaths, marriages, divorces, name changes, adoptions), property records, criminal records, and so forth. Most of the facts in the areas we just listed may be found in government offices, and often they are available online.

## Using Computers for Research

Although originally they were essentially glorified typewriters, computers have become very useful tools for research. The widespread availability of Internet search engines such as Google and Yahoo! is making the computer the tool of choice for gathering information. Most major newspapers, television networks, and databases provide online access to research information. Some companies require you to subscribe and pay a fee to search current issues; others provide current issues for free via a simple registration process. Most Web sites that maintain an archive of their articles charge a fee for usage.

---

*Portfolio Exercise:* **Use one or more computer databases to do the background research for a profile of a fashion or furniture designer. Make a list of questions for potential interviewees. Use the background information you found to write the profile of the person, and quote your interview subject from the online information you found.**

---

## Telling the Story with Accuracy

While it is important to get the facts, correct spelling of names, verifiable numbers, and accurate quotes, it is also necessary to get the context of the story right. You are responsible for conveying the background, the atmosphere, and the tone in the right way.

Every journalist knows that ethical behavior does not allow you to make up stuff. The classic example is the case of a *Washington Post* writer, Janet Cooke. Ms. Cooke was assigned to write about drug use in the public schools and how it ruins lives. Unable to find an actual victim, Ms. Cooke *created* a victim who she called *Jimmy*. But she wrote the story as if Jimmy was a real child. Her compelling story won a Pulitzer Prize, journalism's highest award. After the award was given, her editors learned that she had fashioned Jimmy from her imagination. The prize was returned, Ms. Cooke was fired, and journalists everywhere were reminded that acceptable behavior had been violated. What would have been acceptable in fiction was not allowed in journalism.

### Box 3.1 Examining Numbers and Statistical Data

Using numbers and statistical information in a story adds clarity and helps explain relevant issues. But most reporters say that to do their job successfully, they did not need to have been an expert in math class. Almost every story about business and government requires some type of statistic, but most stories are about people, not mathematical calculations.

One of the most important considerations a writer can give the audience is to show the relationship between the numbers in the news by spelling out what the related figures actually mean. Some examples: If a Donna Karan blouse costs $1,695, how does that compare to the price of a couture or mass-market blouse? Annual retail sales of $500,000 might be a huge amount for a boutique in a small town, whereas it might be just the monthly sales for a large store in Chicago or Atlanta.

Percentages and percent change, the basic building blocks used to explain proportion, are also useful numbers for describing the success of a designer or retailer. Percent changes are useful numbers to help people understand changes in a value over time. Calculating a percent change uses a simple formula. Subtract the old value from the new value, and then divide by the old value. Multiply the result by 100 and slap a % sign on it. That's your percent change:

$$\text{Percent change} = [(\text{New value} - \text{Old value}) \,/\, \text{Old value}] * 100$$

A story that reports sales of $1.2 million means little without a comparison to another benchmark. It would be more understandable to the reader if you report that "retail sales of $1.2 million are 3.6% higher than last year at the same time."

Another useful numbers tool in reporting is the average (also called the arithmetic mean), which can be used to describe a general trend. For example, you might report that "accessory retailers have average hourly sales of $80 per hour, which is 20% below the industry average for apparel retailers of $100 per hour."

$$\text{average} = \text{sum of each example} \,/\, \text{number of examples}$$

Other statistical data that can be used in an article include interest rates, inflation, taxes, budgets, revenues, and expenses. Charts, tables, and diagrams are great visual aids for helping make the numbers make sense.

**CHECKLIST TO HELP YOU ENSURE ACCURACY**

☐   Identify your sources. Include names, and state why these people are appropriate as *authorities.*

☐   Admit ignorance or uncertainty. If you do not know something, admit it. If you speculate or create a scenario, let your readers know that that is what you are doing. Do not be afraid to admit your ignorance to a source. It is better to feel stupid in front of one person than in front of 100,000 readers.

☐   Quote only what you personally have heard. Secondhand information is not reliable, so do not quote what you have not heard.

☐   Reconstruct cautiously. When reconstructing a meeting or a conversation as a narrative, be sure that it represents what occurred, not something you wish had occurred.

☐   Check multiple sources. This will give you a wide range of viewpoints and will help you confirm that the information is consistent.

# STORYTELLING

After the research is completed, the next step is to structure the story. Most journalists learned to use the inverted pyramid format when they first started writing. Although many editors and publishers attempt to put the inverted pyramid to rest, it is still widely used in newspaper articles.

## *The Inverted Pyramid*

The **inverted pyramid** puts the most important information first, arranges the paragraphs in descending order of importance, and requires the writer to rank the importance of information. The first use of the inverted pyramid story structure has been attributed to correspondents using the telegraph during the American Civil War. Newspaper editors supposedly required their reporters to put the most important information first, in case the transmission of information was interrupted. Both space and time were limited. Figure 3.4 shows the inverted pyramid format.

The inverted pyramid format allows the reader to understand the tone and content of the article right away. The format usually begins with a summary lead, which

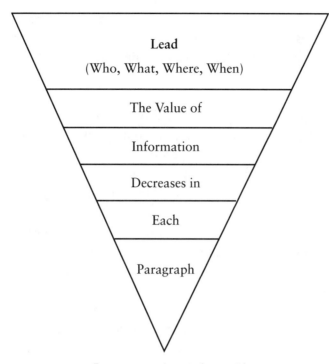

FIGURE 3.4. Inverted pyramid.

tells the reader what to expect in the news story. The reader can assess whether to continue reading. And as in the American Civil War, it still allows editors to shorten a story from the bottom up, because the least important information is at the end of the story.

The story starts with the **lead,** a simple, clear statement in the first paragraph or two of the story. The summary lead contains information broken into four categories: Who, What, Where, and When. Many journalists today add How and Why to the lead. Writers determine the priority and begin with the most important information. Here is an example from the *New York Times*:

---

*Lead example:* **The fragrances are to be displayed behind glass, as if, like their creator's coveted rings and bracelets, they were made of the same diamonds and pavé sapphires. For customers who want a closer look sales clerks will carefully remove each one from the case and present it in a chamois cloth. But they will decline to reveal its name. That might unduly influence the buyer.**

> **This is just one indication of how precious Bergdorf Goodman would like its customers to consider the fragrances in its new JAR boutique, which is to open in its below-street-level beauty department this month (Wilson, 2005, p. E4).**

In the first paragraph, the writer Eric Wilson hinted or teased the reader that the product was something extremely special, a luxury item. This hook led the reader into the second paragraph, where more information was offered. When you are trying to create the lead of the story, looking through your research notes for the Who, What, Where, When, How, and Why will help you focus on getting the important information into the lead.

The next paragraphs provide more information in decreasing importance. If the story is six paragraphs long, the newspaper editor may use all six paragraphs or may cut from the end of the story. A story written in inverted pyramid style does not have an actual ending. It just stops.

The lead of any story, inverted pyramid or not, is important because it creates interest for the reader. The lead is especially important for the writer of the inverted pyramid story because of the need to be brief and still be interesting. Writers using other methods of storytelling have more opportunity to create interest and set the hook for the reader.

## Modify the Inverted Pyramid

The most recognized alternatives to the pyramid structure include Anecdotal, Chronological Order, Foreshadowing, Flashbacks, and Narration and Exposition. These alternatives are part of the **focus structure**, which allows writers to add humanity and creativity to a story while still providing information. We'll explore these methods briefly here. What other methods have you seen?

*Anecdotal* The **Anecdotal** structure allows the writer to concentrate on an individual or a group that represents a bigger population. This tactic allows the writer to make complex issues, large institutions, or complicated numbers meaningful to the reader. Let's say that after doing your research and interviewing, you have found an individual through whom you can tell your story. You can open with an anecdote or a scene that says, "I've got an interesting story to tell." (When using this method, keep in mind that while fiction writers use this technique to create imagined situations, nonfiction writers use it to recreate real circumstances.) Here is an example of an Anecdotal opening, using an individual to introduce the reader to a story about men's wear sizing and fitting problems.

---

*Anecdotal opening example:* **LOS ANGELES—Back in high school in Spring Valley, N.Y., Joe Carbone barely knew the word defeat. As captain of the football team, star of the wrestling team, a power lifter who competed on a national level and an athlete with the kind of physique that tends to be featured on magazines with cover lines like "Perfect Abs in 7 Days," Mr. Carbone was a textbook specimen of American manhood.**

**He even had a tryout with the New York Giants before deciding to take up a career as a strength coach for professional athletes, people like Kobe Bryant, who was Mr. Carbone's exclusive client for nearly a decade, and then as a general strength coach for the Los Angeles Lakers.**

**But there has always been one area of Mr. Carbone's life where failure is a given, and that is at the suit rack of a department store (Trebay, 2005, p. E1).**

---

Next is the transition to the **nut** paragraph (also known as the **nut graph**), which is where you let your reader know what the story is about and why they should read it. Without the transition, many readers will be unable to make the connection between the example used to open the story and the story's theme. A simple way to make the transition would be to say, "This person (or situation, or anecdote) represents many such. . . ." The transition makes the connection explicit. The next two paragraphs in the story about Mr. Carbone give us the transition into the reason for the article.

---

*Nut graph example:* **"Look, I know I'm shorter than most people," said Mr. Carbone, who stands a hair over 5 feet 3 inches in stocking feet. "I've never really had a problem with it, but you just have to accept that you can't buy clothes."**

**You have to accept that in a super-size universe, even the smallest of regular garments tends to be scaled wrong for Joe Carbone and also for the legions of other men under 5-foot-8, a stature that denotes the point below which the term off-the-rack becomes a joke (Trebay, 2005, p. E1).**

---

The nut graph serves the same role as the lead in an inverted pyramid story. It is not the opening paragraph of the focus structure, but it contains the Who, What, Where, When, How, and Why. The nut graph leads to the narrative, which is the body of the story. Here is the nut graph paragraph for this story.

---

*Narrative example:* **Both census figures and common sense suggest that Americans are growing ever larger: the average height of an American male age 20 to 74 increased to 5-foot-9½ in 2002 from just over 5-foot-8 in 1960. Still, according to the most recent census data, an estimated 30 percent of all men between 20 and 60 are under 5-foot-8, a figure that seems to indicate the existence of a hidden-in-plain-sight market to which few in the apparel business have given much serious thought (Trebay, 2005, p. E4).**

---

After the story is reported, the Anecdotal structure wants the author to come full circle and craft a closing. Close the story by returning to someone or something introduced in the opening. The close allows you to tie up any loose ends. Here is how the article by Guy Trebay ends:

---

*Closing example:* **"Face it," Mr. Garcia said, "the world is designed for tall guys."**

**Fashion would certainly seem to be. Or at least it is in coastal America. "In talking to other retailers, I've found that New York and California have more smaller men than anywhere else in the country." Mr. Burke of Bergdorf Goodman said, "This is completely unscientific, but for some reason men are just bigger everywhere else" (Trebay, 2005, p. E4).**

---

The Anecdotal structure differs from the inverted pyramid, which expects an editor to be able to chop off the ending paragraphs of the story. This list shows how the focus structure works:

- Open with an anecdote, a scene, or a situation that illustrates the issue.
- Tease or hook the reader.
- Provide a transition to the nut paragraph.

- Explain the story in the nut paragraph.
- Provide details to support the theme in the body, by using the person or group introduced in the lead.

---

*Portfolio Exercise:* **Using Anecdotal structure, describe an event. Put yourself into the scene you describe. Include your reaction. What is your point of view? Next, rewrite the description, changing the structure to inverted pyramid.**

---

*Chronological Order* A story using **Chronological Order** starts at the beginning and runs through the end. This method is especially useful when a series of events takes place. In the following example, describing how the Internet has changed the availability of information in the modern era lends itself to a chronologically ordered format.

---

*Chronological order:* **In the winter of 1996, back when I was a brunette who wore sensible shoes, a photographer snapped my picture during a rehearsal for a college musical. The production mattered; eating and sleeping did not. The resulting portrait showed a pasty, gaunt girl being swallowed by a XXX-large T-shirt.**

**The only thing more unfortunate than the photo is that nearly a decade after it was taken—a decade in which I became a blonde and graduated to stilettos—it is still the definitive image of me on the World Wide Web, the one that pops up every time my name is entered in a Google search (Rosenbloom, 2005, p. E1).**

---

The article continues, bemoaning the fact that embarrassing moments live forever in cyberspace. The article discusses how to work with the Web in the new era.

---

*Portfolio Exercise:* **Find a short inverted pyramid story about an event, such as the opening of a new retail store or the introduction of a new line of furniture. Rewrite the story as a feature article, consisting of 8 to 10 paragraphs in chronological order. You will have to do some additional research for information that is not available in the original story.**

---

*Foreshadowing* **Foreshadowing** is the technique of giving hints about what is coming next. Movies use trailers to entice you to buy a ticket. Broadcasters use the Foreshadowing technique to encourage you to stay tuned for the next story after a commercial break. Linda Ellerbee uses it to start her story about travel:

---

*Foreshadowing example:* **"I am not supposed to be here" (Ellerbee, 2005, p. 113).**

---

This technique is another way of saying, "The story gets better. Read on." You wonder why Linda Ellerbee was not supposed to be there. So, you read on.

*Flashbacks* Departure from the chronological events allows the writer to take the reader back to earlier times or to another physical space. This departure from the present time or space to the past is known as a **Flashback**. In this form, the chronology is still the main road, but the part taking the reader to another thread offers opportunities to add elements to the story to make it more interesting.

Alex Kuczynski (2007) starts her *Critical Shopper* column about a famous jewelry store by reminding us about *Breakfast at Tiffany's*, the iconic movie and novella. She uses the Flashback technique to take the reader back to the 1960s, when Tiffany's was admired as the perfect place for a romantic flirtation.

---

*Flashback example:* **Tiffany & Company has long enjoyed a gilded reputation, conferred by its association with the happy things in life: engagements, weddings, babies, trophies, retirements, anniversaries and romantic Hollywood movies. Most notable among the last category is "Breakfast at Tiffany's," the 1961 version of Truman Capote's novella. In the movie, Holly Golightly and the writer find the cat and decide to get married and live happily ever after (Kuczynski, 2007).**

---

*Narration and Exposition Formats* **Narration** is the telling of a story, whereas **Exposition** allows the writer to stand between the reader and the information by ordering the facts. Narration arouses emotion, makes you laugh, makes you cry, and is more easily recalled. Exposition is only as interesting as the facts, and is more often forgotten.

Exposition is used to inform. It works best when the information has immediacy and relevancy and is unknown to the reader. Narration is used to entertain as well as to inform. Below is an example of a lead to a story, using both Exposition and Narration, about a skin-care drug that is illegal in the United States:

---

*Exposition example:* **James Rigel, owner of Skin Plus More, a beauty boutique specializing in skin-care products and facial spa services, was arrested today in Miami Beach. Rigel was selling the banned substance, Memoryl, the illegal sunscreen made by the Lyon, France-based cosmetic manufacturer Chez Omlie. The Food and Drug Administration has not yet approved its sale in the United States.**

*Narration example:* **Memoryl is not the most notorious drug on the black market, but a few insiders, mostly women, know its worth. It is one of the most ordinary substances to be bootlegged into the United States. Memoryl, made by the French cosmetic giant Chez Omlie, is an illegal sunscreen in this country, one that is thought to be especially useful in preventing wrinkles. Women in the know find it at certain drugstores or order it online from French pharmacies. Though the F.D.A. does not track down and prosecute individual consumers, it has targeted shop owners selling the illegal substance.**

---

In Exposition, the writer observes and listens, and then interprets what was seen and heard for you. Reading Narration, in contrast, is like watching a movie. You listen directly to the speakers to hear them tell what happened.

The structure and writing techniques presented here are guidelines, not rules. They are presented to stimulate your writing styles. Accomplished writers use these guidelines to find their own way of writing stories. They chart their own course after learning about the established patterns.

## WRITING HEADLINES

In a newspaper story, a **headline** is the title of the article. Headlines summarize the content and entice the reader to glance at the story. Since the headline is designed to attract readers, it should be brief. Every word in a headline, should be meaningful.

According to Timothy Kelley (2007), when you are writing headlines, you should use the present tense and always use short, active verbs. You don't need to say *Celebrities seek rehab after drunken episodes and bigoted rants* when you can say *Britney Needs Help.* You don't need to write exactly the same thing as you write in your news lead; that's wasting a chance to draw readers in.

If you are writing a news article, your headline should summarize in a straightforward manner what is most newsy about it. Don't write *Council of Fashion Designers of America Holds Meeting* when everyone already knew they were going to meet; write something more specific, like *CFDA Announces Size Policy for Models.*

With a feature article, there's more of a place for humor or cleverness—but you still want to convey the main point of your story. You might play off a well-known phrase or something that is going on in popular culture. For a headline on a story about a store that sells natural cosmetics, Mike Albo (2007) used the headline *Save a Face, Save the World.* This was adapted from a promotional line used in a popular television show called *Heroes.* The show's phrase was *Save the Cheerleader, Save the World.* The article went on to discuss the retail store Origins and the firm's mission to provide environmentally friendly natural remedies and ancient healing traditions.

---

*Portfolio Exercise:* **Break into teams of four to five students. Using current newspapers, magazines, and the Internet as research resources, look for five examples of popular phrases, such as *The Devil Wears Prada* or *Are you on the list?* Convert these popular phrases into at least two different headlines that could be used for headlines for feature articles.**

---

## REVISING FOR PUBLICATION

Many beginning writers think the writing is over after the first draft is written. In fact, the story is not ready until it has been read, edited, reworked, and re-edited at least once. What seems like a tedious process is really just a necessary part of the writing process.

### Finding Focus

Here is an opening to the first draft of a story intended to help readers who are interested in buying a new pair of sunglasses. The editor's comments follow the first draft in italics.

All of us remember Mom saying it was important to wear our sunglasses when we left the house. But, how many of us actually remembered to do it? Now that we are older, and the bright sun hurts our eyes, we rarely forget to wear sunglasses.

Despite knowing the practicality of wearing sunglasses, how do we know which glasses to buy? Where do we learn about the styles, materials, and fashion trends to make us feel safe, yet cool at the same time?

There has hardly been a better time to buy new sunglasses as the summer season arrives . . .

*Comment: To tell such a story, you need to find a person who has recently purchased a new pair of sunglasses. This will help you move from speculation to reporting, from exposition to narration. You still need a nut graph with appropriate transition.*

With the editor's comments in mind, the writer found someone who had recently purchased sunglasses. Now the writer had someone to build and to weave the narrative around.

Last week, Sandy Woodall lost her sunglasses after an unexpected rainstorm hit town. She only noticed they were missing the next morning when the sun hit her eyes on the way to work.

Now Sandy needed a new pair of sunglasses, but she didn't know what new styles are available. Why not update her look, as long as Sandy needed to replace the lost glasses?

Contemporary variations of oversized vintage movie-star glasses are as common as designer handbags this season. Eyewear is fashionably massive, just like the current trend for giant metallic bags. Sunglasses are the most sought-after fashion accessory of the season.

If you have not shopped for sunglasses in a while, you will be confronted with an astonishing array of choices, just as Sandy was. An informal survey of stores in Chicago last week turned up wide-temple aviator frames from Gucci, headlight-size wire frames from Marc Jacobs, and embossed tortoiseshell models from Versace. Which style was right for Sandy, and which one is right for you?

With the revisions, the reader knows what to expect from the story. Now the writer can lead the reader through the kinds of sunglasses available and give her information so that she can think about the best way to make a decision about what to buy. A chart could be developed to show the various benefits, costs, and availability for the various trendy items.

## Polishing the Draft

Some stories need polishing more than they need complete revision. The editor may want the story to be shorter or longer. The tone may be inconsistent or the transitions may be weak. An editor can make suggestions to improve the length, voice, and flow. Clarity can be improved with re-reading as well as with input from someone with a different perspective. You should seek out and listen to various perspectives on your writing.

Critiques will help point out ways to improve your writing. Sometimes the review will be discouraging, but sometimes the evaluation will boost your ego. Whatever the reaction, learn from each critique. Use the criticism to continue to improve your writing skills.

### CHECKLIST FOR REVISING YOUR ARTICLE

Timothy Kelly (2007) offers the following guidelines for making an effective article revision:

- ☐ Take a break. Put your article aside for a few minutes and do something else: walk the dog, play a game, have a snack. When you return and take a fresh look at what you've written, you'll probably see things you missed before.
- ☐ Read your article out loud. Sometimes the ear can tell you things the eye doesn't see. If there's a part of your article that your tongue repeatedly stumbles over, that's a clue that there may be awkward writing that needs to be reworked.
- ☐ Is the sequence of ideas clear? If it's a news story, does it give the reader the information needed to understand new concepts by the time they're introduced? If it's a feature article, does it start out with enough to snag the reader's interest, yet save something as a payoff for reading on? When you've completed a draft, you hate to think of changing something as basic as the order in which your points are covered. It feels like throwing away

work. But take the chance and at least consider it. You may find that a different sequence works better, and that the "cutting and pasting" you need to do—on a computer screen, or on paper—really isn't so bad.

□ Put yourself in the reader's shoes. Could your words be misunderstood? Think of the poor guy who wrote the headline about a planned change in Scout uniforms: "Boy Scouts to Drop Short Pants." He knew what he meant. But he forgot to think about what his words might call to mind for others.

□ Does the article you have written seem to you to contain any words that aren't fully necessary to your purpose? Does your article contain unnecessary words? Look at the two questions you've just read. The first one needed pruning; the second is the same question after the pruning has been done. Now do a similar pruning job on your article. Tight writing is usually best.

□ Check your paragraphing. In journalism, short paragraphs of one to two sentences are common. If you find you have changed the subject in mid-paragraph, that's probably a place for a paragraph break.

□ Use spell-checkers and other programs to check your spelling, grammar, and punctuation—but don't rely on them alone. Remember: The best computer for perfecting your writing is the one between your ears!

---

*Portfolio Exercise:* **Find a published story that you think can be improved. Working with four or five other students, critique the story. Compare suggestions that come from each member of the team. Using some of the techniques described in this chapter, have each team member rewrite the story. Point out which techniques were used, such as rewriting the lead; interviewing and incorporating dialogue; or using Chronological Order, Foreshadowing, Flashbacks, or Narration and Exposition. How do the stories differ from each other and the original?**

---

# TRENDS IN THE NEWSPAPER INDUSTRY

A number of issues challenge the publication of newspapers in the United States today. There has been a steady decline in circulation, and fewer people are reading newspapers now than in the past. In the 19th and 20th centuries, many newspapers were consolidated and ownership became more concentrated. The newspaper industry has already faced increased competition from radio and television. Now it faces competition from the Internet as well, which is already revolutionizing the newspaper industry worldwide.

## CONSOLIDATION

The number of newspapers published in the United States is decreasing. Although newspaper publishers estimate that nearly 6 out of 10 adults in the United States and Canada read newspapers every day, and 7 out of 10 read a paper each weekend, that number is declining ("Newspaper," 2005). During the 20th century, strong reader-ship enabled many cities to support multiple newspaper publishers, with morning and evening editions offering many ideas and commentaries. Now, many of those publi-cations have merged or have been acquired by other publishers. For example, New York City once had 20 daily newspapers, but by 1940 that number had decreased to 8 ("Newspaper," 2005).

Today, most U.S. cities have only one newspaper, most likely a morning edition. Many critics of the news media are concerned that without competition, the integrity of news coverage in those cities will be compromised. Without competition, papers may be less likely to publish alternative views and may print the views of the owner as fact, not opinion. Although television and radio can present alternative views, many newspaper publishers also own radio and television stations in the same cities where their newspapers are printed.

## NEWSPAPER CHAINS

Starting with publishers such as William Randolph Hearst and Edward Wyllis Scripps with Milton Alexander McRae, in the late 19th century newspaper ownership began shifting from independent operations to national chains ("Newspaper," 2005).

The first large-scale newspaper chain was the Scripps–McRae League of News-papers, with 23 newspapers by 1914 ("Newspaper," 2005). Hearst constructed an even larger news media empire, with magazines as well as newspapers. Gannett Company, which owns 94 newspapers with a circulation of about 8 million in 2002, is the largest newspaper chain today ("Newspaper"). Gannet also owns numerous television stations.

## MEDIA COMPETITION, THE INTERNET, AND CONVERGENCE

Radio and television, with their instantaneous broadcast capabilities, became a competitive threat to newspapers in the 20th century. Radio reached the height of its influence during World War II (1939–1945) when it carried war news from multiple battlefronts directly to millions of listeners. Television took over audience attention after World War II ended. By the 1990s, cable television, with its 24-hour news programming, took over leadership of breaking news stories. Cable and network television, with the ability to broadcast breaking news within minutes after an event happens, took advantage of getting news to the public faster than newspapers.

Newspapers struggled to maintain their place in news reporting. Realizing that readers had already heard breaking news stories on television, newspapers began covering news in greater detail than they had in the past. Newspaper articles provided historical context as well as in-depth analysis, not done in the broadcast media.

The biggest challenge to newspapers in the 21st century is the rapid and widespread expansion of the Internet. Especially after September 11, 2001, news consumers wanted to have news available "24/7"—and they found it online. Now, almost every newspaper has a Web site that is usually free to Internet users. From May 2004 to May 2005, there was a 12% increase in unique visitors to newspaper Web sites, according to Nielsen/NetRatings (Freierman, 2005). Many readers who get their news primarily from newspapers have turned to Web editions of their favorite newspapers. The *New York Times* attracted 11,300,000 visitors in May 2005, a 25% increase over the same month the previous year (Freierman). Competitive pressure from broadcast media and Internet sources has led some media authorities to predict that printed newspapers will completely surrender to exclusive electronic information sources in the future.

Many newspaper companies have voluntarily joined or involuntarily merged with broadcast and digital media firms, resulting in media convergence. Writers will need to adapt to new techniques and technologies. For example, many newspaper journalists, including Cathy Horyn of the *New York Times*, are writing blogs about the various fashion weeks for the newpaper's Web site. This allows the writer to offer more personal impressions than she could in traditional media. Writing for the new media will be discussed in Chapter 8.

## SUMMARY

Fashion has always been reported in newspapers, whether daily, weekly, special interest, or trade publications. The two most common types of stories are news stories and feature stories. News stories use the inverted pyramid method to present information, addressing the questions of Who, What, Where, When, and sometimes How and Why. The more descriptive feature stories use modifications of the inverted pyramid method, including Anecdotal, Chronological Order, Foreshadowing, Flashbacks, and Narration and Exposition formats.

Reporters are good storytellers. The tools they use to gather information for a story include interviewing, employing traditional research methods, and taking advantage of the Internet. When telling a story, the reporter must portray numbers in a way that readers will understand. Ultimately, the most important element of storytelling is to present the story—both the details and the context—accurately.

The newspaper industry is changing. The number of newspapers continues to decline, and those that have survived are often consolidated. Convergence has also forever changed the way that people get news. Nontraditional sources like the Web are better able to keep us constantly informed.

## KEY TERMS

Anecdotal

Broadsheet

Chronological Order

Daily newspaper

Exposition

Fashion journalist

Feature story

Flashback

Focus structure

Foreshadowing

Headline

Inverted pyramid

Lead

Narration

News story

Newspaper

Newsprint

Nut (nut graph)

Special interest newspaper

Supermarket tabloid

Tabloid

Trade newspaper

Weekly newspaper

CASE STUDY

## *Chicago Fashion Critic Banned from Shows*

Chicago, Illinois, is the center for fashion in the Midwestern part of the United States. With a population of over 2.9 million people and a median age of 32, it can support a prosperous fashion industry. Retail sales of approximately $7.7 billion in apparel and accessories show a significant interest in fashion-related products. Chicago ranks third in retail sales and third in apparel and accessories sales, behind only New York and Los Angeles in the United States.

Chicago is home to a promising and expanding fashion design industry. With four fashion design schools, hundreds of Chicago area fashion designers, the Chicago Apparel Center, and the Apparel Industry Board, as well as numerous merchant and professional associations, the interest in fashion is growing by leaps and bounds in this region. Many of the most significant high fashion retailers, including Nordstrom, Macy's, and Saks, in addition to powerful independent specialty stores are located in Chicago.

With the support of Mayor Richard M. Daley, the city's growing fashion industry is being promoted through its Fashion Focus Chicago program. The multiple-day city-wide fall initiative features fashion shows, shopping events, student designer events, and industry seminars, in addition to many other fashion programs. The Chicago Office of Tourism joined the effort by offering out-of-town guests a Fashion Immersion Weekend, with reservations at a fashionable hotel, front row seats at Macy's gala fashion show, a private party after the show, and a behind-the-scenes tour of the fashion exhibit at the Chicago History Museum. Chicago is becoming a shopping and fashion event gathering place.

With the growing interest in fashion in the region, the *Chicago Tribune*, one of the city's top newspapers, decided to expand its fashion and style coverage. After all, the *Los Angeles Times*, the *New York Times*, and the *Washington Post* all have major fashion coverage. The *Los Angeles Times* has expanded its fashion coverage in print and online through its *Los Angeles Times Image Section*. Cathy Horyn is the Council of Fashion Designers of America, Eugenia Sheppard Award-winning fashion critic for the "Style" section of the *New York Times*. And Robin Givhan is the Pulitzer Prize-winning fashion critic for the *Washington Post*. It was time to join these other prestigious fashion analysts and hire a fashion critic.

A fashion reviewer who works in the fashion industry has a difficult job. The reviewer must balance journalistic ethical standards of reporting both positive and negative comments about the designers that he or she is hired to review, while maintaining a positive working relationship with the designers being reviewed. For example, Cathy Horyn has been banned from some designer shows based upon her less-than-glowing critiques from previous shows.

Terrance Sanders, a graduate of Columbia College of Chicago, had been writing fashion and home furnishings articles for the *Cleveland Plain Dealer* when he heard about the planned expansion of the fashion and lifestyle section at the *Chicago Tribune*. Terrance wanted to return to his roots in Chicago. He was hired to be the *Tribune*'s fashion critic, traveling to New York and Los Angeles twice each year to review the collections, in addition to reviewing the work produced by designers in Chicago.

Terrance was excited to visit New York in his new role as fashion critic. He was generally thrilled with most of the creations, but he thought that the collection by Francisco Costa for Calvin Klein was not up to the firm's usual standards. Terrance wrote, "Costa is continually defeated by his own eye, which is seeing women without the classic Calvin Klein vision. He created interesting visual effects by featuring models as Manhattan call girls with the idea of a chic, yet seedy uniform for all women. But, the trashy-looking evening wear failed to live up to Calvin Klein's sportswear tradition."

After reading this review, the designer was furious. How could this inexperienced fashion critic pan his collection? The other critics complemented Costa's risk-taking innovations. Mr. Sanders was banned from future Calvin Klein fashion collections.

## CASE STUDY QUESTIONS

1. What should Terrance Sanders do? Should he give a positive review, even if he does not believe the collection was up to the designer's standards?
2. How can a fashion journalist maintain his or her ethical standards and provide a non-favorable review?

## INDUSTRY PROFILE

*Teri Agins*

**What is your current job and title? Can you describe the main responsibilities for your job?**

I am a senior special writer at the *Wall Street Journal* covering the fashion and retail industries. I have been writing at the journal for 23 years and I developed the fashion beat here about 18 years ago. My responsibilities are varied. I spin a lot of plates! I cover the public companies on the fashion beat—and the spot news developments that come from them—as well as develop enterprise feature stories. We cover the fashion industry the same way we cover airlines or the auto industry. We look at everything through the prism of business.

**What is a typical day at work like?**

My day begins with reading the local newspapers and trade publications, such as *WWD*. I spend a lot of time on the phone, talking to sources which vary from bankers, designers, analysts, retail sources, etcetera. I'm usually working on two or three features at any given time, I don't have a quota of stories to do. I also spend a lot of time outside of the office, going to stores, doing interviews, meeting with sources, and attending fashion industry events.

**At what point did you decide to pursue a career in writing for a fashion-related business?**

I have always pursued a journalism career—since I worked on the junior high school newspaper back in my hometown, Kansas City, Kansas. Coincidentally, one of my assignments in the 9th grade journalism class was a fashion column, which I called "teri's tips for fashion flair." I began signing my name in lower case letters back then. (I was copying a character played by Susan Hayward in a movie called "Backstreet" where she was a designer and she signed her name as "rae" . . . she said the small letters looked very chic). The column was a 14-year-old girl's view of fashion; I subscribed to *Vogue* magazine back then. I wrote about what the kids in high school wore and a bit about trends such as mini skirts and go-go boots—which were the rage back then. Of course, I put lots of names of students in the column—the ones who had the "cutest knee socks" or sweaters or hairstyles, etcetera.

*Describe your first writing job. What was the most important or interesting thing you wrote for that job/publication?*

My first writing job was a summer internship at the *Kansas City Star*, where I wrote obituaries most of the summer. I also wrote a few spot news features, reviewing a Stan Getz concert, one story I remembered because I had to write it on deadline . . . and I got to go backstage. I loved the newsroom atmosphere—the bustle and excitement. I also liked learning to interview all kinds of people. The following summer my internship (summer of junior year when I was at Wellesley) was at the *Boston Globe*. It was the Watergate summer 1974 . . . Just being in a newsroom that summer that Nixon resigned was exciting. The newsroom crackled as the end approached.

*What are you currently reading (books, magazines, Web sites, newspapers, other media)? Do you have a favorite author or publication?*

In addition to the *Journal*, NYT, *Washington Post* and the fashion publications, I also read the *New Yorker, Vanity Fair, Psychology Today, Consumer Reports,* and the *New York Observer*. I also glance at a number of Web sites. For leisure reading—commuting to work on the bus and on planes—I prefer nonfiction, usually biographies. Lately, I've been on a history kick with bios such as John Adams, Alexander Hamilton, Barak Obama, Langston Hughes. I love business books, too—all of James B. Stewart's books, *Den of Thieves*, etcetera. (he's a former *WSJ* colleague), Roger Lowenstein's bio on Warren Buffett; Michael Lewis, *The New New Thing* . . . like that.

Favorite nonfiction author is Arnold Rampersad.

I lived in Brazil for five years, so I try to keep up Portuguese reading . . . mostly with a news magazine called *Veja*, which I can read on the Web.

*What advice do you have for students interested in a writing career? Do you have any recommendations for students?*

Writers should be voracious readers—it should come naturally . . . and if it doesn't, you're in the wrong profession. Students should get into the habit of reading major newspapers like the *Journal* and NYT. The more you know about the world and how it works, the more sophisticated you will be. You'll be sharper on analysis—and more creative when you approach stories.

Writers become better at what they do when they read so they can learn how stories are conceived . . . which decisions we make about who we interview, the statistics we cite, the anecdotes we include, the research we do . . . .

Writers should also consider keeping a diary/journal. But they should keep in mind that blogging isn't the same as journalism. What professional writers do is more structured—and has academic rigor. We are accountable for what we write. We must prove what we say. We must be objective. We must tell both sides of the story—and allow sources to comment. We use financial documents and legal briefs and other research. There is scholarship in what we do. Blogs are stream of consciousness. They certainly are valuable to the conversation. They contribute to the forum of ideas. But they are not journalism.

Students should vary their course load beyond their major—take courses in history, economics, religion. Learn well at least one foreign language (which helps improve your English). The more curious you are, the better journalist you will be.

## REFERENCES

Albo, M. (2007, March 15). Save a face, save the world. *New York Times*, p. G4.

Byrnes, G. D. (1951). *Fashion in newspapers.* New York: Columbia University Press.

Ellerbee, L. (2005). *Take big bites: Adventures around the world and across the table.* New York: G. P. Putnam's Sons.

Freierman, S. (2005, June 20). Newspapers online. *New York Times.* Retrieved June 20, 2005, from http:www.nytimes.com

Givhan, R. (2005, May 5). Simply Chanel. *Washington Post.* Retrieved June 28, 2005, from http://www.washingtonpost.com

Horyn, C. (2005, June 9). Fashion, the mirror and me. *New York Times.* Retrieved June 9, 2005, from http:www.nytimes.com

Kelley, T. (2007). News writing. *Scholastic.* Retrieved March 26, 2007, from http://teacher.scholastic.com/writewit/news/step4.htm

Kuczynski, A. (2007, February 8). A story in every box. *New York Times*, pp. E1, E4.

Newspaper. (2005). *Microsoft® Encarta® Online Encyclopedia.* Retrieved June 21, 2005, from http://encarta.msn.com

Rosenbloom, S. (2005, June 2). Loosing Google's lock on the past. *New York Times,* pp. E1, E5.

Trebay, G. (2005, June 9). Measuring up: In a world where bigger is better, short men have few fashion alternatives. *New York Times*, pp. E1, E4.

Wilson, E. (2005, June 2). Front Row: A whiff of Paris. *New York Times*, p. E4.

# FOUR

## *Writing for Magazines*

After you have read this chapter, you should be able to discuss the following:

• The purpose of consumer and trade magazines

• Who works for consumer and trade magazines

• How to prepare a magazine article

• How to get a magazine article published

T he influence of top editors from such fashion magazines as *Vogue* and *Harper's Bazaar* is legendary. These powerful editors, starting with Carmel Snow, editor of *Harper's Bazaar*, set the nationwide fashion agenda. In 1947, Mrs. Snow coined the term "The New Look" to describe Christian Dior's inaugural collection that year, making Dior the best-known French designer to *Harper's Bazaar*'s U.S. audience. Diana Vreeland, who wrote the column "Why Don't You . . . ?" for *Harper's Bazaar*, became known for stylish and outrageous fashion ideas that appealed to her readership. Of her many fashion columns, 100 were reprinted in the 21st century, introducing a young audience to her quirky fashion advice (Esten, 2001). These articles seemed just as timely decades after they were written. Later, Mrs. Vreeland set the fashion mood at *Vogue* as its editor-in-chief during the swinging 1960s, bringing a new, young, multicultural look to the magazine.

Grace Mirabella took over leadership of *Vogue* in the 1970s, after Mrs. Vreeland was fired. Ms. Mirabella worked at *Vogue* for 38 years, 17 of them as editor-in-chief

(Mirabella & Warner, 1995). In the cutthroat world of fashion publishing, Ms. Mirabella was fired just as her boss Mrs. Vreeland had been, making way for British-born Anna Wintour to take over the top editorial spot at American *Vogue* in 1988 (Mirabella & Warner, 1995).

Anna Wintour, despite her reputation as being icy and extremely demanding, has had considerable influence over American and worldwide fashion. Runway fashion shows wait for her to take her seat in the front row before the show begins. (See Figure 4.1.) Designers, photographers, fashion trends, and charitable causes succeed or fail due to her patronage or lack of support. Ms. Wintour was named one of the top ten most powerful women in fashion and beauty—the only magazine editor on the list—by *Time Style & Design* (Orecklin, 2004).

FIGURE 4.1. Anna Wintour.

But just what do all of those people listed on the masthead of the magazine actually do? According to Sarajane Hoare, fashion editor for *British Vogue* and *Harper's Bazaar*, "the fact is that we form a part of a global business which generates a multibillion dollar annual turnover—which happens to be called Fashion . . . the fashion editor must find new images that show fashion-obsessed women how to wear them" (2002, p. 1).

This chapter looks at fashion journalism that takes place in the print world of magazines. We'll define consumer and trade magazines and analyze these publication organizations. After discussing people who write for magazines, we'll explore how magazine articles are planned and how a freelance writer can present those plans to a potential publisher.

# MAGAZINES

**Magazines** are print or electronic publications that contain advertising and editorial content. Typical print publications are available on a regular basis, published weekly, monthly, bi-monthly, or quarterly. Electronic magazines may be updated as often as every day. Most often, magazines are printed on glossy paper, with full-color photography. Therefore, magazines typically are read, reread, and passed along to other individuals.

Magazines serve many different informational, educational, and entertainment needs for a wide range of readers. While some magazines, such as *Time* in the news category or *People* in the entertainment field, seek a general audience with a mass appeal, many more magazines try to reach specific audiences. These publications are directed at virtually every type of reader—on the basis of demographics, lifestyle, activities, interests, or fascination. Magazines may target consumers; alternatively, they may focus on issues of interest from one business category to another. The magazines in this second group are considered to be trade publications. Figure 4.2 and Table 4.1 compare the features of consumer magazines to the features of trade magazines.

After declining for years, in 2004 retail sales of magazines rose. The rapid growth of celebrity weeklies, such as *People*, *Us Weekly*, *In Touch*, and *Star Magazine*, led the growth. These four titles, sold primarily in supermarkets, accounted for 20% of audited magazine sales during the second half of 2003 ("Circulation Snapshot," 2005).

Most of today's national magazines are owned by large corporate entities. For example, Condé Nast, which publishes such consumer titles as *Vogue*, *Condé Nast Traveler*,

FIGURE 4.2. Comparison of consumer (top) and trade (bottom) magazines.

and *GQ*, also produces a variety of trade publications, including *BeautyBiz, Footwear News,* and *WWD Beauty Report International.* Hearst Communications, another large media company, owns such magazines as *Harper's Bazaar, Esquire*, and *House Beautiful*, while Meredith Corporation produces *Ladies' Home Journal* and *More* in addition to other niche publications, broadcast media, and Web sites.

---

*Portfolio Exercise:* **Look at the table of contents of at least three magazines from various genres (men's or women's fashion, shelter, beauty, fitness, or other specialty categories). In memo format, identify the specific magazine and analyze the various types of articles offered. For each magazine, address the following:**

- **What tone is used? Is it conversational or more formal? Are slang terms used?**
- **Read the editor's statement and analyze the magazine's content, audience, and tone based upon what the editor has to say.**
- **What types of articles are found in each issue?**

---

## CONSUMER MAGAZINES

**Consumer magazines** are publications that are targeted to the general public or to specialized groups that have specific interests in common—such as fashion, beauty, shelter, shopping, or some other, more narrowly defined niche. Fashion magazines cover wide ranges of consumer interest. For young fashionistas, *Seventeen* is a popular title. It is joined by *Teen Vogue*. (Figure 4.3 shows the cover of a recent edition of *Teen Vogue*.) Well-liked magazines for women include the previously mentioned *Vogue* and *Harper's Bazaar*. There is a lot of competition for fashion coverage from *Cosmopolitan, Elle, Glamour, InStyle, Town & Country, Vanity Fair,* and *W*. Men, too, have a number of publications directed toward their fashion and lifestyle interests. *Details, Esquire, GQ, Men's Vogue,* and *Men's Fitness* are among the popular men's consumer magazines.

While the topic of beauty is almost always featured in women's fashion magazines, a separate category of beauty magazines has gained popularity. *Allure*, for example, focuses on beauty and health. Another new, cool group of magazines is the

**FIGURE 4.3.** Magazine cover from an issue of *Teen Vogue*.

category known as shopping magazines. *Lucky*, first in this genre, was followed by *Domino*, the shopping magazine for home design.

Shelter magazines focus on all things for the home. From interior design to new product development, shelter magazines feature stories on every aspect of the dwelling. Such magazines include *Architectural Digest*, *Better Homes & Gardens*, *Good Housekeeping*, and *O Home*.

Other specialty categories are almost unlimited. As this book is being written, weeklies such as *In Touch*, *People*, *Star*, and *Us Weekly* are prominent selections in the fastest-growing category: entertainment. Another new category is the Spanish-language magazine, with such titles as *Latina*, *Men's Health en Español*, and *Ocean Drive Español*. Virtually any topic or hobby can be the theme of a magazine. From *Brides* to *Wired*, or *Bon Appétit* to *Golf Digest*, any special interest topic may be covered as a consumer magazine.

Regional titles are also examples of consumer magazines. These magazines are directed toward life in various regions. States feature such publications as *Arizona Highways* or *Florida Monthly*, while cities—including Chicago, Los Angeles, New York, Santa Fe, and Tucson—have local magazines (often with more than one title per city) devoted to the lifestyle of that location.

Business magazines focus on editorial content that is of interest from one business to another. For example, general business magazines such as *Business Week*, *Forbes*, and *Fortune* are aimed at executives in all areas of business. These publications may also be considered consumer magazines, because they are directed to a general audience.

## TRADE MAGAZINES

**Trade magazines**, also known as **business-to-business magazines (B2B)**, are published for specific businesses, industries, or occupations. One example of a fashion-related trade magazine is *Stores* (Figure 4.4 shows an example of *Stores* magazine), which is the publication of the National Retail Federation (NRF). Other trade magazines are targeted toward specific categories of business, such as *WWDBeauty Biz*, *Children's Business*, *Home Furnishings News*, *Interiors and Sources*, *Stitches*, *Wearables Business*, and *VM + SD* (*Visual Merchandising and Store Design*). Table 4.1 compares the content of consumer magazines with trade magazines.

**Table 4.1.** Comparison of consumer and trade magazines.

| CRITERIA | CONSUMER MAGAZINES | TRADE MAGAZINES |
|---|---|---|
| Accountability | Editorial review<br>No bibliographies | Editorial review<br>May have bibliographies |
| Advertising | Extensive<br>National and international products and services<br>Significant number of pages | Moderate<br>Products related to the industry |
| Audience | Anyone interested in the category<br><br>Consumers | Professionals within a particular industry or organization<br>Business professionals |

**Table 4.1.** Comparison of consumer and trade magazines. *(continued)*

| CRITERIA | CONSUMER MAGAZINES | TRADE MAGAZINES |
|---|---|---|
| Content | News<br>Information<br>Personalities and<br>celebrities<br>Topics related to the<br>category, such as<br>fashion, beauty, home<br>furnishings, shopping | Industry trends<br>New products<br>How-to<br>Organization news |
| Authors | Articles written by staff<br>or contributing writers<br>May be signed or unsigned | Articles written by staff or<br>contributing writers<br>Articles submitted<br>by freelancers |
| Visual Appearance | Dramatic cover with<br>celebrity or model<br>Glossy paper<br>Photos and illustrations<br>in full color | Industrial setting or executive<br>portrait on the cover<br>Glossy paper or newsprint<br>Photos and illustrations<br>in full color |
| Examples | *Elle*<br>*Glamour*<br>*Men's Fitness*<br>*O Home*<br>*Gourmet* | *Daily News Record*<br>*Home Furnishings Daily*<br>*Stores*<br>*VM+SD*<br>*Women's Wear Daily* |

# WORKING FOR CONSUMER MAGAZINES

National consumer magazines contain editorial content as well as many pages of advertising. Most of the articles in such national publications as *InStyle* and *Vogue* are nonfiction stories created by the editorial staff or a contributing editor. Rarely do national consumer magazines publish fictional short stories or poems. In this section, we'll examine how magazines are put together.

For starters, we'll take a close look at the masthead, where we can see the job titles and names of all the employees who work for a magazine. The masthead also

FIGURE 4.4. *Stores* magazine.

identifies contributors who offer insight into events and issues on a regular basis. Next, we'll consider how a magazine is composed. Based on the editorial calendar, the merchandise to be covered is selected and the pages are edited. Finally, we'll consider how trade magazines are prepared for publication.

## MASTHEAD

The **masthead** is a list much like the credits at the end of a movie. By looking at the masthead, you can get a sense of all the people needed to put together the magazine. The titles may change from one magazine to the next, but each masthead lists the people who create the magazine: from the publisher at the top, to the editors (managing editor or editor-in-chief) and creative editors (fashion, features, beauty, or art), to the editorial assistants and contributors and, in some magazine mastheads, even the interns.

The magazine **publisher** manages the periodical, and is responsible for such issues as advertising revenue and circulation; market share; multimedia initiatives on the

Internet, television, and in film; and brand extension launches. For example, Thomas A. Florio, the vice-president and publisher of *Vogue*, created an in-house ad agency called *Vogue* Studio, served as the executive producer for the fashion documentary *Seamless*, and created the brand extension *Men's Vogue* (Condé Nast, 2006b).

The Condé Nast Web site (2006a) lists a variety of editors, along with typical job responsibilities. In the following paragraphs, we'll summarize the characteristics of the managing editor, beauty editor, bookings editor, copy editor, fashion editor, features editor, and creative director.

The **managing editor** is a senior-level editor, with extensive management experience, who oversees the day-to-day management of the office; supervises staff, editorial, and photography budgets; produces actual pages of the magazine; and controls the editing process and closings. Maintaining calendars and schedules to meet the magazine's deadlines and ensuring smooth and constant communication between all departments are key parts of this individual's job. Establishing an editorial system and working with all of the subordinate editors to plan all deadlines are also part of the managing editor's responsibilities. If freelancers are used, the managing editor hires and supervises them. Some magazines use the title **editor-in-chief** for the job done by the managing editor.

The **beauty editor** is responsible for doing extensive market research within the beauty industry, as well as writing, editing, and producing the magazine's beauty and grooming pages. Further responsibilities include attending press events and representing the magazine to the public. Having contacts with market representatives and writers throughout the industry is critical. Experience in writing and editing and knowledge of the beauty industry and magazines are essential.

Securing models and hair and makeup artists, and finding locations for photo shoots are among the responsibilities of the **bookings editor**. This is a highly professional, solution-driven, problem-solving position. Experience with the model agency business is essential.

Working on tight deadlines, the **copy editor** reviews text for spelling, content, style, word usage, and grammar, and also resolves queries on proofs. The ideal copy editor is familiar with the writing style desired by the publication, knows Quark-Copydesk, has first-rate copyediting skills, and has the ability to line-edit. Familiarity with topics found in the magazine and experience with InDesign are desired characteristics. The position requires the ability to work under pressure, as well as excellent communication and problem-solving skills.

The **fashion editor** works to produce tight, fresh, modern features for the fashion pages. The ideal fashion editor should have extensive experience managing photo shoots, handling market work, generating current story ideas, and managing stylists and prop-closet inventory. Extensive contacts in the fashion world are essential, as is the ability to meet tight deadlines.

**Features editors** generate, edit, and package stories; recruit writers; and participate in all facets of editorial planning and production. A proven history of reporting, editing, and compiling material along with a solid knowledge of copyediting and fact-checking are critical for a features editor. The ability to weave a compelling, literary story that evokes a strong sense of place and captures the essence of an experience or destination is necessary for features editing.

The title **creative director** was invented by Alex Liberman, long-time editorial director of Condé Nast, for Anna Wintour in 1983 (Oppenheimer, 2005). Ms. Wintour came to *Vogue* with the new title, which was vague but had flair and a compelling ring to it. This position was Anna Wintour's stepping stone to her promotion to editor-in-chief for *Vogue*.

Responsibilities, as well as job titles, vary from one publication to another. Where the editor-in-chief of a large fashion magazine has control and decision-making power over which photographers, fashion designs, and formulas are used, the editor of a small regional magazine might also be responsible for writing articles, managing photo shoots, and hiring freelancers.

Entry-level positions for consumer magazines are generally as assistants or interns, with such titles as editorial assistant, editorial secretary, production assistant, fashion assistant, or researcher. In most cases, these entry-level employees handle general office or secretarial duties—everything from getting or making coffee to performing some basic writing tasks. Entry-level applicants should be able to use a computer and may be expected to have working knowledge of particular computer programs used in the magazine industry.

One of the typical assistants at a fashion magazine is called the fashion assistant. The **fashion assistant** supports the fashion department of the periodical with a balance of administrative and creative responsibilities. Assistants manage their editor's office as well as contribute to concept development for fashion pages. Management expects these assistants to be capable of supervising the incoming and outgoing flow of merchandise; organizing photo shoots, before, during, and after; and completing any projects that contribute to the issue's closing. Fashion assistants should be self-motivated, detail- and deadline-oriented, and highly organized. Experience multitasking in a fast-paced, hectic environment is an essential responsibility for any of the assistants.

At many magazines, the staff consists of only three or four people, so opportunities for advancement may require moving to another title. Larger publications, with a staff of 20 or more people, may have regular openings. Again, for a sampling of these types of positions, visit the Condé Nast Web site, which lists the current openings at Condé Nast for jobs in editorial, sales and marketing, production, and human resources for its many different consumer and trade publications.

## CONTRIBUTORS

**Contributors** or **contributing editors** are freelance writers who contribute to the magazine frequently (Harrigan & Dunlap, 2004). As this book is being written, there are 23 contributing editors listed on the *Vogue* masthead.

Joan Juliet Buck is listed on the *Vogue* masthead as a contributing editor. In this position Ms. Buck regularly reviews television programs for the fashion magazine's popular "People are talking about . . ." column. Ms. Buck started her magazine career as a book reviewer for *Glamour* in 1968 ("French Vogue names editor," 1994). She contributed to *Women's Wear Daily* as a European correspondent from London and Rome, and to British *Vogue* on politics, arts, and fashion. Two novels and five screenplays are also on her résumé. She was named the editor-in-chief of French *Vogue*, a position she held from 1994 until 2000 (Socha, 2000). After returning to the United States, Ms. Buck started commenting on various topics for *Vogue* and other U.S. magazines.

The list of 23 contributors at *Vogue* does not include editor-at-large André Leon Talley. The title "editor-at-large" was created for Mr. Talley, who writes a monthly column called "Life with André." A front-row regular at fashion shows in New York, Paris, and Milan for more than 25 years and a former protégé of Diana Vreeland, he has used his influence to champion the work of dozens of designers, such as Stephen Burrows and Tracey Reese, as well as celebrities Jennifer Hudson and Beyoncé Knowles. (Figure 4.5 presents a photo of Mr. Talley.)

André Leon Talley writes each of his columns in the first person. Whether he is writing about the couture shows or the awards season, he writes the column as a diary. For example:

What motivated me, after having already taken up squash, to pick up a Prince tennis racket?

Being in Paris for the couture shows and the idea of new tennis gear! I left the Ritz at 6:30 A.M., grabbed my LV monogram gym bag, towels, and

FIGURE 4.5. Andre' Leon Talley.

water, and took my first-ever lesson (a two-hour drill of hitting the ball) with brilliant coach Bruno Lambert at the Tennis Club de la Châtaigneraie in Rueil Malmaison, 20 minutes outside of the city. The tennis thing is invigorating, and while I saw red at the club—with its *terre battue* (clay court)—spring haute couture 2007 was about to serve up a pretty-in-pink revival (Talley, 2007, p. 110).

## EDITORIAL CALENDAR

Each issue of a magazine typically has a theme. These themes are created and organized into an editorial calendar for the publication. The **editorial calendar** lists the editorial focus for each issue, in addition to any special reports or surveys, products, or events. *Vogue* emphasizes its editorial themes. During June, the magazine features its annual "Escapes" issue. Common editorial themes in the fashion industry are the Power Issue, Fall Fashion, Summer Survival Guide, the Awards Shows, and so forth.

The editorial calendar leads to the creation of various themes and stories. For example, one issue of *Essence* magazine focused on the theme "Be Happy." Articles in the issue spotlighted taking control of your life at age 20, at age 30, and at age 40 in terms of money, health, and relationships.

For a spring issue of *WWDBeautyBiz*, the theme of "The Ultimate Spring Shopping Guide" was created. The magazine features articles about such topics as backstage at the New York Fall collections, hot trends in new products, and the fresh new models from around the world. The following example shows how the top spring trends are introduced.

HOT STUFF
From sexy silver makeup to lychee-infused scents, spring's best products will keep you feeling cool all season long.
*Darling Clementine*
At first glance, orange doesn't seem like the world's easiest color to wear, yet it's proving to be one of spring's most popular shades, nudging out perennial favorites red and pink for the season's top honors ("Hot Stuff," 2007).

## SELECTING THE MERCHANDISE AND EDITING FOR PUBLICATION

Fashion editors attend the runway fashion shows held in Paris, New York, London, and Milan. After viewing the collections and meeting with the designers, fashion editors select the collections to be photographed and included in the editorial pages of their magazines. Clothes are borrowed from the designers. The editors select models or celebrities and photographers, and they book a location for the photographic shoot.

Models recognize that being photographed for editorial pieces will not pay the high fees that are paid for advertising work, but they know that editorial work, especially a cover of a magazine, will lead to other opportunities. Celebrities also like to appear on magazine covers in order to promote a film or other project. The going rate for editorial work is $225 a day for models and celebrities, plus an additional 10% for the model's agency (James, 2005).

Fashion, beauty, fitness, or home furnishing stories are approved or rejected by the managing editor or editor-in-chief. Some editors involve all of the magazine's staff members in the decision, while others make the final decisions themselves.

# WORKING FOR TRADE MAGAZINES

Trade magazines are published in almost every type of industry. These publications rely on experts in the field of the publication and on writers who represent such experts. Technical language and industry jargon are extremely important for establishing credibility in writing for trade magazines.

It is important to recognize that there is a difference between professional or scholarly journals and trade magazines. A professional or scholarly journal is written by and for members of a particular profession or academic discipline. Normally, articles in professional or scholarly journals are about the latest research being conducted in a particular field. The technical and research articles in these publications are written by professionals in the field, and before they're published they are reviewed by other professionals in that field (peer reviewed). The *Journal of Retailing* and *Clothing and Textiles Research Journal* are examples of scholarly publications. Scholarly writing is the topic of Chapter 9.

## EDITORIAL STAFF

The editorial staff for a trade magazine is most likely much smaller than for a consumer magazine. In addition to the managing editor, trade magazines typically employ some staff writers. Trade magazines are more likely than consumer magazines to use **freelance writers,** who write independently and are paid a fee for their contributions.

Freelance writers often work from their homes, creating an "office" in their residence. Besides a desk, a chair, and a computer, freelancer writers need a telephone and a fax machine—basic equipment for use in writing their articles and interacting with a magazine's on-site staff. In addition, freelancers must keep track of all their work-related income and expenses, acting as their own financial agents and keeping track of their financial data so they can handle their IRS obligations themselves.

Freelance writers also must be able to sell their articles. Later in this chapter, we will discuss targeting articles to a particular magazine and writing a query letter.

## EDITORIAL CALENDAR

Trade publications use editorial calendars in a manner similar to consumer publications. For example, *VM+SD*, the trade publication in the fields of visual merchandising, store planning, and store design, publishes its yearly editorial calendar on its Web site (Figure 4.6). The editorial focus for January is typically its *Buyer's Guide*, with a report on *VM+SD*'s Stores of the Year.

The editorial calendar can trigger possible articles from freelancers. Making the theme of the issue available, either on a Web site or in print, is one way that the publication can enable freelance writers to offer story ideas.

| ISSUE | ISSUE FEATURES | SPECIAL COLUMN | PRODUCT MARKETPLACE | BONUS DISTRIBUTION |
|---|---|---|---|---|
| **January**<br><br>Ad reservations: Nov. 22<br>Ad materials: Dec. 4<br>Mail date: Dec. 20 | - Buyers' Guide Issue<br>- Top 50 Retail Design Firms | - A Look Ahead at 2007 | - All Prducts/Services | - The Signage and Graphics Summit, Tuscon, AZ<br>- The National Retail Federation Convention & Expo, New York City |
| **February - RL**<br><br>Ad reservations: Dec. 15<br>Ad materials: Jan. 2<br>Mail date: Jan. 18 | - Annual ISP/VM+SD Design Awards<br>- Holiday Windows Annual Design Firm Survey | - Visual Merchandising<br>-<br>Signage/Graphics | - Signage/Graphics<br>- Furniture | - GlobalShop, Las Vegas<br>- Surfaces, Las Vegas |
| **March**<br><br>Ad reservations: Jan. 23<br>Ad materials: Jan. 31<br>Mail date: Feb. 16 | - The GlobalShop At-Show Issue<br>- Las Vegas Retail<br>- Mannequin Trends | - In-store Marketing<br>- In-store Digital Media | - GlobalShop Exhibitors: All Products and Services | - GlobalShop, Las Vegas |
| **April**<br><br>Ad reservations: Feb. 21<br>Ad materials:Mar. 1<br>Mail date: Mar. 19 | - Retail Lighting<br>- Retail Interiors Expo<br>- PreShow Issue | - Lighting: Trends | - Retail Interiors Expo: All Products and Services | - Retail Interiors Expo, Chicago*<br>- Lightfair, New York |
| **May - RL, EZ**<br><br>Ad reservations: Mar. 22<br>Ad materials: Mar. 30<br>Mail date: Apr. 18 | - The Food Retailing issue<br>- Digital Retailing Expo At-Show Issue<br>- Retail Interiors Expo At-Show Issue<br>- In-Store Digital Media Special Section | - Food & Drug Retail<br>- Store Fixturing: Components | - Digital Retailing Expo Exhibitors<br>- Lighting | - Retail Interiors Expo, Chicago*<br>- Digital Retailing Expo, Chicago*<br>- Food Marketing Institute, Chicago |
| **June**<br><br>Ad reservations: Apr. 24<br>Ad materials:May 2<br>Mail date: May 18 | - The Store Fixture Issue<br>- Annual Store Fixture Industry Survey<br>- Top 50 Fixture Manufacturers<br>- NeoCon Preview | - Store Fixturing: Trends | - Store Fixtures | - NASFM Convention<br>- NeoCon, Chicago |
| **July**<br><br>Ad reservations: May 22<br>Ad materials: May 31<br>Mail date: June 18 | - Atlanta Retail<br>- Digital Retailers of the Year | -<br>Signage/Graphics | - Signage/Graphics | |

FIGURE 4.6. 2007 editorial calendar from *VM + SD* Web site. (*continued*)

| August - RL<br><br>Ad reservations: June 22<br>Ad materials: July 2<br>Mail date: July 19 | - Annual Visual Merchandising Survey<br>- Lightfair Review<br>- International Retail Design Conference Preview | - Visual Merchandising Trends | - Mannequins<br>- Lighting | - VM+SD International Retail Conference, (IRDC) 2006, Atlanta* |
|---|---|---|---|---|
| **September**<br><br>Ad reservations: July 26<br>Ad materials: Aug. 3<br>Mail date: Aug. 21 | - Renovation Competition Winners<br>- Peter Glen Retailer of the Year<br>- NeoCon Review<br>- International Retail Design Conference At-Show Issue | - Retail Construction<br>- Store Fixturing: Materials<br>- Flooring Trends | - Exterior Signage/Graphics<br>- Furniture | - VM+SD International Retail Conference, (IRDC) 2006, Atlanta*<br>- The In-Store Marketing Show, Chicago |
| **October**<br><br>Ad reservations: Aug. 22<br>Ad materials: Aug. 30<br>Mail date: Sept. 18 | - Green Retail Update<br>- Brand-Building Case Studies | - Food and Drug Retail<br>- In-Store Marketing | - Flooring, Lighting, Surfacing Materials | - NASFM Convention Nat'l Association of Convenience Stores Show<br>- Greenbuild International Conference & Expo, Los Angeles |
| **November - RL**<br><br>Ad reservations: Sept. 25<br>Ad materials: Oct. 3<br>Mail date: Oct. 19 | - Annual In-Store Digital Media Survey<br>- New York Retail (Part I)<br>- Convenience Store Update<br>- In-Store Digital Media Special Section | - Lighting: Trends<br>- Store Fixturing: Installation | - In-Store Technology<br>- StoreXpo Exhibitors and Showrooms | - StoreXpo, New York*<br>- National Association of Convenience Stores Show, Atlanta |
| **December - EZ**<br><br>Ad reservations: Oct. 24<br>Ad materials: Nov. 1<br>Mail date: Nov. 19 | - StoreXpo At-Show Issue<br>- New York Retail (Part II) | - A Look Back at 2007 | - Best New Products 2007<br>- StoreXpo Exhibitors and Showrooms | - StoreXpo, New York* |

FIGURE 4.6.

Since freelance writers can look at the editorial calendar, they get ideas for appropriate stories that could be published in a particular magazine. With this in mind, writers can research a topic, compose an article, and submit a query letter to a magazine with the hope of finding the source for publication of their article.

# PREPARING THE ARTICLE

The feature article is said to have been invented in the 19th century. "[N]ewspaper titans Joseph Pulitzer, William Randolf Hearst, and James Gordon Bennett almost simultaneously, but competitively, decided to attract readers with stories about ordinary people doing extraordinary—often bizarre—things" (Harrison, 2002, p. 1). Feature articles of today's magazines continue to focus on interesting individuals, celebrities, current affairs, events, food, homes, travel, and other lifestyle concerns. Each magazine has its own **formula**, or list of topics that editors, writers, and readers can expect in each issue. For example, most women's fashion magazines cover fairly similar ground. Most include such topics as beauty, celebrity profiles, fashion, fitness and health, how-to articles, food, lifestyle information, and sex.

The author of a feature article needs to first consider the tone of the article, which can be refined through the brainstorming process. The author may need to undertake various types of research; interviews with appropriate individuals can add richness to the article. As the article develops, the writer tries to come up with a title that will attract the attention of the editor and readers. Next, the author writes the lead and finishes writing the article. The job is still not complete until the article is rewritten and edited. The final step is proofreading to make sure that grammar and content are correct. All of these steps are examined in the following paragraphs.

## TONE

Most articles in consumer and trade magazines are informal, often quite intimate, in tone. The most intimate form of writing is in the first person, saying, in effect, "I am writing to you." Writing in the first person increases interest and understanding. As we mentioned in Chapter 2, the second person (you) is also used in magazine article writing to create a sense of familiarity between author and reader. Many students are used to writing in the third person for academic papers, which are more formal than magazine articles. Third-person style is detached, providing a cool relationship between the reader and the audience.

The tone used by the staff at *Town & Country* for a fashion article and images that were photographed at Frank Sinatra's Palm Springs house was creative and nostalgic for its target audience. Each of the fashion segments began with a Sinatra theme song. Swimwear was highlighted with, "Nice work if you can get it—and chances are you can in these choices for poolside panache" ("A Swingin' Affair," 2007, p. 148). Evening wear was introduced by "Night and day, you are the one—especially in a glamorous look worthy of an evening with a Sinatra sound track" (p. 151). "The lady is a vamp in this high-contrast ensemble" (p. 155) featured casual attire.

Whatever tone and style of writing is called for, it should be consistent throughout the article. A writing style manual is helpful in making the article uniform throughout. There are many style manuals to use as guides, including the *AP Stylebook*, *Chicago Manual of Style*, *Elements of Style*, and *The New York Times Manual of Style and Usage*. See the "Additional Resources" section at the end of this chapter for further information about these style manuals.

---

*Portfolio Exercise:* **Discover one or two writers of magazine articles whose work you appreciate for tone and style. In memo format, identify the specific magazine and analyze how those authors use direct quotations, narrations, and anecdotes in their stories. Be prepared to share your research orally in class.**

---

# BRAINSTORMING

Brainstorming, or tossing around any and all ideas about a topic, is the starting point of any project. Carrying around a small notebook to jot down article ideas is a good start to the brainstorming process. You can generate ideas by reading articles from a variety of sources; having conversations with friends, relatives, or other writers; watching television or movies; listening to the radio; or surfing the Internet—to name just a few resources.

Once you've completed a list of potential story ideas, you need to narrow the focus. Get rid of the ho-hum ideas. Analyze the theme and decide if it is more appropriate for a consumer publication or for a trade publication.

## CHECKLIST FOR EVALUATING STORY IDEAS

Charles Harrison (2002) suggests applying a six-question test to evaluate ideas that will lead to articles that will sell:

- ☐ Are they fresh and timely?
- ☐ Do they have an angle?
- ☐ Are they tightly focused?
- ☐ Do they truly interest *you*?
- ☐ Are they likely to interest editors/readers of trade/professional publications as well as consumer publications?
- ☐ What research is entailed: Can you gain access to sources, and will you have time to complete all necessary research before writing the article?

# RESEARCH AND INTERVIEWS

Lack of research and documentation is a top complaint from editors about articles submitted by new writers. Research begins with the questions "What information do I need to know?" and "Where do I find it?" Curiosity has led you to the topic, so the first thing to do is ask why the topic is interesting. Second, keep track of information. List some of the data that would be helpful in composing the article. The list might include historical information, statistics, biographical records, case studies, illustrations, examples, and anything else that helps to define the issue.

The Internet is a great resource for finding information. But there are some concerns about the information found in cyberspace. Because anyone, authority or not, can publish on the Internet, information found there may or may not be credible. Print materials undergo more rigorous editing and fact-checking, which makes them more believable resources. If authors and resources found on the Web are credible, their credentials should support this. Using databases for Internet searches and researching the organizations' publishing information can improve the credibility of Internet searches. This topic is covered in Appendix D, "Web Source Location and Evaluation."

Interviewing is another way to find authorities on a subject. The experiences and observations of interviewees add power and personality to a story. As the interviewer, you must prepare before the actual interview. Start by asking yourself, "What information do I want from this person?" Then, select someone who has something to say about the topic and is willing to share information with you. Develop a list of questions. And be sure to ask for permission to quote the interviewee.

*Portfolio Exercise:* **After brainstorming with other class members, determine a topic that could be used for a magazine article. Document some relevant facts from your preliminary research. Conduct an interview with someone who is an authority on the topic. Write a section of a magazine article that includes quotes from the interview to blend narration from your research.**

## CHOOSING A TITLE

A title should let the reader know what the article is about, reflecting the angle or focus of the proposed article. There are some common categories of titles, including How-to, Descriptive, Question, and Statement. The How-to article describes how to perform a task, make a product, or use a product. "Decorating Your Home Office" is an example of the title of a how-to article. The phrase *how to* is not necessary, but may be included.

A Descriptive title is used for an article where the reader is expected to envision a scene, experience an emotion, or examine an object. Such an article might be titled "Healing Scents."

Questions are used when the author wants the reader to think about possible answers. "Where Do You Find the Best Prices on Handbags?" could be an article on outlet shopping.

Statement titles are the most common form and may be used with any type of article. "Fighting Fakes" could be the title of an article about the expanding counterfeit products market. A subhead might clarify the topic and give more clarity to the article—for example, "Chanel Sues Counterfeiters in Los Angeles."

## WRITING THE LEAD

The **lead** is the first few sentences or the first paragraph of the magazine article. We discussed writing leads for newspapers in Chapter 3. Here we look at how to create leads for magazines. The lead helps to explain the title, start the story, and grab the reader's attention. According to Harrison (2002), leads also come in categories, including Anecdote, You, Descriptive, Question, First person, Surprising, and Straightforward.

The Anecdote is a very short, self-contained story with a beginning and an end, written as one paragraph. An Anecdote is usually based upon personal experience of the writer or someone the writer has interviewed. For example, the article might start, "I started looking around the room and noticed everyone was wearing a suit. I looked down at my sweater and slacks and wondered if I had not received the new Friday dress code memo." This could be the start for an article about changing dress code standards in a business working environment.

The You lead is a popular way to directly involve the reader. "To succeed with a weight loss plan, you need to start a comprehensive exercise program." This lead could be used with a how-to article on the benefits of exercise for losing weight.

By painting a picture of an environment, the Descriptive lead asks the reader to visualize a situation. "Imagine running to your seat in the front row as the lights go down and the music starts." This could be the introduction to a story about attending a show during Fashion Week.

The Question lead wants the reader to answer the question or try to get the answer. "Grace Mirabella had been the editor-in-chief of *Vogue* for 17 years. She wondered if the rumors were true, would she soon be replaced?" This could be a lead for the story of how Anna Wintour got her job at *Vogue*.

By offering a hook that catches the reader off guard, the element of Surprise causes interest in the topic. "She heard a voice on the other end of the phone, screaming, 'I have to go, I just heard a loud noise.'" Who was the screaming woman, what was the noise, and where was the woman calling from? The surprises will be explained in the article that follows.

A Straightforward lead provides solid information about the topic, with the hope that the reader will want more information. "This month, daring London theatergoers looking for nostalgia can find it at the Old Vic Theater. *The Philadelphia Story*, starring Kevin Spacey, opens on June 11th." This classic play with a new actor is the subject for this story with a Straightforward lead.

---

*Portfolio Exercise:* **Examine an article of your choice in one consumer magazine and in one trade magazine. Identify the type of lead used in each article. Rewrite the lead in a format different from the existing one. (For example, if the lead is a How-to, rewrite it in the You style.)**

## WRITING THE ARTICLE

Before starting to write the article, read the magazine you want to write for. Notice the style and tone of existing articles. While we do not want you to plagiarize, it is appropriate to imitate the style used by other authors of that publication. All writers learn by reading other authors' work.

Magazine writing allows for a more personal style between the writer and the reader than writing for some other types of publications does. Write your magazine article as if you are having a conversation with your audience.

Unlike more formal writing, magazine articles depend upon direct quotations. Writers with a background in journalism know the benefits of sharing the personal views of others through direct quotation. A direct quote from a person related to the story can add color and sparkle.

The articles in consumer and trade publications often use anecdotes to illustrate a point. Usually, an anecdote is short: no more than one paragraph relating one incident. It may be humorous or quite serious. Anecdotes break up the story by offering illustrations that the reader can visualize.

## REWRITING AND EDITING

Many first-time writers think that once the story is written, their job is done. On the contrary, rewriting and editing are important parts of the writing process. Besides using the grammar and spelling tools in your word processing software, you need to reread the manuscript for yourself, keeping in mind the purpose and the style of the potential publication. Make sure you have not lost track of the original reason for writing the article.

A reexamination helps you to discover missing pieces. As you are writing, cutting, and pasting, it is easy to lose your train of thought. Rereading the article helps you check the flow of the story.

Rereading also allows you to see where you may have overused a particular word. The thesaurus feature in your word processing software offers word options that can help to eliminate worn-out language. (Of course, make sure the word you choose not only helps you avoid overuse but also fits your article's tone and voice.)

**CHECKLIST FOR REWRITING AND EDITING**

Charles Harrison (2002) offers another helpful writing checklist:

- ☐ **Check clarity**—Something that is perfectly clear to you will not be as clear to your reader unless there is sufficient information, explanation, and definition.
- ☐ **Check coherence and unity**—Paragraphs are focused, and words, phrases, clauses, and sentences follow in logical order. You have provided transitions between paragraphs.
- ☐ **Check simplicity**—Help your reader to understand by offering sentences that are not too long or confusing.
- ☐ **Check voice and tone**—Be sure you are coming across in the voice and tone you intended.
- ☐ **Check direct quotes and paraphrasing**—Be sure your direct quotes and paraphrased material are accurate and properly attributed.
- ☐ **Check consistency**—If you start the article in first person and present tense, be sure you do not change it in mid-article. Make sure you did not miss some points or alter your step-by-step format.

# PROOFREADING, PROOFREADING, PROOFREADING

Almost every word processing computer program offers some type of spell-checking tool and grammar-checking tool. While these programs are extremely helpful, they do not replace rereading the article. Some authors find it helpful to read the article out loud. Others ask a friend to read the article. Sometimes, you keep reading the same errors, and you do not even realize it. The article is not finished until you have proofed it.

In Chapter 3, we discussed proofing and revising for newspaper writing. We cannot emphasize enough the need for proofing and checking all of your documents before publication. No matter how many times we've looked at a chapter, we have found mistakes—we hope we catch them all before publication.

# GETTING PUBLISHED

Magazines exist in a highly competitive and crowded information marketplace. Consumers have almost unlimited choices of where to find information. With competition from everywhere—from local newspapers to global cable television networks and the Internet—magazines attempt to attract readers by offering original content and unique presentation.

Because most magazines have a limited number of staff, they rely heavily upon freelance writers. This allows a wide range of topics to be fully developed by an endless pool of writers. Typical magazine freelancers spend a significant amount of time, sometimes as long as several months, researching a topic. At the same time, these freelance authors are checking the market by sending letters to editors to gauge interest in the topic and potential for publication. In the following sections, we'll look at finding the right audience for a writer's content and writing the query letter that a freelance writer would send to a magazine editor.

## UNDERSTANDING THE AUDIENCE

Some writers start with a story idea and then look for an appropriate target publication. Other writers start with a particular publication in mind and develop a story specifically for it.

Reading the magazine you want to write for is a good first step in understanding the audience and that publication's accepted style of writing. You'll gather hints about the audience as well as about the types of topics covered, the treatments, and the length of articles. You can determine the typical length of a paragraph and can discover whether the articles use anecdotes or direct quotes. You can determine whether the editors prefer articles written in the first person, the second person, or the third person, and determine the tone of the writing. Is it light or serious? Each of these issues will help you decide how to write your own material.

Checking the type of advertising used in the magazine will also give you insight into the publication. Does the magazine advertise diapers and baby food? If so, it is targeted toward young parents. Lots of ads for cosmetics and beauty products indicate a predominantly female audience. By being aware of the audience, you can tailor the language you use when you write your article.

# WRITING THE QUERY LETTER

Editors receive hundreds of letters from prospective writers each month. Many of these ideas are inappropriate for the magazine to which they have been sent. In order to attract the attention of a busy editor who has limited time to consider various article submissions, a good-looking and well-written one-page letter can create a positive first impression. The **query letter** is a proposal asking if the editor is interested in your topic. It assesses your ability to write and to create interest in your subject.

Editors need information about your article in a hurry, so you need to get to the point quickly. Let the editor know why the story is important to the readers of the magazine and why the topic is unique. Harrison (2002) offers the following tips to guide the preparation of query letters:

1.  **Know the magazine.** Understand the type of audience (reader demographics and preferences), the kinds of articles published (how-to, personal experience, indepth), and the writing style (light and hip or more formal). This will help you find the best publication for your topic and avoid sending it to the wrong editor.

2.  **Remember, you're writing a business letter.** Use a standard business letter format. Address the letter to a specific editor by name, not just "Dear Editor" or "To whom it may concern." Names are printed on the masthead or are available in such resources as *Writer's Market* or *Bacon's Magazine Directory*. In the salutation, address the editor by last name (use *Ms.* or *Mr.*). Only if you know the editor personally is it appropriate to use the editor's first name.

3.  **Structure your letter.** The one-page letter should contain three parts: the lead paragraph, the summary or explanatory paragraphs, and the paragraph about your qualifications as a writer. Just like in the article you plan to write, the lead paragraph of your proposal letter provides the hook to grab the editor's attention. If it does not do this, the editor will probably stop reading right here and send a rejection letter. The summary or explanatory paragraphs tell the editor how you plan on developing the article from the research you are conducting. It is important to keep this section short, yet informative. Finally, you must tell the editor about your background as a writer and why you are the writer best able to construct this story. Figure 4.7 shows an example of a query letter.

P.O. Box 6589
Kent, Ohio 44240-6589
July 18, 20xx

Ms. Jerry Elliot, Editor-in-chief
*College Woman*
19 Old Town Square, Suite 137
Ft. Collins, CO 80524

Dear Ms. Elliot:

During my sophomore year in school, I was so busy with my class assignments, my job at the DuBois Bookstore, my sorority, and spending time with my boyfriend. I didn't have time to think about my future. I heard my teachers talk about internships, but how could I possibly fit that in with all of my other obligations?

There were so many things to consider. How would I be able to afford moving to another city? How would I go about getting the internship? Is it really worth all of the time and expense? Then, I learned that Nordstrom in Scottsdale, Arizona, was offering an internship in public relations. Aunt Kay lives in Phoenix! The light bulb went off. It was time to think about what I want to do after graduation. I applied and I was offered the position.

My internship was the greatest experience. I learned so much about luxury retailing, merchandising and public relations. My proposed article is about doing an internship. Hopefully, my article will give insight into the decision-making process about whether or not to do an internship, discussing the pros and cons. I plan on reporting how to make the experience of applying for and completing an internship better for any student who decides to do one.

I am currently a senior at Kent State University with a major in Fashion Merchandising and a minor in Journalism and Public Relations. I believe that my experience and current studies give me the experience to write such an article. I have taken some photography courses at Kent and can also provide photos for the article, if you are interested.

Thank you for your consideration, and I look forward to discussing my article with you. You may contact me by phone at (303) 555-5555 or by e-mail at ljp55@kentstate.edu.

Sincerely,

*Liz Patterson*
Liz Patterson

**FIGURE 4.7.** Query letter.

**4. You may submit the same idea to more than one publication.** Simultaneous submissions to two or three magazines are acceptable. Since acceptances are rare, it is a good idea to accept the first offer rather than waiting to hear back from all of the editors. Rejections are more plentiful than acceptances.

**5. Think of different angles and markets for the same idea.** You may increase your chances of getting the article published if you look at alternative angles or come up with another approach to the topic and send your ideas to publications that are dissimilar. For example, a consumer-oriented article may be rewritten for a trade publication.

Every query letter should include a self-addressed, stamped envelope (SASE). As we've said, many magazines have limited staffs. Editors may not respond to each and every query letter. By including a SASE, you are more likely to receive a response from an editor. Even if the response is negative, the editor may provide some insight into improving your work the next time.

As we move into the electronic age, many of you will use the Internet to send query letters and article proposals. This is becoming much more commonplace in the 21st century. Some magazines, traditional as well as online, might actually prefer submissions by e-mail or fax. The contents of a query letter should remain essentially the same whether the letter is submitted through the postal service or e-mail.

---

*Portfolio Exercise:* **Write a query letter to a trade or consumer magazine for an article idea that you develop. Adapt that letter to different types of magazines, one of which is available only online.**

---

## SUMMARY

Writing for fashion magazines is fun and challenging. Opportunities are available in both consumer magazines and trade magazines. To view the makeup of the staff for a consumer magazine, review the magazine's masthead; there you will see the editor-in-chief, editors, contributors, and even interns given credit for their work. Magazines use an editorial calendar to determine the theme for each issue.

Preparing an article for submission to a magazine requires developing a tone that is entertaining to the audience. Reviewing past issues of the magazine can help you establish the correct tone. Brainstorming can help you decide what to write about. Once the topic is selected, research or interviews often help flesh out the article. The lead is intended to get the audience immediately interested in reading the rest of the story. Editing, rewriting, and proofreading are all necessary elements of writing a magazine article. The query letter directs the article proposal to the magazine editor for possible publication.

## KEY TERMS

Beauty editor

Bookings editor

Business-to-business
   magazine (B2B)

Consumer magazine

Contributing editor

Contributor

Copy editor

Creative director

Editorial Calendar

Editor-in-chief

Fashion assistant

Fashion editor

Features editor

Formula

Freelance writer

Lead

Magazine

Managing editor

Masthead

Publisher

Query letter

Trade magazine

## CASE STUDY

## *Model Behavior: Dress Accordingly*

Each year, the executives at Condé Nast sponsor an in-house competition to find new and creative ideas for periodicals. Personnel from each of its divisions, including the various consumer and trade magazines, Web sites, and books, submit ideas and compete to have their idea selected for publication.

For example, *Cookie* magazine was developed into a real publication after it was presented as a new concept for the Condé Nast competition. *Cookie*'s mission statement is that the magazine will showcase all the best for your family, featuring articles about fashion, home, travel, entertainment, and health for parents and children. With a clean, stylish design aesthetic, *Cookie* believes that being a good parent and maintaining a sense of style are not mutually exclusive.

With so many magazine editors and contributors, as well as celebrities such as Gwyneth Paltrow, Kate Hudson, and Maggie Gyllenhaal, having babies and raising children, the time seemed right to start a magazine about stylish moms and kid culture.

This year the interns from the Fairchild Fashion Group organized a team to enter the competition. Lindsey Warren and Stephanie Parker—summer interns at *WWDBeautyBiz*, the monthly trade publication that provides in-depth coverage and analysis on all aspects of the beauty industry—are leading the team.

Lindsey and Stephanie feel they've identified a missing niche market in the magazine industry: There is no national magazine about modeling. Reality television shows such as *America's Next Top Model*, *The Agency*, and *Project Runway* are popular with college students. Other media, including newspapers and entertainment news broadcasts, are covering the models wearing the latest fashion collections in New York, Paris, London, and Milan. Both Lindsey and Stephanie modeled for their college fashion shows, and they fantasized about getting into the modeling industry after their internships. The fashion show at Stephanie's university was even called *Model Behavior: Dress Accordingly*. The rest of the intern group thought this was a good idea, and they started to brainstorm about a potential title and features that would be included in their magazine.

In their mission statement, the interns write that the mission of this new modeling magazine would be to inspire and empower modern, stylish readers who would look to the magazine as their guide to a model's life. Whether covering the latest fashion/beauty trends or presenting pioneering editorials on models' health issues, *Model Behavior* would offer a unique combination of style and substance about this influential industry.

## CASE STUDY QUESTIONS

1. Do you think this is a good idea? What pros and cons are associated with starting a magazine about modeling?
2. What types of articles should be included each month?
3. What types of articles should be featured on an irregular schedule?
4. What kinds of special issues could be created? Develop an editorial calendar for the upcoming year.

## INDUSTRY PROFILE

*Jenny B. Fine*

***What is your current job and title? Can you describe the main responsibilities for your job?***

My current job is Editor of *WWD Beauty Biz*, which is a monthly glossy magazine published by *Women's Wear Daily*, covering the business side of the beauty industry. I am really responsible for the overall content, and the look and feel of the magazine.

***What is a typical day at work like?***

There really is no typical day, which is what I like about my job. I do everything. I cover the market. I oversee photo shoots. I report and write stories, so I am constantly doing something different, and that keeps it both interesting and exciting for me. That is what drew me to journalism in the first place.

When you cover something, you become kind of an instant expert in whatever it is that you cover. You also have the capability to cover so many different things as a journalist. I am somebody that likes to do a lot of different things. I get bored very easily. This is the type of job where you really never get bored because one day is never like the next day.

***At what point did you decide to pursue a career in writing for a fashion-related business?***

While I was growing up in Kentucky, I always loved fashion magazines, which were my link to an outside bigger world. I've been reading magazines for as long as I can remember, probably since age 6 or 7. I always thought I wanted to work for a fashion magazine. I studied art history undergraduate and really only wrote academically.

My first job out of undergraduate was working for a fashion editor, and it quickly became clear to me within the space of a year that wasn't so much my forte. It seemed like everybody else was really creative . . . the designer was creative, the photographer was creative, and the stylist was creative. I began to see that is where my talents lie.

I went back to graduate school for a master's in journalism. I thought maybe I wanted to write about politics. But, I wasn't really sure what I wanted to write about. I sent my résumé everywhere. The first job offer I got was at Fairchild on a magazine called *Salon News*, which doesn't exist anymore. It covered the hair salon industry. I was there for about a year and a half. Fairchild gave me an opportunity to write and learn more about writing. One person does the job of five people, and it is still like that today. Some people thrive in a situation like that. I was one of those people.

A position opened up on *WWD* covering the beauty industry. I was there for about two years and was offered a position at *Self* magazine as the beauty director.

My career kind of happened. It wasn't really preplanned.

***Describe your first writing job. What was the most important or interesting thing you wrote for that job/publication?***

My first writing job after college was the credits editor for *Model* magazine, which doesn't exist anymore. I was actually there only two weeks because I got a job offer at *New York* magazine working for the fashion editor. The editor-in-chief at *Model* magazine was very kind and released me from *Model* to go work for *New York*. She realized that was an amazing opportunity.

What I really remember most of all is the skill of the writing, more than the specific stories that I wrote. At *Salon News* we wrote so much. We wrote everything, no part of the magazine was freelanced out. We wrote stories about how to market a perm, how to sell, or other business-related stories for that market. What I remember as much as the writing itself is the conceiving of story ideas, getting into the head of the reader, and then continually coming up with new ideas to make it fresh every month.

Getting into the head of the reader is key.

***What are you currently reading (books, magazines, Web sites, newspapers, other media)? Do you have a favorite author or publication?***

I'm reading all of the above. Bookwise, I'm reading Calvin Trillin, who I am rediscovering and loving. I am also reading an English writer, a playwright, Alan Bennett. He wrote a play called *The History Boys*. I'm reading an anthology of his writing, something of a diary.

Magazines . . . on a weekly basis I read the *New York Times Sunday Magazine*, which I love. The *New Yorker*. I read every fashion magazine. I read gossip rags. I read it all. Blogs, I read tons of blogs . . . media blogs . . . fashion blogs. I read foreign newspaper sites. I'm reading baby books. [As this interview took place, Jenny Fine was on maternity leave.]

I have tons of favorites . . . Books . . . *The Magus* by John Fowles . . . Favorite writers . . . John McPhee, Paul Theroux, Calvin Trillin, Joan Didion. I just reread *The Year of Magical Thinking*. I read Joan Didion in college, and did not read her for a while. I love the sparseness of her language, but it's so descriptive at the same time. Adam Gopnik writes for the *New Yorker* and wrote *Paris to the Moon*. Bill Buford is an incredible writer and reporter.

### What advice do you have for students interested in a writing career? Do you have any recommendations for students?

If you are a writer, you are doing it. The first thing is to try to write as much as possible. Try to get internships. Get your résumé out there. A lot of young people limit themselves, and think of only wanting to write for XYZ magazines or newspapers.

As I started my career, I asked myself, would I want to write for *Vogue* one day? . . . yes. But, it was more important, especially early in my career, that I write. *Salon News* wasn't the best known or most prestigious magazine. But, what I got from it was a wealth of experience that I really would not have gotten at most other entry-level places.

The other thing I would say is to read a lot. You have to be completely plugged in to what's out there. Read a lot of books. Being out and doing things, journalists are both recorders and participants in some ways. You can't wait for an editor to assign you a story idea. You have to come up with good ideas. You have to be on the pulse of whatever is happening. You also have to do your research about the readership of whoever it is you want to write for. Come up with interesting ideas that the readers are going to like. At the end of the day, it is not necessarily about pleasing the editor or yourself, it is about pleasing the reader.

People underestimate the importance of writing a lot. Depending upon the type of job you get, in certain entry-level magazines, you may not be writing very much at all. If you want to be a writer, as opposed to be an editor, you need to write. You have to be out there. You have to be prepared at an entry-level job, and assisting a lot, which is perfectly normal. You've got to have almost a second full-time job in which you are writing.

Being successful is a matter of being incredibly motivated and really wanting it, especially in New York. If you are not like that, there are plenty of other people who are. There are too many other people who want to write, and they are good at it. Nobody is going to hand it to you.

---

**Box 4.1  What Is WWDBeautyBiz?**

In every issue, the monthly trade publication *WWDBeautyBiz* explores the trends that are driving new products, showcases the professionals and icons behind the business, provides retail and competition analysis, conducts consumer research, explains business strategies and best practices, gives category-specific analysis, presents the celebrities involved, and covers fashion shows. The target audience for this periodical includes top retail managers, beauty industry executives, fashion and women's magazine editors, beauty advisers, stylists, and financial managers.

---

## ADDITIONAL RESOURCES

Goldstein, N. (2004). *AP stylebook*. New York: Basic Books.

Seigal, A. M., & Connolly, W. G. (2002). *The New York Times manual of style and usage: The style guide used by editors and writers of the world's most authoritative paper*. New York: Three Rivers Press.

Staff of the University of Chicago Press. (2005). *The Chicago manual of style* (15th ed.). Chicago: University of Chicago Press.

Strunk, W., Jr., White, E. B., & Angell, R. (2000). The elements of style (4th ed.). Needham Heights, MA: Longman.

## REFERENCES

A Swingin' Affair. (2007). *Town & Country*, 148–165.

Circulation snapshot. (2005, April 29). *Women's Wear Daily*. Section II, p. 4.

Condé Nast Publications. (2006a). *Careers*. Retrieved March 22, 2007, from http://www.condenastcareers.com

Condé Nast Publications. (2006b). *Media kit*. Retrieved March 23, 2007, from http://www.condenastmediakit.com/vog/publisher.cfm

Esten, J. (2001). *Diana Vreeland Bazaar years*. New York: Universe.

French Vogue names editor. (1994, April 11). *New York Times*. Retrieved March 2, 2007, from http://nytimes.com

Harrigan, J. T., & Dunlap, K. B. (2004). *The editorial eye*. Boston: Bedford/St. Martin's.

Harrison, C. H. (2002). *How to write for magazines: Consumers, trade, and web.* Boston: Allyn & Bacon.

Hoare, S. (2002). *Talking fashion.* New York: Powerhouse.

Hot Stuff. (2007, Spring Beauty). *WWDBeautyBiz,* 30–38.

James, S. (2005, April 29). Anatomy of a magazine cover. *Women's Wear Daily,* Section II, p. 14.

Mirabella, G., with Warner, J. (1995). *In and out of Vogue.* New York: Doubleday.

Oppenheimer, J. (2005). *Front row: Anna Wintour, the cool life and hot times of Vogue's Editor in Chief.* New York: St. Martin's Press.

Orecklin, M. (2004, February 9). The power list women in fashion. *Time Style & Design.* Retrieved June 1, 2005, from http://www.time.com/time/2004/020904/power/3.html

Socha, M. (2000, December 8). Buck leaves French Vogue. *Women's Wear Daily.* Retrieved March 2, 2007, from InfoTrac OneFile via Thompson Gale.

Talley, A. L. (2007, April). Life with André. *Vogue,* 110.

# FIVE

## *Writing for Broadcast Media*

After you have read this chapter, you should be able to discuss the following:

• The role of writing in broadcast journalism

• How news stories and features are written for broadcast media

• How documentaries and cable broadcast channels incorporate fashion

• How broadcast scripts differ from other forms of writing

I felt like I was the only teenager who cultishly watched and videotaped *Style* every weekend on CNN in the 1980s. But, many fashion television broadcasters today admit they were drawn to the first weekly television show pioneered and hosted by Elsa Klensch. Her 30-minute show covered fashion, luxury goods, and design. The program became the role model as well as competition for other shows, such as *Fashion Television* (hosted by Jeanne Beker), *Fashion File,* and *House of Style.*

Showing fashion and how to wear it is the primary purpose of such cable shows as *What Not to Wear* and *The Look for Less.* Entire cable networks, such as Fashion Television Channel in Canada and Style in the United States, follow every aspect of fashion. Reality programs, including *America's Next Top Model* and *Project Runway*, have many loyal followers, who anxiously await the next episode (Figure 5.1).

The point of this chapter is to discuss the role of writing in broadcast media. We will look at broadcasting in general. Then, we'll analyze the characteristics that set radio and television apart from print media, the characteristics common to radio and

FIGURE 5.1. *Project Runway.*

television news writing, and the characteristics of story structure. Writing for documentary and cable programs will also be explored.

## BROADCAST MEDIA

The term **broadcasting** refers to the airborne transmission of electromagnetic signals—audio signals for radio and audiovisual signals for television—that are available to a vast audience through widely available receivers. Radio and television are the primary means by which information and entertainment are delivered to listeners and viewers in virtually every nation around the world.

Radio evolved from an earlier medium, the telegraph, which was the first instantaneous form of information available. The telegraph depended upon physical wires to transport messages in a code of long and short electronic impulses standardized as Morse code.

Scientists worked to devise a system that could overcome telegraph's limitations. In 1895, the Italian inventor Guglielmo Marconi transmitted a message in Morse code that was received 3 miles away by a device that had no wire connection to the transmitting device (Schoenherr, 2001). Thus Marconi created the first machine that broadcast widely through space, and the age of broadcasting began. The tool was first used after World War I for transmitting information and entertainment to the general public with commercial purposes. The first radio broadcast by station KDKA in Pittsburgh, Pennsylvania, took place in October 1920 (Schoenherr). As more citizens purchased the receivers, more radio stations were started and began broadcasting. Radio experienced its greatest influence during the first part of the 20th century.

The development of television has been a lengthy, collaborative process. It took several inventions to make the transmission of visual and audio images work. The earliest commercial news and entertainment television broadcasts took place in the 1930s. The British initiated daily experimental broadcasts through the British Broadcasting Corporation (BBC) as early as 1935. The U.S. public got its first look at television at the 1939 New York World's Fair, with coverage of the fair's opening ceremonies and a speech by President Roosevelt, the first televised appearance of a U.S. president (Schoenherr, 2004).

Radio and television programs were developed and transmitted over local channels and national networks. While programming for broadcast media evolved into various entertainment and news shows during the last half of the 20th century, the first broadcast news programs mimicked the print media—with someone reporting a story by reading it aloud. These reporters became the news anchors and newscasters.

News anchors and newscasters present stories and introduce live or videotaped reports on television or radio. Typically, **news anchors** sit behind a desk, serving as a master of ceremonies and introducing stories and fellow newscasters. While the anchor must understand the script and know how to pronounce all of the words and names, the anchor does much more than simply read words from a script or TelePrompTer; she presents the news in a manner that holds the audience's attention. The anchor's performance can make or break a newscast.

Another important requirement of the anchor's performance is that he must gain the trust of the audience. Anchors do this by behaving professionally, providing trustworthy and objective news stories, and having credibility. Credibility is established when an observer or audience member believes or accepts the newscaster's statement, action, or source as truth.

Many broadcast journalists are members of the Society of Professional Journalists (2007), which established a code of ethics. This code emphasizes the Society's members' duty to seek truth and provide a fair and comprehensive account of events and issues. Conscientious journalists from all media and specialties strive to serve the public with thoroughness and honesty. Professional integrity is the cornerstone of a journalist's credibility.

On fashion television programs, the anchor usually stands on the set or sits with other fashion professionals on chairs or sofas. This gives the program a more casual and approachable feeling.

Some **newscasters** are reporters who work in specialized types of news, such as sports or weather, for large television stations; other newscasters work on any topic assigned by the news director. At some stations, reporters cover a beat, which targets a specific topic or field, such as business, consumer affairs, crime, education, health, politics, religion, science, social events, or theater.

In addition to news programming, announcers, actors, and a variety of celebrities are involved in the broadcast media in other ways. Fashion and lifestyle coverage is prevalent on television cable channels, in addition to being part of national media productions, such as talk shows and entertainment venues. Morning television shows, such as the *Today* show, *Good Morning America*, and the *Morning Show*, frequently include fashion and lifestyle topics as a part of their news, information, and entertainment features.

Broadcasting dramatically changed life wherever it was introduced. Radio, and later television, brought news and information from around the world into individual homes. Professionally crafted radio and television programs brought into everyday life performances that audiences once could only expect to see in theaters, concert halls, or movie houses. Instantaneous news made worldwide events a shared experience.

The Internet is also considered to be a broadcast medium, but it is different enough from radio and television to be discussed in a separate chapter. Chapter 8 will cover writing for new media.

# CHARACTERISTICS OF BROADCAST MEDIA

Before radio and television, most news and information was disseminated through print media, such as newspapers and magazines. Live entertainment was presented in theaters and concert halls. The goal of writing for broadcast media is not just to replicate reports from other sources, but to write better stories than the ones you read in the newspaper or the ones you hear/see on other radio/television stations.

Four criteria distinguish radio and television from print sources: timeliness, information more than explanation, news with audio or visual impact, and people more than concepts. We will now look at those characteristics in more detail.

## Timeliness

The news value of timeliness is a priority for radio and television broadcasters. *When* something happens determines what items will be used in a broadcast. A breaking story takes precedence over any other story. Radio and television news is broadcast many times a day. This differs from the print press, where the paper or magazine goes to print at a specific time. If a particularly significant newsworthy story comes up, a regularly scheduled program may be interrupted. A sense of urgency is instilled in the broadcasts.

## Information

Because of the short time they have to tell the story, most radio and television reporters are more concerned about information than explanation. Broadcast narratives are typically 20 to 30 seconds long, and a story almost never runs longer than 2 minutes. During 1 minute of airtime, news that is read out loud consists of about 15 lines of copy, or approximately 150 words. The average length of a half-hour news program is 22 minutes, after the commercial and promotion time is subtracted. That would allow coverage of about one half of the content on the front page of a newspaper.

Announcers rarely have the time to provide in-depth explanation. Even if their audience knows nothing about the story, announcers often assume that listeners or viewers will turn to a newspaper, the Internet, or some other resource for further background and details.

## Audio or Visual Impact

The technologies that are used to report a story differ between print and broadcast sources. If a radio reporter is on the scene and has an opportunity to do a live interview, the story has audio appeal. Press conferences allow radio reporters to pass information on very quickly. And, since press conferences are not that interesting visually, the radio report fills the immediacy needs.

A television crew can provide visual interest. Good pictures from a visually stimulating event often receive prominence in the next newscast. Awards ceremonies such as the Academy Awards, Grammys, and Emmys generate a significant amount of interest in the celebrities at the event and the clothing they wear. Special broadcasts from "the red carpet" are commonplace.

## *People*

In contrast to print media, radio and television more regularly tell the story through people. In classic storytelling, you find a problem. Then, you find a person who is dealing with the problem, and you tell the audience how that person is doing. A representative person or family, someone who is affected by the story, becomes a chief participant, humanizing the story. Rather than using abstractions or concepts with no sound or visuals, television—and radio to a lesser degree—emphasizes the human nature of the story.

---

*Portfolio Exercise:* **Read a copy of a trade publication, such as *Women's Wear Daily* or *DNR*. Make a list of the stories (at least three, preferably five) covering fashion, textiles, retailing, fashion design, or a special event that would make good broadcast stories. Discuss why each of these is appropriate for broadcast media.**

---

# CHARACTERISTICS OF BROADCAST NEWS WRITING

Story structure as well as emphasis of certain characteristics makes writing for radio and television different from other forms of journalistic writing.

## CHECKLIST OF BROADCAST MEDIA WRITING TIPS

- ☐ Write factually and accurately.
- ☐ Write in the *active* voice.
- ☐ Write leads that stress what is happening now.
- ☐ Write the story so that it can be understood the first time it's heard.
- ☐ Write to the video.
- ☐ Be conversational.
- ☐ Be creative.
- ☐ Keep it simple.
- ☐ Make sure the "pronouncers" are included for all hard-to-pronounce names.
- ☐ Avoid pronouns.
- ☐ Avoid clichés.
- ☐ Avoid adjectives and adverbs.

Adapted from: Ohio University. (n.d.). Writing News. *Athens MidDay Manual.* Retrieved July 22, 2005, from http://www.scripps.ohiou.edu/actv-7/writers.htm

Because timeliness is so important in radio and television, radio and television news writers (as well as online writers) must emphasize immediacy. In addition, they must use a conversational style with tight phrasing and clarity. These distinctive styles will be discussed next.

## *Immediacy*

With concern for timeliness and immediacy, news writers use the present tense as much as possible. Note the use of the present tense in the lead for the following story:

AS TEMPERATURES SIZZLE IN THE NINETIES, MANY SHOPPERS *ARE RACING* INTO COOL ENVIRONMENTS . . . MALLS AND RETAIL STORES. THE HIGH OF NINETY-ONE DEGREES IN CHICAGO ON THURSDAY **FELT** LIKE NINETY-EIGHT DEGREES WITH THE HUMIDITY . . . AND MORE OF THE SAME *IS FORECAST* FOR THE WEEKEND.

SALES OF SWIMWEAR *ARE SOARING*. THIS *IS* A DRAMATIC TURNAROUND FROM LAST WEEK, WHEN SALES **WERE** BEHIND PLAN ACCORDING TO JANE BARNEY, GENERAL MANAGER FOR IN THE SWIM AT OLD ORCHARD MALL. SALES *ARE EXPECTED* TO SKYROCKET OVER THE WEEKEND.

In this story, the verbs displayed in *italics* are active and in the present tense, showing the action representative of a timely story. Of course, sometimes the past tense is needed in order to add emphasis to what is currently happening. In the example above, some background information was needed in order to tell the story, and those verbs—the ones in the past tense—are in **bold**. Notice that the broadcast story is printed in all capital letters, which is the standard format for broadcast media writing.

While the past tense will not emphasize action that is currently taking place, it may be needed to lead into new developments. You can update yesterday's story by including some new incident or new facts that have become available. Remember that radio and television are "live." Your copy should give that important sense of immediacy.

## Conversational Style

Writing for radio and television delivery differs from other writing because you are trying to write in the same way that you speak. Conversational style is questionable for most kinds of writing, but it is a requirement for broadcast writing. The best way to see if your copy is written in the broadcast style is to read it out loud, since that is how it will be presented on the air.

Your copy should be constructed of short sentences with active verbs. People rarely use the passive voice when they talk. It sounds clumsy and cumbersome.

---

*Passive Voice:* **I was told by the designer, Jennifer Gold, her line would be sold on QVC in January.**

*Active Voice:* **Designer Jennifer Gold told me her line will be sold on QVC in January.**

---

Another concern about writing in a casual speaking style is the use of contractions. An occasional contraction is acceptable, as long as your pronunciation is clear. We have learned that contractions are not to be used in formal writing, while in oral communication contractions are common. For broadcast media, however, the negative *not* is more clearly understood than the contraction *don't*.

Conversational style—"writing the way you speak"—also permits an occasional use of fragments or incomplete sentences. Still, you must strive to be clear and precise.

Writing in conversational style for broadcast purposes does not mean that you can use slang, colloquialisms, or incorrect grammar. Nor does it allow you to use rude, offensive, or off-color language. Take into consideration that your audience includes people of all ages, backgrounds, and sensitivities.

As you develop stories, you must decide what is ethical to report. Decisions regarding what to air or how to write a story are essential for maintaining credibility. For example, you hear that one of the top fashion designers has entered a rehab clinic due to a drug addiction. Prior to running a story about the situation, you should contact the designer's public relations office for confirmation and a quote. If the story can't be confirmed, you should not run the story if you want to maintain credibility.

## Tight Phrasing

In order to make each word count in a time-crunched story, you must learn to limit the number of words and condense your material. Maintaining a tight conversational style requires cutting down on adjectives and adverbs, eliminating the passive voice, and making each word count.

In order to present the story within the time allotted, you must identify and focus on the most important facts. Often, you will not have time to tell the whole story. Radio and television announcers want good, tight writing that is easy to follow. Here is a look at how a story that was originally written for *Women's Wear Daily* as a print story could be condensed for a radio or television story.

NEW YORK—Saks Fifth Avenue's Oscar-winning run continues.

After Nicole Kidman in 2003 and Charlize Theron last year, Saks secured Hilary Swank as the Entertainment Industry Foundation ambassador to its annual Key to the Cure cancer campaign.

Swank will appear in the campaign wearing a limited-edition T-shirt designed by Diane von Furstenberg, featuring an abstract red heart motif and phrases like "love is life" and "life is love," in DVF's own script. The T-shirt, available at Saks this fall, will retail for $35, of which $33 will be given to the cause. The campaign featuring Swank will break in fashion and lifestyle magazines in October.

Fighting cancer is a cause that's dear to Swank . . . (Karimzadeh, 2005).

The story goes on to quote Swank about how cancer has impacted her family's life. It also explains how much money was raised in previous years and discusses plans for the initiative, including a black-tie gala and a special shopping weekend fund-raiser in October. Benefactors of the event were also mentioned.

Here is how the story could be revised for a radio or television story:

OSCAR WINNER HILARY SWANK IS THE AMBASSADOR FOR THE ENTERTAINMENT INDUSTRY FOUNDATION'S ANNUAL KEY TO THE CURE FOR CANCER CAMPAIGN. SAKS FIFTH AVENUE WILL AGAIN SELL A LIMITED EDITION T-SHIRT DESIGNED THIS YEAR BY DIANE VON FURSTENBERG. MS SWANK WEARS THE SHIRT IN ADVERTISE-MENTS IN FASHION AND LIFESTYLE MAGAZINES IN OCTOBER.

THIS IS THE THIRD YEAR THE CAMPAIGN TAPPED THE CELEBRITY WHO JUST WON THE ACADEMY AWARD FOR BEST ACTRESS, AS ITS SPOKESPERSON. LAST YEAR, CHARLIZE THERON WORE A MARC JACOBS DESIGN, AND THE YEAR BEFORE, NICOLE KIDMAN SPORTED ONE BY STELLA MCCARTNEY.

SAKS KICKS OFF THE INITIATIVE WITH A BLACK-TIE GALA AT ITS MANHATTAN FLAGSHIP ON OCTOBER TWENTY SIXTH. A SPECIAL SHOPPING WEEKEND WILL FOLLOW THIS INTRODUCTION. EACH OF THE FIFTY-EIGHT SAKS FIFTH AVENUE STORES AND FIFTY-TWO OFF 5TH OUTLET STORES, AS WELL AS SAKS-DOT-COM, WILL SELL THE T-SHIRT ON OCTOBER TWENTY-EIGHTH AND TWENTY-NINTH. THE T-SHIRT WILL SELL FOR THIRTY-FIVE DOLLARS, OF WHICH THIRTY-THREE DOLLARS WILL BE GIVEN TO THE CAUSE.

BREAST CANCER IS SAKS' LARGEST CHARITABLE CAUSE. SINCE ITS FOUNDING SEVEN YEARS AGO, KEY TO THE CURE HAS RAISED OVER FIFTEEN MILLION DOLLARS. THIS YEAR THE COMPANY HOPES TO BREAK THE TWENTY MILLION DOLLAR BARRIER.

In the broadcast version, the audience is given basic facts. If they want more information, listeners must visit a Web site or look in the newspaper. The length of one newspaper story typically converts to two or three broadcast stories. Writers for radio and television strive to waste no words. Tight writing is expected. (Notice that the numerals and symbols are spelled out to aid in reading the story aloud.)

## Clarity

The readers of newspapers or online articles have the luxury of being able to reread the print story if they have missed something or they want less ambiguity. Radio and television listeners hear or see the story only once, and their attention is often divided. Therefore, you must try to be clear and precise in addition to being understood.

Clarity requires that you write simple, short sentences filled with commonly understood words. Synonyms, which are often used in print writing, are not necessary. Using smaller words is also a good idea. If a small, simple word conveys the same meaning as a longer, more difficult word, use the small one.

Another rule of thumb is to avoid using pronouns. In oral communication, it is helpful to repeat proper names, because the listener can easily forget the name of the person you are discussing.

Numbers and statistics can also cause problems. If you need to use numerical data, keep it simple and relevant to the audience. Reporting detailed sales figures can easily confuse your listeners. Instead of saying, "INCOME FROM OPERATIONS FELL TO ONE HUNDRED FOURTEEN MILLION DOLLARS FROM ONE HUNDRED NINETY EIGHT MILLION DOLLARS LAST YEAR," it would be better to say, "INCOME FROM OPERATIONS FELL FORTY-TWO POINT FOUR PERCENT TO ONE HUNDRED FOURTEEN MILLION DOLLARS DURING THE YEAR." Have the numbers help you tell the story, not add confusion.

## CHARACTERISTICS OF STORY STRUCTURE

Just as the approaches to writing stories for radio and television are different from those of print and online publications, the structure of the story differs as well. The leads for broadcast stories are constructed differently than the leads for print or online leads. Broadcast writers also must craft unique introductions and conclusions to audio or video segments in order to coordinate their foreword and ending to pre-taped segments. We will look at these approaches next.

## *Writing the Lead*

The lead must grab the listeners' attention, just as it must do for print media. Much of what we learned about writing leads for newspapers and magazines applies to broadcast leads as well. However, while newspaper and magazine readers are generally focused on reading, the audience for radio and television may be doing other things, such as driving a car while listening to the radio, or fixing breakfast while watching television. You have to attract them in different ways.

A common way to grab the audience's attention is to prepare them for what is to come by cueing them. You **cue** your audience by giving them a hint of what is coming next, hoping that they will stay tuned for the piece. You introduce the story with a general statement that will arouse interest, and then you go into the details. For example:

> LEVI STRAUSS WINS A LEGAL BATTLE WITH A FORMER CONTRACT MANUFACTURER IN MEXICO. THE FAMOUS AMERICAN BLUE JEANS MANUFACTURER HAS COME OUT ON TOP. A CIVIL APPELLATE COURT IN MEXICO CITY OVERTURNED A LOWER COURT RULING AND VACATED A FORTY-FIVE MILLION DOLLAR AWARD IN A LAWSUIT FILED BY COMPANIA EXPORTADORA DE MAQUILA COMEXMA ON MAY THIRTY-FIRST.

Cueing is just one of the techniques used for opening a broadcast story. The traditional pyramid lead—discussing Who, What, Where, and When—is also a popular lead for radio and television. Time and place may be included in the lead, if there is time. The Why and How follow later in the story. For example:

> GRAMMY AWARD WINNER AND ACADEMY AWARD NOMINATED ACTRESS QUEEN LATIFAH IS EXPANDING HER PARTICIPATION IN THE WORLD OF LINGERIE FOR THE CURVATION BRAND AT V—F INTIMATES. AT A MEDIA EVENT HELD AT THE V—F INTIMATES

OFFICES TODAY, QUEEN LATIFAH ANNOUNCED SHE WILL SERVE AS A CREATIVE CONSULTANT FOR DESIGNING, PACKAGING, ADVERTISING, AND MARKETING FOR THE ONE HUNDRED MILLION DOLLAR BRAND.

The story goes on to discuss how and why the actress is involved in the project.

It is also helpful to **tee-up,** or identify an unfamiliar name in the lead. By introducing the person, you are preparing the audience for an unknown name. For example:

CELEBRITY MAKEUP ARTIST AND SPA OWNER JOHN NAUGHTON, SIXTY-FOUR, LOST A TWO-YEAR BATTLE WITH CANCER ON TUESDAY.

Opening words should set the tone and mood for the story. You can ask a question without answering it. However, you should not mislead the audience by creating a deceptive lead.

## Writing Lead-ins and Wrap-ups

Television and radio broadcasts often use a videotape that was shot at the event location or an account or interview from another resource, such as a report from a participant. A **lead-in** introduces a prerecorded excerpt from another source or from a remote location. A **wrap-up** helps the audience understand that a story is over before the broadcast goes on to the next story.

The function of a lead-in is to set the scene by briefly telling Where, When, and sometimes What, and to identify the source or reporter. The lead-in may also be called a "toss." This introduction should contain something substantive and generate interest in what is coming next. For example:

SURF COMPANY BILLABONG IS BRINGING ITS BEACH MERCHANDISE TO THE URBAN JUNGLE WITH A NEW FLAGSHIP STORE IN THE HEART OF TIMES SQUARE. REPORTER SAM DERBY IS WITH THE PRESIDENT OF BILLABONG USA, PAUL NAUDE, AT THE NEW LOCATION ON BROADWAY BETWEEN WEST FORTY-FOURTH AND FORTY-FIFTH STREETS.

The lead-in should generate interest but not include too much information about what will come in the story. Just as a headline for a newspaper article entices the reader to read the story, the lead-in should get the reader's attention without robbing the opening words of the reporter or correspondent.

The wrap-up concludes the story, and it is usually delivered by the same person who introduced it. The wrap-up is especially important for radio copy since there are no visuals to show the transition back to the person who introduced the story. Using the previous lead-in, the following example shows how you can wrap up the story:

THANKS SAM. I AM LOOKING FORWARD TO VISITING THE NEW STORE. WE WILL BE RIGHT BACK AFTER THESE MESSAGES.

The wrap-up gives your story an ending and clearly separates it from the next story.

## Writing the Tease

Announcers also use the **tease** as a method to create audience interest for reports yet to come. A broadcast tease would consist of a phrase such as "COMING UP AFTER THE BREAK . . . ," "HERE IS A PREVIEW . . . ," "DO NOT GO AWAY . . . ," "FIND OUT MORE . . . ," or "WE WILL TALK WITH. . . ."

Keep in mind that you should never be satisfied with the first draft of a story. Reviewing, proofreading, and editing are just as necessary for broadcast stories as they are for print stories.

---

*Portfolio Exercise:* **Select two of the articles you found for the Portfolio Exercise earlier in the chapter. Now that you have learned about the techniques for writing for broadcast media, rewrite one of the stories for a radio story and rewrite the other one for a television story.**

---

We have just studied the specialized format that writing for radio and television news takes on. Now, we will look at other forms of writing for broadcast media, including documentaries and cable programs.

# DOCUMENTARIES AND CABLE PROGRAMS

Documentaries and full-length cable television programs are much longer than broadcast news or feature stories, and they provide opportunities to present greater detail. For example, each of the fashion cable networks typically presents 30- to 60-minute programs showing highlights of New York Fashion Week. In addition to showing the latest clothing, these comprehensive programs discuss the hair, makeup, models, and designers—and of course the celebrities attending the shows. The nonfiction coverage highlights the fashion presentations as well as the parties and store openings. This is in contrast to a segment lasting 5 minutes or less on a national network morning television show, during which there is time to present only a brief overview of the event and trends.

## DOCUMENTARIES

**Documentaries** are films or television shows that tell nonfiction stories, analyze news, and explore social conditions through an in-depth yet dramatic or theatrical format. Documentaries may be shown in movie theaters as well as on television. Documentaries are more like movies in that they are produced to cover longer periods of time (30 minutes to several hours), and they provide more content and penetration of the topics than do the lifestyle segments created for television or radio broadcasts (shorter than 10 minutes).

Documentaries require a great deal of time to produce. The first steps in producing a documentary include selecting a topic, writing a proposal, researching the facts, shaping the film, and composing the first draft. After the first draft is completed, the documentary has essentially three stages:

1. In the preproduction stage, the budget and contract are completed and a preproduction survey takes place.
2. During production, the director puts the plan into action. Writers, actors, announcers, and photographers, in addition to other production personnel, are hired. The location is selected and, if necessary, the set is created. Scripts and interview questions are prepared. Wardrobe is planned. The documentary is filmed. Much more time is spent filming the events, people, and locations than will ever be actually shown in the final edited production.

3. After filming is finished, the project goes into postproduction. At this stage, the film is edited, the final narration is written, and whatever else may be required to finish the film takes place.

Writing is an essential part of putting together a documentary, from conception to postproduction.

---

*Portfolio Exercise:* **Break into teams of 4 or 5. Brainstorm for ideas and topics that could make an interesting 15-minute documentary. Discuss the pros and cons about the topic your group favors. Draft a proposal that includes your working hypothesis, your lines of inquiry or research methodology, your point of view on the subject, and the dramatic possibilities. Your purpose is to convince a television editor that you have a great idea, that you know what you want to do, and that you are professional and are capable of completing the film.**

---

## CABLE PROGRAMS

When television first started, the broadcast medium was dominated by national networks with local affiliates. Cable television originated in the United States in the late 1940s to enhance poor reception of over-the-air television signals in mountainous or geographically remote areas. Typically, community antenna towers were erected on mountaintops or other high points, and homes were connected to the towers to receive the broadcast signals. As early as the 1950s, cable operators took advantage of their ability to pick up broadcast signals from hundreds of miles away. These "distant signals" changed the focus of cable's role from one of transmitting local broadcast signals to one of providing new programming choices (National Cable & Telecommunications Association, n.d.). In the 21st century, cable access and its accompanying technological improvements are almost a necessity for viewers who want to watch the wide variety of programming that is available. As this book is being written, many homes use the cable connection as their way to access high-speed Internet.

From the beginning, cable television programming choices have offered viewers almost unlimited alternatives to the local and national network television shows. Subjects from history to home furnishings to music to mysteries—and everything in between—are available to cable audiences. As we learned at the beginning of the chapter, fashion coverage on television began in the 1980s. Today, fashion information is covered on entertainment programs as well as on fashion networks. The cable channel TLC features *What Not to Wear*. The Style® Network broadcasts such shows as *How Do I Look?*, *Look for Less*, *Style Star*, and *Isaac*.

There are opportunities for cable television writers in various capacities. Not only are program script writers needed; the industry needs writers for marketing, public relations, research, and advertising purposes as well.

---

*Portfolio Exercise:* **You have been hired as an intern for The Style® Network. Management is considering who to profile next on *Style Star*. As one of your assignments, you are asked to complete research on two up-and-coming actresses. Determine who you think the next *Style Star* should be. Write a proposal in memorandum format stating why you think that individual should be profiled. Create a profile with images of what she has worn to the most recent red carpet events.**

---

# PREPARING RADIO AND TELEVISION COPY

Writing copy that is easy for the newscaster to read and easy for the audience to understand is the primary goal of preparing radio and television copy. What follows will help you achieve that goal. Figure 5.2 provides a wealth of the terms used to describe different elements of radio and television copy.

## FORMAT

In most newsrooms today, most writers use computerized production systems—such as Electronic News Production System (ENPS), which was created by the Broadcast Technology group of the Associated Press (Associated Press, 2005). ENPS is used to create, manage, and broadcast news content. Some of the features of the ENPS system include program rundowns, scripting, planning, contacts, messaging, archiving, third-party

### Broadcast Media Glossary

**Actuality:** The voice(s) of one or more people, who are experts, newsmakers, or spokespersons for the organization being featured.

**Announcer:** The person hired to narrate introductions and transitions within the broadcast story. This individual may be an individual that works for a broadcast station or a communication professional trained as a broadcast speaker.

**B-roll:** A series of rough supplemental video footage that incorporates a variety of different camera angles with natural sounds [NATSOUND].

**Chryron:** Words shown on a video screen, also known as a super.

**Contact slate:** The name(s) and contact information of the source of video news releases, including a telephone number and e-mail address, in case there are any additional questions.

**CU:** A close-up shot in a TV script. Most frequently, it is a shot of the face of a person.

**Disclaimer:** A standard slate that allows a television station to use any footage supplied on a video news release or electronic media kit. Copy generally states, 'The following material is offered to you for your free and unrestricted use by [name of organization]'.

**Dolly:** The physical forward or backward movement of the camera instead of zooming, panning, or tilting the camera from a fixed location.

**Fade:** In radio, a gradual decrease in volume. In TV or film, a gradual darkening of the scene.

**MS:** A medium shot in a TV or film, frequently of a person shown from the waist up.

**Outcue:** The final few words of the sound bite.

**Page slugs:** Indicators at the bottom of each page. For example, -MORE-, indicates the copy continues on the next page. Alternatively, -30- or ### or -END-, indicates the end of the story.

**Pan:** Movement of a TV camera's lens from left to right or vise-versa without moving the camera from a fixed location.

**Précis:** Background information on news being presented for video news releases or electronic media kits. It is a slate that provides the themes and messages from the sponsoring organization as a link to the news station.

**Pronouncers:** Names or words, with difficult or unusual pronunciations, presented phonetically within parentheses immediately after the name or word is written into the script.

**RT:** Running time that is specified for radio, TV, or film scripts.

FIGURE 5.2. Broadcast media glossary. *(continued)*

**Sequence:** A group of related shots in a TV or film script.

**Script:** The print format of the story. For radio, TV, or film, it is formatted into two columns. On the left are the slates, which indicate video and audio elements, and on the right are words to be spoken, written in capital letters.

**Slate:** A screen that identifies basic information or introduces images that follow. Slates, also known as billboards, are used in TV or film scripts, video news releases, and electronic media kits to show video elements.

**Slug:** A short title for a radio or TV script.

**SFX:** Sound effects.

**SOT:** Sound on tape. Designates natural background sound.

**Sound bite:** A recorded quotation that accompanies a radio news release.

**Tilt:** Movement of a TV camera up or down without moving the camera from a fixed location.

**Under:** A description of quiet background sound or music.

**VO:** Voiceover. Words spoken by an announcer that is not visible.

**WS:** Wide shot in a TV or film script. Frequently a building, a room, or a group of people.

Figure 5.2. Adapted from: Diggs-Brown, B. (2007). *The PR styleguide: Formats for public relations practice* (2nd ed.). Belmont, CA: Thomson Wadsworth; Marsh, C., Guth, D. W., & Short, B. P. (2005). *Strategic writing: Multimedia writing for public relations, advertising, sales and marketing, and business communication.* Boston: Pearson Education.

device control, publishing, news wire management, full text searching, tightly integrated resilience capabilities, and language support (Associated Press). For more information, you may look at the EPNS Web site at http://www.enps.com/.

Radio and television stations with computerized newsrooms may use scripting software that produces a standardized format. The E. W. Scripps School of Journalism's student-operated television station at Ohio University uses ENPS to create the script for its Athens MidDay program that is broadcast each weekday during the school term. The ENPS software program integrates the newsgathering and production process, allowing students in the broadcast newswriting program to learn on state-of-the-art equipment. The Ohio University lab also is used in teaching other broadcast newswriting courses ("E.W. Scripps School of Journalism," 2004).

If you are not using computerized scripting software, the following guidelines will help you produce radio and television copy in an appropriate manner. Figure 5.3 provides a sample of radio copy, and Figure 5.4 demonstrates the format for television copy. Most television and radio producers want copy to be in all capital letters and double- or triple-spaced. This leaves room for notes and edits. Thus, you would also leave two to three inches of blank space at the top of the page and one to two inches at the bottom.

For radio copy, Brooks, Kennedy, Moen, & Ranly (2004), who are known as the Missouri Group, recommend that you set your computer for 70 characters per line. Each line will average about 10 words. The announcer will read, on average, 15 lines per minute. Further, each story should begin on a separate piece of paper. That way, the order of stories can be rearranged, or stories can be added or deleted without difficulty. Use the word "-MORE-" (in capital letters with a dash or hyphen on either side) at the bottom of the page for a story that is more than one page long.

Television copy requires a different format, according to the Missouri Group (Brooks et al., 2004). Audio or video information, which is not read out loud, is placed on the left half of the page. Copy that will be read aloud is placed on the right half of the page, set for a 40-character line. Each line will average about six words, because the announcer will be able to read about 25 lines per minute. Typically, copy that is spoken is presented in uppercase letters. Just as in radio copy, you write the word "-MORE-" at the bottom of the page if the story continues to the next page.

For both radio and television writing, you should end a page with a complete paragraph. Then, if the script gets misplaced in the middle of a newscast, the announcer will at least be able to end with a complete sentence or paragraph. The word -END- shows the conclusion of the story.

Most television stations use a **videoprompter**, also known as TelePrompter, an electronic device that projects copy over the camera lens, so the announcer can read it while appearing to look straight into the camera lens. This helps the announcer appear to have eye-to-eye contact with the viewer.

The first page of the script should include the date, your last name, and the slug. The **slug**, which is typically assigned by the producer, is a word that identifies the story as it is processed.

**Sample Radio Script**

| | |
|---|---|
| **Show:** | Business Edition |
| **Project:** | Where America Shops |
| **Title:** | A Beautiful Mind |
| **Writer:** | Diane Brock |
| **Announcer:** | Jennifer Colter |
| **Guest:** | Linda Wells, Editor-in-chief of *Allure* magazine |

Music:
Theme song from
*Beauty and the Beast*

Colter: BEAUTY MAY BE IN THE EYE OF THE BEHOLDER...BUT CONSUMERS MAKE THE CHOICE WHERE TO SPEND THEIR DOLLARS ON BEAUTY PRODUCTS. . . HELPING RETAILERS AND COSMETIC PRODUCERS FIGURE IT OUT IS ALLURE MAGAZINE. . . EACH YEAR . . . ALLURE CONDUCTS ITS ANNUAL SURVEY OF WHAT INFLUENCES AMERICAN WOMEN'S BEAUTY PURCHASE DECISIONS . . . LINDA WELLS . . . EDITOR-IN-CHIEF OF ALLURE IS WITH ME TODAY TO REPORT SOME OF THE FINDINGS.

Wells: IT'S A PLEASURE JOINING YOU TODAY JENNIFER . . . WE HAVE SOME EXCITING INFORMATION TO SHARE . . . THE ALLURE CATALYST REPORT POLLED MORE THAN TWO-THOUSAND-SIX-HUNDRED WOMEN . . . AGES EIGHTEEN TO SIXTY-FOUR . . . BETWEEN APRIL TWENTY-FIFTH AND MAY ELEVENTH . . . THEY LOGGED MORE THAN ONE-THOUSAND-THREE-HUNDRED HOURS OF WOMEN GIVING THEIR OPINIONS AND SHOPPING HABITS.

Colter: THAT IS A LOT OF INFORMATION ABOUT SHOPPING . . . WHAT KIND OF INFORMATION WERE YOU LOOKING FOR?

Wells: THE REPORT REVEALS THAT WOMEN . . . ON AVERAGE . . . USE THIRTEEN BEAUTY PRODUCTS AT LEAST ONCE A WEEK . . . AND REGULARLY USE SEVEN DIFFERENT BRANDS . . . SHE SPENDS ABOUT FOURTY MINUTES EACH DAY ON BEAUTY . . . NEARLY DOUBLE THE AMOUNT OF TIME SHE SPENDS ON COMMUTING TO WORK.

Colter: WHERE IS SHE MOST LIKELY TO SHOP FOR HER BEAUTY PRODUCTS?

Wells: THE SURVEY TOLD US THAT SHE SPENDS MOST OF HER MONEY AT MASS MERCHANDISERS AND THAT PRICE APPEARS TO BE A KEY FACTOR . . . AS "THE EXPENSE OF PRODUCTS" RANKED FIRST IN A LIST OF THINGS CONSUMERS LIKED LEAST WHEN SHOPPING FOR BEAUTY PRODUCTS . . . WITH FIFTY-FIVE PERCENT REPORTING THAT CONCERN.

-MORE-

FIGURE 5.3. Sample radio script. *(continued)*

Colter:      THE SURVEY ALSO REPORTS THAT MOST WOMEN WON'T LEAVE THE HOUSE WITHOUT FOUR BEAUTY PRODUCTS IN THEIR HANDBAGS . . . AND THEY WERE MOSTLY LIP PRODUCTS.

Wells:      YES . . . LIP BALM TOPPED THE LIST . . . WITH FORTY-FIVE PERCENT . . . HAND/BODY MOISTURIZER WAS IDENTIFIED NEXT WITH THIRTY-FIVE PERCENT . . . LIPSTICK WAS THIRD AT THIRTY-ONE PERCENT . . . AND LIP GLOSS WAS FOURTH AT TWENTY-NINE PERCENT.

Colter:      IT SOUNDS LIKE THE WOMEN NEEDED A GOOD HANDBAG TOO . . .

MORE RESULTS FROM THE ALLURE CATALIST REPORT CAN BE FOUND IN THE APRIL ISSUE OF THE MAGAZINE OR ON THE WEB SITE . . . ALLURE DOT COM.

THANK YOU FOR BEING WITH US TODAY . . . OUR GUEST HAS BEEN LINDA WELLS . . . EDITOR-IN-CHIEF OF ALLURE MAGAZINE.

-END-

FIGURE 5.3

**Sample Television Script**

| | | | |
|---|---|---|---|
| **Show**: | Chic Café | **Writer:** | Pamela Smith |
| **Project:** | International Fashion | **Announcer**: | Lynne Graves |
| **Title:** | Geneva Style | **Producer**: | Tim Goodman |

<u>VIDEO</u>                                                                <u>AUDIO</u>

TABLE OF CONTENTS
    Précis: (insert RT)
    Sound bite: Julia Boege
    Sound bite: Massimo Radaelli
    Sound bite: Harald Wolf
    Sound bite: Melissa Drier
    B-roll:

PRÉCIS: Fashion Week takes place at a new
venue in Geneva Switzerland. The Swiss
city hopes to join the ranks of other famous
fashion cities. Examples of Swiss fashion
designs and designers will be featured.

Slate #1:                                                    NATSOUND
B-roll
(WS) of the Geneva Switzerland
(MS) of the fashion show runway near Lac
Léman (Lake Geneva)

-MORE-

FIGURE 5.4. Sample television script. *(continued)*

| VIDEO | AUDIO |
|---|---|
| Slate #2:<br>(WS) of audience at the show<br>(MS) of model on runway | SOUND OF VOICES AND MUSIC AT FASHION SHOW<br><br>Announcer:  SWITZERLAND'S CITY OF INTERNATIONAL POLITICS IS HOPING TO BECOME THE NEWEST FASHION CENTER IN EUROPE. . . GENEVA IS FULL OF ARTISTS . . . CREATIVE PEOPLE . . . AND GENEVA EVEN HAS SEVEN FASHION SCHOOLS . . . TREND-SETTERS AND GERMAN CELEBRITIES GATHERED AT LAC LÉMAN TO WATCH YOUNG DESIGNERS PRESENT THEIR STUFF ON THE RUNWAY. MODELS WEARING IMMENSE BERETS AND CLEAR PLATFORM SHOES CLOMPED DOWN THE RUNWAY WEARING MINI-DRESSES. |
| Slate #3<br>(CU) of local fashion design firm Q-E-D's model on the runway<br>(MS) of Julia Boege, designer for Q-E-D | SOT #1 Boege: "GENEVA'S WEALTHIEST CITIZENS LOOK TO PARIS . . . LONDON . . . AND MILAN FOR FASHION INSPIRATION . . . OUR OWN PEOPLE DON'T KNOW OUR OWN DESIGNERS. . . IF WE WANT TO GROW . . . WE'VE GOT TO LOOK GLOBALLY." |
| Slate #4<br>B-roll<br>Visuals of models on runway | NATSOUNDS AT THE FASHION SHOW<br><br>Announcer:  INTERNATIONAL ATTENTION FOR GENEVA'S DESIGNERS WILL HELP. . .THE GERMAN AUTOMOBILE MANUFACTURER . . . MERCEDES-BENZ IS THE SPONSOR OF FASHION WEEK GENEVA . . . OVERSEEN BY MEDIA . . . SPORTS . . . AND ENTERTAINMENT GIANT I-M-G . . . THE PRODUCERS OF SUCH INTERNATIONAL EVENTS AS NEW YORK . . . HONG KONG . . . AND AUSTRALIAN FASHION WEEKS. |

-MORE-

FIGURE 5.4. *(continued)*

| VIDEO | AUDIO |
|---|---|
| Slate #5<br>(WS) IMG offices in Geneva<br>(MS) of Massimo Radaelli sitting at his desk<br>(CU) of Massimo Radaelli | SOT #2 Massimo Radaelli: "GENEVA BRINGS TOGETHER WHAT I SEE AS TWO OPPOSING POWERS . . . CREATIVITY AND CAPITALISM . . . WE FELT THAT SWITZERLAND'S POLITIAL CAPITAL HAS THE BEST PLATFORM AND OPPORTUNITY IN EUROPE TO STRIKE THE RIGHT BALANCE OF ART AND COMMERCE." |
| Slate #6<br>(WS) fashion show audience | Announcer: THE HOPE IS THAT GENEVA WILL BECOME KNOWN AS MUCH FOR FASHION AS IT IS KNOWN FOR POLITICS. . . GENEVA POLITICIAN HAROLD WOLF HOPES FASHION WEEK WILL STIMULATE FASHION IN THE CITY. |
| Slate #7<br>(CU) Harald Wolf, Geneva politician | SOT #3 Harald Wolf: "WE HAVE FIVE HUNDRED DESIGNERS IN OUR CITY . . . AND SO THIS EVENT WILL GIVE THEM THE POSSIBILITY TO BECOME INTERNATIONALLY KNOWN AND MAKE CONNECTIONS WITH INTERNATIONALLY KNOWN COMPANIES TO DISTRIBUTE THEIR PRODUCTS." |
| Slate #8<br>(WS) Commercial buildings in Geneva<br>Swiss teens wearing styles from local designers | NATSOUND<br><br>Announcer: MELISSA DRIER IS THE SWISS CORRESPONDENT FOR WOMEN'S WEAR DAILY. . . SHE IS NOT SURE IF GENEVA . . . WITH ITS PREFERENCE FOR HIGH FASHION OVER LOCAL DESIGNER LABELS CAN OR EVER WILL BE THE NEXT PARIS. |

-MORE-

FIGURE 5.4. (continued)

| VIDEO | AUDIO |
|---|---|
| Slate #9<br>(MS) of Melissa Drier | SOT #4 Melissa Drier: "I THINK WE FIRST HAVE TO LET GENEVA BE GENEVA . . . AND LET PEOPLE TAKE ADVANTAGE OF THAT . . . WE HAVE SO MUCH SAMENESS IN THE WORLD . . . ESPECIALLY IN THE DESIGN AND RETAILING WORLDS . . . WE SHOULD BE THANKFUL THAT MAYBE SOMETHING LOOKS A LITTLE BIT DIFFERENT." |
| Slate #10<br>(WS) Swiss Fashion Show | Announcer:  THE FIRST FASHION WEEK GENEVA CONTINUES TOMORROW, JULY 20TH. |

-END-

FIGURE 5.4.

## NAMES AND TITLES

The style used in radio and television allows a well-known person to be identified without their full name, even on the first reference. For example, you may say the following:

SENATOR CLINTON OF NEW YORK WILL ATTEND THE OPENING OF NEW YORK FASHION WEEK.

You do not have to give her complete name and title—Senator Hillary Rodham Clinton, Democrat for New York—as you would in a newspaper article. Note, also, that you should not use middle initials unless they are a natural part of someone's name or are necessary to distinguish two people who have the same first and last names.

In broadcast communication, titles should always be used to introduce formal names. The reason for this is that when the title is announced first, listeners are prepared to hear the name.

PHILLIPS-VAN HEUSEN CHAIRMAN AND CHIEF EXECUTIVE OFFICER BRUCE KLATSKY OFFICIALLY STEPPED DOWN FROM HIS POST TODAY.

In this case, the first name is included because the chair of PVH is probably less well known than Senator Clinton.

## PRONUNCIATION

Not every word is pronounced the way it looks. Names and places in different geographic locations may have difficult or unique pronunciations. To assist the announcer, look up unfamiliar or tricky words in an unabridged dictionary and write out the pronunciation phonetically in parentheses. For example, pronouncing the name *Givenchy* causes fear for many broadcasters. Writing the phonetic pronunciation (zhee VAHN shay) will help. Some stations have their own pronunciation directories.

If you do not find a name in a dictionary or directory, you will need to call the person's office, or try calling someone who knows the person or place. If the name is a geographic location, town, or city, try calling someone who lives there. Because pronunciation is so important, you need to find out the correct way to say the word. Never assume or guess. Find out. If you do not pronounce the name correctly, you will diminish your credibility. Figure 5.5, Fashion Pronunciation Guide, illustrates how to pronounce some of today's most popular fashion names.

## Fashion Pronunciation Guide

In this age of label-mania, none of us want to cause a gaffe riot. Hence, our first ever Fashionista Pronunciation Guide.

Tony Soprano bought Carm some high-quality "Hermeez." *Showgirls*' Nomi Malone gushed about "Ver-sayze." One of our own fashion editors arrived in NYC convinced that DKNY was "Dick-knee." It happens to the best of us . . .

ANDREW GN \jen\
This Singapore-born designer's name rhymes with "Zen"—the antithesis of his opulently embellished clothes.

ANNA SUI \swee\
Maybe it was her cowgirl collection, but her surname did elicit the pig call "sueeee!!!" Think "sweet" sans the T.

AQUASCUTUM \ah-kwa-skew-tum\
As you'll remember from Latin class, this name merges aqua (water) and scutum (shield)—and these British raincoats have lived up to it for well over a century.

BALENCIAGA \ba-len-see-ah-ga\
Today's head designer, Nicolas Ghesquiere \nee-coh-la guess-kee-air\, is also a mouthful. Rather delicious, he is, too!

BEHNAZ SARAFPOUR \ben-oz sah-rafpoor\
This A-list designer is simply "Behnaz"; her clientele—mostly rich-girls-in-a-hurry—rarely have time to manage both her first and last name.

CESARE PACIOTTI \che-sah-ray pa-chotee\
We say *ciao* and get all choked up over his gorgeous footwear.

CHLOË SEVIGNY \sev-en-ee\
This actress/designer's muse is seven times a style icon.

FIGURE 5.5. Fashion pronunciation guide. *(continued)*

DRIES VAN NOTEN \dreez van no-ten\
The first name rhymes with "trees," which is easy to remember: The Belgian scattered gold leaf through his fall collection.

HERMÈS \er-mez\
So, who's going to tell Tony Soprano that the formidable French house ne pronounce pas the "h"? The second syllable rhymes with "fez."

INEZ VAN LAMSWEERDE \in-ez van lams-veerd\ & VINOODH MATADIN \vihnood mat-a din\
Even seasoned fashionistas need travel guides to navigate the bumpy road through these photographers' multisyllabic monikers.

MARCHESA \mar-kay-sah\
Hollywood actresses are more than okay with what this London house offers.

MIU MIU \mew-mew\
No need to get into a catfight over it: Miuccia Prada's nickname is as easy to love as her funky secondary line.

MONIQUE LHUILLIER \mo-neek loo-leeyay\
Rumor is a lot of young actresses send their stylists over to pick up her glam gowns: Her name is a line many of them just can't learn.

NATALIA VODIANOVA \vo-dee-ah-no-vah\
She sounds like a prima ballerina and is grace personified on the catwalk.

PETER SOM \sahm\
Many a psalm has been sung to this young designer's heavenly clothes.

PROENZA SCHOULER \pro-en-za skooler\
"Schoul" rhymes with "drool"—and you might over their fabulous fall 2006 collection.

RODARTE \ro-dar-tay\
This exquisite label's hand-stitching and beading attest to the art of fashion (but pronounce all three syllables).

FIGURE 5.5. (continued)

SCARLETT JOHANSSON \joe-hansen\
She looks Scandinavian—but doesn't go by "yo." It's Jo-hansson.

SONIA RYKIEL \ree-kee-el\
We're really keen on her resort collection.

THAKOON \ta-koon\
Suppress the urge to pronounce this onenamer "tha-koon." You wouldn't go
out for "thigh food," would you?

TIIU KUIK \tee-you kweek\
Estonia exports models with impossibly long legs and impossibly short
names.

TRASTEVERINE \tras-te-ve-reen-eh\
Italians believe all vowels are created equal: Give them their due.

FIGURE 5.5.  Source: Dempsey, M. (2005). Fashion mis-statements. Retrieved July 22, 2005, from
http://lifestyle.msn.com/BeautyandFashion/PersonalStyle/ArticleMC.aspx?cp-documentid=1203054

## ABBREVIATIONS

It is best not to use abbreviations in your copy. It is much easier to read a word that
has been written out than it is to read its abbreviation. Therefore, do not abbreviate
the names of states, countries, months, days of the week, or military titles.

The exception to this guideline is the term *U.S.* When it is used as an adjective, in
broadcasting the letters should be separated by long dashes rather than by periods.
This will prevent the announcer from mistaking the second period for the end of a
sentence. The correct way to write this in your copy is "U—S" with no periods.
Another exception is a person's title, such as *DR, MR, MRS,* and *MS.* You may
abbreviate these terms, but avoid using a period.

## SYMBOLS AND NUMBERS

Symbols and numbers can also cause problems for announcers. It is much easier to read a word than to interpret a symbol. For example, you should never use symbols such as the dollar sign ($) or the percent sign (%) in broadcast copy.

Writing numbers in a style similar to print standards will be helpful for the announcer. Write out the numbers one through nine. Also, write out the number eleven, since the numeral 11 might not be easily recognized as a number. Figures can be used for the numbers 10 and 12 through 999. The eye easily comprehends a three-digit number, such as 525; but you should write out words for *thousand*, *million*, and *billion*. It is effortless to convert "5,982,000" to "5 million, 982 thousand" in your copy, and the result will be much easier for the announcer and the listener. You should also write out fractions (for example, three-and-a-half million) and decimal points (for example, FOUR-POINT-FIVE percent) for clarity.

Another note about numbers: You should use *st*, *nd*, *rd*, and *th* after dates: April 1*st*, May 2*nd*, June 3*rd*, and July 4*th*. (Alternatively, APRIL FIRST, MAY SECOND, JUNE THIRD, and JULY FOURTH could be used. This makes dates easier to recognize and pronounce.

## QUOTATIONS AND ATTRIBUTIONS

In print writing, quotation marks are used to indicate that another person's words are being quoted. It is difficult to translate this to a listener, so broadcast copy usually uses indirect quotes or a paraphrase instead. If a direct quote is used, the quote can be introduced with any of the following: "IN HIS WORDS," "WHAT SHE CALLED . . . ," or "HE PUT IT THIS WAY." Most announcers avoid using the formal "quote" at the beginning of the quoted material followed by "unquote" at the end, although they may clarify by starting the attribution as follows:

> ACCORDING TO DONNA KARAN, QUOTE, "THE NEW LINE IS INSPIRED BY MY TRIP TO ASPEN LAST YEAR."

When a direct quote is used, the attribution should precede the quotation. Many announcers don't bother saying "unquote" at the end of the statement. But, you must remember that the listener cannot see the quotation marks. Other ways to emphasize a direct quote are to conduct a live interview or use a tape recording of the person being quoted.

# PUNCTUATION

Broadcast copy tends to have less punctuation than traditional writing does. The one exception is the comma, which is used to help the announcer pause at appropriate places. This is especially helpful after introductory phrases referring to time and place. For example:

IN PARIS, JOHN GALLIANO SHOWED A DIOR FALL COUTURE COLLECTION CELEBRATING THE ONE HUNDREDTH ANNIVERSARY OF CHRISTIAN DIOR'S BIRTH.

Sometimes, ellipsis points ( . . . ) are used in place of a comma, parentheses, or a semicolon to signal a pause to the announcer. The long dash, typed as two hyphens (--), may also be used.

Writing styles may vary from one television or radio station to another. You will learn the specifics for your station, but the guidelines we just presented will help you prepare. Differences tend to be small, and you will adapt easily.

## SUMMARY

This chapter looked at the role of broadcast media. General broadcast writing was explored. Characteristics that set radio and television apart from print media were presented, in addition to characteristics common to radio and television newswriting. Commonly used ways to format and structure broadcast stories were presented. Writing for documentary and cable programs was also explored.

## KEY TERMS

| | |
|---|---|
| Broadcasting | Slug |
| Cue | Tease |
| Documentary | Tee-up |
| Lead-in | Videoprompter |
| News anchor | Wrap-up |
| Newscaster | |

## CASE STUDY

### *Fashion News!*

The world's largest producer and distributor of entertainment news and lifestyle-related programming is E! Entertainment Television, Incorporated. The company operates E! Entertainment Television, the 24-hour network with programming dedicated to the world of entertainment; The Style® Network, the cable television channel for women age 18 to 49 who have a passion for the best in fashion and in related lifestyle programming; and E! Online, the company's Web site. E! is available to over 87 million cable and direct broadcast satellite subscribers in the United States. The Style Network currently counts 42 million subscribers.

E! News, one of the featured shows on E! Entertainment Television, is a daily program that covers news about television, movie, events, celebrity, music news, and the entertainment industry. The program has anchors as well as reporters. Its format is similar to the format of any of the traditional television network evening news programs.

The Style® Network is planning a new weekly fashion and lifestyle news program. It will air for 30 minutes each Friday night, with rebroadcasts on Saturday and Sunday afternoons. If the launch is successful, the network plans on expanding the show to be shown each weeknight in addition to the weekend edition in a manner similar to E! News.

The new fashion program will have two anchors, who will present stories and introduce taped segments. The topics that will be covered include Fashion Week news, designer news, fashion event news, beauty news, shopping news, and trend news. Reporters will be assigned to each of the categories.

Jennifer March started her career as an intern for Michael Kors, while she was finishing her bachelor's degree. She worked in the public relations department, writing and distributing media releases, preparing and mailing invitations to Michael Kors' fashion shows and store events, assisting with backstage fashion show preparations, and taking care of any other media tasks needed by the firm.

After completing her internship and degree program, Jennifer took a job at the Style.com Web site, which is the online home for *Vogue* and *W* magazines. She was hired as assistant to Candy Pratts Price. Jennifer loved her job at Style.com and learned a lot from her boss and mentor there. It was hard to leave after 18 months, but it was time to move on.

---

### BOX 5.1 A NOTE ABOUT CANDY PRATTS PRICE

Ms. Pratts Price, a popular fashion analyst and trend spotter, is the Executive Fashion Director of Style.com. She has appeared on many television shows, including the *Today Show*, *Good Morning America*, and *Fashion Television*.

Ms. Pratts Price's relationship with *Vogue* began in the late eighties. She spent eight years there as the magazine's well-respected Fashion Director of Accessories. In addition to her print work, she worked in broadcast media as the Executive Producer on a documentary about the Metropolitan Museum's Jacqueline Kennedy exhibit in coordination with E! Networks and was the creative director of the VH1/*Vogue* Fashion Awards.

*Lady Beware*, a film starring Diane Lane, was based on Ms. Pratts Price's early career designing award-winning store windows and displays for Bloomingdale's. Ms. Pratts Price is a graduate of the Fashion Institute of Technology and has been a faculty member at the Parsons School of Design.

---

Jennifer was hired as a designer news reporter for the new *Fashion News!* program at The Style® Network. With her contacts from her job at Michael Kors and from her recent experience as Candy Pratts Price's assistant, Jennifer knew she had the right skills to do the new job. She looked forward to this new responsibility with the network pioneering a fashion news show.

At the launch party for the new Gucci store in the Meatpacking District of New York City, one of Jennifer's contacts pulled her away from the event. The person told her that one of the design finalists for the CFDA/*Vogue* Fashion Fund award had just been arrested for shoplifting at Bloomingdale's at the other end of town. This was extremely timely news. Jennifer could be the first reporter to tell the story on the air.

But Jennifer had been assigned to tape a story about the opening of the new Gucci store and about the head of Gucci design, who was visiting the store. *The Fashion News!* videographer was there to shoot the story. Jennifer thought about diverting the crew to the police station and turning this evening's shoot into the breaking story about the fashion designer being arrested for shoplifting.

## CASE STUDY QUESTIONS

1. What should Jennifer do? Should she play it safe and report on the story she was sent to cover, or should she take the risk to cover the breaking news story?
2. How could Jennifer confirm whether the fashion designer was arrested?
3. What kinds of stories would be interesting to you on the *Fashion News!* program?

## INDUSTRY PROFILE

*Penny Martin*

**What is your current job and title? Can you describe the main responsibilities for your job?**

I have been Editor-in-Chief of the fashion and art broadcasting company SHOWstudio for the past six years. In collaboration with Nick Knight, who owns SHOWstudio, I am responsible for commissioning all projects and writing on our Web site as well as running the live studio space out of which we operate.

**What is a typical day at work like?**

There are live webcams in our working space so it's possible for our international audience to view what every one of our working days is like from several angles! In some senses, most people's days are pretty much the same: meetings, hours spent in front of the computer, phone calls, chats over coffee . . . Add to that fashion shows, press days, studio visits, arts and fashion festivals, live broadcasts, mobile phone blogging, and giving public presentations of what we do, and that pretty much covers it.

**At what point did you decide to pursue a career in writing for a fashion-related business?**

I didn't. My background is in museums and at the time I was approached to become Editor of SHOWstudio in 2001, I was doing a PhD at the Royal College of Art on 80s magazines and fashion photography and probably intended to pursue a career in academia. My specialism is really in fashion imagery but there is such an overlap with fashion design that increasingly, I am being approached to write about that too. SHOWstudio is interested in the shared interests between fashion, photography, film, performance, design, architecture, and so on, so it offers a lot of scope for writers.

**Describe your first writing job. What was the most important or interesting thing you wrote for that job/publication?**

My first paid work as a writer was a catalogue essay for the photographer Melanie Manchot. In those days, I was very influenced by the photographic theorist

Abigail Solomon Godeau so I was probably very indebted to her style. What working in fashion media has allowed me is a certain loosening up of my style: academic writing can be terse and unreadable. I miss how in-depth academia allows you to go, but now I don't think I'd trade the pleasure of the unsolicited commission, which is one of the best aspects of writing for magazines or newspapers.

### What are you currently reading (books, magazines, Web sites, newspapers, other media)? Do you have a favorite author or publication?

I'm reading *The Corrections* by Jonathan Franzen. I sickened myself with fashion magazines a bit. I have a massive collection of *Vogue* since 1964 but since working in fashion, my reading habits aren't the same and I just tend to flick, rather than pore. The only consumer magazine I still read is *Fantastic Man*. My only subscription is to *The New Yorker*. I get frustrated by the tendency toward the shorter article, caused no doubt by the Internet. So the long articles in *The New Yorker* are my antidote to that.

### What advice do you have for students interested in a writing career? Do you have any recommendations for students?

I don't think I realized what kind of writer I was when I started and tried to force myself to write in a way that didn't suit my strengths or temperament. I still find writing hard and extremely painful if I go for a long period without doing any. If a young writer came to me with difficulties, therefore, I would probably advise them to think of themselves as a runner and then ask themselves: "am I a marathon runner?" If the answer is no, then don't approach a PhD or a book. Try a half marathon-type commission instead: maybe a long profile. If that doesn't suit, then have a go at a "400 metres" piece: a "think piece" or a review. If you're more of a 100 metres person, then maybe consider a job in newspapers where the quick initiation of ideas and rapid fire execution will suit your adrenaline-fuelled creativity. There is always room to change your style or average length of pieces, but it's important not to keep forcing yourself to fail at unsuitable tasks in the early stages. That will eventually rob you of your nerve, which is something you need in writing above all else. If you are having a total block, write a diary to keep your internal dialogue flowing.

Finally, it is crucial to bring something different to the field that you are writing about. I see so many wannabe fashion writers who know nothing about/have no interest in literature/art/architecture/history/politics. In truth, it doesn't really matter what it is, but you always need something of your own to distinguish your work from the sea of other writing out there.

# REFERENCES

Associated Press. (2005). *About ENPS: Everything you need to know*. New York: Author.

E. W. Scripps School of Journalism. (2004, September 14). *Broadcast newswriting computer lab*. Retrieved April 2, 2007, from http://scrippsjschool.org/labs.php?story_id=91

Brooks, B. S., Kennedy, G., Moen, D. R., & Ranly, D. (2004). *Telling the story: The convergence of print, broadcast and online media* (2nd ed.). Boston: Bedford/St. Martin's.

Karimzadeh, M. (2005, June 16). Saks taps Swank for "Key to the Cure." *Women's Wear Daily*, p. 3.

National Cable & Telecommunications Association. (n.d.). *History of cable television*. Retrieved March 4, 2007, from http://www.ncta.com/ContentView.aspx?contentId=2685

Schoenherr, S. E. (2001). *History of radio*. Retrieved April 2, 2007, from http://history.sandiego.edu/GEN/recording/radio.html

Schoenherr, S. E. (2004). *History of television*. Retrieved April 2, 2007, from http://history.sandiego.edu/GEN/recording/television1.html

Society of Professional Journalists. (2007). *Code of ethics*. Retrieved April 2, 2007, from http://www.spj.org/ethicscode.asp

## Part Three

# FASHION PROMOTION COMMUNICATION

In Part Three, we will look at the three primary communication channels for making fashion promotion communication come to life: advertising, public relations, and new media. While approaches for writing in each of these exciting areas are similar, they also have many differences.

Fashion promotion communication has the ultimate goal of persuading consumers to take action. Whether that action involves going to a store to purchase new merchandise or attending a fashion show or clothing exhibit, fashion promotion is one of the most creative areas of fashion writing.

Fashion advertising starts with an analysis of the client and product or service that is to be promoted. Analyzing the situation strategically helps the fashion advertiser understand what has been done in the past and recognize what needs to be done in the future. Writing takes place as the situation analysis is put into a document; at this point, the creative message and the media where the message will be presented are considered. Writing also takes place as the advertising message is placed in print, broadcast, or any other medium for the audience to see or to hear. All this is examined closely in Chapter 6, "Writing for Advertising."

Public relations for fashion-related businesses also starts with a critical analysis of the needs of the client. A variety of public relations tools assist the writer in conveying a message to the audience, as we'll show in Chapter 7, "Writing for Public Relations." Among these tools are news releases, media kits, feature stories written for newspapers or magazines, pitch letters, annual reports, speeches, and fund-raising letters. Fashion public relations personnel are also involved with such activities as news conferences and fashion events, from fashion shows to product launch parties and more.

The Internet offers a wide range of fashion writing opportunities. Fashion Web sites promote and sell classic apparel, luxury fashion, and everything in between. Journalists, advertisers, and public relations personnel are among the writers offering exciting, up-to-the-minute information about trends on the Web. Historically, the public had to wait until garments arrived in the retail stores in order to see the hot new styles. The Web has made such information instantaneous. Whether it is haute couture in Paris or ready-to-wear lines in New York, London, Milan, or Los Angeles, fashion trend information is available as the shows happen or within a few hours after the collections are presented to industry insiders. Since every interested fashionista in the world has the opportunity to watch fashion presentations as they occur, there aren't any fashion insiders anymore. Chapter 8, "Writing for New Media," explores the career opportunities related to writing on the Web.

# SIX

## *Writing for Advertising*

After you have read this chapter, you should be able to discuss the following:

• The role of writing for fashion advertising

• What a situation analysis is and how to prepare one

• How to write strategically for print and broadcast advertisements

• How to write strategically for other promotional efforts

The roots of fashion advertising were established during the end of the 19th century. Magazines started to specialize in narrowly defined topics, such as women's issues, fashion, and lifestyle. At the same time, manufacturers were developing technologies to improve production of ready-to-wear. Clothing manufacturers wanted a place to promote their broad arrays of standardized, mass-produced, fashionable products, and the magazine publishers were ready.

These turn-of-the-century magazine publishers continued a practice that had been established in the 1890s. That is, first they built a large circulation for their magazines. Then, with a sizable circulation established, the publishers sold advertising based upon circulation statistics. They made money despite selling the magazines below cost; they made their profits by selling ads (Hill, 2004).

Although a number of magazines were created for women in the 19th century, the first one devoted to fashion was *Harper's Bazaar*, which was started in 1867

(Hill, 2004). Women received regular reports describing international fashion trends from this resource, and advertising was part of this publication. At that time, however, advertising was placed into a single section, typically in the last few pages of the magazine, that looked similar to the classified ads of a contemporary newspaper. These early advertising pages contained little boxes crammed with type, rarely illustrated.

In 1892, *Vogue* was started as a social gazette by Arthur B. Turnure and purchased in 1909 by Condé Montrose Nast. Since that time, under the ownership of Condé Nast, *Vogue* has evolved into one of the world's most influential fashion magazines (Hill, 2004). Under Nast's leadership, September became the key fashion issue each year, with a proportionately evolving amount of advertising. In 1911, *Vogue* contained 51 pages of advertising. By the mid-20th century, the September 1, 1950, issue featured 131 pages of advertising. In 2005, the number of advertising pages in the September issue rose to a record-breaking 691 ad pages (Elliott, 2005).

At this point three forces converged to make the fashion industry successful:

- Ready-to-wear manufacturers provided ever-changing and updated products.
- Fashion journalists wrote about the upcoming fashion trends that were being initiated in major cities by influential designers and worn by societal leaders.
- Fashion advertising developed to help sell these products and to help sell fashion magazines.

We begin this chapter by discussing the role of advertising in selling goods and sharing ideas and information. Next, we will explore the situation analysis: the research and assessment on which an advertising campaign is based. We'll then talk about the strategic writing that is done on the basis of that situation analysis—as it applies to print advertisements, radio advertisements, and television advertisements. The chapter concludes with a discussion of radio and television promotions.

Fashion advertising may have started with simple boxes of classified ads, but these boxes have progressed into visually exciting promotional tools. Let's begin our review of the role of fashion advertising and its various components.

# THE ROLE OF ADVERTISING

Advertising involves creating sponsored messages that are delivered to consumers through controlled media. **Advertising** is defined as "any nonpersonal information paid for and controlled by the sponsoring organization. This type of promotion communication contains information about the organization, product, service, or idea created by the sponsoring firm to influence sales" (Swanson & Everett, 2007, p. 19). These messages are carefully and deliberately created to persuade consumers to take action, usually to buy the sponsor's products or services. Advertising is an exciting and creative field. Imagine being part of the creative team that came up with Nike's "Just do it" slogan, or the Nicole Kidman "mini movie" advertising campaign for Chanel.

The sponsor of the message is the client or the creator of a product or a service. The message is the innovative statement used to attract the potential customer. That message is designed to gain attention and to persuade the customer to take action. The controlled media, usually print or broadcast, are selected to match the characteristics of the target audience. The message may also be delivered in more than one medium, as a campaign. Placement in the media is only one of the expenses of doing advertising. Developing the creative idea and producing the print or broadcast ads are usually the major expenses associated with advertising.

The message is dependent upon several considerations. First, the **target audience**—the viewers and listeners who are intended to use the product or service—is identified. Then, the advertising executives determine which approach will be taken: a product approach or an institutional advertising approach. The objective of **product advertising** is the promotion of specific goods or services; the objective of **institutional advertising** is promotion that is geared toward building the reputation of the sponsor, enhancing civic sponsorship and community involvement, and developing long-term relationships between customers and the sponsor (Swanson & Everett, 2007).

Typically, advertising campaigns are created by a creative team—one that works for a company as an in-house division or one that works for an outside advertising agency. For example, an **in-house promotion division** can be a branch of a large retailing or manufacturing company. A retailing company such as Macy's or Nordstrom may have a promotion division, directed by a vice-president with responsibility for creating the store's advertising, marketing, fashion leadership, public relations, and visual merchandising programs.

If the firm does not produce its promotional materials in-house, it hires an outside agency. A full-service **advertising agency** "is involved in planning, creating and producing advertising; selecting and buying media time or space; and evaluating advertising effectiveness" (Swanson & Everett, 2007, p. 73). The heart of an advertising agency is the creative services group, which is responsible for creating and executing advertisements. This group is led by its creative director, who develops the creative philosophy of the firm.

The creative division typically has two functional areas: visual and verbal. The visual team, which includes designers and graphic artists, creates the art, graphics, and overall layout of ads. The verbal team, which consists of writers and copywriters, creates the written words—from the situation analysis to the headlines, subheadlines, and body copy for ads.

Recent trends in advertising have diminished the role of the copywriter as compared with the graphic designer. Because so many fashion ads are meant to draw an international audience, fashion ads have eliminated most words, depending upon the designer's or manufacturer's name as the sole identifier. This method allows the exact same ad to run in the United States, France, Dubai, and Japan simultaneously. Without headlines or copy, the ad goes beyond traditional borders, traveling easily with just a visual image and a name. See Figure 6.1 for an example of such an ad.

# SITUATION ANALYSIS

Before the creative message is developed, a complete analysis of the sponsor's product or service is conducted and its relationship to the target audience is considered. This examination, called a **situation analysis,** is the research that helps the creative team fully understand the product or service, its benefits and values, and the consumers to whom the message will be directed. From this research and analysis, the creative strategy will focus on the appropriate strategic core message, which will eventually be presented to the target consumer through directed media. Figure 6.2 is an outline for preparing a situation analysis.

## PURPOSE

The document that we call a situation analysis may go by different titles at different advertising agencies or at in-house advertising departments. It is also known as a

**FIGURE 6.1.** Magazine ad without copy.

strategic message planner, a copy platform, a creative work plan, or a strategic statement. The purpose of the document is to create a clear message that has evolved from the research conducted.

The situation analysis is completed before the more creative themes and visuals of the ad are considered. In fact, it is this analysis that directs the more creative ideas and the vision of what the strategic message should be. If the creative process begins before the situation analysis is completed, the vision desired by the client may become distorted.

## TARGET AUDIENCE

The writer of the situation analysis must understand who the target audience is and what benefits or characteristics are desired by the group who will purchase and use the product or service. Does this audience want a practical product, or do they want a

**Situation Analysis Outline**

I. Executive Summary

II. SWOT Analysis

III. Situation Analysis
   a. Client and Product
      i. Who created the product or service?
      ii. Who is the client and what are they selling?
      iii. What is the product or service category? (apparel, accessories, store, beauty services)
      iv. What is the product made from? For services, are there intangible ingredients, such as a type of regimen for treatment?
   b. Target Audience
      i. Although your client will specify the target audience, define the target audience in terms of demographic and psychographic information.
      ii. Conduct original research, such as in-depth interviews, focus groups, or surveys, to help understand who the customer is.
   c. Product Benefits
      i. A benefit is a product feature that appeals to the target audience.
      ii. Consumers seek solutions to three main needs—control, companionship, or confidence.
   d. Current Brand Image
      i. Your target audience's impression of your product.
      ii. Advertising can be used to inform consumers about your product, if the current brand image is unknown or misunderstood.
      iii. Advertising can be used to reinforce the current brand image, if the current brand image is desirable.
   e. Desired Brand Image
      i. Usually the client has specific ideas in mind.
      ii. It is the impression you wish consumers to have of the product.
   f. Direct Competition and Brand Image
      i. Who are the direct competitors in your product or service category? (If you client is Calvin Klein, a direct competitor might be Ralph Lauren or Donna Karan.)
      ii. What features differentiate it from its competitors?
   g. Indirect Competition and Brand Image
      i. These are things that keep your customer from buying your product or service. (Even though your brand is Calvin Klein apparel, an indirect competition might be Bobbi Brown cosmetics or Coach handbags. If a customer does not like the style or color of apparel, she could buy cosmetics or handbags instead of dresses.)
      ii. This is more of a challenge to address. How would your target audience describe the brand image of Bobbi Brown or Coach?

**FIGURE 6.2.** Situation analysis outline. *(continued)*

h. Advertising Objective
 i. What is the objective?
 ii. This section is normally brief, consisting of one sentence or a sentence fragment.
i. Strategic Message
 i. This section is a key part of the situation analysis.
 ii. This is the theme of the ad.
 iii. A good strategic message will provide a unique and positive position in the minds' of your target audience.
j. Supporting Benefits
 i. Supporting benefits are also called selling points.
 ii. A benefit is a feature that appeals to your target audience.
 iii. Supporting benefits supply the evidence for your strategic message previously identified.

FIGURE 6.2. Adapted from Marsh, C., Guth, D. W., & Short, B. P. (2005). *Strategic writing: Multimedia writing for public relations, advertising, sales and marketing, and business communication.* Boston: Pearson Education.

product with sex appeal? Is the product a beauty product, such as moisturizer, that might be promoted as a practical product to heal dry and itchy skin? Or might it be promoted as a product that gives the skin a dewy, sexy appearance? The characteristics of the expected audience will help the creative team direct the appropriate message.

# MEDIA

Media refers to the places where the ads are presented to the target audience, and it includes various print, broadcast, or electronic sources. The decision whether to place the ad in a magazine or newspaper, on television or radio, on a Web site, or as a banner ad for some other Internet site depends on the research completed in the situation analysis.

# SITUATION ANALYSIS FORMAT

The format for the situation analysis differs from one agency to another. The situation analysis normally includes an Executive Summary, a SWOT analysis, and detailed information about the client and the products or services it provides, the target audience, and the firm's competition. The **Executive Summary** is a brief statement, typically one to two pages long, that contains the key elements of the situation analysis. Although it is placed at the beginning of the document, it is written after the other sections are completed. The Executive Summary provides the client with an abstract of the analysis in a format that's easy to read and understand.

The **SWOT analysis** consists of a discussion about the strengths, weaknesses, opportunities, and threats. Box 6.1 illustrates the elements of a SWOT analysis. Information comes from sources inside the organization, including information from the current executives or from company documentation. This internal information may include knowledge about company origins, sales history, products or services offered, distribution methods, pricing policies, and promotional practices. Additional documentation such as annual reports, sales and stock statistical reports, or departmental records should be readily available from internal sources. External data that may be useful includes material and facts from outside sources, often reflecting conditions beyond the control of the firm. This type of information consists of knowledge about the economic, social, political, technological, and competitive environments in which the firm operates. These details are available from government, sociological reports, and economic statistical sources.

---

### Box 6.1 Elements of a SWOT Analysis

- **Strengths**—Positive traits, conditions, and situations, such as growth, which planners can use as leverage in advertising activities for the company, product, or brand.

- **Weaknesses**—Negative traits, conditions, and situations, such as diminishing market share, which planners can address with advertising activities.

- **Opportunities**—Areas in which the company can develop an advantage over its competition, derived from a weakness of another company, and use it as leverage in advertising.

- **Threats**—Trends or developments in the environment, such as competition or new technology, that will erode the business unless the company takes action. Planners need to address the threat if it is a critical factor to the success of the company, product, or brand.

Adapted from Wells, W., Moriarty, S., & Burnett, J. (2006). *Advertising principles and practice* (7th ed.). Upper Saddle River, NJ: Pearson Prentice Hall.

The situation analysis document is concise, yet specific and detailed. The following paragraphs describe the types of information that are standard in a situation analysis and are critical to it effectiveness.

## Client and Product

Important details about the client company and its product or service are discussed in this section of the situation analysis. The Product category refers to the client's product classification. Is it high fashion or junior's apparel? Is it cosmetics (fragrance, color cosmetics, skin care)? Is it a retailer (department, discount, specialty, or some other type of store)?

Details of the Client and Product category include features that distinguish the client's product or service from other products or services in the category, as well as discernable qualities determined by the senses: seeing, hearing, touching, tasting, or smelling. The materials or ingredients used to make the product are also examined. Further, this section provides information about the organization that created the product or service. Finally, in this section, the purpose or intended uses of the product or service are evaluated.

If the client is the department store Macy's, the product is already well known on the East and West Coasts. Acquisition of such stores as Filene's, Robinsons-May, and Marshall Field's by the parent company, Macy's Group, provides an example of an opportunity for an advertiser to reach new shoppers. Macy's needs to persuade people who are familiar with and loyal to their local retailers that Macy's offers the products and services they need. Potentially, Macy's can attract many new shoppers from these acquired geographic regions. Alternatively, Macy's could lose these consumers, if the transition and message are not handled well.

## Target Audience

The client will probably provide some indication of its ideal consumer. But to define and understand the audience, the analysis team must look beyond what the client has provided. The team might conduct its own research to help discover new information about what the consumer really wants. **Demographic information**—such as age, gender, race, income, and education level of the target audience—is presented in this section, in addition to information about how members of the target audience purchase and use the product or service. **Psychographic information** is attitudinal information, such as religious, political, and social beliefs. Primary research methods for obtaining this type of information include in-depth interviews, focus groups, and surveys of people using the product or service. This effort can lead to new research discoveries. For the stores being renamed and restocked as Macy's, customers from Filene's, Robinsons-May, or Marshall Field's become the new target audience.

## Product Benefits

Benefits are product or service features that appeal to the client's target audience. Information compiled in the Target Audience section helps to complete this analysis. Consumers are concerned about "What's in it for me?" That is, many consumers are seeking control, companionship, or confidence. Products or services that appeal to a consumer's need for *control* are expected to save time, save money, simplify a task, make things easier to use, get rid of unpleasant tasks, or alleviate fear or guilt. Products or services that appeal to the consumer's need for *companionship* are expected to improve appearance, increase sexual attraction, increase acceptance and belonging, make the user fashionable, or improve family relationships. Products or services that appeal to the consumer's need for *confidence* are expected to lead to praise and accomplishments, improve skills and knowledge, lead to personal advancement, aid dependability, improve status, protect reputation, give pride of ownership, and give special privileges and recognition.

Macy's (2006) converted its various regional divisions—including such stores as Filene's and Bon Marché, as well as the former May Company divisions—into Macy's nameplate stores. Now with 800 branches throughout the United States, the company knew its first national-level advertising campaign would be important. Macy's tagline, "Way to Shop," was used and highlighted at various locations where the nationwide retailer had stores with a "Dancing in the Streets" theme.

## Current Brand Image

The target audience's existing impression of the client's product or service is the Current Brand Image. This should be the actual impression, as determined by primary research conducted by the strategic writer; it should not be wishful thinking. If consumers do not understand the product or service, advertising can try to improve the current brand image and solve the misunderstanding. If consumers already correctly understand the image that the client wants to project, advertising can be used to reinforce the current brand image.

The current brand image may be positive or negative, especially in geographic markets that are not familiar with the Macy's brand. In Chicago, former Marshall Fields customers, who liked the regional department store, had a negative image of Macy's as it renamed the stores.

## Desired Brand Image

The Desired Brand Image is whatever impression the client *wishes* the target audience would have about the product or service. This section of the analysis consists of a brief statement of how the client would like the target audience to describe the product or service.

In order to introduce Macy's to its new markets, block parties were held in cities throughout the United States where renamed Macy's stores were located. Along with the fun and fresh "Dancing in the Streets" national advertising campaign, Macy's emphasized its latest fashion trends; its store traditions, such as the Thanksgiving Day Parade; and its various charitable activities. The company hoped that consumers would see Macy's as a fashion leader on the national stage, yet accessible locally.

## Direct Competition and Brand Image

Previously, we discussed the Product category. If the client's brand is Macy's department stores, the Direct Competition would probably include Dillard's and Nordstrom. If the client's product is a manufacturer such as Roxy, a direct competitor is Water Girl. For each direct competitor, the situation analysis should include a brief description of that product's current brand image. Understanding how the target audience views the competition's current brand image will help the analysis team know how to distinguish the client's product from that of its competitors.

## Indirect Competition and Brand Image

Identifying indirect competitors is more challenging than naming direct competitors. Indirect competitors may be in a different product category, but they could keep the target audience from buying the client's product. For example, let's say the product is a department store, and the indirect competition is a specialty store. If the target audience is not interested in buying from Macy's, they may shop at the specialty retailer Gap or even at the discount department store Target.

## Advertising Objective

The Advertising Objective for the advertisement is defined by the client. For example, the specific objective might be "To get 18- to 24-year-olds to view Macy's as the fun and fashion-forward place to purchase apparel."

## Strategic Message

The Strategic Message is one of the most important sections of the situation analysis. This is what all the background and the analysis have been moving toward: to provide the theme of the advertisement. From this Strategic Message will come all the creative elements for the ad. A good Strategic Message gives the product a unique and positive position in the mind of the target audience. It makes claims for benefits that no other competing product can make. For example, the Strategic Message might be "Macy's offers the best selection of apparel for 18- to 24-year-olds in the juniors department."

## Supporting Benefits

Supporting Benefits are also known as selling points. These selling points provide supporting evidence to present in the ads. Supporting Benefits involve details about how the product or service meets the needs of the audience. For example, being able to point to a private-label product as a way to show how Macy's meets the consumers' needs can strengthen the Macy's brand name.

Once the situation analysis is complete, the creative team can start developing the creative message. At this point, the team will write a slogan or another creative message, and they'll plan the place or places where the ad will be printed or broadcast. In the next section, we'll look at the specific writing and creative messages that are needed to produce effective ads.

---

*Portfolio Exercise:* **You have been hired by an advertising agency and have been assigned to the situation analysis team for a new line of skin care products targeted toward teenagers with acne. It is your responsibility to do the background research on the cosmetic company and the product. Write the Client and Product section, which includes the history of the client and the product characteristics. This section will be incorporated into the situation analysis. For this assignment, you may select an existing cosmetic firm and analyze current innovations in this product category.**

---

# STRATEGIC WRITING FOR ADVERTISING

Once the situation analysis is completed and the communication message is established, the team can start to think about images, sounds, headlines, slogans, logos— all of the creative aspects that make advertising so much fun. In this part of the chapter, we will put the situation analysis to work by creating advertisements.

Advertisers have used a variety of advertising appeals with great success. After these advertising appeals are introduced, ads may be formatted for print in newspapers, magazines, direct response media, or sales promotion. They may also be formatted for broadcast on radio or television, if that's the medium most directed toward the target audience.

## ADVERTISING APPEALS

**Advertising appeals** are methods used for attracting the target audience's interest in the client's products or services. According to Clow and Baack (2002), the most successful appeals used by advertisers include fear, humor, sex, music, rationality, emotions, and scarcity. Let's take a look at how these appeals might be used in fashion advertising.

## Fear

Fear appeals focus on the negative consequences of using or not using certain types of products or services. For example, you might become a social outcast if you do not use a certain type of shampoo, deodorant, or mouthwash. Many clients with such products have effectively promoted their goods using fear.

Besides using fear, advertisers of health and beauty products often attempt to sell their merchandise by presenting the idea that using a particular product will perform miracles. Losing weight, gaining more beautiful skin, or styling pretty hair are the miracles that result from using the advertiser's products.

## Humor

Humor allows consumers to take a light-hearted, comedic view of life. It is a more upbeat appeal than using fear. Humor allows the audience to watch and listen, laugh, and (the advertiser hopes) remember ads. To do well, the humor should connect the target audience directly to the product's benefits.

In a commercial for a recent VISA advertising campaign, for example, a rather unattractive woman breaks the heel of her dull shoe, which leads to her remarkable transformation. Not only does she get a makeover, with new makeup, a fresh hair-style, and more attractive clothes, she gets to pick a new pair of beautiful shoes—presented to her by several handsome salesmen (Figure 6.3).

## Sex

Fashion merchandise often uses sexual themes to attract customers. A sexy man or woman can be shown in an advertisement for fragrance, implying that you could be as sexy as the model if you wear that cologne or perfume.

Models are often used as decorative elements for ads. Their primary purpose is to act as a sexual or attractive stimulus, drawing attention to the products in that way.

FIGURE 6.3. Visa commercial shows humor.

## Music

Music helps to capture the attention of listeners of broadcast commercials. Music is linked to memories and emotions. Hearing a particular song can bring back memories of experiences that were pleasant for the audience members.

Well-known songs have successfully been used for commercials, even though the rights to use popular music can be very expensive. For example, Zales Jewelers used the song "For Your Love," originally recorded by the Yardbirds, to promote its Valentine's Day campaign.

Special tunes, known as jingles, have also been created to emphasize products or brands. For example, Sears created a series of ads with the theme "Come see the softer side of Sears."

## Rationality

The goal of a rational appeal is to provide the information the consumer needs in order to make a purchase decision. If a consumer wants to purchase a new pair of shorts to wear to the lake, a rational appeal will provide selling points, including the price, the fiber content, and the advantages of the style.

For example, an advertisement for L.L. Bean shorts shows the important rational benefits of purchasing the product. The item is priced at $29.50. The shorts are made from lightweight and quick-drying Supplex ® nylon fabric. They have been redesigned with four pockets with mesh drain panels, a nylon waist belt to provide a place to clip on a cell phone, and an interior key clip. The man wanting a pair of shorts that are ideal for water activities would be exposed to the benefits of this garment.

## Emotions

Emotional attachments can capture an audience member's attention and help connect the consumer to the brand. Emotions about looking and feeling good are common in fashion advertising. For example, you wear clothes from American Eagle Outfitters to fit in with the popular crowd at school—an emotional reaction to belonging to a peer group.

Because weddings, funerals, and graduations invoke emotional reactions, these events are often depicted in emotional appeals. A popular television commercial shows the parents redecorating their home after their son graduates from school. Now that the parents are empty nesters, they feel free to renovate his room to meet their needs.

## Scarcity

When there is a limited supply of a product, the value of the product increases. A limited edition T-shirt designed by a famous designer to support breast cancer charities motivates consumers to purchase the product immediately. If they wait, the shirt will be gone.

Target and H&M have profitably introduced lines with limited supply. Proenza Schouler and Behnaz Sarafpour created capsule collections for Target's Go International promotion, while Karl Lagerfeld, Stella McCartney, and Viktor & Rolf designed limited editions for H&M. These collections, priced much lower than the designers' traditional lines, were extremely popular. When Lagerfeld introduced his collection, consumer demand was high and inventory sold out within days.

# PRINT ADVERTISEMENTS

Print advertisements are persuasive messages that appear in newspapers, magazines, direct response media, and other sales promotion materials. The goal for print ads is to convince a particular group of people to purchase a product or service or at least to seek more information about that good or service by visiting a retail store, calling a telephone number, visiting a Web site, or filling out and returning a coupon. Print ads are typically part of an advertising campaign that includes other forms of advertising, such as radio, television, or other promotional communication.

Print ads most often are categorized as announcement ads, institutional (or image) ads, or product ads. **Announcement ads,** which include grocery ads, one-day sale ads, and special occasion ads (President's Day or the Day after Thanksgiving Early Bird Specials), are found everyday in newspapers. These time-sensitive ads contain very limited copy; usually they just mention price and product names. Think of the institutional ads and product ads that were introduced earlier in this chapter in the section called "The Role of Advertising."

The target audience for print ads is defined in the situation analysis. Effective print ads, placed in newspapers, magazines, or other controlled media, capture the consumer's attention, generate interest and desire for the product or service, and encourage the consumer to take action to obtain the product or service.

The copy you would write for a print ad should flow from the research. Following the generally accepted advertising guidelines of Attention–Interest–Desire–Action (AIDA), you must first get the audience member's attention; and then you must interest her in your product. Finally, you create desire in her to take action by buying the product.

---

*Portfolio Exercise:* **You are an advertising intern with Macy's department stores in San Francisco. The firm is having a special event promoting children's back-to-school apparel in two of its Arizona locations. The event features a fashion show, nutritional snacks prepared by the store's restaurant, and assistance planning a back-to-school wardrobe with merchandising representatives from Baby Phat, Sean John, Polo Ralph Lauren, and Guess? The event, directed toward elementary school children, will be held at noon at the Scottsdale Fashion Square branch of Macy's on Friday, August 15, and repeated**

**at the Chandler store on Saturday, August 16. Plan a theme and prepare the copy for an announcement advertisement for the event.** 

---

## *Newspapers*

Newspaper ads consist of a number of elements, including a visual, a headline, body copy, a logo, a slogan, a tagline, mandatory information, and a call to action. Normally, newspaper ads are reproduced as half-tones, which appear as black and white photography or illustrations on newsprint. Most artwork in newspapers reproduces with a grainy appearance.

Marsh, Guth, and Short (2005) report that two thirds of print ad viewers see the visual part of the ad first. This means that the visual part of the ad—the photographs, illustrations, or graphic designs—is most important for grabbing the viewer's attention. The visual should create a mood, establish a theme, or tell a story that directs the viewer to the ad's message. Thus, it is the visual that leads the consumer to the headline and body copy.

The headline is created to promote the ad's key message, which was defined in the situation analysis. Within approximately eight words, the headline should be direct, contain a key benefit, command the consumer's attention, and guide him to the ad's message. The headline should answer the consumer's question, "What's in it for me?" This is an appeal to the consumer's self-interest.

Subheadlines, which are optional, are secondary to the main headline and help clarify the main headline.

Body copy starts with an opening sentence that swings the reader from the headline into the body copy, persuading that person to continue reading. You want the reader to get into the body copy where the specific information about the product or service is explained. The body copy includes the key benefits, which are the heart of the ad. As discussed in the situation analysis, this is where the reader learns how this product or service will fill her needs. The body copy starts with the strongest selling point, followed by a dramatic feeling that your consumer will get by using the product. It ends with a snappy, witty, memorable punch line that imparts a sense of urgency to take action. This ending may be a fragment, not even a complete sentence.

Print ads may also contain other elements known as logos, slogans, and taglines. **Logos** are visual images that serve as a visual identifier, such as the Nike swoosh or

Target's red and white circles. Logos may also be a specific font or typeface used as a visual image. Most fashion retailers and manufacturers use a distinct typeface with a symbol for visual identity. **Slogans** or **taglines** are phrases that state the promotional theme for the firm. Kohl's uses the phrase "Expect great things" as a slogan for its advertising. The phrase is placed near the sans serif typeface the store uses for its logo. It helps the client identify with the product. The cosmetic brand Maybelline includes the tagline "Maybe she's born with it. Maybe it's Maybelline" with its print ads.

Some situations and industries may include items that are required by law. For example, copyright symbols, registration marks, and fairness statements such as "Equal opportunity employer" may be required for an agency or a legal entity.

The ad ends with a call to action. It asks the potential consumer to stop by a store, call a phone number, or go to a Web site.

---

*Portfolio Exercise:* **Your next assignment for Macy's is to create a headline for a new line of sweaters that will be sold in the junior apparel department and will be featured in a newspaper advertisement. The sweaters are made by XOXO and the collection includes a lambswool cowl neck, a belted sweater, an acrylic wavy stripe pullover, and an acrylic crochet inset cardigan. Write four different headlines for this fall collection. Circle the one you think is the best.**

---

All of the elements, visual as well as verbal, are put together in a pleasing format by a layout artist or graphic designer. The final ad is placed in a newspaper. Figure 6.4 is an example of a newspaper ad that puts all of the components together.

## Magazines

Magazine advertisements are similar to newspaper ads. Many of the same characteristics, including visual and verbal building blocks based upon the situation analysis, are used for magazine ads. Magazines have one strong advantage over newsprint: the printing process is much more sophisticated. Magazine artwork is reproduced as black and white or by a four-color process, which brings a more realistic, professional look to photographs and drawings.

# Grand Opening
# Serenity Spa!!!

## August 1

### Located in the Red Mountain Promenade

### Southwest corner of Power and McDowell in Northeast Mesa

# For all your beauty needs!

# Serenity Spa

Come in between August 1 and August 31 for a complimentary gift!

Open Monday through Saturday
8 a.m. to 8 p.m.

480-225-4965
serenity@spa.com

FIGURE 6.4. Newspaper advertisement.

Fashion magazine ads typically are more visual and image-oriented, and, therefore, these ads are more dependent upon photography and logos. Print ads placed in fashion magazines are less likely to use extensive copy. The name of the designer, manufacturer, or retailer may be the only words on the page.

Trade or business-to-business magazine ads follow a format similar to those used for newspaper ads. Headlines, subheadlines, body copy, logos, slogans, and calls to action are common elements in the ads that are placed in trade magazines.

## Direct Marketing Media

Direct marketing media send persuasive messages directly to a consumer via a traditional mailing list or an electronic mailing (e-mail) list. This form of promotion attempts to raise money, to expand membership for an organization, to educate consumers, to increase sales of products or services, or to increase sales of subscriptions. Direct marketing media, which requires a response for the receiver, differs from other forms of advertising in several ways:

- It is targeted to a specific audience member.
- It is delivered to the consumer through traditional or electronic mail.
- It is personalized and speaks directly to the consumer.
- It is timely.
- It is produced with the intent to provide measurable results.

Traditionally mailed direct response media consists of several parts that are presented as a package. These parts include the envelope, a sales letter, and a response card. Optional promotional materials typically include a brochure that restates the offer in a visual format—as well as other teaser devices, such as testimonials, product samples, free gift offers, or coupons.

The outer envelope is used to attract attention in a manner similar to the headline for a print ad or just like a store window created to bring the customer inside a retail store. The envelope asks your customer to open it and look inside to see additional materials. You have approximately three seconds to create a positive first impression and tempt the customer to open the envelope and look inside (Marsh, Guth, & Short, 2005).

Inside, the customer will find a sales letter and perhaps a brochure that explains the offer in detail, with benefits and a call to action. Sales letters are frequently longer than one page, and may even use an 11-by-17-inch page, which is folded to be four 8½-by-11-inch standard pages. Sales letters often begin with a teaser: a headline that appears in the upper left corner of the page, above the date and salutation. Teasers are formatted to fit into the upper corner, in a larger font, in a typeface that's different from the rest of the letter, and in color. Teasers frequently ask a question, mention a problem, provide an interesting statistic, or make a sales pitch. This is where you, the copywriter, try to grab the reader's attention.

In the next section of the direct mail piece, you try to create a sense of need or desire. You remind the reader that something in her life could be better, invoking a desire to learn that your product could be the solution. This section does not have to be lengthy.

Next, you offer reasons why your product in fact does offer a solution to the problem. Here you discuss the benefits of your product in detail and discuss how your product improves your addressee's life. This section is several paragraphs long. Add emphasis by using various combinations of colored ink, boldface type, italics, all capital letters, underlining, and various font styles.

Now that the consumer is aware of the benefits, you ask for the sale. For example, tell the reader, "Order yours today and save 20% on your first purchase." Then provide details about how to buy your product. Remind your reader how the product will help solve the problem identified at the beginning of the letter. Create a sense of urgency with a special benefit, such as "and if you respond within 30 days, you will receive . . ."

After you close the letter with a standard "sincerely" sign-off, you will probably want to add a postscript, or "P.S." Almost all sales letters include a postscript that contains one final incentive for the consumer to purchase the product. Frequently, the postscript uses a script typeface that appears to be handwritten, as a personal appeal.

In addition to the letter, the package may include a brochure, a direct-response catalog, product samples, address labels, and even money in the form of a discount check or cash. A specialized response or reply card asks for the sale and lets the consumer know how to respond.

Electronically delivered interactive media relies on technology to reach the target audience. With the increased costs for printing and mailing, many firms have moved toward e-mail lists, offering targeted messages to the individual. Writing strategic messages for electronic delivery is discussed more fully in Chapter 8, "Writing for New Media."

*Portfolio Exercise:* **Your third task for Macy's is to create a direct marketing flyer that will be included in the firm's September billing statement. The product that Macy's wants to promote is a line of Christmas cards that can be printed with the sender's personal holiday greeting and name. Customers must order these cards by October 1 in order to assure delivery to the customer by the middle of November. Prepare a direct marketing flyer that will fit into an envelope measuring 3 ½ by 7 inches. Include an illustration of the product, a headline, a sales pitch, a price list, and the ordering information.**

## Sales Promotion

In this book, the term **sales promotion** refers to activities that provide extra value or incentives. Sales promotion activities that are commonly directed toward consumers who are product end-users include "contests, coupons, gift-with-purchase, purchase-with-purchase, point-of-sale displays, refunds, rebates, sweepstakes, and sampling" (Swanson & Everett, 2007, p. 348). Other sales promotion activities are directed toward members of the trade, such as wholesalers, distributors, or retailers; these activities typically include "promotion and merchandising allowances, price deals, sales contests, special counter displays or sales fixtures, and trade show discounts" (p. 359). Our discussion will concentrate on consumer-oriented sales promotion incentives.

The oldest type of consumer sales promotion started in 1895 with the cents-off coupon. C. W. Post created the coupon to encourage consumers to buy his new Grape-Nuts cereal (Belch & Belch, 2007). Since then, a variety of sales promotion techniques have offered value to consumers. Fashion retailers learned the value of coupons from other industries, offering discount coupons to help introduce the new season's fashion and cosmetics lines, as well as to help clear end-of-the-season merchandise from the sales floor. They have also adapted airline frequent-flyer programs into loyalty programs of their own. Retail chains like Victoria's Secret and Chico's offer discounts to holders of store-branded credit cards or to members of their frequent-buyer clubs, such as Chico's Passport Club.

Retail coupons that are placed in newspaper ads typically list the discount amount as a percentage, describe any restrictions for products not covered, and provide a UPC code that can be scanned by a sales associate when the coupon is redeemed. The headlines and body copy are part of the newspaper ad. Other incentives combine a photograph with the information about the value of the coupon: "Take $25 off your purchase of $100 or more." The other side of the coupon is where the copywriter provides additional information and clarification about the sales promotion.

The message presented as sales promotion comes from the situation analysis. Is the consumer looking for a discount or a sample of the product prior to investing in a big purchase? Is she looking for a gift-with-purchase, or will she be willing to purchase something extra to get the gift? All questions such as these should be answered before the creative approach is developed.

---

*Portfolio Exercise:* **Macy's is offering a beach tote bag with the purchase of any new swimsuit selling for $75 or more. The tote bag has a retail value of $40. Prepare a newspaper advertisement, with a headline, selling points, the firm's logo, and a visual image of the merchandise that will entice customers to purchase a swimsuit and receive the gift-with-purchase sales promotion.**

---

## RADIO ADVERTISEMENTS

Radio advertisements, also known as radio spots, are commercials that are broadcast via the radio to motivate the listener to take an action desired by an ad's sponsor. Radio ads are a generally low-cost method of distributing the message to a specifically targeted audience, since radio stations have extensive information about the demographic and psychographic statistics of their audience. Radio ads commonly are used as a supplement to advertising messages that have been delivered via another medium.

Time on the radio is equivalent to space in print media. Radio ads are prepared in standard time lengths of 10, 15, 20, 30, or 60 seconds. These measurements are precise, and the copy must fit into the time the advertiser has purchased. A media planner and buyer decide which radio station to use, based upon the situation analysis. Then, the creative approach is planned.

The copywriter creates the radio script. Figure 6.5 shows an example of a radio advertisement script. The upper left corner of the form contains the traffic information: the title of the spot, the name of the client or sponsor of the message, the time

| Agency | All Advertising | Writer | Amanda Hobbs |
|--------|-----------------|--------|--------------|
| Client | Serenity Spa | Producer | Amanda Hobbs |
| Project | Radio Spot | Medium | Radio |
| Title | Serenity Radio Spot | | |

AMBIENT SOUND IN BACKGROUND

ARE YOU LOOKING FOR A RELAXING, FUN ATMOSPHERE TO PICK UP YOUR FAVORITE BEAUTY PRODUCT OR GET THAT MASSAGE YOU'VE BEAN YEARNING FOR? STOP INTO SERENITY SPA...OPENING AUGUST FIRST AND LOCATED IN THE RED MOUNTAIN CORNER OF POWER AND MCDOWELL...SERENITY SPA OFFERS QUALITY BEAUTY PRODUCTS AND SERVICES IN A COMFORTING ATMOSPHERE WITH A CARING SMILE...SO COME ON IN...AND MAKE ALL YOUR BEAUTY DREAMS COME TRUE...

Page #1

FIGURE 6.5. Radio advertisement script.

length of the spot, and the dates on which the spot is scheduled to be broadcast. This information is similar to the heading on an office memorandum; it is intended to make certain that the right people use the proper paperwork at the right time.

A radio advertising script is typically created as an announcer continuity script or as a production script. The **announcer continuity script** contains only the words that the announcer will read during a live, real-time broadcast. While this appears to be the easiest format to create, the script should be formatted so it is easy for the announcer to read, with the copy presented in a large, easy-to-read typeface. It should be double-spaced and limited to one page. Further, none of the words or key phrases should be divided onto different lines of copy—that is, no end-of-line hyphenation. A guide for pronouncing an unusual or difficult-to-pronounce word is provided in parentheses immediately after the word.

A **production script** is provided for prerecorded spots that different broadcasters will play at various times. Production scripts provide a consistent presentation, which has the advantages of distinctive voices, sound effects, and music. A two-column format is used. On the left-hand side of the sheet, production instructions discuss the use of voice, sound effects, and music. The right-hand side contains the script to be read by announcers or actors. Like the announcer continuity script, the production script should be presented in a large, easy-to-read typeface, with pronunciation guidance provided as needed.

The situation analysis drives the content and organization of the radio spot, and radio spots vary widely. Despite the different approaches that might be taken to achieve the goal, all radio commercials are seeking to stand out from the crowd. You want to grab your listeners' attention and keep them interested. Because the success of radio ads depends upon how well the audience hears the message, key information can be reinforced by repetition. If you want the consumer to call or come to the store, repeat the telephone number or address a couple of times. If you are focusing on a product, be sure to mention the name of the product at least three times in a 30-second ad (Marsh, Guth, & Short, 2005).

Radio commercials can use special effects techniques, including voices, music, and sound effects, that take your listener to a place, time, or atmosphere that you desire. With all of these elements in place, you ask your listener to take action, such as "Come to Victoria's Secret today and meet Heidi Klum!"

*Portfolio Exercise:* **In order to attract new female and male customers between the ages of 18 and 24 to the store, Macy's will be sponsoring a party in the junior department. The party will feature free pizza and sodas, as well as dance music that will be played by the town's most popular DJ. Write a 30-second radio spot targeted to this audience. Determine the best radio station in your community to broadcast the spot.**

## TELEVISION ADVERTISEMENTS

Television advertisements, also known as television commercials, are created to motivate viewers to take action. Television has a major advantage over radio commercials in that visual elements can be added to the sound, creating a dynamic impression. Television ads are the most expensive types of ads to produce, with costs for commercial production as well as costs for placement.

Television ads are classified in terms of distribution:

- Local or spot advertising is produced by an individual station or cable provider. These ads are targeted to the local community, and generally they are the least expensive to produce and place.
- National advertising is created by advertising agencies for distribution through nationwide networks, such as ABC, CBS, NBC, or FOX, or through their affiliate stations.
- Syndicated advertising is linked to contract programming for such television shows as *Oprah* or *Sex and the City,* depending upon the media planner's and buyer's recommendations.

The creative message, developed from the situation analysis research, is composed by the strategic writer. A detailed narrative, called a treatment, describes the look, location, and other logistical requirements for the commercial. Scripting follows this step. Scripts may be presented as a written script, as a storyboard, or sometimes in both formats.

Written television advertising production scripts are similar to radio production scripts. The document starts with traffic information and is presented in a two-column format, just like radio scripts. In addition to a production description, the left-hand column has visual directions to accommodate the added dimension for a television production. This description includes such elements as camera angles, lengths and widths of shots, and any special effects. The right-hand column includes script and audio information. Figure 6.6 shows a television commercial production script.

**Storyboards** are visual representations of how the words and pictures will be combined into a single persuasive message. These visual interpretations are used to give the client a sense of the finished product. Accompanying the drawings is relevant audio information, forcing writers to think visually while writing a television commercial. A television commercial isn't just a radio commercial with pictures; it's an integrated persuasive message. A storyboard can help bring the various elements into a cohesive product. Figure 6.7 illustrates a television commercial storyboard.

Most television commercials have 10, 30, or 60 seconds to accomplish their objective.

---

*Portfolio Exercise:* **Macy's is offering a new line of menswear, inspired by Tim Gunn, the Chief Creative Officer for Liz Claiborne Company. The launch of the new brand is occurring during the same week that a new season of the television show *Project Runway* starts. The reality television show features Mr. Gunn as the designers' mentor. Write the script for a 30-second television commercial for this new line at Macy's.**

---

## RADIO AND TELEVISION PROMOTIONS

Most radio and television stations use their own announcers to promote programming and establish an image for the station through announcements commonly referred to as "promos." The purpose of **promos** is to build and maintain a target audience through announcements that are directed to attract the audience to a particular program, to nurture the relationship between the audience and the station, or to demonstrate that the station operates in the public interest according to government licensing demands.

| Agency | All Advertising | Writer | Amanda Hobbs |
| Client | Serenity Spa | Producer | Amanda Hobbs |
| Project | TV Spot | Medium | Television |
| Title | Serenity TV Spot | | |

| VIDEO | AUDIO |
|---|---|
| Ambient/NAT sound<br>VO of Beauty products and treatments | LOOKING FOR A NEW PLACE TO FIND YOUR FAVORITE BEAUTY PRODUCTS AND TREATMENTS? |
| Ambient/NAT sound<br>VO of Northeast Mesa/ Store<br>VO of Phoenix and Scottsdale<br>VO of Serenity Spa | COME TO SERENITY SPA! LOCATED IN NORTHEAST MESA…MILES FROM THE BUSY PHOENIX AND SCOTTSDALE AREA, SERENITY'S CALM SETTING IS THE IDEAL PLACE TO FIND YOUR FAVORITE PRODUCT OR GET THAT TREATMENT YOU'VE BEEN WANTING! |
| Ambient/NAT sound<br>VO of Red Mountain Promenade | SERENITY SPA IS PART OF THE RED MOUNTAIN PROMENADE…ON THE SOUTHWEST CORNER OF POWER AND MCDOWELL… |
| Ambient /NAT sound<br>VO of products and spa services offered | WE OFFER THE LATEST QUALITY BEAUTY PRODUCTS AND SERVICES…ALL IN A COMFORTING ATMOSPHERE WITH A CARING SMILE… |
| Ambient /NAT sound<br>VO of store setting | SO COME ON DOWN TO SERENITY SPA!!! |

Page #1

FIGURE 6.6. Television commerical production script.

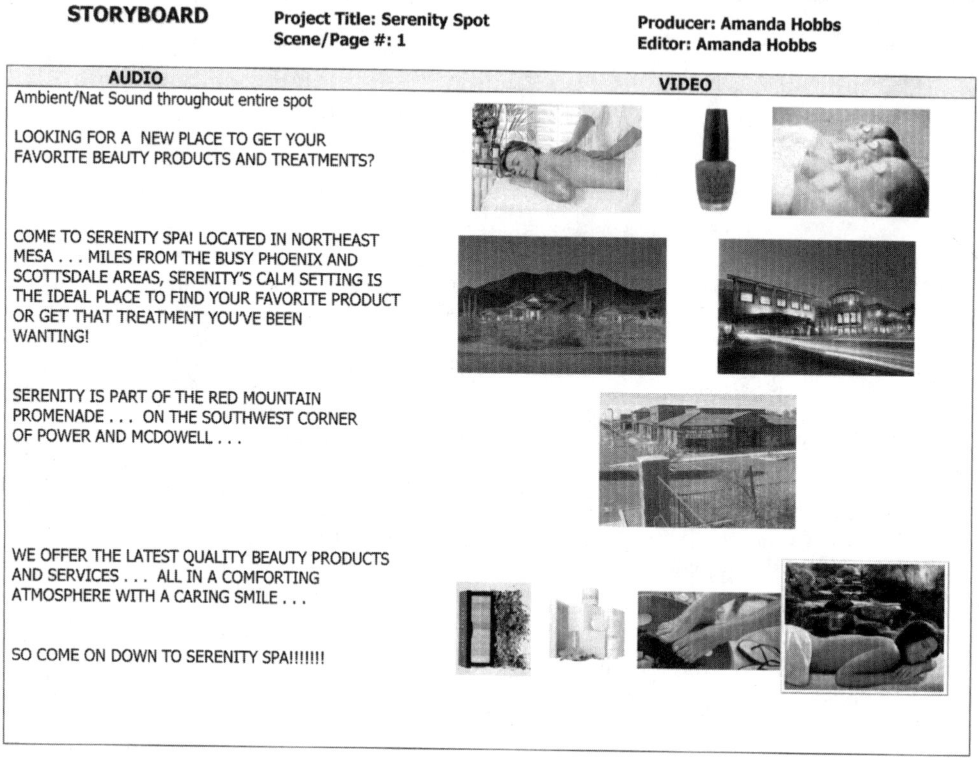

**FIGURE 6.7.** Television commerical storyboard.

Promotion of particular media and programs has become increasingly important in the era of media convergence, in which many media outlets are owned by a single company. This involves **cross-promotion**, in which an integrated promotional message is presented across multiple media. For example, television announcers from the national television network NBC may promote programs that will be broadcast on MSNBC or CNBC, the cable channels owned by NBC. Announcers from ABC promote a more complete analysis of a story by encouraging viewers to visit its Web site for further information. Media outlets with Internet Web sites are able to strengthen their relationships by offering program synopses, biographies of participants, contests, or the ability to purchase promotional items such as books, DVDs, or apparel. This is an integrated marketing approach, promoting the show, providing additional information, and extending product offers to consumers.

Radio and television on-air promotions follow script formats similar to those used in radio and television advertising. Here the client is the radio or television station rather than an advertising sponsor.

Before a promo is created, preliminary research should be conducted to determine which type of promo would be more effective: a topical promotion or a generic one. This research is similar to the research that is done in the situation analysis.

**Topical promos** provide information about a specific program that will air at a definite time. For example, a topical promo invites the listener to hear more information about a special designer preparing a ready-to-wear collection. This promo would be aired during Fashion Week on National Public Radio. This type of promo has a limited shelf-life. Once the program has aired, the promo has no further use.

**Generic promos** are designed to air at any time, reminding the audience of when and where to find their favorite programs, rather than focusing on a specific episode. For example, the Style Network reminds viewers to watch new episodes of *The Look for Less* with host Yoanna House every Sunday at 8 p.m. As long as new episodes with Yoanna as the host are shown at that time, the promo can continue to be broadcast.

Figure 6.8 illustrates a radio promotion script. Whether the promo is topical or generic, certain key information must be included and regularly repeated. First, the audience needs to know the name of the program. They also need to know the day of the week, the time, and the channel on which the program is broadcast. Stating key information a second time reinforces the information as well as attracting additional or new viewers and listeners. Even if the Who, What, and When are introduced at the beginning of the spot, the audience member who tunes in during the middle of the spot needs the information as well. And repeating the information a third time as the spot closes reinforces the point.

| **Agency** | KMLE Camel Country | **Writer** | Amanda Hobbs |
| **Client** | Serenity Spa | **Producer** | Amanda Hobbs |
| **Project** | Radio Promo for Remote | **Medium** | Radio |
| **Title** | Serenity Radio Promo | | |

MUSIC BED:                    LISTEN UP, EVERYONE...K-M-L-E CAMEL COUNTRY WILL BE
BROADCASTING LIVE ALL MORNING TOMORROW FROM
SERENITY SPA IN NORTHEAST MESA...

YOUR OFFICIAL MORNING CREW, DAVE AND KATY, WILL BE
TALKING WITH THE OWNERS AND HOSTING SPECIAL
GIVEAWAYS WHILE, AS ALWAYS, GIVING YOU THE MOST
MUSIC IN THE MORNING!

SO GET UP...AND GET GOING...WITH DAVE AND KATY IN THE
MORNING...LIVE AT SERENITY SPA!

Page #1

FIGURE 6.8. Radio promotion script.

## SUMMARY

Advertising is a sponsored message presented through the media to consumers. It plays an important role in today's culture. The creativity that we see on television or in print begins with a situation analysis. This document defines the purpose, target audience, and media that the advertisement is being created for. Once a situation analysis is completed, it is used to develop the advertising material that will be presented in newspapers, magazines, direct response media, sales promotions, and radio and television commercials.

## KEY TERMS

Advertising

Advertising agency

Advertising appeal

Announcement ad

Announcer continuity script

Cross-promotion

Demographic information

Executive Summary

Generic promo

In-house promotion division

Institutional advertising

Logo

Product advertising

Production script

Promo

Psychographic information

Sales promotion

Situation analysis

Slogan

Storyboard

SWOT analysis

Tagline

Target audience

Topical promo

## CASE STUDY

### *Fuhgeddaboudit!*

Despite being identified as one of the top 25 firms on *Fortune* magazine's Annual List of Most Admired Companies in the United States, Wal-Mart met significant resistance as it attempted to open branches in such large cities as New York (Manhattan), Chicago, Cleveland, and Los Angeles. During the battle to open a branch of the world's largest retail store in New York, Wal-Mart's chief executive officer, H. Lee Scott, Jr., told the editors and reporters from the *New York Times* that it was not worth the effort to conduct business there. He said that it is too expensive and it is too exasperating to open a store there.

The opposition to Wal-Mart locating in New York was led by unions and Democratic members of the city councils. Labor organizations feared that having low-priced merchandise being sold by non-union workers—who earn modest wages and receive limited health benefits, compared to union workers—would undermine the unionized competitors. The image of Wal-Mart, known for dowdy cheap merchandise, was the antithesis of New York City, the iconic center of cutting-edge style and fashion innovation.

Critics of Wal-Mart cite that Wal-Mart's prices are so low because its wages and benefits leave many workers with an income below the federal "poverty threshold" and without health care. Other threats to communities where Wal-Mart wants to build stores include discrimination against female employees, environmentally unfriendly practices, driving local stores out of business, and unethical relationships with local governments and suppliers.

The campaign used by those opposing Wal-Mart in New York was given the theme "WAL-MART FREE NYC." Political, union, and community groups worked together to prevent the store from opening there—for now, at least.

Chicago was not able to prevent Wal-Mart from opening in that urban area. The company opened a store in Chicago that attracted thousands of job applicants and performed stronger than the firm had anticipated. Benefits for city-dwellers, such as lower prices due to the chain's enormous purchasing power and efficient distributions systems, were emphasized as reasons for the firm's success there. Grocery prices at Wal-Mart are typically 10 to 30% lower than prices charged by competitors that employ union workers.

Wal-Mart has long considered New York City a tantalizing prize. After all, the city is home to more than eight million consumers and it's the place to find the best attention-grabbing stores for just about every major retailer in the country.

## CASE STUDY QUESTIONS

1. Do you think that Wal-Mart will really give up the hope of opening stores in all of the boroughs of New York?
2. What are the current pros and cons of having a Wal-Mart store in Manhattan?
3. What theme would you use in an ad campaign to support opening a branch of Wal-Mart in New York?
4. What theme would you use in an ad campaign to protest the opening of a branch of Wal-Mart in New York?

## INDUSTRY PROFILE

*Deby Green*

**What is your current job and title?**

Creative Director of Dillard's, Texas Division

**Can you describe the main responsibilities for your job?**

I am responsible for directing all the creative that we produce in our division. That includes newspaper design, preprint design, and any special publications or direct mail. In this division, we produce all newspaper ads for the state of Texas.

**What is a typical day at work like?**

Each morning I check to see how our ads are developing to see if they are missing art or information. I basically make sure all jobs are flowing in a timely manner. We try to have ads completed and ready to send to each newspaper by mid afternoon for the next day. I check with our in-house studio to make sure they are aware of any design ideas and are photographing needed merchandise on the correct models. We try to coordinate the age of the model to the age of the customer buying the apparel. My job includes putting out a lot of fires. In retail advertising, things are constantly changing. We have to be flexible and ready to adapt ads at a moment's notice.

**At what point did you decide to pursue a career in writing for a fashion-related business?**

I have always been interested in fashion. I guess it was just a natural progression. I first worked for a newspaper in their ad department. I wrote and designed fashion ads for the local women's stores. When my husband and I moved to Fort Worth, Dillard's had an opening in the advertising department. I was thrilled to advance my career and my focus on fashion by working for a leading fashion retailer.

**Describe your first writing job. What was the most important or interesting thing you wrote for that job/publication?**

I wrote fashion advertising for that newspaper. It was challenging and fun to create copy that would catch the customers' attention and cause them to stop and read the ad. That is our main focus today: attracting the reader's attention and pulling them into the ads. Most people scan the paper. If we can stop someone for an instant with a catchy headline or intriguing image, then we have accomplished our goal. Hopefully, we can sell them on the merchandise shown and make them want to come into the store, either to look for that piece of clothing or to want to see more options.

*What are you currently reading (books, magazines, Web sites, newspapers, other media)? Do you have a favorite author or publication?*

I always read our local papers. The *Dallas Morning News* and the *Star Telegram*. One of my favorite magazines is *InStyle*. They have great style ideas and clothing trends. We keep ongoing subscriptions to *Marie Claire*, *Vogue*, *GQ*, *Women's Wear Daily*. Reading is one of my joys. I love fiction and have quite a varied taste. I love Isabel Allende and Robert Tannenbaum, Amy Tan. I am planning to start reading some of the classics again.

*What advice do you have for students interested in a writing career?*

Be completely involved in the world around you. Read the newspapers and magazines. Watch style channels, documentaries, biographies on TV. The more knowledge you have within you, the more you will be able to contribute to your writing.

*Do you have any recommendations for students?*

While in college, try to get involved in community projects. You meet a lot of interesting people, and everyone has a life story. It's amazing to learn what some people have experienced in their lifetime. That opens you up to so many different ideas and beliefs. Makes for a well-rounded writer. Also, some businesses have internships. That enables a student to experience the working environment. And it can lead to connections within the industry for job placement.

## REFERENCES

Belch, G. E., & Belch, M. A. (2007). *Advertising and promotion: An integrated marketing communications perspective* (7th ed.). New York: McGraw-Hill/Irwin.

Clow, K. E, & Baack, D. (2002). *Integrated advertising, promotion & marketing communications.* Upper Saddle River, NJ: Pearson Education.

Elliott, S. (2005, August 22). The cover models may not be fatter, but the issues are. *New York Times*. Retrieved August 22, 2005, from http://www.nytimes.com

Hill, D. D. (2004). *As seen in Vogue: A century of American fashion in advertising*. Lubbock, TX: Texas Tech University Press.

Macy's Group. (2006). *Macy's launches national advertising, marketing campaign*. Retrieved April 11, 2007, from http://www1.macys.com/catalog/syndicated/remote/remotesyndication .ognc?Brand=PRESSRELEASE

Marsh, C., Guth, D. W., & Short, B. P. (2005). *Strategic writing: Multimedia writing for public relations, advertising, sales and marketing, and business communication*. Boston: Pearson Education.

Swanson, K. K., & Everett, J. C. (2007). *Promotion in the merchandising environment* (2nd ed.). New York: Fairchild Books.

# SEVEN

## *Writing for Public Relations*

After you have read this chapter, you should be able to discuss the following:

• The role of public relations in fashion communication

• How to strategically write news releases for print and broadcast resources

• Media kit contents and how to prepare backgrounders, fact sheets, and photo opportunity sheets

• How to write newspaper articles and magazine stories from a public relations point of view

• How to strategically write pitch letters, annual reports, and fund-raising letters

Can you imagine having a great job, working hard, and loving it—for over 60 years? That is just exactly what Eleanor Lambert (Figure 7.1) did. During the 1930s, Miss Lambert moved to New York, where she became the first fashion publicist. Her public relations innovations included creating the International Best Dressed List in 1940 for her client the New York Dress Institute, as a publicity stunt to encourage people to think about clothes and buy even more. In addition, she started a week of fashion shows for the press in 1943, a precursor to today's New York Fashion Week. She also founded the Council of Fashion Designers of America (CFDA) in 1962. According to her many business associates and friends, Miss Lambert—starting in the 1930s and continuing until just before her death at the age of 100 in 2003—was never high-pressure while promoting fashion and fashion designers (Zilkha, 2004).

FIGURE 7.1. Eleanor Lambert.

This chapter focuses on the role of public relations within the fashion industry. We will look at public relations (sometimes referred to as "PR") as a profession, as well as demonstrate several strategic writing formats used by individuals involved in writing for public relations.

# THE ROLE OF PUBLIC RELATIONS

An important part of a company's promotional communication mix includes public relations and publicity. Although these processes are related, we need to recognize their differences. "**Public relations** (PR) is the management function that establishes and maintains mutually beneficial relationships between an organization and the public on whom its success or failure depends (Cutlip, Center, & Broom, 2005, p. 5). This definition recognizes that public relations involves evaluating public attitudes, using that knowledge to identify policies and procedures for an individual or organization with public interest, and executing a plan of action to earn public understanding and acceptance.

"**Publicity** is communication by the initiating party seeking to tell others about a product, service, idea, or event and is delivered to the public at the discretion of the media" (Swanson & Everett, 2007, p. 372). Public relations has broad objectives, whereas publicity is more narrow in focus—establishing and maintaining a positive image of a company or an individual to its various publics. Public relations uses publicity—along with a variety of other tools, such as special publications, participation in community events, fund-raising, and event sponsorship—to enhance the image of an organization or an individual.

Publicity and advertising share some similarities, yet they have many differences as well. Like advertising, publicity involves nonpersonal communication to a mass audience. Unlike advertising, publicity is not paid for by the sponsoring organization. Instead, the company tries to get the media to cover a story about a product, service, cause, or event in a favorable manner—although how the story is presented in the media is controlled by the media.

One of the first public relations practitioners was Ivy L. Lee, who worked for John D. Rockefeller (Scott, 2005). After reformers and activists campaigned forcefully to expose the excesses of big business, which had operated with little regard for public welfare, Rockefeller and other American industrialists of the early 20th century realized they needed to promote a positive public image for themselves. Edward L. Bernays also influenced early public relations activities by linking public relations to research, psychology, and the social sciences (Scott).

Public relations practices in contemporary society help institutions to build prestige for individuals or groups, to promote products or services, and to help win elections or legislative battles. Most of today's public relations practitioners work for corporations or for public relations counseling firms.

According to Professors James Grunig and Todd Hunt (1984; cited in Marsh, Guth, & Short, 2005, p. 30), there are four different models of public relations:

1. The *press agentry model* focuses on gaining favorable publicity from the news media.

2. The *public information model* focuses on distributing accurate information to those who request it, such as members of the news media.

3. The *two-way asymmetrical model* focuses on researching and communicating with target publics to get them to agree with an organization.

**4.** The *two-way symmetrical model* focuses on researching and communicating with target publics to build productive relationships that benefit both sides. In this model, the organization recognizes that sometimes it needs to change in order to build a productive relationship.

## PUBLIC RELATIONS PLAN

The practice of public relations follows the process that is also used in advertising, business communication, as well as sales and marketing communication. The process consists of four stages: research, planning, communication, and evaluation. This is a fluid model. Sometimes we create a plan based upon our research, only to discover that we need more information. Before we can complete our plan, we need to conduct more research. As we start the communication stage, the situation changes and we have to go back and adjust the plan. In general, we conduct research and develop a plan prior to communicating. The final stage, evaluation, is fundamental to determining whether we took the right plan of action, and the entire process will help us adjust to changing conditions in the future.

Public relations specialists are experts in communication arts and persuasion. Their work involves a sequence of actions such as the following (Scott, 2005):

1. **Develop a program.** Analyzing problems and opportunities, defining goals, and determining the audience to be reached, as well as recommending and planning activities and actions.

2. **Write and edit.** Preparing materials such as news releases, speeches, annual reports, product information, and employee publications.

3. **Place information.** Working with newspaper, magazine, broadcast, or interactive media editors to place information in the most advantageous mediums and media vehicles.

4. **Organize special events.** Coordinating and staging events such as press conferences, award programs, fashion shows, product launches, exhibits, and displays.

5. **Set up face-to-face communication.** Including preparing and delivering speeches.

6. **Provide research and evaluation.** Documenting the background of the situation by examining reference materials, conducting interviews, and completing various surveys in order to recommend a course of action and also be able to assess the success or failure of the action.

7. **Manage resources.** Using strategies to plan, budget, recruit, and train staff to attain the organization's goals.

A range of various skills is required to execute a public relations program successfully. These skills include completing public opinion research, handling media relationships, conducting direct mail programs, implementing institutional advertising, writing for various print publications and electronic media productions, and coordinating special events.

## RELATIONSHIP TO NEWS MEDIA

As we learned in the journalism chapters, writers, editors, and producers have a responsibility to report about events, products, and people in the news. Journalists always work on short deadlines and look for stories with newsworthy information from a variety of sources, including creative businesspeople and experts in the topics that they cover. Some of these story ideas and contacts come from ideas pitched by public relations professionals. Although not every idea makes it into the media, journalists depend upon information and story ideas provided via public relations.

What sets some stories apart from others is their newsworthy nature. But, what is newsworthy to a reporter? There is no magic list or set of guidelines, but incorporating some of the following criteria will definitely help (Laermer, 2003):

- **Emphasize a local angle.** Bed Bath & Beyond is a large chain retailer that sells products for the home. In attempting to get a story about the opening of a branch in your town, determine what is happening specifically in your town. Is this a new category of retailer in your community? Is the store remodeling a space vacated by a retail store that went out of business? Is a new shopping center being built? Is the store manager a well-known local citizen?

- **Relate to a larger story.** After Hurricane Katrina devastated New Orleans and the Gulf Coast, did someone in your town get involved in the rescue and recovery operations? What products, expertise, or logistical support did the individual offer? Did a retailer from that region relocate to your town?

- **Associate with celebrities.** Do you make jewelry or handbags? Send a gift to a celebrity. If you get someone like Oprah, Gwyneth, or J. Lo to say something nice about your product, it gives you an opportunity to name-drop to the local media. Mere mentions of various products on Oprah Winfrey's talk show have sparked buying frenzies. Web site hits went up 400% the day after an Eileen Fisher waffle-weave merino cardigan was mentioned on Oprah's "Favorite Things," and a $995 linen and rhinestone tunic by Tory by TRB sold out after it appeared on the *Next Big Thing* show ("Oprah's Midas Touch," 2005).
- **Find the right journalist.** Start your research by picking up the past five to ten issues of a particular magazine or newspaper and get better acquainted with it. Are there specific journalists who cover companies like yours? Is a certain writer more a reporter, covering in-depth stories with local emphasis? Or is the writer more a columnist, working on stories about people and places with the writer's own opinion or outlook? Be sure to ask, "Are you the right person to tell this story?" Once you've found the right writer, tell that journalist your story.

## Press Conferences

A **press conference** is a staged forum where journalists are invited to view a new product or hear an important announcement firsthand. It is the generally accepted way that companies, politicians, government workers, sports figures, and celebrities announce something important to a number of print or broadcast journalists simultaneously. A press conference also allows journalists to pose questions directly to the person making the presentation.

For journalists, the big draw of press conferences is the speakers: people who are well known in the industry. Here is an opportunity to interview top individuals in a particular field. If a celebrity model such as Tyra Banks or Heidi Klum is the spokesperson at the press conference, the journalists are likely to come so that they can ask questions about *America's Next Top Model* or *Project Runway* or other projects involving the supermodels.

Another way to get journalists involved is by product sampling. Many apparel, cosmetic, and accessory firms offer samples of their products to members of the press. At a press conference, Bob Mackie might launch his latest scarf designs or perfume collection by giving out scarves or perfume in addition to media kits and refreshments. The event will also create photo opportunities. Press photographers or videographers will be invited to personalize the event for their media outlet.

## Special Events

"A **special event** is a one-time occurrence with planned activities, focused on a specific purpose—to bring attention to a brand manufacturer, retailer, or organization, or to influence the sale of merchandise" (Swanson & Everett, 2007, p. 23). Many of these events are coordinated with product launches; magazine anniversaries or previews; store openings; gallery exhibitions; award programs; or musical, theatrical, or sports performances. The range and variety of events are almost endless.

Special events are planned to fulfill business and social goals. For example, the event could be created to enhance the image of an individual, a brand, or a company to the general public; reach specific target customers; give back charitably to the community that one's customers come from; contribute to the economic development within the community; enhance VIP relationships with preferred and potential customers; and, of course, sell new or existing products.

During Fashion Week, special events are commonly coordinated with the fashion presentations. Typically, after-fashion-show parties take place at chic restaurants and clubs, such as Francisco Rodriquez's party at the Rose Bar of the Gramercy Park Hotel, Diane Von Furstenberg's dinner at Indochine in New York, or Donatella Versace's Walk of Style event in Los Angeles. Other special events timed to coincide with Fashion Week have included perfume launches, new store openings, book signings, and museum exhibits.

New York specialty retailer Bergdorf Goodman scheduled the unveiling of its revamped designer collections on the third floor to overlap Fashion Week, when many designers and celebrities would be in town. Guests were treated to canapés of caviar and foie gras, while admiring the transformation. The event drew such designers as Donna Karan, Michael Kors, Derek Lam, Matthew Williamson, and Doo-Ri Chung, among others. Italian designer Roberto Cavalli was able to view his own shop-within-a-shop at BG at the opening of the renovated designer floor.

These various public relations ideas encourage public awareness about products and services. But, some PR ideas have been taken to an extreme. Box 7.1, titled *A Good PR Idea Gone Bad*, looks at of out-of-control gift bags.

---

*Portfolio Exercise:* **As the special event planner for the public relations firm hired by the publisher Hyperion, it is your job to plan the launch party for the much anticipated sequel to Candace Bushnell's book *Lipstick Jungle,* called *One Fifth Avenue*. Brainstorm to come up with at least three different ideas for introducing the author and her book to the public. Select one of these ideas and develop it into a special event-planning portfolio. Complete the following tasks:**

- **Determine the location.**
- **Prepare a sample invitation.**
- **Write a news release about the event.**
- **Discuss the venue atmosphere with decorations and signage.**
- **Plan food and beverages.**
- **Create a floor plan and seating chart, if necessary.**
- **List the steps necessary to bring the event to a close.**

---

# STRATEGIC WRITING IN PUBLIC RELATIONS

Strategic writing is one of the foundations of successful public relations. Much of the communication is created to build positive relationships between the groups that have messages to distribute and the public to whom the messages are directed. Much of the communication is written in news releases, newsletter stories, broadcast or in-person scripts, and the many other tools that are available to public relations practitioners. In this section, we will look closely at some of these public relations tools.

## NEWS RELEASES

"A **news release** is a document that conveys newsworthy information about your organization to the news media" (Marsh et al., 2005, p. 31). Because most of us now get

## Box 7.1  A Good PR Idea Gone Bad

Fashion shows, press conferences, and awards shows have enticed celebrities and journalists to attend by offering **gift bags**, also known as **goodie bags**. Instead of being a small token of appreciation for attending or presenting awards, the product enticement has evolved into "swag suites" full of long tables of iPods, digital cameras, exotic trips, designer clothes, extravagant jewelry, and lavish accessories, which are loaded into luxury luggage. The bags and their contents have grown to excessive proportions in order to lure stars to attend award shows, post-fashion show social gatherings, and product launch parties.

At the party celebrating the 10th anniversary of *Allure* magazine's "Best of Beauty" awards (Figure 7.2), the gift bag was filled to the brim with over 100 full-size products, weighing 35 pounds (Shi, 2005). The beauty executives attending the event were overwhelmed by the gift, which was featured along with a special performance by Joss Stone at the Rainbow Room.

The popularity of this trend motivated the industry insider Hilary De Vries to write a novel called *The Gift Bag Chronicles* (2005). And the Fashion Institute of Technology offers an academic course called "The Art of the Goodie Bag"—taught by Jane Ubell-Meyer, a former television producer who owns the goodie bag company Madison & Mulholland (Weinstein, 2005). Ubell-Meyer teaches publicists how to procure "goodies" with ingenuity and creativity, sharing

FIGURE 7.2. *Allure* magazine, October 2005 cover.

with her students what she has learned from designing gift bags for such events as the Oscars, Emmys, Grammys, and Tonys, in addition to VIP events during Fashion Week. With each event trying to top every other event, each bag must have three essentials: the *WOW* factor (a BlackBerry), the *Oh My God I Need That* factor (Bose headphones), and the *Filler* (candy, pens, gift certificates, makeup). Even the Live 8 event, a free concert to battle African poverty, gave participants gift bags valued at $4,000 (Weinstein).

## Box 7.1 (continued)

One of the downsides of this gift bag proliferation involves the greedy individuals who want something or everything for free. At many events, there is just too much excess. Almost everyone attending these events has seen stingy partygoers who are not satisfied with just one goodie bag, or who later claim that they did not get one when in fact they did. To avoid the perception of unethical behavior, many stars, including Clint Eastwood and Keanu Reaves, did not accept gifts for participating at the Oscars or the Sundance Festival.

The Internal Revenue Service (IRS) sought to deter the practice, notifying gift recipients that they are responsible for paying taxes on the ever-more-lavish gifts received during awards season (Waxman, 2007). Gift bags as well as other goods and services given to celebrities in association with award shows are considered to be income and must be reported to the IRS. At the Golden Globes, a tax accountant handed out IRS 1099 forms at an unofficial gift-giving suite.

According to Waxman (2007), the newest twist on swag, created by Hollywood marketers to avoid tax issues, is to give celebrities "branded retreats." One example: An upscale meal, complete with fine food and elegant wines, was presented in a private club setting. The invitation-only retreat focused on the pleasures of food, drink, entertainment, and spa treatments, and was provided to certain celebrities gratis. One of these retreats was held during Oscar week at Soho House, a gracious stone manor mansion overlooking Los Angeles. The budget for the retreat was about $1 million dollars, paid by such sponsors as Delta Airlines. But, Delta exhibited the seats used for the airline's first-class service instead of providing give-aways.

### REFERENCES

De Vries, H. (2005). *The gift bag chronicles*. New York: Villard Books.

Shi, J. (2005, September 20). Allure's big 10 bash. *Fashion Week Daily*. Retrieved September 21, 2005, from http://www.fashionweekdaily.com/fullstory.sps?iNewsid=244237&itype=8488

Waxman, S. (2007, February 23). Let them eat foie gras (Gift bags are so last year). *New York Times*. Retrieved May 16, 2007, from www.nytimes.com

Weinstein, F. (2005). Booty-licious. *New York Post*. Retrieved July 20, 2005, from http:www.nypost.com

our news from a variety of media outlets—from broadcast and electronic media as well as from print sources—some professionals think the term *news release* fits all media while technically *press release* applies only to print media and thus has become outdated. Both terms are still widely used in the industry. (Although news releases and media kits have adopted new terminology, oral news presentations are still primarily known as *press conferences*. A few firms embrace the updated term *news conference*.)

### NEWSWORTHINESS CHECKLIST

A key component of any news release should be that the story is newsworthy. It should have at least one, and probably more, of the following elements (Marsh et al., 2005):

- □ **Timeliness**—New information is available in the story.
- □ **Impact**—Journalists, readers, viewers, or listeners are affected by the story.
- □ **Uniqueness**—There is a difference from similar stories.
- □ **Conflict**—A clash of people and/or forces of nature is involved in the story.
- □ **Proximity**—Events are geographically close to the targeted readers, viewers, or listeners of the story.
- □ **Celebrity**—A famous person, such as a business leader, a politician, a sports figure, or an entertainer, is involved in the story.

# NEWSWORTHINESS

A variety of situations or events can stimulate a newsworthy story idea. The following are just a few of the ideas that could be developed into a news release: opening a local branch of a regional or national retailer; sponsoring an athletic team or a special event; changing the name of a business; moving to a new location; introducing a new product line; hiring or promoting a new manager; supporting a local charity; reaching a milestone, such as an anniversary of the business or of a member of the management team; expanding the business; obtaining a new contract; or, earning an award.

"News releases are probably the most recognized of all public communications products" (Diggs-Brown, 2007, p. 129). News releases are written as ready-to-publish stories, in the hope that journalists will take the story and publish or broadcast it as you wrote it. Thus, *your* story will reach hundreds or thousands of people, maybe even more. But not every story is published or broadcast verbatim. You cannot expect that it will be and you must not be disappointed if the information is revised. Journalists often use the news release as a story idea of their own, making it into a story with a different emphasis by adding more information than you provided. As long as the journalist does not introduce something negative, your news release was successful in getting your message out to the public.

News releases may be written in one of three typical styles: an announcement, a feature story, or a hybrid story. An announcement is a straight news story, and a feature story is a combination of information and entertainment. A hybrid story is a mixture of an announcement and a feature story.

A straight news story begins with a headline that summarizes the story's main point, similar to a journalist's news article. The lead contains the Who, What, Where, and When. The rest of the narrative explains Why and How as part of the descending order of importance. This is the inverted pyramid style we discussed in Chapter 3, "Writing for Newspapers."

Feature stories are similar to news stories, but they also entertain. Thus, storytelling skills are important. The writer teases or charms the reader into wanting to read more of the story. Instead of writing about the one millionth customer to enter a retail store, the writer could compare that angle with how long the checkout line would be for one million customers. The conclusion has a more dramatic spin in a feature story than in a straight news story, which ends with the least important facts. The end of a feature story provides a sense of closure to the narrative.

Hybrid stories are a compromise between a straight news story and a feature story. The hybrid could begin with a lead similar to a feature story lead, and then move into the straight news. The conclusion of a hybrid is more like a straight news story, without a dramatic finish.

Because the audience for your news release is a journalist, you must write in a style that will attract a member of that group. Journalists like concise stories, with specific information. They prefer reputable sources with appropriate attribution. Journalists want honesty and candor with objective facts, not promotional writing, so they are likely to ignore documents that sound more like advertising than news. Unfortunately, many news releases are prepared with the message sponsor, not the journalist, in mind.

News releases are presented in a variety of formats, often written on paper and sent through the mail. In attempts to capture the attention of journalists in an atmosphere crowded with information, a variety of creative methods have been introduced. Some news releases have been placed on Web sites, while others have been sent via e-mail messages or burned onto CDs and mailed to journalists through the postal service. Some imaginative writers have sent news releases written on champagne bottles or boxes of chocolates to get noticed. Below, we will look at the traditional formats used for print, radio, and video press releases.

## Print News Releases

Print news releases are prepared as hard copy that will be mailed, sent as an e-mail attachment, or delivered in person. News releases are used independently or as part of a media kit. If possible, these documents should be presented on the organization's letterhead stationery. The letterhead will most likely contain the organization's logo and contact information, including the mailing address and the telephone and fax numbers. The first page should be printed on the organization's letterhead; if the release is longer than one page, subsequent pages should be printed on plain paper of the same color and a similar quality. Some organizations generate specialized news release stationery, clearly documenting that the text is a news release. Margins for a news release should be one to one-and-a half inches on all sides. Figure 7.3 shows the formatting for a print news release. Figure 7.4 provides an example of a print news release in announcement style. Note: The media kit examples that follow are based on student work and do not necessarily reflect actual Lucky Brand Jeans lines, stores, or personnel.

If you are using regular letterhead stationery, type "News Release" in big letters—usually 24-point boldface type—underneath the letterhead data. Below that, create headings that specify (1) "FOR IMMEDIATE RELEASE" with the date, and (2) "FOR MORE INFORMATION," which identifies a specific contact person with his or her contact information. These sections are single-spaced.

Leave about two inches between these headings and the headline, which is similar to a newspaper-style headline. The **headline** is a statement, written in present or recent past tense, to generate interest and summarize the story's main point. Using the organization's name in the headline, whenever appropriate, is advantageous. For example, the headline "The Phoenix Art Museum celebrates the Pucci Exhibit" means that the museum recently celebrated the opening of the exhibit, probably yesterday. If the museum has not yet opened the exhibit, future tense is required, and the headline would be "Pucci Exhibit will open at the Phoenix Art Museum."

After the headline comes the text. Double-space the text, providing room for journalists to edit the copy. The text should tell the story concisely in one page or at most

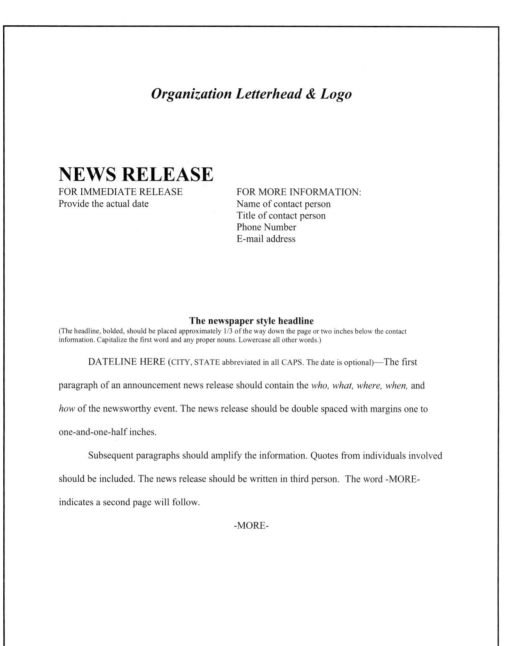

*Organization Letterhead & Logo*

# NEWS RELEASE
FOR IMMEDIATE RELEASE              FOR MORE INFORMATION:
Provide the actual date             Name of contact person
                                    Title of contact person
                                    Phone Number
                                    E-mail address

**The newspaper style headline**
(The headline, bolded, should be placed approximately 1/3 of the way down the page or two inches below the contact information. Capitalize the first word and any proper nouns. Lowercase all other words.)

DATELINE HERE (CITY, STATE abbreviated in all CAPS. The date is optional)—The first

paragraph of an announcement news release should contain the *who, what, where, when,* and

*how* of the newsworthy event. The news release should be double spaced with margins one to

one-and-one-half inches.

Subsequent paragraphs should amplify the information. Quotes from individuals involved

should be included. The news release should be written in third person.  The word -MORE-

indicates a second page will follow.

-MORE-

FIGURE 7.3. Example of a print news release in standard format. (*continued*)

Abbreviated title/page 2

If an additional page is necessary, the next page should contain a condensed two- or three-word heading repeating important words from the headline. This is called a slug and should be placed in the upper left corner of the page with the page number.

Paragraphs should never be split between pages. News releases should not be more than 2 pages in length. If there are two pages, staple the news release together.

The news release should end with ### or -30- placed on the center of the page to signify the end of the release.

-###-

FIGURE 7.3.

# LUCKY BRAND JEANS

**4290 S. Beaver St. Flagstaff, AZ 86001**

## NEWS RELEASE

FOR IMMEDIATE RELEASE
April 30, 20xx

FOR MORE INFORMATION:
Michelle Marchi
Public Affairs Director
Office: (928) 555-5555
E-mail: Michelle@email.com

**Lucky Brand Jeans introduces new lines for 'tweens**

FLAGSTAFF, AZ—One of the leading men's and women's clothing lines Lucky Brand Jeans will introduce their new Lucky Kids boy's and girl's lines of clothing on May 12, 20xx at their newest store located at the Fashion Square Mall, Scottsdale, Arizona.

"We are very excited to be part of this important launch," said Store Manager Lindsey Haldeman. "The children's market, both girl's and boy's, is rapidly growing and Lucky Brand Jeans sees great potential in serving these markets."

The Lucky Kids lines include shirts, jackets, and skirts for girls, as well as the durable denim the company is known for. Size ranges for boy's are 8 – 18; size ranges for girl's are 7 – 14. The styles in both lines will have many pieces that can be mixed and matched. The clothes are designed for children that are interested in fashion and concerned with what they wear.

-MORE-

**FIGURE 7.4.** Example of a print news release in announcement style. (*continued*)

Lucky Brand Jeans/page 2

In store displays will be designed to entice children to bring their parents into the stores and to buy the fashionable clothes. Bright colors and bold prints which are visually stimulating to children will create interest in the clothes Lucky Kids has to offer. "We have a topnotch forecasting group that really understands the children's market," Haldeman said, "We are ready to make our mark with 'tweens'."

Many child celebrities, including Abigail Breslin, nominated for an Academy Award for her role in *Little Miss Sunshine*, have been waiting for Lucky Brand Jeans to design clothes for them. In a quote from her publicist, Ashley Sloan, "Abigail can hardly wait! She is really excited to see the Lucky Kids line for girls."

The Lucky Kids lines will be available at all Lucky Brand Jeans stores by the end of May.

For media inquiries contact Michelle Marchi at (928) 555-5555 or Michelle@email.com.

-###-

FIGURE 7.4.

two. News releases are rarely longer than two pages. Always make sure a complete paragraph is on one page. Never split a paragraph across two pages. Paragraphs are usually indented with double spacing between paragraphs. If the paragraphs are not indented, insert a triple-space between paragraphs to indicate to the reader where paragraph breaks should occur.

If the news release is longer than one page, type "-more-" or "-over-" at the bottom of the page. This indicates that more information follows. Beginning on the second page, place a **slug**—a condensed version of the headline and the page number—in the upper-left corner: for example, "Phoenix Art Museum/page 2." After the last line of the text, space down one line and type "-30-" or "-###-" to signify the end of the story. Staple the pages of the news release together.

The text may begin with a **dateline**, which gives the location of the story. It is written with the name of the city followed by a dash, such as "SAN FRANCISCO—." The date of the story may also be included, for example, "SAN FRANCISCO, Sept. 24—."

The first sentence of the text should establish local interest and move right in to the news. An appropriately newsworthy story should convey the Who, What, Where, and When, similar to a lead in a news story. As we learned in earlier chapters, most traditional news stories are formatted as an inverted pyramid, with the most important information at the beginning of the story. Then, less and less significant information follows.

---

*Portfolio Exercise:* **Write a traditional print news release to your local newspaper, announcing the opening of a new branch of Old Navy in your town.**

---

## PRINT NEWS RELEASE CHECKLIST

- ☐ **Select an appropriate contact person.** A club or organization president may not have the specific information a journalist needs. The contact person should have intimate details about the event.
- ☐ **Use a phone number that is available 24 hours a day/7 days a week.** The contact person should have a cell phone and voice messaging to guarantee that journalists have immediate access.

- **Avoid using the words** *today,* *yesterday,* **and** *tomorrow.* Journalists will almost always have to change those words, since your "today" will be incorrect by the time your story is published or broadcast. It is better to use an actual date.
- **Use past tense verbs to attribute quotes.** In print-oriented news releases, the director of the museum *said* instead of *says.*
- **Be precise and concise.** Journalists use streamlined and clear statements.
- **Emphasize local interest.** Spotlight local importance by finding a hometown angle.
- **Be objective.** By avoiding promotional language, you increase your chances of having the information published.
- **Clear the news release with your client or boss before distributing it.** If necessary, remind your client that the news release should be unbiased and objective. Keep your supervisor's comments in mind, and revise as necessary to address them.

## Radio News Release Scripts

**Radio news release scripts** are created for radio broadcast with the same purpose as print news releases: to generate publicity for organizations. The difference is that radio news releases provide radio journalists with newsworthy information in a virtually ready-to-use format. Still, a release is a *starting point* for broadcast stories. Just as they do with print sources, journalists may use a radio news release as is, change it, or not use it at all.

Two types of radio news releases are most common: the radio reader and the sound bite. The **radio reader** is a script for an announcer to read. A **sound bite** story is a news release that contains taped comments from an organization representative, presented much like a quote in a print story. Taped or digitized comments are generally 6 to 20 seconds long. Prerecorded material often includes a series of sound bites with suggested announcer lead-ins, which gives anchors or announcers increased flexibility. Suggestions and flexibility can greatly improve the chances that the material will be used.

Radio news releases may be presented as announcer's script, a prerecorded package, or a combination of both. They are distributed through various channels, with a dial-up toll-free telephone number as the most popular method.

Radio news release scripts use broadcast-style writing techniques. In addition, they are printed in large, easy-to-read fonts with wide margins, and they are double-spaced. Like other broadcast scripts, radio news release information in script format is capitalized. Headers similar to the ones used in print news releases—such as date of release, contact information, and headline—are included.

Radio reader scripts typically last 20 to 30 seconds, which amounts to approximately 5 to 7 lines of copy. The story should include the necessary basics of any news story: Who, What, Where, and When. The story's purpose and essential information must be reported clearly and concisely.

A sound bite runs a little bit longer, lasting 40 to 50 seconds. The sound bite format requires a prescribed format consisting of the following:

- **Lead**—This must grab the attention of the listeners and orient them before getting into details.
- **Body**—This details information not covered in the lead.
- **Lead-in**—This is where you identify the speaker by name.
- **Sound bite**—This runs 6 to 20 seconds and is identified by a short title, its length, and its outcue (that is, the final few words of the sound bite).
- **Close**—This is additional information that concludes the story and helps the listener avoid confusion regarding the ending of one story and the beginning of the next one.

Figure 7.5 is an example of a radio reader news release, and Figure 7.6 is an example of a sound bite news release.

---

*Portfolio Exercise:* **Prepare a radio reader news release announcing the production of a fund-raising fashion show that will be held at your school.**

---

## Video News Release Scripts

**Video news releases** (VNRs) are the video version of printed news releases (Diggs-Brown, 2007). Organizations use VNRs for major announcements, such as the introduction of a new product or to reach out to stakeholders during a crisis. While critics

# LUCKY BRAND JEANS

**4290 S. Beaver St. Flagstaff, AZ 86001**

## RADIO NEWS RELEASE

FOR IMMEDIATE RELEASE
April 30, 20xx

FOR MORE INFORMATION:
Michelle Marchi, Public Affairs Director
Office: (928) 555-5555
E-mail: Michelle@email.com

**LUCKY BRAND JEANS HIRES NEW MANAGER WITH LOCAL TIES**

**ANNOUNCER:** LUCKY BRAND JEANS WILL HAVE A NEW MANAGER AT THE RECENTLY OPENED STORE AT THE FASHION SQUARE MALL, SCOTTSDALE, ARIZONA. LINDSEY HALDEMAN...AN ARIZONA NATIVE...WILL START HER NEW JOB AS STORE MANAGER ON JUNE 15TH. THE ANNOUNCEMENT WAS MADE BY C-E-O...CHRISTINE DOKKEN (DOE-KEN) AT THE CLOSE OF FASHION WEEK IN NEW YORK.

FOR THE PAST TWO YEARS...HALDEMAN SERVED AS THE ASSISTANT MANAGER OF THE LUCKY BRAND JEANS STORE LOCATED AT FASHION SHOW MALL IN LAS VEGAS...NEVADA. HALDEMAN GRADUATED FROM DESERT HILLS HIGH SCHOOL IN TWO-THOUSAND-AND-TWO. SHE COMPLETED A BACHELOR OF SCIENCE DEGREE AT NORTHERN ARIZONA UNIVERSITY IN TWO-THOUSAND-AND-SIX. HALDEMAN SUCCEEDS SARAH TRAVIS, WHO WILL BE MOVING TO NEW YORK AS PART OF THE DESIGN TEAM FOR THE BOY'S AND GIRL'S LINES.

-###-

FIGURE 7.5. Example of a radio reader news release.

# LUCKY BRAND JEANS

**4290 S. Beaver St. Flagstaff, AZ 86001**

## RADIO NEWS RELEASE

FOR IMMEDIATE RELEASE
April 30, 20xx

FOR MORE INFORMATION:
Michelle Marchi, Public Affairs Director
Office: (928) 555-5555
E-mail: Michelle@email.com

**LUCKY BRAND JEANS HIRES NEW MANAGER WITH LOCAL TIES**

**ANNOUNCER:** LUCKY BRAND JEANS WILL HAVE A NEW MANAGER AT THE

RECENTLY OPENED STORE AT THE FASHION SQUARE MALL, SCOTTSDALE,

ARIZONA. LINDSEY HALDEMAN…AN ARIZONA NATIVE…WILL START HER NEW

JOB AS STORE MANAGER ON JUNE 15TH. THE ANNOUNCEMENT WAS MADE BY

C-E-O CHRISTINE DOKKEN (DOE-KEN) AT THE CLOSE OF FASHION WEEK IN NEW

YORK.

SOUNDBITE: (HALDEMAN (12 seconds) "I'm thrilled to be returning to Arizona. My family and so many of my friends still live here. I want to make more people aware of Lucky Brand. I plan on taking some of my personal time taking pictures. Arizona is such a beautiful state, and photography was my minor in school."

**ANNOUNCER:** FOR THE PAST TWO YEARS…HALDEMAN WAS THE ASSISTANT

MANAGER OF THE LUCKY BRAND JEANS STORE LOCATED AT FASHION SHOW

MALL IN LAS VEGAS…NEVADA. HALDEMAN GRADUATED FROM DESERT HILLS

HIGH SCHOOL IN TWO-THOUSAND-AND-TWO. SHE COMPLETED A BACHELOR OF

-MORE-

FIGURE 7.6. Example of a sound bite radio news release. (*continued*)

Lucky Brand Jeans/page 2

SCIENCE DEGREE IN MERCHANDISING AT NORTHERN ARIZONA UNIVERSITY IN

TWO-THOUSAND-AND-SIX. HALDEMAN SUCCEEDS THE OPENING MANAGER

SARAH TRAVIS…WHO WILL BE MOVING TO NEW YORK AS PART OF THE DESIGN

TEAM FOR THE BOY'S AND GIRL'S LINES THAT WERE LAUNCHED AT THE

SCOTTSDALE STORE.

For media inquiries contact Michelle Marchi at (928) 555-5555 or Michelle@email.com.

-###-

FIGURE 7.6.

denounce VNRs as fake news, the charge is unfair. Journalists decide whether to use VNRs, just as journalists decide whether to use other types of news releases.

The target for a VNR is a television or cable station. Television journalists are looking for VNRs that address issues that are important to their demographic audience. They also look for stories that can be used on slow news days or amusing stories that offer something different from hard news.

VNRs are typically distributed via DVD, videotape, or satellite. Originally, videotapes were used with traditional media kits that were circulated at news conferences, annual meetings, or some other newsworthy event. Satellites are used when a shorter lead time or broader distribution is required. With the increasing capabilities of digitizing video, DVD and Internet downloads are becoming more commonplace.

Some stations want complete news packages, whereas others may only want short sections of a video or a brief sound bite. The writer for the production of a VNR produces a two-column script, similar to those used in television scripts and advertisements, as shown in Figure 7.7. The visual elements are indicated in the left column and the script is shown in the right column.

VNRs are self-contained; that is, the video contains all the information a reporter or editor needs. Writers convey critical information through a **slate**—a screen that identifies or introduces the images that follow (Diggs-Brown, 2007). This written information is scrolled on the screen to alert the journalist about what comes next. The video, which is designed to stand on its own, generally contains five parts (Marsh et al., 2005):

1. **Opening slate**—Background information about the news story is presented, identifying the organization that is producing the story and providing contact information for follow-up. It identifies speakers by name and title, as well as provides a suggested lead-in; the running time; and the outcue, or closing.

2. **Video news release**—This is a 60- to 90-second news story, with an announcer voiceover, sounds on tape (SOT), and sound bites.

3. **Video news release without announcer voiceover**—This is similar to the previous content but without an announcer. This allows the station to use their own personnel. A brief slate reveals that the voiceover has been deleted from this section.

4. **Sound bites**—This section includes a variety of sound bites that were not included in the VNR. A slate identifies the speaker, specifies the length of the sound bite, and offers a suggested lead-in before each sound bite.

5. **B-roll**—This is additional footage that journalists can use to illustrate the story. A slate specifies content and running time in this part.

**Lucky Brand Foundation**                          **Total Running Time:**

**Date: April 30, 20xx**                            **Producer: Alissa Bush**

<u>VIDEO</u>                                         <u>AUDIO</u>

DISCLAIMER: The following material
is offered for your free and unrestricted
use by Lucky Brand Jeans.

TABLE OF CONTENTS
    Précis: (insert RT)
    Interview with Gene Montesano
    Interview with Ryan Mandino
    Interview with Lindsay Haldeman
    Interview with Abigail Breslin
    B-roll:

PRÉCIS: Lucky Brand Jeans is offering
a new line of apparel targeted to the
'tween market. The Lucky Kids lines
include shirts, jackets, and skirts for
girls, as well as the durable denim in
boy's sizes 8 – 18 and for girl's sizes
7 – 14. The products are being
introduced at the Lucky store at Fashion
Square Mall in Scottsdale, Arizona.
Event profits will be donated to the
Lucky Brand Foundation.

                             NATSOUND

Slate #1:
B-roll
(WS) of the Lucky Brand Store in
Scottsdale, AZ
(MS) of Abigail Breslin and her mother
entering the store
(MS) of Lindsay Haldeman with Abigail
Breslin

-MORE-

FIGURE 7.7. Example of a video news release, or VNR. (*continued*)

Lucky Brand Foundation VNR
page 2 of 4

<u>VIDEO</u>

<u>AUDIO</u>

Slate #2:
(MS) of Ryan Mandino
Lucky Brands Special Events
Coordinator

SOT#1 Mandino: "TODAY...WE ARE
HERE WITH GENE MONTESANO,
ONE OF THE FOUNDERS OF
LUCKY BRAND JEANS. THE STORE
IS LOCATED IN SCOTTSDALE
FASHION SQUARE MALL. THE
FIRM IS INTRODUCING A NEW
LINE OF LUCKY KIDS APPAREL
FOR BOYS AND GIRLS."

Slate #3:
(MS) of Gene Montesano
One of the founders of Lucky Brand

SOT#2 Montesano: "I AM SO HAPPY
TO BE HERE IN THIS BEAUTIFUL
LOCATION TO PRESENT OUR
LATEST KIDS PRODUCT LINES. WE
ALSO ARE PROUD TO DONATE
ALL OF THE PROFITS FROM THIS
SPECIAL EVENT TO THE LUCKY
BRAND FOUNDATION."

Slate #4:
(CU) Ryan Mandino

SOT #3 Mandino: "CAN YOU
EXPLAIN WHAT THE
FOUNDATION IS AND DOES?

Slate #5:
(CU) Gene Montesano

SOT #4 Montesano: "THE LUCKY
BRAND FOUNDATION IS A
CHARITABLE ORGANIZATION
COMMITTED TO BRINGING
HAPPINESS...COMFORT AND HOPE
TO DISADVANTAGED AND
DISABLED CHILDREN. WE HAVE
RAISED APPROXIMATELY
$6 MILLION...THROUGH OUR
ANNUAL BLACK TIE & BLUE
JEANS GALA...SINCE 1996."

Slate #6:
Dream Street Foundation
B-roll
Visuals of children playing
(WS) Children at a campground
(MS) Children enjoying ice cream
(CU) Two children smiling

SOT # 5 Mandino: "DREAM STREET
FOUNDATION IS ONE OF THE
MANY ORGANIZATIONS THAT
THE LUCKY FOUNDATION
SUPPORTS."

-MORE-

FIGURE 7.7. *(continued)*

Lucky Brand Foundation VNR
page 3 of 4

| <u>VIDEO</u> | <u>AUDIO</u> |
|---|---|
| Slate #7:<br>B-roll<br>Visuals of children setting up tents, boating on a lake in canoes, and playing softball. | SOT #6 Montesano: "CHILDREN SUFFERING FROM ILLNESSES INCLUDING CANCER…AIDS…AND OTHER BLOOD DISORDERS ARE GIVEN THE OPPORTUNITY TO ENJOY ACTIVITIES THEY WOULD NORMALLY BE RESTRICTED FROM PARTICIPATING IN…DUE TO THEIR ILLNESSES. CAMPING TRIPS ARE AMONG THE FUN ACTIVITIES DREAM STREET PROVIDES." |
| Slate #8:<br>(MS) Ryan Mandino and Lindsey Haldeman, Store Manager | SOT #7 Mandino: "THIS IS THE STORE MANAGER, LINDSEY HALDEMAN. WHAT IS GOING ON AT THE LUCKY STORE TODAY?" |
| Slate #9:<br>(WS) Ryan Mandino, Lindsey Haldeman and Abigail Breslin. | SOT #8 Haldeman: "ABIGAIL BRESLIN IS HERE, WEARING THE LATEST LUCKY KID JEANS. ABIGAIL…WHO WAS NOMINATED FOR AN ACADEMY AWARD FOR HER ROLE IN *LITTLE MISS SUNSHINE*… FELL IN LOVE WITH LUCKY BRAND KIDS." |
| Slate #10:<br>(CU) Abigail Breslin | SOT #9 Breslin: "I TOLD MY MOM THAT I COULDN'T WAIT TO WEAR THESE JEANS…AND NOW I'M HAPPY TO BE HERE AND SUPPORT THE LUCKY BRAND FOUNDATION. I KNOW I AM SO LUCKY AND OTHER KIDS NEED SOME HELP." |
| Slate #11:<br>(CU) Ryan Mandino | SOT #10 Mandino: "ABIGAIL WILL BE AT THE STORE UNTIL 6 PM. HER FANS CAN MEET HER AND TODAY'S SALES WILL BE DONATED TO THE LUCKY BRAND FOUNDATION…HELPING OTHER CHILDREN IN NEED." |

-MORE-

FIGURE 7.7. *(continued)*

Lucky Brand Foundation VNR
page 4 of 4

| VIDEO | AUDIO |
|---|---|
| Slate #12:<br>B-roll<br>(WS) Visuals of kids and parents looking at merchandise in the store and interacting with Abigail Breslin. | NATSOUND |
| Slate #13: For more information, contact: Michelle Marchi, Public Affairs Director, (928) 555-5555 or by e-mail: Michelle@email.com. For video information, contact: Alissa Bush, (928) 555-5556. | NATSOUND |
| Slate #14:<br>Additional B-roll footage will be available on Monday, May 15, 20xx from noon until 3 p.m. MST Galaxy 9 / Transporter 12 Audio 7.2+7.8. | |

-END-

FIGURE 7.7.

# PUBLIC SERVICE ANNOUNCEMENTS

Have you heard an announcement about a museum exhibit, a benefit fashion show, or some other special event on your local television or radio station? Persuasive messages that are carried without charge by radio and television outlets to promote social causes sponsored by nonprofit and charitable organizations are called **public service announcements** (PSAs). Federal licensing requires broadcast stations that serve the public interest to provide PSAs. Although many PSAs are produced to sound like television or radio commercials, they are targeted communications that contain a call to action.

PSAs are different from advertisements. First, PSAs are not placed in controlled media—in contrast to advertisements, which are created, timed, and placed in specific media by the message sponsor. The media outlet decides whether and when to use a PSA. These social interest announcements are not guaranteed to receive airtime. Second, advertisements normally are created to promote a product or service for marketplace transaction, whereas PSAs typically promote social causes and behavior changes. Many broadcast stations present anti-drug, anti-teen pregnancy, or stay-in-school PSAs to promote healthy lifestyles.

Because broadcasts of PSAs are at the mercy of the media outlet, you should include a cover letter and/or pitch letter along with the prebroadcast materials, to help make it easy for the outlet to contact you for additional information and agree to provide time to air your PSA. A package of PSA materials, giving the media outlet flexibility and immediately usable announcements, will increase the likelihood of the PSA being broadcast.

The PSA package should include a cover letter, written as a sales letter, explaining why the message is relevant to the media outlet's audience and tactical interests. Additional materials should be organized and presented as a list, similar to a table of contents. The list makes it easier for the program director to find what she or he is looking for. Scripts of the messages provided, in combination with recorded messages in a variety of lengths (10-second, 15-second, 20-second, 30-second, and 60-second versions), provide options for program directors.

The creation of PSAs should follow the guidelines for writing broadcast media. Figure 7.8 shows a sample production script for a public service announcement.

Goodwill PSA
page 1 of 4

| **Goodwill Industries PSA** | **Total Running Time:** |
|---|---|
| **Date: June 30, 20xx** | **Producer: Marty Baker** |
| <u>VIDEO</u> | <u>AUDIO</u> |

DISCLAIMER: The following material is offered for your free and unrestricted use by Goodwill Industries International

TABLE OF CONTENTS
    Précis: (insert RT)
    Interview with Vince Barr
    B-roll:

PRÉCIS: Goodwill Industries enhances the quality and dignity of life for individuals, families, and communities on a global basis, through the power of work, by eliminating barriers to opportunity for people with special needs, and by facilitating empowerment, self-help, and service through dedicated, autonomous local organizations.

Each year Goodwill recognizes a Goodwill Industries "Graduate of the Year". Victor Barr is the recipient this year.

| | |
|---|---|
| Slate #1:<br>B-roll<br>(WS) of a motor cycle accident<br>(MS) of Vince Barr in a wheelchair | Sound of tires screeching |
| Slate #2<br>B-roll<br>(WS) Vince Barr learning to walk after the accident | NATSOUND |

-MORE-

FIGURE 7.8. Example of a public service announcement, or PSA. (*continued*)

Goodwill PSA
page 2 of 4

| VIDEO | AUDIO |
|---|---|
| Slate #3:<br>(MS) of Announcer<br>Bill Finley | SOT#1 Finley: "AFTER VINCE BARR'S TERRIBLE MOTORCYCLE ACCIDENT, HE WORRIED ABOUT HOW HE WOULD BE ABLE TO SUPPORT HIS FAMILY." |
| Slate #3:<br>(WS) at Vince's church<br>(MS) Vince and Sam Singleton | SOT#2 Singleton: "I AM SO SORRY ABOUT YOUR ACCIDENT. I KNOW YOU ARE CONCERNED ABOUT YOUR FUTURE. HAVE YOU HEARD ABOUT THE GREAT TRAINING PROGRAMS AT GOODWILL? MY COUSINS GOT HELP THERE AFTER HIS BOATING ACCIDENT." |
| Slate #4:<br>B-roll<br>Goodwill store footage<br>(MS) Vince training at store | NATSOUND |
| Slate #5:<br>(CU) Vince Barr | SOT #3: " LIVING THROUGH THE INJURY WAS TRAUMATIC . . . BUT NOT WORKING WAS EVEN HARDER. THE HARDEST THING WAS WATCHING MY FAMILY GO WITHOUT THE SIMPLEST THINGS, LIKE EATING OUT OR WATCHING A MOVIE ULTIMATELY INFLUENCED ME TO GET SOME ASSISTANCE IN MOVING AHEAD." |
| Slate #6:<br>(WS) Goodwill Banquet<br>(MS) Vince Barr accepting award | SOT #4 Barr: "I AM PROUD TO ACCEPT THIS AWARD FOR THE GOODWILL INDUSTRIES INTERNATIONAL GRADUATE OF THE YEAR. GOODWILLHAS DONE SO MUCH FOR ME AND MY FAMILY. THE PROGRAM HAS HELPED ME BE A PRODUCTIVE MEMBER OF MY COMMUNITY. I AM FOREVER GRATEFUL" |

-MORE-

FIGURE 7.8. (continued)

Goodwill PSA
page 3 of 4

| VIDEO | AUDIO |
|---|---|
| Slate #7:<br>Announcer Bill Finley | SOT #5 Finley: "AFTER A SIX-MONTH HOSPITAL STAY AND MANY MONTHS OF PHYSICAL THERAPY, BARR LEARNED TO WALK AGAIN. IN SPITE OF HIS SERIOUS CONDITION, HIS GREATEST CONCERNS WERE ALWAYS FOR THE WELFARE OF HIS FAMILY. HE WENT TO GOODWILL INDUSTRIES IN JULY 2003, WHERE HE ATTENDED A CUSTOMER SERVICE REPRESENTATIVE AND COMPUTER TRAINING CLASS." |
| Slate #8:<br>(MS) Vince Barr at the Pointe Hilton Resort | SOT #7 Barr: "IN EARLY 2004 I FOUND THE JOB THAT PERFECTLY MATCHED MY SKILLS AND PREFERENCES…I BECAME THE COMMUNICATIONS OPERATOR FOR THE POINTE HILTON RESORT. TWO YEARS LATER…I WAS PROMOTED TO OMMUNICATIONS SUPERVISOR… NOW I OVERSEES AND TRAINS NEW EMPLOYEES." |
| Slate #9:<br>Announcer Bill Finley | SOT #8 Finley: "AS A VOLUNTEER MEMBER OF GOODWILL'S BUSINESS ADVISORY COUNCIL, BARR CAPITALIZES ON THE MANY OPPORTUNITIES HE HAS TO SHARE HIS PERSONAL EXPERIENCES WITH OTHERS…HE IS AN INSPRIRATION." |
| Slate #11:<br>(WS) Goodwill offices<br>Vince Barr | SOT #9 Barr: "THE PEOPLE AT GOODWILL HELPED ME TO GAIN MY SELF CONFIDENCE BACK." |

-MORE-

FIGURE 7.8. (continued)

Goodwill PSA
page 4 of 4

| VIDEO | AUDIO |
|---|---|
| Slate #12:<br>B-roll<br>(WS) Visuals of Vince with his wife and kids | NATSOUND |
| Slate #13:<br>Announcer Bill Finley | SOT #10 Finley: "THE GRADUATE OF THE YEAR AWARD HONORS AN OUTSTANDING PERSON WHO HAS COMPLETED A GOODWILL INDUSTRIES CAREER PROGRAM AND IS NOW COMPETITIVELY EMPLOYED BY A NON-GOODWILL EMPLOYER IN HIS OR HER COMMUNITY. GOODWILL PUTS PEOPLE TO WORK." |
| Slate #14: For more information, contact: Marty Baker, Public Affairs Director, (928) 555-5555 or by Email: MBaker@email.com. | |

-END-

FIGURE 7.8.

# MEDIA KITS

**Media kits** are public communication techniques used to generate news stories about a company or group through its newsworthy initiatives. They are prepared to provide important news, background information, facts, perspectives, research, historical information, biographies of the people involved, and other items so that members of the media have information to use in preparing print, broadcast, or online media stories. Media kits contain at least one news release in addition to other supporting documents. These supporting documents typically include backgrounders, fact sheets, biographies of personnel, photo opportunity sheets, captioned photographs, media coverage from previous events, business cards, product samples, videos, and other items that help tell the story. Clearly, a media kit provides journalists with more information than a simple news release does. (Media kits may also be called press kits. But, similar to the reason for choosing the term *news release* over *press release*, *media kit* is becoming the preferred term.)

Journalists are the audience for media kits, just as they are for news releases. Therefore, writing styles should be similar to those described previously for news releases.

Media kits are developed in a variety of formats. Typically, they are organized into folders, sometimes called **shells**, with internal pockets for documents and other support materials. (Slots for business cards are commonly built into the folders.) As shown in Figure 7.9, the cover of the shell should clearly identify the organization for which the media kit is written or provide other pertinent information. Some media kits are sent in small boxes with CDs, DVDs, and videotapes, in addition to product samples, gifts, novelties, and documents. The next sections describe cover letters, backgrounders, fact sheets, and photo guidelines—items frequently included in a media kit.

The most important pieces (primary information), such as the cover letter and news releases, should be placed in the right-hand pocket of the shell. The cover letter should be placed in front, followed by the most important news release, so they will be read first. Other news releases and fact sheets are usually considered primary information and should also be placed in the right-hand pocket in order of importance. The left-hand pocket should contain secondary information that will amplify the news element of the media kit. Photographs with captions should be placed in front, followed by backgrounders, biographies, and any other supplemental information that will help the journalist in reporting about your organization or event.

FIGURE 7.9. Example of a media kit shell cover.

## *Cover Letters*

A **cover letter** identifies the purpose and the contents of the media kit. It includes the names of the persons to contact for further information, and it explains why the information is being sent. It should be written in a tone that generates excitement and interest—to entice the reader to want more information and to review the remaining contents. In essence, the cover letter serves as a pitch to the editor or producer. A cover letter is shown in Figure 7.10.

## *Backgrounders*

A **backgrounder** is a supplement to a news release that includes such information as a biography of a key individual mentioned in the news release or the history of the organization. News releases generally do not require a backgrounder, but backgrounders often appear in media kits. They supply interesting or relevant background information, but they do not provide news, leads, or news headlines.

An organization's letterhead may be used for a backgrounder, just like those used for news releases. Instead of "News Release" in large bold type, the heading should be "Backgrounder." A headline, identifying the subject matter, should be included. This might be the name of the person or organization.

The backgrounder follows the format of news releases, using "-more-" or "-over-" to indicate a second page. The slug and the page number are included on pages after the first page. And, the last line of information is followed by "-30-" or "###" to indicate the conclusion of the backgrounder.

The backgrounder is not another news release; it provides historical information about the story or individuals involved in the story. While some overlap of information between the news release and backgrounder is bound to occur, the news release must stand on its own. The backgrounder provides additional information that is rarely published. A journalist may use information from the backgrounder to ensure audience understanding. Figure 7.11 is a sample backgrounder.

---

*Portfolio Exercise:* **Prepare a backgrounder for the news release you prepared earlier in the chapter.**

---

# LUCKY BRAND JEANS

**4290 S. Beaver St. Flagstaff, AZ 86001**

April 27, 20xx

Mr. Jake Guerrero, Publicist
*Seventeen* Magazine
300 W. 57th St.
17th Fl.
New York, NY 10019

Dear Mr. Guerrero:

Lucky You! Lucky Brand Jeans has exciting news and information to share with you. In the coming month, Lucky Brand Jeans is introducing their new Lucky Kids boy's and girl's lines of clothing.

As you may be aware, Lucky Brand Jeans is an established trendsetter for men and women ages 18 – 34. The 'tween population, both boys and girls, is rapidly growing and Lucky Kids sees great potential in serving these markets. This demographic coincides with the demographic your magazine targets. We believe your readers will be just as excited about our new Lucky Kids lines as we are.

In this media kit you will find the following:

- News release introducing Lucky Kids
- Backgrounder
- Fact sheet
- Publicity photos

Please review the enclosed media kit. I believe you will feel lucky after reviewing the materials. If you have further questions about Lucky Kids or Lucky Brand Jeans please do not hesitate to call me at (202) 555-5555 or by e-mail at Ryan@email.com.

Sincerely,

Ryan Mandino
Special Events Coordinator

**FIGURE 7.10.** Example of a media kit cover letter.

# LUCKY BRAND JEANS

**4290 S. Beaver St. Flagstaff, AZ 86001**

## BACKGROUNDER

FOR IMMEDIATE RELEASE
April 30, 20xx

FOR MORE INFORMATION:
Rachel Gray, Communications Director
Office: (928) 555-5555
E-mail: Rachel@email.com

### Gene Montesano and Barry Perlman

Founded in 1990 by Gene Montesano and Barry Perlman, Lucky Brand Jeans was established with the goal to create a denim company without compromise, about great quality and good humor.

As childhood friends, Gene and Barry always possessed a thrill for blue jeans and rock and roll. During the 1970s, the two friends envisioned opening a jeans shop in Florida and Gene recalled spending late nights at the Laundromat, "with our pockets full of coins and some bleach. A few hours later, we had a stack of great washed jeans – one of a kind and 100% authentic!" Through the next several years, Gene and Barry explored different business ventures.

Before Lucky Brand Jeans was founded, Gene Montesano had created another denim

-MORE-

**FIGURE 7.11.** Example of a backgrounder. *(continued)*

Montesano and Perlman/page 2

company, Bongo Jeans. After 15 years working for Bongo, Montesano wanted to experience a new business project. Gene left Bongo in 1990 to launch his dream, Lucky Brand Jeans, and asked Barry to become his business partner once again. In the same year the first order of Lucky Brand Jeans was shipped and immediately became known for their great-fitting, vintage-inspired jeans.

As the business took off, Lucky Brand Jeans was faced with many competitors. Gene and Barry made a risky business move to personalize their jeans for customers. They included a humorous signature message "Lucky You" stitched into each pair of jeans. While this was a risky business decision in its beginning, it is now customers demand it.

Lucky Brand Jeans was built by two friends who had a vision and then and now do not compromise.

-###-

FIGURE 7.11.

## Fact Sheets

A stripped-down presentation of the Who, What, Where, and When outline of the news release is traditionally called a **fact sheet**. Facts are presented in a list, with only the essential data; they are not written in newspaper style. Editors like fact sheets because information is presented without any subjectivity. Fact sheets only appear as part of a media kit.

Fact sheets are presented in a manner similar to news releases. Instead of the heading "News Release" on the letterhead, the term "Fact Sheet" is presented. Ideally, a fact sheet is limited to one page. But, if you need more than one page, follow the multiple-page techniques discussed under the sections about news releases and backgrounders earlier in this chapter. Figure 7.12 shows how a fact sheet may be prepared.

*Portfolio Exercise:* **Prepare a fact sheet for the news release you prepared earlier in the chapter.**

## Photo Guidelines

Actual photographs or photo opportunity sheets may be included in a media kit. One to three photographs can be included as prints or on CDs, with captions that support the materials in the news release.

Publicity photographs are normally sized to 5-by-7 or 8-by-10 inches. Alternatively, photographs can be sent as digital images. Photographs of significant people mentioned in the news release, products being presented for a product launch, and window or in-store displays are included for visual stimulation. Figure 7.13 is an example of a publicity photograph and caption.

# LUCKY BRAND JEANS

**4290 S. Beaver St. Flagstaff, AZ 86001**

## FACT SHEET
FOR IMMEDIATE RELEASE
April 30, 20xx

FOR MORE INFORMATION:
Michelle Marchi
Public Affairs Director
Office: (928) 555-5555
E-mail: Michelle@email.com

**Lucky Brand Jeans**

- Lucky Brand Jeans has a personalized brand image, a humorous signature message "Lucky You" stitched into every pair of jeans.

- According to business founders Gene Montesano and Barry Perlman, the "Lucky You" signature was a risky business decision at first but is now in demand by consumers.

- Lucky Brand Jeans believes it is important to stay involve with the community by giving back through the Lucky Brand Foundation.

- The Lucky Brand Foundation is a charitable organization committed to bringing happiness, comfort, and hope to disadvantaged and disabled children.

- The Foundation was founded in 1996 by Gene Montesano and Barry Perlman.

- The Foundation has been successful in raising approximately $6 million through an annual Black Tie and Blue Jeans Gala.

- The Lucky Brand Jeans business has expanded beyond denim to offer sportswear, knits, wovens, outerwear, T-shirts, and active wear.

- The company currently has 150 company-owned stores in the United States and Puerto Rico and 3 company-owned stores in Europe.

-###-

FIGURE 7.12. Example of a fact sheet.

# LUCKY BRAND JEANS

**4290 S. Beaver St., Flagstaff, AZ 86001**

**PHOTO CAPTION**

FOR IMMEDIATE RELEASE     FOR MORE INFORMATION:
April 30, 20xx     Ryan Mandino,
    Special Events Coordinator
    Office: (928) 555-5555
    E-mail: Ryan@email.com

Featured items include Lucky plaid shirt, Triumph spade T-shirt, and vintage straight jean. These items will be available as part of Lucky Kids launch at the Scottsdale Fashion Square location on May 12, 20xx.

FIGURE 7.13. Example of a publicity photograph (top) and caption on reverse side (bottom).

## PUBLICITY PHOTOGRAPH CHECKLIST

Like news releases, photos have specific requirements that should be followed for ease of printing. General requirements that assist the publication of publicity photographs are as follows:

- ☐ Black and white photography is preferred.
- ☐ Portraits should be 8"×10" or 5"×7" glossy stock; news photographs should be 4"×5" glossy stock.
- ☐ Photographs should emphasize people or fashions, de-emphasizing backgrounds.
- ☐ Fingerprints should not be left on photographs.
- ☐ Photographs should be identified on the back; use a preprinted label or a felt tip pen to avoid making an impression on the photograph.
- ☐ Each photograph should be accompanied by a simple caption, with or without the association of a news release.
- ☐ A caption should be five or six lines long, written following the same stylistic guidelines as for a news release.
- ☐ If the captions are accompanying a news release, they should be typed using the same identification lines as the news release.

**Photo opportunity sheets** are designed to attract photographers to an event you are publicizing, especially when there is a visual component that will help publicize the occasion. Not all events deserve a photo opportunity sheet. For example, a news release announcing a quarterly financial report probably does not stimulate a visual. However, if your organization is sponsoring the appearance of a well-known celebrity for a product launch at your store, you have a photo opportunity. Photo opportunity sheets may be included in a media kit, or they may be sent directly to a photojournalist.

The format of a photo opportunity sheet is similar to the format of a news release. Figure 7.14 is an example of a photo opportunity sheet.

---

*Portfolio Exercise:* **Create a photo opportunity sheet for a costume exhibit opening at a museum.**

---

# NEWSLETTERS AND MAGAZINE STORIES

Public relations has another great tool that needs strong writing skills. Stories written for newsletters and magazines are narratives that deliver facts on important subjects

# LUCKY BRAND JEANS

**4290 S. Beaver St. Flagstaff, AZ 86001**

## PHOTO OPPORTUNITY SHEET

FOR IMMEDIATE RELEASE
April 30, 20xx

FOR MORE INFORMATION:
Michelle Marchi
Public Affairs Director
Office: (928) 555-5555
E-mail: Michelle@email.com

**Lucky Brand Jeans Personal Appearance**

**What:** Gene Montesano and Abigail Breslin will make a personal appearance at the Scottsdale Fashion Square Lucky store.

**Who:** Gene Montesano is one of the founding partners of Lucky Brand Jeans. Abigail Breslin is the young actress, who was nominated for an Academy Award for her role in *Little Miss Sunshine.*

**When:** Montesano and Breslin will be available at the retail store between 4 p.m. and 6 p.m. on May 12, 20xx for photographs.

**Where:** The Lucky Brand Store is located in the east wing of Scottsdale Fashion Square Mall. The mall is located at 7000 East Camelback Road, near the intersection of Scottsdale and Camelback roads.

**Why:** The new line of Lucky Brand Kids will be sold. All sales from the day will be donated to the Lucky Brand Foundation, which is a charitable organization committed to bringing happiness, comfort, and hope to disadvantaged and disabled children.

-###-

FIGURE 7.14. Example of a photo opportunity sheet.

directed toward a specific audience. **Newsletters** are niche publications that are prepared for members of an organization, members of a profession, or people with a common interest. For example, Fashion Group International (FGI), a nonprofit organization for professionals in the fashion industries, publishes two newsletters that it distributes to all of its members. First is the *FGI Bulletin*, a member-only worldwide newsletter, reporting on industry news, business insights, FGI events, and career advice. Second is a newsletter called *Trend Reports*, which provides the latest fashion and trend information from the European and American RTW collections, including coverage of apparel, accessories, and beauty by Marylou Luther of International Fashion Syndicate. (Recall the Industry Profile in Chapter 1, "Effective Fashion Communication.") At the chapter or branch level, FGI newsletters may be printed as documents or distributed to the membership via e-mail. Figure 7.15 shows the cover of an issue of *FGI Bulletin*.

Public relations practitioners also write magazine articles that may be published in the organization's magazine, in trade magazines, or in consumer-oriented magazines. Chapter 4 provides more detail about writing for magazines.

Depending on the organization's resources, a newsletter or magazine may be formatted by a publication designer or by the newsletter editor. Articles are submitted to an editor as a file attached to an e-mail message, and they follow whatever format is preferred by the production designer or editor.

At the top of page 1, start with a proposed headline, a subheadline if necessary, and a byline (your name). The text of the story should be double-spaced, making your narrative easier for the editor to read and edit. The actual story will probably be converted from your format to fit the space allocated in the publication. That is why many publications set a format, so that an editor can easily change your line-spacing or other formatting.

Paragraphs should be indented, but should not have extra space between them. There should be only one letter space, not two, after periods and other punctuation marks. Thus, sentences have only one letter space between them, not two. If your piece is longer than one page, put "-more-" at the bottom of each page and use a slug and page number in the upper right corner of each additional page. At the end of the story, type "-30-" or "###" or some other closing symbol to let the editor know that he or she has reached the end of the story.

Since space in most newsletters is limited, stories typically are short and concise. Most stories are categorized as straight news, announcements, feature stories, or hybrid stories, as in our earlier discussion of news releases. For additional information, refer to Chapter 4, "Writing for Magazines."

THE PUBLICATIONS COMMITTEE

**Chair**
Adrienne Youngstein Gruberg
*Creative Strategist, AY & A*

**Co-Chair**
Wendi Winters
*Freelance Writer, Reporter and Public Relations Consultant*
*QuantumStep, Inc.*

**Committee**

Wendy D'Amico
*Creative Consultant*

Diana Dolling-Ross
*Town & Country Apothecary*

Ariene Eisner
*Cover New York*

Joyce Kauf
*Creative Content Strategist*

Katie Kretschmer
*Departments Editor, Women's Day SIPs*

Dominique Pasqua
*Creative Director, PasquaDirect*

**Foreign Correspondents**
Christine Jackson
Yolanda Serra

**Graphic Design**
Debora DeCarlo

THE fashion GROUP INTERNATIONAL INC.

# FGI Bulletin
## 2006

### Beauty's New Balance: Science vs. Nature
*"There are science and the applications of science, bound together as the fruit to the tree which bears it."*
Louis Pasteur

Will Baby Boomers' aging skin benefit from the modern technological advances that the scientists and cosmetic chemists have discovered, or should Boomers (and their offspring) become more environmentally supportive by using the natural products that Mother Nature has bestowed? Exactly how natural is a natural beauty product? What is an organic moisturizer? Recently, Fashion Group International hosted an enlightening beauty symposium to discuss "Beauty's New Balance, Science vs. Nature." The distinguished panel included: Joseph Gubernick, chief marketing officer, Estée Lauder Companies Inc.; Howard Kreitzman, V.P., Cosmetics & Fragrances for Bloomingdale's; **Betsy Schmalz**, EVP creative & technical innovation for Beauty Avenue, a division of Limited Brands; Lauren Thaman, global director for Procter and Gamble; and Stephane Wilmet, general manager, SkinCeuticals, L'Oreal USA. The moderator was **Carol A. Smith**, SVP and publishing director, Elle Group.

The room was filled with anticipatory energy as FGI members eagerly awaited the beauty experts' advice on whether they, themselves, should be choosing between natural products or technologically advanced skincare. According to *Elle* magazine's beauty report, "What Women Really Want," presently, the nation is obsessed with the two extremes.

The American consumer is having it both ways, buying high tech as well as organic. Eighty-three percent have bought organic, while 78 percent have bought high tech. The consumer is content with the results from both: Organic gives her a sense of "inner beauty," while technology gives immediate, recognizable results.

Joseph Gubernick pointed out technology is moving at the speed of light. The beauty consumer depends on marketing information from industry professionals to keep abreast of the latest advances and what is beneficial for her skin.

Betsy Schmalz mentioned the importance of integrative concepts, both in skincare and in medicine; traditional, combined with natural. According to Ms. Schmalz, spirituality and simplicity are relevant factors for achieving emotional wellness. Those factors are important to the female consumer today.

She mentioned the highly successful Dove beauty campaign in which women of all ages and sizes were showcased. The highly-publicized campaign celebrated the reality that beauty comes in all sizes and the importance of self-acceptance.

The panelists agreed the market is flooded with products and information.

This deluge confuses the consumer. For starters, she's unclear about the distinctions between natural and organic products. According to the experts, natural products have guidelines and are controlled by the FDA, while organic products are not under FDA guidelines. Many so-called "natural" products are actually derived from a natural source, though they use preservatives to enhance shelf life.

As the retail expert, Mr. Kreitzman pointed out the crossover between nature and technology.

CONTINUED ON PAGE 2 ➡

1

FIGURE 7.15. Front page of *FGI Bulletin* newsletter.

---

*Portfolio Exercise:* **Prepare a newsletter for a student organization. Emphasize what is happening at the school. Prepare an article about a field trip to a regional fashion market, such as MAGIC or the Dallas Market Center. Include the student organization's logo and other appropriate photographs or artwork.**

---

## PITCH LETTERS

To attract the interest of a specific journalist, a public relations writer creates a **pitch letter,** which pitches or promotes a story idea. The pitch letter is used as an alternative to a news release in attempting to persuade a particular journalist to write the story described. Since pitch letters are shorter than news releases and the story is not yet written, some journalists may actually prefer a pitch letter over a news release. The letter is quick to read, and the journalist can personalize the information. Another way a pitch letter differs from a news release is that it is sent to just one targeted journalist rather than several media writers.

When writing a pitch letter, follow the guidelines for writing a business letter (covered in Chapter 11, "Writing Business Communications"). A pitch letter starts with a hook or a fascinating story, much like the lead of a news story. For example, you could pitch a story about Chicago accessory designer Amy Malloy by asking a question. Since journalists are storytellers, capture their attention with an irresistible introduction.

How did well-known massage therapist Amy Malloy come to create a line of fashionable tote bags? Many of Amy's clients complained about sore backs and shoulders. Amy determined that they were carrying tote bags that were too heavy. So, she set out to make a better bag.

The next paragraph states the purpose of the letter. For example, you might write, "I think you should do a story for the *Chicago Tribune* on accessory designer Amy Malloy." Go on to explain why you think that journalist is the perfect writer to tell the story about Malloy, who was introduced in the first paragraph of the letter. In this paragraph, also provide more information about the designer and her products.

You have supported many new Chicago designers and are part of the Fashion Focus Chicago initiative. I know you would enjoy meeting Amy. After years of working with her massage clients, Amy designed a pretty tote bag made from fashionable fabrics with two straps created to be worn over both shoulders instead of one. This design, similar to a backpack but more attractive than the traditional nylon ones, distributes weight more evenly. The result is less pain in the neck and shoulder areas.

The third paragraph makes clear that you are offering this story exclusively to the letter recipient. You hope that this information will capture the journalist's interest. Offer your assistance in setting up an interview and providing additional contacts.

The *Chicago Tribune*'s Style section would be an ideal place for an article about Amy Malloy's wonderful bags. I am contacting you first and the article is exclusive to you. After the success of her tote bags, Amy branched out to design other attractive, functional bags for carrying essentials.

In the final paragraph, provide closure by mentioning that you will call the journalist in a few days to see if she is interested. If the pitch letter successfully creates interest, the journalist will probably call you before the deadline you presented, so be sure to include your contact information, including a phone number and an e-mail address. End the letter by thanking the journalist for her consideration, and sign off using a standard "Sincerely" complimentary close.

Amy's bags are available at Macy's on State Street and at Whole Foods Market in Deerfield, near her home. I will call you next week to set up an appointment with Amy and the public relations director at Macy's. I can arrange for you to visit Macy's for a photo shoot.

---

*Portfolio Exercise:* **Create a pitch letter about a jewelry designer who has just been named a "Rising Star" by the local chapter of Fashion Group International. Make the pitch to a local television channel anchor.**

---

# ANNUAL REPORTS

Companies that publicly trade on any of the U.S. stock markets—for example, the New York Stock Exchange—are required by the Federal Securities and Exchange

Commission to issue an annual financial report to their stockholders. **Annual reports** consist of recent financial records, a year-to-year comparison of financial figures, a description of the organization's upper management team, and a discussion of the firm's goals and objectives. Thus, many firms use their annual report to meet their legal obligation to disclose financial information to the public. For example, the manufacturer Quiksilver posts its quarterly and annual financial reports as pdf files on the firm's Web site. To see the latest Quiksilver financial report, go to http://www.quiksilverinc.com/investor_anualreports_04.aspx.

The primary audience for annual reports is the firm's stockholders. But, the annual report may be attractive to a larger audience, which includes potential investors, investment analysts, employees, potential employees, and government regulators.

Nonprofit organizations prepare annual reports just like profit-making firms do. "Nonprofits" create annual reports to inform their current donors as well as to attract potential donors. The reports also document the activities the organization has undertaken to achieve its mission.

While some annual reports are bare-bones paper documents, with lots of facts and figures, many annual reports look like glossy magazines, with CDs, DVDs, and videotapes as well as samples of the firm's products. As mentioned above, annual reports may even be published on the firm's Web site. Thus, the format of an annual report varies widely from company to company.

In order to meet legal obligations, however, annual reports generally have five traditional sections (Marsh et al., 2005):

1.  **Opening charts and graphs with basic financial information**—Bar graphs and pie charts are used to show financial information. This section is often just one page long. The writer is concerned about editing the financial terminology to make the information clear and reader-friendly.

2.  **Message from the Chief Executive Officer (CEO)**—This message is frequently written as a letter, focusing on the organization's achievements over the past year and thanking employees, stockholders, and others who have helped the firm work toward its goals. Although this is the CEO's message, it frequently is written by a member of the public relations staff, upon the direction given by the CEO. The writer is responsible for integrating the CEO's personality and the theme of the annual report into this letter.

3.  **Information on the company**—This longer section of the report is much like a feature story in a magazine or newsletter, making it the section in which to present the firm as an attractive investment opportunity. Smaller insets or sidebars may be

used to highlight key information and provide relevant quotes. Photographs and artwork regularly are incorporated into this section.

4. **Management's analysis of the financial data**—Financial data, with accompanying technical explanations, are presented in this section. Financial personnel from the company are responsible for writing this section, in cooperation with an outside accounting agency that has verified the information. Some of the language may seem boring and unnecessarily complex, but the language is used for complying with disclosure laws and is written to meet standard financial reporting guidelines.

5. **Who's who in the company**—The board of directors and other high-ranking company officials are discussed in the closing section of the annual report. This section may be a simple listing of individuals with their titles, or it may include in-depth profiles of the people who run the firm. Photographs and quotes from the individuals make this section more interesting.

## SPEECHES

Strategic public relations writers may be asked to create a **speech,** which is a scripted oration to be delivered by an individual in front of an audience. Many other types of written communication are also accompanied by oral presentations. Oral presentations and speech writing are covered in Appendix E, "Making Oral Presentations."

---

*Portfolio Exercise:* **Tyra Banks, popular fashion model, television celebrity, and entrepreneur, has been invited to deliver a speech to a group of young women attending the Young Business Women's Conference in San Francisco. These women, who are between 20 and 30 years old, are interested in starting their own businesses. As Tyra's speechwriter, develop a 20-minute speech on becoming an entrepreneur for her to deliver to the nearly 500 members of the audience.**

---

## FUND-RAISING LETTERS

Public relations specialists are frequently asked to write fund-raising letters. Nonprofit organizations, for example, often use **fund-raising letters,** which are unsolicited business letters sent to current or potential donors to raise money, identify new donors, increase organization visibility, boost public relations, identify potential volunteers, or publicize new programs (Marsh et al., 2005). Mailing lists are used in much the same way as direct-response media. Response rates are higher when a specifically targeted mailing list is used to deliver an emotional, benefit-driven message, showing the reader how he can make a difference. Frequent mailings to the target audience are used in effective, ongoing fund-raising campaigns.

Figure 7.16 presents an example of a fund-raising letter. Fund-raising letters use a business letter format, with elements such as boldface type, color printing, capital letters, underlining, and headings to gain attention. Take care to avoid preparing fund-raising letters that look too flashy, as they may be seen as frivolous or extravagant and thus a waste of donors' money. The fund-raising letter might be part of a package, containing an attention-grabbing outer envelope, a personalized fund-raising letter, a personalized reply form, a reply envelope, and a brochure.

The fund-raising letter sometimes begins with a teaser headline, which appears in the upper left corner of the page, above the date and salutation. The teaser headline, usually in a different typeface and color from the rest of the letter, typically asks a question, mentions a problem, states an eye-opening statistic, or refers to a solution, to capture the reader's attention.

The next step is to present an emotional description of the need by describing a social problem in specific terms. This helps the reader identify with the cause or issue. An appropriate news story or a real-life story that stirs empathy shows the reader that something can be made better. In this section, focus on the problem, not the solution.

Once the reader is aware of the problem, introduce your organization as a solution to the problem. This is where you point out how your organization's programs have had a positive impact on the problem. This section may be several paragraphs long, highlighting the strengths and successes of your organization. Visual elements such as the boldface type, color printing, capital letters, underlining, and headings mentioned previously may be used here.

At this point, ask for a donation. You have built a case for what your organization has done and that the work has made a difference. Suggest an amount, and state what the reader's money can do to help even more. Offer a receipt for a minimum donation. Create a sense of urgency by giving a reason to respond now.

Close the letter with a sense of need. Remind the reader about the problem and how your organization is part of the solution, which can be achieved with a donation. End the letter with a straightforward complimentary close, such as "Sincerely," followed by a signature. If the letter uses colored ink, using blue-colored ink for the

# LUCKY BRAND FOUNDATION

**4290 S. Beaver St. Flagstaff, AZ 86001**
**(928) 555-5555**

**Can a trip to summer camp really boost a sick kid's life?**

May 18, 20xx

Dear Ms. Debbi Dyke:

Jenny Packard, age 11, has experienced more than most kids her age. She was diagnosed HIV positive two years ago. Jenny's dad left before she was born. Her mother died last year from AIDS. Now, Jenny's grandmother, Betty, is raising her. It is hard for Betty to keep up with her granddaughter, and it is difficult for her to give her special opportunities on a limited income.

Debbi, I can think of a way to help Jenny and her grandmother. It's a summer camp provided by DREAMSTREET FOUNDATION, which is a charitable organization that Lucky Brand Foundation sponsors. Children suffering from illnesses including cancer, AIDS, and other blood disorders are given the opportunity to enjoy activities they would normally be restricted from participating in due to their illnesses. Camping trips are among the fun activities DREAMSTREET provides sick kids.

> *"I've always dreamed of going away to camp," Jenny says. "I can't think of a better way to spend time this summer. Grammy says she went to camp when she was my age. I want to do the same things that Grammy did!"*

**Make a Difference!** The Lucky Brand Foundation seeks out charitable organizations, such as DREAMSTREET, that are led by people dedicated to making the lives of children happier and more hopeful. The tireless efforts of these organizations remain true to the heart of the Lucky Brand Foundation.

You can help Jenny and many kids just like her! Please visit our Web site at: www.dreamstreet.com or call us a 1-800-555-5555 to make a donation of $50, $75, $100, or more. Please help us provide summer camping trips and boost a sick kid's life!

Sincerely,

*Marty Baker*

Marty Baker, Foundation Director

P.S. Governor Janet Napalitano just endorsed the DREAMSTREET FOUNDATION. She called it, "the best program I've seen for kids with such horrible diseases."

FIGURE 7.16. Example of a fund-raising letter.

signature will give the appearance of a personally signed letter. Letters asking for significant donations should be signed manually, not printed. A **postscript,** or **P.S.**—an emphasis statement appearing *after* the signature—may be added to reinforce the need to give now.

---

*Portfolio Exercise:* **Prepare a fund-raising letter, asking for donations to your school's scholarship fund.**

---

## SUMMARY

Public relations has broad objectives for establishing and maintaining a positive image of a company or an individual to its various publics. Public relations uses publicity—along with a variety of other tools—to enhance the image of an organization or an individual. These tools include writing special publications, such as news releases, media kits, and annual reports; preparing pitch letters; participating in community events; raising funds for charitable activities; and sponsoring events.

## KEY TERMS

Annual report

Backgrounder

Cover letter

Dateline

Fact sheet

Fund-raising letter

Gift bag

Goodie bag

Headline

Media kit

News release

Newsletter

Photo opportunity
    sheet

Pitch letter

Postscript (P.S.)

Press conference

Publicity

Public relations (PR)

Public service announcement
    (PSA)

Radio news release script

Radio reader

Shell

Slate

Slug

Sound bite

Special event

Speech

Video news release (VNR)

CASE STUDY

## Overcoming Amy's Negative Media Coverage

After Amy Jackson graduated from Oregon State University with a Bachelor of Science in Communication, she enrolled at the Fashion Institute of Design and Merchandising in San Francisco. Amy completed the one-year program in fashion design and returned to her home in Portland, Oregon, with her husband and young son. She started designing a collection of young, hip clothing that appealed to her 18- to 25-year-old target customers. Along with building her fashion design business, Amy joined the local chapter of Fashion Group International.

Amy met several other innovative fashion designers in Portland who were attracting a lot of attention from the local media. Despite being away from the traditional centers for fashion design, such as New York or Los Angeles, these designers created a niche market for their innovative designs. In order to promote the avant-garde designers, Amy put her communication knowledge to work by starting a publication, Web site, and fashion show production team called LabelHorse with her college roommate Jenny James, who was also a communication graduate. LabelHorse included a print directory of people working in fashion-related businesses in the Portland area, as well as a network of enthusiastic models, hairstylists, disk jockeys, photographers, and stage designers who produced fashion shows at various venues around Portland. LableHorse became a clearinghouse for many fashion events in Portland, in addition to producing many of the local fashion shows.

The Portland chapter of Fashion Group International sponsors an annual "Rising Star" event to honor entrepreneurs in fashion, accessory, and interior design. This competition is a way for the group to honor young designers, promoting their businesses to the public. The fashion design finalists present four of their outfits in a gala fashion show, held at the Portland Art Museum.

Amy presented her garments as part of the extravaganza, and Amy and Jenny, as co-owners of LabelHorse, produced the show for the FGI chapter. To her surprise, Amy was named the "Rising Star for Fashion Design in 2007." At first she was reluctant to accept the award, not wanting to give the appearance of a conflict of interest. Members of the FGI Board convinced Amy to accept the acknowledgment for her creative efforts.

A journalist from the weekly arts and politics newspaper, *The Portland Exchange*, asked Amy and Jenny for an interview. The writer, Pat Swope, planned an in-depth article about the growing fashion design scene. Excited about the potential for publicity for both the fashion design business and LabelHorse, Amy and Jenny eagerly met with Pat and shared their plans.

When the article was published, Amy and Jenny were dumbfounded. Pat had turned the article into a negative exposé of the local fashion industry, painting Amy and Jenny as self-promoting cranks. Pat attacked Amy and the other fashion designers. He said that if they had any real talent, they would move to one of the centers for fashion in the United States and stop wasting their time in Portland. He also attacked Amy for accepting the Rising Star award, saying that receiving an award from an organization she belonged to and created fashion shows for was nepotism.

## CASE STUDY QUESTIONS

1. What should Amy Jackson and Jenny James do now?
2. Could they have anticipated the negative angle of the story?
3. Does the Fashion Group International chapter have any public relations responsibility?

## INDUSTRY PROFILE

*Lisa Pagel*

***What is your current job and title? Can you describe the main responsibilities for your job?***

Public Relations Manager, Neiman Marcus Scottsdale. Local store event planning and execution, marketing, public relations, charitable nonprofit liaison for Scottsdale store, media spokesperson, and community outreach.

***What is a typical day at work like?***

There are no typical days when you work in retail public relations. One day might be spent pulling fashions, shoes, and accessories for an upcoming fashion show; one day may be distributing event schedules or media releases to our media partners about future designer appearances; one day I may be in strategic meetings for the next season; another I might be attending a charity luncheon or black-tie function; and yet another might include setting up for an in-store special event.

***At what point did you decide to pursue a career in writing for a fashion-related business?***

Most of my background has been in retail sales management. I was a fashion merchandising major in college and have worked in the past for leading luxury retailers as a selling or department manager. I have been with Neiman Marcus for over 15 years, and 4 years ago I applied for and was hired in my current position.

***Describe your first writing job. What was the most important or interesting thing you wrote for that job/publication?***

This is my first "writing" job.

***What are you currently reading (books, magazines, Web sites, newspapers, other media)? Do you have a favorite author or publication?***

It is a full-time job to keep up with the top fashion publications such as *Vogue*, *W*, and *Bazaar*, including the local and regional magazines and newspapers. I subscribe to the *New York Times* on the weekends for their Sunday Style section and the *Times Magazine*. I also get e-mail notices and updates from our regional magazines, as well as Style.com from *Vogue*.

***What advice do you have for students interested in a writing career? Do you have any recommendations for students?***

1. Excel in English! Work hard at it if it doesn't come naturally, as it will serve you well throughout your life. 2. "Spell-check" doesn't exist everywhere.

## REFERENCES

Cutlip, S. M., Center, A. H., & Broom, G. M. (2005). *Effective public relations* (9th ed.). Upper Saddle River, NJ: Pearson Prentice Hall.

Diggs-Brown, B. (2007). *The PR styleguide: Formats for public relations practice* (2nd ed.). Belmont, CA: Thomson Wadsworth.

Grunig, J. E., & Hunt, T. (1984). *Managing public relations*. New York: Holt, Rinehart, Winston.

Laermer, R., with Prichinello, M. (2003). *Full frontal PR: Getting people talking about you, your business, or your product*. Princeton, NJ: Bloomberg Press.

Marsh, C., Guth, D. W., & Short, B. P. (2005). *Strategic writing: multimedia writing for public relations, advertising, sales and marketing, and business communication*. Boston: Pearson Education.

Oprah's Midas touch. (2005, September 19). *People, 64,* 183.

Scott, A, (2005). Public Relations. *Microsoft® Encarta® Online Encyclopedia*. Retrieved August 25, 2005, from http://encarta.msn.com

Swanson, K. K., & Everett, J. C. (2007). *Promotion in the merchandising environment* (2nd ed.). New York: Fairchild Books.

Zilkha, B. (2004). *Ultimate style: The best of the best dressed list*. New York: Assouline Publishing.

# EIGHT

## *Writing for New Media*

After you have read this chapter, you should be able to discuss the following:
• New Media
• Web writing for journalists
• Web writing for promotional communication
• Web writing for books
• Writing for blogs

Paris—2006

Louis Vuitton, Christian Dior, Elie Saab, and Yves Saint Laurent were just a few of the big-name fashion houses to unveil their fall 2006 collections last week in Paris. Dior showed a little attitude with headscarves, sunglasses, biker boots, and pin-straight hair on the runway, while Vuitton had some fun with heaps of fur, including eye-catching handbags featuring multicolored LV logos (sure to be a must-have next autumn). All the shows were edgy, modern, and the perfect end to a brilliant debut of fall fashion lines ("Best of Paris," 2006, ¶ 1).

The paragraph above is from the "Best of Paris" link on the Fashion Week Fall 2006 report on glam.com's Web site. Figure 8.1 shows a screen capture of that site. While this information was retrieved much later in the month, anyone interested could have read such a report about the fashion shows during the actual shows or immediately after the glamorous presentations in London, Paris,

**FIGURE 8.1.** Example of the instantaneous reporting of fashion trends from Paris collections that is possible on the Internet.

Milan, or New York. Some of the fashion shows could be watched in real time. This is the type of information that at one time rarely got to the average consumer until the garment and its knockoffs were available in retail stores. Today, we're much more active consumers, and we're more influential than ever before when it comes to making fashion decisions.

The focus in this chapter is to learn about the New Media and how to write for various online applications. We will take a general look at writing for the Web, and then take a closer look at journalistic, promotional communication, and book writing for the Web. The developments in creating Web logs, also known as blogs, will also be discussed. This chapter will not attempt to teach you Web coding. That should be learned in a computer class. The chapter concludes with a brief discussion about the future of writing for the New Media.

# THE NEW MEDIA

The **Internet,** a computer-based global information system, emerged from a U.S. military communication network created in the late 1960s ("Internet Developments," 2004). Various academic, governmental, and information technology communities contributed advancements that moved the closed information system to an openly shared, widely available communication source.

One of the first advancements came in the 1980s, when the National Science Foundation started a network and allowed everyone to access it ("Internet Developments," 2004). At that time, the network was being used primarily by computer-science graduates and professors, known as "techies." Then, the first commercial **Internet Service Provider (ISP)** came along and made the system available to a greater variety of users. (An ISP allows its customers Internet access for a fee, usually paid on a monthly basis.) At first, customers used a dial-up connection that linked them to the Internet via a telephone line. Most large businesses were able to set up dedicated, high-capacity connections, making their response time over telephone lines quicker than the response time that was available for individual customers. The desire for speed soon led to better technologies, such as **digital subscriber lines (DSL)** or cable modems, for everyone. Next came **Wi-Fi** technology, or wireless access to the Internet. Niue, a self-governing Pacific island, became the first country to offer free nationwide wireless access to the Internet using Wi-Fi technology ("Internet Developments"). Even as this book is being written, availability and use of Wi-Fi is becoming increasingly widespread.

By 1990, the British physicist and computer scientist Tim Berners-Lee had invented the **World Wide Web (WWW** or **Web)** as an Internet environment where scientists could share information ("Internet Developments," 2004). This opened the system that gradually evolved into a sophisticated medium in which text, graphics, audio, animation, and video can be shared with virtually anyone around the world who has Internet access. As as work started work on this chapter, an e-mail message arrived from a friend in Denmark. This shows how we are able to share information almost instantaneously with almost anyone in the world due to continually updating and improving technology.

The Internet has been compared to a highway system, whereas the Web is more like a package that is being shipped via a highway from one city to another. The Internet is the roadway over which Web traffic and traffic from other applications move from one computer to another. That is why you often hear the Internet and Web described as an information superhighway.

Accessing information on the Internet is accomplished by using a **Uniform Resource Locator (URL)**, which is the address for a Web site. For example, a business URL could be formatted as follows: http://www.nameofbusiness.com. This is the top level of the organization's Web site. From the URL, you can obtain an overview of the site contents and what additional information or products are available on the site. If you do not know the URL, you can use a search tool, such as Google (www.google.com) to locate it.

This technology faces several challenges, including battling spam and viruses, addressing heightened security and privacy issues, and providing enough capacity to meet the needs resulting from the Web's phenomenal growth rate. Believe it or not, the first spam, or junk e-mail message, was sent in 1978 ("Internet Developments," 2004). By 2003, spam was estimated to account for half of all e-mail, clogging and slowing access to the Internet ("Internet Developments"). Computer viruses that spread via the Internet have infected countless computers, shutting many of them down and causing billions of dollars of damage.

On the Internet, people are now able to purchase almost anything from a commercial site; to conduct personal and commercial banking; and to communicate with businesses and governments. **E-commerce** is the use of the Internet as a way to transact business, providing products or services to customers via the Web. As a result, personal, business, and credit card information is more widely available—and vulnerable. Companies doing business over the Internet need sophisticated security measures to protect their customers' information from being shared with unauthorized sources.

During the early years, e-commerce was dominated by sales of technology products such as computers and printers, and by sales of books, airline tickets, and hotel reservations. Online sales of apparel seemed too risky to both retailers and consumers. But, according to Corcoran (2006), online sales of apparel grew by 61% in 2006 compared with the previous year, moving sales of apparel, accessories, and footwear to the number one spot for online product sales. Contributing to these sales were traditional brick-and-mortar stores, such as Neiman Marcus and J.C. Penney, as well as stores that are exclusively online, such as Bluefly and NET-A-PORTER.

Table 8.1 illustrates the 12 most-searched apparel brands in February 2007 (Hall, 2007). The original research was conducted by San Francisco-based Stylophane.com, an Internet apparel design and marketing firm that counts the number of times that apparel brands that the firm tracks monthly are entered into search engines. According to Stylophane, six brands—Louis Vuitton, Nike, Adidas, Gucci, Chanel, and

**Table 8.1.** The WWD List: Brand Power.

| RANK | BRAND | SEARCH VOLUME |
|------|-------|---------------|
| 1 | Louis Vuitton | 315,126 |
| 2 | Nike | 252,875 |
| 3 | Adidas | 158,656 |
| 4 | Gucci | 154,237 |
| 5 | Chanel | 147,716 |
| 6 | Speedo | 137,236 |
| 7 | Prada | 119,895 |
| 8 | Juicy Couture | 113,835 |
| 9 | Ugg Boots | 112,280 |
| 10 | The North Face | 112,100 |
| 11 | Converse | 99,438 |
| 12 | Guess | 97,621 |

Adapted from Hall, C. (2007, April 5). The WWD list: Brand power. *Women's Wear Daily*, p. 12.

Prada—reappeared on the list from the previous year. The firm noted that each brand had lower search volume figures than it had had the year before. Next, we will look at some of the concerns associated with the New Media.

## NEW MEDIA CONCERNS

Without the principles established by practitioners in traditional media, anybody can post anything he wants on the Internet. Anyone posting to a Web site, chat room, or blog can be a publisher or columnist. Digital articles are filled with commentary, personal opinion, rumors, or gossip. Web writers expand the boundaries of what was previously considered newsworthy, pushing the standards of traditional journalistic ethics. The Web has flexible boundaries and a lack of rules for users to follow.

The reliability of various resources on the Web can and should be questioned. If you are working for a particular media publication, your employer may have a list of reliable URLs. Information presented with a **byline**, which is a line identifying the author of the story, is considered to be more trustworthy. That is especially true if the byline is from someone you have referenced and found trustworthy previously. Appendix D, "Locating and Evaluating Sources on the Web," offers suggestions for finding information that is valid and sources that are reliable.

Another concern about information found on Web sites has to do with accuracy. Material written by Web authors does not go through the copyediting and fact-checking that print-based resources routinely do. Therefore, readers find a lot of mis-spelled names, wrong titles, wrong dates, and incorrect information.

Additionally, the Web contains massive amounts of information, some of it out-dated. A story might read as if the information is current, but it might actually be sev-eral years old. To overcome this concern, it is important to be able to determine the creation date of material that is accessed online.

Concern over potential use of the Internet by terrorists has led the U.S. Congress to pass new laws. Individuals who cause or attempt to cause death by disrupting computer systems can be criminally penalized. The laws also allow ISPs to reveal subscriber infor-mation to government officials without a court-approved warrant, if there is a risk of death or injury. Nothing shared via the Internet is private, and under specific conditions, government authorities may trace any interactions that take place over the Internet.

# CONVERGENCE

One of the biggest buzzwords in the media industry today is **convergence**, which involves alliances among print media (newspapers or magazines), broadcast media (broadcast or cable television and radio), and other forms of electronic media (the Internet and wireless communication devices). "Convergence is the practice of shar-ing and cross-promoting content from various media, some interactive, through news room collaborations and partnerships" (Brooks, Kennedy, Moen, & Ranly, 2004, p. 19). This process of bringing together and sharing information from a variety of media sources is changing the face of media in the 21st century. Today, you can watch a news story on television, immediately get more information from a newspa-per Web site, and then ask for updates to be sent to your wireless communication device (also known as a **personal digital assistant**, or **PDA**).

One of the first converged media companies in the United States, based in Tampa, Florida, was the Media General Communications Company, initiated in 2000 (Brooks et al., 2004). Much larger today, it first consisted of the *Tampa Tribune* (a newspaper), WFLA (a radio station), and Tampa Bay Online (a news Web site). The converged newsroom in Tampa uses all three platforms to present routine as well as breaking news. Crossover reporting, which means that the news is presented in more than one medium, has become commonplace in Florida and in many other markets. Today, most television stations and newspapers—as well as radio networks, such as National Public Radio—have Web sites.

# WEB WRITING DIFFERS FROM WRITING FOR PRINT

Although writing for print and writing for the Web are similar in many ways, there are significant differences as well. Like writing for print media, Web writing requires understanding the target audience. Give the reader an identity, general age group, interests and desires, technological proficiency, type of Internet connection; this helps you to put yourself in his shoes. One other matter to consider is the international nature of the audience. You probably will not know if your reader is in the United States, France, or Japan.

Web readers want information quickly. They are impatient and they move through pages more quickly than readers of print do. They interact with information and take detours when they are bored or do not find what they are looking for on a Web page. Web sites should provide current content-driven data in an easy-to-navigate format.

## LINEAR VERSUS NONLINEAR WRITING

People read information from a computer screen more slowly than they read material in print. Typically, when reading on the screen, they do not read every word—instead, they skim, scan and skip through a page for items that interest them. Internet readers scan headlines, article summaries, and captions. If the text is too long, these readers either move on or print a hard copy to read later. They may also keep several browsers or windows open simultaneously and switch among them regularly. Understanding who the reader is and what she or he is looking for will help you to organize your writing.

Traditional print media writers use a linear pattern, stringing together a long structured story. These writers want the reader to read the whole story in the order the writer has chosen to present it. Online readers, on the other hand, do not necessarily want to follow the author's outline or have to scroll down the screen to read all of the material. These readers prefer to scan the article and click on hyperlinks in the text or on other elements on the Web page to jump to information that truly interests them. Web sites are considered to be nonlinear, allowing a reader to decide what to read and where to go to get the information he or she is seeking. The key, then, is to organize the Web site to make it easy for the reader to navigate.

## ORGANIZE AND STRUCTURE

The inverted pyramid style of writing used by journalists is one well-known way to structure and organize a story. It allows the reader to move through the content in essentially a straight line, starting with the most general information and moving toward more specific information.

By contrast, writing for the Web allows the writer to move the reader through content hierarchically rather than linearly. As Web writers create Web sites, the whole Web site is commonly organized like an organizational chart rather than a pyramid. Establishing a hierarchy is an ideal way to organize material for Web-based writing. Information is structured into information units, known as **chunks**. This allows information to be offered in portions that can stand alone or be linked to other portions as part of a more comprehensive document. We have learned that online readers do not like long documents, so making smaller sections will make an article more attractive to that type of user.

At the top of the hierarchy is the home page. From there, you need to decide how readers will make their way through the information. Will the structure be relatively flat, allowing users to move directly between tiers? Or, will the structure be deep, making users browse more pages to get to the content desired? While both structures have advantages and disadvantages, the choice is most likely determined by the number and variety of focused topics, the amount of content, and the content's intended application. For example, a reader finds a fashion story on the *New York Times* Web site by first going to the paper's Home Page. From there, the reader can find various topics from a menu. Once the reader locates the Style section, she or he has a choice of looking at articles in subsections called Fashion &

Style, Dining & Wine, Home & Garden, Weddings/Celebrations, and T Magazine. This is an example of a structure that enables the reader to move easily among pages.

If you are looking for a new pair of shoes, some e-commerce Web sites allow you to narrow your viewing range by choosing from among various characteristics, such as end-use, heel height, popularity, brand, size, and color. Some accessory Web sites do not offer the ability to focus on special characteristics; instead, they require you to look at a lot of unrelated products to get to the ones you might want. A frustrated consumer is more likely to give up a search than plow through unrelated products.

A **Webmaster** is an individual who authors, designs, develops, markets, or maintains a Web site. This person may also be called the system administrator, the author of the Web site, or the Web site administrator. When establishing the hierarchy, the Webmaster should prevent or at least minimize the possibility of dead ends. If the hierarchy does not contain navigable and intuitive paths for the user to follow, the user will get frustrated and move to another site.

## GUIDELINES FOR WRITING ONLINE

Now that we have some basic knowledge about online sources, it is time to look at the specific strategies for putting information onto a Web site. Since we know that most online users are skimmers, scanners, or skippers, we want to learn how to captivate those users and make them willing readers of our information. Ideally, the following strategies will hold the reader's attention long enough to get your message across.

### Deliver Information in a Timely Manner

The Internet is capable of delivering information as soon as it is available. Writing for the Internet is like writing stories for the wire services that provide the most updated news to the media, making everyone who uses the Internet similar to a wire service subscriber. The challenge is to make sure that the information posted to the Internet is accurate, up-to-date, and well written, and has an appropriate depth of coverage.

## Be Clear

Internet users do not want to waste time looking for information. The best way to save users time is to be clear and concise with your information. Choose simple words and language. Keep sentences and paragraphs short. Emphasize key words by highlighting them through visual techniques, such as using boldface type, underlining, different fonts, and color.

Some guidance regarding the possible international nature of your audience: Using simple words and sentences assists the auto-translation programs that some search engines use to translate a page. Also, when simple words are used, a foreign language translation has a much better chance of being accurate and understandable.

## Make Information Quick and Easy to Get

If a Web site has good organization and structure, the reader should be able to find and read information rapidly. Because it is so easy for a user to click something else, users should not be confused or led astray. Know your audience, and guide your readers to what they want to know. Make it easy for them to find information.

## Provide Visual Images in Addition to Textual Information

Since the Web is as much a visual medium as a verbal one, you need to consider how visual images will enhance your written information. Photos, illustrations, and graphics make the Web an interesting and entertaining medium. Previously, writers were concerned strictly with the written word. As our culture has become more visually literate, and less interested in complex narrative, the visual elements have become more significant to telling the story. Web writers collaborate with photographers, artists, and graphic designers to find ways to emphasize the text with visual elements.

Fashion brands are particularly dependent upon visual elements. People want to see the products more than they want to read about them. In an attempt to make its Web site more artsy, Prada provided access to PDF images and a production movie, as well as links to events, special objects, and exhibits. According to Ilari (2007), selling online is the next step for Prada and will be available at a future date. Until then,

FIGURE 8.2. A PDF from the Prada Web site.

the company offers visuals in the non-conventional Prada spirit. Figure 8.2 presents a page from the Prada Web site.

## Cut Excess Copy

The writing that is done for online presentation must be concise. A good goal would be to cut your copy by half. Editing your material from four pages down to two may seem impossible, but most online readers will ignore long stories.

## Use Lists and Bullets

A common way to help cut that copy is to put the information into list format. Information presented in lists or bullet points gets more attention from the reader than ordinary narrative does, as well as enabling better comprehension and retention. Bulleted and numbered lists are easy to skim, which is what most Web users want.

## Write in Chunks

As we mentioned previously, presenting information in chunks is an effective way to make the information easier to read and understand. Readers will read more if you break up the information into small portions. A sidebar or box can help draw the reader's attention to supporting documentation. Presenting the information in chunks can help improve the reader's comprehension of the subject.

Think of how your story might make sense if it were divided into parts. Perhaps each segment of the story could be organized into a separate, independent story. Carefully crafted transitions—with subheads to act as titles for the separate stories— would enable you to retain all the parts. In this way, the coverage could still be comprehensive and the user could still gain a well-rounded understanding.

## Use Hyperlinks

**Hyperlinks** are connections to places where the reader can learn more about the topics in the story. Being connected means being interactive, a characteristic that is highly desirable to Web users. Hyperlinks take users to audio, video, or pictures that enhance the text content.

Rather than defining words, going into long explanations, or elaborating on the story, you can stick to the essential information and insert links that lead the reader to additional documentation and support. For example, the story about a new fashion design can link to another Web site where the technique is described more fully.

## Provide for Feedback

Web users like to be interactive and to communicate with the Web site owners. In fact, users feel they have the right to write back to the author of an article. Feedback opportunities include responding to the writer or communicating with other readers. Many articles provide the author's e-mail address or a link to a chat line where readers can offer their points of view. This interactivity gives the reader a reason to come back to the Web site again and again.

The writer and Webmaster get feedback in ways never thought possible before. Reaction and comment typically can occur instantly, and readers really like to respond. Never has it been so easy to find out what is on the minds of your readers. Figure 8.3 shows a place where a Web site viewer can contact the author or Web site owners.

## Keep the Human Touch

When you're writing on a computer, it is easy to lose touch with humans. People are part of most Web stories. Facts are simply facts unless they are related to people. People are involved in the news. People make buying decisions as consumers. Human beings still count.

FIGURE 8.3.  Where a viewer can contact an author or Web site owner on an Internet Web site.

# WEB WRITING FOR JOURNALISTS

Let's look at writing for the Web as it relates to writing for journalistic and promotional communication. After we cover those types of writing, another area that deserves discussion is writing books for the Web.

Journalists were among the first writers to be influenced by the New Media. Newspapers, seeing the benefits of posting articles on a Web site, placed exact text versions of newspaper articles on their Internet sites. Traditional consumer and trade print magazines also saw the benefits of developing Web sites, especially as places where consumers could find supporting materials as well as ways to purchase subscriptions to the original print version. Independent magazine publications started as Web-only productions. This section of the chapter discusses how journalism has been evolving under the changing electronic environment.

## NEWSPAPERS

Most newspapers today publish two versions of a story: one for the print newspaper and the other for the paper's Web site. Newspapers have become 24-hour-a-day news machines, with updates and additional information published to the Web site within minutes of a major story breaking.

The lead in a newspaper story, which was discussed in Chapter 3, "Writing for Newspapers," is especially important for online newspaper articles. The lead is used to link the story to various search engines. Therefore, the lead should contain key words that provide opportunities for readers to find your story. For example, a story about Italian jeweler "Bulgari" opening a store in "Tokyo" should have those key words in the lead. The lead might read as follows:

Milan—Bulgari is opening its biggest store in the world, a 10-story tower in Tokyo's Ginza shopping district.

After the lead, the story continues. Embedded into an online newspaper story are hyperlinks. In the previous example, a hyperlink could take the reader to Bulgari's Web site or to a place where the reader could learn more about Tokyo's Ginza area. The reader decides where to go. He can finish reading the entire story at the newspaper's

Web site, or he can click a hyperlink and be diverted to a site where he can learn more about the jeweler or the shopping district.

The trend-oriented fashion stories that were commonly published about the current season are still being written, but now they are presented to a sophisticated audience eager to learn about the latest trends *before* the products are even in mass production. For example, newspapers normally have a special Sunday edition, with current fashion emphasis, at the start of fall and spring. The *New York Times* print edition presents its interpretation of spring fashion in March and of fall trends in August. But that's not fast enough for current fashionistas.

The fashion-forward audience of today is tuned into the industrial practices of the fashion industry and knows that fashion collections, introducing the new lines, are presented during the various international Fashion Weeks. These events take place during September and October for the following spring, and during February and March for the following fall. This industry-savvy audience reads about the shows in daily newspapers and in trade publications such as *Women's Wear Daily*, and for the most up-to-date looks it turns to various online resources. During New York's Fashion Week, held in February, anyone interested could turn on the computer and watch the fall shows from New York live, as they occurred in real time. Figure 8.4 shows the home page for *Women's Wear Daily*, wwd.com.

---

*Portfolio Exercise:* **Locate a fashion-related article from a recent print issue of the *New York Times*, *Wall Street Journal*, *Washington Post*, or *L.A. Times*. Visit the newspaper's Web site and compare the treatments of the article. Is the same exact article used in both places, or has it been modified for the Web site? Discuss the advantages and disadvantages of each medium. If the article is the same, rewrite it as an online version.**

---

## MAGAZINES

Most popular magazines have Web sites. To attract subscribers and new readers, many of them offer content that differs from the print editions. Magazine readership would certainly suffer if the content of the two media were exactly the same. The

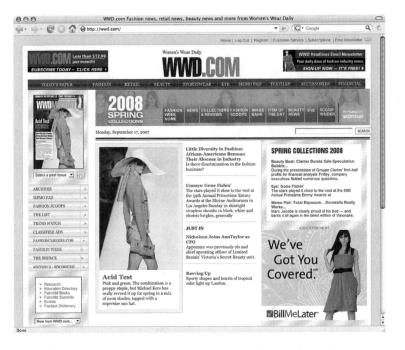

FIGURE 8.4. The Internet Home page for *Women's Wear Daily.*

publications that simply "shovel" the content of their print source to an online source are said to be providing **shovelware.** Having the articles on a magazine's Web site be identical to those in the magazine's print form might drive readers away from the New Media. Such duplication fails to take advantage of the unique characteristics of online media. Figure 8.5 shows the home page of the Style.com Web site, which is the online site for *Vogue* and *W* magazines. While some of the content is shared with the print magazines, much of the content on the Web site is original.

Magazines that are published exclusively in cyberspace are called **e-zines.** These publications are available online via Internet or e-mail. E-zines are unique entities, bearing almost no resemblance to traditional consumer or business magazines. Generally, e-zines are Internet sites based upon some original print source; alternatively, they may be an Internet-only source in the form of a newsletter, or they may be a private organization's Web site.

In order to remain competitive, most traditional print magazines maintain Web sites in addition to their long-established print format. E-zines based upon original print sources may provide short versions of original articles, provide some articles

**FIGURE 8.5.** The Internet Home page for Style.com.

that appear only online, or provide interactive articles through which the publisher can do market and audience research. They are virtually certain to provide information about how to subscribe, and they may limit access to individuals who have print-edition subscriptions. The range of online approaches is practically limitless.

*Salon* magazine in San Francisco is credited with being the first professionally staffed, Internet-based magazine (Harrison, 2002). According to information on the Salon.com Web site, "the Salon Media Group, Inc. is an Internet media company that produces 7 original content sections as well as two online communities—Table Talk and the WELL." Salon.com was founded in 1995 ("Press Information," 2005, ¶ 1).

Hundreds of e-zines have appeared overnight and have disappeared just as quickly in the rapidly changing cyber world. Some of these sources are for-profit;

others are not. Many e-zines are self-published, to promote the ideas or products of the publisher. In that way, an e-zine is closely related to a blog, which will be discussed later in this chapter.

---

📂 *Portfolio Exercise:* **Visit six different magazine Web sites. Three should be traditional print magazines and the other three should be e-zines. Pick the top traditional print magazine Web site and the top e-zine Web site. These are the sites that do the best job of using online writing techniques. Write a report discussing your reasons for selecting these as the best.** 📂

---

# WEB WRITING FOR PROMOTIONAL COMMUNICATION

This section looks at the role of the Web in the changing environment of promotional communication. Not surprisingly, the Web quickly became a place for electronic commerce. Advertising has become a significant way for Web sites to gain revenue, as well as a place for other in-depth promotional information to be presented. As we introduced in Chapter 6, direct marketing media have found ways to reach target customers via electronic mail alerts, in addition to retail sales of traditional or innovative firms. Public relations professionals have used business communication as well as news release postings, taking PR into a new media world.

## ADVERTISING

The Super Bowl has long been the event where new commercials debut, and some commercials are created to be shown only once. It remains as one of the few television shows to capture a large audience, and many viewers watch just to see the commercials. The price tag to run just one 30-second spot has increased continually, reaching an estimated $2.5 million in 2006 (Elliott). Most television and radio stations critique the ads and rate them to determine which ones were the most popular. Fashion products and fashionable themes, although limited, have regularly been a part of this event.

But many of the commercials prepared for the Super Bowl run only once, since they are so expensive to produce and to broadcast. The latest trend has been to show the video clips of the spots on various Web sites—such as AOL, MSN, and Yahoo!—in addition to the advertiser's Web site. Many Super Bowl advertisers have even created **microsites:** special Web sites with unique addresses to catch the attention of a post-event audience. These sites are different than a firm's traditional Web site and are designed to build on the excitement generated for Super Bowl ads. For example, the Dove line of personal care products set up campaignforrealbeauty.com, and Master-Card created priceless.com to enhance its image.

There's no question that the New Media is changing advertising. In fact, many advertising professionals ask if the 30-second spot is dead.

Writing for advertising to be presented on the Internet follows many of the guidelines presented earlier in this chapter. Keeping headlines creative yet simple is key to writing successful Internet advertising. Working with the visual artists to develop interesting collaborations is also a necessity.

---

*Portfolio Exercise:* **Create a series of 10 advertising headlines that could be used to promote a new sunscreen called "Montana Sun." Collaborate with a visual artist to incorporate images for each of the specific headlines.**

---

## DIRECT MARKETING MEDIA

Did you receive a message from Victoria's Secret in your e-mail inbox today? If so, you are like thousands of other Web alert subscribers. Direct marketing retailers have found the Internet to be a great resource. Direct advertising makes it very easy for a retailer to reach a target audience that particularly wants to receive messages from that retailer. Figure 8.6 is the home page for Zappos.com, the online retailer of shoes and accessories.

Many retailers know how to attract more sales from what they adapted from such online stores as Amazon.com. Amazon started as a book retailer, offering discounts on most books and free shipping with a minimum order. Amazon quickly learned that consumers purchased more books, music, or DVDs when the company offered recommendations based upon previous acquisitions. As we are writing this book, Amazon has expanded from its traditional roots to over 32 categories of products; to international sites in Canada, the United Kingdom, Germany, Japan, France, and

FIGURE 8.6. The Internet Home page for Zappos.com.

China; and to partnerships with such retailers as Target, Nordstrom, Macy's, Urban Outfitters, and Polo.

*Portfolio Exercise:* **For a product (of your choosing), create a direct marketing media communication that will be inserted into an e-mail message. Your message should include appropriate visual images in addition to promotional copy. Since one of the advantages of presenting direct marketing appeals online is the ability to use hyperlinks, you should include hyperlinks in your finished product.**

## PUBLIC RELATIONS

Traditional public relations specialists depended upon building relationships with media representatives, using telephones and media releases to get information out. Now, public relations specialists have come to prefer e-mail and other new media to accomplish their communication. (The role that e-mail is playing is discussed more fully in Chapter 11, "Writing Business Communications.")

Web-based newswires are becoming a popular method for distributing information. These fee-based services will send your news release to thousands of journalists, targeted to your industry and interests. Because it is so easy to send these mass messages, it is also easy to send bland, uninteresting announcements. If you have something interesting and real to announce, it will be worth the cost of between $100 and $3,000 to deliver a release in this manner.

Two popular wire services are Business Wire (www.businesswire.com) and PR Newswire (www.prnewswire.com) (Laermer & Prichinello, 2003). These services allow the writer to send messages to targeted editors; select the exact time for release; and attach visuals, such as photographs or graphics, for illustration. Releases are posted on the wire site and delivered to journalists who have registered to receive announcements from particular industries via e-mail. These releases are also archived, so that reporters writing about a specific industry or topic can look up and view previously posted releases.

---

*Portfolio Exercise:* **Write an online news release for the launch of a new line of apparel designed by Zac Posen for J.C. Penney. Posen follows Ralph Lauren, who successfully introduced "Chaps" at Kohl's, and Isaac Mizrahi, who successfully launched his line for Target. The moderately priced collection will feature apparel, accessories, and eyeglasses in the $20 to $200 price range and in sizes 2 to 16. The line is called "Just Zac." Include hyperlinks as appropriate.**

---

# WEB BOOK WRITING

A relatively new method of publishing a book is through electronic media as an **e-book**. If you're interested in writing a book, now you can do it through an e-book publishing company or as a self-published e-book.

E-books are just as dependent upon quality writing and good marketing strategies as are traditionally printed books. An interesting topic, a well-composed narrative, good editing, and use of appropriate visuals are just as important in an e-book as they are in conventional media. Advantages of publishing an e-book include lower production costs and an increased likelihood of getting published. You will save money on printing costs, especially if the book is downloaded and printed by the purchaser. You must be able to write the book in a word processing program and convert it to a printable format, such as an Adobe Acrobat **portable document format (PDF)** file. E-books can also be sold on CDs or DVDs that the user can read on a computer screen or print out.

The second edition of *Contemporary Fashion* by Taryn Benbow-Pfalzgraf and Richard Martin (2002) is available both in the traditional hardback format and as an e-book.

Of course, the disadvantages should be considered as well. E-books are easily copied, which limits your profits through sales or royalties. It may also be difficult to get bookstores to carry your book in this format. You will still need to find ways to promote your book, and so far, sales of e-books have been limited. Since this is a relatively recent, unproven method of publishing books, finding a reliable e-book publisher could also be a challenge.

Among the important issues for an author and her or his publisher to agree upon prior to signing a contract is the granting of rights. Primary rights are how the work will be published—in hardcover, in paperback, or in some other format. These rights also include translation rights and international distribution, among other concerns. Rights make up most of the deal points in a book contract. Book contracts will be discussed further in Chapter 10, "Writing Books."

You need to negotiate with the publisher to determine who (you or the publisher) has the rights to publish materials in electronic media. **Electronic rights** is a term, with various implications, used in book publishing contracts. Because electronic media is changing so rapidly, a legal definition has not yet been established. Care should be taken when entering into any book publishing contract.

**Publishing-on-demand**, also known as **printing-on-demand**, is a computer-based system for distribution of books (Embree, 2003). In some cases, this means that a reader can order a book from an online catalog, and the online distribution company prints and binds the book and sends it to the purchaser. In other cases, it means that the reader finds a resource on the Web, orders the book from that resource and pays for the book by credit card, and then the book is made available to the purchaser in a form that he or she can download and either read on-screen or print out.

# BLOG WRITING

**Blogs** or **Web logs** are personal journals published on the World Wide Web. *Blog* is an abbreviated term for *Web log*. Blogs frequently include philosophical thoughts and views about various social issues; they also provide a "log" of the author's favorite Web links. Blogs are usually presented in journal style and are updated each day. Since blogs are personal and tend to advocate the interests of the author, blogs are not considered journalistic sources. They are created to promote the interests or views of the blogger.

Cathy Horyn, the *New York Times* fashion critic, writes a blog called "On the Runway." The blog covers all things about fashion, from the front row of fashion shows to behind the scenes at ateliers and houses around the world, to inside the minds of designers. Cathy Horyn's narrative contains hyperlinks to related stories as well as links to reader's comments, and the site gives readers the opportunity to forward the story to someone via e-mail.

According to Luman, by 2006 there were approximately 27 million blogs in the world (2006). Many of them relate to each other through hypertext links. Since most bloggers do not advertise, links are the chief way that visitors find new blogs.

But, how does anyone make money with a blog? Gawker.com, a very popular gossip Web site, was pioneered by founding writer Elizabeth Spiers and high-tech publisher Nick Denton (Thompson, 2006). Spiers developed a distinctive online writing style that attracted a large Manhattan media world audience. Denton estimated that the site received about 200,000 "page views" a day from readers (Thompson). The firm ran approximately two big ads on each page of the Web site and charged advertisers between $6 and $10 for every 1,000 page views, which was similar to a midsize newspaper rate during the same period. There also were a few one-line text ads bringing in a few hundred dollars each day. With income from ads bringing in nearly $4,000 per day, Gawker probably had revenues of at least $1 million a year (Thompson). First-movers have a significant edge over competition, and Gawker towers over more recent entries into the field. According to Technorati, a research firm that tracks blogs online, about 70,000 new blogs are created daily; and according to a study called the Pew Internet & American Live Project, prepared by the Tides Center, about 11% of Internet users read blogs regularly (Corcoran, 2006).

During Fashion Week, fashion bloggers bring information about the fashion shows to their audience almost instantaneously. Some fashion industry experts feel that this trend is changing the way fashion is reported and is giving the consumer more control and ownership of fashion.

Most fashion bloggers view the shows, but do not post live. They post their comments later from home. This practice of getting the fashion message out via blogs is having a small but rapidly increasing influence in the fashion industry. According to Technorati, in 2006, the number of fashion- and shopping-related blogs was approximately 2 million (Corcoran, 2006). The first blogger to comment live from inside the tents was Julie Frederickson of "Almost Girl."

Bloggers see themselves as independent reviewers who can tell the truth in a world where truth is not always easy to find. A writer in traditional media would find it difficult to express any negative comments about a show, a designer, or a celebrity attending the fashion events. But, as a self-employed writer, a blogger has more freedom. Bloggers are their own boss.

Designer Nanette Lepore created her own blog from her studio and posted it on Glam.com. Lepore described the grueling hours she spent getting ready for and presenting during Fashion Week. The designer also wrote about makeup artist Polly Osmond of MAC, who created the look for Lepore's show.

Glam Media (2007), which runs Glam.com, is the number one women's Web property. Glam Media runs lifestyle Web sites and an online media network of publishers with more than 17 million unique visits a month in the United States. Glam Media comprises the company's flagship Web site, Glam.com; other Glam-owned sites; the Glam Publisher Network of more than 350 popular lifestyle and fashion Web sites, blogs, and magazines; and select syndicated content from leading media companies. Registered members of Glam Media can link their blogs to the firm's Web site. Figure 8.7 shows Glam.com's home page.

Bloggers also take their readers to the international shows. *Marie Claire*'s editor-in-chief Lesley Jane Seymour reported from Milan and Paris as part of fashion coverage on MSN Lifestyle (2006). Seymour's messages were titled *Postcards from the (Cutting) Edge*, and they were posted daily. Her reports made her readers feel like they were reading her personal journal and were a part of the frantic Fashion Week carousel.

---

*Portfolio Exercise:* **Do a Web search and find five different blogs about fashion. Write a memorandum about the blogs and their contents. For each of the sites, answer these questions: What is the featured story? Did the blogger use visuals? What did you like or dislike about the site?**

---

FIGURE 8.7. The Internet Home page for Glam.com.

# THE FUTURE OF WRITING FOR NEW MEDIA

It is hard to picture what the future influences of the New Media will be. This information highway has taken us from a slow, text-based communication tool into a new, rapidly changing society. Approaches to communication problems and technological advances will certainly change further, even by the time this book goes to print.

What do you imagine happening to communication in our future? Will we have three-dimensional (3-D) TV and computer screens? Will voice-activated computers become commonplace, eliminating the need for a key pad or a mouse? Will Virtual Reality (VR) be fully integrated into our lives, making it possible to "attend meetings" without travel, to practice surgical techniques without a patient, or to produce "clones" to act on our behalf in a virtual world? One thing is certain: There will be lots of changes in communication in our future.

## SUMMARY

This chapter provided background about the New Media and how to write for various online applications. The chapter presented broad tips for writing for the Web, in addition to taking a closer look at writing for journalistic, promotional communication, and at writing books for the New Media. Web logs, also known as blogs, are growing and linking the global consumer in ways not imagined in the past. Web coding is a technical aspect of the New Media that should be learned from a specialist, knowledgeable about writing computer code. The chapter concluded with a brief discussion about the future of writing for the New Media.

## KEY TERMS

Blog
Byline
Chunk
Convergence
Digital subscriber lines
   (DSL)
E-book
E-commerce
Electronic rights
E-zine
Hyperlink
Internet
Internet Service Provider
   (ISP)
Microsite

Personal digital assistant
   (PDA)
Portable document format
   (PDF)
Printing-on-demand
Publishing-on-demand
Shovelware
Uniform Resource Locator
   (URL)
Web log
Webmaster
Wi-Fi
World Wide Web (WWW or
   Web)

## CASE STUDY

### *To Web or not to Web*

Thredz is a casual women's apparel store located in Durango, Colorado, which is in the southwestern corner of the state. The store carries merchandise that is fashionable to wear in this tourist town, or to wear during outdoor activities, such as hiking and camping in the summer or skiing in the winter.

Durango, located near the Animas River, originally developed as a rough cattle town that grew with the arrival of the Denver & Rio Grande Western Railroad in 1880. Today, it is a college town, home to Fort Lewis College, and a tourist destination, with such attractions as the Durango & Silverton Narrow Gauge Railroad, the San Juan Symphony, San Juan National Forest, and the Animas Museum. Just north of town is Durango Mountain, a popular winter ski area. With all of the summer and winter recreational opportunities, it is a year-round tourist destination.

Over the past 25 years, Thredz owner Sally Francis developed a loyal customer base from among the locals and the students at Fort Lewis College. In addition to her local client base, many tourists shopped at her store, which is located on Main Street.

Sally followed a typical promotional strategy for a small business in a rural area. She placed a modestly sized weekly advertisement in the *Durango Herald*, the town's local newspaper. Other than that, Sally depended on word-of-mouth and her display windows to draw people into the store.

A few of her regular customers were retailing students at Fort Lewis College. They were studying promotional strategies in the retailing program, and some of the students were also enrolled in computer classes. As a community outreach, retailing instructor Jennifer Edwards got Sally's permission for the program's students to do a promotional plan for Thredz. The class was divided into three teams. Each group was asked to plan a creative message and prepare at least three different ads. The first team, called the Lucky Belles, named after a nearby ghost town, planned three print ads with an Old West theme. The next group, named the City Cyclists, planned a print ad and a series of radio spots, aimed at the mountain bike community that lives in Durango. The third group, which consisted of some international exchange students from London, England, called themselves the Stilletos. Their idea was to show a more high-fashion, designer image directed at the tourists. This third group created a Web site that could be linked to via Durango's tourism Web site or Chamber of Commerce Web site. It included a fashion blog, a story about the Thredz merchandise, and a history of the store.

Sally was impressed with all of the campaigns. She had to select one as her top choice, but she did not know which one to pick.

## CASE STUDY QUESTIONS

1.  What are the pros and cons of each theme and type of advertisement?
2.  What are the pros and cons of each medium (print, radio, Web)?
3.  What message would you recommend to Sally?
4.  What other themes or media can you suggest?
5.  What medium would you recommend to Sally?

## INDUSTRY PROFILE

*Amy Swift*

**What is your current job and title? Can you describe the main responsibilities for your job?**

Copy Writer and Brand Communications Specialist (see http://www.ladieswholaunch.com/)

My primary responsibility as a (freelance) copy writer is to create communications, either internally or externally, that illuminate and express the identity of a brand's products or services. It is also my job to push the brand/company to distill their message to a degree that a consumer could digest and synthesize pertinent information in a finite amount of time. I lived in New York for many years but base myself out of Los Angeles now and go to New York when necessary.

**What is a typical day at work like?**

Meet with a creative agency about a client. Workshop approaches and ideas about this client (let's say it's the brand Christian Dior). Talk about the "story," which is incredibly important; even though the consumer does not know every detail of a brand's story, the people who tell the story (including creative director, graphic designer, identity people) need to understand down to the last pore who this brand is, and who they are talking to.

Return to office.

Wait for "creative brief," which outlines everything discussed in our meeting, or in other meetings where I was not present (marketing/design, anything.) Ask any outstanding questions to any team member to gain further clarification.

Begin getting inspiration for the project through film (usually old and very stylized) or books, other projects, random ideas. Ideate these in a "downloading" type of fashion before articulation begins.

Start writing.

Distill.

Write.

Distill.

And so forth.

*At what point did you decide to pursue a career in writing for a fashion-related business?*

I had gotten a job working for the model and entrepreneur Christy Turlington, which was my first big exposure into fashion. After being on sets with amazing artists, photographers, stylists, makeup/hair people, I began to understand fashion in a different way. Fashion, to me, is a business. It's style that really interests me more, although I do stay on top of and involved in fashion in order to write to it or about it.

*Describe your first writing job. What was the most important or interesting thing you wrote for that job/publication?*

My first published piece of work was in *New York* magazine on the Style page. I wrote a short piece about a beauty product, which was not that significant, but gave me the confidence to go after articles that I really wanted. My next contribution was to *Contents* magazine (now closed), and because they had so many high-caliber writers, I knew I couldn't get accepted right away. So, I asked my friend Robert F. Kennedy, Jr., if he would make himself available for me to profile him for the magazine, if they accepted my pitch to do a story on him. I called *Contents*' Editor in Chief and said, "Hey, I've got RFK Jr. here—can I write a piece on spec?" They said yes. They loved it. I became a contributing editor and stylist.

*What are you currently reading (books, magazines, Web sites, newspapers, other media)? Do you have a favorite author or publication?*

I read constantly. I always read the *NYT* Thursday and Sunday papers, *The New Yorker*, *New York* magazine, all of the fashion bibles, *Domino*, the Web site Love-Marks.com, various articles I pluck from places like *Harvard Business Review*, or different trend sites. I love information.

*What advice do you have for students interested in a writing career? Do you have any recommendations for students?*

Facing a blank page is the hardest thing. I just interviewed the best-selling author Jackie Collins, and one thing she said about writers is that you need to write about what you know. I agree. I think you can write about what you don't know, but a reader can sense if you're not authentic or not speaking from a place of credibility. You have to just start writing sometimes—and see where it goes. Don't be too intellectual or highbrow about it. One of my favorite writers, Jen Sincero—who writes a column called "Living in Sin" (www.jensincero.com)—is hilarious, unruly, and totally engaging. My writing is very different. But try not to compare voices. Just WRITE and don't talk about writing. Do it.

## REFERENCES

Benbow-Pfalzgraf, T., & Martin, Richard (Eds.). (2002). *Contemporary fashion* (2nd ed.). Farmington Hills, MI: St. James Press.

Best of Paris, Fall 2006. (2006). *Glam.com*. Retrieved March 26, 2006, from http://www.glam.com/g/p/3014655/117567972/5/49757036/2001/32252767/

Brooks, B. S., Kennedy, G., Moen, D. R., & Ranly, D. (2004). *Telling the story: The convergence of print, broadcast and online media*. Boston: Bedford/St. Martin's.

Corcoran, C. T. (2006, February 6). The blogs that took over the tents. *Women's Wear Daily*, p. 30.

Elliott, S. (2006, February 7). Can you TiVo to see just the ads? *New York Times*, p. C3.

Embree, M. (2003). *The author's toolkit: A step-by-step guide to writing and publishing your book*. (Revised ed.). New York: Allworth Press.

Glam Media, Inc. (2007). About us. Retrieved June 18, 2007, from http://www.glam.com/app/site/loadServicePage.act?id=5357927&pageId=5357942

Hall, C. (2007, April 5). The WWD list: Brand power. *Women's Wear Daily*, p. 12.

Harrison, C. H. (2002). *How to write for magazines: Consumers, trade and web*. Boston: Allyn & Bacon.

Ilari, A. (2007, April 23). Prada enhances Web site with artistic feel. *Women's Wear Daily*, p. 2.

Internet Developments. (2004). *World almanac & book of facts*. Retrieved Monday, March 20, 2006, from the Academic Search Premier database.

Laermer, R., & Prichinello, M. (2003). *Full frontal PR: Getting people talking about you, your business, or your product*. Princeton, NJ: Bloomberg Press.

Luman, S. (2006, February 20). Linkology. *New York*. Retrieved February 20, 2006, from http://nymag.com

Press Information. (n.d.). *Salon.Com*. Retrieved June 6, 2005, from http://www.salon.com/press/fact/

Seymour, L. J. (2006, March 3). Postcards from the (cutting) edge. Retrieved March 6, 2006, from http://lifestyle.msn.com/SpecialGuides/IntlFashionWeek/Article.aspx?cp-documentid=242791&GTI=7910

Thompson, C. (2006, February 20). Blogs to riches: The haves and have-nots of the blogging boom. *New York*. Retrieved February 20, 2006, from http://nymag.com

*Part Four*

# OTHER FORMS OF FASHION WRITING

In this last section of *Writing for the Fashion Business*, we discuss other forms of fashion writing. Research is one form of writing that is undertaken in the fashion business. Research is the investigation of a subject in order to understand it in a detailed, accurate manner based on the scientific method. Fashion research covers historic and cultural aspects of dress, anthropology, consumer behavior related to fashion, retailing, textiles, aesthetics and design, fiber arts, merchandising, advertising, social and psychological aspects of dress, and on and on. In order for a researcher to have her or his work published and disseminated to other professionals, that work must be written in an accurate, detailed, systematic manner. We cover scholarly writing in Chapter 9, "Scholarly Writing."

Writing books on fashion is another avenue that may interest readers of this book. This is the topic of Chapter 10, "Writing Books." Enter the word *fashion* as the subject of a book search in Amazon.com and you will likely get over three hundred thousand hits. Those hits can be narrowed to fiction, biographies and memoirs, fashion design, fashion history, and many more topics. People inside and beyond the fashion industry read fashion-related books for entertainment.

Essential elements and techniques of office writing within the business environment are necessary in the fashion industry. Good writers within the corporate environment express themselves clearly and professionally with powerful writing skills. Solid business writing includes proper presentation of letters, memos, reports, proposals, and the like. All these elements are covered in Chapter 11, "Writing Business Communications."

In order to get a job in fashion, you need to prepare a strong résumé, write an effective application letter, and have strong interviewing skills. We discuss this aspect of fashion writing in Chapter 12, "Writing Employment Messages."

# NINE

## *Scholarly Writing*

After you have read this chapter, you should be able to discuss the following:
- The research process
- The written research report

D id you know that retailers can communicate fit through window displays (Sen, Block, & Chandran, 2002)? And speaking of fit, did you know that fashion innovators rely on fit, rather than price, when making fashion purchases (Muzinich, Pecotich, & Putrevu, 2003)? And speaking of price, did you know that researchers are currently working on price optimization systems to price staple and fashion merchandise according to their position on the fashion life cycle, a great help to retailers (Levy, Grewal, Kopalle, & Hess, 2004)? This information is a very small sampling of the research that has been conducted and reported as scholarly writing.

This chapter discusses scholarly writing and examines the three stages of the research process. In the first stage of the process, you formulate the research problem you want to explore, leading you to a review of literature. In the second stage of the research process, you conceptualize the research study, leading you to the development of a research proposal. The last stage of the research process is where data collection and analysis take place. It is not until this stage that the research report is actually written. We'll finish the chapter with a discussion specifically about writing the research report.

**Scholarly** or **academic writing** means writing a research report to detail the findings and implications of a research study. As noted above, writing the research report takes place in the final stage in the research process. In your research report, you'll be able to share with others the quality and amount of work you put into all the stages of your research study. Obviously, after all this work, it is critical that the report be well written (Kumar, 2005).

Scholarly writing may take the form of a research proposal, a thesis, a dissertation, a presentation at a conference, a journal article, or an abstract.

- A **research proposal** is the conceptualization of the total research process that you propose to undertake (Kumar, 2005). You write the proposal and submit it to your academic supervisor or the sponsor of contractual research before you conduct the actual study.

- A **thesis** is a written document representing and reporting original research. Researching and writing a thesis is one of the requirements for earning a master's degree; it is conducted and written from an approved research proposal.

- A **dissertation** is also a written document representing and reporting original research. Researching and writing a dissertation is one of the requirements for earning a doctorate degree; it is conducted and written from an approved research proposal.

- Many researchers present their research findings at regional, national, or international conferences sponsored by organizations within academic disciplines. These are termed **paper presentations**. Two fashion-related organizations where papers may be presented are the International Textile and Apparel Association (ITAA) and the American Collegiate Retailing Association (ACRA). ITAA meets once a year and offers opportunities for graduate students and academic faculty to present research. Research from this organization is available through the organization Web site at www.itaaonline.org. ACRA meets twice a year; the winter conference is always held in New York City to coincide with the National Retail Federation meeting. Additionally, this organization holds a spring conference. Faculty are encouraged to present their research during these conferences, and the papers are distributed to members on CD-ROM.

- Submitting a research report to a scholarly journal, in the form of a **journal article**, is a permanent way to disseminate your findings and ideas (Leedy &

Ormrod, 2005). The audiences for scholarly journals are other researchers and professionals. Figure 9.1 is a listing of journals where fashion articles may be published. Scholarly journals contain articles covering research projects, methodology, and theory.

- Some journals and organizations ask authors to submit a summary of the article or research study before submitting the final paper. Such a summary is called an **abstract.**

International Journal of Consumer Studies

International Journal of Retail and Distribution Management

Journal of Consumer Marketing

Journal of Family and Consumer Science

Journal of Fashion Marketing and Management

Journal of Leisure Marketing

Journal of Retailing

Journal of Retailing and Consumer Services

Journal of Shopping Center Research

Journal of Travel and Tourism Marketing

Journal of Travel Research

Psychology and Marketing

Textile and Clothing Research Journal

Tourism Management

FIGURE 9.1. Journals where fashion articles may be published.

---

**BOX 9.1 PEER REVIEW PROCESS**

Accountability is very important in scholarly journals. Articles in these journals have been peer-reviewed, and they include reference lists that identify works used by the researcher from other authors who have provided relevant background information. For a manuscript to be **peer-reviewed** or **refereed** means that members of a review board who are experts in the field examine the manuscript before the article is accepted for publication. A manuscript may be accepted for publication, returned to the author to be revised and resubmitted, or rejected. The reviews are often intentionally anonymous, in which case the review is termed a **blind review**.

---

*Portfolio Exercise:* **Find and read a research article from an academic journal. After you have read the article, answer the following questions and be ready to discuss your article and answers in class.**

1. **Where did you find the article?**
2. **What was the topic of the article? What problem was the researcher trying to solve?**
3. **What topics or themes were discussed in the review of literature?**
4. **Describe how the researcher conducted the study. Who was the sample? How were data collected? What statistics were used? Do you have questions after reading this section?**
5. **Read the conclusion. Write one or more paragraphs interpreting the information. What stood out to you as important, and why? How is this research of benefit to professionals in the fashion industry?**

---

According to Kumar (2005), the difference between other types of writing and research writing is the "degree of control, rigorousness and caution required" (p. 266). Research writing is controlled through extremely careful writing, word choice, ideas expressed, and validity and verifiability of the conclusions that are drawn. Rigor involves writing that is absolutely accurate, clear, concise, and free of ambiguity or bias. As with other types of writing, quality is based on strong written communication skills, clear and concise thoughts, the ability to express ideas in a logical and sequential manner, and a good working knowledge of the subject matter (Kumar).

# THE RESEARCH PROCESS

In order to write a research report, it is necessary to understand the research process. **Research** is "the systematic investigation of a subject aimed at uncovering new information (discovering data) and/or interpreting relations among a subject's parts (theorizing)" (Vogt, 1999, p. 246). Conducting research means to become involved in a process that requires you to think critically, evaluating and interpreting ideas explored in other sources to formulate your own ideas (Kirszner & Mandell, 2005). In broad terms, research methodology can be defined as quantitative or qualitative. **Quantitative research** provides a numerical description of trends, attitudes, or opinions of a population, obtained by studying a sample of that population (Creswell, 2003). **Qualitative research** focuses on **phenomena** (observable facts or events) that occur in natural settings; this research involves studying the phenomena in all their complexity (Leedy & Ormrod, 2005).

Kumar (2005) divides the research process into three stages, with multiple steps within each stage (see Figure 9.2):

1. In the initial stage of the research process, the researcher determines a topic and produces a working bibliography and a review of literature. This stage is the *What* stage, where the researcher decides *what* to study.

2. The middle stage of the research process is the *How* stage. During this stage, the researcher plans *how* to conduct the study. This stage includes developing the research design, constructing an instrument for data collection, selecting a sample, and producing the research proposal.

3. In the final stage of the research process, the *Doing* stage, the researcher collects, processes, and analyzes data and, produces the research report.

## FORMULATING THE RESEARCH PROBLEM

Choosing a research topic may be the most difficult part of the entire research process. Your instructor may offer suggestions for research, or he or she may prefer that

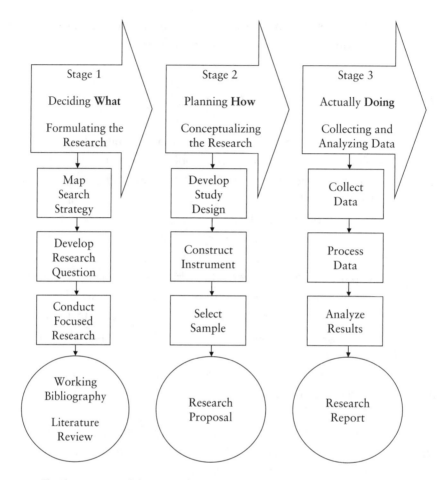

**FIGURE 9.2.** The three stages of the research process. Adapted from Kumar, R. (2005). *Research methodology* (2nd ed.). London: Sage Publications.

you select a topic on your own. If you select your own topic, you should consider a topic that you are genuinely interested in that will keep your interest during the research and writing processes. Your topic should be neither too broad nor too narrow. "What influenced the need for fashion photography?" may be too broad and vague to be adequately covered in a research study, while "The influence of the shrug in children's wear" may be too narrow to develop into a research study. Additionally, when you are choosing a topic, you should be sure that there is adequate information available about the topic from academic journals and other credible, verifiable sources.

## Map Out a Search Strategy

Once you have settled on a topic, the next step in the research process is mapping out a search strategy. A **search strategy** is the process you will use to locate and evaluate source material (Kirszner & Mandell, 2005). Figure 9.3 illustrates the search strategy. The process begins with **discovery research**, looking for general references that give you a broad overview of the topic. The process progresses to **focused research**, which includes consulting other scholarly writing, specialized reference works, and books that relate to your topic. The references that are used in the final research report will be listed in a bibliography. Refer to Appendix D, "Evaluating Resources on the Web," for information on locating and evaluating sources through the Internet.

---

*Portfolio Exercise:* **Select a research topic that interests you and map out a search strategy for the topic. Be specific in identifying academic journals and other references that will assist you in writing about the topic.**

---

## Develop the Research Question

The goal of exploratory research is to develop a research question. A **research question** is the problem to be investigated in a study, stated in question format (Vogt, 1999). Examples of research questions include the following:

- What are the online buying patterns of adolescent girls?
- Can networking strategies help small apparel retailers?
- Are vitamins and minerals beneficial in skin care products?

The focus of the research study will be to answer the research question. Formulating the research question enables you to determine which sources will be helpful and should be examined in depth, and which sources should be eliminated as you plan the research proposal.

Some studies include hypotheses. A **hypothesis** is a logical supposition or reasonable guess that provides a tentative explanation for a phenomenon under investigation (Leedy & Ormrod, 2005). If a research question asks, "What is the relationship

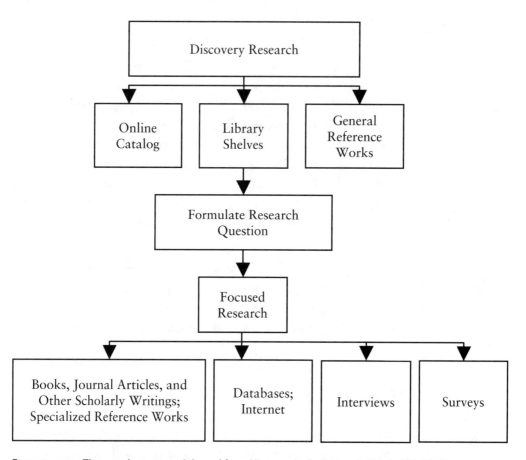

**FIGURE 9.3.** The search strategy. Adapted from Kirszner, L. G., & Mandell, S. R. (2005). *The Wadsworth handbook* [Instructor's Edition]. Boston: Thomson Wadsworth.

between A and B?," a research hypothesis might tentatively explain that "Increases in A lower the incidence of B" (Vogt, 1999, p. 247).

## Conduct Focused Research

Once you have determined the research question, you can begin to do more **focused research,** looking for specific details to help develop and support your research study. Details may include information to more fully explain the problem you intend to solve with your research or to support your research question when you are writing a review of literature. Details may also include identifying specific variables, research designs, research instruments, or statistical procedures.

## Assemble a Working Bibliography

As part of the research process, you need to collect journal articles and other scholarly research that will help you formulate your own research ideas. As you read journal articles, abstracts, books, or other works that you believe are helpful, you need to take accurate notes from these sources (see Appendix B, "Documentation Formats"), or photocopy or print important information from the source and record complete and accurate bibliographic information. A **bibliography** is an alphabetized list of all the sources you used when conducting your research. Each entry in a bibliography is

---

**BOX 9.2 INDEXING REFERENCES**

A big challenge of collecting sources is determining a retrieval system. It is not enough to find a relevant article; you must also be able to retrieve it later when you are writing a review of literature or developing your methodology.

Some researchers choose to index articles by key words. To use this method, you write key words at the top of each article and also index the key words in a separate file. File the article under one primary key word. When you want to retrieve an article, you consult the key word index, and then go to the primary key word topic in your files to find relevant articles. This method works best if your subject can be easily categorized into relevant topics. With this method, articles will have multiple listings based on multiple key words or topics, but you file them under only one key word.

Other researchers file articles alphabetically by author's last name. This method works when the volume of information becomes too large to manage efficiently by topic, or when the topics are too broad and shallow for efficient indexing. Whatever method you choose, make sure that it makes sense to you. You don't want to waste valuable time looking for an article you already have or photocopying or printing the same article numerous times.

written in full citation format (refer to Appendix B for documentation format). Keep the bibliography as a separate file on your computer, so you can easily add each new reference as you locate and determine its usefulness.

## Write the Review of Literature

Research proposals, research reports, theses, and dissertations always include a section or chapter that reviews related literature; this section is termed the **review of literature**. The review of literature is a discussion of other studies, research reports, and scholarly writings that have direct relevance to your own study (Leedy & Ormrod, 2005). It is an essential tool in the research process. Kumar (2005) states several functions of the review of literature:

- Provides a theoretical framework for your study
- Reviews the means by which you establish links between what you are proposing to examine and what has already been studied, to help you refine your research methodology
- Allows you to show how your findings have contributed to the existing body of knowledge in your profession
- Enables you to contextualize your findings

The two broad functions of the review of literature are (1) to provide a theoretical background to your study and (2) to enable you to contextualize your finding in relation to the existing body of knowledge and refine your methodology (Kumar, 2005). Your review of literature will reflect these functions. Before you write the review of literature, you should identify key words or issues that have emerged from the work of others. These issues may provide subheadings within the review of literature that will help you outline and organize the information. As part of the review of literature, you should develop a theoretical framework. The **theoretical framework** is the main theme or theory that your research will be built on. You may identify and include more than one theme or theory if they are relevant to your study. The framework highlights agreements and disagreements among other authors, and it identifies unanswered questions or gaps in the literature (Kumar, 2005).

A **theory** is a statement or group of statements about how some part of the world works, often explaining relationships among phenomena (Vogt, 1999). For example, fashion adoption is made up of fashion theories (downward-flow, upward-flow, or horizontal-flow) that explain how fashion is diffused from fashion leaders to fashion followers.

In the review of literature, give each theory a subheading and describe it according to its relevance to your study. When writing about the theoretical background, you should list previously identified themes and give each a subheading. Under each subheading, include a description of the theme, arguments for and against the theme as reported by other researchers, and gaps and issues relative to the theme. When writing about the context of your findings, systematically compare your findings with the findings of others. Again, start with meaningful subheadings, and then write by summarizing, paraphrasing, or quoting from others' studies to confirm, contradict, or add to the existing literature.

Similarly, if you will be analyzing several variables or attributes in the study—such as age, education, satisfaction, or effectiveness—each of these variables should have a subheading in the review of literature and should be discussed thoroughly in relation to the proposed study. Additionally, throughout the review of literature, systematically include the findings of others so that when you write about your findings and conclusions, you can confirm or contrast your findings to those of others.

The review of literature is ongoing. It begins when you find the first article relevant to your topic, and it concludes when you complete the research proposal or report. The review of literature contributes to every step of the research process—from helping you formulate your research question, to establishing theoretical roots of your study, to helping integrate your findings and conclusions with the existing body of knowledge. Leedy and Ormrod (2005) suggest the following guidelines to write a clear and cohesive literature review:

1. Be clear in your thinking about what a review of literature is. It may help you to think of the review of literature as a discussion with the reader about what others have to say about your topic.

2. Have a plan. Before you begin writing, prepare an outline. Start by writing your problem at the top of the page, and then develop each theme as a major point in the outline. For each major point, you should identify relevant research articles; include correct citations for development of the bibliography. The outline and subsequent review of

literature should begin from a wide-ranging point of view and move to more specific ideas that focus in on your study.

3. Emphasize relatedness. The literature review is not just a chain of isolated summaries; rather, it is a discussion that constantly lets the reader know how the literature from others directly relates to your topic. If you cannot show a relationship between a study and your own work, you should not use the study in your review of literature.

4. Always give credit to another author whose ideas you are using. Footnotes or parenthetical citations are acceptable ways to give credit. Not giving credit where credit is due results in plagiarism.

5. Review the literature, do not reproduce it. What others have to say about the topic is important; however, what you have to say is more important.

6. End the review of literature with a summary. Summarize all that has been said and describe its importance in terms of your research problem.

7. Realize that you will edit and rewrite the review of literature numerous times before it is complete.

8. Ask others for feedback.

---

*Portfolio Exercise:* **Once you have selected a research topic, write a review of literature for the topic. To begin, write your research question at the top of the page. Then list important themes as subheadings, developing an outline. Continue writing by filling in under the subheadings. As you write, make sure that you accurately document others' research using a style guide such as the *MLA Handbook for Writers of Research Papers* or the *Publication Manual of the American Psychological Association.***

---

## CONCEPTUALIZE THE RESEARCH STUDY

Twice a year, prominent fashion designers present their latest collections at New York Fashion Week. Presenting the collection is the culmination of many months of planning and organization. Each collection requires conceptualization of the overall line and development of detailed garment specifications before actual production takes place. Planning a research study is similar to planning a collection. Before the study can be conducted, it must be completely thought through and meticulously detailed.

Certain features are common to all research projects and should serve as guidelines as you conceptualize your research study (Leedy & Ormrod, 2005):

- **Universality**—The research study should be able to be carried out by any competent person. As the researcher you collect, organize, and report your findings, but any other individual who is equally capable should also be able to carry out the study.
- **Replication**—The research should be repeatable with similar results.
- **Control**—In order to be able to replicate a study, you must isolate or control factors that are central to the research problem. Control is particularly difficult in fields like fashion where people and circumstances are always changing.
- **Measurement**—The data should be able to be measured in some way.

Concept and details are shaped during the middle stage of the research process. At this stage, the researcher determines *how* to find answers to the research question. The planning of procedures for conducting studies is termed **research design** (Vogt, 1999). Research design is the blueprint for how the research study will be completed. It provides all the details that you, your supervisor, and other readers will need to know about the procedures you plan to use and the tasks you are going to perform to obtain answers to your research question. Good research design ensures that procedures are adequate to obtain valid, objective, and accurate answers to the research question.

## CHECKLIST FOR RESEARCH DESIGN

According to Kumar (2005), a research design should do certain things. Consider these points as you do your own research. This chapter examines them in detail:

- ☐ Name the study design.
- ☐ Detail who will make up the study population and how they will be identified.
- ☐ Detail how the sample will be selected, contacted, and their consent given.
- ☐ Detail the method for data collection and explain why.
- ☐ Ensure that ethical procedures are in place.

## Develop a Study Design

**Study design** is the basic structure of the study. Study designs are commonly classified by the number of contacts with the study population, the reference of the study, or the nature of the investigation. For example, you may want to survey a group of people about your topic. If you contact this group once, the type of study design is a **cross-sectional study** in which data are gathered at one point in time from a cross-section of the population to find out about an issue or a problem. If you want to contact this group of people more than once, the study design is a **longitudinal study** and is used to determine a pattern of change in relation to time.

Study design can also be based on a reference period. **Historical research** concentrates on the meanings of events and is an example of research based on a reference period. In fashion, much historical research has been conducted on textiles, silhouettes, garments, or products of a certain time period.

The third type of study design centers on the nature of the investigation. For example, you may want to determine the cause-and-effect relationship between two variables. If the two variables can be studied in the laboratory, such as the effects of sunlight on cotton, the study design is **experimental design**, in which the researcher considers many possible causes that might affect an outcome. If the two variables can be studied in a natural setting, the study design is **quasi-experimental**. One study example at the beginning of this chapter discusses window display and fit. This is an example of a quasi-experimental design. There are many other types of study designs that are beyond this scope of this chapter. You may need to refer to a research methodology book to provide you with adequate information to help you design your study. A variety of research methodology books are listed as additional resources and references at the conclusion of this chapter.

## Construct an Instrument for Data Collection

Once you have designed the study, next you must think about how to collect the data. There are two types of data you can use: primary data and secondary data. **Secondary data** is information collected by others that you extract for research purposes. Census data is an example of secondary data. The U.S. government has collected the data, but you might extract certain information for your own study. Cotton Incorporated®

regularly collects secondary data and reports its findings through the Lifestyle Monitor™ and publishes this research in *Women's Wear Daily* and other sources.

**Primary data** is information that you collect yourself for purposes of your study. This primary data can be collected through observation, interviews, or questionnaires. **Observation** is a systematic, selective way of watching or listening to an interaction (Kumar, 2005). A common observation method in fashion is the fashion count. A **fashion count** is an organized plan for counting and classifying apparel components, used to forecast fashion trends. The components can be viewed on consumers or in fashion magazines and then summed up to do a quantitative analysis of current trends. A leading observation researcher in the field of shopping is Paco Underhill, founder and managing director of Envirosell. He has written about his observations in two books: *Why We Buy: The Science of Shopping* (Simon & Schuster, 2000) and *Call of the Mall* (Simon & Schuster, 2000).

Another type of data collection is an **interview**, which is a person-to-person interaction with a specific purpose. In-depth interviews and focus groups are types of interviews. **In-depth interviews** are repeated interviews with a participant to learn about a topic in detail. **Focus groups** are planned discussions with six to twelve participants to learn people's perceptions about a topic in a nonthreatening environment.

**Questionnaires** are lists of questions on which respondents record their answers. As data collection instruments, questionnaires differ from interviews in that you generally are not present to answer participants' questions during questionnaire data collection as you would be during an interview.

Once an instrument has been developed, a **pilot study** must be conducted. A pilot study is like a dress rehearsal in which you test the procedure to discover problems before the study begins. Based on what you learn from the pilot study, you can modify the research design to improve the overall study.

Data collection instruments must be valid and reliable. **Validity** means the instrument measures what it is supposed to measure (Vogt, 1999). **Reliability** means the instrument is consistent in what it measures. When measurements of the same thing are repeated, they should give very similar results if they are valid and reliable. Validity and reliability control (1) the extent to which you can learn something about the topic you are researching, (2) the probability of obtaining statistical significance in your data collection, and (3) the degree to which you can draw meaningful conclusions from your data (Leedy & Ormrod, 2005).

Again, there are too many details about instrument design to discuss here. A research methodology book can provide adequate information to help you with your study.

---

*Portfolio Exercise:* **Once you have selected a research topic, do one of the following: Conduct a fashion count, develop interview questions, or write a questionnaire that will help answer questions about your research topic.**

---

## Select a Sample

After you have designed an instrument for data collection, it is necessary to determine who or what you are going to collect the data from. **Sampling** is the process of selecting a few (a sample) from a bigger population to become the estimate for predication of an unknown piece of information. The way you select your sample will influence the accuracy of your findings. According to Kumar (2005), "the basic objective of any sampling design is to minimize, within the limitation of the cost, the gap between the values obtained from your sample and those prevalent in the population" (p. 23). The goal is to select a sample that is representative of the population at large.

Two types of samples are evident in research: probability samples and nonprobability samples. **Nonprobability samples** are samples in which every person or every item does not have the same chance of being selected. For example, if you take a random survey of students in your class, only those students who are in class on that day will be sampled, excluding all students who were not in class that day. Nonprobability samples are good for exploring a topic prior to developing a research question. **Probability samples** are samples in which every person or every item has the same likelihood of being chosen. Probability samples are preferred if the researcher wants to use inferential statistics during data analysis. Research methodology books can give you a full explanation of sampling theory to assure accuracy for your study.

## Write a Research Proposal

At this point you are ready to write your research proposal. Proposals follow a simple, logical format, telling the reader exactly what you intend to do in your study.

1. The problem and its setting
    a. Statement of problem
    b. Hypotheses
    c. Limitations of the study
    d. Definition of terms
    e. Importance of the study
2. Review of related literature
3. Data and treatment of data
    a. Study design
    b. Data collection
    c. Sample
4. Qualifications of researcher
5. Outline of proposed study
    a. Steps to be taken
    b. Timeline
6. References
7. Appendices

**FIGURE** 9.4. Example of an outline for a quantitative research proposal. Adapted from Leedy, P. D., & Ormrod, J. E. (2005). *Practical research* (8th ed.). Upper Saddle River, NJ: Merrill Prentice Hall.

Figure 9.4 is an example of an outline for a quantitative research proposal. Figure 9.5 is an example of an outline for a qualitative research proposal. The proposal is written to demonstrate that you are able to think clearly about the research study you plan to undertake. Strong proposals are written with a clear focus, they are well-organized, and they include details essential to understanding the study. Nonessential information, or "creative writing," is not part of the proposal. Thoughts are expressed in simple sentences and paragraph form, using precise word choice and headings and subheadings to guide the reader to the next major point.

*Portfolio Exercise:* **Write a research proposal based on your research topic and review of literature. You may have to review a research methodology book to determine details about research design, data collection, and sampling.**

1. Introduction
   a. Background for the study
   b. Purpose of study
   c. Guiding questions
   d. Limitations
   e. Significance of study
2. Methodology
   a. Theoretical framework
   b. Type of design
   c. Role of researcher
   d. Selection and description of site and participants
   e. Data collection strategies
   f. Data analysis strategies
   g. Methods for achieving validity
3. Findings
   a. Relationship to literature
   b. Relationship to theory
4. Management plan
   a. Feasibility
   b. Timeline
5. References
6. Appendices

FIGURE 9.5. Example of an outline for a qualitative research proposal. Adapted from Leedy, P. D., & Ormrod, J. E. (2005). *Practical research* (8th ed.). Upper Saddle River, NJ: Merrill Prentice Hall.

# DATA COLLECTION AND ANALYSIS

Your research proposal has been accepted. Now you are ready for the final stage in the research process: the *Doing* stage. As the researcher, you collect, process, and analyze data and produce the research report.

## Collect the Data

Collecting data is just that: actually collecting the data. It is critical to a research study and must be done following ethical principles of conduct. Before asking a respondent to answer questions through an interview, a questionnaire, or some other means of data collection, you must obtain the respondent's **informed consent**. This means that the respondent has been told the nature of the study and has been given the choice to participate or not participate.

Researchers should not expose participants to undue physical or psychological harm. In general, the risks of participating in a research study should be no greater than risks associated with day-to-day living. Participants should not be subjected to abnormal stress, embarrassment, or loss of self-esteem. In studies where it has been determined that physical or psychological risk may occur, participants should be fully informed beforehand and should be allowed to stop participating at any time during the research study. Additionally, respondents should be offered counseling or debriefing immediately following the study.

Participants also have the right to privacy. Confidentiality of respondents' answers should be maintained at all times. When possible, participants' responses should be anonymous. When that is not possible, respondents' responses should not be presented in oral or written form that would in any way disclose who the specific respondent is.

Colleges, universities, and research institutions have **Internal Review Boards (IRB)** to evaluate all proposals that involve collecting data from human subjects. These boards make sure that no unnecessary harm is inflicted on potential participants. Any student conducting research on human subjects for theses, dissertations, or other research projects must have approval from her university's IRB at the proposal stage, before any research is conducted.

## Process the Data

Once data have been collected, the researcher needs to process the data so that the findings can be interpreted and reported. Processing data includes reviewing completed research instruments to identify and minimize errors, incompleteness, misclassification, and gaps in the information obtained from the respondents (Kumar, 2005). In-depth discussion of data processing is beyond the scope of this book. A basic research methodology book can help you in this step of the research process.

## Analyze the Data

Data can be analyzed manually or by computer. If the number of respondents is small and the number of variables is limited, then the researcher may decide to manually compute the results. Realize that even a small sample with minimum variables may be time-consuming to calculate manually. If the sample is large or the variables are complex, you can use computer programs such as Microsoft® Excel or Statistical Package for the Social Sciences (SPSS) to analyze the data and compute the statistics.

When you are analyzing data, statistics serve two major functions. First, statistics describe what the data look like—for example, where the midpoint is or how spread the data are (Leedy & Ormrod, 2005). These are called **descriptive statistics**. Second, statistics can allow the researcher to make inferences about larger populations by collecting data on smaller samples; this is known as **inferential statistics**. Many different types of statistics can be computed to understand data. Refer to a general statistics textbook for help in understanding the type of statistics you should run to interpret your data correctly.

As part of data analysis, you should determine the best way to present the data so that your findings can be effectively understood by the reader. Tables are a common method used to describe data in scholarly writing. **Tables** present data in columns and rows. Data that are presented in any form other than a table are presented as a figure. **Figures** are graphical representations of data and include pie charts, bar charts, flow charts, illustrations, maps, photographs, or other pictorial representations of the data. Consult your style guide (APA, MLA, or others) for proper formatting of tables and figures. Formatting of tables and figures for business presentations is discussed in Chapter 11.

## Write the Research Report

The last step in the research process is writing the research report. According to Leedy and Ormrod (2005), a research report should achieve four objectives:

- Give the reader a clear understanding of the research problem and why it justified an in-depth investigation.
- Describe exactly how data were collected in an attempt to resolve the problem.
- Present the data completely and precisely. The data presented in the report should substantiate all the interpretations and conclusions included in the report.
- Interpret the data for the reader, and demonstrate exactly how the data resolve the research problem.

The research report is a straightforward document that tells the reader clearly and precisely what the researcher has done to solve the research problem. Similar to a research proposal, it is factual, logical, and comprehensive and is not a work of "creative writing." The following section will explain the components of the written research report in detail.

# COMPONENTS OF THE WRITTEN REPORT

Figure 9.6 is an example of an academic journal article. This article is the written result of a study conducted to investigate fashion innovativeness among adolescents. The article will be used to illustrate written components of a research report.

Just as with other types of writing, it is good to start writing a research report by developing an outline. In research reporting this is called chapterization (Kumar, 2005). During this process you decide how to divide your report into chapters and what content will be included in each chapter. For example, a traditional quantitative study would generally have five sections or chapters:

Chapter I: Introduction
Chapter II: Review of Literature
Chapter III: Method
Chapter IV: Results and Discussion
Chapter V: Summary, Conclusions, and Recommendations

Journal editors may refer to these chapters as headings that will appear in the published paper. Most journals have published guidelines for authors, and common headings are included in the author guidelines; or you can determine them by reviewing an article published in the journal. For example, the *Journal of Fashion Marketing and Management* requires that an author address the following headings when submitting an abstract to the publisher:

- Purpose of the paper
- Design/methodology/approach
- Findings
- Research limitations/implications (if applicable)
- Practical implications (if applicable)
- What is original to/value of paper

The Emerald Research Register for this journal is available at
http://www.emeraldinsight.com/researchregister

The current issue and full text archive of this journal is available at
http://www.emeraldinsight.com/1361-2026.htm

ACADEMIC PAPER

# Fashion innovativeness, fashion diffusion and brand sensitivity among adolescents

Pierre Beaudoin
*Consumer Sciences Programme, Laval University, Québec, Canada*
Marie J. Lachance and Jean Robitaille
*Department of Agricultural Economics and Consumer Sciences,
Laval University, Québec, Canada*

**Keywords** Young people, Fashion, Product innovation, Consumer behaviour,
Brand awareness

**Abstract** *Using Rogers' theory of diffusion of innovation, this paper reports the results of a study that had two objectives: the first objective was to compare the number of male and female adolescents in each of Rogers' five categories of consumer adopters. The second, was to verify if there were differences among the five distinct categories of adopters with respect to brand sensitivity. Results show that, as with other market segments, there are more female than male adolescents in the categories "innovators" and "early adopters", and more male than female adolescents in the categories "late majority" and "laggards". Further, it appears that brand sensitivity is an increasing function of fashion "adoptiveness" among adolescents.*

## Introduction

Even if, in the fashion history, men have played a significant role as fashion creators, fashion consumption has generally been associated with women. In most societies, women are more expected than men to be concerned with beauty, appearance and fashion (Kaiser, 1990). As a result, taking care of their image is becoming a kind of second nature or a "natural duty" for most females (Paoletti and Kregloh, 1989). Men, on the other hand, were rather regarded suspiciously if they seemed to attach too much importance to their looks or to fashion in general (Kaiser, 1990). Not surprisingly, past research has consistently found that there were more female fashion innovators than males. However, the large majority of researchers that have investigated fashion innovativeness in the past used respondents over 20 years of age in their sample. In fact, we could not find any research that studied fashion innovativeness and fashion diffusion with a sample strictly composed of adolescents. This is surprising since, of all social groups, adolescents are those that attach the most importance to fashion and beauty in general (Francis and Liu, 1990; Koester and May, 1985; Ossorio, 1995), it is also well-established that it is among young fashion consumers that we usually find the majority of fashion innovators (Beaudoin *et al.*, 1998; Goldsmith *et al.*, 1991; Gutman and Mills, 1982; Horridge and Richards, 1984).

Emerald

Journal of Fashion Marketing and
Management
Vol. 7 No. 1, 2003
pp. 23-30
© MCB UP Limited
1361-2026
DOI 10.1108/13612020310464340

FIGURE 9.6. Example of an academic journal article. *Source:* Beaudoin, P., Lachance, M J., & Robitaille, J. (2003). Fashion innovativeness, fashion diffusion and brand sensitivity among adolescents. *Journal of Fashion Marketing and Management, 7,* 23–30. *(continued)*

JFMM
7,1

24

Nowadays, male adolescents are increasingly taking care of their looks and do not seem to give the impression of being afraid of projecting this fashion image that used to be so "risky" for males of past generations. They also seem to be more creative in developing their own fashion style leading one to believe that males are now playing a more significant role than they used to have in the process of fashion diffusion.

*Adolescents and brand sensitivity*

In the last few years, adolescents' interest in fashion brand names has increased to the extent that even criminal acts associated with this infatuation have been reported (O'Neil, 1998). However, this growing interest, which has been increasingly discussed by parents, teachers and mass media, has not received much attention from academic researchers.

During adolescence, peers are seen as being an important source of influence on clothing purchases (Shim and Koh, 1997) and brands (Kaiser, 1990). In this context, and since brand names seem so popular for adolescents, it is highly possible that adolescents acting as models for later adopters in the process of fashion diffusion – those who are the first to buy and adopt new clothing products and fashion tendencies – should also be more brand sensitive.

The first purpose of the study was to assess the representation of male and female adolescents in the different categories of adopters in the process of fashion diffusion. More specifically, we wanted to verify whether significant differences exist between the number of males and females in each of the five categories of consumer adopters given by Rogers (1983) in his well-known model of diffusion of innovation, namely:

(1) innovators;

(2) early adopters;

(3) early majority;

(4) late majority; and

(5) laggards.

The second purpose of the study was to evaluate whether there are differences among categories of adopters with respect to the level of brand sensitivity. In other words, are adolescents who share greater interest in fashion also more likely to be brand sensitive?

**Methodology**

This research was conducted during the spring of 2000 with a convenience sample of 1,034 high school students aged between 12 and 17 years. The adolescents came from three secondary schools in the Quebec city area. Respondents had to complete a self-administered questionnaire, which included 89 items intended to measure several distinct constructs, such as:

FIGURE 9.6. *(continued)*

- brand sensitivity;
- perceived clothing deprivation;
- innovativeness level; and
- consumer competence, to name but a few.

The different scales were validated during a pilot study.

For the purposes of this study, and in order to respond to our specific research questions, the only measures needed were the ones purporting to innovativeness to determine the five different categories of fashion adopters and the measure of brand sensitivity. These two instruments are described below.

*Measure of brand sensitivity*
Brand sensitivity is a psychological construct that refers to a buyer's decision-making process (Kapferer, 1992). The author explains that an individual is brand sensitive if the brand plays a significant role in the psychological process that precedes his/her purchase. Kapferer and Laurent (1983) developed a short instrument comprising seven items to measure brand sensitivity. One of the questions asks the respondent to rank from one to five, the importance of the five following criteria:

(1)  colour;
(2)  price;
(3)  motif;
(4)  fabric; and
(5)  brand.

The rest of the instrument comprises of six Likert-type items. One reads: "When I buy a clothing product, I prefer to buy well-know brands." Hence, scores on this scale could range from 7 to 35, where higher scores reflect higher brand sensitivity.

*Measure of fashion innovativeness*
Fashion innovativeness was measured by the six-item domain specific innovativeness scale (DSI) (Goldsmith and Hofacker, 1991). This scale which contains six summated rating scale items, has been evaluated by its authors for:

(1)  dimensionality;
(2)  reliability;
(3)  convergent and discriminant validity;
(4)  nomological validity;
(5)  criterion validity; and
(6)  freedom from social desirability.

FIGURE 9.6.  *(continued)*

JFMM
7,1

26

Results of these tests showed that the scale was a unidimensional measure with high reliability and possessed a very good validity of all types (Beaudoin *et al.*, 1998; Flynn and Goldsmith, 1993; Goldmith and Flynn, 1992; Uray and Dedeoglu, 1997). One item reads: "Compared with my friends, I own few new fashion items." Scores to the DSI range from 6 to 30 and higher scores indicate greater fashion innovativeness.

*Classification of fashion adopters*
Using Rogers' theory of diffusion of innovation and its adopters classification (Rogers, 1983), the sample of adolescents was divided into five different categories namely:

(1)    innovators;

(2)    early adopters;

(3)    early majority;

(4)    late majority; and

(5)    laggards.

In order to divide the sample into five different categories of fashion adopters, and considering that we wanted to retrieve the closest percentages of adopters per category to those in the Rogers model, we examined the distribution of the scores on the DSI and identified natural breaks in the data to determine each range of scores that best fits the theoretical percentages given in the Rogers model. For instance, Rogers evaluates that about 2.5 per cent of consumers are fashion innovators. In our sample, 14 respondents (1.4 per cent) had a score between 28 and 30, and 35 (3.4 per cent) between 27 and 30. Since the latter range of scores represents the closest percentage to the one of the Rogers model (2.5 per cent), respondents that had a score of 27 and higher on the DSI were chosen to represent the group of fashion innovators. The exact same procedure was used to determine the other four categories of adopters. Table I describes the slight differences between the theoretical percentages of adopters per category (Rogers model) and the ones that resulted from our classification based on the sample distribution on the DSI. Needless to say, we could hardly

| Category of adopters | Theoretical percentage of adopters by category (Rogers) | Percentage of adopters by category (sample) | *n* | Score ranges on the DSI[a] |
|---|---|---|---|---|
| Innovators | 2.5 | 3.42 | 35 | 27-30 |
| Early adopters | 13.5 | 15.47 | 158 | 23-26 |
| Early majority | 34.0 | 30.16 | 308 | 19-22 |
| Late majority | 34.0 | 32.71 | 334 | 15-18 |
| Laggards | 16.0 | 18.21 | 186 | 06-14 |
| | | | 1,021 | |

**Table I.**
Comparison between percentages of adopters per category according to the Rogers model and the ones based on the scores distribution on the DSI[a]

**Note:** [a] Scores to the DSI range from 6 to 30

FIGURE 9.6. *(continued)*

divide the sample by using the very same percentages given in the Rogers model because many respondents with the same scores to the DSI would have been placed in different categories of adopters.

### Analysis of data
*Sample*
A total of 1,034 questionnaires were completed. However, 13 were unusable for a variety of reasons. This left 1,021 questionnaires completed by adolescents ranging mostly from 12 to 17 years of age (only three respondents were 18 years old).

To answer our first research question, simple Pearson's chi-square tests were used to verify if there were differences between the number of male and female adolescents in each of the five categories of adopters (Table II).

As shown in Table II, in the group of "fashion innovators", there are about three times more females than males, and in the group of "early adopters" almost two times more females than males. These differences are both significant. As a result, and obviously, males are significantly more represented than females in the last two categories (i.e. "late majority" and "laggards").

To answer our second research question, a one-way analysis of variance was performed in order to determine if there were a significant relationship between the type of fashion adopters and their degree of brand sensitivity. This Analysis of Variance was found to be statistically significant, $F(4, 1016) = 24.39$, $p < 0.001$, $\eta^2 = 0.09$. Accordingly, pairwise multiple comparisons were used to compare means on brand sensitivity for the five types of fashion adopters. In total, ten comparisons were conduced. Since Levene's $F$ test permitted to confirm that the error variance of the dependent variable was equal (i.e. homogenous) across the five groups of fashion adopters (i.e. $F(4, 1016) = 0.338$, $p = 0.853$), Tukey's method for multiple comparisons was employed to perform the *post-hoc* analysis in conjunction with Holm's sequential Bonferroni method to control for type I error across multiple hypothesis tests. Results of this analysis are reported in Table III.

From the results reported in Table III, it is interesting to note that brand sensitivity clearly appears to be related to the type of fashion adopters.

| | Gender | | |
| --- | --- | --- | --- |
| | Male | Female | Chi-square |
| Innovators | 6 (17.1%) | 29 (82.9%) | 15.11*** |
| Early adopters | 54 (34.4%) | 103 (65.6%) | 15.29*** |
| Early majority | 139 (46.3%) | 161 (53.71%) | 1.613 |
| Late majority | 184 (55.9%) | 145 (44.1%) | 4.62* |
| Laggards | 120 (65.6%) | 63 (34.4%) | 17.75*** |

**Notes:** * $p < 0.05$; ** $p < 0.01$; *** $p < 0.001$
[a] Sample was composed of 501 females and 503 males; 17 respondents did not report their gender

**Table II.**
Chi-square analysis by gender and categories of fashion adopters $(n = 1,004)$[a]

FIGURE 9.6. *(continued)*

JFMM
7,1

28

Particularly, abstracting from the group of adolescents identified as fashion innovators, pairwise comparisons of mean scores recorded on the brand sensitivity scale across the five types of fashion adopters defined by the DSI scale suggests that brand sensitivity is an increasing function of fashion "adoptiveness" among adolescents.

This is to say that adolescents who lag in the process of fashion adoption (i.e. laggards) are significantly less brand sensitive than those in the late majority of fashion adopters, adolescents making up the late majority of adopters are significantly less brand sensitive than those identified in the early majority, and adolescents in the early majority of fashion adopters are significantly less sensitive to brands than those identified as early fashion adopters. Here the only exception to this tendency among adolescents of being more brand sensitive with increasing levels of fashion adoptiveness arises from the group of adolescents identified as innovators in the process of fashion adoption. As such, although fashion innovators are found to be significantly more brand sensitive than laggards, results from the pairwise comparisons do not indicate that adolescents identified as fashion innovators are significantly more brand sensitive than those making up the other categories of fashion adopters (i.e. early adopters, early majority, late majority).

From a statistical perspective, this result was somewhat expected considering the relatively small number of adolescents identified as innovators in contrast to those in the other categories of fashion adopters. Furthermore, since innovators and early adopters have very similar means with respect to brand sensitivity (i.e. 24.10 and 24.47, respectively), it shall be clear that the mean of innovators would have been also significantly greater than those of the early majority and late majority if the number of innovators had been larger.

**Table III.**
Results of Tukey's multiple comparisons conduced on the five levels of the independent variable "type of fashion adopter" in relation to the dependent variable "degree of brand sensitivity" ($n = 1{,}021$)

| Type of adopter ($n$) | Mean[a] (SD) | Innovators | Early adopters | Early majority | Late majority | Laggards |
|---|---|---|---|---|---|---|
| Innovators (35) | 24.10 (7.02) | NA[b] | $p = 0.998$ | $p = 0.496$ | $p = 0.021$ | $p = 0.000$ |
| Early adopters (158) | 24.47 (6.53) | NS[c] | NA | $p = 0.004$ | $p = 0.000$ | $p = 0.000$ |
| Early majority (308) | 22.17 (6.71) | NS | ** | NA | $p = 0.012$ | $p = 0.000$ |
| Late majority (334) | 20.47 (6.65) | NS | *** | * | NA | $p = 0.000$ |
| Laggards (186) | 17.95 (7.04) | *** | *** | *** | *** | NA |

**Notes:** [a] Possible scores on the brand sensitivity scale ranged from 7 to 35; [b] NA = not applicable; [c] NS = not significant using Holm's sequential Bonferroni method for controlling type I error across multiple hypothesis tests; * = significant at $p < 0.05$ using Holm's sequential Bonferroni method for controlling type I error; ** = significant at $p < 0.01$ using Holm's sequential Bonferroni method for controlling type I error; *** = significant at $p < 0.001$ using Holm's sequential Bonferroni method for controlling type I error

FIGURE 9.6. (*continued*)

### Results and discussion

The first objective of the study was to compare the representation of male and female adolescents in each of the five different categories of fashion adopters. More specifically, we wanted to assess if males were better represented than females in the most important categories of adopters in the diffusion of innovations, namely fashion innovators and early adopters. Given that these two groups of fashion adopters are mostly composed of females, we must conclude that the relationship between fashion innovativeness and women appears to be as strong among the specific market segment of adolescents as it seems to be for the other fashion consumer market segments. This result was not expected since, as discussed earlier, male adolescents seemed to be as interested in fashion as their female counterparts. This finding is interesting however for consumer psychologists, clothing theorists and fashion marketers who all study fashion innovativeness and fashion diffusion for different purposes. As such, it seems that, regardless of the age group in which they belong, females play a significantly greater role than males in the process of fashion diffusion. Consequently, it appears that there is no need to include both genders in a sample when the objective of a study is to gather general information about fashion innovativeness, unless, of course, specific information related to men is needed.

The second objective of the study was to verify if there were differences among the five distinct categories of adopters with respect to brand sensitivity. Innovators and early adopters are the most important groups in the process of fashion diffusion because of the role they play as models for later fashion consumers. To this extent, our findings tend to corroborate the idea that these two groups are the most brand sensitive. This could indeed partially explain the adolescents' infatuation for clothing brand name that has been noticed in recent years. Even if there is no evidence that innovators and/or early adopters are intentionally promoting brand names, it is clear that they do influence later fashion adopters by at least providing exposure to brands.

The results of this study are limited by the "convenience" of the sample and, therefore, generalization of its findings should be approached with caution. Nevertheless, the clear differences between the number of males and females in the categories of "innovators" and "early adopters" found in this study lead us to believe that replication of this research should provide similar results.

Finally, our findings seem to show a direct relation between brand sensitivity and fashion innovativeness. However, very little is known regarding adolescents' brand sensitivity. Further studies should be focussed on characteristics such as gender, age, self-esteem, susceptibility to group influence to name but a few, which may be related to this construct, in order to evaluate more specifically the real impact of fashion innovativeness as a determinant factor on brand sensitivity.

FIGURE 9.6. (*continued*)

JFMM
7,1

**30**

References

Beaudoin, P., Moore, M.A. and Goldsmith, R.E. (1998), "Young fashion leaders' and followers' attitudes toward American and imported apparel", *Journal of Product and Brand Management*, Vol. 7 No. 3, pp. 193-207.

Flynn, L.R. and Goldsmith, R.E. (1993), "Identifying innovators in consumer service markets", *Service Industries Journal*, Vol. 13 No. 3, pp. 97-109.

Francis, S.K. and Liu, Q. (1990), "Effects of clothing values on perceived clothing deprivation among adolescents", *Perceptual and Motor Skills*, Vol. 71, pp. 1191-9.

Goldsmith, R.E. and Flynn, L.R. (1992), "Identifying innovators in consumer product markets", *European Journal of Marketing*, Vol. 26, pp. 42-54.

Goldsmith, R.E. and Hofacker, C.F. (1991), "Measuring consumer innovativeness", *Journal of the Academy of Marketing Science*, Vol. 19, pp. 209-21.

Goldsmith, R.E, Heitmeyer, J.R. and Freiden, J.B. (1991), "Social values and fashion leadership", *Clothing and Textiles Research Journal*, Vol. 10, pp. 37-45.

Gutman, J. and Mills, M.K. (1982), "Fashion life style, self-concept, shopping orientation, and store patronage: an integrative analysis", *Journal of Retailing*, Vol. 50 No. 2, pp. 64-86.

Horridge, P. and Richards, L. (1984), "Relationship of fashion awareness and apparel economic practices", *Home Economics Research Journal*, Vol. 13 No. 2, pp. 138-52.

Kaiser, S.B. (1990), *The Social Psychology of Clothing*, 2nd ed., Macmillan, New York, NY.

Kapferer, J.N. (1992), *La Sensibilité Aux Marques*, Les éditions d'Organisation, Paris.

Kapferer, J.N. and Laurent, G. (1983), "La sensibilité aux marques", *Adolescence*, Vol. 18 No. 71, pp. 659-74.

Koester, A.W. and May, J.K. (1985), "Profiles of adolescents' clothing practices: purchase, daily selection, and care", *Adolescence*, Vol. XX No. 77, pp. 97-113.

O'Neil, G. (1998), "Study of teen's 'dangerous dress' prompts call for smaller schools uniforms", available at: www.hec.ohio-state.educ/admin.epdnews/oneal study2.html

Ossorio, S. (1995), "Teen spending soars to $96 billion in 1994", *Tucson Citizen*, 12 April, p. 13.

Paoletti, J.B. and Kregloh, C.L. (1989), "The children's department", in Kidwelland, C.B. and Steele, V. (Eds), *Men and Women: Dressing the Part*, Smithsonian Institution Press, Washington, DC, pp. 22-41.

Rogers, E.M. (1983), *Diffusion of Innovations*, 3rd ed., The Free Press, New York, NY.

Shim, S. and Koh, A. (1997), "Profiling adolescent consumer decision-making styles: effects of socialization agents and social-structure variables", *Clothing and Textiles Research Journal*, Vol. 15 No. 2, pp. 50-9.

Uray, N. and Dedeoglu, A. (1997), "Identifying fashion clothing innovators by self-report method", *Journal of Euromarketing*, Vol. 6 No. 3, pp. 27-46.

FIGURE 9.6.

In the following sections, we will discuss specific inclusions within each chapter.

# INTRODUCTION

As the first section of a research report, the Introduction is a general overture to the study. The Introduction includes several components: statement of the research problem; purpose of the study; research objectives, questions, or hypotheses; limitations to the study; and definition of terms. The order of these components may vary slightly, depending on the researcher's writing style or the requirements of the academic journal or organization to which the report is being submitted.

## Statement of Research Problem

To begin the report, in a few introductory paragraphs you should create reader interest in your study. Provide background and a foundation for your study. Following the introductory paragraphs, shape the **problem statement**, which tells the reader what you intend to research. The study on fashion innovativeness and adolescents provides the following problem statement:

> . . . However, the large majority of researchers that have investigated fashion innovativeness in the past used respondents over 20 years of age in their sample. In fact, we could not find any research that studied fashion innovativeness and fashion diffusion with a sample strictly composed of adolescents. (Beaudoin, Lachance, & Robitaille, 2003, p. 23)

## Purpose of the Study

The problem statement may be written in general terms, followed by a more specific sentence that articulates the purpose of the study in a clear and concise manner. Often the purpose sentence begins with the phrase "The purpose of this study is to . . ." to explicitly tell the reader the reason for the study. The purpose of the study in Figure 9.6 begins this way: "The first purpose of the study was to assess the representation of male and female adolescents . . ." (Beaudoin et al., 2003, p. 24).

## Research Objectives, Questions, or Hypotheses

Research questions, objectives, or hypotheses are also included in the Introduction chapter. Research questions use the question form to state the problem to be investigated. **Research objectives** are the goals the researcher sets out to achieve in the research study (Kumar, 2005). The main objective is the overall statement of the study, showing associations or relationships the researcher seeks to discover. Objectives develop out of research questions. Objectives transform research questions into behavioral aims by using action-oriented words such as "to find out" or "to determine" (Kumar, p. 46). Subobjectives are more specific aspects of the topic, to be investigated within the main framework of the study. When you write subobjectives, each one should contain only one aspect of the study.

In the Beaudoin et al. (2003) study, the word *purpose* is used in place of the word *objective*. However, a very specific objective is implied: "More specifically, we wanted to verify whether significant differences exist between the number of males and females in each of the five categories of consumer adopters . . ." (p. 24).

## Limitations of the Study

Research often emerges from larger problem areas or contexts. Therefore, the research problem that you will study and write about often requires limitations. The limits of the problem should be carefully defined, and the reader should know exactly what the researcher intends to do and does not intend to do.

## Definition of Terms

The last section of the Introduction precisely defines terms in the problem that may be unfamiliar to the reader or that have a specific meaning relative to the study. For example, in Figure 9.6, *process of fashion diffusion* is defined as "those who are the first to buy and adopt new clothing products and fashion tendencies" (Beaudoin et al., 2003, p. 24).

## REVIEW OF LITERATURE

Reviewing the literature is central to the entire research process, contributing to nearly all operational steps. In the example study, several major themes and theories were discussed in the Review of Literature section, including adolescents and brand sensitivity, and the model of diffusion of innovation theory.

## METHOD

In this section of the research report, you explain the method you used to collect your data. The section should include selection of the sample, the instrument used to collect data, and the procedures used. This section should be very precise so that other researchers may duplicate your methods if necessary. Beaudoin et al. (2003) explained the time frame of the study and the use of a convenience sample of 12- to 17-year-old high school students. They go on to describe that respondents completed a self-administered questionnaire that included 89 items intended to measure brand sensitivity, perceived clothing deprivation, innovativeness level, consumer competence, and others. These researchers also stated that "the different scales were validated during a pilot study" (p. 25).

Very specific breakdowns of the concepts measured on the instrument are common in many scholarly articles. Often researchers explain where the concepts were identified in the literature and how items on the scales will be evaluated. The research team whose work we are examining here specifically discussed measure of brand sensitivity, measure of fashion innovativeness, and classification of fashion adopters, and they presented a table that illustrated the differences in the theoretical percentages of adopters and the ones the researchers found in their study (Beaudoin et al., 2003).

The last component to be included in the Method section is the analysis of data. In this section researchers report their response rate and the results of statistical computations. Beaudoin et al. (2003) reported response rate, Pearson's chi-square test results, and one-way analysis of variance test results, among other data analysis. Some of these data were presented in table form to make them easier for the reader to understand.

# RESULTS AND DISCUSSION

The Results and Discussion section of the written report focuses on the researchers' interpretation of their data. Within the Discussion, researchers again use findings of other researchers, as reported in the review of literature, to verify or contradict their own findings. As Beaudoin et al. (2003) did, researchers often develop the Discussion by first refreshing the reader's memory about the objectives of the study and then reporting what they expected to find and what they actually did find. Here, also, limitations of the study are presented as part of the Discussion. In this section, the researchers defend their work and justify their conclusions.

# SUMMARY, CONCLUSIONS, AND RECOMMENDATIONS

Some academic papers end with a Summary, Conclusions, and a Recommendations section that distill in a few paragraphs precisely what the research study accomplished (Leedy & Ormrod, 2005). The article by Beaudoin et al. (2003) does not include this section. Conclusions that are drawn in this section should be completely supported by the data. This section should end with recommendations for future research to be conducted by the research team or others. A complete reference list follows the conclusion of the written report.

## SUMMARY

This chapter has concentrated on the research process. The process comprises three stages. The first stage of the research process involves formulating the research problem and producing a review of literature. The second stage involves conceptualizing the research study and writing the research proposal. The third stage involves data collection and analysis and concludes with writing the research report. When written, the formal research report includes an introduction; a review of literature; a description of the methodology; results and discussion; and finally a section consisting of a summary, conclusions, and recommendations.

## KEY TERMS

Abstract
Academic writing
Bibliography
Blind review
Cross-sectional study
Descriptive statistics
Discovery research
Dissertation
Experimental design
Fashion count
Figure
Focus group
Focused research
Historical research
Hypothesis
In-depth interview
Inferential statistics
Informed consent
Internal Review Board (IRB)
Interview
Journal article
Longitudinal study
Nonprobability sample
Observation
Paper presentation
Peer-reviewed
Phenomena

Pilot study
Primary data
Probability sample
Problem statement
Qualitative research
Quantitative research
Quasi-experimental
Questionnaire
Refereed
Reliability
Research
Research design
Research objective
Research proposal
Research question
Review of literature
Sampling
Scholarly writing
Search strategy
Secondary data
Study design
Table
Theoretical framework
Theory
Thesis
Validity

CASE STUDY

## *Eddie, You're Outa' Here*

Alyx Nystrom, a fashion reporter for *Sacramento Today*, has been given the assignment to write a story about tattoo removal. This is a growing trend among women particularly, but facts about the procedure are limited. So Alyx has to do some background research before she can start writing.

She first contacted Gina Granger, an account executive for a local retailer, whom Alyx recently befriended in a kickboxing class. When Gina was 18, she had the name of her then-boyfriend tattooed on her upper arm. Ten years later she is engaged to someone else, and she wants to have the name of her ex erased before she walks down the isle in a spaghetti-strap wedding dress. Gina was excited to share her story, recounting the pros and cons of getting the tattoo in the first place, and describing her research to find a local physician who could remove the tattoo.

Gina also offered to contact Dr. John Wilcox, a local dermatologist and expert in tattoo removal, whom Gina had already met with concerning the tattoo removal. Dr. Wilcox granted Alyx an interview and described the procedure, giving general details about the price and time line necessary to have the tattoo completely removed.

Alyx has two good interviews for the article. However, she feels that she still needs more information to provide a balanced, informative story. Her next resource is the Internet.

## CASE STUDY QUESTIONS

1. Where should Alyx start her search on the Internet?
2. Where should Alyx continue her Internet search?
3. What keywords might be helpful for Alyx in her Internet search?
4. What criteria should Alyx use to determine if an Internet source is reliable?

## INDUSTRY PROFILE

*Valerie Steele*

**What is your current job and title? Can you describe the main responsibilities for your job?**

I am the Director and Chief Curator of the Museum at the Fashion Institute of Technology (FIT). At FIT I'm in charge of a staff of more than 30. I am in charge of putting on four major fashion exhibitions a year plus about eight more student and faculty exhibitions. Of the four main fashion exhibitions, two of them are special exhibitions usually on contemporary fashion and two are thematic exhibitions in our fashion history gallery, which looks at 250 years of style. So, for example, before this interview I was working on the brochure copy, writing the brochure copy for our forthcoming fashion history exhibition on "Luxury," so I was writing about our changing definition of luxury and the development of particular luxury brands such as Hermes.

We are also responsible for trying to make the museum at FIT into a kind of think-tank for fashion studies, so to that end we organize once a year a fashion symposium where we bring in curators and scholars and artists and fashion designers from all over the world to talk about a particular theme. So one annual symposium was on "Art and Fashion," so I wrote a paper about fashion and art and presented that to the symposium.

I am also slowly in the process of writing a book called *Museum Quality: The Rise of the Fashion Exhibition*, which will look at how museums have become increasingly interested in doing exhibitions on fashion designers, exhibitions about fashion as a concept, about art and fashion, etc.

In the special exhibition gallery, as well, I am working on refining the concept for the exhibition we will be doing on "Lanvin," and on future exhibitions such as "Gothic: The Dark Glamour" for which I will also be writing a full book with Yale University Press, not just a brochure. I can't do a book for every single exhibition but I try to do them as often as I can.

I am also founder and editor-in-chief of *Fashion Theory: The Journal of Dress, Body and Culture*. Back in 1996, I was at a conference of the Costume Society of America and I met a publisher, Katherine Earle, who asked me if I would be willing to serve as an advisor for a book series that they were doing about fashion. I told her, "Of course I would be willing to do that, but you know you are a small publisher and you are going to lose out on a lot of good books to other bigger and richer publishers so what you really ought to do," I said, "was to start a journal that would publish scholarly articles about fashion." That way you could get articles by scholars and curators from a wide variety of fields and create a kind of interdisciplinary forum where people could see what their colleagues all around the world were working on, whether they were art historians or philosophers or curators—everybody working on fashion; it would be a place to bring it together. She came back to me the next day and said, "Right! We can do it and why don't you be the founding editor?" That was the beginning of *Fashion Theory*.

Our first issue came out in 1997. It's continued to grow; we have four issues a year. Every year one of them is a special issue which usually somebody else guest edits. But the rest of them I edit. I get many articles. People will send me articles. Very often I have to solicit articles. If I go to a conference and hear a good paper, I'll ask the presenter if he or she would be willing to expand on that and turn it into an article for the journal.

I am very pleased with it because it has given more intellectual credibility to fashion as a field of study. For example, a younger colleague of mine describes how when she was working on her Ph.D. at Columbia University she wanted to write her dissertation on fashion and her professor said, "No, no, that's not serious," and when *Fashion Theory's* first issue came out she went running into the faculty lounge waving the issue saying, "Look, there is a scholarly journal on it. That means it is a valid topic for me to write about!" So they agreed and now she has published several books on the history of fashion and contemporary fashion.

### What is a typical day at work like?

A typical day . . . well, let me see . . . I'll look at my calendar . . . it's full and most of it is full of boring stuff, regrettably. It's full of things having to do with human relations. Working with all of the people who are at an institution takes up a lot of the time of an administrator. Also, fund-raising takes up a huge amount of the time of a museum director. Then, there are various kinds of meetings because the museum is part of a university system, so there's that.

Fortunately, there are also some fun things involved with having meetings about the exhibitions that we're working on. There might be a meeting where we'll be talking about having such and such clothes ready for a show but we are still missing important pieces so who are the different designers, companies that I should be calling. Can we find out the name of their press person and the phone number so I can call and see if I can solicit a donation?

I might be doing an interview, for example, like with you, or with a magazine or a newspaper. For example, just the other day I did an interview with the *Wall Street Journal* about current fashion trends. And then another journalist's interview and then in the evening I went to see a film produced by my friend Ruben Toledo called *Fashion Nation*, which was about fashion and luxury brands in Paris that included period footage of old fashion shows, Dior shows from the 1940s, as well as his own really beautiful fashion illustrations, which were animated. So that was a fun thing that I did. More of the time it is things like budget meetings and staff performance meetings.

*At what point did you decide to pursue a career in writing for a fashion-related business?*

My very first term in graduate school at Yale I was in history class. I had gone there to study European cultural and intellectual history and a classmate of mine, Judy Coffin, gave a presentation about two scholarly articles in a feminist journal about the significance of the Victorian corset and one of them said the corset was oppressive to women and the other said it was sexually liberating and it was just like a light bulb went on in my brain and I realized fashion is a part of culture. I can work on the history of fashion, and I never turned back from that point on. With the exception of one class, I managed to force all of my professors to let me do all of my research papers on fashion and my doctoral dissertation was on fashion. That became my first book. I got a post-doc at the Smithsonian where I worked at the National Museum of American History on fashion and on exhibition. Then I came and started teaching fashion history at FIT. I created my own fashion journal and kept on writing fashion books. I became chief curator of the museum here and ultimately also director doing various fashion exhibitions. I never turned back. Once I had that epiphany that fashion was for me, that was it!

*Describe your first writing job. What was the most important or interesting thing you wrote for that job/publication?*

Well, I had written my doctoral dissertation on erotic aspects of Victorian fashion. I had actually wanted to write about the corset but I heard that this other professor was already doing a book on the corset, so being young and naive I thought, "Well, I'm scooped. I'd better do something else." I did have a long chapter in my dissertation on the corset, but the book was basically on fashion and eroticism during the Victorian era. Then I took off and revised the dissertation and turned it into my first book, *Fashion and Eroticism*. Over the years, with my fifth book *Fetish: Fashion, Sex and Power*, I did another chapter on the corset, on really kinky corsets, and finally with about my tenth book, I actually bit the bullet and did an entire book called *The Corset: A Cultural History*. At that point I had also done a big exhibition, called "The Corset: Fashioning the Body" so there has been a lot of corset stuff in my work over the years.

**What are you currently reading (books, magazines, Web sites, newspapers, other media)? Do you have a favorite author or publication?**

Wow, what am I currently reading . . . Hold on a second. I'll go and get some of the books that are strewn around the office . . . Well, for the luxury brochure of course I am looking at a lot of books on luxury—*Trading Up*, *Living It Up*, old classics like *Luxury and Capitalism*, and then for my Gothic book I'm looking at books like *Contemporary Gothic*, *Fashioning Gothic Bodies*, and just plain *Gothic*. You have to see what has already been done and also sort of assess the competition.

I just joined www.IQONS.com so that's amusing, sort of like FaceBook or something—MySpace for fashion people. And I am starting to carve out a little bit of time in my day to look at some fashion blogs because that has been a whole new medium. I am inundated with paper. I have about five issues of *Women's Wear Daily* piled up on my desk, but I am cognizant of the fact that there is a lot of interesting stuff going on on the Web; I am trying to catch up on some of that too. Everybody's doing blogs now.

**What advice do you have for students interested in a writing career? Do you have any recommendations for students?**

Writing is something that you have to learn how to do. So I think you have to approach it with a certain amount of modesty and determination that you are going to really analyze the books that you read. You have to be a reader in order to be a writer. You really have to look at them and see what you can learn from different authors that you like.

Well, coming out of a history background, you have to have evidence and you have to have an argument that you are presenting. You have to learn how to do research and you have to learn how to assess the research. I have told students, "You wouldn't believe everything you read in the *National Enquirer*, so why should you believe everything you read in a fashion magazine just because it is a hundred years old?" You have to be able to exercise critical judgment about your sources. You're interviewing someone. What they say may not be true. An awful lot of fashion writing is hagiography books about the lives of the saints: "Oh, this designer is a genius . . . he/she has invented everything . . . greatest thing since sliced bread." There is no kind of critical awareness.

## ADDITIONAL RESOURCES

Gay, L. R. (2006). *Educational research: Competencies for analysis and application* (8th ed.). Upper Saddle River, NJ: Merrill Prentice Hall.

Kerlinger, F. N., & Lee, H. B. (2000). *Foundations of behavioral research* (4th ed.). Boston: Wadsworth.

Salkind, N. J. (2004). *Statistics for people who think they hate statistics*. Thousand Oaks, CA: Sage Publications.

Underhill, P. (1999). *Why we buy: The science of shopping*. New York: Simon & Schuster.

Underhill, P. (2004). *Call of the mall*. New York: Simon & Schuster.

## REFERENCES

Beaudoin, P., Lachance, M J., & Robitaille, J. (2003). Fashion innovativeness, fashion diffusion and brand sensitivity among adolescents. *Journal of Fashion Marketing and Management, 7*, 23–30.

Creswell, J. W. (2003). *Research design* (2nd ed.). Thousand Oaks, CA: Sage Publications.

Kirszner, L. G., & Mandell, S. R. (2005). *The Wadsworth handbook* [Instructor's Edition]. Boston: Thomson Wadsworth.

Kumar, R. (2005). *Research methodology* (2nd ed.). London: Sage Publications.

Leedy, P. D., & Ormrod, J. E. (2005). *Practical research* (8th ed.). Upper Saddle River, NJ: Merrill Prentice Hall.

Levy, M., Grewal, D., Kopalle, P. K., & Hess, J. D. (2004). Emerging trends in retail pricing practices: Implications for research. *Journal of Retailing, 80*, xiii–xxi.

Muzinich, N., Pecotich, A., & Putrevu, S. (2003). A model of the antecedents and consequences of female fashion innovativeness. *Journal of Retailing and Consumer Services, 10*, 297–310.

Sen, S., Block, L. G., Chandran, S. (2002). Window displays and consumer shopping decisions. *Journal of Retailing and Consumer Services, 9*, 277–290.

Vogt, W. P. (1999). *Dictionary of statistics and methodology* (2nd ed.). Thousand Oaks, CA: Sage Publications.

# TEN

## *Writing Books*

After you have read this chapter, you should be able to discuss the following:

• Research and the idea behind a fashion book

• The differences between fiction and nonfiction

• The writing environment

• Writing a book proposal and query letter

• Using a literary agent

• Negotiating a book contract

• Working with a publisher or self-publishing a book

When Judith Krantz started writing her first novel, which became the *New York Times* bestseller *Scruples,* she did not know that she would become one of the best-known authors of her era. *Scruples* is a story about a young woman who lived in Paris where she learned about fashion, retailing, and love before opening a luxury boutique on Rodeo Drive. Judith Krantz went on to write 10 best-selling novels, with varying themes covering fashion, shopping, art, and romance, before writing her own autobiography (2000).

In that autobiography, Judith Krantz reveals that when she started writing she was not sure there was an audience for her fiction. "It had been a once-in-a-lifetime experience to write my first novel on spec, in freedom and privacy, with courage and hope but without clear expectations, without an advance, without an agent or publishers or PR people breathing down my neck" (2000, p. 257). Krantz also clarifies what many writers feel about the process of writing: "The chief joy of my career has . . . been the process of writing itself. To settle down in the morning in front of my computer, with an entire day of uninterrupted work ahead of me, to turn on my machine knowing what I hope to achieve in the scene I'm about to write, is as richly satisfying a state as I've ever experienced in a lifetime" (p. 257).

Currently, themes of fashion, shopping, and love are widely used in novels with contemporary heroines, such as Becky Bloomwood in the *Shopaholic* series of books by Sophia Kinsella or Andrea Sachs in Lauren Weisberger's *The Devil Wears Prada*. Author Candace Bushnell created a legion of fans with her novels, such as *Sex and the City*, *Trading Up*, and *Lipstick Jungle*, as did Jennifer Weiner with her books, including *In Her Shoes*, and *Goodnight Nobody*. Many of these popular novels have been converted into television shows or movies, which reflects the crossover of media in the 21st century.

This next example takes a popular television show and converts it into a nonfiction book. Stacy London and Clinton Kelly, the hosts of the popular television show *What Not to Wear*, used their fashion knowledge in the book publishing world with their book *Dress Your Best: The Complete Guide to Finding the Style That's Right for Your Body* (2005). This book builds upon tools the authors presented during the real-life makeovers that take place on the television program.

Whether your goal is to become the next best-selling novelist, like Sophie Kinsella or Jennifer Weiner, or to write nonfiction books about fashion, there are many opportunities for writers to have their works published. This chapter looks at the process of writing a book, whether it is fiction or nonfiction; finding an agent; preparing a query letter and book proposal; and taking the project through the publication process.

# RESEARCH AND THE IDEA

Writing a book starts with an idea. Once you have decided that you want to write a book, jot down a short sentence or two describing what you want to write about. This serves as the first attempt at explaining your project to a potential publisher or target audience. Do you have a particular interest that other people also want to know more about? Have you created a new design approach or product development strategy that might be of interest to others in your field? Do you have a great idea for a new novel?

Mary Embree, who wrote *The Author's Toolkit*, has this to say: "It is my belief that if you have ever written anything—business proposals, technical manuals, poetry, or even a daily journal—you can learn to write a book. Talent can't be taught but craft can" (2003, p. viii).

Research, the search for more background information and data about your topic, is essential for every writer. Whether you are writing a fictional story or reporting how to proceed with that new design approach, research keeps you current and helps to improve and maintain your credibility, even if you are the expert in the subject. No matter what the subject is, information and technology are changing at a rapid rate. Writing with current and accurate information is essential.

If you are writing a novel about the fashion magazine publishing industry, you will need to investigate current practices. How are magazines organized? What are the responsibilities of various editors? Who will be the villain or the hero? If your retail executive heroine is based in London, you will need to know about the people, geography, customs, climate, stores, and competitive environment of that city in order to make your novel more convincing. Research is needed so that you will be accurate about places, dates, the spelling of names, historical events, recent developments in the field, and so forth. Consider this example: As the cell phone became popular, characters in contemporary fiction started using that tool. As text messaging entered mainstream use, writers inserted text messages into the plot. Yet one popular writer has set her storyline in the 1980s. That means that despite the technological changes that have taken place later in the 20th century, her characters cannot use the Internet or cell phones as the plot is developed. The amount of attention you pay to detail such as this can make you look like an expert or like an amateur. Do your research.

The Internet has become a major resource for research in recent times. That resource was not even available to writers during most of the 20th century. Now we can access all kinds of information from all over the world from our homes and offices. Even though this is a valuable resource, you must be aware that not all information provided at Web sites is accurate and nonbiased. You will need to analyze which resources on the Internet are reliable and which ones are not. For further information about assessing the reliability of an Internet resource, see Appendix D, "Web Source Location and Evaluation," where this topic is covered in greater detail.

Another great tool for your research is the public library or a specialized library. Books and other reference materials are widely available. A librarian can help you locate your subject matter and help you use interlibrary loan to get copies of books that might not be available at your local library. This is especially helpful if you need to conduct historical research outside the traditional centers for fashion, such as New York, Los Angeles, or Chicago. Plus, just being around books can inspire you.

A specialized library might be part of a museum collection or part of an academic environment. For example, the Phoenix Art Museum has an extensive collection of fashion resources in its Fashion Design Gallery and its Fashion Design Collection, as does the Metropolitan Museum of Art in New York. A writer doing research in fashion may be able to schedule an appointment to search the archives of these and other museums. Several colleges and universities also have special library collections. Fashion Institute of Technology has the Gladys Marcus Library and Kent State University has the June F. Mohler Fashion Library as part of the Shannon Rodgers and Jerry Silverman School of Fashion Design and Merchandising.

*Portfolio Exercise:* **Visit a special collections library at a school or museum near where you live. Select a historical time period that interests you. Conduct some preliminary research about the time period, keeping good notes and a list of appropriate references. Write a two-page proposal for a novel based in that time period. What additional information will would you need to find before creating an outline?**

**Reference books** that contain general information about a wide variety of subjects are resources for quick answers to common questions. Most writers have some general reference books in their personal library—such as an encyclopedia, a desk dictionary, a thesaurus, a handbook of synonyms and antonyms, an almanac, and a fact finder. Also included in most writers' reference collection are books on writing and manuals on writing style, such as the *Publication Manual of the American Psychological Association*, the *MLA Handbook for Writers of Research Papers*, or the *Chicago Manual of Style*. Another popular reference tool for writers is a classic: *The Elements of Style*, by William Strunk, Jr., and E. B. White.

While, reference books are necessary tools for authors, they are often dry and lack appeal to younger writers. English author and journalist Lynne Truss took a humorous look at punctuation in her book *Eats, Shoots & Leaves: The Zero Tolerance Approach to Punctuation* (2003). Maira Kalman, a fabric, watch, and accessories designer and an illustrator of children's books, was the sole artist that the estate of E. B. White trusted to illustrate *The Elements of Style*. The result was *Elements of Style Illustrated*, a book that gives a fresh jolt of energy to the classic work, directed toward contemporary readers and writers (2005).

It is helpful to have physical copies of various reference books, but the computer age has brought authors' reference materials to writers at the touch of a few computer keys. A thesaurus is built into most common word processing programs, including Microsoft Word, or Corel's WordPerfect. And there's always www.Dictionary.com

Subject-specific books also belong in a writer's library. The fashion writer's library should contain a number of useful historical references, such as *Survey of Historic Costume* (2005), *Fashion: The Century of the Designer 1900–1999* (1999), and *As Seen in Vogue: A Century of American Fashion in Advertising* (2004). These are time-tested reference books about what, where, and how to wear fashion; shopping, retailing, and merchandising practices; and promotional strategies. Other valuable references include a fashion dictionary, such as *The Fairchild Dictionary of Fashion*; biographies, such as *Who's Who in Fashion*; or encyclopedias, such as *The Fairchild Encyclopedia of Fashion Accessories*. Figure 10.1 presents a list of reference books that would be appropriate for a fashion writer's personal library.

Keeping up with what is going on in the world and your industry is essential for a fashion writer. Reading newspapers, magazines, and journals is a great way to keep up with happenings on a daily basis. Major newspapers, such as the *New York Times, Washington Post, Wall Street Journal,* and *Los Angeles Times*, provide news and commentary daily. They provide news of the fashion industry in addition to other general news. A side note: Be aware that some publications have a particular political slant. You should take the possible bias of a specific publication into consideration before using and citing that publication in your own work.

Participating in professional organizations is an excellent way to keep up with current trends in the field. Groups such as Fashion Group International (FGI) provide opportunities for networking with other professionals in the fashion industry. Executive members are often called upon by writers and journalists to offer insight into the workings of the fashion industry. It is fun and professionally stimulating to be around other people with interests that are similar to yours. Other major organizations that might interest a fashion and retail writer are the Costume Society of America and the National Retail Federation. Writing groups and book seminars also provide the opportunity to interact with other writers.

American Psychological Association. (2001). *Publication manual of the American Psychological Association* (5th ed.) Washington, DC: Author.

Calasibetta, C. M., & Tortora, P. G. (2003). *The Fairchild dictionary of fashion* (3rd ed.). New York: Fairchild Books.

Everett, J. C., & Swanson, K. K. (2004). *Guide to producing a fashion show* (2nd ed.). New York: Fairchild Books.

Farrell-Beck, J., & Parsons, J. (2007). *Twentieth century dress in the United States*. New York: Fairchild Books.

Gibaldi, J. (2003). *MLA handbook for writers of research papers* (6th ed.). New York: Modern Language Association of America.

Hill, D. D. (2004). *As seen in Vogue: A Century of American fashion in advertising*. Lubbock, TX: Texas Tech University Press.

Laver, J. (2002). *Costume and fashion: A concise history* (4th ed.). London: Thames & Hudson.

Mendes, V., & de la Haye, A. (1999). *20th century fashion*. London: Thames & Hudson.

Seeling, C. (1999). *Fashion: The century of the designer 1900–1999*. Cologne: Könemann.

Stegemeyer, A. (2004). *Who's who in fashion* (4th ed.). New York: Fairchild Books.

Strunk, W., Jr., & White, E. B. (2000). *The elements of style* (4th ed.). Needham Heights, MA: Allyn & Bacon.

Tortora, P. G. (2003). *The Fairchild encyclopedia of fashion accessories*. New York: Fairchild Books.

Tortora, P. G., & Eubank, K. (2005). *Survey of historic costume* (4th ed.). New York: Fairchild Books.

Tortora, P. G., & Merkel, R. S. (1996). *Fairchild's dictionary of textiles* (7th ed.). New York: Fairchild Books.

University of Chicago Press. (2003). *Chicago manual of style* (15th ed.). Chicago: Author.

FIGURE 10.1. Fashion writer's reference library.

**BOX 10.1  ACKNOWLEDGING INFORMATION FROM OTHER RESOURCES**

If you do seek guidance and information from an authority or another published author, citing that person is critical to maintaining credibility. A **citation** is a method of giving credit to the original author or expert in written works. More information about creating appropriate attributions is found in Appendix B, "Documentation Format." If an expert offers opinions, knowledge, or advice, you should cite that expert if you're preparing a nonfiction work or acknowledge them if you are writing a fictional work. Plagiarism, which is the use of another author's ideas or writings as your own, is an unethical behavior and can tarnish and possibly ruin your reputation as a writer.

A **copyright** is a legal authorization that allows the author or artist to publish or sell a literary or artistic piece with protection from unauthorized use or duplication by others. If someone else uses, copies, or publishes a work that is protected by copyright, the original author or artist has the right to seek damages from the person who has violated the copyright without permission. Getting permission to use copyrighted materials is most likely less expensive and less embarrassing than being sued and humiliated by the holder of the copyright.

There's more about copyright in the section of this chapter called "Negotiating a Publication Contract."

An added benefit of such networking is that other authors and experts are frequently open to and available for consultation. For example, if you're planning a fictional story to be set in a television studio or a retail store, working with an expert who has worked for a television station or a specialty store can help you gather information and experience that will provide authenticity to your story.

Once you have completed your research, you will be to put together an outline or plan of how the idea will be developed. Outlines are discussed at length in Chapter 2, "The Writing Process."

Producing an authoritative, informative, and interesting book is dependent upon the research that you, the author, have conducted. The research can also add credibility to the storyline in fiction or enable you to add convincing facts and data in a nonfiction work. It can make the difference between a book that gets published and one that does not.

# FICTION AND NONFICTION

Elsa Klensch, who pioneered fashion and style commentary on cable television, applied her fashion knowledge to writing both fiction and nonfiction. Her first book, *Style*, built upon her experience as the host of CNN's *Style with Elsa Klensch* (1995). In this nonfiction book, Klensch used her journalism background and professional contacts in the fashion industry to focus on teaching her readers about wearing clothing and accessories with a sense of style to fit their individual lives. Later, Klensch used her fashion journalism experience in writing a mystery novel, *Live at 10:00, Dead at 10:15* (2004). This story involved a fictional television producer named Sonya Iverson, who investigates a murder that takes place at a fashion industry event.

According to Mary Embree, **nonfiction** is the broadest category of written works. It includes histories, biographies, and how-to books, as well as any narrative that offers opinions based upon facts and reality (2003). Accuracy and truth are key elements for nonfiction publications. This is the opposite of **fiction**, which involves stories that the author creates from her imagination with the intention of entertaining the reader. While many authors have more experience in one genre than the other, authors such as Judith Krantz and Elsa Klensch have experience writing in both categories.

# FICTION

Writing fiction is telling an imaginary story. The **plot** is the story's outline or plan of action. In the first draft of a work of fiction, the plot essentially details how the story begins, notes the major events, and defines how the story concludes. It gives you a map of where the tale is headed. However, the first draft of this plan is not written in stone. As you develop the characters and write about the events, the story and characters may develop or change from your original idea.

There are various categories of fictional works. Some stories may be developed from historical events, whereas other stories may be centered around some mystery or as a romantic story.

The story is developed around the various characters. The main character of a novel is known as the **protagonist**. The story is centered on this person, who might also be called a hero. Another important character is the **antagonist,** who is the figure in opposition to the protagonist. If the protagonist is the "good" person, the antagonist is the "bad" individual. Other characters are developed to help tell the story. It is recommended that your protagonist not be completely "good" and your antagonist not be completely "bad." Readers will not be able to identify with a completely virtuous person or an utterly viscous and evil person with no redeeming qualities.

Characters, main and secondary, tell the story through dialogue. **Dialogue** is the discussion or interchange of ideas that takes place between two or more of the characters. Through their speech, we learn about what the characters want or are looking for, who or what is standing in their way, and how and why they are different from each other. The personalities of these characters are revealed through their conversations, as well as through the author's introduction of each character. Is he arrogant? Is she innocent? How are they similar to or different from each other?

Lauren Weisberger uses her protagonist to introduce the antagonist in her novel *The Devil Wears Prada*, in the following manner:

Since I'd never seen so much as a picture of Miranda Priestly, I was shocked to see how *skinny* she was. The hand she held out was small-boned, feminine, soft. She had to turn her head upward to look me in the eye, although she did not stand to greet me. Her expertly dyed blond hair was pulled back in a chic knot, deliberately loose enough to look casual but still supremely neat, and while she did not smile, she did not appear particularly intimidating. She seemed rather gentle and somewhat shrunken behind her ominous black desk, and although she did not invite me to sit, I felt comfortable enough to claim one of the uncomfortable black chairs that faced her. And it was then I noticed: she was watching me intently, mentally noting my attempts at grace and propriety, with what seemed like amusement. Condescending and awkward, yes, but not, I decided, particularly meanspirited (2003, p. 21).

A good character description contains more than a physical portrayal; it shows suggestions of personality, traces of motivations, and foreshadowing of things to come. Weisberger gives us a feeling that Miranda Priestly is very controlled and extremely powerful, although those words are not directly used. Could this entry mean that Priestly is really meanspirited? The reader can find out only by reading more.

The novel can be written in the first person or the third person. If the first person is used, the point of view comes from one of the characters. Then the story is narrated by one of the main characters: by the protagonist, as in the case of *The Devil Wears Prada*, or by an observer, such as a friend in *The Great Gatsby*. Other successful novels are told in the third person. Elsa Klensch uses this point of view in her novel *Live at 10:00, Dead at 10:15*. Her lead character is introduced in the third person as follows:

> Sonya Iverson raced up the rain-soaked red carpet as fast as her high heels would allow. She was late and that was something she hated. It was not her idea of what a TV producer should be—especially not a producer for the *Donna Fuller Show* (2004, p. 19).

Although some authors are able to combine first-person voices and third-person voices, most readers prefer to follow the story from one point of view. It is difficult for the reader to follow the story if they are confused by the writing style. If you are a new novelist, you might find it easier to write in the third person, until you learn to write as one of your characters in the first person.

The story may be written in the present tense or the past tense. Using the past tense allows the writer to tell the story as if it has already happened. You can foreshadow events to come and you can look back on events in the past.

Formulating the story is similar to developing a musical piece. There needs to be varying intensity. Just as daily activity has calm periods, it has harried and tension-filled moments as well. The flow of the story should have variety in its pace and level of intensity. There should be some minor turning points, as well as a major turning point to resolve the question or concern introduced in the beginning of the tale.

The story builds to a climax, which is the peak of interest or excitement. It is often the key turning point of the story. This leads to the ending where the winner is identified or the solution to the problem is found. How has the protagonist changed? What happened to the antagonist? You may not know how the story will end until you finish writing the book. Some authors start with the ending in mind, while others search for the conclusion as the characters are developed.

There are as many ways to write a story as there are writers. Each book that you write can take a different voice and tense. But, the tense and voice you have chosen for a manuscript should be used consistently throughout that work.

# NONFICTION

Writing nonfiction can be as exciting and rewarding as writing fiction. While you are not creating characters and inventing events when you are writing nonfiction, you have a broad variety of topics and genres to explore. Common nonfiction books include histories, which involve recording and analyzing events that have already occurred; biographies, which provide an accounting of another person's life; "how-to" books, which explain the steps required to accomplish what is desired; and art and coffee table books, which feature the artistic works of fashion designers, fashion illustrators, or photographers. Since most books are nonfiction, the list of subjects is almost unlimited.

Research and accuracy are essential for nonfiction. Some writers create fictional events to make a point, but when you're writing historical nonfiction it is unethical and inappropriate to change the time and place of an incident.

Besides drawing from print and recorded documents, you should interview people who have first-hand knowledge of the person or topic you're writing about. If you are writing a contemporary biography, you should interview quite a few different people who know the individual being profiled. Each person you interview can offer his view on the person or subject. Keep in mind that eyewitnesses to an event see that event from their own perspectives. When police detectives ask eyewitnesses what they saw, they do not all report exactly the same details. To be able to properly analyze an aspect of your topic, you need to interview as many people as possible.

Biographers, including Jerry Oppenheimer, conduct extensive research and interviews in order to write about such subjects as Anna Wintour, Martha Stewart, Ethel Kennedy, and Barbara Walters. Oppenheimer's biographies, meticulously researched, have been written without the support of many of his subjects. For his book on Anna Wintour, Oppenheimer states, "I was faced with the enormous task of tracking down scores of knowledgeable, credible sources—her schoolmates, friends, family members, colleagues, employees, lovers—because little was known about Anna's pre-*Vogue* life, private and professional . . . Anna Wintour declined to cooperate with me" (2005, p. 363).

Interviews frequently start with common questions. What was she like as a child? Did she have any brothers or sisters? Did she have a good relationship with her parents? Where did she go to school? If the person being interviewed likes the subject, the interviewee will most likely compliment the person or place the person in a favorable light—just as interviewees will point out flaws if they do not like the subject.

Interesting stories can be difficult to get. The person being interviewed may answer questions cautiously. Mary Embree, a former researcher and writer for the television show *This Is Your Life*, learned to wait and listen. She let the interviewee think about what to say, especially when that person was reticent about divulging private information. Embree says, "I simply stopped talking and waited. It always worked. That's when I got my best material" (2003, p. 40).

If the person you are interviewing allows you to tape-record the discussion, you will have a better and more complete verification of the testimony provided. You might have a hard time trying to take notes and formulate follow-up questions while listening to what the speaker has to say. If the interviewee agrees to let you tape-record the conversation, you will not have to rely on your memory or on sloppy, illegible handwritten notes.

---

*Portfolio Exercise:* **Select a fashion designer, a retail executive, or another person who interests you. Conduct some preliminary research about the person before you ask for an interview. Prepare a list of questions you would like information about. Ask for an interview and take notes on the answers the interviewee offers. Write a five-page biography about the person you interviewed. Include information you learned in the preliminary research, comments from the person you interviewed, and comments from someone who knows the individual.**

---

After the research and interviews are completed and the outline is drafted, you are ready to start writing the book. Keep in mind that you will probably reorganize the outline and conduct additional research as you are putting the project into manuscript form.

# YOUR WRITING ENVIRONMENT

Where and how to work are up to you. Some writers feel that all they need is a pad of paper and a pencil, whereas others have a separate room or office space devoted to their writing. Styles are as individual as authors. Right now, the author is sitting on an airplane, working on the first draft of this chapter. When she started writing books, she wrote her first chapter in longhand and then typed it into her desktop computer. Her co-author laughed at her and said it would not be long before she started composing at the computer. She was right. At that time, the author was still trying to figure out how to use the word processing program on her computer, but now she is trying to figure out how to type on her laptop during a long, rough airplane ride.

In reality, if you want to become a published author, you will need some tools. The manuscript that you send to an agent or publisher will have to be typed, most likely on a computer so that you can submit electronic files as well as a paper copy. See the "Checklist for Equipping Your Writing Environment."

## CHECKLIST FOR EQUIPPING
## YOUR WRITING ENVIRONMENT

You may want to collect all or some of the following as tools for your writing process:

- ☐ Computer or word processor
- ☐ Laser or inkjet printer
- ☐ Telephone
- ☐ Internet connection
- ☐ Scanner
- ☐ Fax machine
- ☐ Flat workspace, such as a table or desk, which is reserved for your writing (You don't want to have to take it down and put things away on a daily basis.)
- ☐ Comfortable, ergonomic chair
- ☐ Good light
- ☐ Research tools, including Internet connection, reference books, dictionary, thesaurus, and subject matter references
- ☐ Supplies, such as paper (pads and computer paper), ink or toner cartridges, pens (black or blue plus a contrasting color for editing), highlighters, paper clips, stapler and staples, adhesive tape, a three-hole punch, and any other general office supplies
- ☐ Media storage and backup devices, such as disks, CDs, or flash drives

# THE BOOK PROPOSAL

After some initial planning, you should have an idea about the type of manuscript you want to write. Will it be fiction or nonfiction? Who is the target audience? What type of publisher publishes your type of book? Will you need an agent? What is a copyright, and who will maintain the copyright?

You will need to decide how you want to put together your materials. Should you write an outline and a sample chapter to send to a publisher before completing the manuscript? Or, like Judith Krantz, should you write the entire novel before searching for an agent and a publisher? (For our first book, *Guide to Producing a Fashion Show*, we wrote a book proposal, an outline, and one chapter, which we sent to various publishers of fashion-related textbooks before we wrote the entire book. What if no publisher had wanted our manuscript? Luckily for us, that was not the case. If we had not found a publisher, would we have been willing to risk self-publishing and self-marketing our book?)

This section looks at all the elements that go into preparing a book proposal.

## SOME INTRODUCTORY THOUGHTS

You have already spent time gathering information and determining the type of book you propose to write. Now it is time to prepare the idea for presentation. A **book proposal** is a document, outlining your idea and the market potential for your book, that you prepare and send to a literary agent or publisher. Your book proposal is the first impression that you make to the literary agent or publisher. Professionalism and appearance are just as important for this presentation as they are for a job interview. First impressions count, and you need to present as a professional, whether you are a first-time author or a seasoned veteran writer.

Frequently, how your proposal looks will determine whether the project will be accepted. The query letter should be presented in a single-spaced business letter format, as discussed in Chapter 11, "Writing Business Communications." Other parts of the proposal, such as the sample chapter, should be double-spaced with wide margins—at least one inch to one and a half inches on the top, bottom, and sides of the paper. Not only are the pages easier to read when they're presented this way, but there is room for the reviewer to add comments and editing symbols.

Each publisher you send to should receive a fresh copy of the proposal. It is not appropriate to send copies that have been turned down by other publishers, especially if those copies have written critiques, look shopworn, or are damaged. They will look recycled, and publishers want to think that they are your first choice.

Read and reread the proposal and edit its presentation fearlessly. Your proposal should be clear, to-the-point, and free of typos and grammatical errors. The print should be clear and dark. This is not the time to skimp on printer quality or try to make that ink cartridge last just a little longer. Use an easy-to-read font and font size; Times New Roman in type of font size 12 is easy for people to read.

After you have completed the proposal, read and edit it again. Then, wait at least a day and read and edit it one last time to be sure you are sending the best proposal you can, one that is clearly written, concise, and properly edited.

Part of your research should be evaluating publishers. Does the publisher you are planning to send the proposal to publish your kind of book? Many misdirected proposals are sent to publishers that do not work in the genre of a particular book. Even if they are impressed with your manuscript, they will not publish something outside their category.

Copying and mailing the proposal can be quite expensive. Therefore, it is a waste of money to send your package to a publisher (or literary agent) that does not represent your category of book. It is better to target the type of publisher that works with your type of project.

## PROPOSAL FORMAT

While there is not just one standard format that will lead to a successful book contract, there are some common elements that will help sell your idea to a publisher. If you are writing a nonfiction book, you can think of the idea, do some research, organize the material, write an outline, draft a chapter or two, and prepare the book proposal and query letter to send to potential publishers—all before you actually write the book.

If you are writing a work of fiction, the proposal will consist of a title page; a **synopsis**, which is a brief narrative description of the book; and an author biography. If you have published other works of fiction, your bio should contain a list of prior publications as well as sales documentation of the previous books. Most agents and publishers want to see the entire manuscript of the novel, rather than just a few chapters. Selling a novel is considered to be more challenging than selling a nonfiction book.

Whether you are writing fiction or nonfiction, the following information will help you format your proposal. The desired format may differ from one publisher to another. For example, some publishers accept materials only through an agent. (We will discuss the role of a literary agent later in this chapter.) Some publishers want you to put your name on each page; others do not. Some publishers want a single chapter; others want three or more. There are a number of ways to learn the formats required by various publishers:

- Check *The Writer's Market* or *The Writer's Handbook* to see if the publisher is listed and provides guidelines for proposals.
- Write directly to the publisher to see if they have guidelines for submission.
- Visit the publisher's Web site and try to identify the acquisitions editor who appears most likely to handle books in the field of study that your proposed book fits into. (The **acquisitions editor** is the employee at the publishing company who is responsible for bringing in new works.) Then contact the acquisitions editor via email or by telephone.

It will be worth the time and effort to modify your proposal to meet the preferences of the specific publisher you are interested in approaching. Your ideal publisher may even accept a book proposal via email. That will certainly save money on copying and mailing.

Now we will discuss the various elements that should be included in the proposal.

## *Title Page*

The title page serves the same purpose as a title page for an academic paper, but its format is not as restricted as in academic research. It gives the title of the work and the names and contact information of the author or authors. Figure 10.2 shows an example of a title page for a book proposal, which may be modified to fit your purpose.

Your title should be short, yet capture the interest of a potential publisher and potential readers. Most publishers prefer short titles, because readers find them easier to remember. The titles of several books on the best-seller lists have no more than two or three words. For example, *Everyone Worth Knowing*, *In Her Shoes*, and *Lipstick Jungle* all made the *New York Times'* Best Sellers List.

Title Page

*Bugs and Beads*

**Bugs and Beads:**

**How Jeanne Hudson became**

**the Accessories Designer of the Year**

By Sara Jane Sedgwick

A scientist, with a Ph.D. in biology, enters the cutthroat world of fashion and gains success and

fame as a jewelry designer.

Number of words: 45,000

FIGURE 10.2. Example of a title page for a book proposal.

Many books make use of a subtitle to convey more information about the book. Jerry Oppenheimer used the title *Front Row: Anna Wintour, the Cool Life and Hot Times of Vogue's Editor in Chief*. That title certainly did not meet the guidelines of a short title. But, the author thought a more descriptive title was necessary to convey his topic.

Check *Books in Print* and *Forthcoming Books*, which are published annually by R. R. Bowker & Company, to see if there are any new or upcoming books on the subject you have chosen to write about. In these resources you will also be able to see what titles have already been used. You want a title that is not published by another author. (The title we proposed for our fashion show production book was already used by another author for a novel. While we were writing the manuscript, our publisher asked us to change the title of our nonfiction book so that it would not be confused with the novel.)

In addition to containing your title and subtitle (if used), your name(s) and contact information, and a short outline of the manuscript, it is helpful to include a brief description of your book. This is the short and intriguing sales pitch about your topic.

It is also helpful to include the approximate number of words you have written or expect to write. Depending on the margins, font style, and font size, the average double-spaced page of text has about 300 to 350 words. Most nonfiction works are between 170 and 300 pages long. The title page should also provide some documentation about the number and types of visual illustrations that will be included.

## Table of Contents

If you have not included a table of contents (TOC) on the title page, it would be appropriate to provide a TOC as part of the proposal package. The TOC serves as a map or an overview of what you have provided. Figure 10.3 is an example of a TOC for a book proposal. This section has the major headings identified with the page numbers where the various documents are located.

## Numbering Pages

It is helpful to number the pages. You may start page one with the title page or the first page of actual contents, depending upon your personal preference or the preference of your potential publisher. (For our examples, we start numbering on the title

TABLE OF CONTENTS

Book Proposal

***Bugs and Beads:***

***How Jeanne Hudson became***

***the Accessories Designer of the Year***

By Sara Jane Sedgwick

Sara Jane Sedgwick
1459 East Huron Road
East Moriches, New York 11940
Phone: (631) 555-6666
Fax: (631) 555-6667
sjsedgwick@author.com

**FIGURE 10.3.** Example of a table of contents for a book proposal.

page, as the *American Psychological Association* does.) A page header provides a brief title, as well as the page number. Your word processing program should provide these capabilities.

## Description and Chapter Outline

The description section of the proposal provides a **synopsis** or brief overview of the book. This section should be approximately one to two pages long. The lead paragraph should grab the interest of the reader, as a newspaper story does. The reader is, most likely, the publisher's acquisitions editor. In this section of your proposal you tell the purpose of the book by describing how the book begins, what it is about, and how it ends.

The synopsis should describe the type of book you are writing. Is it fiction or nonfiction? If it is fiction, is it a romantic story or a mystery or something else? If it is nonfiction, is it a how-to, history, biography, or another genre? What is interesting or unique about your approach?

After the synopsis is presented, the chapter outline is offered. The chapters may be presented in an actual outline form or as a brief narrative describing what is covered in each chapter. Figures 10.4a and 10.4b show examples of both types of chapter outline techniques.

## Sample Chapter

Depending upon the publisher's requirements, for a nonfiction book you will send one to three sample chapters. Some authors advise sending the first chapter, while other authors suggest sending a chapter that demonstrates your expertise, knowledge, and writing style. The publisher of a fiction book may require a complete manuscript instead of some sample chapters. Whether you are sending mock chapters or a complete manuscript draft, you need to provide materials that will help sell your concept and writing style to the publisher.

If you know how the work of fiction ends, you should provide it, especially if the ending is dramatic. Do not worry about giving away the ending. You are trying to sell the manuscript, not keep the publisher's reader in suspense.

**Traditional Book Outline**

***Bugs and Beads* by Sara Jane Sedgwick**

1) **Glamour and Glitz**
   a) Jeanne Hudson shows her jewelry to the Council of Fashion Designers Award (CFDA) judges
   b) She trys on gowns designed by Alice Roi and Dana Buchman to wear to the CFDA ceremony
   c) Arriving at the New York Public Library
   d) The CFDA paid tribute to the winners and honorees of the CFDA Fashion Awards in the Celeste Bartos Forum of The New York Public Library
   e) Jeanne Hudson was among the winners, named the Accessories Designer of the Year
2) **Glamour and glitz**
   a) Jeanne Hudson went to New York University
   b) She studied biology, intending to become an environmental biologist
   c) Her long term goal was to become a university professor, spending summers doing field research
   d) School was expensive and stressful
   e) How could Jeanne relieve stress and relax?
3) **Learning to Make Jewelry**
   a) She learned to make necklaces and bracelets during a field study at the Grand Canyon between completing her bachelor's and master's degrees
   b) This relaxing diversion was so much fun, Jeanne enrolled in a jewelry making class at NYU
4) **A New Obsession**
   a) Using discipline learned in biology, Jeanne was embraced her new hobby
   b) Jeanne made exotic bug shaped jewelry for her family, classmates, professors, and friends
5) **Meeting Mentors**
   a) Stephanie Smith, owner of Trendz, the hip store in Soho fell in love with Jeanne's jewelry
   b) Stephanie started carrying Jeanne's jewelry line in her store
   c) Stephanie introduced Jeanne to Jade Jagger, who was then the Creative Director and jewelry designer for Garrard, the British Crown Jeweler

FIGURE 10.4a. Example of chapter outline format technique.

### Narrative Book Outline

#### *Bugs and Beads* by Sara Jane Sedgwick

**Chapter 1: Glamour and Glitz**
Jeanne Hudson is thrown into the glamorous world fashion as an award nominee the Council of Fashion Designers of America. She is invited to submit her designs for the prestigious Accessory Designer of the Year competition. Both Alice Roi and Dana Buchman offer her dresses to wear to the event, where she is honored as the winner of the award.

**Chapter 2: Becoming a Biologist**
When Jeanne was growing up in upstate New York, she dreamed of becoming an environmental biologist. She worked hard to get into New York University, where her skills and interests were challenged. On a field study at the Grand Canyon, she met other biologists and loved the work. As a way to relax, her friend Deb Rivera taught her how to make beaded necklaces.

**Chapter 3: Learning to Make Jewelry**
Upon returning from her field study, Jeanne entered the master's degree program in biology at NYU. But, for fun, she took a jewelry making class. This is where she learned to make jewelry in the shape of the exotic bugs she studied in biology.

**Chapter 4: A New Obsession**
Jeanne was obsessed with her new creative art. She started making gifts for her friends at school. Naturally, she gave her jewelry to her family as presents. Her professors also enjoyed her work, asking to buy the jewelry as gifts for their families and friends.

**Chapter 5: Meeting Mentors**
The owner of Trendz, the hip store in Soho, Stephanie Smith fell in love with Jeanne's jewelry. Stephanie started selling Jeanne's jewelry line in her store, where it became a best-seller. Stephanie introduced Jeanne to Jade Jagger, who was then the Creative Director and jewelry designer for Garrard, the British Crown Jeweler. The two unlikely new friends started working together.

FIGURE 10.4b. Example of chapter narrative format technique.

## Market Potential

As you have been doing research about your subject, you probably discovered statistics about your target audience. This section of the proposal is where you share that data with the potential publisher. Here you outline the demographic and psychographic characteristics of the audience you've identified as your target—the potential purchasers and readers of your book.

Who will read your book? Is your book directed toward women? Toward men? What are the ages of your readers? Are they children? Teens? Young adults? Mature adults? Knowing your audience will help define the market potential.

Another key piece of defining the market potential is identifying potential outlets for distribution of your book. If you are writing a book on how to apply make-up or how to wear accessories, an ideal outlet might be personal appearances at a cosmetic or an accessories store, where you can give demonstrations and sign books. You may be able to make outlet recommendations that the publisher did not even think of.

The ideal place for a book launch might be a real location that is featured in your book. For example, a shop or business where characters in the novel meet could be used as the site for a book launch or special event. If the book's characters met at Bloomingdales, and the executives from Bloomingdales are supportive, the book could be introduced at several branch locations throughout the United States. This emphasizes the story and provides an interesting double promotion for the book and the store.

Market potential also considers other books in your genre. What is the competition for your book? How is your book different from the others? Read the books written by your competition so that you can answer these questions and promote your project. This section of the proposal should include a complete publication reference, similar to the References at the end of each chapter of this textbook. After a source is cited, provide a brief synopsis in which you reveal the competitor's strengths and weaknesses. Here is your opportunity to differentiate your work from the work of other authors.

## Author Biography

What makes you qualified to write your book? Here is where you provide pertinent information about why you are the ideal candidate to write this book. This section of the proposal is called the author biography, or more simply the author bio.

This narrative section tells the publisher about you. If you have written other books, list them here. Include any special experiences or skills that make you an expert on the topic. Here is where you tell the publisher about any promotional skills that you have, such as your public speaking, television, or radio experience or seminars or classes that you have taught on the subject of your book. You can suggest other authorities who might endorse or review your book.

### CHECKLIST FOR YOUR AUTHOR BIO

Consider the following checklist for the content of your author bio:

- ☐ Education, related academic credentials, and any specialized training
- ☐ Professional work experience in the field you are writing about
- ☐ Other books, articles, scripts, or papers you have written
- ☐ Public speaking, teaching, acting experience, or seminar presentations
- ☐ Personal information, when applicable to what you are writing about
- ☐ Promotional experience, especially media experience
- ☐ Personal reasons for writing this book
- ☐ Professional reviews or prior endorsements
- ☐ Résumé or curriculum vita

Not all of the elements in the "Checklist for Your Author Bio" may be necessary or applicable to your book. For instance, having a university degree in fashion may not be as important for a novelist as it is for a nonfiction writer. A curriculum vita is essential for a university professor.

# QUERY LETTER

Once you feel your proposal is ready to send to a potential publisher or literary agent, you will write a query letter to accompany your proposal. The **query letter**, which is similar to the cover letter discussed in Chapter 7, "Writing for Public Relations," is the document that brings all the elements of the package together. It contains an extremely condensed version of the book proposal. You hope that the publisher or agent will want more information and want to publish your book. The query letter is a key element in finding the right publisher.

The query letter is generally a single-spaced, one- to one-and-a-half-page business letter that contains an opening paragraph, the body of the correspondence, and a closing paragraph. The first step in developing a query letter is to determine an appropriate publisher for your book. You may find publishers by looking through your personal library and identifying publishers of similar types of books. As we mentioned earlier in the chapter, the *Writer's Market* and *The Writer's Handbook* are good sources for identifying potential publishers. Additionally, online sources such as Amazon.com list publishers and the types of books a publisher would be interested in. These references and individual publisher Web sites provide the background information you need.

After you have determined appropriate publishers, get the name and address for the current acquisitions editor for each. This is the person to whom the query letter is directed, unless the publisher indicates that it accept manuscripts only from literary agents. That process is described in the next section of this chapter.

Once you have identified the acquisitions editor, be sure to get that person's official title and the correct spelling of their name. Published directories become outdated rather quickly, and some editors have been known to toss letters addressed to their predecessor or letters with excessive typographical or grammatical errors. Why should they work with someone who does not pay attention to details the way a successful published author does?

The tone of your query letter should be upbeat and positive. Be enthusiastic and prepare the letter in a manner that will sell your ideas and project to the publisher.

The opening paragraph should include the title of the book and the hook, or selling point, of the work. This is the most important paragraph of the query letter.

---

*Opening Paragraph Example:* **How did a scientifically trained biologist end up as the winner of the Council of Fashion Designers of America Award for Accessories Designer of the Year? The story is about the unusual career path of Jeanne Hudson, who made jewelry to help pay for her college expenses. I look at her remarkable success in the jewelry business in my book,** *Bugs and Beads.* **Let me explain how the two unrelated topics merge into one.**

---

The next section, the body of the letter, should consist of several paragraphs that describe the contents of your book. In addition to describing your text, include some statistical data, unknown facts, or interesting passages. You can also discuss why you are interested in writing the book and why you are the right person to do it.

The body of the letter also includes a concise explanation of the target audience and how the book could be promoted. This section also provides an overview of the book proposal, highlighting the most important parts.

The concluding paragraph describes your next action. Based upon your research and your knowledge of what specific publishers want, you will accompany your query letter with a whole manuscript, a book proposal, or a synopsis. For example, you could say, "I am sending you a proposal for *Writing for the Fashion Business,* a how-to book for up-and-coming authors in the fashion field. My book proposal, extended outline, and one sample chapter with a list of illustrations consists of 60 pages." Be sure to thank the editor for his time in reviewing your material as you close the query letter.

Check the draft of the letter after you have completed it.

### QUERY LETTER CHECKLIST

- ☐ Take time to edit it, just as you do all of your writing projects.
- ☐ Be sure you have the current acquisition editor's name and title.
- ☐ Proofread the letter for the correct spelling of the publisher and the accurate address.
- ☐ Check the grammar and spelling of the letter content.
- ☐ Make sure that you have included your current contact information, including full name, address, telephone number, and e-mail address. More and more publishers are using e-mail for contacting and communicating with authors.
- ☐ Put together a complete package, which typically includes the query letter, the book proposal, and a self-addressed envelope for a response.
- ☐ Remember to sign the letter, and be sure to provide adequate postage.

*Portfolio Exercise:* **Using the preliminary research you have done at a special collections library for the brief biography that you have already written, prepare a query letter and book proposal to an actual publisher. Find out the name of the acquisitions editor and the current address of the publisher, and put together a proposal package for your book idea.**

Some publishers will not accept unsolicited manuscripts, preferring to work directly with agents, not authors. Next, we will look at the role of literary agents and will define when they are required and when they are not.

# LITERARY AGENTS

An agent is a person with the authority to act on behalf of another person. Therefore, a **literary agent** represents the author of a book while negotiating the terms of a book contract with a potential publisher. There are good literary agents and bad literary agents, just as there are good authors and bad ones. How do you know if you need an agent? If you do need an agent, how do you find a good one?

Whether you need an agent or not depends upon the type of book you are writing and the type of publisher you are working with. If you have access to publishers in your field, you may not need an agent. Most fiction authors want an agent who works with established major publishers—to negotiate the best possible contract details, obtain a respectable advance, and arrange for an experienced marketing department to promote the book.

A literary agent's primary responsibility is to get you a book contract. An experienced agent should be able to get you a better contract, with a larger advance and higher royalty rates than you could negotiate on your own. A literary agent would also know what type of publisher is looking for authors such as you. If an agent has an ongoing relationship with a publisher, she can work effectively to get you the contract you desire. Good agents frequently become friends with their authors, offering career guidance and a nurturing environment for new authors.

As compensation, the literary agent typically receives 15% of the book advance and royalties. While this may not be a huge amount of money, it can be. If you do use an agent, you enter into a contractual agreement with the agent. You want an agent who will provide a positive relationship as well as positive results. Once you have started working with an agent, publishers probably will not want to work directly with you until a publishing contract is signed. If you sign an agreement with an agent, but that agent does not provide the services for you, you may still find it difficult to get out of the agreement with the literary agent to represent yourself. So be careful when selecting an agent. You want an agent who is appropriate for your needs.

Agents may specialize in specific categories of books, just as some publishers specialize in specific categories of books. You may find an agent in books such as *Guide to Literary Agents*, which is published by Writer's Digest Books, or *Literary Market Place*, published by R. R. Bowker. Another way to find an agent is to seek recommendations from other authors. For the best chance of a good working relationship, make sure you feel a positive rapport with the agent you choose.

Once you have agreed to work with an agent, a legally enforceable contract is normally drafted. It takes time to complete an agreement. Before signing any agreement, you should ask important questions and seek advice from a lawyer, other authors, or a professional organization such as the Association of Authors' Representatives (AAR), a nonprofit organization that has established a Canon of Ethics for members to use (Association of Authors' Representatives, 2006a). According to AAR, you and the agent you are considering should fully discuss the nature and extent of the agent's responsibility. Members of AAR are prohibited from charging a reading fee, which is an upfront charge to the client for reading and evaluation by an agent.

AAR suggests asking an agent the following questions before you sign an agreement (Association of Authors' Representatives, 2006b, ¶ 11):

- Are you a member of the Association of Authors' Representatives?
- How long have you been in business as an agent?
- Who in your agency will actually be handling my work? Will the other staff members be familiar with my work and the status of my business at your agency? Will you oversee or at least keep me apprised of the work that your agency is doing on my behalf?
- Do you issue an agent–author agreement? May I review the language of the agency clause that appears in contracts you negotiate for your clients?
- How do you keep your clients informed of your activities on their behalf?
- Do you consult with your clients on any and all offers?
- What are your commission rates? What are your procedures and time-frames for processing and disbursing client funds? Do you keep different bank accounts separating author funds from agency revenue? What are your policies about charging clients for expenses incurred by your agency?
- When you issue 1099 tax forms at the end of each year, do you also furnish clients upon request with a detailed account of their financial activity, such as gross income, commissions and other deductions, and net income, for the past year?
- In the event of your death or disability, what provisions exist for my continued representation?
- If we should part company, what is your policy about handling any unsold subsidiary rights to my work?

Basically, a literary agent is responsible for seeking publishers for your work, and it is your obligation to pay the commission when the agent fulfills that obligation.

You probably want to set a specified period of time during which the agent represents your work. Agent and author agreements are typically set for one year, which should be enough time for an agent to seek a publisher for your work. Either you or the agent may want a longer period of time, and you can extend an agreement.

If you do not feel that things are working out, you may want to be able to get out of the agreement. Some agents will agree to negotiate a termination clause that allows you to end the relationship with a 30-day notice. But, the agent may insist that the contract contain a post-termination clause stating that the agency is owed a commission if the work is sold within 90 days of your terminating the contract. That clause protects the agent who has worked to sell your manuscript.

You will feel more confident about signing any agreement, for a literary agent or directly with a publisher, if you are able to speak with another author who has worked with that agent or publisher. You should ask for some contacts and have a list of questions prepared to ask those contacts. Some questions you would want to ask: Has the other author had any problems with the agent in the past? If so, what were they and how were they resolved? Understanding the process and knowing what to ask can lead to a mutually beneficial agreement, one in which both the author and the agent understand the conditions and in which the details are well documented.

---

*Portfolio Exercise:* **Assume that a publisher has responded to your book proposal in a positive manner, but has sent you a letter stating that an agent is required for negotiation. Prepare an inquiry letter to send to a potential literary agent.**

---

# NEGOTIATING A PUBLICATION CONTRACT

Changes in technology and how works are delivered to the reader are causing publication contracts to become more and more complex. Whether you negotiate your own contract with a publisher or you use the services of a literary agent, you should understand what the contract means. If there are any terms or issues you do not understand, it would be advisable to hire a lawyer to assist you with negotiations.

## TERMS OF AGREEMENT

If the publisher likes your proposal and topic, and sees the market potential, the publisher may offer you a contract. The **terms of agreement** are the fundamental deal points, which are the elements considered essential to the people making the book contract. Deal points include such things as authorship credit, rights, distribution, author compensation, delivery of the manuscript, publication details, and plans for future editions.

## GRANT OF RIGHTS

The **grant of rights** is the section of a book contract where an author grants the publisher the rights to publish the author's work. This typically includes a term or time period, which is typically for the life of the copyright. It also covers the geographic scope. Can the work be published worldwide or limited specifically to a region? For example, the publication could be limited to the United States and its possessions.

The primary rights grant the format of the publication. Will it be published as a hardcover, a paperback, a trade paperback, mass market, or an e-book. Secondary rights, also called subsidiary rights, include publishing the work as a periodical, through a book club, dramatic rights, film/TV rights, radio rights, commercial tie-in (merchandising) rights, new technologies, or foreign translation rights.

## COLLABORATION

Some authors prefer to write alone, while other authors like to collaborate. **Collaboration** involves working with a ghostwriter, a partner, or group of writers. The agreement specifies the names of all the authors, with the lead author first. It also states the percentage of work that is expected to be contributed by each other. This will impact the distribution of royalties to each author.

A **ghostwriter** is an experienced writer who is hired to help an individual put ideas into publication format. If you are hired as a ghostwriter, you may be helping a famous person write his autobiography or helping an expert put an idea into a format that the public will understand. Whether you are hired as a ghostwriter or you hire a ghostwriter to work with you, you must agree on terms of payment and author credit. The ghostwriter may receive author recognition or not.

If the ghostwriter is given credit, the authorship may be listed as "*Fashion Author Name* with *Ghostwriter Name.*" Another way the ghostwriter is identified: "by *Fashion Author Name* as told to *Ghostwriter Name.*" The credit should reflect what each of the authors contributed. Sometimes a ghostwriter is not even identified or given credit on a book's title page.

If the book is published by an established publisher, the contract may be written so that the ghostwriter gets the full advance plus 50% of the royalties. If the book is self-published, the ghostwriter will likely negotiate an hourly rate or a per-page rate. It would be appropriate for you to investigate the current rates for ghostwriters before agreeing to any arrangement.

**Equal partner collaboration** involves two authors with equivalent responsibilities. Writing responsibilities as well as proceeds are shared in the same way. Because each person's tasks, expenses, and rewards are detailed in the agreement, a clause defining what will happen if the project is not completed by one or both authors should also be included. Each author should retain the rights to turn what she has written into a complete work of her own.

## AUTHOR COMPENSATION

How the author is paid and how much the author is paid are covered by author compensation. There are two issues you should consider:

1. Is there some form of advance or signing bonus?
2. How and when will the royalties be sent to you?

The publisher may offer an **advance**, which is a cash payment that the publisher pays the author prior to publication. This advance, which is paid against future royalties, may be enough to allow the author to quit her job and concentrate on writing. But do not quit your day job yet. The size of an advance for a first-time author generally does not permit that kind of luxury. An advance against royalties is usually paid in thirds: one third upon signing the agreement, one third upon delivery of the manuscript, and the final one third when the book is published. Again, this is not a straight gift from the publisher. The amount of the advance will be deducted from any future royalties the book earns. Other publishers may offer a **signing bonus** or **grant,** which is a cash payment that directly supports the author and does not have to be repaid from future royalties.

**Royalties** are the share of the book sales that is paid to the author. This amount is normally set as a percentage. If author royalties are negotiated for 10% of the cover price and the book sells for $25.00 a copy, the author will receive $2.50 for each book sold. But, some publishers negotiate royalties as a percentage of **invoice prices**, which is the amount that the publisher is paid by bookstores and wholesalers. Thus, a publisher that offers bookstores and wholesalers a 40% discount will receive only $15.00 from the sale of each book with a cover price of $25.00, and the author would receive only $1.50 on each book. It is important for you to know whether royalties are paid on the cover price or on the invoice price.

It is also important to agree to the accounting terms. This is where the publisher establishes a formal system to credit the author for sales of the book. It also defines when and how the author is paid. If an agent is involved, royalty checks may be distributed to the agent. Then, the agent pays the author. If an agent is not involved, the publisher pays the author directly. Royalties are commonly paid twice each year.

## MANUSCRIPT DELIVERY

The manuscript delivery section of the contract deals with the delivery due-date and format of the completed manuscript. Once the delivery date is established, the format is negotiated. Some publishers want both a hard copy (printout) and a computer disk containing the manuscript prepared in a word-processing program; other publishers want chapters to be sent electronically via e-mail.

A complete manuscript may include artwork, illustrations, charts, photographs, preface, table of contents, bibliography, index, and other essentials. This section of the contract will also outline any other expectations, such as who—the publisher or the author—will obtain permissions, authorizations, or endorsements.

The publisher will probably include a clause called "publisher's rights upon delivery." This allows the publisher to back out of the agreement if the manuscript or any of its parts arc not acceptable. The publisher may give the author an opportunity to revise and resubmit the project or terminate the contract. This clause also allows the publisher to terminate the contract if the manuscript is not delivered by the due date.

In addition to the contract being terminated, if the manuscript is not delivered on time or in an acceptable condition the author will be asked to return the advance. If the publisher decides to terminate the contract upon delivery of the manuscript due to some outside conditions that adversely impact the ability to sell the work, the author is usually allowed to keep the advance.

## COPYRIGHT

A copyright is the name (publisher or author) that is used to register the work, and it protects the publisher or author from other writers using the written or other creative work without permission. If someone copies, adapts, or publishes a copyrighted work without permission from the copyright holder, the copyright holder's rights are violated. These violations can lead to serious civil and possibly criminal penalties.

Copyright law protects the work from reproduction, preparation of derivative works based upon the copyrighted work, distribution of copies, or performance or display of the work. However, other persons may still be able to use certain parts of the work. For example, other authors and artists are permitted to quote sections of the work (of a specific length) without your permission through the doctrine of **fair use**. Some of the purposes that are considered fair use include criticism, news reporting, teaching, and research.

Copyrights may be held by the publisher or by the author. This point is also negotiated before the parties sign the publication agreement. Typically, first-time authors allow the publisher to hold the book's copyrights. The publisher registers the work with the U.S. Copyright Office.

## PUBLICATION

The publication section of the contract lays out how the publisher will prepare the manuscript for print form. This involves editing and revising the manuscript, designing the page layout and cover, setting the price, and planning a promotional package. This section will also define the terms for future editions of the book. If the publisher wants to publish a second edition or additional revisions, usually it is the original author who is asked to produce the revisions. If the author does not want to do another edition, terms will define the role of another author brought in to revise the work.

You need to become familiar with the various elements of a publication agreement, copyrights, literary agents, and publishers. You cannot depend upon anyone else to do that for you. Many authors seek advice from other authors and lawyers before signing any legal contracts.

# WORKING WITH A PUBLISHER

After you have signed a contract with a publisher, it is time to get to work. If your work is a novel, the manuscript may already be written. If you are producing a nonfiction book, you probably have an outline and one or more sample chapters. Either way, you now have a partner in producing the book: your publisher. You and the publisher share a common goal of producing a high-quality book with potential for commercial success.

Both the author and the publisher have responsibilities to make this happen. Keep in mind that you will probably have to negotiate and compromise as you work toward your goal. It is hard to hear someone tell you that you need to remove a section of your work or move it to another chapter, but a professional working relationship with mutual respect is the ultimate hope for authors and editors.

The author is responsible for producing a work that is edited for grammar and punctuation and is free of spelling errors. The work should provide accurate information with proper credit given to other references, to avoid any possible claims of plagiarism or factual error. The work should be prepared and submitted in the format requested by the publisher, whether that is hard copy, electronic files, or both.

Most publishers provide guidelines for formatting the manuscript, such as what margins and font and font size to use; what word processing programs are acceptable; how to organize headings; how to reference figures and tables; and which writing style manual to follow. You will find these guidelines extremely helpful. Their purpose is to get the manuscript into a format that will be easy for the editor and designer and typesetter to convert into final book form.

Typically, the publisher assigns one of its employees, the **developmental editor**, to read the work and offer suggestions as well as professional criticism regarding the content and form of the book. After it is edited, the work is returned to the author for comment and adjustment. This process may involve more than one pass between the development editor and the author. The development editor may also be involved in the copyediting, or the manuscript may be sent to a copyeditor for that part of the work. **Copyediting** is checking for grammar, spelling, consistencies, and facts. Meanwhile, the design team prepares an attractive, functional page format and cover design. Once the design has been approved and the editorial work has been substantially completed, the book is sent for typesetting. **Proofs**, which are the typeset pages, are sent to the author for final corrections—and to potential reviewers, if their comments are desired for promotional purposes. The cover design is finalized and approved. In today's book market, page proofs and cover designs may be transmitted between the editor and author electronically as PDFs.

Once the final corrections are made, the electronic version of the page proofs is sent to the printer. One last check: The printer sends the publisher final proofs called "bluelines." After bluelines are approved, the book is printed and bound (has its cover attached) and is shipped to the publisher's warehouse. From here, the copies of the book are distributed to the author, bookstores, and wherever the author and publisher have arranged for sale or editorial review.

The publisher's responsibilities range from providing editorial review, guidance, and encouragement to producing a professional-quality publication. It is hoped that you and the publisher have worked well together and have listened to each other's ideas and desires along the way—leading to a book published according to schedule, with shared excitement at the results. Of course, one other responsibility of the publisher is to meet the contractual financial agreement and pay the author the royalties that are due.

# SELF-PUBLISHING

What if you do not find an agent or a publisher willing to take on your project? All is not lost. There are other ways to get your work to readers. Some authors take the project into their own hands and publish their work themselves. Are you willing to take the risk and put in the time and effort to self-publish?

The risk is in putting your own money into publishing the work. Many authors simply want to get their work into book format and are not interested in any financial rewards. Still, many self-publishers have been financially successful with their projects.

## BASIC STEPS

If you choose to publish your book yourself, the following steps will help you complete the process. You start by creating a company, which is necessary to sell your book through bookstores and other retail outlets (Embree, 2003).

1. The first step in setting up a publishing company is selecting a name and registering it with your county clerk's office. After checking with the clerk's office to be

sure the name is not already being used, you file a Doing Business As (DBA) form and publish the DBA in a local newspaper for a period of time.

2. You need a sales tax permit, which you obtain from your state's Board of Equalization. Depending on the state in which you register your company, you may need other government approvals as well. Research these through your local and state government offices.

3. Once you have established your company, you need to purchase a block of at least ten International Standard Book Numbers (ISBNs) and get your copyright registered. The minimum number of ISBNs that you may order is 10. For current prices, a copy of the application form, and more information, check the Web site www.isbn.org. Although you do not have to register with the U.S. Copyright Office to use the © symbol, registering will ensure greater legal protection.

4. You also need a Library of Congress Control Number (LCCN). Look at the Library of Congress Web site (www.lcweb.loc.gov/faq/catfaq.html) for more information.

5. By completing an "Advance Book Information Form," you will be listed in the databases for *Forthcoming Books* and *Books in Print*, which provide information to libraries and book sellers. R. R. Bowker publishes both of these books.

6. If you plan on selling through traditional retail stores, you need bar codes.

7. Once you have obtained the preceding items, you can apply for Publisher's Cataloging in Publication (PCIP). An established larger publisher gets Cataloging in Publication (CIP) from the Library of Congress, whereas a small publisher must purchase it from Quality Books (www.quality-books.com). Librarians need this PCIP information in order to process your book. You will need to check with the various agencies to find out the current prices for the required registrations.

Figure 10.5 shows an example of a copyright page, which contains the book's title, LCCN, PCIP, ISBN, the copyright symbol and the year of publication, and the author's name. This page is placed on the reverse side of your title page.


## OTHER CONSIDERATIONS

There are many additional costs associated with self-publishing. You must consider the expenses for editing, proofreading, designing the cover and page layouts, typesetting, and printing. You can complete some of these elements yourself, but you should not skimp on editing and proofreading. Every writer benefits from review by outside

Director of Sales and Acquisitions: Dana Meltzer-Berkowitz
Executive Editor: Olga T. Kontzias
Senior Development Editor: Jennifer Crane
Development Editor: Cate DaPron
Art Director: Adam B. Bohannon
Production Manager: Ginger Hillman
Senior Production Editor: Elizabeth Marotta
Photo Researcher: Erin Fitzsimmons
Copy Editor: Cate DaPron
Cover Design: Adam B. Bohannon
Text Design: Nicola Ferguson

**Focus Strategic Communications, Inc.**
Project Managers: Adrianna Edwards, Ron Edwards
Formatter: Carol Magee
Proofreader: Linda Szostak
Indexer: Carol Roberts

Library of Congress Catalog Card Number: 2007934509
ISBN-13: 978-1-56367-439-6
ISBN-10: 1-56367-439-4

GST R 133004424
Printed in USA

FIGURE 10.5. Example of a copyright page.

critics. If you can do the typing and typesetting yourself, you can save on those costs, as long as the printer can translate your work to the printing process. Most self-typeset works are completed in desktop publishing packages such as Quark, InDesign, or Adobe Acrobat software to convert your document to a PDF file.

You must decide what price to charge for your completed book, taking into consideration the price range for competitive works. A price that is too high will probably eliminate the book from consideration from your potential readers. If you price it too low, potential readers may think that the book is worth less than the competition. Before settling on a selling price, you must also consider the price of having the book printed.

Once the price for printing has been negotiated with the printer, you can place your first order. Many first-time authors are optimistic and want to order 1,000 copies, which was the minimum order in the past. Now, in the digital age, fewer copies can be printed cost-effectively. Take into consideration how you will sell your book. If it has a limited target audience, and you plan to sell it only at seminars or workshops that you present, print a small number of copies. If you print 100 copies, you will have an opportunity to see how the book sells, and you can make any changes prior to printing more. Endorsements and reviews can also be added to a second printing. With a smaller first printing, you do not have to tie up so much money in advance or be stuck with unsold inventory in your basement or garage.

## SUMMARY

This chapter looked at the world of writing and publishing books. We defined fiction and nonfiction, recognizing that a nonfiction book on a topic of interest to a wide readership may be easier for a first-time author to get published. Competition for publishing fiction is much greater. The first steps in getting any book published are to develop a book proposal and write a query letter. Representation by a literary agent may or may not be part of the negotiation with a potential book publisher. Once a publisher has expressed a desire to publish a book, negotiations between the author and the publisher will lead to a book contract. For authors who do not find a publisher, self-publishing is a viable option. The techniques as well as the pros and cons were evaluated.

## KEY TERMS

Acquisitions editor

Advance

Antagonist

Book proposal

Citation                        Invoice price
Collaboration                   Literary agent
Copyediting                     Nonfiction
Copyright                       Plot
Developmental editor            Proofs
Dialogue                        Protagonist
Equal partner collaboration     Query letter
Fair use                        Reference book
Fiction                         Royalties
Ghostwriter                     Signing bonus
Grant                           Synopsis
Grant of rights                 Terms of agreement

## CASE STUDY

### Nancy's Negotiation

After graduating from college with a degree in fashion design and a minor in English, Nancy Sanchez spent three years working for the *Los Angeles Times* as a fashion reporter. Her exciting job entailed visiting the fashion capitals of the world and reporting on up-and-coming trends and the business of fashion to readers in Southern California and nationwide.

During this time, Nancy met and interviewed most of the top fashion designers and public relations specialists in the fashion field. Nancy loved doing her job and meeting all kinds of new people. But then she married her college sweetheart, and she quit her job at the *Los Angeles Times* to relocate to the small Oregon town where her new husband had a teaching job. Nancy still loved fashion, read every top fashion magazine, and looked at several fashion blogs online everyday. What could she do with her fashion and journalism background, living in a small rural community without much of a tradition in fashion?

Nancy's other dream was to write books. She had several ideas for fiction books based upon some of the people she had met during her travels for the newspaper. Could she turn writing into a new career? Just thinking about that tough, demanding designer she met in Milan got her love of story-telling going! Wouldn't a good story revolve around the assistant who is really creating the fabulous designs? The well-known fashion designer is stealing the assistant's ideas and taking credit for them.

Then, the assistant is found murdered. Who did it? The designer? The assistant's lover? The designer's public relations agent? Oh, it could make a great mystery novel, with the fashion industry in the background.

Nancy put her writing skills to work. Within six months she had created the first draft of a fashion–fiction–mystery novel. Three months later, Nancy felt it was time to put her book proposal out to several publishers. She asked her friends in Los Angeles for the name of a literary agent, since she knew this was important for works of fiction.

Upon the recommendation of her former boss, Nancy hired Joan Dysart as her literary agent. Joan took the manuscript to several small publishers, and Bluenote Mystery Books expressed interest in her story. Nancy was overwhelmed by all of the details in the book contract.

Bluenote wants a Grant of Rights, which is where the author grants the publisher the right to publish the work, as protected by copyright law. For most authors this means giving the publisher exclusive worldwide rights, including the rights to all derivative works. While it's not in the interest of the author to give up anything without negotiation, the publisher is frequently in a better position than the author to exploit these rights (such as publishing translations), which will result in further payments to the author. If the author believes the work is likely to become a smash movie or TV hit, the derivative rights could be the plum of the book contract. But, turning over those rights would prevent Nancy from using the material from her book with any other future opportunities. Nancy thinks that her story just might be a good plot for a TV movie. She also thinks that international audiences will want to read her novel.

Other points of negotiation that concern Nancy include advances, royalties, and foreign rights. The publisher offered her $2,000 as an advance, 5% for royalties, and 1% for foreign rights. Although she is a new writer, Nancy believes these are minimal.

## CASE STUDY QUESTIONS

1. Where should Nancy go for advice?
2. Is it unrealistic to expect a first-time author to be able to negotiate with a publisher?
3. What is the role of the literary agent in the book negotiations?
4. Are contracts a take-it-or-leave-it proposition?

## INDUSTRY PROFILE

*Robyn Waters*

***What is your current job and title? Can you describe the main responsibilities for your job?***

I am currently self-employed. I am president of RW Trend, LLC. I am an author, keynote speaker, and trend consultant. I am the only employee of my company. My primary income is derived from my keynote presentations at conferences and to businesses.

***What is a typical day at work like?***

There is not typical day, per se. Each day however, I probably spend two to three hours on e-mail, answering questions for clients, conference calls with events managers, making travel arrangements, preparing my PPT presentations, and doing interviews for various media. Then, two to four times a month on average, I catch a plane in the evening, fly to another city, present at a conference the next day, and fly home that evening.

Note: Some months I may not speak or present at all. Some months I'm gone more than I'm home. When my second book *The Hummer and the Mini* launched last October, I was in 12 cities in 25 days, including Helsinki, Finland.

***At what point did you decide to pursue a career in writing for a fashion-related business?***

After 28 years in the corporate retail world, I was ready for a change. I felt I had become a "talking head" for my company. I knew what I was expected to say, but had lost touch with my personal values and my authentic self. I wrote my first book and self-published it as a way to clear my head. I wrote it on my sabbatical in between leaving Target and forming my own consulting company. I wrote it in my language, shared my stories, and hired a designer to "bring it to life" visually. My first self-published version of *The Trendmaster's Guide* was written in part to help put a little soul back into the $.

***Describe your first writing job. What was the most important or interesting thing you wrote for that job/publication?***

My first writing job was for myself. (See above.) *The Trendmaster's Guide from A to Z* was written, designed, and printed within a year after leaving the corporate world. The most important thing about the book was that it was my experience, my language, my story, my viewpoint. It wasn't something someone else asked me to write. The only objective I had was to share my personal trend philosophy. It was also a bit of a backlash to the corporate world that at the time was declaring that everything had to be a process. I am quick to stress that my first book is a philosophy, not a process. i.e., it's not linear, it's more organic.

### What are you currently reading (books, magazines, Web sites, newspapers, other media)? Do you have a favorite author or publication?

I have a voracious appetite for knowledge, and as such, read a lot. *WSJ* is my home page on my computer. I read the *NY Times* every Sunday. I most often pick up *USA Today* in my travels. I subscribe to and pick up selectively many magazines, including fashion and shelter magazines, as well as business magazines and other general interest. We subscribe to *Fortune, Business Week, Smithsonian, National Geographic*, and *Tricycle*. My favorite trend publication is *Viewpoint* by MODE INFO. It's published in Europe and comes out two times a year. I subscribe on the Internet to *Cool News/Reveries* by Tim Manners, *MorningNewsBeat* by Kevin Coupe, the *NRF* (National Retail Federation) newsletter, *Retail News* newsletters, *Iconoculture, Trendwatching*, and *Springwise* by Reiner Evers, and Tom Peters and Tim Sanders newsletters. I do not blog.

Recent books: *The Fellowship* (Frank Lloyd Wright's biography), and a biography on Mary Jane Elizabeth Colter. Also just completed *13 Moons, Made to Stick, German Boy*, and *Golf for Enlightenment*.

All-time favorite business books: *Orbiting the Giant Hairball* by Gordon MacKenzie; *The Age of Paradox* and *The Elephant and the Flea* by Charles Handy, *The World Is Flat* by Thomas Friedman, *A Whole New Mind* by Daniel Pink, *The Art of Possibility* by Rosamund and Ben Zander, and *Purple Cow* by Seth Godin.

### What advice do you have for students interested in a writing career? Do you have any recommendations for students?

There's a great book that helped me get through writing my second book: *Bird by Bird*, by Anne Lamott. It's sort of the Nike version of writing. . . . i.e., "Just Write It."

Specific writing advice: Know who you are and what's important to you before you start writing. It's the only way you can write authentically.

Lastly, avoid clichés.

# REFERENCES

Association of Authors' Representatives. (2006a). *About the AAR*. Retrieved January 28, 2006, from: http://www.arr-online.org

Association of Authors' Representatives. (2006b). *Frequently asked author questions*. Retrieved January 28, 2006, from: http://www.arr-online.org

Embree, M. (2003). *The author's toolkit: A step-by-step guide to writing and publishing your book*. (Rev. ed.). New York: Allworth Press.

Kelly, C., & London, S. (2005). *Dress your best: The complete guide to finding the style that's right for your body*. New York: Three Rivers Press.

Klensch, E., with Meyer, B. (1995). *Style*. New York: Perigee.

Klensch, E. (2004). *Live at 10:00, dead at 10:15*. New York: Forge.

Krantz, J. (2000). *Sex and shopping: Confessions of a nice Jewish girl*. New York: St. Martin's Press.

Oppenheimer, J. (2005). *Front row: Anna Wintour, the cool life and hot times of Vogue's editor in chief*. New York: St. Martin's Press.

R. R. Bowker & Co. (2005). *Books in print*. Oldsmar, FL: Author.

R. R. Bowker & Co. (2005). *Forthcoming books*. Oldsmar, FL: Author.

Strunk, W., Jr., & White, E. B. (2000). *The elements of style* (4th ed.). Needham Heights, MA: Allyn & Bacon.

Strunk, W., Jr., White, E. B., & Kalman, M. (2005). *The elements of style illustrated*. New York: Penguin Press HC.

Truss, L. (2003). *Eats, shoots & leaves: The zero tolerance approach to punctuation*. New York: Gotham Books.

Weisberger, L. (2003). *The devil wears Prada*. New York: Doubleday.

Writer's Digest Books. (2005). *Guide to literary agents*. Cincinnati: Author.

# ELEVEN

## *Writing Business Communications*

After you have read this chapter, you should be able to discuss the following:

• Writing business communications

• Types of business messages

• Message formats

survey of 120 major American corporations employing nearly 8 million people concluded that in today's workplace writing is a "threshold skill" for hiring and promotion among salaried (that is, professional) employees ("National Commission on Writing," 2004). The report went on to say that in large American companies approximately two thirds of all employees have some writing responsibility and that 80% of service-oriented companies assess writing during the hiring process. Over half the companies reported that they "frequently" or "almost always" produce technical reports, formal reports, memos, and other business correspondence. Further, they reported that e-mail and PowerPoint presentations are universal business communication tools. E-mail particularly has caused employees to write more often, and businesses are now required to document much more information.

This chapter focuses on writing business communications. The chapter begins by discussing how to write business communications. Next, the chapter concentrates on the types of business messages found in the workplace. The chapter concludes with a discussion about the message formats that are used.

# WRITING BUSINESS COMMUNICATIONS

Communication in the workplace is escalating. We are expected to send more messages to more people at a faster rate than ever before. Effective communication in today's work environment is crucial. Effective business communications involve shaping written messages to respond to the needs of **stakeholders**—those people who may be affected by actions of the organization: managers, supervisors, employees, customers, clients, vendors, media, stockholders, government, the public at large, or other important groups. Business messages should be written in a manner easily understood by the stakeholder. Chapter 2, "The Writing Process," discussed planning and preparing written messages. Briefly, the steps include:

1. Planning
2. Shaping
3. Drafting
4. Revising
5. Editing
6. Proofreading

Systematically following these six steps can help you develop effective business communications that contribute to the productivity of the organization and enhance your credibility as a professional within the organization.

Business writing requires special adaptations to ensure the message fits the specific needs of the audience. Lehman & DuFrene (2005) include the following adaptations:

- Focusing on the receiver's point of view
- Communicating ethically and responsibly
- Building and protecting goodwill
- Conveying a positive, tactful tone
- Writing concisely

## FOCUS ON RECEIVER'S POINT OF VIEW

Capable business writers use a writing style that focuses on the receiver's point of view, often termed the "you attitude" (Lehman & Dufrene, 2005, p. 89) rather than a "me attitude." The message is written to reflect the receiver's needs and interests (receiver-centered) rather than the sender's needs and interests (sender-centered). An easy way to make business messages receiver-centered is to remove the first-person "I" and replace it with the second-person "you" or use the receiver's name.

---

*Sender-centered Example:* **I want to congratulate you on your promotion to Footwear Buyer.**

*Receiver-centered Example:* **Congratulations, Ashley, on your promotion to Footwear Buyer.**

---

Instead of writing "I want to . . . ," as in the sender-centered example, remove the "I" to focus on the receiver and write "Congratulations, Ashley, . . . ," as shown in the receiver-centered example. This makes the receiver the center of attention and allows the reader to feel as though the message was written specifically to them.

---

*Portfolio Exercise:* **With a partner, compose 10 sentences that would apply to a business setting. Review the sentences to determine if the tone is sender-centered or receiver-centered. For each sentence that you identify as sender-centered, rewrite the sentence to focus on the receiver.**

---

# COMMUNICATE ETHICALLY AND RESPONSIBLY

All writing should be composed and delivered in an ethical and responsible manner. However, particularly in business, where many decisions are power-driven and can affect many people, writers must be advocates for ethical and responsible messages. All information presented in business communications should be truthful, honest, and fair. The receiver should be offered all relevant information. The information should not be exaggerated or embellished, and ideas should be supported with objective facts (Lehman & Dufrene, 2005).

# BUILD AND PROTECT GOODWILL

**Goodwill** is defined as the favor or prestige that a business has acquired beyond the mere value of what it sells (Merriam-Webster, 2000). To put it another way, goodwill is the value of intangible assets of the company. Poorly written business messages that show thoughtlessness to the receiver diminish the goodwill of the sender and the company the sender represents. The following are examples of poor goodwill represented in writing:

- **Condescending or demeaning expressions**—Expressions that give the sender a tone of superiority over the receiver
- **Sarcasm**—Expressions hidden in wit intended to hurt an individual
- **Biased language**—Discriminatory language that may include **stereotyping** (oversimplified perception of a characteristic or behavior of a group)
- **Excessive euphemisms**—Considerate words substituted for offensive words. Use **euphemisms** to present negatively connoted words in a better light, but do not over use them.

It takes much longer to build goodwill than to destroy it. Writers should always be aware of the receiver's sense of self-worth and write messages that represent interest in and concern for the recipient.

---

*Portfolio Exercise:* **Collect five writing examples (e-mail messages, memos, letters, reports, other written correspondence) from your workplace. Trade your examples with a partner. Review the writing examples to determine if the tone illustrates goodwill (no evidence of demeaning expressions, sarcasm, biased language, or excessive euphemisms). Rewrite the sentence or passage as needed to promote goodwill on the part of the sender.**

---

# CONVEY A POSITIVE, TACTFUL TONE

All business writing should convey a positive, forward-looking tone, focusing on the pleasant rather than the unpleasant. Even when you are delivering bad news, express the issue in an encouraging manner. In business writing, negative messages are often written in the passive voice to try to lessen the negative reaction that will be evoked in the receiver.

## WRITE CONCISELY

Business writing is not creative writing. It is direct, simple, and to the point. Sentence structure is short and simple, and precise words are used to replace vague words or phrases. Excessive adjectives and unnecessary information are omitted. After having been trained to fill page limits for term papers, students sometimes have a difficult time adapting to the concise, simple, short style of writing required in business. In business writing, you will never be told how long a message should be. As the sender, you must determine the appropriate length of the message by including all relevant information and omitting any unnecessary information.

# TYPES OF BUSINESS MESSAGES

This section of the chapter will focus on the specific types of messages commonly written in the workplace. These include routine or goodwill messages, bad news messages, and persuasive messages. You will select the type of message based on the reaction you expect from the reader.

## ROUTINE MESSAGES

If the reader is interested in the message, the tone of the message is neutral, and the message does not generate an emotional response, you are writing a **routine message**. Most business correspondence consists of routine messages. Requests for information or action or responses to those requests, merchandise orders or claims, and letters of recommendation are types of routine messages. You should consider the following points (Bovée & Thill, 2006) when writing a routine request:

- Pay attention to tone. You want a favorable reply to your request, so do not sound demanding. Use a pleasant tone, and always include the word *please* in your request.

- Assume that the receiver will comply; do not sound impatient in the request.
- Avoid beginning the message with a personal introduction such as "I am the senior visual merchandiser for . . . ," which comes across as authoritarian and so may cause the message to be lost.
- Differentiate polite requests from direct questions with the appropriate punctuation. A polite request ends with a period: "Would you help us to determine if the merchandise was delivered on Friday as promised." A direct question, such as "Was the merchandise delivered on Friday as promised?," ends with a question mark.

One common routine message is a request. To write a request or other routine message, follow a **direct writing strategy**. Deliver the main idea of the message first, followed by details and explanation. Use a direct strategy when the receiver is receptive to the idea and needs no education on the topic. A direct strategy puts the reader in the proper frame of mind and thus saves the reader time and frustration. An example of a routine message is shown in Figure 11.1. Guffey (2007) offers the following plan for writing a routine request:

- **Opening**—Ask the most important question first, or politely express a command.
- **Body**—Explain your request logically and courteously, followed up by additional questions if necessary.
- **Closing**—Request a specific action with an end date if appropriate and show appreciation.

Routine messages let readers know what you want from them directly in the opening sentence of the message. This way a reader can quickly act on your request.

---

*Weak Letter Opening Example:* **I have been given the task of locating a suitable location for a spring fashion show for my organization. I have checked a number of locations around Loveland and your mall looks possible.**

*Stronger Letter Opening Example:* **Will you please answer the following questions regarding use of Centerra Mall for a fashion show in June coinciding with the North America Wool Market held in Estes Park.**

---

# E & S Event Specialists

2323 Niwot Road     Niwot, Colorado 80503
PHONE: (303) 555-5555
FAX: (303) 555-5556

January 20, 20xx

Ms. Janice Morales, Manager
Red Rock Inn
813 S. Stonecreek Road
Lyons, CO 80540

Dear Ms. Morales:

Can the Red Rock Inn provide a meeting room and accommodations for approximately 50 event planners from June 22 to June 24?

Your hotel has received strong recommendations because of its beautiful location and excellent catering services. We are planning a retreat for the Association of Event Planners in Colorado (AEPC) in June and I am collecting details for the AECP president, Jean Morrison.  Please answer these additional questions about the Red Rock Inn:

- Is a meeting room for 50 available?

- Are audio visual equipment and other computer equipment available for electronic presentations in the meeting room?

- What type of dining arrangements can be made for 50 people?

- Is parking at your location easy to navigate?

Answers to these questions and other information that you might provide will help us decide if your facility will work for your needs. Your response by February 15 would be most appreciated since Ms. Morrison will be traveling on business for the remainder of the month of February.

Sincerely,

*Bethann Mabley*

Bethann Mabley
Destination Marketing Manager

**FIGURE 11.1.**    Routine message.

Within the body of the message, provide pertinent details that will encourage the reader to respond. If you make your request in a clear and logical manner, the reader is more likely to respond. If you bog the reader down with unnecessary information and superfluous detail, the reader will likely put the request aside and leave it unanswered.

Close the message by reminding the reader of the request and asking them to take action. Readers prefer end dates with reasons so they can prioritize the request within their workload. Always show appreciation at the end of the message. At the same time, try to avoid trite closings like "Thank you for your consideration." Try to personalize the message to show you are sincere in your request.

---

*Weak Letter Closing Example:* **Thanks for taking the time to provide me with any information you can.**

*Stronger Letter Closing Example:* **Your answers to our request by January 31 will help us determine if Centerra Mall is the right location for our event.**

---

Another common routine message is a **claim,** which is a request for an adjustment such as a refund, a replacement product, or a correction to a billing statement. The writing plan for a claim is similar to the writing plan for a request for information (Guffey, 2007):

* **Opening**—Describe the desired action clearly.
* **Body**—Explain why you are making the claim, justify your claim, and provide details regarding the requested action.
* **Closing**—Always end the message pleasantly with a goodwill statement and an end date if appropriate.

When writing a message concerning a claim, be sure to limit your message to a single idea, presented in the first sentence. This way the receiver can act specifically on your request and not have to guess at what solution you are after.

---

*Portfolio Exercise:* **Think of a product or service you recently purchased that did not work the way you expected or did not provide the service you** expected. Write a claim message asking for a refund, a replacement product, or an adjustment to your account. Use the direct writing strategy. When you have finished writing, exchange your message with a partner. Edit your partner's message as needed to make it as clear as possible so the receiver will respond in a positive manner. Your partner will do the same to your message.

## GOODWILL MESSAGES

If the reader will be pleased with the message, you are writing a **goodwill message**. These messages present pleasant information to the reader, such as congratulations and expressions of appreciation. They are also appropriate for expressing condolences. Like a routine message, a goodwill message uses a direct writing strategy. A goodwill message is shown in Chapter 12, "Writing Employment Messages," in Figure 12.9. The message opens with the pleasant idea, is followed by detail and explanation, and closes by reminding the receiver of the good news or a future-oriented closing thought. Goodwill messages are sent to show appreciation for an act of kindness, to recognize the accomplishments of others, or to express grief. In addition to sending the message in a timely manner, you will want to follow Guffey's (2007) "five Ss" when writing a goodwill message:

- **Selfless**—The message should be completely receiver-centered.
- **Specific**—The message should include specific occurrences or characteristics of the receiver with verified names and facts.
- **Sincere**—The message should be genuine, avoiding pretentious, formal, or extravagant language.
- **Spontaneous**—The message should be fresh and enthusiastic, natural and direct in language.
- **Short**—The message should convey your sentiment in a few sentences rather than being long, drawn-out, and wordy.

*Portfolio Exercise:* **Think of a friend or co-worker who was recently recognized (recognized as employee of the month, elected as a club officer, promoted, broke a sports record, or other examples). Write a letter of congratulations using the five Ss as described above. When you have finished writing,**

**exchange your message with a partner. Edit your partner's message as needed to make sure the message is receiver-centered.**

## BAD NEWS MESSAGES

While it is not pleasant, there are times in business when you must convey bad news. It is best to give someone bad news in person. However, some situations require written documentation. When you expect that the reader will react negatively toward the message, you are writing a **bad news message**. Delivering bad news face-to-face or in writing is difficult. Lehman & Dufrene (2005) offer the following suggestions for delivering bad news:

- Convey the bad news as soon as possible to show respect for the receiver and to avoid rumors.
- Give the receiver a complete, rational explanation, providing detail to establish your credibility concerning the problem.
- Show empathy toward the receiver. Allow the receiver adequate time to react to the news, and listen attentively to his concerns.
- Follow up by letting the receiver know what will happen next, what is expected of her, and what the company is going to do. Plan additional meetings as necessary to keep everyone informed of the situation.

An **indirect writing strategy** is used to deliver bad news messages. In this strategy, explanation and details are presented before the main idea (which is the bad news) to help the audience accept the bad news. Giving the explanation before the bad news keeps the reader's attention and allows the receiver to be persuaded toward the idea before being met with it directly. A bad news message is shown in Figure 11.2. Bovée & Thill (2006) offer the following plan for writing a bad news message:

- **Opening**—Start with a buffer statement.
- **Body**—Continue with a logical, neutral explanation for the bad news, followed by a concise, diplomatic statement of the bad news.
- **Close**—End with a positive, forward-looking statement that shows respect for the receiver.

**MEMORANDUM**

Date:        November 10. 20xx

To:          Matt Connor
             Manager, Marketplace Gourmet Food Boutique

From:        Jason Henderson *JH*
             Director, Human Resources

Subject:     Request to attend the Winter Fancy Food Show

The owner, Reed Maxwell, and other Marketplace associates are extremely pleased with the job you have done creating the new Marketplace Gourmet Food Boutique. Your creative ideas, particularly the *Haunt Chocolate* event for Halloween, made your division the top selling division for the month of October. Because of your genuine interest in the gourmet food market, I can understand your desire to attend the Winter Fancy Food Show being held in San Diego from January 13 to 15.

This time directly coincides with a management retreat the Marketplace executives have been planning for several months. We have reserved this time in January for evaluation and long term planning for the future. As you know, we are planning to expand the Marketplace and develop four branch locations within the next three years. We need you here during this important planning session.

If your schedule permits in April, we are willing to pay your travel to the Spring Fancy Food Show in Chicago. You're a valuable member of the Marketplace team and we are grateful for your contributions to making the Marketplace a success.

FIGURE 11.2. Bad news message.

A **buffer statement** is a neutral, noncontroversial statement that both sender and receiver can agree on. The buffer statement should be delivered in a kind, courteous, sincere manner using respectful language. Guffey (2007) describes possible buffer openings for bad news messages:

- **Best news**—Deliver the best news first.
- **Compliment**—Offer praise for the receiver's accomplishments or efforts.
- **Appreciation**—Offer thanks to the receiver for his contributions.
- **Agreement**—Make a relevant statement that both the receiver and the sender can agree on.
- **Facts**—Provide objective information for the bad news.
- **Understanding**—Show that you care about the receiver.
- **Apology**—If an apology is warranted, present it early, briefly, and sincerely.

In the body of the bad news message, cover the more positive points first followed by the less positive points. Your goal is to explain *why* you reached the decision you did before you explain *what* the decision is (Bovée & Thill, 2006).

After the reasoning has been laid out, it is time to state the bad news. When writing the bad news, tell the receiver what you *did*, instead of what you *did not do*. The bad news should be de-emphasized visually and grammatically. The bad news should be placed in the middle of a paragraph halfway through the message in a longer sentence. Better writers place the bad news in a subordinate clause.

---

*Emphasizing the Bad News Example:* **Our company does not hire interns.**

*De-emphasizing the Bad News Example:* **Although our company is not currently hiring interns, we are pleased that you considered us when you started your internship search.**

---

End the message with a positive outlook. You can achieve this by offering an alternative to the refusal, a forward look, or good wishes. When closing the bad news message, avoid endings that sound canned, insincere, inappropriate, or self-serving. Remember to show respect for the receiver. The following guidelines from Bovée & Thill (2006) suggest how to close a bad news message:

- **Keep it positive**—Do not refer to, repeat, or apologize for the bad news.
- **Limit future correspondence**—Encourage further discussion only if you really *are* willing to discuss it further.
- **Be optimistic about the future**—Do not go on about additional problems.
- **Be sincere**—Avoid clichés and two-faced comments.
- **Be confident**—Do not show doubt about keeping the person as a client or a customer or in some other role in the future.

---

*Portfolio Exercise:* **Write a message refusing the claim that you wrote about in the earlier Portfolio Exercise. Use the indirect writing strategy. When you have finished writing, exchange your message with a partner. Edit your partner's message to make sure it is written in a positive, sincere, and optimistic manner.**

---

## PERSUASIVE MESSAGES

**Persuasive messages** are messages written to attempt to change someone's attitudes, beliefs, or actions (Thill & Bovée, 2005). Figure 7.16 in Chapter 7, "Writing for Public Relations," is an example of a persuasive message. Examples of persuasive messages include sales, fund-raising, advertising, and public relations messages. Persuasive messages are different than routine messages in that they are aimed at audiences that are of a mind to resist what is being said. Persuasive messages also are longer and more detailed than other types of messages. They require careful preparation so that you understand the specific needs of the audience you are making the appeal to.

But why should your reader be persuaded to listen to what you have to say? Because you have earned respect from your audience—called credibility. **Credibility** is your ability to be believed because you are reliable and worthy of confidence (Bovée, Thill, & Schatzman, 2003). Establishing credibility is a process that takes time. Ways to gain credibility include the following (Bovée et al.):

- **Support your message with facts.** Make use of testimonials, statistics, research, guarantees, or other pieces of evidence.

- **Name your sources.** Be specific about where your information came from. If these sources already have credibility with your audience, it will enhance your credibility too.
- **Be an expert.** Use your expertise about the subject matter to give your audience quality information so they can make a better decision.
- **Establish common ground.** Use values, beliefs, attitudes, or experience to find something in common with your audience so they will identify with you.
- **Be enthusiastic.** Excitement is infectious!
- **Be objective.** Show your audience all sides of the issue.
- **Be sincere.**
- **Be trustworthy.** High ethical standards are critical to successful persuasion.
- **Have good intentions.** Your willingness to consider the best interests of your audience helps you create persuasive messages that are believable.

Most persuasive messages use the direct writing strategy, in which you define the main idea first and then use details and explanation to make your point in a meaningful way. A common method to write persuasive messages is to use the **AIDA** (attention, interest, desire, action) organizational plan (pronounced "A-I-D-A"). Sales associates may know AIDA as a personal selling technique used to encourage a customer to reach a buying decision about a product or service (Swanson & Everett, 2007). In writing a persuasive message you are doing the same thing: encouraging the reader to reach a decision. The steps include:

1. **Getting the *Attention* of your reader**—Make the reader hear your problem or idea amid the clutter of other messages.

2. **Creating *Interest* in the message**—Show your reader the relevance of your issue so she will begin thinking about it.

3. **Forming *Desire* by the reader**—Show the reader how accepting the problem, idea, or issue will directly benefit him.

4. **Stimulating reader *Action***—This is the most important step: telling your reader what specific action you want her to take immediately.

Another way to persuade your audience to listen to your message is through emotional or logical appeals. **Emotional appeals** use human feeling to make the argument. The message may be brought to light through suggestions of patriotism, compassion, anger, love, or other poignant sentiments intended to arouse action in the reader. **Logical appeals** use human reason to make the argument. Three types of reasoning are used in persuasive messages:

- **Analogy**—Infer that if two or more things agree with one another in some aspects, they will probably agree with one another in other aspects.
- **Induction**—Infer a general conclusion based on the specifics of a particular situation.
- **Deduction**—Infer a specific conclusion based on generalizations.

Two distinct types of persuasive messages are sales messages and fund-raising messages. Sales messages are discussed here. (Advertising and public relations writing—including fund-raising letters—are also persuasive messages; they are discussed in Chapters 6 and 7, respectively.)

Sales messages use product knowledge in the form of **selling points**—features and characteristics of the merchandise that make it desirable—to sell the product or service to the reader (Swanson & Everett, 2007). To make a persuasive pitch for the item, it is essential that you determine which characteristic is the most important selling point in the eyes of the reader. Design, reputation of the manufacturer, versatility, or price may be the outstanding feature that encourages the reader to buy the product.

---

*Portfolio Exercise:* **New trends are always flooding the fashion scene. Identify a current fashion trend and write a sales message to prospective customers. Follow the AIDA model to create interest in your product, and be sure to tell your reader how to respond. When you have finished writing, exchange your message with a partner. Edit your partner's message to make sure it demonstrates credibility.**

---

# MESSAGE FORMATS

Your goal in business communication is to get your message read. A sloppy message with little care given to format and style will give the impression that your message is not very important. On the other hand, a professional-looking document that uses conventional style and format and is easy to read and understand will give the impression that you are intelligent and proficient.

Some firms train new employees on the standard documents to be used for the firm's business correspondence. Other businesses may expect new hires to come prepared with this knowledge. Either way, business writers are encouraged to look at model documents from their organization and other sources to understand format and style.

Business communications sent to recipients outside the organization are considered **external messages**. **Internal messages** are sent to recipients within the organization. Specific formats are used to send business communications within and outside the organization. Common formats include e-mail, memorandums (memos), letters, reports, and proposals. Letters, memos, and e-mail messages are used for short communications (two pages or less; one page for e-mail messages). Letters are more formal in tone, structure, and format, while memos and e-mail messages are less formal. Reports and proposals require the most formal tone and structure. Also, they generally are longer than two pages.

The beginning of this chapter focused on writing a concise business message. However, before the content of the message is read, it must grab the reader's attention by its appearance. Stationery is the first consideration for appearance. Most organizations use high-quality stationery for business documents. Two types of paper are used. **Printed letterhead stationery**, which is a heavier paper (20–24 pound) is preprinted with the company's official name, street address, Web address, e-mail address, telephone and fax numbers, and the company logo. Letterhead is used for all external correspondence and more important internal documents. Lighter-weight paper (16-pound; used in printers or copy machines) is acceptable for internal documents such as memos.

A second point for consideration is the placement of the message on the page. You want the message to appear balanced on the page. The easiest way to place messages on a page is to use the default settings in your word processing programs. Margins setting are generally 1 inch on the left, right, and bottom, and 1 inch at the top unless modifications are required to accommodate a printed letterhead. For very short messages, under 200 words, it is acceptable to use 1½-inch left and right margins.

The last thing to consider in appearance is justification. **Justification** means aligning text at the margin. It is customary to have the text "justified," or aligned, along the left margin. You may also choose to align the text on the right margin (in word processing programs, if both sides are aligned the text is said to be **full-justified**). Or you can set the right margin to be unjustified, leaving a **ragged edge** in which each line ends at the end of a word. This "ragged right" justification is easier to read than full justification.

# E-MAIL

E-mail messages are the most common form of business communication. The use of e-mail has surpassed the use of memos and other forms of communication, because it reduces paper waste, "telephone tag," and interruptions. Unlike telephone calls, which are disruptive, e-mail messages permit people to respond at their convenience. With e-mail, quick questions and answers can be sent with no time wasted waiting for phone replies. E-mail has also eliminated the problem of communication across time barriers by allowing communication to take place between users at various locations and time zones. During part of the year, the authors of this book are located three time zones away from the book's editors, yet with e-mail it is not necessary to try to calculate when someone will be at their desk and available. E-mail also allows the same message to be sent to many people at once, creating a more efficient workplace.

Both e-mail messages and memos should be very concise. Each e-mail message should address only one topic. It is better to send two separate e-mail messages than to discuss two unrelated topics in one message. Show courtesy to the receiver by including a **salutation** (greeting), such as "Hi, Heather" or "Good Morning," and an ending, such as "Thanks" or "Regards," to show goodwill. Finish the message with a **signature file** so the reader can contact you. The signature file should include your name, mailing address, e-mail address, phone and fax numbers, Web address, and other useful information. You may prefer to create different signature files for work and personal messages.

Keep the length of your e-mail messages to one screen. Busy people may not take time to scroll through longer messages. Send longer messages as attachments. Keep sentence length short. Single-space the message. Double-space between paragraphs rather than using indented paragraphs. Use bullets and/or line breaks to make messages easier to read. Use standard grammar rules and punctuation, as you would with any other type of message; this shows courtesy to the reader and enhances your credibility. Try not to use all capital letters for emphasis; this is the equivalent of shouting at someone in person. Try to find features in your e-mail software that allow you to use formatting such as boldface or a change in font color to show emphasis. If you do

---

**Box 11.1  E-Mail: Some Critical Information UP FRONT**

The heading, an important part of any e-mail message, generally is preformatted by the e-mail program. Most e-mail programs provide the following headings:

- **To:**—This line contains the receiver's e-mail address. Many e-mail programs allow you to set up an address book so you can simply click on the name of the person you want to send a message to. If you are typing in an address, make sure you type it correctly or the message will be returned undeliverable.
- **From:**—This line contains the sender's address. E-mail programs automatically fill in your name and e-mail address when you create a new message. Your e-mail program may or may not show a From: field when you're sending a message, but you will see one on any message you receive.
- **Cc and Bcc:**—On this line, you may type in names or e-mail addresses of anyone besides your main recipient who needs to receive the message. *Cc* stands for "Copy" and *Bcc* stands for "Blind Copy." If you want to send a message to someone without the other addressees knowing, use the Bcc line.
- **Subject:**—In this line, you identify the subject of your e-mail message. The subject line should be meaningful to the reader because it allows her to see what the message is about and to organize and retrieve the message at a future date. Some e-mail programs prompt the sender to add a subject if nothing has been entered in that line.
- **Attached:**—This line shows the recipient that a document has been attached to the e-mail message. Most e-mail packages allow the recipient to click the attached file name to upload the document on their computer.

---

use all capital letters, let your reader know this is your only way of formatting—not that you are shouting at them.

Some last words of e-mail advice:

- Never respond to an e-mail message when you are angry. E-mail is an easy form of communication, but it should be used only when the message is intended in a friendly manner.

- If you expect that your message could generate heated or negative emotions, it is better to stop e-mail communication and talk to the person face-to-face.
- E-mail should not be used to avoid personal contact.
- Consider that all e-mail may be monitored, and do not send anything that you would not want published for others to see.

## MEMORANDUM

A **memorandum** (plural, *memoranda*)—a memo or interoffice communication—is an essential format for correspondence inside an organization. Generally, this communication format is best used between people who already have established contact, and memos are conversational in tone. In addition, they provide formal records of transactions and thus allow for the hardcopy paper trail that many situations require. The "bad news" message shown in Figure 11.2 also provided a good example of standard memo format.

Most memos begin with the title *Memo (Memorandum, Interoffice Communication)* at the top of the page. Every memo contains a header with the same basic information as an e-mail message: TO, FROM, DATE, and SUBJECT. The heading is double-spaced for easy reading. The content of the memo is single-spaced, with a double space between paragraphs; there are no indented paragraphs. You should initial next to your name in the header to show that you approve of the content. Memos do not include an inside address or a complementary close, and they are never signed at the bottom.

---

### Memo Heading Example

**[MEMO] or [Memorandum] or [Interoffice Communication], centered**

TO:          **recipient's name and job title or department name**

FROM:      **your name and job title or department name;** *sign* **or** *initial* **to right of name**

DATE:       **use month–day–year format (June 23, 20xx)**

SUBJECT: **subject line should be very specific (sometimes [RE], short for** *regarding***)**

---

The main objective of memos is to convey internal business information in a clear, brief, tactful manner. The first sentence of a routine or goodwill message memo should repeat the subject line and inform the reader of the purpose of the communication. If the subject of the memo is bad news, the subject line is repeated after a buffer.

In the body of the message, present the information in an easy-to-read format. Use bulleted lists, numbered lists, tables, headings, and other formatting tools to assist the reader. Close the memo with a friendly, positive note.

When a memo is longer than one page, a second-page heading should be included on the second and successive pages. Position the heading 1 inch from the top of the page, single-spaced, at the left margin. Include the name of the person or company to whom the memorandum is being sent, the page number, and the date. Triple-space after the heading before continuing the body of the memo. The heading may be vertical or horizontal:

---

**Second Page Heading Horizontal Example:**
**Mr. Ephraim Scott**                 **2**                 **June 23, 20xx**

**Second Page Heading Vertical Example:**
**Mr. Ephraim Scott**
**Page 2**
**June 23, 20xx**

---

## LETTER

**Letters** are more formal messages than e-mail or memos. They are written to individuals outside of the organization. The parties generally do not know each other. Letters are the preferred format when a formal record for an inquiry, response, or complaint is needed. The "routine message" in Figure 11.1 also provided a good example of a standard business letter.

Most business letters can be formatted in either block or modified block format.

- With **block letter format**, all letter parts and paragraphs start at the left margin. Paragraphs are not indented five spaces; instead, the text is single-spaced and there is double-spacing between paragraphs. Many companies are adopting this format because it is easy to learn and is cost-efficient when the company is producing a high volume of documents.

- **Modified block letter format** is the more traditional format. The dateline, complementary close, and signature block begin at the horizontal center of the page. Paragraphs are single-spaced both within and between paragraphs, and the first line of each paragraph is indented five spaces.

Letters using letterhead stationery should have a 2-inch top margin on the first page. All subsequent pages should have a 1-inch top margin. All business letters are left-justified and ragged right. The text should have pleasing vertical placement on the page. To achieve balance on the page, use one to nine blank lines between the date and the inside address. Letters that continue to a second page should use a second-page header.

## The Parts of a Letter

Business letters follow a conventional sequence of standard parts, as shown in Figure 11.3:

- **Letterhead or Sender's address**—On plain paper, the sender's address consists of the following single-spaced lines: (1) the sender's street address and (2) the sender's city, two-letter postal state abbreviation, and five- or nine-digit ZIP code. The sender's name is omitted because it appears in the signature block. If letterhead stationery is used, the sender's address is omitted.

- **Dateline**—On plain paper the dateline appears on the line immediately following the sender's city, two-letter postal abbreviation, and ZIP code. On letterhead stationery the dateline appears two lines below the letterhead or two inches from the top, whichever placement is lower on the page. The American English format (most common in the United States) is *June 23, 20xx*. The month should be spelled out completely, and a comma and letter space should follow the date; ordinal endings such as *st, nd, rd*, or *th* should not be used. European and military formats use the following: *23 June 20xx*; the date precedes the month and no commas are used.

**Sender's address**  E & S Event Specialists          do not include sender's name, it will
or letterhead         2323 Niwot Road                  appear on the signature line
                      Niwot, Colorado 80503
**Dateline**          January 20, 20xx                 with letterhead 2 inches from top or
                                                       2 lines below letterhead whichever
                                                       position is lower on the page

                                                       1 to 9 blank lines to balance page

**Inside**            Ms. Janice Morales, Manager
**Address**           Red Rock Inn
                      813 S. Stonecreek Road
                      Lyons, Colorado 80312
                                                       1 blank line
**Salutation**        Dear Ms. Morales:
                                                       1 blank line
**Body**              This letter illustrates block letter style.  All typed lines begin at the left
                      margin. In business writing, punctuation after the salutation is a colon (:),
                      not a comma.

                      Paragraphs are single spaced with a double space between paragraphs.
                      When a letter is longer than one page, a second-page heading should be
                      included on the second and successive pages.

                      The complimentary close appears one blank line below the end of the last
                      paragraph.
                                                       1 blank line
**Complimentary**     Sincerely,
**Close**
                                                       3 blank lines to allow space for
                                                       signature
**Signature**         Bethann Mabley
**Block**             Destination Marketing Manager
                                                       1 blank line
**Enclosure**         Enclosure
**Notation**

FIGURE 11.3. Parts of a letter.

- **Inside address**—This is the complete address of the person or organization receiving the letter. It should include some or all of the following components: on the first line, the courtesy title, full name, and professional title (note: the recipient's professional title may follow the name or be placed on the line below); on the second line, the department name (if necessary); on the third line, the company name; on the fourth line, the street or mailing address; on the fifth line, the city, two-letter postal abbreviation, and five- or nine-digit ZIP code. The inside address appears from one to nine lines below the dateline depending on the length of the message. Shorter messages should use more spaces to balance the message on the page.

- **Salutation**—This greeting opens the letter. It is placed one double-space below the inside address. The format of the salutation depends on the degree of familiarity between the sender and receiver. For more formal letters, a person's personal or professional title (*Mr.*, *Ms.*, *Dr.*, or *Professor*) is included in the salutation followed by their last name (no first name is included). For more informal salutations, the first name alone can be used. In business writing the salutation is completed with a colon (:) (not a comma as is used in personal correspondence).

- **Body**—This is the message of the letter. It begins one double-space below the salutation. Paragraphs are single-spaced with a double-space between paragraphs. Keep whole paragraphs together; avoid breaking across pages. Similar to a memo, when a letter is longer than one page, a second-page heading should be included on the second and successive pages.

- **Complimentary close**—This begins one double-space below the last line of the body. This is a phrase to close the letter and create goodwill. *Sincerely* is considered a neutral phrase and is appropriate for the majority of business situations. Other common courtesy closings include *Cordially* and *Respectfully*. The complimentary close finishes with a comma (,).

- **Signature block**—This is the sender's name, typed and signed. Three blank lines are placed between the complimentary close and the sender's typed name. The sender's name is signed legibly in the space above the typed name. A business or professional title may be placed under the typed name if desired.

- **Enclosure notation**—If additional items—such as a résumé, price list, or brochure—are included in the same envelope, the word *enclosure* should be typed one double-space below the last line of the signature block.

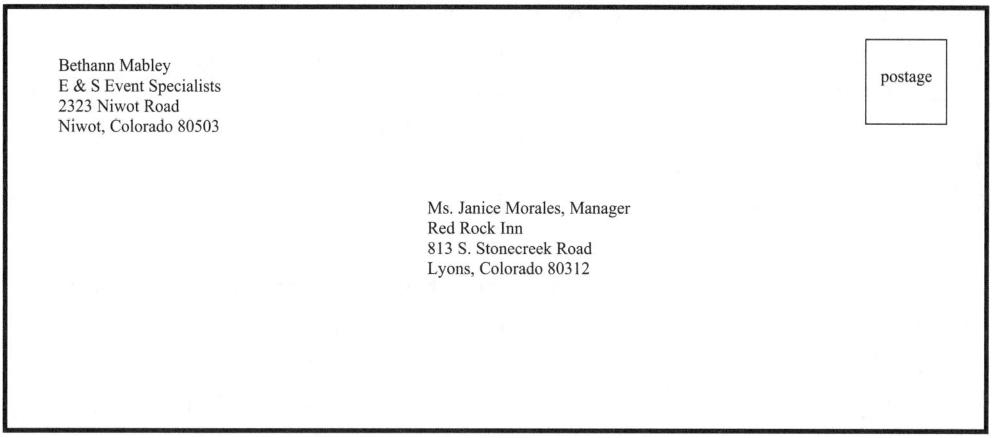

Bethann Mabley
E & S Event Specialists
2323 Niwot Road
Niwot, Colorado 80503

postage

Ms. Janice Morales, Manager
Red Rock Inn
813 S. Stonecreek Road
Lyons, Colorado 80312

FIGURE 11.4. Envelope format.

# ENVELOPES

Envelopes should be of the same quality and color of stationery as the letter. Standard parts of an envelope include the following (see Figure 11.4):

- **Return address**—This is printed in the upper left corner of the envelope using the same information as is printed in the letterhead or the sender's address. Word processing packages usually allow the sender's address to be captured and sent to the label and envelope wizard. The address should be single-spaced, $1/2$ inch from the top and left sides of the envelope.
- **Mailing address**—On legal-sized No. 10 envelopes ($4^1/2 \times 9^1/2$ inches), the mailing address starts $4^1/4$ inches from the left edge of the envelope on line 13. For smaller-sized No. $6^3/4$ envelopes, the mailing address starts $3^1/2$ inches from the left edge on line 12.

# REPORTS AND PROPOSALS

Many management decisions are made on the basis of information that has been submitted in the form of a report or a proposal. Business **reports** are systematic attempts to answer questions or solve problems. According to Bovée & Thill (2006), reports serve one or more of six general purposes:

1. To oversee and manage company operations
2. To carry out company rules and ways of doing business
3. To obey government and legal requirements
4. To inform others of what is being done on a project
5. To guide decisions on particular issues
6. To get products, plans, or projects accepted by others

Firms rely on several different types of reports to conduct business. **Information reports** present data and facts without analyses or recommendations. Figure 11.5 is an example of an information report written in memo format. The example is based on student work and does not necessarily reflect actual Neiman Marcus opportunities or financial standings. Progress reports are an example of informational reports. **Analytical reports** provide supporting information, analyses, and recommendations to help managers to make informed decisions.

**Proposals** are a special type of analytical report. They are persuasive offers presented to others to solve problems, provide services, or sell equipment. **Solicited proposals** are prepared at the request of a party who needs a service or product. Businesses or individuals are invited to submit a **request for proposal (RFP)** to bid for a contract. **Unsolicited proposals** are written by firms or individuals to obtain business or funding without a prior invitation to submit a proposal. **Internal proposals** are submitted to decision-makers within one's own firm. **External proposals** are submitted from outside the organization.

## Planning Reports and Proposals

Like other messages, reports should be drafted using a writing strategy based on the response expected from the reader. When writing a report or a proposal, you should follow the same writing plan as was described in Chapter 2, "The Writing Process." You need to have a good understanding of your audience and the purpose of your report or proposal. You should define the problem that needs resolution and write this as a statement of purpose. An example might be "To develop promotion goals and objectives for the next six months." Sometimes your supervisor or other authority will define the problem for you. Other times you will need to define the problem for the decision-maker. The purpose statement for an analytical report is much more complex than the purpose statement for an informational report. If someone has asked you to write the report, review the purpose statement with that person before continuing.

**Memorandum**

Date:   April 2, 2007

To:    Kris Swanson

From:   Tiffany Carlyon  *TAC*

Subject:   Information Report on retailer Neiman Marcus

The following is an information report on the retailer, Neiman Marcus. In conducting research for this report, information was used from the company websites and through searchable databases. This report will outline the company profile, opportunities at Neiman Marcus, human resources, financial information, and conclude with a summary.

**Company Profile**

**Corporate Mission**

Neiman Marcus makes it known who it is, what it stands for, and where it came from. "Neiman Marcus is a renowned specialty store dedicated to merchandise leadership and superior customer service…offering the finest fashion and quality products in a welcoming environment" (Neiman Marcus, 2007b, ¶ 1). Neiman Marcus prides itself as being an elite store that sells the highest quality merchandise. Neiman Marcus targets the top 2% in household income in the United States; their clients are well educated, possess advanced degrees, are well traveled and sophisticated. Neiman Marcus truly is a store of wants rather than needs, and they strive to portray that.

One of the most important aspects to Neiman Marcus is its customer service. According to Neiman Marcus (2007f) the best service ideals come from having ordinary day-in-and-day-out interactions with its cliental. Neiman Marcus prides itself on having, what it says, are some of the best trained associates in the industry. As stated on the firm's webpage, "Throughout our history, Neiman Marcus has always been a company with a unique, if not unconventional, approach to retailing" (Neiman Marcus, 2007f, ¶ 2).

**Organization**

Neiman Marcus has stores located in 19 states and the District of Columbia. The states with the most stores are California and Texas. Like many high end stores the company also offers clearance center sales at their *Last Call* stores which are located in almost all 19 states. Neiman Marcus also runs a higher end store called Bergdorf Goodman, which stands on the corner of Fifth Avenue and 58th Street in New York City. According to Hoovers (2007) Bergdorf Goodman is a store known worldwide for its luxury, elegance and superior service. It operates two stores that are directly across from one another. The smaller store is targeted toward men and has high end fashion designers such as Giorgio Armani and Oscar de la Renta.

**FIGURE 11.5.** Information report. *(continued)*

Kris Swanson
Page 2
April 2, 20xx

Neiman Marcus offers its clients the opportunity to shop away from the store. For convenient at home shopping one could go online and shop Neiman Marcus at www.neimanmarcus.com or clients can shop their catalogs. Bergdorf Goodman also offers both of these amenities. Bergdorf Goodman launched its website, www.bergdorfgoodman.com, in 2004 and also has a catalog for additional at home shopping.

### Opportunities at Neiman Marcus

**Working for Neiman Marcus**

What an individual wants to do as a career is the determining factor in where she would work. Working for Neiman Marcus offers several areas of opportunity. There are the Central Offices located in Dallas along with 38 other Neiman Marcus stores. There are also 19 last call clearance centers, along with Bergdorf Goodman in New York.

Other job opportunities include working for Neiman Marcus direct. This is where Neiman Marcus and Horchow comprise the online and catalog business of both Neiman Marcus and Bergdorf Goodman. Lastly, the newest opportunity for employment is with Cusp. According to Neiman Marcus (2007c) Cusp is a retail venture that premiered in 2006; working for a Cusp store means being involved in knowing and selling the hottest and hippest trends.

The most career opportunities lie in working for the central offices of Neiman Marcus. Located in downtown Dallas, Texas are the executive and buying offices, human resources, public relations and marketing, and visual presentations offices. Also located nearby are the advertising, accounting, store planning, and credit division offices. In total, Neiman Marcus has over 1500 associates in their Dallas offices (2007g). Working for the central offices also means a wide array of employment options. Opportunities include working in:

- advertising, public relations, marketing, or merchandising
- credit services and financial planning
- customer programs
- accounting and accounts payable
- food services (overseeing the restaurants within the Neiman Marcus stores)
- human resources
- information technology
- loss prevention
- operations (providing logistical and administrative support)
- property and new store development, and
- visual planning among other opportunities.

FIGURE 11.5. (*continued*)

Kris Swanson
Page 3
April 2, 20xx

**Executive Development Program**

Upon being hired at Neiman Marcus each employee is given an orientation on the firm's history, values, and expectations. Employees are also given a Business Leadership tool. According to Neiman Marcus (2007d) employees have access to curriculum that includes communication, strategic planning, conflict resolution, and more. All of these are available through a classroom setting, web conferences, along with online and library resources. The Neiman Marcus Executive Development Program is an intensive twelve-week course, for college graduates that exposes employees to store management, buying, and merchandise planning. By incorporating each of these Neiman Marcus (2007d) believes that it helps employees to have a better understanding of the roles and responsibilities involved in their future careers. The program involves both in the classroom and on the job experiences.

Once the Executive Development Program is completed there are two paths that can be taken. The first career option is as an Assistant Buyer. According to Neiman Marcus (2007e) the duties of an Assistant Buyer include, overseeing vendor support and store communication, executing marketing events and advertising processes, recapping and analyzing sales trends, assisting the buyer in achieving sales and gross margin plans, overseeing product receipts, assisting the buyer in product selection and identification of fashion trends, and managing operations of the buying office.

The second career option is as an Assistant Merchandise Planner. According to Neiman Marcus (2007d) the duties of an Assistant Merchandise Planner are setting up locker stock and replenishment programs, recapping and analyzing sales trends, overseeing purchase order mechanics, assisting buyer in achieving sales and gross margin plans, overseeing inventory management, developing strategic plans, budgets, and recaps, and lastly managing operations of the buying office. There are several career options after successfully completing one of these first executive positions, and the path and success of each depends on the individual's performance.

## Human Resources

**Benefits**

The benefits to working for Neiman Marcus are vast. Neiman Marcus (2007a) lists benefits including:

- paid holidays and vacations
- direct paycheck deposit
- federal credit union membership
- education assistance plans
- basic life insurance
- short term disability and long term disability, and
- business travel insurance.

FIGURE 11.5. *(continued)*

Kris Swanson
Page 4
April 2, 20xx

Employment at Neiman Marcus also provides benefits for your future including a 401K savings plan, a pension plan, and seminars on financial planning. Another distinct factor of employment at Neiman Marcus is the opportunity it gives you to benefit your community through their matching gift program as well as volunteer and fundraising opportunities.

Working for Neiman Marcus also provides benefits to your family. Neiman Marcus (2007a) lists family benefits including: medical and dental plans, same-sex domestic partner benefits, mail-order pharmacy benefits, employee assistance program, accidental death and personal loss insurance. optional term life insurance, adoption benefits, health care spending account, dependent care spending account, scholarship award program for dependent children, prenatal/well-baby care programs, FMLA-family and medical leave program, discounts on store and catalog merchandise, and a computer purchase program.

**Recognition**

As stated by Neiman Marcus (2007e) the Neiman Marcus Group is committed to honoring its employees that demonstrated excellence in sales and customer services on both an individual and group level. As found on the Neiman Marcus (2007e) webpage, service awards include; NM Best, Neiman Marcus' most prestigious employee honor, awarded annually to associates nominated by their peers; *"You're What We're Famous For"* Award, for excellent customer service, a positive attitude, and other legendary Neiman Marcus attributes; Star Awards, for exemplary achievement. Also, available on the webpage are the merchandising awards which include Buyer of the Year, Assistant Buyer of the Year, Chairman's Risk Taker's Club, Merchant Team of the Month, Merchant of the Quarter, Planner of the Year, and lastly Star Awards, for exemplary achievement.

**Financial Information**

Neiman Marcus Group (2007a) provides financial information for the 2006 fiscal year that can be seen on Figure 1.

Figure 1

NEIMAN MARCUS FINANCIAL INFORMATION FOR THE 2006 FISCAL YEAR

|  | Total Sales ($MM) | Specialty Retail | NM Direct | Total |
|---|---|---|---|---|
| 1st Quarter | 946 | 8.8% | 10.4% | 9.0% |
| 2nd Quarter | 1,195 | 4.5% | 13.2% | 6.0% |
| 3rd Quarter | 992 | 5.7% | 16.5% | 7.3% |
| 4th Quarter | 897 | 5.8% | 13.2% | 7.0% |
|  |  |  |  |  |
| Total | 4,030 | 6.1% | 13.3% | 7.3% |

FIGURE 11.5. *(continued)*

Kris Swanson
Page 5
April 2, 20xx

The Neiman Marcus Group (2007a) states that the information listed has been adjusted to exclude the revenues of Gurwitch Products, L.L.C., which was sold in July 2006 and Kate Spade LLC, which was sold in December 2006.

In 2006 The Neiman Marcus Group broke its sales down by percentages of major merchandise categories making up its merchandise mix. The information is available on the Neiman Marcus Group (2007b) webpage and the sales are as follows (see figure 2): 35% of the sales were made in woman's apparel; 19% in woman's shoes, hand bags and accessories; 12% in men's apparel and shoes; 11% in cosmetics and fragrances; 10% in designer and precious jewelry; 8% in furnishings and home décor; and 5% in other merchandise.

Figure 2

NEIMAN MARCUS SALES BY CATEGORY FOR THE 2006 FISCAL YEAR

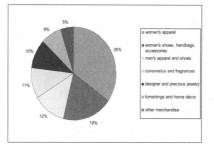

**Summary**

Neiman Marcus is an apparel retailer that is committed to their clients. The firm is willing to provide the best customer service and have some of the best trained associates in the industry. Employees succeed because of the commitment that Neiman Marcus has to them. They are well trained and have the option to enter into their executive development program giving their employees the options to succeed however they want.

Working for Neiman Marcus employees have several career paths to consider. Neiman Marcus also offers great benefits to its employees and their families along with benefiting the community. Also, Neiman Marcus is a firm believer that their employees should be recognized for their hard work. That is why the company offers many options for recognition in their annual awards.

Lastly, the Neiman Marcus Group along with Neiman Marcus itself is experiencing successful financial growth. Sales have already increased over the 2006 fiscal year, and Neiman Marcus is anticipating continual growth. It truly seems that Neiman Marcus is a great company to work for.

FIGURE 11.5. *(continued)*

Kris Swanson
Page 6
April 2, 20xx

**Reference Page**

Hoovers. (2007). *Bergdorf Goodman, Inc.* Retrieved March 16, 2007 from
http://www.hoovers.com/bergdorf-goodman/--ID__116849--/free-co-factsheet.xhtml

Neiman Marcus. (2007a). *Benefits.* Retrieved March 16, 2007, from
http://www.neimanmarcuscareers.com/working/benefits.shtml

Neiman Marcus. (2007b). *Corporate mission.* Retrieved March 16, 2007, from
http://www.neimanmarcuscareers.com/story/mission.shtml

Neiman Marcus. (2007c). *CUSP.* Retrieved March 16, 2007, from
http://www.neimanmarcuscareers.com/where/cusp.shtml

Neiman Marcus. (2007d). *Executive development program.* Retrieved March 16, 2007, from
http://www.neimanmarcuscareers.com/working/edp.shtml

Neiman Marcus. (2007e). *Recognition.* Retrieved March 16, 2007, from
http://www.neimanmarcuscareers.com/working/recognition.shtml

Neiman Marcus. (2007f). *The Neiman Marcus story.* Retrieved March 16, 2007, from
http://www.neimanmarcuscareers.com/story/index.shtml

Neiman Marcus. (2007g). *Where to work.* Retrieved March 16, 2007, from
http://www.neimanmarcuscareers.com/where/index.shtml

Neiman Marcus Group. (2007a). *Financial information.* Retrieved March 16, 2007, from
http://phx.corporate-ir.net/phoenix.zhtml?c=118113&p=irol-monthly2006

Neiman Marcus Group. (2007b). *Merchandise mix.* Retrieved March 16, 2007, from
http://phx.corporate-ir.net/phoenix.zhtml?c=118113&p=irol-merchandisemix

FIGURE 11.5.

Depending on your writing style, you may outline your report or proposal first and then conduct research. Or you may reverse the order, researching information first and then outlining the report. It does not matter which you do first as long as both are completed accurately and thoroughly. Appendix D, "Web Source Location and Evaluation," offers assistance in finding and evaluating sources for research purposes. Remember to document all sources to avoid plagiarism (see Appendix B, "Documentation Format").

After researching the information, you need to interpret your research findings for the reader. Depending on the purpose of the document, you may summarize, draw conclusions, or make recommendations from your research results. A **summary** is a brief restatement of the main ideas from the research you have collected (Kirszner & Mandell, 2005). The summary, though written in your own words, is unbiased and free of your opinion or recommendations. It is strictly a report of fact.

A **conclusion** is a logical interpretation of the facts from your research (Bovée & Thill, 2006). Developing analytical skills that allow you to draw good conclusions based on the evidence presented is a critical business skill. Conclusions must directly fulfill the original purpose of the report or proposal and must be based strictly on the information that you found and reported on in the rest of your report. It is important to draw conclusions from all the information presented, not just the information that supports your conclusion. Finally, the conclusion is not the place to introduce new material. All information should have previously been discussed in the body of your report or proposal.

A summary restates facts, a conclusion interprets facts, and a recommendation suggests what to do about the facts. **Recommendations** are suggestions for action (Bovée & Thill, 2006). Good recommendations are practical, they are acceptable to the reader, and they include enough detail for the reader to take action.

---

*Summary Example:* **Department stores reported that bestsellers during the last holiday season included coats, dresses, contemporary men's and women's sportswear, handbags, shoes, fine jewelry, and children's wear.**

*Conclusion Example:* **On the basis of last year's bestsellers, I conclude that coats, dresses, handbags, and shoes should be considered for a larger percentage of our open-to-buy for the upcoming holiday season.**

*Recommendation Example:* **I recommend that we contact our top coat vendor, and offer to carry their line exclusively for the upcoming holiday season.**

---

## Organizing Reports and Proposals

Reports and proposals are organized using one of four formats: memo, letter, manuscript, or preprinted form. You should select the format based on your relationship with the audience, the subject of the report or proposal, its purpose, and its expected length.

- **Memo format** is used for reports that are circulated within an organization and are fewer than 10 pages long. Figure 11.5 provided an example of an information report written in memo format. These reports should include the normal parts of a memo, internal headings, and, if necessary, graphics to help the reader understand the information.
- **Letter format** is used for reports of eight or fewer pages that are circulated outside the organization. These reports should include the standard parts of a letter plus internal headings and graphics as necessary.
- **Manuscript format** (also referred to as **formal report format**) is used when the audience will be more receptive to a formal structure and tone, regardless of the page length. Formal reports contain specific elements before the text (prefatory parts) and after the text (supplementary parts) (see Figure 11.6). The formal report example that follows is based on student work and does not necessarily reflect actual Lucky Brand Jeans lines, stores, or personnel.
- **Preprinted forms** are used for fill-in-the-blank reports that are routine in nature, such as time sheets, records of absences, or monthly inventory sheets. These forms are often available online and in some cases can also be filled out online.

There is not one uniform, conventional way in which to organize the content of a report or proposal. For example, the report in Figure 11.6 is an abbreviated example of a promotion plan, and the body of the report contains headings specific to this type of report.

Organization is based on the specific purpose and content of your report, so you should present the information in a logical order that makes sense to your audience. Bovée, Thill, and Schatzman (2003) offer common topics covered in a report body:

- Explanations of an opportunity or problem
- Facts, statistical evidence, or trends
- Results of a study, investigation, or experiment
- Discussion/analysis, advantages/disadvantages, costs/benefits of a potential course of action

- Procedures or steps for a process
- Methods or approaches
- Criteria for evaluating alternatives or options
- Supporting reasons, conclusions or recommendations

The introduction should prepare the audience by tying the report or proposal to the problem, introducing the purpose of the report or proposal and indicating why it is important, previewing the main ideas and the order in which topics will be covered (roadmap the report or proposal; this tool is described below), and establishing the tone of the document and your relationship to the audience (Bovée & Thill, 2006).

The body of your report contains the substance of your report or proposal and is dependent on the type of report you are writing. Information reports are written to present facts. Using one of the organizational patterns discussed in Chapter 2 (for example, chronological, topical, or geographical), present your facts so that readers will understand the information easily.

The body of a proposal generally includes a more detailed explanation of the background, purpose, or problem of the proposal, and it provides supporting facts and evidence to support your conclusion. In the proposal you lay out a plan or schedule for the reader, along with a detailed description of the staffing needs, the budget or cost analysis, and the qualifications of the individuals connected to the project.

In the final section of the report or proposal, you want to leave your reader with a strong and lasting impression. The closing should emphasize the main points of your message, summarize reader benefits if you are drawing conclusions or making recommendations, and suggest action about what should be done next.

---

*Portfolio Exercise:* **Visit your favorite retail store. You are acting as if you are an ordinary customer, but in fact you are a detective for the owner. After your visit, write the owner an informal report in memo format explaining what you did, what you observed, what the store does well, and what recommendations you have for improvement.**

---

A **formal report or proposal** is organized into three major sections: prefatory parts, body, and supplemental parts. We have already discussed the body of the report or proposal, which includes introduction or background; discussion of findings; and summary, conclusions, or purpose. One additional element that should be included after the introductory paragraph is the **roadmap paragraph**, which is a brief paragraph telling the reader how the information in the report or proposal is organized. The beginning of each chapter of this textbook includes just such a roadmap paragraph. Transition words are used in the paragraph to link sentences together.

---

*Transition Word Examples:*

- **Next, additionally, finally . . .**
- **For the following reasons . . .**
- **As shown below . . .**
- **If . . . then . . .**
- **This section outlines . . .**
- **First . . . second . . . third . . .**
- **Begins . . . concludes . . .**

---

## BOX 11.2 HOW ANALYTICAL REPORTS ARE DIFFERENT

Analytical reports are more complex, and the body of the text is formulated around the reaction you expect from your audience. According to Bovée and Thill (2006), the three most common analytical reports are focused on one of the following:

- **Conclusions**—When readers are likely to accept your conclusions, structure your report around the conclusions. Use the direct approach, presenting your conclusions first, and then give supporting detail and explanation for your conclusions.

- **Recommendations**—When you are asked to solve a problem, structure your report around the recommendations using the direct approach. This includes the following steps: (1) establish the need for action in the introduction, briefly describing the problem or opportunity; (2) without providing much detail, introduce the benefit that can result; (3) using action verbs, list the steps (recommendations) required to achieve the benefit; (4) explain each step fully, giving all necessary details—including costs; and (5) summarize your conclusions for the reader.

---

**Box 11.2** *(continued)*

- **Logical arguments**—Encourage your reader to weigh all the facts before you present your conclusions or recommendations. Use the indirect approach, presenting the detail and explanations before stating your conclusion and recommendations. The detail and explanation should logically lead your reader to your conclusions.

---

*Portfolio Exercise:* **Select your favorite fashion item (apparel item, accessory item, or beauty item). Take the role of an employee for the manufacturer of this item. You have been given the responsibility of getting a local retailer to carry the product. Write an unsolicited proposal (letter or formal format) to be sent to the owner of the retail store asking to carry the product. When you have finished writing, exchange your message with a partner. Edit your partner's message as needed so that it demonstrates thorough knowledge of the product and summarizes the benefits of carrying this item.**

---

The first page of the body of the report contains the title of the report, printed two inches from the top of the page. Headings should be used to inform the reader of major sections. This is page 1 of the document if you are using arabic numerals for your page numbering system. The prefatory material is numbered with lowercase roman numerals, then the numbering switches to arabic numbers in the body of the document.

---

*Levels of Heading in Reports or Proposals Example:*

## REPORT, CHAPTER, AND PART TITLES

*First-Level Subheading*
**[centered, uppercase and lowercase letters, bolded, title case]**
**After a first-level heading, text begins on a new line.**

*Second-Level Subheading*
**[left margin, uppercase and lowercase letters, bolded, title case]**
**After a second-level subheading, text begins on a new line.**

### *Third-Level Subheading*

**[left margin, uppercase and lowercase letters, bolded, sentence case, period punctuation and letter space at end] After a third-level subheading, text begins on the same line as the subheading.**

---

**Prefatory parts** appear before the body of the report. These include a transmittal letter or memo, a title page, a Table of Contents, and an Executive Summary or abstract. The **transmittal letter or memo** introduces the report or the proposal to the recipient. It is written like any other letter or memo. Some writers prefer the transmittal letter to be bound into the document itself, immediately following the title page; others present it as a separate document. In Figure 11.6, the transmittal memo is a separate document. If the letter or memo is bound in the document, do not include a printed page number on this document (even though it is page 2, roman numeral ii). In addition to presenting the report or proposal to the recipient, the transmittal letter presents an overview of the report, suggests how to read and interpret the report, acknowledges others who assisted the writer, makes an offer to discuss the report personally, and expresses appreciation for the opportunity to write the report or proposal.

The title page is arranged with four evenly balanced areas: report title, recipient name, report writer, and date—all centered. The page number is omitted on the title page but is counted as page 1 in lowercase roman numerals [i]. The report title is generally in all capital letters and boldfaced. For long titles, break the title into several lines, and place longer lines over shorter lines. The words *Prepared for* appear on a line above the recipient's name, and the words *Prepared by* appear on a line above the writer's name. The date is spelled out: for example, *January 23, 20xx.*

The Table of Contents page follows the title page and shows major headings and page numbers in lowercase roman numerals. This is either page ii or page iii depending on whether the transmittal letter is bound in the document. All entries on the Table of Contents page start after this page, so in most cases the Executive Summary is the first heading on the Tables of Contents page. Leader dots should be used to guide the eye to the page number.

The Executive Summary is a summary condensing the entire report in case the report is not fully read. The Executive Summary provides an overview of all main points of the report. In research, this document is called an abstract. The page numbering follows the sequence of roman numerals for other prefatory parts of the report. This document is one to two pages long for a shorter document; it may be as long as five pages for a longer document (200+ pages).

**MEMORANDUM**

Date: August 12, 20xx

To: Kris Swanson

From: Rachel Gray

Subject: Lucky Brand Jeans Promotion Plan

The attached promotion plan describes the overall communication strategy developed by the team of Lindsay Haldeman, Ryan Mandino, Michelle Marchi, and Rachel Gray for Lucky Brand Jeans for the 6-month period February – July, 20xx. We are confident you will find the results of this plan beneficial.

The promotion plan specifically examined the following:

- Situation analysis

- Communication process

- Promotion mix recommendations

Preliminary findings indicated that Lucky Brand Jeans has strengths including quality, long-lasting products, but also weaknesses including a price that competes at the better price zone. The "Lucky You" insignia presents a good opportunity as a positioning strategy that our competitors do not have. Finally, a threat that must be overcome is the perceived overbearing image of select sales associates.

Two key problems were identified including a focus on quality and originality. Four promotion objectives were presented to create awareness and communicate about Lucky Brand Jeans and the Lucky Brand Foundation.

Decisions concerning each promotion mix element were also discussed including Web, advertising, personal selling, sales promotion and a featured fashion show at Central Park to create awareness for the Lucky Brand.

We would be pleased to discuss this plan and its conclusion with you at your request. We thank you for your confidence in our team in developing this promotion plan for Lucky Brand Jeans.

FIGURE 11.6a. Formal report format: Transmittal memo.

**LUCKY BRAND JEANS PROMOTION PLAN**

Prepared for
Dr. Kris Swanson
Flagstaff, Arizona

Prepared by
Rachel L. Gray
Lindsay M. Haldeman
Ryan A. Mandino
Michelle C. Marchi

August 12, 20xx

FIGURE 11.6b. Formal report format: Title page.

## TABLE OF CONTENTS

ii

**FIGURE 11.6c.** Formal report format: Table of Contents. (*continued*)

**LIST OF FIGURES**

Figure

iii

FIGURE 11.6c.

## EXECUTIVE SUMMARY

The promotion plan describes the overall communication strategy for Lucky Brand Jeans for the 6-month period February–July, 20xx.

Lucky Brand Jeans targets male consumers ages 18–34, who want to be stylish and comfortable. They are well-educated men, single or married, with or without children, with an average household income of $30,000–$50,000 who want to be stylish and comfortable.

Lucky Brand Jeans designs and produces denim, sportswear, knits, wovens, outerwear, T-shirts, and active wear, and it licenses swimwear and accessories for men and women. Better department stores and specialty stores carry Lucky Brand Jeans. The product is sold at 110 company-owned stores nationwide and 3 international retail outlets.

Selected internal factors that affect this promotion plan are (1) brand awareness, and (2) awareness about the Lucky Brand Foundation. Selected external factors that currently affect Lucky Brand are current oil prices, inflation, and the stock market.

A SWOT analysis identified strengths (a long-lasting product, exceptional brand image, perfect fit); weaknesses (better price point); opportunities ("Lucky You" personalized insignia); and threats (perceived sales associate image) that Lucky Brand Jeans faces during the next planning period. This analysis resulted in the identification of two key focuses of the promotion: quality and originality.

Four promotion objectives were presented to create awareness and communicate about Lucky Brand Jeans and the Lucky Brand Foundation. The Lucky Brand Jeans customer perceives the brand as a high-quality product with an easy-going image. The brand is positioned as one that is unique, offering originality meeting a variety of casual needs for men. The long-lasting nature of the product is positioned in the mind of the consumer as a good alternative to less expensive and equally less durable products in the marketplace.

The company has two recognized two trademarks, the "Lucky You" written on the inside of the fly of every pair of jeans and the four-leaf clover present on all things related to the brand.

Promotion mix recommendations include a web presence at www.luckybrandjeans.com. Print advertising continues to be strong in various consumer fashion magazines including *InStyle* among others. Personal selling efforts are focused on getting customers into the product. Sales promotion efforts focus on database development for marketing efforts to increase brand loyalty among consumers. Lastly, Lucky Brand Jeans will produce a fashion show at Central Park in New York City to display our new clothing lines.

iv

**FIGURE 11.6d.** Formal report format: Executive Summary.

**LUCKY BRAND JEANS PROMOTION PLAN**

**INTRODUCTION**

This promotion plan was designed to analyze the overall communication strategy developed for Lucky Brand Jeans for the 6-month period February–July, 20xx. Specifically, the report will address the situation analysis, communication process, and promotion mix recommendations. Review of the marketing plan, current trend forecast, and target market were conducted prior to the development of the promotion plan.

**Target Market**

For this promotion plan, Lucky Brand Jeans targets male consumers ages 18–34. The Lucky Brand customer wants to look stylish while being comfortable. They are laid back and casual dressers and want quality clothes that will hold up while they participate in numerous activities. They are well-educated men, single or married, with or without children, with an average household income of $30,000–$50,000. They hold a wide variety of occupations, usually wearing Lucky Brand clothes away from work. They can be found shopping with their significant other or skateboarding with their friends. They might also be having a backyard party with family and friends all while wearing Lucky Brand jeans.

**Product**

Lucky Brand Jeans designs and produces denim, sportswear, knits, wovens, outerwear, T-shirts, and active wear, and it licenses swimwear and accessories for men and women. Better department stores and specialty stores carry Lucky Brand Jeans. Additionally, the product is sold at 110 company-owned stores nationwide and 3 international retail outlets (Lucky Brand Jeans, 20xx).

**SITUATION ANALYSIS**

The procedure for developing a situation analysis was conducted in three phases: (1) conduct background research, (2) prepare a SWOT analysis, and (3) identify key problems or opportunities to be solved with promotion.

**Background Information**

Many factors go into a promotion plan. Important elements that have an effect on a promotion plan arc:

- Internal factors which focus on the company, brand and product, and

- External factors which focus on the consumer, competition and environment.

1

**FIGURE 11.6e.** Formal report format: Report body. (*continued*)

**Internal Factors**

Selected internal factors that affect this promotion plan are (1) brand awareness, and (2) awareness about the Lucky Brand Foundation. Brand awareness is the most important element in creating customer loyalty. Success involves getting more consumers into our denim. If we don't let the consumer know who and what our brand is and what our brand stands for, we won't be able to meet this objective.

Another internal factor is the Lucky Brand Foundation. The Lucky Brand Foundation is a charitable organization committed to bringing happiness, comfort and hope to disadvantaged and disabled children (2007). It is essential that we bring awareness of our foundation to our customers, showing how much of a consumer's purchase goes to the disadvantaged children.

**External Factors**

Selected external factors are also important. External features that currently affect the apparel market in general and Lucky Brand specifically are: current oil prices, inflation, and the stock market.

The first external factor affecting the industry and Lucky Brand is current oil prices. Oil prices per barrel are currently rising affecting the cost of gas. With an increase in gas prices, consumers are not as willing to spend money on apparel products. In 2006 the National Retail Federation's Gas Price Consumer Intentions and Actions Survey found that 69.3 percent of shoppers with household incomes of $50,000 or higher said gas prices were negatively affecting their spending, compared to 59.1 percent in 2005 (Poggi, 2006). The survey indicates that when gas prices increase consumer spending drops.

The next external factor that can affect the brand is inflation. Just as oil prices are increasing, inflation is also rising. Although the rate that inflation is rising can be viewed as a small percentage, it can still affect the consumer market. According to *USA Today*, food costs in January 2006 grew 0.7% and consumer prices rose 2.1% from January 2005 ("Consumer Price Index," 2007). These numbers are small increments but if a customer spends more money on food and other basics, he may have less disposable money to spend on apparel, including Lucky Brand jeans.

The third external factor affecting the economy in general and Lucky Brand specifically is the stock market. Because there is so much fluctuation within the stock market, it can effect how the public views the economy. If there is a 400 point drop, even when we are trading on 12,000 plus points, economist still view this as a huge drop. Although this is a low drop percentage wise, the media portrays it as a big drop in the market. This portrayal can lead to consumer buying patterns dropping as well, due to apparel customers worrying about the market and if it is going to continue to drop. This can affect Lucky Brand due to the decreasing purchasing power of the customer.

2

FIGURE 11.6e. (*continued*)

### SWOT Analysis

A SWOT analysis has developed to identify selected strengths, weaknesses, opportunities and threats Lucky Brand Jeans faces during the next planning period.

#### Strengths

Lucky Brand Jeans provides a quality, long-lasting product. Lucky Brand Jeans takes pride in the fact that our jeans last. When people walk into retailers that offer the Lucky product, they are not always aware of the caliber of jeans that Lucky offers. Through the brand knowledge of highly trained sales associates, we are confident that the product strengths, features, and benefits will be made clear to each consumer.

Another strength of Lucky Brand Jeans is an exceptional brand image. The Lucky Brand founders, Gene Montesano and Barry Perlman, have always believed in the philosophy that every customer leaving the store with a Lucky product will feel stylish and comfortable. This philosophy has translated into a successful business and continues to be a major strength for the brand today.

Finally, another valuable strength of Lucky Brand Jeans is the perfect fit that Lucky offers to every customer, no matter their shape or size. Jean walls behind the cash register make it convenient for sales associate to help guests pick out the right pair of jeans for their body type. Furthermore, customers are encouraged to step out of the fitting room to model jeans for associates who are trained to make customers feel superb every moment they are in the Lucky atmosphere. Associates can identify fit positive fit characteristics and offer alternative styles that will decrease negative fit issues, ensuring the perfect fit.

#### Weaknesses

Weaknesses must also be addressed. A potential weakness is placement in the better price zone. Jeans range from $65 to $120 for a pair of jeans. The founders wanted to "create an upscale line of blue jeans that was not geared to the mass market, instead they wanted to individualize their jeans" (Belgrum, 2001, p. 3). More specifically, they wanted to create a line "that used better fabrics, had pocket liners and unusual stitching techniques" (p.3). Higher quality and finer fabrics has resulted in a higher price point.

Through customer research, Lucky Brand Jeans has learned that once skeptical customers are pleased with their decision to spend a little more on Lucky Brand Jeans based on the quality they have derived from the product. One consumer said "although I was very hesitant to spend $80 on a pair of jeans, I decided to take a chance and see if this brand of jeans was the one for me. Six months later, my Lucky jeans are my favorite pair of jeans and still have not shown any signs and wear and tear. I am completely satisfied with my Lucky Brand Jeans experience" (A. Sloan, personal communication, March 6, 2007). Our company believes that our target market is willing to spend a bit more for quality goods.

FIGURE 11.6e. (continued)

**Opportunities**

The Lucky Brand Jeans company is a humorous company that likes to have fun. Lucky personalizes each pair of jeans with the message "Lucky You" stitched into the fly of jeans. Our target markets, generations X and Y, like to have things designed just for them. They like to feel special and unique. Through the "Lucky You" insignia and the signature green four-leaf clover, Gene Montesano and Barry Perlman have ensured great brand identification through personalization.

**Threats**

The final element of the SWOT analysis identifies key threats to the brand. One potential threat the brand faces is the image that some sales associates are over bearing and scare customers away from entering stores. Through customer research we have become aware that customers sometimes feel threatened by our associate's overly friendly and positive attitudes. We recognize this complaint and have addressed this with sales associates through training. The Lucky brand name never has the intention of being over bearing to our consumers and we believe that our sales associates are simply excited about informing our customers of our brand. We believe that by addressing this threat with our associates, the problem will diminish. Customers will feel comfortable in our stores and purchase our product.

## Key Problems

The next step in the promotion plan is to identify the few key problem(s) that can be solved with promotion.

- **Focus on quality**. We believe that through a focus on quality, consumers will realize the benefit of spending more on a long-lasting pair of jeans now, allowing them to not have to spend this money later. We believe that after trying our product, skeptical consumers are pleased with their purchase.

- **Focus on originality**. Our brand stands out as something original; a desirable product for our consumers. Leveraging quality and originality will allow consumer to feel like they are one-of-a-kind and they are wearing something that suits their individual personality.

## COMMUNICATION PROCESS

The communication process defines how Lucky Brand Jeans will communicate with consumers, utilizing information gained from the situation analysis. The process includes establishing promotion objectives, identifying the positioning strategy, and establishing brand communication.

**Promotion Objectives**

Promotion objectives state what is to be accomplished by the promotion program. The following promotion objectives are recommended:

4

FIGURE 11.6e. (*continued*)

- To create a 25% gain in awareness of Lucky Brand Jeans among 18–24 year-old males during the next 6 months.

- To communicate the distinct elements of quality featured in every pair of Lucky Brand Jeans to 50% of the target market audience to interest them in the brand during the next six months.

- To communicate the benefits of the Lucky Brand Foundation—that it supports charitable organizations for disadvantaged children—to 60% of the target market audience to encourage purchase of the brand during the next six months.

- To create a 40% increase in positive interaction between Lucky Brand sales associates and customers during the next six months, to encourage customers to make repeat visits to a Lucky Brand store.

**Position Strategy**

The Lucky Brand Jeans customer perceives the brand as a high-quality product with an easy-going image. The brand is positioned as one that is unique, offering originality meeting a variety of casual needs for men. The long-lasting nature of the product is positioned in the mind of the consumer as a good alternative to less expensive and equally less durable products in the marketplace.

**Brand Communication**

The Lucky Brand Jeans brand is communicated in a variety of ways. The company has two recognized two trademarks, the "Lucky You" written on the inside of the fly of every pair of jeans and the four-leaf clover present on all things related to the brand. The brand is fun-loving and humorous, attracting the same kind of customers. Lucky Brand Jeans is part of an easy-going lifestyle appealing to consumers that want to make a good impression and like to be active. The promise that we make to our customers is for a high quality, long-lasting pair of jeans that are stylish and fashion forward at the same time. Our promise is what keeps our consumers loyal. They know that when they spend money on our jeans they are going to last a long time and they will look good wearing them.

## PROMOTION MIX RECOMMENDATIONS

Decisions concerning the role of each promotion mix element are the focus of the past section of this promotion plan. Lucky Brand Jeans is focused on presenting a simple, easy-to-remember message to the consumer. Lucky Brand Jeans are known for their high quality and easy-going image. The promotion team is charged with developing new strategies that help the consumer recall the brand when they are shopping for their next pair of jeans.

5

FIGURE 11.6e. *(continued)*

**Web**

Lucky Brand Jeans continues to have a presence on the web, providing brand reinforcement and e-commerce opportunities at www.luckybrandjeans.com.

**Advertising**

Print advertising for Lucky Brand Jeans have been placed in the following magazines:

- *Fit Pregnancy*
- *Marie Claire*
- *InStyle*
- *Lucky*
- *Men's Fitness*
- *Cookie*
- *Self*
- *Teen Vogue*

Additionally, *InStyle,* May, 2007 featured editorial credit for Lucky Brand Jean's embroidered tops as shown in figure 1.

Figure 1

**Personal Selling**

One of the main objectives of Lucky Brand Jeans during the next promotion period is to get the customers to try on a pair of Lucky Jeans when they come into the store. Consumers often are challenged to find a pair that fits, feels, and meets their individual standards. If Lucky Brand Jeans is able to persuade the potential customer to try the jeans on for fit, we are confident they will believe their standards are met resulting in purchasing the product.

Personal selling is a positive way to reach this goal. At each Lucky Brand store, the employees will be specially trained to know every silhouette, style, attributes and features that each pair of Lucky Brands Jeans has to offer. This way, the customer will be cared for and attended to during the search for their perfect pair of jeans. High standards in training and incentive programs will encourage sales associates to be attentive to the customer.

6

FIGURE 11.6e. (continued)

**Sales Promotion**

Sales promotion is a good way to attract customers and get the brand name out to the public. When consumers hear the words "discounts" and "contests" it will immediately grab their attention, even if they are not a regular Lucky customer.

One of the promotional strategies will be directed towards the customer. Anyone who purchases an item at a Lucky store will be asked to put their general information into the computer system which includes; name, address, e-mail address, and phone number. The computer will store this information as well as what the customer purchased on that day. As follow-up we will be able to see what the individual customer's interests are and send thank you cards and discounts back to the purchaser. Depending on the prices and items that the customer purchases, they will receive discounts accordingly. This will encourage returning customers and potential brand loyalty.

Lucky coupons will be sent to the general public of the suburban areas where Lucky stores are located , as well as at college campuses. This will encourage those who receive the coupons to enter the Lucky stores in order to redeem their discount and attract potential new customers.

Lucky Jeans accumulates business by offering benefits of purchasing a certain number of Lucky Jeans. This will help counteract the fact that Lucky Jeans are known to be a bit more expensive than their direct competitors.

**Fashion Show**

Since there are limited silhouettes for male jeans, we want them to be aware of how to mix and match to create various looks. In order to obtain awareness we will conduct an annual fashion show in August for men's and women's clothing. Our theme is "A Walk in the Park" and the show will be held at Central Park in New York City and display our new clothing lines.  Since this is a major fashion city, this will create interest with the general public and they will become more aware of the Lucky Brand.

By implementing these approaches, we think that our target customer will be influenced to purchase our brand of jeans instead of our competitors. We think we have a well-rounded promotional mix with personal selling encouraging customers to try on merchandise, sales promotion through the mail offering discounts, and an annual fashion show making the public aware of our campaigns all while creating brand retention.

## CONCLUSION

Through the elements of our promotion plan, we believe that we have addressed any external and internal issues that could affect our brand and by creating our SWOT analysis, we have developed ways in which to reach our target consumers.  Additionally, we are confident in the strategies of our promotion mix, communication process and promotion program evaluation that we have a strong promotion plan that will ensure our brand name success.

7

FIGURE 11.6e. (*continued*)

**REFERENCES**

Belgrum, D. (2001, August 21). Denim brand wears well. *Los Angeles Business Journal*, pp. 3, 50.

Consumer Price Index. (2007, February 21). *USA Today*. Retrieved June 22, 2007, from
http://libproxy.nau.edu:2168/universe/document?_m=13af3a82e5aa464536c1f4549eb004
00&_docnum=8&wchp=dGLbVtz-zSkVb&_md5=0b5a832a61285b953136cfc0c09fb21c

Lucky Brand Foundation. (2007). Lucky gives back. Retrieved June 22, 2007, from
http://www.luckybrandjeans.com/Foundation/LBF_mission.htm

Lucky Brand Jeans. (2007). *About Gene and Barry.* Retrieved June 22, 2007, from
http://www.luckybrandjeans.com/about_gene_barry.aspx?g=8

Poggi, J. (2006, June 12). Analysts expect drop in consumer spending. *Women's Wear Daily*,
*191*(123), 13-13. Retrieved March 7, 2007 from Business Source Premier.

FIGURE 11.6e.

After the report itself, insert any additional pages, known as **supplementary parts.** These include a **reference page,** which is a listing of the actual works cited in the document formatted according to your preferred writing style (APA, MLA, or other). A bibliography may also be included; this is a list of additional works that might be useful to the reader. Each of these documents starts at the top of a new page and is numbered consecutively in Arabic numbers following the body. Additional supplementary parts may include appendices. **Appendixes** are supplemental information needed to clarify the report or proposal. They may consist of survey instruments, letters, maps, optional tables, brochures, or other information.

## VISUAL ELEMENTS

Sometimes it is true that a picture is worth a thousand words. This is certainly true in business communications, where a chart or table or figure can convey more easily what several paragraphs of words cannot. Illustrative data in reports, proposals, memos, and letters can make the message more effective and thus make your audience more receptive. Illustrative data helps clarify the content, summarize important ideas, emphasize facts, and provide focus. And, of course, it adds visual interest to the written document.

Figure 11.7 provides examples of the different types of graphics that can be used in a report. The most frequently used visual element in a report is the table. Tables show exact figures and data in a systematic order of rows and columns. Rows and columns should be labeled clearly and units of measure (such as percentages or dollars) should be identified. Tables generally are numbered separately from figures, and the label (Table 1) and title are placed at the top of the table. If the data for a table or a figure were obtained from another source, be sure to give the original source proper credit, using your preferred style guide for direction.

All other visual elements used in a written document are referred to as *figures*. These include charts, photographs, illustrations, and other visual elements. A **pie chart** is used to visualize a whole unit, with its proportional parts represented as wedges in the pie. It is best to limit a pie chart to four to eight segments and distinguish each wedge with a different color or cross-hatching. Labels should read horizontally. A **bar chart** allows items to be compared to one another using vertical or horizontal bars. The length of each bar should be proportional and should start at the zero mark (dollars or percentage).

| Who is responsible if a garment falls apart after first wearing? | | | | |
|---|---|---|---|---|
| | 16-24 | 25-34 | 35-55 | 56-70 |
| Retailer | 39% | 46% | 61% | 63% |
| Manufacturer | 48% | 51% | 42% | 40% |

FIGURE 11.7a. Visual element example: Table—Shows exact figures and values.

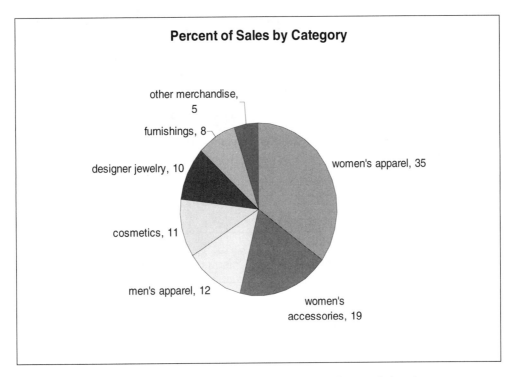

FIGURE 11.7b. Visual element example: Pie chart—Visualizes a whole unit to parts.

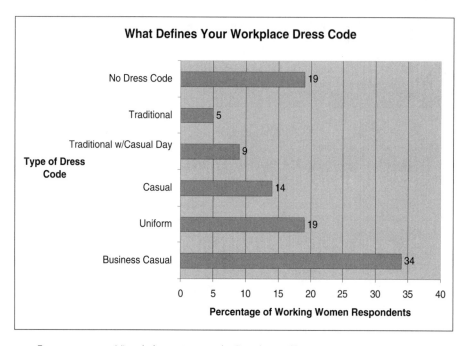

**FIGURE 11.7C.** Visual element example: Bar chart—Compares one item to others.

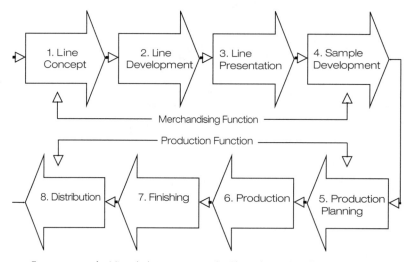

**FIGURE 11.7d.** Visual element example: Flow chart—Displays a process.

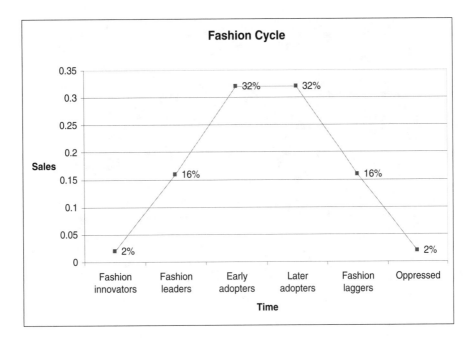

**FIGURE 11.7e.** Visual element example: Line chart—Demonstrates changes over times.

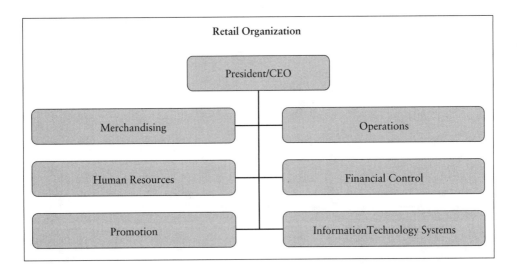

**FIGURE 11.7f.** Visual element example: Organization chart—Defines a hierarchy of elements.

FIGURE 11.7g. Visual element example: Photograph—Creates authenticity or spotlights a location.

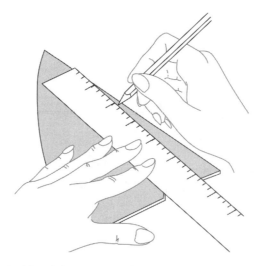

FIGURE 11.7h. Visual element example: Line drawing—Shows an item in use.

**Flow charts** display a process or procedure. Ovals designate the beginning or end of the process, diamonds denote decision points, and rectangles represent major activity or steps (Guffey, 2007). **Line charts** demonstrate changes in quantitative data over time. **Organization charts** define a hierarchy of elements or a set of relationships. Photographs provide authenticity to a presentation. Maps help to spotlight a location. **Line drawings** show how an item might be used.

As you can see, in developing effective visual aids, there are many choices. You should choose the visual aid that most represents your objective. The contents of the visual aid should be clearly identified with a meaningful title and appropriate labels. Try to keep the visual aid in a vertical direction so the reader will not have to rotate the page to understand the visual.

The text should refer the reader to the visual aid by location and table number or figure number. Additionally, the visual aid should be talked about in the text of the message; it should not just appear on the page with no discussion. If a visual aid is smaller than an 8½-by-11-inch page, it should be located as close to its text reference as possible. If the visual aid is larger than one page, consider placing it at the end of the report in the appendix.

In today's workplace it is also common to present your findings in the form of a presentation to an audience. Many times these presentations are accompanied by electronic tools. Appendix E, "Oral Presentations," can assist you with making these important business presentations.

## SUMMARY

This chapter has concentrated on writing business communications. Every aspect of business requires at least minimal communication through writing. Business writing involves focusing the message on the receiver's point of view in an ethical, positive, concise way that builds goodwill.

The expectations of the reader should always be considered when you are writing business messages. Routine messages are neutral in nature and do not affect the reader emotionally. In reading bad news messages, however, the reader is likely to become emotionally charged; you should try to anticipate this when you are composing the message. We all like to be appreciated or thanked, which is the purpose of a goodwill message. Persuasive messages are written to convince an often unreceptive reader to take action toward a cause or product.

Fashion business communications take many shapes. Memos and e-mail messages are informal, internal communications, while letters, reports, and proposals are more formal types of external communications.

## KEY TERMS

AIDA

Analytical report

Appendix

Bad news message

Bar chart

Block letter format

Buffer statement

Claim

Conclusion

Credibility

Direct writing strategy

Emotional appeal

Euphemism

External message

External proposal

Flow chart

Formal report format

Formal report or proposal

Full-justified

Goodwill

Goodwill message

Indirect writing strategy

Information report

Internal message

Internal proposal

Justification

Letter

Letter format

Line chart

Line drawing

Logical appeal

Manuscript report format

Memo report format

Memorandum

Modified block letter format

Organization chart

Persuasive message

Pie chart

Prefatory part

Preprinted form

Printed letterhead stationery

Proposal

Ragged edge

Recommendation

Reference page

Report

Request for Proposal (RFP)

Roadmap paragraph

Routine message

Salutation

Selling point

Signature file

Solicited proposal

Stakeholder

Stereotyping

Summary

Supplementary part

Transmittal letter or memo

Unsolicited proposal

## CASE STUDY

### *Safari's Choice*

Notable Fashion Worldwide (NFW) is a renowned forecasting service that provides clients with a network of resources, information, and services for a comprehensive view of the global fashion market. Clients can choose from a menu of offerings, including trend and color forecasting services, industry resources and manufacturing reports, and retail and market analyses.

Analysts with NFW regularly shop major retail centers, including all of the fashion capitals in Europe, as well as U.S. centers New York and Los Angeles, to update clients on colors, fabrics, silhouettes, and accessories. They also cover international trade shows and provide clients with city reports covering the latest fashion shows, store window displays, and trendy hotspots to view fashion. Analysts profile manufacturers to assist retailers with sourcing issues. The products and special capabilities of specific manufacturers are reported on to give clients an overall sense of the manufacturer's business and available resources. Additionally, personnel with NFW keep clients updated on the current climate in retailing, marketing, and merchandising around the globe.

NFW is competing against several other firms for a large contract with Safari, an upscale retailer with locations in London, Paris, Tokyo, and New York. Since the founding of the company in 1979, Safari has relied on its own in-house research and marketing division to provide (1) merchandise trend analysis and (2) business and market analysis. The owner of Safari, Mr. Thom Henriksen, has always believed that an in-house research team is time- and cost-efficient and can provide company leaders with greater control and coordination over all business activities.

Lena Henriksen, Wharton School of Business graduate and daughter of Thom, recently joined the company as Chief Operating Officer. She has recommended that Safari consider using an outside agency for merchandise trend analysis and business and market analysis. She believes that an outside agency can be more objective and can provide a larger scope of services that will benefit Safari as the company grows.

Diane Dewong is the VP for Sales and Marketing at NFW and is responsible for acquiring new clients. Ms. Dewong wants to make sure that NFW's proposal stands out against the competition. She believes that to win the contract, NFW must win over both Thom and Lena.

## CASE STUDY QUESTIONS

1.  What type of business report/proposal should Diane prepare for Thom and Lena?
2.  Should she use a direct writing strategy or an indirect writing strategy?
3.  What components should be included in the report?
4.  What type of visuals should be included in the report?
5.  What type of oral presentation should accompany the report?

## INDUSTRY PROFILE

*Melissa Turner*

***What is your current job and title? Can you describe the main responsibilities for your job?***

Title: Director of Fashion Arts & Events, Chicago Department of Cultural Affairs

Responsibilities: Project Manager for fashion for the City of Chicago

Includes: Liaison for the City to the Mayor's Fashion Council, developing year-round programming to help support and promote designers and local retailers in the City and coordinating Chicago's Fashion Week, Fashion Focus Chicago 2007.

***What is a typical day at work like?***

I don't have a typical day. I usually start my day at 5:00 a.m. I may be in the office in the morning or in meetings right away. Some days, my meetings last all day, and I come back to the office at night to work through e-mails and phone messages. During event times, I spend much of my day on the phone and e-mail to get things arranged for the events, with frequent site meetings and partner meetings. I spend a lot of time meeting with designers. I meet with them in the Chicago Cultural Center, or I meet with them in their studio or production spaces to learn how they are working. Also, I work with media to spread the word about the amazing things that are happening in the industry here.

***At what point did you decide to pursue a career in writing for a fashion-related business?***

While I don't have a career in writing, writing is very much part of my career. Much of my work is done in letter and e-mail correspondence. Communicating in this manner requires thought about word usage, grammar, and controlled discourse so that you make your points accurately and your message is properly conveyed. People cannot hear your tone of voice in writing. I am reminded of that occasionally!

***Describe your first writing job. What was the most important or interesting thing you wrote for that job/publication?***

My first writing professionally involved legal writing. I used to practice law, and legal writing required development of a different skill set and techniques. I worked for an attorney who was a wonderful writer and a great teacher. He handed letters back to me with red ink all over the page but told me I did a great job in spite of all of the ink corrections. I learned most about writing clearly and concisely from him. Although I still edit every time I write, even short letters and e-mails. I've learned that the first round is usually just getting thoughts on the page. The edit is creating a clearer version of what I am trying to say, and generally, the communication gains much more clarity and effectiveness with editing.

**What are you currently reading (books, magazines, Web sites, newspapers, other media)? Do you have a favorite author or publication?**

I don't have a favorite author or publication. I just finished reading *The Culture Code*, by Clotaire Rapaille. The book is a fascinating approach to consumer behavior. I also enjoy reading historical fiction and nonfiction. I read many different magazines, including *I-D*, *Surface*, *Architectural Digest*, *Vogue*, *Women's Wear Daily*, *Chicago* magazine, *CS* magazine, *TimeOut*, *Chicago Tribune*, *New York Times*, and so many more I can't even recall at the moment.

**What advice do you have for students interested in a writing career? Do you have any recommendations for students?**

My advice to students is to read everything you can. Look at different styles of writing and word choice that writers and authors use. Write frequently even if it's stream of conscious. If you are writing to someone, particularly for business, always think about the who, what, where, when, and how questions and add from there if needed, and always edit before you send it out to someone.

## REFERENCES

Bovée, C. L., & Thill, J. V. (2006). *Business communication essentials* (2nd ed.). Upper Saddle River, NJ: Prentice Hall.

Bovée, C. L., Thill, J. V., & Schatzman, B. E. (2003). *Business communication today* (7th ed.). Upper Saddle River, NJ: Prentice Hall.

Guffey, M. E. (2007). *Essentials of business communication* (7th ed.). Mason, OH: Thomson South-Western.

National Commission on Writing. (2004). *Writing: A ticket to work . . . or a ticket out.* New York: College Entrance Examination Board.

Kirszner, L. G., & Mandell, S. R. (2005). *The Wadsworth handbook* [Instructor's Edition]. Boston: Thomson Wadsworth.

Lehman, C. M., & Dufrene, D. D. (2005). *Business communication* (14th ed.). Mason, OH: South-Western.

Merriam-Webster. (2000). *Merriam-Webster's collegiate dictionary (Version 2.5).* Springfield, MA: Author.

Swanson, K. K., & Everett, J. C. (2007). *Promotion in the merchandising environment* (2nd ed). New York: Fairchild Books.

Thill, J. V., & Bovée, C. L, (2005). *Excellence in business communication* (6th ed.). Upper Saddle River, NJ: Prentice Hall.

# TWELVE

## *Writing Employment Messages*

After you have read this chapter, you should be able to discuss the following:

• The employment process and interview skills

• Writing an effective employment message

• Résumés and follow-up correspondences

I n a report written by the National Commission on Writing (2004) and published by the College Entrance Examination Board, the Commission stated that "writing is a ticket to professional opportunity, while poorly written job applications are a figurative kiss of death" (p. 3). Employment messages—résumés, application letters, appreciation letters—may be the most important written communications you prepare. Effective employment messages *will not get you the job*; however, they *will get you an interview* so you can prove you are the right person for the job.

This chapter discusses employment messages. But, before you can write an effective message you need to understand yourself and the job market. These are the topics of the first two sections of this chapter. Next, we will discuss planning a résumé. This may be the most important written message you write, so take time to develop a good one. Once the résumé is created, you need to introduce the résumé with an

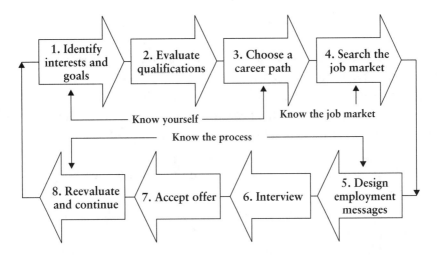

FIGURE 12.1. Employment search process. Adapted from Guffey, M. E. (2007). *Essentials of business communication* (7th ed.). Mason, OH: Thomson South-Western.

application letter and follow up with an appreciation letter. The final segment of this chapter briefly discusses what to expect in the interview process.

## PLANNING YOUR CAREER

What is a **career**? Stone (2004) defines a *career* as "a profession for which one trains and which is undertaken as a permanent calling" (p. 467). In planning your fashion career, you should learn about yourself, the job market, and the employment search process. Figure 12.1 summarizes this learning in a multiple-step process.

Many professionals will tell you that when they were getting ready to start their first full-time career position, they had a long list of jobs they *didn't want to do*, but they really couldn't tell you what they *did want to do*. You may find yourself in the same position. One way to move away from this feeling of uncertainty is to identify those things that will give you happiness and satisfaction at your job. The first step is to explore yourself and discover your interests.

# SELF-EXPLORATION

Self-exploration is not an easy task. It involves taking time to systematically learn about your own qualifications and capabilities so that you can meet the needs of a potential employer. By analyzing yourself, you will be better prepared to write a résumé and an application letter and to answer an interviewer's questions. The following questions are offered to help you learn about yourself:

- What kind of person are you? Do you take on leadership roles? Are you a good team player? Do others consider you dependable? Take time to inventory the positive personality traits that you can bring to a job.
- What skills do you have? Are you good at problem-solving or decision-making? Do you have analytical or verbal skills? Are you a left-brain thinker or are you a right-brain thinker?
- What would you like to do everyday? Ask your friends, relatives, and current or past employers what their typical workday is like. What do they like about their day? What don't they like about their day? By speaking with many people, you can get a feel for what different jobs are like (Bovée, Thill, & Schatzman, 2003).
- How would you like to work? Do you prefer working with people or with data? With ideas or with products? Do you prefer a close working environment or independence? Do you want variety in your job? Fashion is constantly changing, but some fashion jobs are more stable than others. You may need to determine the amount of upheaval you want to deal with on a daily basis.
- What is your ideal job? Can you obtain that job right out of school or is there a career ladder that you must take? A **career ladder** is the upward progression of jobs, each job building on the experience, responsibilities, and financial compensation of the previous job (Stone, 2004).
- What size company would you prefer to work for? The fashion industry offers many small entrepreneurial opportunities as well as careers in large corporations.
- Where would you like to be located? Fashion is global. Opportunities are available in small towns and large cities throughout the United States and internationally.

- How important are salary, benefits, and job security to you? How important are power or prestige? You should consider each of these elements before seeking a career in any industry. Knowing which of these is most important to you can help you at decision-making time (Guffey, 2007).
- What sort of corporate culture are you most comfortable with? **Corporate culture** is the mixture of values, traditions, and habits that give a company its atmosphere or personality (Thill & Bovée, 2005). Do you want a casual workplace or a formal one? Do you want defined communication channels or a team atmosphere? You will spend a great deal of time at work, so you should enjoy the atmosphere at your place of work and be receptive to the company's corporate culture.

---

*Portfolio Exercise:* **Write a report to your instructor answering the questions from this section.**

---

## CAREER EXPLORATION

After you have analyzed your strong points and your desires, it is time to explore potential career opportunities. Your job search for prospective employers should start months in advance of your graduation date. Procrastinating may affect your ability to find a satisfying job—not to mention that it could bring sleepless nights and an onslaught of questions from well-meaning friends and family.

Track your contacts using a **job search log**. Keeping a log will give you confidence that you have started the job search. More important, it will allow you to refer back to information you collected from earlier contacts. According to Lehman & Dufrene (2005), in a job search log, you should include the following information for each organization you contact:

- Company name
- Complete address
- Telephone number
- Date of each contact you make to and receive from the company
- Information you learned from each contact
- Complete name of each person who you contacted and who contacted you
- Date you sent your résumé, application letter, appreciation letter, and so forth

You can maintain the log as a paper file or a computer file. Expandable files or three-ring binders are possible paper file solutions. The goal is to make the file easy to use and easy to add information to when necessary. The log should be accessible when you receive a contact from an organization so you can use the log to help you respond efficiently to the call or e-mail.

*Portfolio Exercise:* **Design a job search log, as either a paper file or a computer file, and begin using it.**

Your job search will probably include both traditional and electronic job search sources. Traditional sources include print sources, employment agencies, and other services that are long-established methods for finding a job. Electronic sources are found on the Internet.

## Traditional Sources

The first place you should go for career assistance is your campus career center or employment services center. Colleges and universities want students to succeed after graduating, so they provide these centers to help students market themselves for employment. Some services centers require students to register prior to using the services. Check with your school's center to learn its procedure. Typical services include the following:

- Workshops for writing résumés and application letters
- Interview information and skills, including sample questions and the opportunity to practice interviewing
- Ability to upload résumés
- Networking to help to find employers and jobs
- Information about employers
- On-campus interview scheduling
- Career fairs or events
- Job and internship postings

Schools typically offer these services free to graduates up to a year after they graduate, and for several years after graduation for a small fee.

Employment agencies are a traditional search source. Government employment agencies offer services for free or at a minimal cost. These agencies often record phone messages stating available jobs within the city, county, state, or federal government offices they represent. Private agencies charge for services and accept payment after employment based on the first month's salary (Lehman & Dufrene, 2005).

The classified ads in newspapers from communities you are interested in are a good job search source. Employers use local newspapers or larger regional newspapers when time is tight and they want the position filled rapidly. Résumés can be received quickly, and review of applicants can begin immediately.

Don't forget the opportunities that networking through professional organizations can offer. Fashion Group International (FGI) allows student memberships and is a good resource for meeting professionals in the field. Any local, regional, or national organization that you have the opportunity to join can assist you in the job search. Members of professional organizations know the skills their profession require and the job positions that are open within their companies. They can help you contact the right person to inquire about a job.

## Web Sources

The Internet is increasingly becoming a good place to search for jobs. However, employment experts suggest that electronic searches should complement rather than replace traditional job search sources (Lehman & Dufrene, 2005). Human resource divisions use the Internet because it is cost-effective and it reaches a large applicant pool.

The Internet is useful for researching potential employers. Web sites such as CollegeGrad.com, JobWeb.com, Hoovers.com, and WetFeet.com help students locate information about potential employers. Using this information, you can write a résumé that directly addresses the company's needs and you can effectively prepare for an interview with the company.

The Internet is also a useful tool for finding available jobs. Web sites like CareerBuilder.com, CareerJournal.com, and Monster.com allow users to find open positions and post résumés. Salary information and job hunting advice are also available on the Internet.

Many companies post job opening on their Web sites. If you are interested in working for a particular company, go to their corporate Web site and find the tab for Careers. Open positions are often posted along with information on how to apply.

# PLANNING A RÉSUMÉ

Whether you are entering the job market or changing career directions, you need a **résumé**: a structured, written summary of your education, employment background, and job qualifications. A recruiter typically takes 45 seconds to decide whether to accept or reject a résumé. Therefore, your objective in writing a résumé is to generate immediate interest about you from the recruiter. Most recruiters scan résumés rather than reading the résumé from top to bottom. Your résumé must look sharp and grab the recruiter's attention even before your qualifications are judged. An example of a less-than-effective résumé is shown in Figure 12.2.

---

**BOX 12.1 HONEST AND ETHICAL—ALWAYS**

Presenting information in an honest and ethical manner is the most important consideration when you are developing a résumé. Guffey (2007) points out unethical practices that you should be aware of:

- Inflated education, grades, or honors
- Enhanced job titles
- Exaggerated accomplishments
- Altered employment dates

All of these are dishonest representations. If you use them and they are discovered, your reputation will be permanently stained.

---

Amy Carmichael

P.O. Box 4567

Flagstaff, Ariz. 86011

555-5555

ditzyblonde@hotmail.com

EDUCATION I am currently a senior at Northern Arizona University, working toward a BS degree in Merhcandising with a minor in Advertising.

PREVIOUS EMPLOYMENT 1997-2002 Gap Inc. at Metro Center Mall in Phoenix, Ariz. Duties included cash register, window displays, floor moves, arranging new merchandise on the floor, marking downs, changing the store layout, customer service, placing orders for customers and cleaned the store.

CONTACT: John Hartman, Store Manager. (602) 555-5555

ACCOMPLISHMENTS I set my mind on attending college and completing my area of study successfully. I have remained focused on my goals and motivated to continue working hard until I graduate next December. This is an achievement for me because I have taken advantage of the opportunities that have come my way successfully.

SKILLS I have excellent people skills. My previous jobs have given me the ability to talk to anyone in different environments. I am organized, punctual, and flexible and am able to multi task. I am also creative, enthusiastic, honest and hard working. I take pride in my work; I believe it is a direct reflection of who you are.

INTERESTS In my spare time I enjoy shopping.

FIGURE 12.2. Ineffective résumé.

There are many different ways to write a good résumé. Some résumé components (for example, identification) are conventional; others (for example, objective statement) are optional. Look at a variety of résumé models as you prepare your résumé. Professionals have opposing opinions about effective résumé design. Ask your professors, career counselors, and people you respect in business to provide you with feedback about your résumé. Listen to what they say, and decide which components and résumé type best suit your qualifications. Résumé models can be found later in this chapter in Figures 12.5 and 12.6.

The first element of résumé design that experts disagree on is length. Some experts prefer one-page résumés. Their reasoning is time; recruiters can look at a one-page résumé and decide in 30 seconds if the candidate is worth considering (Guffey, 2007). Experts who prefer two-page résumés believe they get a better idea of the candidate by seeing a more complete summary of skills and abilities (Guffey).

## ESSENTIAL ELEMENTS

An effective résumé should be neat, simple, and accurate. Essential information on a résumé includes

- Identification
- Education
- Experience
- Activities, awards, honors, and other such elements

Professionals expect all these elements to be on a résumé to provide critical information about the job candidate's credentials. These components will be discussed in the following section.

### *Identification*

**Identification** is the contact information you provide on your résumé. As the topmost section of your résumé, it should contain your first and last name, complete address, and telephone number with area code. Adding your middle initial gives the document a more professional appearance. E-mail and Internet addresses are optional. If your résumé is more than one page long, carry over your name and a page number as a header on consecutive pages.

The Identification section should be simple and uncluttered so that your name stands out. The word *Résumé* at the top of the page is redundant and should be omitted. The word *Identification* is also unnecessary. You may choose to include both your school address and your parents' address with the dates during which you can be reached at each address. This makes it easier for potential employers to contact you when school is not in session. Some experts caution students not to include two addresses because it draws attention to the fact you are a student with limited job experience. Alternative: Include whichever of the two addresses you believe is more reliable.

Your e-mail address should sound professional. An e-mail address like "Dittsyblonde@provider.net" does not present a professional image of you to prospective employers. If you are currently employed, you should use a personal e-mail address to show you are not using company resources to conduct your job search. If you are using a school-provided e-mail address, make sure you are aware of your school's policy for purging e-mail addresses after graduation. You do not want to provide an employer an invalid e-mail address.

The message on your answering machine should also present a positive image to prospective employers. Speak your full name clearly, and avoid music or any loud, distracting noises. The potential employer should not be subjected to crude language, jokes, shouting, or other amateurish behavior.

## *Education*

Under the heading **Education**, you provide details about your schooling. Include the following information:

- Name of institution, city, state
- Degree
- Major, minor, or certificate program if applicable
- Dates of attendance
- GPA if above 3.0 (with scale)
- Special abilities or experiences

Begin with your most recent degree. List the full name of the institution and the city and state where the institution is located. Use the common two-letter state abbreviation (for example, *MN, FL*). Next, list the degree(s) you have earned or will earn. The degree may be spelled out (for example, *Bachelor of Science degree in merchandising*) or displayed using initials (for example, *B.S. degree*). The name of the degree is capitalized. *Bachelor, Master,* and *Doctor* are used in singular form when written on a résumé. The word *degree* is not capitalized. Common college degrees include:

- **A.A.**—Associate of Arts
- **B.A.**—Bachelor of Arts
- **B.F.A.**—Bachelor of Fine Arts
- **B.S.**—Bachelor of Science
- **M.A.**—Master of Arts
- **M.B.A.**—Master of Business Administration
- **M.F.A.**—Master of Fine Arts
- **M.S.**—Master of Science
- **Ph.D.**—Doctor of Philosophy

Follow the degree with your minor (for example, *Minor in advertising*), certificate (for example, *Certificate in customer service*), or specialization (for example, *Specialization in CAD*) if these elements are part of your graduation requirements. Be sure to use official program titles on the résumé. Within departments, students and faculty may use lingo to refer to a discipline or program, but this is not appropriate for formal writing. If you are unsure of the program title, look it up in your school catalog. If you are attending college, do not include information about high school.

The dates you have attended the institution follow the degree. If you have already graduated with a degree, the year of graduation is sufficient. If you are still attending college, you should use *degree expected* or a similar phrase. Include the month and year to indicate to the employer when you are available for hire.

Your grade point average (GPA) or class ranking may be a strong selling point. Some professionals say to list your GPA only if it is above 3.0 (on a 4.0 scale). Other professionals believe that leaving your GPA off the document automatically signals to a recruiter that it is below 3.0. Always list the scale next to your GPA, such as *GPA: 3.5/4.0 scale*. A 3.5 on a 4.0 scale is much better than a 3.5 on a 5.0 scale. Identifying the scale reflects your academic achievements more accurately.

Your GPA in your major may be stronger than your overall GPA. You may use this figure on your résumé as long as you indicate it (*GPA: 3.75/4.0 in major*).

Hold back on listing courses you have taken. As Guffey says, "This makes for dull reading" (2007, p. 386). Refer only to classes that you can directly relate to the position being sought. Of more relevance may be specialized skills, honors earned, or membership in key educational organizations that set you apart from the competition.

## *Experience*

The next major heading of your résumé will be **Work Experience**: a listing of your employment history. Specific elements required under this section include the following:

- Employers' names, cities, states
- Most significant job title
- Dates of employment
- Related job duties and resulting skills; accomplishments

As in the Education section, you start with your immediate employer first, creating a backward timeline, resulting in your earliest job at the bottom on the list.

If you have been employed less than one year, include the months and years of employment (*March 20xx–December 20xx*). Once you have been employed by an organization for over one year, some recruiters believe the years are enough, while other recruiters become suspicious if they do not also see the months. For your current position, state the dates of employment from the month and year you were hired to the present (for example, *March 20xx to present*).

In this section you want to concisely tell the reader your responsibilities, skills, and accomplishments. Generally, to ensure that these statements are easy to read you place them in a bulleted list. General statements are not effective. Concrete statements that accurately reflect your tasks and skills will allow you to stand out in the applicant pool. Using active verbs will help you to make a more persuasive argument about your skills. See Figure 12.3 for a list of active verbs. Avoid using personal pronouns such as *I* or *me*. Concentrate on the skill, not the fact that *you have the skill*. Whenever possible, quantify the statements.

| | | | |
|---|---|---|---|
| Acquired | Created | Integrated | Set up |
| Administered | Delegated | Launched | Shaped |
| Advertised | Demonstrated | Managed | Simplified |
| Advised | Designated | Marketed | Solicited |
| Aided | Designed | Measured | Solved |
| Allocated | Developed | Monitored | Sorted |
| Analyzed | Devised | Motivated | Specified |
| Applied | Directed | Organized | Spoke |
| Appointed | Distributed | Oversaw | Stimulated |
| Appraised | Documented | Performed | Streamlined |
| Approved | Documented | Persuaded | Strengthened |
| Arranged | Elaborated | Planned | Studied |
| Assembled | Enabled | Prepared | Submitted |
| Assessed | Encouraged | Presented | Suggested |
| Assigned | Enforced | Prioritized | Summarized |
| Assisted | Engineered | Produced | Supervised |
| Attained | Established | Promoted | Surveyed |
| Built | Evaluated | Provided | Trained |
| Calculated | Examined | Publicized | Unified |
| Collaborated | Executed | Recommended | Updated |
| Communicated | Explained | Recruited | Upgraded |
| Compiled | Facilitated | Referred | Utilized |
| Computed | Forecasted | Reinforced | Validated |
| Conceptualized | Formulated | Represented | Valued |
| Conducted | Guided | Researched | Verified |
| Consolidated | Identified | Reviewed | Visualized |
| Consulted | Illustrated | Revitalized | Wrote |
| Contracted | Implemented | Scheduled | |
| Contributed | Improved | Secured | |
| Coordinated | Increased | Selected | |
| Counseled | Initiated | Set goals | |

FIGURE 12.3. Active verbs.

*Poor Statement Example:*

- **I ran the men's side of the store.**

*Effective Statement Examples:*

- **Managed sales for the men's division for 18 months before being promoted to store manager.**
- **Supervised 8 employees, including 1 assistant manager.**
- **Motivated sales associates to exceed monthly sales goals for 8 of 12 months in 20xx.**

*Poor Statement Example:*

- **Handled customer questions and concerns regarding store operations.**

*Effective Statement Examples:*

- **Handled merchandise returns, credit, and cash refunds.**
- **Played a key role in resolving customer complaints.**
- **Decreased customer wait time by 12% over 12 months by applying efficient customer service skills.**

The space on a résumé is limited; therefore, you should select only the most important responsibilities, skills, and achievements that directly relate to the job you are applying for.

## Activities, Awards, Honors, or Other Elements

Somewhere on your résumé, you should include honors, activities, or awards that enhance your qualifications. If you have three or more items that can be listed together, include them under a section heading such as Activities and Awards. Otherwise, include these elements where they are most appropriate, under Education or Work Experience. These items show that you are a productive, well-rounded individual. Common elements in this section include the following:

- Scholarships
- Dean's list
- Recognition at work (for example, Employee of the Month)
- Honors (for example, Outstanding Student in Retail Management)
- Volunteerism (for example, Senator for Associated Students)
- Competitive review (for example, designs featured in a juried show)

Personal data (age, marital status, gender, national origin, religion, race, children, or disabilities) are not included on a résumé. Recruiters are not allowed to ask personal questions and may not use this information to make a selection or hiring decision. Interests not related to work (singing in a church choir, reading science fiction) should not be listed on a résumé. On the other hand, if you have talents that can help on the job or that are a good conversation starter in the interview (for example, photography, sewing skills), include them in your résumé. Additional items that do not belong on a résumé are your Social Security number and a photograph of yourself.

## References

**References** are individuals who can discuss your qualifications. These are professional contacts made through school or employment—such as teachers, employers, and colleagues who know you and are willing to talk about your employment potential. Neighbors, family, and friends are considered personal references. Recruiters are reluctant to use personal references because the person may not be aware of your job performance.

Ask references in advance if they are willing to speak about your employment potential. Do not assume the person you ask is willing to give you a reference. Give the person an opening to decline the request graciously if they do not believe they can give you a strong recommendation. No reference is better than a negative reference. Provide a minimum of three references.

References can be handled on the résumé in two ways:

- Some recruiters prefer a brief statement "On request" printed on the résumé.
- Other recruiters believe this statement is old-fashioned; they prefer that applicants leave the statement off. Instead, they suggest listing the references

on a separate page. This page is not sent with the résumé. Rather, it is given to the recruiter during the interview.

As you review model résumés, make note of this detail to help you decide which format to follow.

Figure 12.4 is an example of a References page. The heading is made to duplicate the Identification section of your résumé. Following the Identification section, list your references including first and last name, job title, mailing address, and telephone numbers. Including an e-mail address allows the recruiter to make initial contact through e-mail followed by a formal reference check by telephone.

---

*Portfolio Exercise:* **Design a Reference page to match your résumé.**

---

## OPTIONAL ELEMENTS

Optional elements provide additional ways to strengthen a résumé. They are considered optional because business writers have mixed opinions regarding inclusion on a résumé. Two optional categories are

* Objective
* Summary of Qualifications

### *Objective*

An **Objective** is a statement specifying the job the applicant is seeking. Advocates for inclusion of an Objective Statement believe it helps a recruiter quickly identify your qualifications and interests. Opponents believe it can limit your ability to be considered for a wider variety of opportunities. If you use an Objective Statement, it should effectively articulate a specific objective. Consider these examples (McKinney, 2002).

**Janet Lynn Webb**
E-mail: jwebb1210@aol.com

**Current Address**
2222 W. University Ave.
Flagstaff, AZ 86001
(928) 555-5555
August 15 – May 15

**Permanent Address**
5555 N. 15th Street
Tempe, AZ 85333
(480) 555-5555
May 16 – August 14

Nancy Wagner
District Manager
Victoria's Secret
5555 W. Metro Boulevard
Phoenix, Arizona  85333
(602) 555-5555

Michael Powell
Store Manager
Gap Inc.
3345 Bell Avenue
Phoenix, Arizona  85333
(602) 555-5556

John Lindstrom
Store Manager
Aeropostale
1717 34th Street
Phoenix, Arizona  85333
(602) 555-5557

FIGURE 12.4. Résumé reference page.

*Poor Objective Statement Example:* **To be given an opportunity to work in a fast-paced environment with merchants, or specialized teams, or individually for a summer internship.**

*Poor Objective Statement Example:* **To obtain a visual merchandising position with a medium- to large-sized business.**

*Effective Objective Statement Example:* **To contribute sales, training, and motivational abilities in a retail management position where my experience in high-volume sales environments will be beneficial to the company and where adaptability to constantly changing situations is desired.**

*Effective Objective Statement Example:* **To contribute to an organization that can use an outgoing individual who offers versatile experience in sales, customer service and business management.**

## Summary of Qualifications

A **Summary of Qualifications** is a rundown of your strongest points, presented in three to eight bullet points to allow recruiters to immediately review your credentials. Some writers also call this a *career summary*. Consider your education, experience, and unique skills as you prepare the statements. These bullet points should provide a smooth transition from the objective, if it has been included. A Summary of Qualifications is more likely to be used by experienced job applicants and less likely to be used by students right out of college. If you use an Objective Statement or a Summary of Qualifications, place it immediately after the Identification section of your résumé.

To some writers, the Objective and the Summary of Qualifications serve the same purpose on the résumé. Other writers believe that they serve two different functions and that both should be included. Yet another group of business writers believes that neither element is necessary; they recommend against including either element on the résumé. Again, you have to make a choice.

## RÉSUMÉ STYLE

Times have changed! When the authors of this textbook first entered the work force, they each had one version of their résumé, which had been typeset at the local print shop for mass distribution to all potential employers. Today, individuals use word-processing software and laser printers to create one-of-a kind résumés to fit the particular needs of a potential employer.

Times continue to change. Career counselors suggest that to take advantage of the computer technology used by many organizations, students prepare three versions of their résumé: (1) a traditional print-based résumé; (2) a scannable résumé; and (3) an embedded résumé.

Some companies prefer traditional print-based résumés. This style is delivered in person or mailed to the potential employer. Bring an extra copy of your print-based résumé (and references page) to your interview, to refer to and/or to leave with the interviewer if he requests an additional copy. Print-based résumés use an outline format and bullets to highlight information. The arrangement of information on each line depends on the amount of content you need to provide. Page layout should be easy to read and uncluttered, with ample white space between elements. Always use the TAB button to align parallel elements. Using the SPACE bar may be easier, but it will cause elements to be uneven and unprofessional.

Traditional résumés are organized as chronological résumés or functional résumés. The style you select is based on the strengths you want to highlight. According to Thill and Bovée (2005), employers look for seven qualities in potential employees:

- Think in terms of results
- Know how to get things done
- Are well rounded
- Show signs of progress
- Have personal standards of excellence
- Are flexible; willing to try new things
- Possess strong communication skills

Keep these seven qualities in mind as you organize the information on your résumé.

## Chronological Résumé

A **chronological résumé** is the traditional organization format for résumés (Figure 12.5). This résumé style focuses on stable work history. Recruiters prefer this style because information is easy to find and because growth, career potential, employment continuity, and stability can be assessed quickly and efficiently (Thill & Bovée, 2005).

You should determine the order of the Work Experience and Education headings. If your work experience directly relates to the position you are applying for, Work Experience should come before Education. If you are a recent graduate and the jobs you held in college were not related to the position you are currently seeking, you should list Education before Work Experience.

## Functional Résumé

A **functional résumé** is more general and focuses on skills rather than work history (Figure 12.6). Headings highlight what you can do for the employer as opposed to when and where you did it. This type of résumé works well if you have limited experience or are changing careers. Under each heading, you can draw on both work and educational experiences to provide support. The advantage of this style includes the ability to show a potential employer what you can do for her without emphasizing breaks in employment or lack of career progression.

*Preparation Guidelines for a Print-Based Résumé* When preparing a traditional print-based résumé, consider the following guidelines:

- Use correct grammar, spelling, punctuation, and parallel structure.
- Use a clean typeface; avoid italics or other hard-to-read typefaces.
- Use ample margins and white space on all sides.
- The resume can be one or two pages long. If two pages are used, the content should look balanced over both pages.
- Use a simple, direct writing style; use short, crisp phrases instead of whole sentences.
- Avoid using "I."

**Janet Lynn Webb**
E-mail: jwebb1210@aol.com

**Current Address**
2222 W. University Ave.
Flagstaff, AZ 86001
(928) 555-5555
August 15 – May 15

**Permanent Address**
5555 N. 15th Street
Tempe, AZ 85333
(480) 555-5555
May 16 – August 14

EDUCATION     Bachelor of Science, Northern Arizona University, Flagstaff, Arizona.
Expected graduation May, 20xx. Grade-point average 3.35 (4.0 scale).
**Major**: Merchandising     **Minor**: Advertising
**Related courses**: Textiles, Merchandise Promotion, Visual
Merchandising, Merchandising Math, Copy and Layout

EMPLOYMENT    Sales Director, Victoria's Secret, Phoenix, Arizona, 2000 – present.
- Provided excellent customer service
- Executed floor moves
- Processed shipment
- Contributed to a constant increasing sales status
- Received first ever full time selling position in current location

Sales Supervisor, Gap, Inc., Phoenix, Arizona, 1998 – 2000.
- Opened and closed store
- Prepared bank deposits
- Motivated team towards increasing sales
- Provided a dynamic example to sales associates and served as a part of management team

Assistant Store Manager, Aeropostale, Phoenix, Arizona, 1997 – 1998.
- Charged with all interviewing, hiring, and training of new sales associates
- Completed all new hire paperwork involved in hiring and firing process
- Supervised an excellent staff of 9–15 people

OTHER SKILLS  Operating systems: Windows 95/98
Applications: Access, Word, Excel, and PowerPoint

FIGURE 12.5. Chronological résumé.

**Bethany Jean Robinson**
**7445 S. Bend Street**
**Flagstaff, AZ 86001**
**(928) 555-5555**
bjr55@dana.ucc.nau.edu

**Summary of**
**Achievements:** Mastered professional core skills in Microsoft Word, Excel and Access. Applied both marketing and E marketing skills while completing cooperative education. Developed management skills and visual merchandising skills while attending school. Prepared proposals, reviews, reports, and analysis's to develop management skills.

**Education:** Bachelor of Science degree in Merchandising, minor in Public Relations. Northern Arizona University. To be conferred December 200x. Grade-point average: 3.4 (4.0 scale). Financed 90 percent of education with loans and part-time work.

**Public Relations**
**Skills:** Learned listening and communication skills in the nursery industry. Commended by management for presentation, diplomacy, and speaking skills. Displayed dependable, consistent, and reliable behavior. Maintained the ability to convey diplomacy during high demand.

**Dependability:** Reported promptly when needed for work. Attended classes regularly while working 30+ hours weekly.

**Learning Capacity:** Commended for learning plant, insect, and native species identification quickly. Developed self-teaching skills pertaining to social and environmental issues. Commended for adaptability to learn different writing skills quickly. Trusted to teach rock-climbing, hiking, and backpacking skills to others.

**Work Experience:** **Warner's Garden Center**, Flagstaff, Arizona. Part-time since 2000. **Department Manager: Tasks included**: ordering merchandising for specific department, overseeing the department and its' employees. **Sales Associate**: Tasks included: customer service, plant, insect, and native species identification, yard and garden counseling, plant care and maintenance, tree and shrub identification, and office clerk.

**Outback Steakhouse**, Flagstaff, Arizona. Full/part-time, 1998-2000. **Server: Tasks included:** serve and wait tables. Greet, sit, and offer menu options. Responsible for opening, closing, bartending, and sidework.

**The Color Spot**, Longmont, Colorado, Part-time 1996-1997. **Sales Associate**: duties paralleled those of Warner's Garden Center.

FIGURE 12.6. Functional résumé.

- Use high-grade, letter-size (8½ × 11 inches) bond paper in white or some light earth tone with matching envelopes.
- Print the résumé on a high-quality laser printer.

---

*Portfolio Exercise:* **Design a traditional print-based résumé using either a chronological résumé style or a functional one.**

---

## Scannable Résumé

A **scannable résumé** is a computer-friendly résumé that can be scanned by the potential employer (Figure 12.7). When scanned, the résumé can be "read" electronically by an employer's optical character recognition (OCR) hardware and software. An OCR converts the characters from a printed page into text that is stored in a database. Employers then use special software to search for keywords, phrases, or skills targeted for a position. Companies may use electronic applicant tracking systems to scan incoming résumés, to create databases, and possibly to rank candidates for positions (Lehman & Dufrene, 2005).

Look on a company's corporate Web site to determine if they scan résumés electronically. Some organizations provide advice on how to prepare résumés for optimum effectiveness. If the Web site is not helpful, call the company and ask. If you send a scannable résumé, follow up by sending a traditional résumé via U.S. mail, more easily read by human reviewers who will select the final applicants to be interviewed.

## Embedded Résumé

An **embedded résumé** sent in the body of an e-mail message, is completely devoid of formatting. Some companies refer to this as a **plain-text** or **electronic résumé.** This style is preferred because the document is immediately searchable and does not require the receiver to open attachments that might carry a computer virus or be incompatible with the receiver's software (Guffey, 2007).

Effective scannable or embedded résumés use keywords effectively. When a scanner recognizes a keyword in your résumé, it's called a "hit." Your résumé will be ranked according to the number of keyword hits. Only résumés with targeted keywords will be selected for review. To increase the number of hits, use keywords and

**Janet Lynn Webb**
2222 W. University Ave.
Flagstaff, AZ 86001
(928) 555-555
jwebb1210@aol.com

EDUCATION
Bachelor of Science in Merchandising
Northern Arizona University, Flagstaff, Arizona, expected in May, 20xx

EMPLOYMENT
Sales Director
Victoria's Secret, Phoenix, Arizona
2000 – present.
- Provided excellent customer service
- Executed floor moves
- Processed shipment
- Contributed to a constant increasing sales status
- Received first ever full time selling position in current location

Sales Supervisor
Gap, Inc., Phoenix, Arizona
1998 – 2000.
- Opened and closed store
- Prepared bank deposits
- Motivated team towards increasing sales
- Provided a dynamic example to sales associates and served as a part of management team.

Assistant Store Manager
Aeropostale, Phoenix, Arizona
1997 – 1998.
- Charged with all interviewing, hiring, and training of new sales associates
- Completed all new hire paperwork involved in hiring and firing process.
- Supervised an excellent staff of 9-15 people.

OTHER SKILLS
Operating systems: Windows 95/98
Applications: Access, Word, Excel, and PowerPoint

FIGURE 12.7. Scannable résumé.

skill-focused words that apply to your career. Substitute descriptive nouns and skills for vague language. Strong keywords may include job titles (for example, *Merchandise Coordinator*), skills and responsibilities (for example, *five year's experience, key holder*), words that are familiar to the industry (for example, *patternmaker*), and education (for example, *B.A in fashion design*). Study job postings in your field to learn what keywords potential employers may use to evaluate scannable résumés.

*Preparation Guidelines for a Scannable or Embedded Résumé* Traditional résumés focus on verbs (for example, *coordinated, evaluated,* and *presented*), while scannable and embedded résumés focus on nouns (for example, *supervisor, manager, B.S.*). When writing a scannable or embedded résumé, include both nouns specific to the profession and verbs specific to interpersonal skills.

When preparing a scannable résumé, consider the following guidelines:

* List your name on the top of every page of your résumé.
* Provide each item of contact information on a separate line on the first page.
* Do not fold or staple the résumé.
* Avoid columns, graphics, and shading.
* Avoid using headers and footers, italics, and bolding.
* Use a sans serif font such as Arial in 12-point or 14-point size; 10-point Times Roman is too small, and the letters will touch and be scanned together.
* Substitute asterisks for bullets.
* Avoid boxes or horizontal or vertical lines.
* Use capital letters to distinguish section headings.
* Print on white paper using a laser jet printer to obtain clean, crisp copies.
* Utilize white space effectively.

## CHECKLIST FOR PREPARING
## EMBEDDED RÉSUMÉS

Guffey (2007) offers these additional guidelines for preparing an embedded résumé:

☐ Format the content to very short lines—less than 60 characters per line—to avoid wrapping to the next line.
☐ Left-justify all text.

☐ Save your résumé in plain text (.txt) or rich text format (.rtf) to ensure that it can be read when pasted into an e-mail message.

☐ Before sending your résumé to the employer, test it by e-mailing it to yourself to see if the formatting and other elements in the message you receive appear as you intended when you prepared the résumé.

Finally, in the e-mail message that contains the embedded résumé, on a separate line above the résumé include a brief note such as "Original to follow via U.S. mail." Then, as was suggested for scannable résumés, send a traditional résumé via U.S. mail. The human reviewers who will select the final applicants to be interviewed will find it much easier to read.

---

*Portfolio Exercise:* **Using the same information that you provided in a traditional print-based résumé, design a scannable or an embedded résumé.**

---

# PLANNING AN APPLICATION LETTER

A résumé is introduced with an **application** (or **cover**) **letter,** written after the résumé to provide a more personal sales message that is specific to the position you are applying for at the moment. The goal of the application letter is to encourage the potential employer to read your résumé. In the application letter you highlight your strengths and the benefits you can provide the company.

Use the letter as an opportunity to make important points not covered in your résumé or to lend support to your résumé without directly repeating information from the résumé. The application letter also functions as a transmittal for your résumé. Strong letters are written using key words and vocabulary directly from the job announcement.

Experts disagree on the appropriate length of an application letter. Some want a short letter that can be quickly read and understood. Others want a longer letter that indicates your strengths, going into some detail about particular connections between the job and your résumé. This second group believes that the interview process is time-consuming and expensive, and they want as much information as possible before beginning that process. Whatever length you determine, the content should be meaningful to the reader.

Application letters are general or targeted. **General application letters** are used to apply for an unsolicited position or for a position that you are not sure is open. **Targeted application letters** are written in response to a specific position that has been advertised.

## ESSENTIAL INFORMATION

Essential information in an application letter includes relevant qualifications, accomplishments, desirable personal qualifications, and references to your résumé (Figure 12.8). The letter should be prepared using the guidelines described for a business correspondence letter in Chapter 11, "Writing Business Communications." Whenever possible, address the letter to a real person rather than a job position.

The AIDA persuasive selling model discussed in Chapter 11 can help you write an application letter. Recall the points that AIDA represents:

- **Attention**—Gain favorable attention and express your interest in the position.
- **Interest**—Market your qualifications; identify specific strengths and attributes.
- **Desire**—Describe selected accomplishments that show how you can benefit the company.
- **Action**—Request an interview or propose a future meeting; make it easy for the recruiter to contact you to schedule a meeting.

The first paragraph is the most important part of the letter. Here you alert the reader to your interest in the position and motivate the reader to read the letter. An effective opening paragraph gets the reader interested in your qualifications and creates a desire for the reader to consider hiring you. Your first paragraph should convince the potential employer that you fit the job requirements and that hiring you will benefit the company. In this paragraph also tell the reader how you found out about the position you are applying for. This helps the business evaluate the effectiveness of their job announcement strategies.

Use the main body of the letter—one or more paragraphs as necessary—to describe your most outstanding accomplishments that relate directly to the job announcement. Use work experience, special expertise, or educational accomplishments to illustrate your strengths and how they meet the job requirements. Read the

P.O. Box 06462
Flagstaff, AZ 86011
April 26, 20xx

Ms. Karen Warner
Skin Essentials, Inc.
5555 Royal Avenue, Unit A
Sacramento, CA 93044

Dear Ms. Warner:

I am applying for the Assistant Manager position at the Skin Essentials Scottsdale, Arizona location. The position was advertised on HotJobs.com on April 20, 20xx. I am familiar with your company and the Scottsdale store specifically. The Assistant Manager position would be a good opportunity to begin my career at Skin Essentials, and become involved with a company whose philosophy and products fit my lifestyle.

As you can see by my attached resume, my past job experiences have provided me with a good understanding of the retail environment. As the Cash Office Associate for Ross Stores, Inc., I was able to learn about the financial side of the business. The responsibility of counting and preparing all registers, making bank deposits, and recording financial information was a valuable experience that exposed me to the 'bottom line' of business. As a Sales Associate at Old Navy for the past two years, I have been able to experience interaction with customers and the fast-paced energy of the sales floor. Additionally, experience in processing shipments, doing inventory counts, and visually merchandising products give me a comprehensive understanding of retailing.

With a B.S. in Merchandising from Northern Arizona University to be completed in 20xx, 1 also have the education to complement my work experience. Classes have focused on merchandise buying, retailing management, and marketing practices. One class in particular gave me the opportunity to dress windows for local businesses; this hands-on visual merchandising experience was very beneficial. My education has been specifically targeted toward the world of retail.

Skin Essentials, self-described as a "hot, new, fast growing, girly-girl specialty retailer," is a company very similar to my interests and experience. As Assistant Manager, I would excel in driving sales, visually promoting the merchandise, developing staff, and serving the consumer.

Thank you for your consideration, and I look forward to meeting with you. You may contact me by phone at 928-555-5555 or by e-mail at bjr55@dana.ucc.nau.edu.

Sincerely,

*Bethany Robinson*

Bethany Robinson

FIGURE 12.8. Cover letter.

job advertisement carefully when you write a targeted letter. Use words in the letter that fit both you and the language of the ad.

In the closing paragraph you want to motivate the potential employer to take action—to read your résumé and invite you for an interview. The best way to get an interview is to ask for it directly in a positive, pleasant manner. Make it easy for the employer to invite you, by including your telephone number and e-mail address. Offer to be at the employer's office at his convenience, or make a point to call in one or two weeks to check the status of your application. Taking the initiative to follow up—when expressed courteously—is not likely to offend; in fact, a potential employer may perceive it positively. Other closing comments should express thanks for consideration or indicate that you look forward to a response. Use stationery that matches the résumé, and always remember to sign your application letter.

## PLANNING AN APPRECIATION LETTER

You'll want to write an **appreciation (thank-you** or **follow-up) letter** immediately after the interview (Figure 12.9). The letter should be brief, cordial, and typed as business correspondence, not as a handwritten note. The letter lets the business know that you are still interested in the position. Even if you are no longer interested in the position, you should send an appreciation letter as a courtesy. You never know what the future holds; you may find yourself applying for a job with that business in the future.

Letters of appreciation should be sent immediately, no more than one or two days after the interview. This way you reinforce your candidacy for the position one more time before final decisions are made. You should send an appreciation letter by e-mail only if the company has previously corresponded with you by e-mail.

In the first paragraph, express your appreciation for the interview. Remind the reader of something memorable about your interaction. In the second paragraph, reinforce how your experience matches the qualifications of the position. In the third paragraph, show courtesy and provide information so the business can contact you easily. Writing thank-you letters is rapidly becoming a lost art. Do not forget this important point of etiquette when you are seeking a career.

P.O. Box 06462
Flagstaff, AZ 86011
May 2, 20xx

Ms. Karen Warner
Skin Essentials, Inc.
5555 Royal Avenue, Unit A
Sacramento, CA 93044

Dear Ms. Warner:

Thank you for taking the time to talk with me on Thursday, May 1, about the Assistant Manager position at the Scottsdale Skin Essentials.

Hearing about the rapid growth of Skin Essentials, and the opportunity to work in a newly opened store were particularly appealing to me. As you recommended, I have purchased the book, *Don't Go to the Cosmetics Counter Without Me*, and am familiarizing myself with competing products within the skincare field.

Thank you again for your time and consideration. I would welcome the opportunity to work for your company and be involved with this fast-paced retailer. I look forward to hearing from you next week.

Sincerely,

*Bethany Robinson*
Bethany Robinson

FIGURE 12.9. Thank-you letter.

# INTERVIEWING FOR A CAREER IN FASHION

So, your well-written résumé and application letters have landed you an interview! Now what do you do? This last section briefly discusses the interview process and what you should expect.

In a sense, your goal during the interview is to convince a total stranger that you are the answer to her company's problems. In fact, the interview is a time of mutual evaluation. Both the recruiter and the job applicant are intent on making a good impression on one another. You need to sell yourself in a professional manner and express to the interviewer the abilities you will bring to the job. In this interview you want to learn not only whether you are right for the job but whether the job is right for you.

To prepare for an interview, you should research the company as described earlier in this chapter. Also study the job description and decide how your skills and accomplishments fit the position. Be ready to answer questions that might arise from your résumé. Typical interview questions are shown in Figure 12.10. Practice answering these questions. If possible, videotape yourself in a practice session to see how you come across. Guffey (2007) suggests five areas that employers will probe:

- **Communication skills**—How well do you present yourself and your ideas?
- **Attitude**—Do you have a positive attitude about yourself and your career?
- **Aptitude**—Do your training and life experiences qualify you for this position?
- **Potential**—How do your attitude and aptitude combine to contribute to this company?
- **Motivation**—What are your short- and long-term career goals? Why do you want this job?

## TELEPHONE INTERVIEWS

Many businesses today conduct telephone interviews as a way to cut down on the expenses associated with interviewing and with pre-screening individuals before an in-person interview. Prepare for a telephone interview just as you would prepare for

What would you like to tell me about yourself?

Why do you want this job?

What best qualifies you for this job?

What are your key strengths? weaknesses?

What did you like and dislike about your last job?

Do you consider yourself a team player? Why?

What are your career goals?

Where do you expect to be five years from now?

What can I tell you about the company?

FIGURE 12.10. Standard interview questions.

an in-person interview. You can build your confidence for a phone interview by dressing professionally. Have a copy of your résumé and the telephone numbers of your references close at hand for easy recall during the interview. Additionally, have a calendar available and know your schedule for the following weeks in case the interviewer asks you on the spot about your availability for a face-to-face meeting. Experts agree that you should do approximately 80% of the talking during a phone interview.

In addition to dressing professionally (no pajamas or fuzzy slippers, even at home), you can sound more confident and energetic by standing during the interview. Try to show expression using your voice. Practice ahead of time so your voice does not come across flat or squeaky.

## IN-PERSON INTERVIEWS

The day of an interview is not the day to practice crisis management. Set your alarm early, plan enough time to dress and groom, and eat a nutritious breakfast. Dress in a professional manner and arrive early to the interview. Introduce yourself to the receptionist, and wait to be seated. Be courteous and congenial to everyone.

Greet the recruiter with confidence. Be ready to shake her hand at the beginning and end of the interview. Have a firm handshake—not tense or limp; but also not so firm that it is painful for the other person. Release the tension in your hands before you shake hands so the grip will be relaxed. If you are uncomfortable shaking hands with others, practice. Wait for the interviewer to offer you a chair. When you speak, show interest, enthusiasm, and sincerity.

During the interview it is important to control your body movements. Make frequent eye contact with the interviewer but do not get into a staring contest. Use the interviewer's name so that you can remember it after the interview. Remember to smile and convey a positive attitude. Your hands should be relaxed and still. Avoid clutching the arms of the chair, knotting your hands into fists, or crossing your arms defensively. Avoid fidgeting.

Learn to control your voice during an interview. When we get nervous the pitch in our voices gets high, particularly for women. Try to stay relaxed and confident during the interview to help you keep your voice well-modulated. Keep a check on your voice during the interview to be sure it is not too high, too loud, or too soft.

Body language often speaks louder than words. Maintain body language that conveys confidence and a positive attitude. Use good standing and sitting posture. Avoid slouching, but also do not be ramrod-straight. Both men and women should keep their knees together when sitting, with legs crossed at the ankles or not.

To fight the nerves that come along with interviewing, take deep breaths, particularly before the interview; practice as much as you can, particularly in real interviews with real companies (as opposed to staged interviews at career services or in classes); and rehearse a closing statement. Be ready to share your success stories, and know how you will answer most frequently asked questions. You will gain confidence if you remember that you are also evaluating the interviewer and his organization.

At the close of the interview, thank the interviewer and shake her hand again. If she has not already offered you her business card, ask for one at this time. This card will provide you with the correct spelling and address of the interviewer for the appreciation letter you will write immediately. Be polite and say goodbye to everyone. Take notes on the interview as soon as you leave. Alert your references that they might be called.

## SUMMARY

This chapter has concentrated on important employment messages: résumés and application and appreciation letters. Before you can write an effective employment message, you need to understand yourself and the career that you are seeking. Answering questions about yourself is difficult sometimes, but it will help you accurately assess what you want to do. Once you know yourself and know the market, you are ready to proceed through the process by writing effective resumes and cover letters, going on interviews, and writing follow-up messages that reinforce your commitment to the potential employer. While interviewing skills are not necessarily writing, they accent your written materials and are important to the entire employment process.

## KEY TERMS

| | |
|---|---|
| Application letter | General application letter |
| Appreciation letter | Identification |
| Career | Job search log |
| Career ladder | Objective |
| Chronological résumé | Plain-text résumé |
| Corporate culture | References |
| Cover letter | Résumé |
| Education | Scannable résumé |
| Electronic résumé | Summary of Qualifications |
| Embedded résumé | Targeted application letter |
| Follow-up letter | Thank-you letter |
| Functional résumé | Work Experience |

## CASE STUDY

### Sara's Sensitivity

Sara Yost is graduating from Colorado State University at the end of this semester. Sara grew up in Cleveland, Ohio. When it came time to select a college, she knew she had to go where they had real mountains and snow. You see, Sara loves to snowboard. Sara has been on the six-year plan, taking two spring semesters off to hone her snowboarding craft.

Sara has always been quick to say in her merchandising and manufacturing classes that for female enthusiasts snowboarding apparel is limited. Many times she has had to purchase items from the men's line and make adjustments and alterations.

Sara knows that when she graduates she would like to combine her love for snowboarding and her merchandising degree in a meaningful way. One time when she was surfing the Web, she came across the Patagonia site. She was familiar with the brand because her grandmother had given her a Patagonia hoodie for her last birthday and she really liked it. It fit her female figure well and had a roomy hood.

Sara did further research on the company at www.hoovers.com and www.patagonia.com. She learned that Patagonia is an outdoor apparel company that makes and sells rugged clothing and gear to mountain climbers, skiers, and other extreme-sports lovers as well as to environmentalists. The company provides clothing for climbing, skiing, snowboarding, surfing, fly-fishing, paddling, and trail running. It sells the clothes, gear, accessories, and luggage through specialty retailers, a catalog, a Web site, and its own stores.

On its Web site, Patagonia states that it provides clothing and gear for all silent sports. That is, none of the sports that Patagonia carries clothing and gear for requires a motor or a cheering crowd. The rewards from these silent sports come in the form of hard-won grace and moments of connection between enthusiasts and nature. The company values a minimalist style, and it takes this approach toward product design with a bias for simplicity and utility.

Patagonia also values wild and beautiful places, and it demands participation in the fight to save them and to help reverse the steep decline in the overall environmental health of the planet. Patagonia as a company donates time, services, and at least 1% of its sales to grassroots environmental groups all over the world that work to help reverse the tide.

As a company, Patagonia is aware that conducting business—from lighting stores to dyeing shirts—creates pollution as a by-product. The company works hard to reduce these harms. The company uses recycled polyester and only organic, rather than pesticide-intensive, cotton in the manufacturing of clothing.

Under the Jobs tab at the Patagonia Web site, Sara learned that Patagonia is looking for motivated people, especially those who share a love of the outdoors, a passion for quality, and a desire to make a difference. The instructions told potential applicants where to mail a résumé with a cover letter. The last paragraph really caught Sara's attention. It said:

> Lastly, we work very hard to minimize our impacts on the environment, and we strongly believe that one person's actions can make a difference in the health of our environment. In keeping with these values, we'd appreciate some sensitivity to environmental concerns in the preparation of your résumé materials. Please be environmentally responsible in the presentation of your information.

## CASE STUDY QUESTIONS

1. How should Sara begin preparing her résumé and cover letter?
2. What specific skills and experiences should she include in her résumé?
3. What should Sara say in her cover letter to spark interest from Patagonia representatives, so they will fully consider her résumé?
4. What actions should Sara take to show sensitivity to environmental concerns in preparing her résumé and cover letter?
5. If Sara is contacted for an interview, what should she say to further show that she was environmentally responsible in the presentation of her materials?

## REFERENCES

Bovée, C. L, Thill, J. V., & Schatzman, B. E. (2003). *Business communication today* (7th ed.). Upper Saddle River, NJ: Prentice Hall.

Guffey, M. E. (2007). *Essentials of business communication* (7th ed.). Mason, OH: Thomson South-Western.

Lehman, C. M., & Dufrene, D. D. (2005). *Business communication* (14th ed.). Mason, OH: South-Western.

McKinney, A. (Ed.). (2002). *Real-résumés for retailing, modeling, fashion and beauty industry jobs.* Fayetteville, NC: PREP Publishing.

National Commission on Writing. (2004). *Writing: A ticket to work . . . or a ticket out.* New York: College Entrance Examination Board.

Stone, E. (2004). *The dynamics of fashion* (2nd ed.). New York: Fairchild Books.

Thill, J. V., & Bovée, C. L, (2005). *Excellence in business communication* (6th ed.). Upper Saddle River, NJ: Prentice Hall.

# APPENDIX A
## *Grammar Mechanics*

This appendix is offered as a quick review of grammar and mechanics associated with writing. The entries have been placed in alphabetical order for ease of use.

If your question has not been answered at the conclusion of this appendix, you may need to refer to one of the stylebooks or English-language guides listed in the "Additional Resources" section at the end of this appendix.

## ABBREVIATIONS

An abbreviation is a shortened form of a word or phrase used in place of the whole word or phrase after first use. Abbreviation styles vary according to the style manual you are using.

Common abbreviation types include measurements, locations, and titles. Measurement abbreviations are used with numbers and are given without periods (for example, 3 *in* of lace; 5 *yd* of silk). An abbreviation that looks like a word—such as *Fig.* for the word *figure*—should be followed by a period to avoid confusion.

Locations include the official two-letter U.S. Postal Service abbreviations (for example, AL for Alabama). U.S. Postal Service abbreviations are used in addressing letters and envelopes. In the text of a document, the state should always be spelled out.

Title abbreviations include courtesy and personal titles; academic degrees and professional designations; and names of well-known businesses, education institutions, government organizations, professional organizations, and television and radio stations. Use abbreviations only when you are confident that the reader understands their meaning. If in doubt, spell out the word. Most style guides have lists of commonly used abbreviations.

> The Council of Fashion Designers America (CFDA) awards were presented last month. The CFDA has been presenting the awards for many years.

Note: In the example above, the type of abbreviation—formed from the initial letter of each of the main words of the title—is called an *acronym*. Commonly, these phrases are spelled out the first time they are used in print, followed by the abbreviation in parentheses. After the first instance, the acronym can be used alone. Abbreviate and capitalize courtesy titles and personal titles.

Mr. William Strunk, Jr., is an authority on writing.

With a few exceptions, academic degrees and professional designations are separated by periods. One exception is Certified Public Accountant (CPA). While this designation is also an acronym, it is well-known enough that it does not need to be spelled out the first time it is used.

Marilyn Floyd, CPA, will lecture on the financial aspects of retail entrepreneurialism.

Direct your questions about this book to Judith Everett, M.B.A., or Kristen Swanson, Ph.D.

Abbreviations of well-known names of businesses, education institutions, government organizations, professional organizations, and television and radio stations are not separated by periods.

International Business Machines Corporation (IBM)

California State University (CSU)

Federal Trade Commission (FTC)

National Retail Federation (NRF)

American Broadcasting Corporation (ABC)

# CAPITALIZATION

The first word of a sentence, a quoted sentence, an independent phrase, a line of poetry, or an item in an outline should be capitalized.

According to the sales receipt, "Merchandise may be returned within 14 days for a full refund."

Now, for the announcement you have all been waiting for.

1. Important employment messages
   a. Cover letter
   b. Résumé
   c. Thank-you letter

Capitalize proper nouns.

Tommy Hilfiger

Paris, France

However, if the noun has developed a common meaning through popular usage, it should not be capitalized.

The home fashions department displayed two dozen different *china* patterns.

Do not capitalize the first word following a colon unless it is a proper noun, consists of two or more sentences, or begins a vertical list.

To create a trend forecast, the following elements need to be researched: color, fabric, silhouettes, accessories, and looks.

To create a trend forecast, you will need to research the following elements:
1. Color
2. Fabric
3. Silhouettes
4. Accessories
5. Looks

Capitalize courtesy titles, such as *Mr.*, *Mrs.*, *Ms.*, and *Dr.* Capitalize a title representing a person's profession, company name, military rank, religious station, or political office when it immediately precedes the person's name. Titles showing family relationships should be capitalized.

Two long-time employees, Mr. Ralph Gonzales and Ms. Anita Burton, will retire at the end of the year.

Please turn your papers into Professor Laura Cunningham.

Vice President Jonathon Gibson will conduct the board meeting in the absence of President Brianna Smothers.

The ceremony will be jointly performed by Rabbi Levin and Reverend Whalen.

This business was first established in 1827 by Grandpa and Grandma Hoskins.

Do not capitalize a title after a person's name in running text.

Jean Harrison, fashion director, has developed several innovative special events for the holiday season.

Do not capitalize a person's title if it takes the place of their name in a sentence.

The governor will give the graduation address on Friday.

Capitalize the first letter of every principal word in the title of a published or artistic work. Some principal verbs are short but still should be capitalized; for example, *be*, *is*, *are*, and *was*. Articles (*a*, *an*, *the*), conjunctions (*and*, *or*, *but*, *nor*) and prepositions with three or fewer letters (*of*, *in*, *on*, *to*) are not capitalized unless they are the first or last word of the title. Capitalize the first word of a subtitle following a colon. Capitalize the names of numbered courses and specific course titles. Do not capitalize the names of academic subject areas. Do not capitalize academic degrees unless they are used after and in conjunction with the name of the person.

> After trying several different books for Merchandising Fundamentals 131, Professor Smith has found that *InFashion—Fun! Fame! Fortune!* is a favorite of students.

> *Beyond Design: The Synergy of Apparel Product Development* has an excellent appendix for design students.

> Jonas will be awarded a bachelor of science degree in merchandising in December.

> Shelley Harp, Doctor of Philosophy, will address the graduates.

# NUMBERS

Just like abbreviation style, number style varies; your style guide will provide definitive answers regarding number style. The most common dilemma writers face when using numbers is determining when to spell out the number and when to use a numeral. In non-technical writing, numbers up to one hundred are spelled out, and numbers greater than one hundred are rounded. When a spelled-out number is three or four words long, use numerals.

> Approximately sixty-five new students entered the fashion program this fall, out of a freshman class of approximately six hundred students.

> This fall's freshman class has 435 more students than last year's incoming class.

In business writing, numerals are used for all numbers greater than ten and for exact measurements.

## WHEN TO SPELL OUT NUMBERS

For all types of writing, spell out numbers when they are the first word in a sentence. If the number is not easily understood in spelled-out format, rewrite the sentence so that the number appears in the middle of the sentence.

> Thirty-seven designers were nominated for the Fashion Group International (FGI) "Rising Star" award.

> Fashion Group International (FGI) nominated 37 designers for the "Rising Star" award.

Spell out numbers one through ten if no larger number appears in the same sentence. Use all numerals rather than mixing numerals and spelled-out words, when they are part of the same paragraph.

> We need to hire three additional sales associates.

> Respondents returned 124 usable questionnaires.

> Inventory was decreased from 48 cases to 5 cases during the sale.

If two numbers occur consecutively in a sentence and both modify the noun, spell out the second number. If the first word cannot be spelled out in one or two words, use a numeral for that number also. Use a hyphen to join the second number with the word that follows it.

> The letter required two 41-cent stamps.

> The experiment required three 2-inch by 2-inch squares of muslin.

> The stage was lit with 360 60-watt light bulbs.

## WHEN TO USE NUMERALS

Numerals are used in writing so the reader can locate them easily. Numerals are always used to express dates, sums of money, mixed numbers and decimals, distance, dimension, cubic capacity, percentage, weights, temperatures, and chapter and page numbers.

> September 25, 2008

> 14 ounces

> $13 million

> Chapter 7, page 17

> 7% [Use the percent symbol when a numeral precedes it; use the word *percentage* when a number is not given.]

When referring to dates, use the ordinal (*st, nd, rd, th*) only when the number precedes the month.

> The anniversary celebration is planned for the 27th of September.

> The anniversary celebration will be September 27.

To express amounts of money less that $1, use numerals followed by the word *cents*.

> One first class stamp costs 41 cents.

Amounts of money $1 or more are expressed as numerals. When expressing a whole dollar amount, omit the decimal and zero—even if mixed dollar amounts also appear in the sentence. Use a dollar sign ($) before every amount of money $1 or greater.

> Ticket prices were $5 in advance, $8.50 at the door.

Use a combination of numerals and numbers when writing about numbers over 1 million.

> 1 million [not 1,000,000]

> 2.7 billion

Numbers over 1 million should be rounded if doing so does not change the meaning of the sentence.

> First-quarter sales were $1.3 million. [instead of $1,327,876, if the shortened version does not change the meaning of the sentence]

**Table A.1.**   Examples of nontechnical and technical symbol use.

| NONTECHNICAL EXAMPLE | TECHNICAL EXAMPLE |
| --- | --- |
| 5 percent increase | 5% increase |
| 24 cents a yard | 24¢ / yd |
| 12 dozen at $20 per dozen | 12 dozen @ $20 / dozen |
| Policy No. 251 | Policy #251 |

## WHEN TO USE SYMBOLS

Symbols are tricky. In nontechnical writing, spell out the terms rather than using the symbol form (%, ¢, #, @). In technical or business writing, you may use symbols when space is limited. In both types of writing, you may use abbreviations and symbols in tables, graphs, and charts. In all types of writing, symbols are always used for the following three terms: the dollar sign ($), when used to show an actual dollar amount; the ampersand (&), when used in the name of a company; and the asterisk (*), used in unnumbered footnotes. Regardless of style, it is important to be consistent. If you spell out a term in one sentence, do not switch to the symbol in the next sentence if the usage is the same.

## PARTS OF SPEECH

Eight parts of speech are evident in the English language.

### ADJECTIVES

Adjectives modify nouns or pronouns; they answer questions such as *What kind? How many?* and *Which one?*; and they use the articles *a*, *an*, and *the*.

The *damaged* merchandise was sent back to *the* vendor.

*Two* sales associates applied for *the manager* position.

*Katie's* presentation was excellent.

*Your* idea will be incorporated into *the* sketch.

Cathy Horyn wrote *a* book about Karl Lagerfeld.

*The* product developer provided *an* answer to *the* problem.

### ADVERBS

Adverbs modify verbs, adjectives, or other adverbs; they answer questions such as *When?, Where?, How?,* and *To what extent?* Most adverbs end in *-ly*.

Angela *accidentally* deleted the file.

The order was processed *quickly*.

You may place an order *directly* online or call the toll-free number provided.

John lives *closer* to work than Shirley does.

Birmingham has been mentioned *most often* as the location for a new store.

Adverbs should be placed as close as possible to the word they modify. If this is not done, the meaning of the sentence will be changed and can result in an awkward sentence.

*Only* the design team was required to stay to finish the project. [The adverb *only* is modifying *design team*.]

The design team was required to stay *only* to finish the project. [Here the adverb *only* modifies *to finish the project*, giving the sentence a different meaning than in the first example.]

## CONJUNCTIONS

Conjunctions connect words or groups of words, such as *and, but,* and *or*.

Polyester, nylon, *and* acrylic are all synthetic fibers.

The graphic designer position has been filled, *but* you are welcome to leave a résumé for future openings.

Buyers can see the new line at either the Dallas Market *or* the Atlanta Market.

## INTERJECTIONS

Interjections express strong feelings.

*Absolutely not!* No one is allowed to see the line before it is presented on the runway.

## NOUNS

Nouns identify persons, places, things, or ideas.

Please have the *financial director* fax over the figures.

The *anger* in Mr. Dillon's voice was evident to everyone in the room.

The magazine headquarters will be located in *Burlington*.

Your *teamwork* is appreciated.

*Alexandra Smith* will become the new CEO on November 1.

Note: For information about nouns in their role as the subject of a sentence, see the discussion of subjects and verbs under Drafting in Chapter 2, "The Writing Process."

## PREPOSITIONS

Prepositions join nouns or pronouns to other words in a sentence. The most common prepositions are *of* and *for*.

Our staff *of* textile archivists is available to assist you when the garments have been recovered.

She left *for* the exhibit opening *before* traffic got bad.

There is a difference *between* consumer magazines and trade magazines.

Themes are organized *into* an editorial calendar.

## PRONOUNS

Pronouns substitute for nouns. The most common pronouns are *he, she, him, her, it,* and *they*.

News anchors sit behind a desk and introduce each story. *They* act as master of ceremonies for the broadcast.

Meagan won the design competition. *She* was extremely pleased with *her* work.

Coach had a strong third quarter. *Its* performance in the fourth quarter should be equally as strong.

## VERBS

Verbs show the action of the subject.

Adam and Amanda *opened* their boutique six years ago.

Come *visit* the Tribal booth at MAGIC.

The company *has been involved* in merger talks for six months.

The order *was processed* last week.

Note: For more information about verbs, see the discussion of subjects and verbs under Drafting in Chapter 2, "The Writing Process."

## PERSON

Person indicates whether the subject of the sentence is speaking (*first person*), is being spoken to (*second person*), or is being spoken about (*third person*).

## FIRST PERSON

In the first person form, the subject of the sentence is the writer or speaker, and that person is speaking.

*I am* honored to be here . . .

*We are* pleased to present this book for publication.

## SECOND PERSON

In the second person form, the subject of the sentence is the receiver, and that person is being spoken to.

*You are* invited to attend the opening tomorrow evening.

## THIRD PERSON

In the third person form, the subject of the sentence is the person being spoken about.

*She has* many creative ideas.

*They will* attend the event tomorrow evening.

*It is* a very long story.

# PUNCTUATION
## APOSTROPHE

Add an apostrophe and the letter *s* (*'s*) to form the possessive case of a singular noun that does not end in *s*.

Alison*'s* position

employee*'s* benefits

Do not use an apostrophe to form the possessive of a pronoun.

ours (not *our's*) [Using an apostrophe here would imply *our is*—a construction that does not make sense.]

its (not *it's*, which is a contraction for *it is*)

Add an apostrophe and an *s* (*'s*) to form a plural noun that does not already have a pronounced *s*.

children*'s* clothing

women*'s* wear

If a word ends in a pronounced *s*, add only the apostrophe (*'*).

six months' vacation benefits

Grand Falls' location

If a singular noun ends in a pronounced *s* and an additional s sound can be pronounced easily, an apostrophe and an *s* (*'s*) may be added.

class*'s* project

boss*'s* opinion

Use an apostrophe to indicate ownership. To indicate separate ownership, add an *'s* to each name. To indicate joint ownership, add an *'s* to the last name only.

> Ali's BlackBerry

> John's car

> Michele's and Nicole's boutiques [indicates separate ownership of two boutiques]

> Michele and Nicole's boutique [indicates joint ownership of the same boutique]

Use an apostrophe to show the omission of a preposition.

> last month's financials [meaning the financial reports of last month]

Use an apostrophe with possessive nouns when referring to time.

> tomorrow's schedule

> three years' experience [The word ends in a pronounced *s*, so add only the apostrophe (').]

## COLON

Use a colon after an independent clause that introduces a list if items. This rule applies whether the items are run into the text or separated in a list format.

> Costs involved in manufacturing apparel products include the following: materials, labor, and transportation.

> Fashion journalism focuses on three media types: newspapers, magazines, and broadcast. [The introduction of the list is implied in the preceding clause.]

Do not use a colon following a "to be" verb or when the listed items are the object of the verb.

> The costs involved in manufacturing apparel products are materials, labor, and transportation. [Do not use a colon after the verb *are*.]

> Fashion journalism writing styles are discussed for newspapers, magazines, and broadcast. [Do not use a colon after the preposition *for*.]

> The store will be closed on Thanksgiving Day, Christmas Day, and New Year's Day. [Do not use a colon between *on* and *Thanksgiving*.]

Use a colon to separate two sentences when the second sentence explains, illustrates, or supplements the first sentence.

> The new promotional campaign is directed toward accessory consumers: it will feature handbags, shoes, belts, and watches.

## COMMA

Commas are used to separate items in a series. In formal writing, a comma is used after the final conjunction. In newswriting (that is, in Associated Press, or AP, style), a comma in not used after the final conjunction.

> A place setting for dinnerware includes a dinner plate, a salad plate, a cup, a saucer, and a bowl.

Do not use commas when all parts of the series are joined by conjunctions.

> Designers can be classified *as* high fashion designers *or* stylist designers *or* freelance designers.

Use a comma to separate two independent clauses in a compound sentence.

> We have not purchased any fabric from that supplier within the last six months, nor have we requested trims or findings.

Use a comma to separate two or more independent adjectives.

> Retailer Web sites can offer shopping convenience 24 hours a day, 7 days a week.

A comma should follow an introductory clause.

> After Scott registered for the conference, he made his airline reservations.

Dependent clauses or short independent clauses should be set off with commas.

> Next week, when you have returned from the conference, please submit a zero balance statement to the budget officer.

## EXCLAMATION MARK

Use an exclamation mark at the end of a sentence to express strong emotion.

> Bravo! The designers took their bows on the runway as the audience shouted accolades for the new line.

## PARENTHESES

Parentheses are a pair of punctuation symbols used to indicate explanatory material that could be left out of the sentence.

> Three branch stores (Columbus, Cleveland, and St. Louis) will be remodeled in the next eighteen months.

Parentheses are also used to contain the type of abbreviation known as an acronym.

> Modern Language Association (MLA)

> State University of New York (SUNY)

## PERIOD

Use a period to end a statement, a command, an indirect question, or a polite request. A polite request (most often seen in technical or business writing), although similar in structure to a question, ends with a period instead of a question mark.

> Whether trimmed in gold for a nautical effect or chicly unadorned, navy blue is the color of choice for pre-spring cocktail dresses and separates. [End a statement with a period.]

> Would you please inventory the number of navy blue dresses and separates in stock and report back to me this afternoon. [End a polite statement with a period.]

Also use periods after abbreviations and initials. When a period is used after an initial or at the end of an abbreviation, a letter space separates the period from the next word. When the period occurs in the middle of the abbreviation, no extra letter space is left after the period. If a sentence ends with an abbreviation, use only one period—this denotes both the end of the abbreviation and the end of the sentence.

> At 7:30 p.m. the curtain will rise on this season's newest fashions. [There is no space after "p"; it is in the middle of the abbreviation.]

> Mr. E. B. White is the timely authority on writing. [Note the space after "Mr." and between "E." and "B."

When placing items in a list, use periods only if the items form complete sentences.

> Steps in outlining include the following:
> 1. List your ideas.
> 2. Categorize your ideas.
> 3. Prioritize your ideas. [Complete sentences finish with a period.]

> Steps in outlining include the following:
> 1. Brainstorming
> 2. Categorizing
> 3. Prioritizing [Sentence fragments do not finish with a period.]

When the words in parentheses form a complete sentence, place the period inside the closing parenthesis. When the words in parentheses are not a complete thought, place the period outside the closing parenthesis.

> Vendors expect embellishments such as sequins, pearls, rhinestones, ribbons, lace, and bows to be top-sellers. (Lingerie has not been this exciting in several years.) [period inside the closing parenthesis]

> The visual display team developed a promotion calendar for the next six months (February through July). [period outside the closing parenthesis]

## QUESTION MARK

Use a question mark to conclude a direct question that requires an answer.

How many employees will be receiving a bonus?

An indirect question should be finished with a period rather than a question mark.

Ms. Bridges, the store manager, asked how many employees will be receiving a bonus.

Polite requests finish with a period.

Would you let me know by Monday how many employees will be receiving a bonus.

When a complete question is contained within quotation marks or parentheses, the question mark is placed within the closing quotation mark or closing parenthesis.

"Will the complete fall line be presented at the trunk show?" asked the reporter.

We sent out the media kits yesterday (did you receive yours?) stating that the complete line would be presented.

## QUOTATION MARKS

Quotation marks enclose the exact wording used by a writer or a speaker. For one- or two-sentence quotations, place the quote within quotation marks. Use a comma to introduce a quote outside of the quotation marks or to finish a quote inside the quotation marks.

"It's all about color," said the executive vice president of design, speaking about the upcoming holiday season.

The executive vice president of design insisted, "It's all about color" when asked by the reporter to comment on the coming holiday season.

Different style guides handle longer quotes in different ways. In business writing, a long quote is three or more lines. In American Psychological Association (APA) format, a long quote is more than 40 words. Check your specific stylebook for clarification. Long quotes are presented without quotation marks. They are indented 0.5 inches from the left margin. If the copy is single-spaced, a blank line separates the quote from the text above and below the quote.

Elaine Roberts, the regional brand manager, went on to say this:

Regional brands are products and distributors located in one region or district of the United States. These products may gain widespread recognition, and consumers in that region may think these products are as strongly positioned as many national brands. Retail stores with strong regional brands concentrate in various parts of the country where they have an established favorable identity.

Short expressions such as jargon, technical words, or words used to express humor or irony are also placed in quotation marks.

"The cat's in the bag" or rather on the bag this season as feline motifs are popping up everywhere.

Titles of books, magazines, pamphlets, newspapers, and other complete published or artistic works are typically italicized in writing. However, the specific title of a newspaper or magazine article, a chapter title in a book, the titles of the acts in a play, or the titles of songs are placed in quotation marks.

The chapter "The Writing Process" contained in *Writing for the Fashion Business* was helpful in explaining how to organize your thoughts before writing any type of document.

Accessory manufacturers are hoping that hats will be the must-have accessory for fall. To make a point at market, male and female models stormed the convention center wearing hats of all varieties as "You Can Leave Your Hat On" by Joe Cocker played over the loudspeakers.

Always place commas and periods *inside* the closing quotation mark; place semicolons and colons *outside* the closing quotation mark.

## SEMICOLON
Use a semicolon to join two independent clauses when the conjunction is omitted.

In 2005 Marc Jacobs presented a history-making line; the press had mixed reactions.

A semicolon is also used when two independent clauses are separated by a transitional expression.

The *New York Times* is available free of charge on the Internet; however, *Wall Street Journal* readers must purchase a subscription in order to be able to access the *Journal* on the Internet.

Items in a series are usually separated by commas; but if one of the items has a comma within it, all of the items are separated by semicolons.

Winners of the design competition represented Colorado State University, Ft. Collins, Colorado; Kent State University, Kent, Ohio; and Texas Tech University, Lubbock, Texas.

## SINGULAR AND PLURAL AGREEMENT
### SUBJECT–VERB
The verb of a sentence must agree in person and number with the subject. To identify the subject, omit any prepositional phrases that separate the subject from the verb.

*Two buttons* on the blouse *were* lost in shipping. [more than one button—plural; to see this, omit *on the blouse*]

*The class* of juniors and seniors *is going* to the exhibit at the Phoenix Art Museum. [*the class* is one—singular; to see this, omit *of juniors and seniors*]

## SUBJECT–PRONOUN

A pronoun representing a subject must agree in number and gender with the subject. Compound subjects are joined by and generally require a plural verb.

*Ms. March* submits *her* travel plans at the beginning of the month. [singular]

*Candace and Jennifer* always submit *their* changes to the lineup just before the show. [two women —plural]

The *company* promoted the designer from within because *it* had to move forward after the previous designer left. [*It* refers to *the company*, which is singular.]

## TENSE

Tense indicates time. Tense is referred to as simple present, past, or future and as compound (perfect) present, past, or future. Use the present tense when something *was* true and *still is* true. Use the past tense when something has already occurred. Use the future tense when something has yet to occur.

### SIMPLE PRESENT TENSE

Simple present tense tells the reader what is happening right now.

I *see* your window display.

Do you *see* the design detail in the embroidery?

He *sees* the mannequin from across the room.

### SIMPLE PAST TENSE

Simple past tense tells the reader what has already happened.

I *saw* your window display yesterday.

You *saw* the design detail in the embroidery?

He *saw* the mannequin from across the room.

### SIMPLE FUTURE TENSE

Simple future tense tells the reader what is yet to happen.

I *will see* your window display tomorrow.

You *will see* the design detail in the embroidery.

He *will see* the mannequin from across the room.

## PRESENT PERFECT TENSE

Present perfect tense tells the reader about past action that extends to the present.

I *have seen* your window display.

You *have seen* the design detail in the embroidery?

He *has seen* the mannequin from across the room.

## PAST PERFECT TENSE

Past perfect tense tells the reader about past action that was finished before another past action.

I *had seen* your window display before it was taken down.

You *had seen* the design detail in the embroidery before it was sold?

He *had seen* the mannequin from across the room before the photographers blocked his view.

## FUTURE PERFECT TENSE

Future perfect tense tells the reader about action that will be finished before a future time.

I *will have seen* your window display before it is taken down next week.

You *will have seen* the design detail in the embroidery before it is sold next month.

He *will have seen* the mannequin from across the room before the guests are allowed to enter the hall.

## ADDITIONAL RESOURCES

American Psychological Association. (2001). *Publication manual of the American Psychological Association* (5th ed.). Washington, DC: Author.

American Psychological Association. (2005). *Concise rules of APA style*. Washington, DC: Author.

Clark, J. L., & Clark, L. R. (2007). *HOW 11: A handbook for office professionals* (11th ed.). Mason, OH: South-Western.

Guffey, M. E. (2007). *Essentials of business communication* (7th ed.). Mason, OH: South-Western.

Kirszner, L. G., & Mandell, S. R. (2007). *The Wadsworth handbook* (8th ed.). Boston: Thomson Wadsworth.

Lehman, C. M., & Dufrene, D. D. (2005). *Business communication* (14th ed.). Mason, OH: South-Western.

Maimon, E. P., Peritz, J. H., & Yancey, K. B. (2007). *A writer's resource: A handbook for writing and research* (2nd ed.). New York: McGraw-Hill.

Gibaldi, J. (2003). *MLA handbook for writers of research papers* (6th ed.). New York: The Modern Language Association of America.

Pfeiffer, W. S. (2004). *Pocket guide to technical writing* (3rd ed.). Upper Saddle River, NJ: Pearson Prentice Hall.

Strunk, W., Jr, & White, E. B. (2000). *The elements of style* (4th ed.). Needham Heights, MA: Longman.

Woolever, K. R. (1999). *Writing for the technical professions*. NY: Addison Wesley Longman.

# APPENDIX B
## *Documentation Format*

All writers are ethically responsible for properly documenting the data reported in their written work. Documenting data is referred to as *citing sources*. Citing sources accomplishes the following:

- Allows the reader to easily cross-reference your sources
- Provides for a consistent format across the publication
- Gives credibility to you as the writer
- Avoids plagiarism

The *MLA Handbook* offers this explanation for the use of one documentation style instead of another:

> Documentation styles differ according to discipline because they are shaped by the kind of research and scholarship undertaken. For example, in the sciences, where timeliness of research is crucial, the date of publication is usually given prominence. Thus in the style recommended by the American Psychological Association (APA), a typical citation includes the date of publication (as well as the abbreviation *p* before the page number). . . . In the humanities, where most important scholarship remains relevant for a substantial period, publication dates receive less attention: though always stated in the works-cited list, they are omitted in parenthetical references. (Gibaldi, 2003, p. 143)

In much of fashion writing, information is very timely and APA style is an appropriate choice. In other fashion writing, Modern Language Association (MLA) format or Chicago Manual of Style (CMS) format is appropriate. For example, a writer reporting on the trends shown at this year's Fashion Week may use APA, while a writer chronicling a particular type of clothing worn over several decades may use MLA. A researcher reporting on a new technology in textile science may use CMS. Whichever format is chosen, the primary goal is to supply adequate information so that the reader can find the source.

The original source is called the source document. Cross-referencing allows your readers to locate publication information about the source document you used. This is important to readers who may want to locate the source for their own research. It also helps you as the writer keep track of your sources as you build documentation. Proper citation of sources is also necessary to avoid plagiarism, which is a serious offense. At school, plagiarism can result in failing a class or being expelled from school. In your professional career, plagiarism is considered literary theft and can result in loss of your reputation and the reputation of the publication you represent. Plagiarizing sources can get you fired or sued.

## DOCUMENTATION STYLES

The two most common documentation styles for general writing are found in the *Publication Manual of the American Psychological Association* (5th ed.), published by the American Psychological Association (APA), and the *MLA Handbook for Writers of Research Papers* (6th ed.), published by the Modern Language Association (MLA). Some journals refer to Harvard style, which is very similar to APA style. Publications or writers preferring to use footnotes instead of in-text citations use the *Chicago Manual of Style* (CMS). Journalism publications prefer the *Associated Press Stylebook* (AP) documentation style; additionally, newspapers such the *New York Times* may distribute their own stylebook or style guide to provide general rules for referencing sources. Writers are responsible for learning the documentation style required by the publication they are writing for.

Again, the primary goal is to supply adequate information so that the reader can find the source.

## NOTE-TAKING

To be effective and efficient at documenting sources, you need to take good notes! Taking good notes when you read an original source will save you valuable time later when you use the information in your fashion message. Before you begin reading the original source, you should routinely record the following information:

- Type of publication
- Author's last name, first name, middle initial
- Date of publication (year, month, and day as available)
- Complete title of article
- Complete title of publication (include volume number and issue number if given)
- Page numbers
- For books, publication information (publisher; city and state where published)
- For online sources, complete URL address and retrieval date
- For materials retrieved from a searchable database, name of database, URL address for main page of database, and retrieval date

It is critical that you record the type of publication—newspaper, academic journal, magazine, journal from a searchable database, and so forth. Each type of publication is cited differently on a References page or a Works Cited page, in a Bibliography, or in an endnote or footnote, so it is important to know what type of publication your source is. Some reference styles (such as MLA) require that an author's first name be written out, while

---

### BOX B.1 TO QUOTE OR NOT TO QUOTE

As you take notes from an original source, you need to consider how you will use the information. Will it be enough to summarize the information? Maybe you need to paraphrase the information? Or, is the information so important that you need to quote it directly? You should think about these options as you are taking notes.

- Summarizing information from an original source means that you take ideas from a large passage and condense the information into a brief restatement of the information, using your own words.
- Paraphrasing material from another source means that you use the ideas from the original source but express the content in your own words. When you paraphrase data or facts from another source, it is important not to change the meaning of the information. The paraphrased passage must still represent the original author's intention.
- Directly quoting an original source means that you repeat the text word-for-word, surround the quoted text with quotation marks to indicate that it is a quotation, and identify the original source author as the writer or speaker.

---

others (such as APA) require only the author's first and middle initials before the author's last name. If the source is published annually, only the year is needed. However, if the materials are published monthly (such as consumer magazines) the month is needed. If a publication is a weekly or a daily one (such as a newspaper), the date is also needed. Volume number and issue number are needed for citing academic journals. It is better to retrieve all possible information when you are first researching the source rather than having to go back and find a detail later.

In fashion messages, writers use two types of notes: source notes and explanatory notes. *Source notes* are in-text citations, footnotes, or endnotes that acknowledge the contributions of other authors. *Explanatory notes* provide information about a topic that does not easily fit into the text. (If explanatory notes are taken directly from another source, they require a source note as well.)

## DOCUMENTATION FORMAT

Whether presented as in-text citations or note citations, those source notes that acknowledge the contributions of other authors must follow a standard documentation format.

- In-text citations are brief parenthetical citations within the document; they contain just enough information so that the reader can locate the complete source in the References or Works Cited—an alphabetical listing of all sources used in the document—at the end of the document.
- Note citations (whether footnote or endnote) are marked in the text with superscript numerals (for example, [1]). The numerals correspond to footnotes at the bottom of the page where the quoted material appears, or to endnotes at the end of the document. Endnotes are listed numerically in the same sequence as in the text, rather than being listed in alphabetical order. The page(s) containing the endnotes is followed by a Bibliography that lists all of the endnote or footnote sources in alphabetical order.

## TYPES OF SOURCES

In general, sources belong to three broad categories: periodicals, nonperiodicals, and online sources. Materials that are published periodically with a fixed interval between the issues or numbers (daily, weekly, monthly, yearly, and so forth) are termed *periodicals*. Trade and consumer newspapers, trade and consumer magazines, and academic journals are common periodicals.

*Nonperiodicals* are publications that are published once or at irregular intervals. Books, book chapters, brochures, technical and research reports, meeting proceedings, master's theses, doctoral dissertations, reviews, and audiovisual media are types of nonperiodicals.

*Online sources* are electronic media on the Internet. These sources include periodicals and nonperiodicals that are presented on the Internet instead of or in addition to print form. Data or information from newsgroups, forums, and discussion-type groups posted on the Internet is also considered an online source. Additionally, articles retrieved from a searchable (aggregated) database, from data files, or from computer software are types of online sources.

Many periodicals are available (1) as printed periodicals, (2) as online sources from an organization's Web site, or (3) from a searchable database (for example, ScienceDirect, Academic Search Premier, LexisNexisAcademic). Although the content is the same for each format, the source for each of these three formats is different and is cited in a slightly different manner. For example, an article retrieved directly from the print edition of *Women's Wear Daily* (Figure B.1) would be cited in APA format this way:

Lockwood, L. (2005, June 6). Karl: I'll take Manhattan. *Women's Wear Daily*, pp. 6–7.

The same article retrieved from a searchable database (Figure B.2) would be cited in APA format this way:

Lockwood, L. (2005, June 6). Karl: I'll take Manhattan. *Women's Wear Daily*, 6–7. Retrieved September 30, 2007, from the Business Source Premier database.

According to *Concise Rules of APA Style* (American Psychological Association [APA], 2005), when you are referencing materials that you obtained from searchable databases,

WWD, MONDAY, JUNE 6, 2005   **7**
WWD.COM

# Karl: I'll Take Manhattan

**By Lisa Lockwood**

**NEW YORK** — Karl Lagerfeld's dream of designing three different collections in three international cities is about to become a reality, thanks to his growing love affair with lower prices.

"My idea was always New York, Paris and Rome," said Lagerfeld, describing his design roles for Chanel in Paris, Fendi in Rome, and now a brand-new, less expensive line to be called Karl Lagerfeld, based here.

In a joint interview, Lagerfeld and Ann Acierno, president of new business development at Tommy Hilfiger Corp., which owns the Lagerfeld business, outlined plans for the global launch of the new contemporary women's and men's lifestyle collection. The line will be introduced in February for fall 2006 retailing and will be priced 50 percent below Lagerfeld Gallery, his designer collection.

"I'm very much into large distribution," said Lagerfeld, from his expansive new showroom at 601 West 26th Street here. "With haute couture, I proved that I can design the most expensive things, and with H&M, I can do the less expensive things. This will be in the middle of all that."

Lagerfeld's wildly successful collection for H&M last fall proved he not only had the ability to design at less expensive price points, but that he also was a household name. The collection featured $19.90 T-shirts with the designer's silhouette, $49 blouses and $149 wool-cashmere overcoats, and it helped buoy H&M's fourth-quarter profits by 23.9 percent. At the other end of the spectrum, Lagerfeld took a trip to Tokyo several weeks later, where he inaugurated the opening of the largest Chanel store in the world and was mobbed by fans.

His popularity hasn't gone unnoticed by the Hilfiger organization.

According to Acierno, the Lagerfeld line will be geared to the contemporary departments of top-tier department and specialty stores. "It will be young and spirited, with denim, sportswear, Ts, tanks and jackets. It will be a full lifestyle assortment," she said. She explained that women today like to pair an expensive jacket with an inexpensive tank, but have to run from store to store to put a look together. The new line will be housed near such resources as Marc by Marc Jacobs and Theory and will offer "more variety and breadth."

Melanie Ward has been named creative director of Karl Lagerfeld and will collaborate with him on the design. Ward, a former Helmut Lang consultant, continues as senior fashion editor of Harper's Bazaar. "She has a flawless reputation. People like her, respect her, and she's modern," said Lagerfeld.

This will be accessible fashion for women and men, with a tremendous amount of style," added Acierno. Pants, for example, will retail for $175; denim, for $150; shorts and shirts, for $100 and up; dresses, for $250; jackets, for $385, and leather outerwear, for $425 and up.

Acierno said the Lagerfeld business will use Hilfiger's infrastructure "where it makes sense," such as legal and finance, but won't be using the same factories or fabrics. She declined to give a first-year sales projection because Hilfiger is in a quiet period before releasing its numbers. However, she said they're expecting Lagerfeld to be a "large business."

Hilfiger and Lagerfeld announced their odd pairing back in December, and the industry has been awaiting word on what Hilfiger was planning to do with the business.

Acierno said her first priority was to get through the fall market for the Lagerfeld Gallery designer line, which was shown on the Paris runways to positive reviews, and to lay out a financial plan for the business. They opened several new specialty store accounts, such as Mix in Houston, Razook's in Greenwich, On Sunset in Los Angeles and Capitol in Charlotte, N.C., in addition to continuing the business with Bloomingdale's. And Lagerfeld shot the Gallery ad campaign featuring Erin Wasson.

"We continue to evolve the Lagerfeld Gallery business," said Acierno. "The quality's extraordinary. The details, the number of seams, the fabric, the construction...it's for someone with a lot of confidence." The collection is produced in France, but Hilfiger is seeking new factories in Italy and Asia. The Lagerfeld Gallery store in Paris remains open, but the one in Monaco has closed.

Since signing the deal, Lagerfeld said he and the Hilfiger executives started to get to know each other "to see what everybody could do."

Although he intimated in December that he didn't expect to renew his contract with Fendi when it expired, he apparently had a change of heart and signed a new long-term deal last month. "I had to continue with Fendi. There was a clause in my contract that I didn't see that I had to give them a year's notice," he claimed.

Still, Lagerfeld believes he has enough time to devote to his own brands, even though historically, he hasn't been able to give them much attention.

"I can give more time than ever before. I'm not a business person," said Lagerfeld, noting that he's happy to leave all the production, sales and distribution decisions to Acierno

and her team. In fact, while Acierno was talking about factories, Lagerfeld said, "This is a subject I want to know nothing about."

Over the years, Lagerfeld has made numerous attempts at developing a less expensive ready-to-wear line, but with little success. He had a licensing deal with Bidermann Industries USA for Karl Lagerfeld women's wear and KL by Karl Lagerfeld sportswear in the Eighties, which never really took off and ended in January 1987. That same year, he signed with the German apparel firm Klaus Steilmann GmbH & Co. to manufacture his KL by Karl Lagerfeld sportswear collection, and that deal lasted eight years. In 1995, Lagerfeld signed a five-year agreement with Italy's Seleme SpA for a signature collection, but there were problems with production and delivery. The agreement was discontinued in 1997, the year Lagerfeld bought his name and company back from the former Vendôme division of Compagnie Financière Richemont SA for a symbolic franc. He then signed a line with an undisclosed Italian company for a signature business, Lagerfeld, for spring 2001.

Asked to describe the consumer for whom he'll now be designing, Lagerfeld declined to put that woman into words.

"A designer proposes, and it's up to people to find it. I have to design a collection and hope it will be right for the market we're supposed to be designing for. You propose an image, a vision and a style. Designing is a proposition. I want it to reflect the energy you find in New York."

Lagerfeld agreed with Acierno that Lagerfeld Gallery shouldn't become too big. "Karl Lagerfeld is better for today's lifestyle. It's meant to be big. Gallery is something intimate," he said. Although Lagerfeld Gallery has been well received the past few years, Lagerfeld has had difficulty building it into a major business. He said there has been a lot of infighting. "It's difficult to make a business in France," he added.

The Lagerfeld line will have a large jeans component. "Life without jeans doesn't exist anymore. Vintage tops with jeans suddenly becomes modern," said Lagerfeld.

And does he envision a lot of black in the Lagerfeld line? Lagerfeld turned to his entourage and a visitor, who were all dressed in black, and replied: "Your question is an answer. I have nothing against color, but look at what everyone's wearing."

In comparison with Lagerfeld's collection for H&M, the Karl Lagerfeld line's "quality and materials will be a few steps up," said the designer.

One thing he's certain of is that he doesn't plan to make personal appearances on behalf of the Karl Lagerfeld line. "That's not a good thing. You lose the kind of mystery if you show up too much. Personal appearances in the stores are very much the Seventies and Eighties. I don't see myself as a young, struggling designer. You have to be careful of overexposure. It can play against you."

Rather, Lagerfeld said he's a big fan of advertising. "Today, advertising is as important as editorial in magazines. You have the essence and spirit of the line, and you can show the image of the collection." He will photograph the Karl Lagerfeld ad campaign, as well.

Plans call for Lagerfeld's business to have an e-commerce component, direct sales and, eventually, freestanding stores, said Acierno.

Despite his full plate, Lagerfeld seems eager to take on another big challenge, including establishing a New York home. In fact, Lagerfeld's love affair with New York appears to be in full bloom.

"I didn't like the Eighties in New York. Suddenly, the mood is different. It's the first time I feel at home in New York." He said he never wanted to have an apartment here and would always go to a hotel, but suddenly, finding a permanent home in Manhattan became a priority. In fact, he recently bought an apartment in Gramercy Park that he'll move into next year. "The apartment is proof I really wanted to be a part of it," he said.

Lagerfeld couldn't say how much time he'll spend in New York, or in Paris or Rome, for that matter, but he said these days, he can do things through e-mail and can even do fittings via videoconferencing.

He was in New York last week celebrating the ad campaign he photographed for the 1998 vintage of Dom Pérignon and a related art book. Meanwhile, he's got the Chanel couture show coming up July 7, and will be appearing in a movie, "La Doublure," by French director Francis Veber. "The couture show is part of the movie. I play myself," said Lagerfeld. "The director is an old friend of mine."

Lagerfeld said he enjoys keeping busy with all his assorted projects, whether it's shooting ad campaigns, photographing for magazines (he was scheduled to shoot Donna Karan and Nicole Richie last week for a magazine), designing Chanel, Fendi or Lagerfeld Gallery, owning a bookstore or being the author of several photography books, "because you always stay in touch with everything.

"It's a constant dialogue, and you're always with people," said Lagerfeld. He said designers can have their points of view, but you have to stay current with the times.

"Fashion is about change, and it suits me perfectly well," he concluded. "It's not what you did, but what you will do."

Ann Acierno and Karl Lagerfeld at the new Lagerfeld offices in New York on Thursday.

Two looks from the fall Lagerfeld Gallery.

**FIGURE B.1.** An article retrieved from the print edition of *Women's Wear Daily*.

**Back**

3 page(s) will be printed.

**EBSCO Publishing   Citation Format: APA (American Psychological Assoc.):**

> **NOTE:** Review the instructions at http://libproxy.nau.edu:3116/help/?
> int=ehost&lang=en&feature_id=APA and make any necessary corrections before using. Pay
> special attention to personal names, capitalization, and dates. Always consult your library
> resources for the exact formatting and punctuation guidelines.

**References**

Lockwood, L. (2005, June 6). Karl: I'll Take Manhattan. *WWD: Women's Wear Daily, 189*(119), 6-
  7. Retrieved October 20, 2007, from Business Source Premier database.

<!--Additional Information:
Persistent link to this record: http://libproxy.nau.edu:3854/login.aspx?
direct=true&db=buh&AN=17336816&site=ehost-live
End of citation-->

**Karl: I'll Take Manhattan**
Dateline: NEW YORK

Karl Lagerfeld's dream of designing three different collections in three international cities is
about to become a reality, thanks to his growing love affair with lower prices.

"My idea was always New York, Paris and Rome," said Lagerfeld, describing his design roles
for Chanel in Paris; Fendi in Rome, and now a brand-new, less expensive line to be called
Karl Lagerfeld, based here.

In a joint interview, Lagerfeld and Ann Acierno, president of new business development at
Tommy Hilfiger Corp., which owns the Lagerfeld business, outlined plans for the global
launch of the new contemporary women's and men's lifestyle collection. The line will be
introduced in February for fall 2006 retailing and will be priced 50 percent below Lagerfeld
Gallery, his designer collection.

"I'm very much into large distribution," said Lagerfeld, from his expansive new showroom
at 601 West 26th Street here. "With haute couture, I proved that I can design the most
expensive things, and with H&M, I can do the less expensive things. This will be in the
middle of all that."

Lagerfeld's wildly successful collection for H&M last fall proved he not only had the ability to
design at less expensive price points, but that he also was a household name. The
collection featured $19.90 T-shirts with the designer's silhouette, $49 blouses and $149
wool-cashmere overcoats, and it helped buoy H&M's fourth-quarter profits by 23.9 percent.

FIGURE B.2.  The same article as in Figure B.1 retrieved from a searchable database.

you should follow the format appropriate to the work retrieved and add a retrieval statement that gives the date of retrieval and the proper name of the database.

Similarly, academic journal articles can appear in three different formats: in a print edition, as an electronic version retrieved from the Internet and downloaded as a PDF file, or as an electronic version retrieved from a searchable database. Even if a PDF file is retrieved from the Internet, it looks identical to the print edition, so it is cited in the same format as the print edition. For example, if you are using MLA format, an article from the *Journal of Retailing* (Figure B.3) that you retrieved from the Internet and downloaded as a PDF file would be cited in the following way:

> Levy, Michael, Dhruv Grewal, Robert A. Peterson, and Bob Connolly. "The Concept of the 'Big Middle.'" Journal of Retailing 81.2 (2005): 83–88.

If you were to cite the print edition of this article, the citation would look exactly the same as the citation for the pdf file. If you are using MLA format, the same article retrieved from a searchable database (Figure B.4) would be cited in the following way:

> Levy, Michael, Dhruv Grewal, Robert A. Peterson, and Bob Connolly. "The Concept of the 'Big Middle.'" Journal of Retailing 81.2 (2005): 83–88. ScienceDirect. Northern Arizona University, Flagstaff, Arizona. 30 Sept. 2007. <http://libproxy.nau.edu:2122>.

According to the *MLA Handbook for Writers of Research Papers* (Gibaldi, 2003), references for materials from searchable databases should include the name of the database, the name of the university, the city and state where the document was retrieved, the date of retrieval, and (in angle brackets) the electronic address of the source.

Fashion writers are aware of the "Thursday Styles" section of the *New York Times*. An article in this section can be retrieved from the print edition of the newspaper. It can also be downloaded from a searchable database or retrieved from the *New York Times* Web site. When retrieved from the *New York Times* Web site, the article (Figure B.5) would be cited this way in APA format:

> Horyn, C. (2005, August 18). Vogue answers: What do men want? *New York Times.* Retrieved August 18, 2005, from http://www.nytimes.com

Pay attention to the retrieval method you use when researching sources, and accurately reflect the method in the citations for your fashion message. The previous section has discussed the importance of taking notes and understanding exactly what type of material an original source is. The following sections will discuss the specific formatting styles.

# AMERICAN PSYCHOLOGICAL ASSOCIATION FORMAT

APA documentation style is the preferred documentation style for writers in the social and physical sciences. Many fashion- and merchandising-related disciplines have also adopted

ELSEVIER

Journal of Retailing 81 (2, 2005) 83–88

Journal of Retailing

Editorial

# The concept of the "Big Middle"

Michael Levy [a], Dhruv Grewal [a,\*], Robert A. Peterson [b], Bob Connolly [c]

[a] *Marketing Department, Babson College, Babson Park, MA 02468, USA*
[b] *University of Texas at Austin, USA*
[c] *Wal-Mart Stores, Inc., Bentonville, Arkansas, USA*

### Abstract

Although several hypotheses have been proffered to explain changes in the structure and evolution of retailing institutions, none provides a comprehensive explanation of how and why retail institutions evolve. This editorial first introduces the concept of the "Big Middle," the marketspace in which the largest retailers compete in the long run. It then hypothesizes that these large retailers generally originate as innovators or low-price retailers that focus on a particular niche but migrate into the Big Middle in search of greater revenues and profits. The goal of this editorial is to suggest an initial framework for investigating those factors that create the structure and motivate the evolution of retailing institutions.
© 2005 Published by Elsevier Inc on behalf of New York University

*Keywords:* Big Middle; Marketspace; Retail institutions

## Introduction

From time to time, it grows instructive to reflect back on the progress that has been made in addressing important and interesting topics in retailing. The recent passing of Professor Stanley Hollander, a retailing theoretician, marketing historian, outstanding colleague, and dear friend, has given rise to such an occasion. Two of Stan's best known contributions to the retailing literature — "The Wheel of Retailing" (Hollander 1960) and "Notes on the Retail Accordion" (1966) — both addressed hypotheses relating to the structure and evolution of retailing institutions, and together, they stimulated the substance of this editorial. Because examining the past often provides the best insights into the future (Savitt 1989), this editorial begins with a brief historical account of Stan's two hypotheses.

*The wheel of retailing*

One of the first, and perhaps the most famous, attempts to explain changes in retailing institutions was the wheel of retailing hypothesis; note the schematic diagram in Fig. 1. The

\* Corresponding author. Tel.: +1 781 239 5629.
*E-mail addresses:* mlevy@babson.edu (M. Levy), dgrewal@babson.edu (D. Grewal).

0022-4359/$ – see front matter © 2005 Published by Elsevier Inc on behalf of New York University
doi:10.1016/j.jretai.2005.04.001

wheel hypothesis apparently first was proposed by Malcolm P. McNair in a speech in 1957; this speech later appeared as a book chapter (McNair 1958). Hollander's (1960) article on the wheel of retailing succinctly summarized its major tenet:

> The wheel of retailing ... hypothesis ... holds that new types of retailers usually enter the market as low-status, low-margin, low-price operators. Gradually they acquire more elaborate establishments and facilities, with both increased investments and higher operating costs. Finally they mature as high-cost, high-price merchants, vulnerable to newer types who, in turn, go through the same pattern. (p. 37)

The evolution of the department store aptly illustrates the wheel of retailing hypothesis. In its entry phase, as Fig. 1 shows, the department store was a low-cost, low-service venture. After World War II, department stores moved into the trading-up phase, during which they upgraded their facilities and increased their stock selection, advertising, and service. Today, department stores sit in the vulnerable phase. They are vulnerable to various types of low-cost, low-service formats, such as full-line discount stores and category specialists.

Despite the intuitive appeal of the wheel hypothesis, Hollander (1960, p. 37) posed three rhetorical questions regarding its generality and usefulness: "Is this hypothesis valid for all retailing under all conditions? How accurately does it describe total American retail development? What factors

FIGURE B.3. Article from the *Journal of Retailing* retrieved from the Internet and downloaded as a PDF file.

FIGURE B.4.   The same article as in Figure B.3 retrieved from a searchable database.

**The New York Times**
nytimes.com

PRINTER-FRIENDLY FORMAT
SPONSORED BY

---

**August 18, 2005**
Vogue Answers: What Do Men Want?
**By CATHY HORYN**

MEN have never exactly been alien to Vogue. Winston Churchill posed in the uniform he wore to the coronation of Queen Elizabeth II, Ernest Hemingway lounged bare-chested in Cuba, and the clowns of "Monty Python's Flying Circus" did the full monty. We saw Hitchcock's pear-shaped profile and Mick Jagger's lips - or, as Tom Wolfe put it around the time that he himself was photographed in Vogue, by Irving Penn: "This boy has exceptional lips. He has two peculiarly gross and extraordinary red lips. They hang off his face like giblets."

You can't say that Vogue has ever neglected distinguished men. Still, the news that Big Mama has spawned an offspring called Men's Vogue may come as a surprise to even the more liberal-minded sons (and daughters; let's be fair) of the feminist generation. Men's Vogue, which arrives on newsstands Sept. 6, joins Teen Vogue as the latest spinoff of this Condé Nast title under its editor, Anna Wintour, who is already brooding on Vogue Living.

Jay Fielden is the editor of Men's Vogue. A soft-spoken, likable Texan, Mr. Fielden, 35, began his career in 1992 in the typing pool at The New Yorker, which was sort of the literary equivalent of the mailroom at William Morris. "All I had to do was learn how to type," he said in a yonder-lies-the-cottonwood drawl.

He eventually became an editor, and in 2000 Ms. Wintour hired him to be the arts editor of Vogue. She said that Mr. Fielden was her first choice to run Men's Vogue after S. I. Newhouse Jr., the chairman of Advance Publishing, the parent company of Condé Nast, suggested to her last fall that there was an audience for such a magazine.

"I mean, he's sort of the target reader, Jay," Ms. Wintour said in her flower-laden office on the 12th floor of the Condé Nast building in Times Square. The target reader is a man over 35 who earns more than $100,000 a year, is already living the life he wants rather than merely chasing it, and presumably isn't too embarrassed to be seen reading a magazine that for more than a century has been associated with women.

"When people ask me, 'Who is this magazine for?' I say, 'Well, did you ever wonder who are the guys on the arms of the women who read Vogue?' " Thomas A. Florio, the publisher, said. Although the first issue is considered a trial until Mr. Newhouse gives the go-ahead for a second one (probably next April), Mr. Florio said it had the highest number of advertising pages (164) for a Condé Nast introduction, more than double what he expected.

The advertisers also reflect the editorial content, which is about lifestyle and accomplishment rather than trendy fashion and how to get a date. They include Hinckley yachts, Kiton suits and distillers of rare Scotch. Bergdorf Goodman and Barneys New York bought multipage spreads that emphasize their specialized brands, and, Mr. Florio said, Gucci agreed to shoot an advertisement that looked less "slick" than its usual campaigns.

Just who is on the arm of the Vogue reader represents, if nothing else, an interesting anthropological study of men and masculinity at the beginning of the 21st century.

The articles Mr. Fielden commissioned - a number of them from New Yorker writers like John Seabrook, Nick Paumgarten and Michael Specter - suggest a robust appetite for a literate, adventuresome life. There is a profile of the painter Walton Ford, who each summer takes a 250-mile walk from his New England front porch to his printer's; a feature called "Life Studies" that opens with a photographic portrait of John Currin in his TriBeCa studio; an article and fashion spreads about the English obsession with weekend shooting parties; a look at Roger Federer and the contents of his tennis bag; and a feature on the New York town house that the architect David Chipperfield designed for Nathaniel Rothschild. There are front-of-the-book pieces on wine, cellphones equipped with G.P.S. tracking systems and a quirky piece by Jeffrey Steingarten about his favorite meat slicer.

George Clooney is on the cover, photographed on the set of the Edward R. Murrow biopic he directed. And though

http://www.nytimes.com/2005/08/18/fashion/thursdaystyles/18VOGUE.html?_r=1&oref=slogin&pagew...   10/20/2007

**FIGURE B.5.** Article retrieved from the *New York Times* Web site.

this format. The *Clothing & Textiles Research Journal* requires the use of either APA or CMS format. Complete APA documentation can be found in the *Publication Manual of the American Psychological Association* (5th ed.) or in *Concise Rules of APA Style,* both from the American Psychological Association, Washington, DC.

## IN-TEXT CITATIONS

In-text parenthetical citations are brief citations within the document, containing information to enable the reader to locate the source on the reference list. Examples of APA in-text citations are shown below:

> *Salon* magazine is considered the first Internet-based magazine (Harrison, 2002). According to the Salon.com Web site, "the Salon Media Group, Inc. is an Internet media company that produces 7 original content sections as well as two online communities" (2005, ¶1). The content sites feature news, politics, opinion, technology, business, arts & entertainment, and more.
>
> Salon.com's arts and entertainment site has attracted many advertisers from the entertainment industry. "Salon A&E features provocative reviews, aggressive reporting and thought provoking essays in the fields of movies, music and television" (Salon.com, 2005, Sites section, para.1).

The in-text citation may immediately follow the passage or it may appear at the end of the sentence. In-text citations may be part of the sentence content or may appear only as a citation.

> *Salon* magazine is the first Internet-based magazine (Harrison, 2002).

> According to Harrison (2002), *Salon* magazine is the first Internet-based magazine.

In APA format, paraphrased or summarized in-text citations include the author's last name and the year of publication.

> Harrison (2002) *or* (Harrison, 2002)

In APA format, if a directly quoted source contains *fewer* than 40 words, its in-text citation must include the author's last name, the year of publication, and the page number or paragraph number where the direct quote can be found in the original source.

> (Salon.com, 2005, ¶ 1)

A direct quote of *more* than 40 words is treated differently in APA format. The following is an example of a quote that is more than 40 words long:

> The following observation was made about the Chanel exhibit:
>> One morning earlier this week, a particular Manhattan archetype climbed aboard a crosstown bus that was headed toward the Metropolitan Museum of Art. She was a discreet blonde dressed in a short black overcoat, crisp khaki trousers and a pair of taupe and black ballet flats. From some distance away, it was possible to make out the embossed interlocking C's on the cap of

her shoes. She was a Chanel lady. One quickly assumed that her crocodile handbag was real. Could she be a fan heading to a sneak peak at the Met's Chanel exhibition? (Givhan, 2005, ¶ 1)

The quotation is indented at the left margin, and quotation marks are not used. The in-text citation is generally placed at the end of the block quote. The in-text citation is not contained within the block punctuation.

## Guidelines for In-Text Citations

The following are selected guidelines for developing in-text citations in APA format:

- In most cases it is easier to write an accurate in-text citation after you have correctly recorded the source on your References page. Review the sections of this appendix titled "Note-Taking" and "References Page" for specific details.
- When a citation has more than three authors, cite all authors the first time the reference occurs; in subsequent citations of the reference, include only the surname of the first author followed by *et al.* and the year if it is the first citation of the reference within a paragraph.
- If the publication does not have an author, substitute the first few important words of the title in place of the author's name, and follow this with a comma. (The first few words used for an in-text citation should be identical to the title used in the author position in the references page entry.) Use double quotation marks around the title, and insert a comma before the closing quotation mark to finish the entry.

    ("Circulation snapshot," 2005, p. 4)

- If you are directly quoting an electronic source and the source material was retrieved as a pdf file, the page numbers should be easy to determine.
- If you are directly quoting an electronic source with no page numbers but paragraph numbers are visible, use the paragraph number in place of the page number. Use the ¶ symbol or the abbreviation "para."

    (Salon.com, 2005, ¶ 1) *or* (Salon.com, 2005, para. 1)

- If you are directly quoting an electronic source and no page numbers or paragraph numbers are visible, but there are headings in the document, cite the heading and the number of the paragraph to direct the reader to the location of the quoted material.

    (Salon.com, 2005, Sites section, para.1)

- The URL address (for example, http://www.nytimes.com) is never acceptable as an in-text citation.

## REFERENCES PAGE

In APA format, references listed at the end of the document appear on a References page (see Figure B.6). The reference list is an alphabetized list of the source documents used in preparing the manuscript.

References

Bonamici, K. (2004, June 14). Tag! You're the it bag. *Fortune, 149*, 50. Retrieved June 19, 2004,

from Academic Search Premier database.

Circulation snapshot. (2005, April 29). *Women's Wear Daily.* Section II, p. 4.

Deitch, L. I. (1989). The impact of tourism on the arts and crafts of Indians of the Southwestern

United States. In V. L. Smith (Ed.). *Hosts and guests: The anthropology of tourism*

(pp. 223-235). Philadelphia: University of Pennsylvania Press.

Fashion Group International. (2005). *Membership directory.* New York: Author.

Horyn, C. (2005a, June 9). Fashion, the mirror and me. *The New York Times.* Retrieved June 9,

2005, from http:www.nytimes.com

Horyn, C. (2005b, August 18). Vogue answers: What do men want? *The New York Times.*

Retrieved August 18, 2005, from http://www.nytimes.com

Mower, S. (2005, March). She means business. *Vogue, 195,* 355, 358, 362.

Oomingkak Musk Ox Producers' Co-operative. (n.d.). *Tundra & snow collection* [Brochure].

Anchorage, AK: Author.

Ravoli, P. (2005). *The travels of a T-shirt in the global economy.* Hoboken, NJ: John Wiley &

Sons.

Salon.com. (2005). *Press information.* Retrieved June 6, 2005 from,

http://www.salon.com/press/fact/

Wilson, R., Hanks, T., Goetzman, G. (Producers), & Zwick, J. (Director). (2002). *My big fat*

*Greek wedding* [Motion picture]. United States: Gold Circle Films.

FIGURE B.6. Sample References page in APA format.

## *Periodical*

The general References form for a periodical is shown below:

> Author, A. A., Author B. B., & Author, C. C. (20xx). Title of article. *Title of Periodical, xx,* xxx–xxx.

### *Journal article*

Khakimdjanova, L. & Park, J. (2005). Online visual merchandising practice of apparel e-merchants. *Journal of Retailing and Consumer Services,* 12, 307–318.

### *Magazine article*

Mower, S. (2005, March). She means business. *Vogue,* 195, 355, 358, 362.

### *Newspaper article*

Circulation snapshot. (2005, April 29). *Women's Wear Daily,* p. 14.

In the References section, a periodical citation includes the following:

- **Name**—Last name, followed by first and middle initials; include a period and a space after each initial. Follow same format for all authors. Separate authors with a comma. The authors' names must appear in the same order they appear in the original source. The ampersand symbol (&) is used in place of the word *and* to connect the last name entry. Complete the entry with a period. If the source does not have an author, move the document's title to the author place before the date, omitting articles (*the, a, an*) that are the first word of the title.
- **Date**—Place year in parentheses, followed by month if necessary, followed by day if necessary. If no date is given, write "n.d." in place of the date. Finish with a period outside the closing parenthesis.
- **Title of article**—Use sentence case capitalization, which means that only the first word of the title, the first word after a colon, and proper nouns are capitalized. Complete the entry with a period.
- **Title of publication**—Italicize the name of the publication. Use title case capitalization, which means that the first word and all important words are capitalized. Finish with a comma.
- **Volume number**—Italicized. Use for magazines, journals, and newsletters. In a print edition magazine, the volume number generally can be found on the last page of the table of contents, or on the page on which the trademark appears. For journals, the issue number does not have to be included unless each issue of the journal starts with page one. Finish with a comma.
- **Page numbers**—Give inclusive page numbers. If pages are discontinuous, list all page numbers and separate them with commas. For newspaper articles, use *p.* or *pp.* in front of the page numbers. Finish with a period.

## *Nonperiodical*

The general References forms for a nonperiodical are shown below:

Author, A. A., & Author, B. B. (20xx). *Title of work* (Xth ed.). Location: Publisher.

Author, A. A. (20xx). Title of chapter. In A. Editor & B. Editor (Eds.), *Title of book* (pp. xxx–xxx). Location: Publisher.

Deitch, L. I. (1989). The impact of tourism on the arts and crafts of Indians of the Southwestern United States. In V. L. Smith (Ed.), *Hosts and guests: The anthropology of tourism* (pp. 223–235). Philadelphia: University of Pennsylvania Press.

Fashion Group International. (2005). *Membership directory*. New York: Author.

Oomingkak Musk Ox Producers' Co-operative. (n.d.). *Tundra & snow collection* [Brochure]. Anchorage, AK: Author.

Ravoli, P. (2005). *The travels of a T-shirt in the global economy*. Hoboken, NJ: John Wiley & Sons.

Swanson, K. K., & Everett, J. C. (2007). *Promotion in the merchandising environment* (2nd ed.). New York: Fairchild Books.

Tortora, P. G., & Merkel, R. S. (2000). *Fairchild's dictionary of textiles* (7th ed.). New York: Fairchild Books.

Wilson, R., Hanks, T., Goetzman, G. (Producers), & Zwick, J. (Director). (2002). *My big fat Greek wedding* [Motion picture]. United States: Gold Circle Films.

In the References section, a nonperiodical citation includes the following:

- **Name**—See Periodical explanation. Spell out the full name of a group author, capitalizing all words. In a reference with editor(s) but no author(s), place the editor name(s) in the author position and enclose the abbreviation *Ed.* or *Eds.* (not italic) in parentheses after the last editor name.
- **Date**—See Periodical explanation. Use year only.
- **Title of work**—Italicize the name of the publication. Use sentence case capitalization (see Periodical explanation). Finish with a period. For editions other than the first edition, after the title in parentheses include the edition number and the ordinal (*nd*, *rd*, and so forth) followed by the abbreviation *ed.*, not italicized.

    For nonroutine works, enclose a description of the form of the work in brackets after the parenthetical information, not italicized. Examples include [Brochure], [Motion picture], [Videotape], [CD], and [Computer software].

    In an edited book, the title of the specific article or chapter replaces the title of the book, not in italics, ending with a period. This is followed by the word *In,* capitalized, then by the editor's first initial, middle initial, and last name and the abbreviation *Ed.* (or *Eds.* if more than one editor) in parentheses followed by a comma. The book title follows in sentence case in italics. The title is followed by the abbreviation *pp.*, not italicized, and the page numbers of the article or chapter. The *pp.* and page numbers are enclosed in parentheses. Finish with a period outside the parentheses.

- **Publication information**—Give the city, and give the state if the city is not well known such as New York, Boston, or Los Angeles. (You will need to review an APA style manual for a complete list.) Use the official two-letter U.S. Postal Service abbreviations for the states (also see Appendix A). If the publisher is a university and the name of the state appears in the name, do not repeat the state name in the location. Use a colon after the location.

  Then give the name of the publisher in brief form (omit words such as *Publisher, Incorporated,* and *Company*). Retain the words *Books* and *Press.* If two or more locations are listed, record the first location or the location of the publisher's home office. If the author is the publisher, use the word *Author* as the name of the publisher. Finish with a period.

## *Online Sources*

The general forms for an online source are:

Author, A. A., Author, B. B., & Author, C. C. (20xx). Title of article. *Title of Periodical, xx*, xxx–xxx. Retrieved month day, year, from source.

Author, A. A. (20xx). *Title of work.* Retrieved month day, year, from source.

Author, A. A., & Author, B. B. (20xx). *Title of work.* Location: Publisher. Retrieved month day, year, from source.

Benbow-Pfalzgraf, T. (Ed.). (2002). *Contemporary fashion* (2nd ed.). Farmington Hills, MI: St. James Press. Retrieved June 19, 2004, from http://libproxy.nau.edu:2169/Reader/

Bonamici, K. (2004, June 14). Tag! You're the it bag. *Fortune, 149*, 50. Retrieved June 19, 2004, from Academic Search Premier database.

Broadcasting, radio and television. (2005). *Microsoft® Encarta® Online Encyclopedia.* Retrieved July 6, 2005, from http://encarta.msn.com

Givhan, R. (2005, May 5). Simply Chanel. *Washington Post.* Retrieved June 28, 2005, from http://www.washingtonpost.com

Horyn, C. (2005a, October 20). Fashion, the mirror and me. *New York Times.* Retrieved June 9, 2005, from http:www.nytimes.com

Horyn, C. (2005b, August 18). Vogue answers: What do men want? *New York Times*. Retrieved August 18, 2005, from http://www.nytimes.com

Levy, M., Grewal, D., Peterson, R. A. & Connolly, B. (2005). The concept of the "Big Middle." *Journal of Retailing, 81*, 83–88. Retrieved August 15, 2005, from the ScienceDirect database.

Lockwood, L. (2005, October 20). Karl: I'll take Manhattan. *Women's Wear Daily*, pp. 6–7. Retrieved August 15, 2005, from the Business Source Premier database.

Orecklin, M. (2004, February 16). Women in fashion: The power list. *Time Style & Design*. Retrieved October 13, 2007, from http://www.time.com/time/style_design

Salon.com. (2005). *Press information*. Retrieved June 6, 2005, from http://www.salon.com/press/fact/

The reference citation includes the following:

- **Name**—See Periodical and Nonperiodical explanations.
- **Date**—See Periodical and Nonperiodical explanations. (Note: Many corporate Web sites are copyrighted (©), and this date can be used as the publication date. The retrieval date should not be used as the publication date.)

    References that have the same author(s) are arranged by year of publication, the earliest first. References that have the same author(s) and the same year of publication are arranged alphabetically by the first important word of the title of the article. A lowercase letter (a, b, c, and so forth) is placed immediately after the year within the parentheses. (See the *Horyn, C.* examples above.) This is particularly necessary for online sources from private organizations that are considered a corporate author.
- **Title of work**—See Periodical and Nonperiodical explanations.
- **Publication information**—See Periodical and Nonperiodical explanations. Publication information of the print version is necessary for e-books.
- **Volume**—See Periodical and Nonperiodical explanations.
- **Page numbers**—See Periodical and Nonperiodical explanations.
- **Retrieval statement**—Provides the date on which the information was retrieved. The word *Retrieved*, capitalized, is followed by the date, a comma, the word *from*, and finally the complete URL address. (Note: The URL address should not be underlined.) If information is retrieved from an aggregated database, the name of the database is sufficient; no further URL address is necessary. When the entry finishes with a URL no period is used at the end. Compare the *Benbow-Pfalzgraf* and *Bonamici* entries above.

## MODERN LANGUAGE ASSOCIATION FORMAT

MLA documentation style is the preferred documentation style for writers in the humanities. Complete MLA documentation can be found in the *MLA Handbook for Writers of*

*Research Papers* (6th ed.), by Joseph Gibaldi. MLA style is similar to APA style in that the in-text information is kept brief and is keyed to the Works Cited list (or References list, as it is called in APA style), where full bibliographic information is provided.

## IN-TEXT CITATIONS

In-text citations should contain enough information to enable the reader to locate the source in the Works Cited. Examples of MLA in-text citations are shown below. (Note: The same materials are used in the MLA examples as in the APA examples, to give you a direct view of the differences.)

In MLA style, in-text citations require the author's last name; if the text contains a direct quotation, the citation also provides the page number where the information can be found. The year of publication is not included. The reader can expect to find the full citation information in the Works Cited list.

> *Salon* magazine is considered the first Internet-based magazine (Harrison). According to the Salon.com Web site, "the Salon Media Group, Inc. is an Internet media company that produces 7 original content sections as well as two online communities" (par. 1). The content sites feature news, politics, opinion, technology, business, arts & entertainment, and more.

In the preceding example, the paraphrased or summarized opening statement is adequately credited by the author's name in parentheses. (Generally, the in-text citation appears at the end of the sentence.) If the source's name is worked into the text, no parenthetical citation is needed at that point. For example,

> Harrison notes that Salon magazine is considered the first Internet-based magazine.

Further into the paragraph, while "Salon.com" would be presented in the author position on the Works Cited page, because the text is a direct quote the reader also needs to know where the particular quoted text appears in the Salon.com citation. This information is placed in the in-text citation.

In MLA format, if a directly quoted source is no more than four lines long when typed out in the text, its in-text citation must include the author's last name and the page number or paragraph number where the direct quote can be found in the original:

> A news release is "a document that conveys newsworthy information about your organization to the news media" (Marsh et al. 31).

> According to the Salon.com Web site, "the Salon Media Group, Inc. is an Internet media company that produces 7 original content sections as well as two online communities" (par. 1).

If a direct quotation is longer than four lines of text, the quote is indented at the left margin, and quotation marks are not used. The in-text citation appears at the end of the block quote just outside the block's closing punctuation.

The following observation was made about the Chanel exhibit:

> One morning earlier this week, a particular Manhattan archetype climbed aboard
> a crosstown bus that was headed toward the Metropolitan Museum of Art. She
> was a discreet blonde dressed in a short black overcoat, crisp khaki trousers and a
> pair of taupe and black ballet flats. From some distance away, it was possible to
> make out the embossed interlocking C's on the cap of her shoes. She was a Chanel
> lady. One quickly assumed that her crocodile handbag was real. Could she be a
> fan heading to a sneak peak at the Met's Chanel exhibition? (Givhan par. 1)

## *Guidelines for In-Text Citations*

The following are selected guidelines for developing in-text citations in MLA format:

- In most cases it is easier to write an accurate in-text citation *after* you have
  correctly recorded the source on your Works Cited page. Review the sections of
  this appendix titled "Note-Taking" and "Works Cited Page" for specific details.
- When a citation has more than three authors, follow whatever form is used in the
  Works Cited; that is, either give the first author's last name followed by *et al.*
  (not italicized) without any intervening punctuation or give all the last names.
- When the author's name is in the text, give only the page number(s) in the
  parenthetical reference.
- If the publication does not have an author, in place of the author's name
  substitute the publication's full title (if it is brief) or a shortened version of the
  title. (The first few words in the in-text citation should be identical to the title
  used in the author position in the Works Cited page entry.)

     Underline—not italicize—the title, and follow it with a page number if a direct
  quote is being cited. [Note: Depending on the font being used, italic type is not
  always easy to distinguish from regular type. Therefore, in the in-text citations
  and the Works Cited (as well as for any other text that should be italicized), MLA
  style calls for underlining in the manuscript so that it will be very clear to the editor
  and publisher when italics are required in the published version.]

  (<u>Circulation Snapshot</u> 4)

- If you are directly quoting an electronic source and the source material was
  retrieved as a pdf file, the page numbers should be easy to determine.
- If you are directly quoting an electronic source with paragraph numbers rather
  than page numbers and the numbers are visible, use the paragraph number(s) in
  place of the page number(s)—abbreviated "par." or "pars." Further, add a
  comma after the author's name to clearly separate the name from the word *par*.

  (Salon.com, par. 1)

- If you are directly quoting an electronic source and no page numbers or
  paragraph numbers are visible, but there are headings in the document, cite the

heading and the number of the paragraph to direct the reader to the location of the quoted material.

(Salon.com, Sites: par. 1)

- The URL address (for example, http://www.nytimes.com) is never acceptable as an in-text citation. The author's name, the title of the article, or the name of the overall Web site—whatever is used in the Works Cited—would be an appropriate in-text citation.

## WORKS CITED PAGE

In MLA format, references are listed at the end of the document on a Works Cited page (see Figure B.7)—an alphabetized list of the source documents cited in the manuscript.

### *Periodical*

The general Works Cited forms for a periodical are shown below:

Author last name, first name, Author first name, last name, and Author first name, last name. "Title of Article." Title of Periodical day month, year: xxx–xxx.

#### *Journal article*

Khakimdjanova, Lola, and Jihye Park. "Online Visual Merchandising Practice of Apparel E-Merchants." Journal of Retailing and Consumer Services 12 (2005): 307–318.

#### *Newspaper article*

"Circulation Snapshot." Women's Wear Daily 29 Apr. 2005: I4.

#### *Magazine article*

Mower, Sarah. "She means business." Vogue Mar. 2005: 195+.

In Works Cited, a periodical citation includes the following:

- **Name**—Whenever possible, give the first name(s) in full rather than using initials. For a single author, give the last name, followed by a comma, then the first name. For two or more authors, present the first author's name inverted as above followed by a comma, then the second author's first name and last name. For subsequent authors, continue the first name–last name format. The word *and* is used to connect the last name entry to the preceding entries. End with a period. The authors' names must appear in the same order as they appear in the original. Complete the entry with a period. If the source does not have an author, move the document's title to the author place, omitting articles (*the, a, an*) that are the first word of the title.
- **Title of article**—Use title case capitalization, which means that the first word and all important words are capitalized. Put the title in quotation marks. Complete the entry with a period (inside the closing quotation mark).

Works Cited

Bonamici, Kate. "Tag! You're the it bag." <u>Fortune</u>. 149 (2004): 50. <u>Academic Search Premier</u>.

    19 June 2004 <http://library.mtsu.edu/libdata/page.phtml?page_id=32>.

"Circulation Snapshot." <u>Women's Wear Daily</u> 29 Apr. 2005: 14.

Deitch, Lewis. "The Impact of Tourism on the Arts and Crafts of Indians of the Southwestern

    United States." <u>Hosts and Guests: The Anthropology of Tourism</u>. Ed. Valene Smith.

    Philadelphia: U of Pennsylvania P, 1989. 223-35.

Fashion Group International. <u>Membership Directory</u>. New York: Fashion Group International,

    2008.

Horyn, Cathy. "Fashion, the Mirror and Me." <u>New York Times on the Web</u>. 9 June 2005. 9 June

    2005 <http:www.nytimes.com>.

—. "Vogue Answers: What Do Men Want?" <u>New York Times on the Web</u>. 18 Aug. 2005. 18

    Aug. 2005 <http:www.nytimes.com>.

Mower, Sarah. "She Means Business." <u>Vogue</u> Mar. 2005: 195+.

<u>My Big Fat Greek Wedding</u>. Dir. Joel Zwick. Prod. Rita Wilson, Tom Hanks, and Gary

    Goetzman. Gold Circle Films, 2002.

Oomingkak Musk Ox Producers' Co-operative. <u>Tundra & Snow Collection</u>. Anchorage:

    Oomingkak Musk Ox Producers' Co-operative.

"Press information." <u>Salon</u>. 6 June 2005. 18 Aug. 2005 < http://www.salon.com/press/facts/>.

Ravoli, Pietra. <u>The Travels of a T-shirt in the Global Economy</u>. Hoboken: Wiley, 2005.

FIGURE B.7. Sample Works Cited page in MLA format.

- **Title of publication**—Underline—not italicize—the name of the publication. Use title case capitalization. No ending punctuation follows.
- **Date**—For newspapers and magazines, after the publication's Title give the complete date: the day (if the publication is other than a monthly one), then the month in abbreviated format (except for May, June, and July, which are spelled out completely), then the year. Follow the year with a colon.
- **Volume number**—For scholarly journals, after the publication Title, give the volume number followed by the year of publication in parentheses followed by a colon. If each issue of the journal starts with page one, include both the volume number and the issue number. Separate them with a period—for example, *Title* 50.4. For newspapers and magazines, do not give the volume and issue numbers even if they are listed.
- **Page numbers**—For scholarly journals, give inclusive page numbers for the article you are referencing; if pages are discontinuous, list all page numbers and separate them with commas. For magazines and newspapers, if the article is not printed on consecutive pages, provide the first page number and a plus sign. Finish with a period.

## *Nonperiodical*

The general Works Cited forms for a nonperiodical are shown below:

Author last name, first name, Author first name, last name, and Author first name, last name. Title of Book. Xnd ed. Location: Publisher, Year of publication.

Author last name, first name. "Title of Chapter." Title of Book. Ed. A. Editor and B. Editor. Location: Publisher, Year of publication. xx–xx.

Deitch, Lewis. "The Impact of Tourism on the Arts and Crafts of Indians of the Southwestern United States." Hosts and Guests: The Anthropology of Tourism. Ed. Valene Smith. Philadelphia: U of Pennsylvania P, 1989. 223–235. [Note the abbreviated publisher name.]

Fashion Group International. Membership Directory. New York: Fashion Group International, 2008.

Oomingkak Musk Ox Producers' Co-operative. Tundra & Snow Collection. Anchorage: Oomingkak Musk Ox Producers' Co-operative, n.d. [Treat a brochure as you would a book. In this example, the author is also the publisher and the date of publication is not known.]

Ravoli, Pietra. The Travels of a T-shirt in the Global Economy. Hoboken: Wiley, 2005.

Swanson, Kristen, and Judith Everett. Promotion in the Merchandising Environment. 2nd ed. New York: Fairchild Books, 2007.

Tortora, Phyllis, and Merkel, Robert. Fairchild's Dictionary of Textiles. 7th ed. New York: Fairchild Books, 2000.

My Big Fat Greek Wedding. Dir. Joel Zwick. Prod. Rita Wilson, Tom Hanks, and Gary Goetzman. Gold Circle Films, 2002.

In Works Cited, a nonperiodical citation includes the following:

- **Name**—Whenever possible, give the first name(s) in full rather than using initials. For a single author, give the last name, followed by a comma, then the first name. For two or more authors, present the first author's name inverted as described above, followed by a comma, then the second author's first name and last name. For subsequent authors, continue the first name–last name format. The word *and* is used to connect the last name entry to the preceding entries. End with a period. The authors' names must appear in the same order as they appear in the original. If the source does not have an author, move the document's title to the author place, omitting articles (*the, a, an*) that are the first word of the title.

- **Title of work**—Underline the name of the publication. Use title case capitalization. Finish with a period. For editions other than the first edition, after the period that ends the title put the edition number and the appropriate ordinal (*nd, rd,* and so forth). Follow this with the abbreviation *ed.*, lowercase (not italicized), then a period.

  In an anthology or other edited book, present the title of the chapter or article in title case and in quotation marks with a period inside the closing quotation mark. Follow this with the book title, underlined and in title case, then a period. Next is the abbreviation *Ed.* (or *Eds.* if more than one editor), capitalized, not italicized, then the editor's first name and last name.

- **Publication information**—Give the city (do not give the state name or postal abbreviation), followed by a colon. Give the name of the publisher in brief form. (That is, omit words such as *Publisher, Incorporated,* and *Company*; retain words such as *Books* and *Press*—but see the *Deitch, Lewis* example above for treatment when a university press is the publisher.) If the publisher is the author, use the publisher's name in both the Author position and the Publisher position. Follow this with a comma.

- **Date**—Use the year only. End with a period. In an anthology, after the date and final period, give the inclusive page numbers of the article that is being cited and close with another period. (See the *Deitch, Lewis* example above.)

## Online Sources

The general Works Cited forms for an online source are shown below:

### An entire book online

Author's last name, first name, or editor's/translator's/ last name, first name, followed by *ed.* or *trans.* Title of the work. City, publisher, year of publication for the print version. Name of Internet site, date of electronic publication, date of access, URL in angle brackets.

*Article in a journal, published both in print and online*
Author A's last name, first name, Author B's first name last name, and Author C's first name last name. "Title of Article." Title of periodical volume number and issue number, separated by a period, year of publication in parentheses followed by a colon, name of online version of journal, date of access, URL in angle brackets.

*Article in an online magazine or newspaper*

> Author's last name, first name. "Title of Article." Title of magazine or newspaper, day month year published, day month year of access, URL in angle brackets.

> Bonamici, Kate. "Tag! You're the It Bag." Fortune 149 (2004): 50. Academic Search Premier. 19 June 2004 <http://library.mtsu.edu/libdata/page.phtml?page_id=32>.

> "Broadcasting, Radio and Television." Microsoft® Encarta® Online Encyclopedia 6 July 2005 <http://encarta.msn.com>.

> Givhan, Robin. "Simply Chanel." Washington Post 5 May 2005. 28 June 2005 <http://www.washingtonpost.com>.

> Horyn, Cathy. "Fashion, the mirror and me." New York Times on the Web 9 June 2005. 9 June 2005 <http://www.nytimes.com>.

> ———. "Vogue Answers: What Do Men Want?" New York Times on the Web 18 Aug. 2005. 18 Aug. 2005 <http://www.nytimes.com>.

> Levy, Michael, Dhruv Grewal, Bob Connolly, and Robert A. Peterson. "The Concept of the 'Big Middle.'" Journal of Retailing 81 (2005): 83–88. 30 Sept. 2007 ScienceDirect. <-http://www.sciencedirect.com/>.

> Lockwood, Lisa. "Karl: I'll take Manhattan." Women's Wear Daily 6 June 2005. 30 Sept. 2007. <http://www.wwd.com/search/article/98945>.

> Orecklin, Michele. "Women in Fashion: The Power List." Time Style & Design. 16 Feb. 2004. 13 Oct., 2007 <http://www.time.com/time/style_design>.

> "Press Information." Salon.com. 6 June 2005 <http://www.salon.com/press/fact/>.

In Works Cited, an online source citation includes the following:

- **Name**—See Periodical and Nonperiodical explanations.
- **Date**—See Periodical and Nonperiodical explanations. (Note: Many corporate Web sites are copyrighted (©), and this date can be used as the publication date. The retrieval date should not be used as the publication date.)

    References that have the same author(s) and the same year of publication should be arranged alphabetically by the first important word of the title of the article. (See the *Horyn, Cathy* example above.) This is particularly necessary for online sources from private organizations that are considered a corporate author.

- **Title of work**—See Periodical and Nonperiodical explanations.
- **Publication information**—See Periodical and Nonperiodical explanations. Publication information of the print version is necessary for an e-book.
- **Volume**—See Periodical and Nonperiodical explanations.
- **Page numbers**—See Periodical and Nonperiodical explanations.
- **Retrieval statement**—Provide the date on which the information was accessed and then the complete URL address in angle brackets. (Note: The URL address should not be underlined.) If information is retrieved from a database, after the print information for the article state the name of the database; follow with the date of access and then the URL in angle brackets. End with a period.

# CHICAGO MANUAL OF STYLE FORMAT

Complete CMS documentation information is found in *The Chicago Manual of Style: The Essential Guide for Writers, Editors, and Publishers* (15th ed.), published by the University of Chicago Press. CMS covers these two basic systems of citation in depth:

1. Numbered footnotes or endnotes (referred to as *notes* in the following text) usually accompanied by a Bibliography, and

2. Author–date in-text citations—similar to the ones used by the Modern Language Association (MLA) and the American Psychological Association (APA)—accompanied by a References page.

The Notes–Bibliography style is most often used by writers in literature, history, and the arts, as well as in various scholarly books and journals. The Author–Date system is used primarily in the physical, natural, and social sciences. (Among scholarly journals that deal with aspects of fashion, the *Clothing & Textiles Research Journal* requires the use of either APA or CMS format.)

This appendix has already presented detailed coverage of the APA and MLA Author–Date systems. After a brief presentation of CMS Author–Date documentation style, we will focus our CMS presentation on the Notes–Bibliography system.

## CMS AUTHOR–DATE SYSTEM

Examples of the CMS version of the Author–Date System are shown below. This system works best where all or most of the sources are easily convertible to author-date references.

### In the text

As Kirszner and Mandell (2005, 33) have said, this is a time to "re-see" what you have written and write additional drafts. [When the author's name is part of the text, the publication date and citation page number appear in parentheses.]

Previously we talked about tone, which is very similar to style. *Style* is defined as "the way something is written" (Woolever 1999, 91). [In this instance, the author's name, publication date, and citation page number all appear in parentheses.]

### In the References list
Kirszner, Laurie G., and Mandell, Stephen R. *The Wadsworth Handbook* [Instructor's Edition]. (Boston: Thomson Wadsworth, 2005).

Woolever, Kristin R. *Writing for the Technical Professions*. (New York: Addison Wesley Longman, 1999).

## CMS NOTES–BIBLIOGRAPHY SYSTEM
Anonymous works, manuscript collections, or other sources that are less easy to convert to Author–Date parenthetical in-text citations can be presented more clearly in notes. In that case, the Notes–Bibliography system is a better choice for presenting the documentation.

The CMS version of the Notes–Bibliography system uses superscript numerals, accompanying numbered notes, and detailed bibliographic entries. Examples are shown below.

### In the text
As Kirszner and Mandell have said, this is a time to "re-see" what you have written and write additional drafts.[1] [Put the note number at the end of the sentence or the end of a clause, after the punctuation.]

### In the notes
1. Kirszner, Laurie G., and Mandell, Stephen R., *Wadsworth Handbook*, 33.

*In subsequent citations of this work in the notes:*
6. Kirszner and Mandell, *Wadsworth Handbook*, 40.

7. Ibid., 43. [To help keep the notes brief, if the very next note refers to the same source, you can use *Ibid.*—the abbreviation for the Latin word *ibidem*, which means "in the same place"—to represent the bibliographic information.]

### In the notes if there is no Bibliography
1. Kirszner, Laurie G., and Mandell, Stephen R., *The Wadsworth Handbook* [Instructor's Edition] (Boston: Thomson Wadsworth. 2005), 33.

### In the Bibliography
Kirszner, Laurie G., and Mandell, Stephen R. *The Wadsworth Handbook* [Instructor's Edition]. Boston: Thomson Wadsworth, 2005.

## Some Guidelines for the Notes
- Just as for APA and MLA styles, in most cases it is easier to write an accurate CMS note after you have correctly recorded the source in your Bibliography.

Review the sections of this appendix titled "Note-Taking" and "Bibliography" for specific details.

- In a heavily documented work, it is acceptable to use the Author–Date form for source citations and use numbered notes for substantive comments.
- Readers often prefer footnotes, because in footnotes the citation information and other commentary are close by during reading. On the other hand, when a document has many notes, moving them out of the way to an endnotes section can make the page less distracting for the reader. Also, endnotes obviously are easier to handle in page makeup.
- Because CMS-style notes are quite detailed, it is acceptable to prepare a document without a formal Bibliography. (See "In the notes if there is no Bibliography" in the examples above.) A citation in the notes can be shortened after the first time it appears, to help control overall length. However, in a Bibliography the reader can get an overview of all the sources used and can easily find full references to individual sources that were cited.

## The Notes–Bibliography Combination

In CMS style, at times the amount of information provided in a note is as detailed as the information in the Bibliography. However, the most complete reference information appears at the end of the document in a Bibliography—an alphabetized list of the source documents referenced in the manuscript (see Figure B.8). The style for entries in the Bibliography is slightly different from the style for entries on the References page of the Author–Date system.

## Periodical

The general Note and Bibliography forms for a periodical are shown below:

*Note:*

X. First author's first name last name and second author's first name last name, "Title of Article," *Title of Periodical* xx (20xx): xxx–xxx.

*Bibliography:*

First author's last name, first name, and second author's first name last name. "Title of Article." *Title of Periodical* xx (20xx): xxx–xxx.

### Journal article

*Note:*

6. Lola Khakimdjanova and Jihye Park, "Online Visual Merchandising Practice of Apparel E-Merchants," *Journal of Retailing and Consumer Services* 12 (2005): 307–318.

*Bibliography:*

Khakimdjanova, Lola, and Jihye Park. "Online Visual Merchandising Practice of Apparel E-Merchants." *Journal of Retailing and Consumer Services* 12 (2005): 307–318.

Notes

1. University of Chicago, *The Chicago Manual of Style Online*, 15 ed. (Chicago: University of Chicago Press, 2003), http://www.chicagomanualofstyle.org/home.html.

2. Fashion Group International, *Membership Directory* (New York: Fashion Group International, 2008).

3. Laurie G. Kirszner and Stephen R. Mandell, *The Wadsworth Handbook* [Instructor's Edition] (Boston: Thomson Wadsworth, 2005), 33.

4. Lola Khakimdjanova and Jihye Park, "Online Visual Merchandising Practice of Apparel E-Merchants," *Journal of Retailing and Consumer Services* 12 (2005): 307–318.

5. Kirszner and Mandell, Wadsworth Handbook, 40.

6. Ibid., 43.

7. Sarah Mower, "She Means Business," *Vogue*, March 2005, 355.

8. Lewis Deitch, "The Impact of Tourism on the Arts and Crafts on Indians of the Southwestern United States," in *Hosts and guests: The Anthropology of Tourism*, ed. Valene Smith, 36 (Philadelphia: University of Pennsylvania Press, 1989).

9. Levy, Michael, and others, "The concept of the 'Big Middle'," *Journal of Retailing* 81 (2005), http://www.sciencedirect-.com/.

FIGURE B.8. Sample Notes and corresponding Bibliography page in CMS format. *(continued)*

Bibliography

Deitch, Lewis. "The Impact of Tourism on the Arts and Crafts of Indians of the Southwestern
       United States." In *Hosts and Guests: The Anthropology of Tourism*, edited by V. L.
       Smith, 24–45. Philadelphia: University of Pennsylvania Press, 1989.

Fashion Group International. *Membership Directory*. New York: Fashion Group International,
       2008.

Khakimdjanova, Lola, and Jihye Park. "Online Visual Merchandising Practice of Apparel
       E-Merchants." *Journal of Retailing and Consumer Services* 12 (2005): 307–318.

Kirszner, Laurie G., and Stephen R. Mandell. *The Wadsworth Handbook* [Instructor's Edition]
       Boston: Thomson Wadsworth, 2005.

Levy, Michael, Dhruv Grewal, Bob Connolly, and Robert A. Peterson. "The Concept of the 'Big
       Middle'." *Journal of Retailing* 81 (2005): 83-88. http://www.sciencedirect.conv.

Mower, Sarah. "She Means Business." *Vogue*, March 2005.

University of Chicago. *The Chicago Manual of Style Online*. 15th ed. Chicago: University of
       Chicago Press, 2003. http-d/www.chicagomanualofstyle.org/home.html.

FIGURE B.8.

### Newspaper article

A newspaper article usually would not be cited in the Notes or the Bibliography; rather it would be cited in the text. For example:

In an article on magazine circulation rates (*Women's Wear Daily*, April 29, 2005), there was an increase in advertising pages.

If it is necessary to include the citation for a newspaper article in the Bibliography, it should be cited as follows:

*Women's Wear Daily*, "Circulation Snapshot," April 29, 2005. [This is an example of an unsigned article—no author is given.]

### Magazine article

*Note:*
10. Sarah Mower, "She means business," *Vogue* 195 (March 2005): 355, 358, 362.

*Bibliography:*
Mower, Sarah. "She Means Business." *Vogue* 195 (March 2005): 355, 358, 362.

## Nonperiodical

The general Note and Bibliography forms for a nonperiodical are shown below:

*Note:*
X. A. A. Author and B. B. Author, *Title of Work* (Location: Publisher, 200x).

*Bibliography:*
Author, A. A., and B. B. Author. *Title of Work*. Location: Publisher, 200x.

*Note:*
5. Kristen Swanson and Judith Everett, *Promotion in the Merchandising* Environment, 2nd ed. (New York: Fairchild Books, 2007).

*Bibliography:*
Swanson, Kristen, and Judith Everett. *Promotion in the Merchandising* Environment. 2nd ed. New York: Fairchild Books, 2007.

*Note:*
12. Lewis Deitch, "The Impact of Tourism on the Arts and Crafts of Indians of the Southwestern United States," in *Hosts and Guests: The Anthropology of Tourism*, ed. Valerie Smith, 36 (Philadelphia: University of Pennsylvania Press, 1989). [In a Nonperiodical note, the exact page number of the citation appears after the editor's name.]

*Bibliography:*
Deitch, Lewis. The Impact of Tourism on the Arts and Crafts of Indians of the Southwestern United States." In *Hosts and Guests: The Anthropology of Tourism*, edited by V. L. Smith, 24–45. Philadelphia: University of Pennsylvania Press, 1989.

[In a Nonperiodical Bibliography entry, the range of page numbers of the entire article appears after the editor's name.]

*Note:*

2. Fashion Group International, *Membership Directory* (New York: Fashion Group International, 2008).

*Bibliography:*

Fashion Group International. *Membership Directory.* New York: Fashion Group International, 2008.

## *Online Sources*

Online journals, magazines, and newspapers include the same bibliographic information as print journals, magazines, and newspapers. In addition, they contain the URL and, especially for time-sensitive articles, the date the material was last accessed. The general Note and Bibliography forms for an online source are shown below:

### *Online book*

*Note:*

1. University of Chicago, *The Chicago Manual of Style Online,* 15th ed. (Chicago: University of Chicago Press, 2003) http://www.chicagomanualofstyle.org/home .html.

*Bibliography:*

University of Chicago. *The Chicago Manual of Style Online.* 15th ed. Chicago: University of Chicago Press, 2003. http://www.chicagomanualofstyle.org/home .html.

### *Online journal article*

*Note:*

15. Levy, Michael, and others, "The Concept of the 'Big Middle,'" *Journal of Retailing* 81 (2005), http://www.sciencedirect.com/.

*Bibliography:*

Levy, Michael, Dhruv Grewal, Bob Connolly, and Robert A. Peterson. "The Concept of the 'Big Middle.'" *Journal of Retailing* 81 (2005): 83–88. http://www.sciencedirect.com/.

### *Online newspaper article*

*Note:*

9. Robin Givhan, "Simply Chanel," *Washington Post,* May 5, 2005, http://www.washingtonpost.com (accessed June 28, 2005).

*Bibliography:*

Givhan, Robin. "Simply Chanel." *Washington Post,* May 5, 2005. http://www.washingtonpost.com (accessed June 28, 2005).

*Online magazine article*
Note:
8. Orecklin, Michele, "The Power List: Women in Fashion," *Time Style & Design*, February 16, 2004, http://www.time.com/time/style_design.

*Bibliography:*
Orecklin, Michele. "The Power List: Women in Fashion." *Time Style & Design*. February 16, 2004. http://www.time.com/time/style_design.

## ASSOCIATED PRESS FORMAT

The Associated Press is a U.S.-based news agency. Its format, as set out in its style guide, is the standard for news writing in the United States and is widely used by writers in print and broadcast journalism, particularly newspapers. Complete AP documentation can be found in the *Associated Press Stylebook and Briefing on Media Law*, edited by Norm Goldstein.

The *AP Stylebook* does not cover reference and bibliographic style in the same way that APA, MLA, and CMS do. Newspaper reporters are doing primary, not secondary, research. They are obtaining quoted material directly from a source as an event is taking place. Of course, if the reporter quotes from already-published material, the author and source of the work are always given.

The chapter in the *AP Stylebook* that deals most directly with documentation concerns is titled "Briefing on Media Law." Especially note the chapter's discussions of copyright infringement and "fair use."

The *AP Stylebook* includes a list of the reference books that were used in the preparation of the stylebook. They are the "accepted reference sources for material not covered by the Stylebook" (Associated Press [AP] Stylebook, 2007, p. ix). The first two resources on the list are the most general ones. In your newspaper writing, they can serve as reliable style references if you need to look beyond the extensive style information given in the AP Stylebook:

- First reference for spelling, style, usage, and foreign geographic names:
  *Webster's New World College Dictionary*. (4th ed.). (2000). Hoboken, NJ: Wiley.
- Second reference for spelling, style, and usage:
  *Webster's Third New International Dictionary*. (2000). Springfield, MA: Merriam-Webster.

## OTHER SOURCES FOR JOURNALISTIC DOCUMENTATION STYLE

Different newspapers often develop their own house style. The *New York Times*, for example, has an extensive house style guide called *The New York Times Manual of Style & Usage*. Like the *AP Stylebook*, it is available to the public.

Consider the following guidance on newspaper documentation needs from the *New York Times Manual* (Siegal & Connelly, 2002). The sections presented below are especially directed toward how to handle attribution: giving credit to the person being quoted—the person whose words are being documented.

### Texts and Excerpts

A verbatim text or transcript, or an extract, begins with an italic introduction explaining the material's nature and source. The introduction specifies any excerpting (and attributes it . . . ), and credits the translation, if any, specifying the original language. If the full document is available on the World Wide Web . . . , readers will welcome a Web address.

*Transcript* denotes a literal rendering of speech. . . . *Text* . . . denotes reproduction of a written document. *Excerpts* . . . may apply to written or spoken material. . . .

A formal introduction (for a document in current news) normally begins *Following is a transcript of* or *Following is the text of* or *Following are excerpts from.* . . .

When excerpts are used, editors should select one or a few substantial, coherent sections rather than a larger number of short bites too fragmented to convey the tone of the whole. . . .

Self-contained texts, transcripts and excerpts are not enclosed in quotation marks. Spelling, punctuation and indentions in a verbatim document (though not grammar or word usage) should conform to The Times's style unless literal reproduction is necessary to convey the significance. . . . (Siegal & Connelly, 2002, p. 329)

### Quotations

Readers have a right to assume that *every word* between quotation marks is what the speaker or writer said. . . . Unless the writer has detailed notes or a recording, it is usually wise to paraphrase long comments, since they may turn up worded differently on television or in other publications. "Approximate" quotations can undermine readers' trust. . . .

The writer should, of course, omit extraneous syllables like "um" and may judiciously delete false starts . . . .In every case, writer and editor must both be satisfied that the intent of the speaker has been preserved. Except in verbatim texts and excerpts, do not add material in brackets or use ellipses ( . . . ) to clarify or abridge the quoted material; those devices divert attention to the editing process. . . . (Siegal & Connelly, 2002, pp. 280–281)

## ADDITIONAL RESOURCES

American Psychological Association. (2001). *Publication manual of the American Psychological Association* (5th ed.). Washington, DC: Author.

Goldstein, N. (Ed.). (2000). The *Associated Press stylebook and briefing on media law*. Cambridge, MA: Perseus.

Guffey, M. E. (2007). *Essentials of business communication* (7th ed.). Mason, OH: South-Western.

Kirszner, L. G., & Mandell, S. R. (2005). *The Wadsworth handbook* [Instructor's Edition]. Boston: Thomson Wadsworth.

Lehman, C. M., & Dufrene, D. D. (2005). *Business communication* (14th ed.). Mason, OH: South-Western.

Woolever, K. R. (1999). *Writing for the technical professions.* New York: Addison Wesley Longman.

## REFERENCES

American Psychological Association. (2005). *Concise rules of APA style.* Washington, DC: Author.

Associated Press. (2007). *The Associated Press stylebook* (42nd ed.). New York: Basic Books.

Gibaldi, J. (2003). *MLA handbook for writers of research papers* (6th ed.). New York: Modern Language Association of America.

Siegal, A. M., & Connelly, W. G. (2002). *New York Times manual of style & usage* (Rev. and exp. ed.). New York: Three Rivers Press.

University of Chicago Press. (2003). *The Chicago manual of style: The essential guide for writers, editors, and publishers* (15th ed.). Chicago: Author.

# APPENDIX C
## *Effective Document Design*

T his appendix will concentrate on the visual image of your document. What good is a well-written fashion message if the physical appearance is so poor that the reader ignores the message? Creative document design is a necessary feature of effective writing.

Visual style is developed through document design—principles that help a writer determine how to design a piece of written work (Kirszner & Mandell, 2005). Writing fashion messages involves visual structure and creativity. Just as designers use the principles of art and design to create and structure beautiful garments, writers use design principles to help create and structure attractive fashion messages. If words are put on a page with no visual stimulation, readers are less likely to get excited about what they are reading. Using visual enhancements in a document increases the likelihood that the message will be read and understood. Of course, visual enhancements should be used only if they improve readability. If they distract the reader from the written message they should be omitted.

The goals of effective document design include the following:

1. Making the document easy to read
2. Showing the reader what is most important
3. In longer fashion messages, allowing for smooth transitions between sections

While the types of written fashion messages range from fashion journalism to fashion promotion to academic and business writing, all well-designed print messages share some general style characteristics, whether the message is a magazine article or a scholarly work or a Web page. These characteristics are discussed in detail below.

## WHITE SPACE

All documents should have some white space on each page. **White space** is the area that is intentionally left blank on a page. Some designers refer to this as negative space, or background. White space eliminates clutter and allows the reader's eyes to rest periodically.

Margins, indentations, and space around charts, graphs, and photographs create white space.

## MARGINS

**Margins** frame a page to keep it from looking overcrowded. Too much text on one page can cause reader fatigue. Generally, margins are at least one inch on all sides. Highly technical information will have wider margins to allow for eye rest and for space to make notes. Magazines and newspapers have narrower margins for cost savings.

## JUSTIFICATION

Alignment of text along a margin is called **justification**. Text aligned along the left margin only, with a "ragged" right edge, is **left-justified**. Readers of English-language materials are accustomed to left-justified text. Conversely, text that is aligned along the right margin with a ragged left edge is **right-justified. Center-justified**, or simply "centered," text is centered at the midpoint of a typed line. Centered text is often used for headings. Text aligned on both the right and left margins with no ragged edges is **full-justified**. Manuscript text is most often left-justified for the editing process and full-justified in print.

## INDENTATION

White space can also be created by **indentation**. For example, indenting the text one-half inch or five spaces is common at the beginning of a new paragraph. It is used as a visual transition, to alert readers that they are about to start reading about a new idea. Some writing styles, such as technical or business writing, call for extra line spaces instead of indentation.

## LINE SPACING

**Line spacing** is the amount of space between lines. Lines that are too far apart vertically lack unity, while lines that are too close together vertically appear crowded. **Single-spacing** means that no blank lines appear between rows of type. **Double-spacing** means that one blank line appears between lines of type. Most published materials are single-spaced, while, draft manuscripts are almost always double-spaced. **Triple-spacing** (two blank lines occurring between lines of text) is used very specifically in letter format between the complementary close and the typed signature.

## TYPEFACE AND TYPE SIZE

A **typeface** is a specifically designed set of letters, numbers, and punctuation marks. Readability is the most important characteristic for typeface selection. Typefaces are either serif or sans serif. **Serif** type, which is distinguished by small lines or tails that finish the ends of letters, is the better choice for readability. For this reason, Times New Roman is the default typeface for many word processing programs.

```
Times New Roman
Times New Roman
Arial
Arial
```

FIGURE C.1. Typeface and type size examples.

**Sans serif** type is characterized by bold, clean strokes without serifs. Arial is an example of a sans serif typeface. Although not as readable as serif typefaces, sans serif typefaces are often selected because of their modern appearance. Sans serif typefaces are often used on Web sites.

**Type size** is the size of the typeface, measured in "points." One inch has 72 points, so 1 point is equal to 1/72 of an inch. Font sizes can be changed within a document to add emphasis and interest. When fashion messages are reproduced in advertisements, brochures, Web pages, or other promotion messages, a wide variety of typefaces and types sizes may be used. For most draft messages, a 10-point or 12-point type size is preferred.

A **font** refers to the complete range of capital letters, small capital letters, lowercase letters, numerals, and punctuation marks for a particular typeface in a particular type size. Figure C.1 shows the fonts for two different typefaces—one serif and one sans serif—in two type sizes.

## TYPOGRAPHICAL EMPHASIS

In addition to using a variety of typefaces and types sizes to create emphasis in a written document, you can use such typographical elements as underlining, italics, and boldface. Underlining draws the eye to a word. *Italics* and **boldface** can convey special meaning to words. Italics are also commonly used in writing to identify names of publications (*Women's Wear Daily*), movies (*Breakfast at Tiffany's*), and television shows (*America's Next Top Model*).

## HEADINGS

**Headings** direct the reader among sections of the document. They're arranged hierarchically, with major headings receiving more attention than minor headings. If you have developed your document from an outline, your headings are already developed.

Most style guides dictate levels of headings. Figure C.2 shows five levels of headings in the style used in the American Psychological Association (APA) style guide.

Headings should not be confused with page headers.

## PAGE HEADER OR FOOTER

This visual enhancement is used on longer documents to help readers quickly recall where they are in the document. Also called a **running head**, a **page header** is an abbreviated title

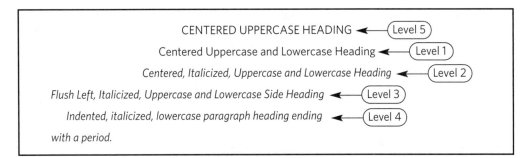

**FIGURE C.2.** Five levels of headings in the style used in the American Psychological Association (APA) style guide.

that, along with the page number, is typed usually one-half inch from the top of the page within margin guidelines.

This textbook has a running head. On even-numbered pages, the part title appears as the running head. On odd-numbered pages, the chapter title appears as the running head. Another book might have the book title on the even-numbered pages and the chapter title on the odd-numbered pages. Again, the purpose is to help readers quickly recall where they are in the document.

Some publications put this information at the bottom of the page instead of at the top, in which case the visual enhancement is referred to as a **footer** or **running foot**. *Vogue* magazine, for example, uses footers. The name and the issue date appear along the bottom of the page at the outside margin, and www.vogue.com appears near the inside margin.

## PAGE NUMBERS

**Page numbering** is the consecutive numbering of pages throughout the document. Style guides offer standard guidelines. Often, page numbers appear either at the outside corner of the page when a page header is used or at the bottom center of the page in a footer. A page number may or may not be used on the first page of a document. The American Psychological Association (APA) and Modern Language Association (MLA) style guides consider the title page to be the first page of the document, using the arabic numeral 1. In business writing and book publishing, the front matter (the portion of the book that includes the Table of Contents, Preface, and several other items) is numbered in lowercase roman numerals (starting with *i*); then the arabic numbering begins on the first page of the main text (starting with *1*).

## BULLETS AND LISTS

When you are writing about items in a series or when you show a list that is set off from the text, place a numeral, letter, or bullet before each element. Use letters or numerals if items are listed in order of most important to least important. Using the letter *A* implies that an item is more important than the item lettered *B*; the numeral *1* implies that an item is more important than the item numbered *2*. If all items in the series are of equal importance, use bullets or similar symbols (for example, •, ✓, ◊, +).

## KEY TERMS

| | |
|---|---|
| Center-justified | Page numbering |
| Double-spacing | Right-justified |
| Font | Running foot |
| Footer | Running head |
| Full-justified | Sans serif |
| Headings | Serif |
| Indentation | Single-spacing |
| Justification | Triple-spacing |
| Left-justified | Type face |
| Line spacing | Type size |
| Margins | White space |
| Page header | |

## REFERENCE

Kirszner, L. G., & Mandell, S. R. (2005). *The Wadsworth handbook* [Instructor's Edition]. Boston: Thomson Wadsworth.

# APPENDIX D

## *Web Source Location and Evaluation*

Global acceptance and adoption of the World Wide Web (WWW, or simply "the Web") has been almost astronomical. Since virtually anyone can post information to the Web, a big concern is the reliability and validity of the information that is available. More information about reliability and validity is provided in Chapter 9, "Scholarly Writing."

Before the use of the Internet became widespread, journalism and other forms of writing required documentation of facts; they also followed specific writing standards. Now, anyone can post opinions and beliefs that do not have to meet any particular set of writing standards. For example, how do we evaluate an authority on the Web? According to Fischler (2007), a new crop of beauty advisors has appeared on such Web sites as YouTube. Anyone, whether the person has beauty training or not, can create videos about makeup application or virtually any other topic, then upload those videos for the world to see. Opinion can easily become interpreted as fact.

Students who are writing term papers or conducting research find many Web sites that offer historical information and what appear to be facts. Sometimes the author of a historical Web site can be identified, but how credible is the site when the author fails to list the original sources of his information. Some of the information may appear valid, but what if the contents cannot be verified? Appendix D looks at the way we locate information, and it provides some guidance on how to determine whether a Web site is acceptable for research purposes.

## LOCATING SOURCES

We have all become quite adept at using personal computers. Almost anyone can find information, use it in creating a document, and share the results almost instantaneously. Posting documents online puts information in a user's hands with just a few keystrokes.

For conducting research, we have two main tools to work with:

- Search engines that are familiar to most Internet users
- Scholarly resources that are found through searchable databases

## SEARCH ENGINES

A **search engine** is a software program that allows an Internet user to look for information by topic. Examples of currently popular search engines are Google, MSN, Yahoo!, and Ask.com.

Search engines locate information from various kinds of resources—from newspaper articles to blogs, Wikis (sites designed for online collaborations), group discussions, and chat rooms (real-time electronic exchanges between individuals). Some of these sources are reliable, while others supply only opinions, without much research credibility. Since search engines cannot type or think, most are simply subject directories—sometimes offering good suggestions and other times offering irrelevant information.

## SEARCHABLE DATABASES

Our second tool for conducting research is searchable databases. Specialized searchable databases find information differently than search engines do. **Searchable databases** find citations (and sometimes full text articles) and other materials that are delivered to the researcher as Web pages generated exclusively in response to a search. Searchable databases are generally a collection of citations that are linked to publishers, academic libraries, or other scholarly resources. These specialized databases for various subjects or topics are typically located on library Web sites.

**Academic databases** contain information from books, newspapers, journals, reports, and other scholarly resources. These sources are more closely aligned with traditional research methodology. Also, academic searchable databases are generally considered to be more credible resources than the more generally available search engines. The primary way to use a searchable database is to enter subject headings (descriptors) and keywords.

The following are some of the most popular searchable databases:

- **EBSCOhost**—Consists of multiple databases. Two popular ones are the Academic Search Premier database and the Business Source Premier, which make available full-text articles from scholarly publications in all academic subjects.
- **Education Resources Information Center (ERIC)**—Education publications are listed in this database.
- **Government Documents Catalog Service (GDCS)**—This resource, which is updated monthly, contains records of all publications printed by the United States Government Printing Office since 1979.
- **InfoTrac Web**—This Web-based service searches bibliographic and other databases, such as *the General Reference Center Gold*, *General Business File*, *ASAP*, and *Health Reference Center*.
- **LexisNexis Academic**—This online service provides full-text access to over 6,000 newspapers, professional publications, legal references, and congressional sources; it is updated daily.
- **ScienceDirect**—This database for scientific research contains the full text of more than 1,000 Elsevier Science journals in the life, physical, medical, technical, and social sciences.

---

### Box D.1 Google It

During the time this book is being written, Google is considered to be one of the most popular search engines. It has even moved into popular language as a verb. According to Cole and Schickman (2007), to *Google* a name or other word means to research for the word through Internet sources.

Simply speaking, using a search engine such as Google is about locating information on the Web. Yet, Google is also one of the best search engines in the *business* of search. Google is a business enterprise. To make money, it sells space for advertisers to post small text ads alongside the search results. According to Helft and Sorkin (2007), due to its search and search advertising technology Google makes more money in a fiscal quarter than Yahoo makes in a year.

---

# EVALUATING SOURCES

You need to evaluate sources based upon your writing needs and your audience. Are you preparing a response to an entry in an online chatroom or a blog? Are you doing research for your clothing history class? Each of these endeavors requires different levels of resource credibility.

When you are evaluating sources, there are two primary points to consider:

- Whether the source is based upon popular characteristics or scholarly ones
- Whether the Web site's content meets certain quality criteria

## POPULAR OR SCHOLARLY SOURCES

When determining whether a source is popular or scholarly, consider the audience and purpose of the publication. You may start your research with popular resources, but you need to look at scholarly resources in order to become fully informed. Maimon, Peritz, and Yancey (2007, p. 216) identify characteristics that define a source as popular or scholarly.

### *Popular Sources*

- Are widely available on newsstands and in retail stores
- Accept advertising for a wide range of consumer goods
- In the case of books, are themselves widely advertised
- Are printed on magazine paper with a color cover
- Are published by a commercial publishing house or media company (such as Time Warner)

- Include a wide range of topics in each issue, from international affairs to popular entertainment

## Scholarly Sources

- Are found generally in libraries, not on newsstands
- Include articles with extensive citations and bibliographies
- Are refereed, which means that each article has been reviewed, commented on, and accepted for publication by other scholars in the field
- List article titles and authors on the cover
- Include articles mostly by authors who are affiliated with a college, a museum, or some other scholarly institution
- Are published by a scholarly or nonprofit organization, often in association with a university press
- Focus on discipline-specific topics

## EVALUATING THE QUALITY OF A WEB SITE

Unlike the content of journals, magazines, and newspapers found in research-oriented libraries, on many Web sites the content has not been conscientiously examined by experienced editors or peer evaluators. The following checklist, "Assessing the Quality of a Web Site," will help you evaluate the value and acceptability of Web sources:

### CHECKLIST FOR ASSESSING THE QUALITY OF A WEB SITE

## Authority

- ☐ Is the site trustworthy? (Is it based upon a credible print source, such as an authoritative magazine or newspaper?)
- ☐ Are the author and her credentials clearly identified?
- ☐ Is the source known? (Does it have support from a trusted media company, educational institution, or research organization?)
- ☐ Is the site free from grammar and spelling errors?
- ☐ Are hyperlinks functional?
- ☐ Does the site have a credible domain (.com, .org, .edu, .gov, .net)?

## Currency

- ☐ How old is the information?
- ☐ Is some of the information obviously out of date?
- ☐ What is the date of the Web page?

## Accuracy

- ☐ Does the site provide evidence for its assertions?
- ☐ Is the argument and use of evidence apparent and reasonable?

☐ Is the site detailed, with text in full paragraph form?
☐ Is the site comprehensive, including archives, links, and additional resources?
☐ Does the site value completeness and accuracy?

## *Substance*

☐ What is the purpose of the site (to entertain, to provide information, to persuade, or to sell)?
☐ How is the page classified (popular or scholarly, news or personal opinion, information or commerce)?
☐ Is the site fair, balanced, and objective?
☐ Does the site make its purpose clear?
☐ Is the site easy to navigate?

## *Support*

☐ Does the site list sources for its information (providing links where available)?
☐ Does the site clarify which content it is responsible for and give credit to links created by unrelated authors or sponsors?
☐ Does the site provide contact information for its authors and/or sponsors?
☐ If the site is an academic resource, does it correctly follow a citation style (APA, MLA, or another accepted style)?

Adapted from: Maimon, E. P., Peritz, J. H., & Yancey, K. B. (2007). *A writer's resource: A handbook for writing and research* (2nd ed.). New York: McGraw-Hill.

## KEY TERMS
Academic database
Search engine
Searchable database

## REFERENCES

Cole, P., & Schickman, M. I. (2007, March 26). Yahoo for Google! *New York Times*. Retrieved June 21, 2007, from LexisNexis Academic Database.

Fischler, A. S. (2007, June 21). Putting on lip gloss, and a show, for YouTube viewers. *New York Times*, p. E3.

Helft, M., & Sorkin, A. R. (2007, June 20). After shake-up, what now for Yahoo? *New York Times*. Retrieved June 21, 2007, from NewsBank Database.

Maimon, E. P., Peritz, J. H., & Yancey, K. B. (2007). *A writer's resource: A handbook for writing and research* (2nd ed.). New York: McGraw-Hill.

# APPENDIX E

## *Oral Presentations*

This appendix is offered to assist you in making oral presentations. Oral presentations are used in many situations. For example, public relations specialists are called on to make speeches, scholarly writers present findings as oral presentations at professional meetings, and business professionals are often asked to make oral presentations during business meetings.

## SPEECHES

A **speech** is a scripted oration to be delivered by an individual in front of an audience. In many cases, the speaker is not the writer. Therefore, the writer must study the speaker and help make the oration sound like the speaker, not the writer, at her best. The speaker is the medium through whom the message is delivered.

The audience for a speech is a group of people interested in what the speaker has to say. For example, the CEO of a nonprofit agency speaks to an audience of potential volunteers, or a corporate business leader addresses stockholders about the company's successes and failures during the past six months. Effective speeches are well organized and short, focused upon the interests of the audience.

## PREPARING AN EASY-TO-USE MANUSCRIPT

Most speeches are printed on paper as a manuscript for the speaker. In some venues, the speech is typed into a computer where it is delivered to a transparent screen, known by the brand name "TelePrompTer," from which the speaker can read the speech. Other speakers prefer to speak from an outline, from note cards, or from a Microsoft Power-Point® presentation. The PowerPoint software allows the speaker to print a notes page, which shows the slide viewed by the audience as well as personal notes for the speaker. Figure E.1 shows an example of a speech manuscript.

A speech script should be easy for the speaker to read, so that he can look up from it and make frequent eye contact with the audience. The copy should be typed in a large font size with triple or even quadruple spacing between the lines. Wide margins are also helpful. If the text is typed on only the upper two thirds of the sheet of paper, the speaker's chin will not dip too low as she reads.

If a manuscript is used, pages should be numbered in the upper right corner; they should be clearly separated from the text, so the speaker will be able to keep the pages in order and avoid accidentally reading the page number out loud. Type the term "-more-" at the bottom of each continuing page, and type "-end-" below the last line of the speech (this is similar to the format used for a news release).

Leave the pages of the manuscript unstapled, so they can be turned easily and quietly. Any one of a variety of binding methods may be used, depending on the speaker's preference. For example, a paper clip can hold the pages together, and the speaker can simply remove the clip when he reaches the lectern. Another speaker might prefer to place the manuscript in a thin three-ring binder.

If the speaker will be using visual aids—such as PowerPoint slides, an easel, or posters—make a notation in the speech manuscript to indicate where the next visual should be accessed or where a gesture should be made. Highlight these signals in the text by using a color highlighter, placing a notation in the margins, or inserting a note in capital letters in parentheses—for example, "(POINT TO GRAPH)"—in the body of the speech.

## ORGANIZING THE SPEECH

Although there are many ways to organize a speech, almost all speeches have an introduction, a body, and a conclusion.

- The introduction builds up to the main point of the message to be delivered. You might begin by thanking the audience for attending or by sharing a brief anecdote. Consider opening with a provocative question or an outrageous statement to capture the audience's attention.
- The body is the elaboration of the main point: the reason for listening to the speech. Using visual aids, if appropriate and available, will improve the audience's retention of the materials presented orally.
- The conclusion is a brief reiteration of the message, with a dramatic or memorable spin.

## REHEARSING THE SPEECH

Speechwriting strategies include writing for the ear, not the eye. Read the speech out loud prior to delivery and listen to how the message sounds. Sentences should be short. Instead of using conjunctions such as *and* to unite two sentences into one, use two sentences. Keep the language simple, and avoid big, pretentious words. Avoid technical terms unless you are sure the audience knows and understands them. As is done in radio or television scripts, spell out numbers and phonetically spell tough words or names. Keep the speech memorable by focusing on no more than two or three key ideas.

**KIDS NEED YOUR HELP!**

I CAN'T THANK YOU ENOUGH FOR INVITING ME HERE TO SPEAK WITH YOU TONIGHT…AND… I CAN'T THINK OF A BETTER TOPIC THAN HELPING KIDS. I REPRESENT THE LUCKY BRAND FOUNDATION AND BRING GREETINGS FROM LUCKY BRAND JEANS FOUNDERS GENE MONTESANO AND BARRY PERLMAN.

GENE AND BARRY ARE COMMITTED TO BRINGING HAPPINESS…COMFORT AND HOPE TO DISABLED CHILDREN. THE FOUNDATION BELIEVES THAT ITS DONATIONS CAN TRULY IMPACT THE QUALITY OF LIFE AND WELL-BEING OF CHILDREN, AND MAKE A DIFFERENCE IN THEIR LIVES.

SINCE ITS INCEPTION IN NINETEEN-NINETY SIX…THE FOUNDATION HAS BEEN SUCCESSFUL IN RAISING OVER SIX MILLION DOLLARS THROUGH ITS ANNUAL BLACK TIE AND BLUE JEANS GALA.

THE PROCEEDS FROM THIS EVENT AND OTHER SIMILAR EVENTS HELD AROUND THE COUNTRY GO DIRECTLY TO HELP KIDS IN NEED. OUR MISSION STATEMENT FOLLOWS: THE LUCKY BRAND FOUNDATION IS A CHARITABLE ORGANIZATION COMMITTED TO BRINGING HAPPINESS…COMFORT AND HOPE TO DISADVANTAGED AND DISABLED CHILDREN. DONATIONS MADE BY THE FOUNDATION ARE DESIGNATED FOR THE IMMEDIATE AND SPECIFIC NEEDS OF THE SELECTED CHARITY OR FOR THE PURCHASE OF SPECIFIC ITEMS ON BEHALF OF THE CHARITY…AND MAY NOT BE USED IN ANY PART FOR ADMINISTRATIVE COSTS.

- MORE -

**FIGURE E.1.**   Example of a speech manuscript. *(continued)*

2

I CALL ON YOU TO INCREASE YOUR INVESTMENT IN OUR YOUNG PEOPLE.
BY BIDDING ON OUR SILENT AUCTION ITEMS AND SPONSORING FUTURE
EVENTS…YOU CAN MAKE A DIFFERENCE!

ENJOY THE EVENING…KNOWING THAT YOUR SUPPORT HERE TONIGHT AT
THE BLACK TIE & BLUE JEANS GALA HELPS KIDS THAT REALLY NEED YOUR
HELP!

-END-

FIGURE E.1.

# PLANNING THE DETAILS

In addition to strategically writing speeches, you should be aware of the needs of the speaker and the limitations of the venue. Before the speech is delivered, both the speech-writer and the speaker should consider the items in the following checklist.

### CHECKLIST FOR SPEECHES

☐ **Research**—Analyze the purpose or main reason for the speech, the expected audience, and the media or technology available at the venue. How much time is the speaker allowed? Will there be questions from the audience at the end of the presentation?

☐ **Plan**—Write an outline based upon the strategic message. How much time is allowed for the speech? Where will the speech be given? Is the venue inside or outside? Is there a lectern and microphone? Will a glass of water be available? Consider whether it is appropriate to use visual aids, depending upon availability. Have a backup plan if the technology does not work.

☐ **Rehearse**—Read the speech aloud before giving it to the speaker. Ideally, the speaker will have time before the actual presentation to rehearse in front of colleagues who will evaluate the speech and offer suggestions for improving it. It is better to learn about errors or timing problems before the actual performance. Have more than one copy of the speech in the room, in case the main copy gets lost. If possible, test the technology before the audience arrives.

☐ **Communicate**—Deliver the speech with confidence. Smile, if it is not inappropriate. (Delivering news about illness or business failure requires a more somber mood.) Maintain eye contact. If media fail, move with assurance to the backup system, without hiding the problems. The audience will respect your having had the foresight to anticipate problems.

☐ **Evaluate**—Relax and enjoy the results of your work. But, ask yourself what worked well and what did not. Analyze how the technology worked and whether the timing worked out as planned. Did anything happen that you did not expect? Learn from successes and failures, and build upon them for future presentations.

Take a look at two sections later in this appendix—Nonverbal Messages and Using Visuals. They may have value for a speech as well as a business presentation.

# MAKING BUSINESS PRESENTATIONS

**Business presentations** are opportunities—such as sales presentations, informational and motivational presentations, briefings, status reports, training sessions, and interviews—where you, as the writer and the presenter, are commanding the attention of the audience though your public speaking skills.

In addition to having expectations about their staff's writing ability, employers want employees who can speak to an audience of customers, clients, team members, or management about the topics they have been writing about. Business presentations in fashion include trend reports, promotion strategies, buyer reports, and a myriad of other fashion-related topics. Business presentations allow multiple people to hear the information simultaneously and provide immediate feedback. Presentations can greatly reduce the message distortion that can occur when sender and receiver are not face-to-face.

Preparing a business presentation is similar to preparing other business communications. You need to identify your purpose, know your audience, and organize the content thoughtfully. Keep this in mind as you write: People comprehend information at a faster rate when they read it than when they hear it. Therefore, in order to remember important facts from a presentation, the audience should hear the information three times. This may seem repetitious to the presenter, but it is very helpful to the listener.

Effective presentations are organized into three parts: introduction, body, and close.

1. **Introduction**—Briefly tell the audience what you are going to say.
2. **Body**—Expand on the points you set up in the introduction.
3. **Close**—Summarize the points that you made in the body of the presentation.

## INTRODUCTION

Giving a business presentation is much like putting on a fashion show or other theatrical performance. The show's opening is critical to the show's success because it gets the audience involved right away. This is where you present your purpose statement and preview the main points of your presentation. An effective introduction also captures the audience's attention, and it establishes rapport between you and your audience. Lehman & Dufrene (2005) suggest a few techniques for getting your audience's attention:

- A shocking statement or startling statistic
- A quotation by an expert or a well-known person
- An open-ended question, or a rhetorical question that generates discussion
- A humorous sketch or joke (if it is appropriate and if you can carry it off)
- A demonstration or dramatic presentation
- A related story or anecdote
- A personal reference, a compliment to the audience, or a reference to the occasion of the presentation

## BODY

A typical business presentation lasts 20 to 30 minutes. As the presenter, you need to determine the three to five most important points to be delivered to the audience and limit your presentation to these. After you have determined your major points, decide what evidence you will use to ensure that the audience understands your points. Lehman & Dufrene (2005) suggest these techniques for use in the body of the presentation:

- Use easy-to-understand vocabulary and sentence structure in order to sound conversational and interesting.
- Avoid jargon or technical terms that the audience may not understand.

I. Introduction

    A. Your name (spoken clearly and loud enough for everyone to hear)

    B. Attention-getter

    C. Purpose of the presentation

    D. Preview of what you will say

II. Body of Presentation

    A. Main idea 1

        i. Evidence

    B. Main idea 2

        i. Evidence

    C. Main idea 3

        i. Evidence

III. Conclusion

    A. Summary of what you have presented (do not present new
information in the Summary)

    B. Memorable close

FIGURE E.2. Speaking outline.

- Provide relevant statistics that are easy for the audience to understand when they hear them. For example, if sales were $64,831 for the month of November, the audience will better understand "Sales in November were nearly sixty-five thousand dollars." In a written report you would report actual sales, but in a spoken presentation the audience will more easily understand the rounded-off number.
- Use quotes from well-known people. Be aware, though, that you can read faster than the audience can comprehend, so read slowly to make sure your point is made.
- To make your points more easily understood, use presentation visuals such as handouts, whiteboards, flip charts, transparencies, electronic presentations, or demonstrations.

## CLOSE

Returning to the fashion show example, the end of every show should be well coordinated and powerful, leaving the audience satisfied and applauding with a great last impression. Closing a business presentation should accomplish the same thing (although wild applause may be too much to expect). Your close provides unity to the presentation when you repeat the main points of your presentation one last time. You should develop a close that supports and refocuses the audience's attention on the opening purpose statement. The following techniques from Lehman & Dufrene (2005) can help you accomplish this:

- Do not wait until the end to prepare your conclusion. Commit time and energy to developing a creative, memorable conclusion.
- Tie the conclusion to the introduction to bring your presentation full circle.
- Use transition words to let the audience know you are moving to the conclusion.
- Practice your conclusion so that you can deliver it with confidence.
- Smile, stand back and say "Thank you," and accept the audience's applause. Be sure that you have said "Thank you" or made some other closing statement so the audience knows you have finished.

## NONVERBAL MESSAGES

Although you might think your message is compelling enough to keep your audience's attention, you also need to have command of the nonverbal messages you send when giving a business presentation. This includes your image, your voice, and the gestures you use during the performance. Guffey (2007) provides the following suggestions to ensure that your presentation is well received:

- **Look sharp.** You will be judged by your appearance, so look professional and act in a professional manner. See Chapter 12, "Writing Employment Messages," for specific examples of professional dress.
- **Show enthusiasm with your body.** Stand up straight. Do not lean on the podium or grasp the sides of the podium. Use gestures to make points, and show confidence in what you are saying. Convince the audience that you are enjoying yourself.
- **Vary the tone, pitch, volume, and pace of your speaking voice.** Be sure to pause often so the audience can think about what you have said and can catch up with your next point.
- **Get out from behind the podium.** Movement makes you look natural and like you feel at ease with your audience.
- **Vary your facial expressions.** Smile and make eye contact with various people in the audience. Change your expression to mimic what you are speaking about. Be serious, or light-hearted, depending on the point you are making.

## USING VISUALS

A business presentation that is accompanied by visual aids is more likely to be remembered. A variety of visuals aids are available for use. Before deciding on a visual aid, find out what your audience's preferences are and what equipment is available for use. Consider theses options:

- **Electronic presentation**—A series of electronic slides created and stored on a computer (As mentioned previously, PowerPoint is a common software package used for electronic presentations.)
- **Overhead transparencies**—Clear plastic sheets that contain words or graphics shown on an overhead project and projected onto a large screen
- **Whiteboard or chalkboard**—Writing surfaces that allow for brainstorming (may be too informal for some presentations)
- **Flip chart**—Large sheets of paper attached to a tablet-like easel (allows ideas to be recorded during a discussion)
- **Other visual aids**—For example, 35-millimeter slides, television or videotapes, movies, CDs, DVDs, and other digital media

## CREATING VISUALS FOR ELECTRONIC PRESENTATIONS

Electronic presentations and overhead transparencies are the two most popular visual aids used in business. Many of the same techniques can be used to create either one of these visual aids. A good visual aid will direct the audience to major points but not *every* point. As the presenter, you need to determine what the major points are and limit the visuals to those points. A visual aid is also a good tool for clarifying or illustrating complex information. Statistics that are difficult to comprehend when the audience is simply listening can be made comprehensible through the use of a pie chart or a table. Do not read your visual aids word-for-word, as they become boring. They should accent the presentation, not replace it.

Limit the number of visuals you use during a presentation. Having too many visuals can detract from your message. Bovée and Thill (2006) recommend one slide for every 90 seconds you speak. So, for a 30-minute presentation you should have about 20 slides. However, if you are going to provide discussion with each slide you should use fewer than that. The only way to determine how many slides to use is to practice, practice, practice.

The slides should have a simple, clean design that creates a sense of continuity and consistency. Consistent use of text alignment, typeface and size, graphics, color, and other design elements will help create a sense of continuity. Do not clutter your slides. Present only one main idea on each slide. Too much detail causes the audience to focus on less important facts. To engage the audience, the title of a slide should reflect the exact content of the slide; limit the title to four words if possible. If you use bulleted or numbered lists, use parallel construction in the text of those items. Use capital letters sparingly. If words written in all capital letters are too long, the audience will see not the word as a whole but rather each individual letter. Generally, when you are creating slides omit the punctuation unless it is necessary. You may need a comma at some point in a sentence, but probably not the period at the end of the sentence. Be sure to punctuate direct quotes with the usual quotation marks. Avoid abbreviations; they present the same problem as jargon if the audience is not familiar with the abbreviation.

Finally, select a font that is easy to read from a distance. For the entire presentation, limit the number of different fonts to no more than three and limit the number of different colors to no more than four. Do not fill more than 75% of the slide; leave some white space. Finally, try to use the $7 \times 7$ rule: no more than 7 lines to a page and no more than 7 words per line.

## KEY TERMS
Business presentations
Speech

## REFERENCES

Bovée, C. L., & Thill, J. V. (2006). *Business communication essentials* (2nd ed.). Upper Saddle River, NJ: Prentice Hall.

Guffey, M. E. (2007). *Essentials of business communication* (7th ed.). Mason, OH: Thomson South-Western.

Lehman, C. M., & Dufrene, D. D. (2005). *Business communication* (14th ed.). Mason, OH: South-Western.

# GLOSSARY

This Glossary contains brief definitions of the boldfaced terms presented in each chapter. For further reference, the chapter or appendix in which a term is introduced appears in parentheses at the end of the definition.

**Abstract** Summary of an article or research study before it is submitted in final form. (Ch. 9)

**Academic database** A type of searchable database that contains information from books, newspapers, journals, reports, and other scholarly resources. (App. D)

**Academic writing** *See* Scholarly writing.

**Acquisitions editor** The employee at the publishing company who is responsible for bringing in new works. (Ch. 10)

**Active voice** Sentences that emphasize the person or thing performing an action. (Ch. 2)

**Advance** A cash payment that the publisher pays the author prior to publication. (Ch. 10)

**Advertising** Any nonpersonal information, paid for and controlled by the sponsoring organization, that contains information about the organization, product, service, or idea created by the sponsoring firm to influence sales. (Ch. 6)

**Advertising agency** A full-service firm that is involved in planning, creating, and producing advertising; selecting and buying media time or space; and evaluating advertising effectiveness. (Ch. 6)

**Advertising appeal** Method used for attracting the target audience's interest in the client's products or services. (Ch. 6)

**AIDA** A type of organizational plan; the letters stand for Attention, Interest, Desire, and Action. (Ch. 11)

**Analytical report** Documents that provide supporting information, analyses, and recommendations to help managers make informed decisions. (Ch. 11)

**Anecdotal** A type of journalistic story structure that allows the writer to concentrate on an individual or a group that represents a larger population. (Ch. 3)

**Announcement ad** Grocery ad, one-day sale ad, and special-occasion ad (such as President's Day or Day after Thanksgiving Early Bird Specials) that is found everyday in newspapers. (Ch. 6)

**Announcer continuity script** A script that consists of only the words that the announcer will read during a live, real-time broadcast. (Ch. 6)

**Annual report** A document that consists of recent financial records, a year-to-year comparison of financial figures, a description of the organization's upper management team, and a discussion of the firm's goals and objectives. (Ch. 7)

**Antagonist** One of the main characters in a story; the figure, often "bad," who stands in opposition to the protagonist. (Ch. 10)

**Appendix(es)** Supplemental information needed to clarify a report or proposal; can include survey instruments, letters, maps, optional tables, brochures, and other information. (Ch. 11)

**Application letter (cover letter)** A letter written to accompany a résumé; used to provide a personal sales message that is specific to the position the job applicant is applying for. *See also* General application letter; Targeted application letter. (Ch. 12)

**Appreciation letter (thank-you or follow-up letter)** A brief letter that an interviewee writes and sends immediately after an interview to let a business know that the interviewee is still interested in the position. (Ch. 12)

**Audience** The particular viewer or group of readers that a piece is targeted to. (Ch. 2)

**Auxiliary level** The fashion press, research and consulting services, trade associations, and other services that support the work of the primary, secondary, and retail levels simultaneously. (Ch. 1)

**Backgrounder** A supplement to a news release that includes such information as a biography of a key individual mentioned in the news release or a history of the organization. (Ch. 7)

**Bad news message** Message to which the reader is expected to react negatively. (Ch. 11)

**Bar chart** A figure or graphic that compares items to one another using vertical or horizontal bars. (Ch. 11)

**Beauty editor** The person who is responsible for doing extensive market research within the beauty industry, as well as writing, editing, and producing the magazine's beauty and grooming pages. (Ch. 4)

**Bias-free** Word choice and expressions that are free of prejudice toward gender, sexual orientation, racial or ethnic group, disability, or age. (Ch. 2)

**Bibliography** An alphabetized list of all the sources a writer uses when conducting research. (Ch. 9)

**Blind review** Anonymous members of a review board, experts in the field, who examine a manuscript before the article is accepted for publication. (Ch. 9)

**Block letter format** All letter parts and paragraphs start at the left margin. Paragraphs are not indented five spaces; instead, the text is single-spaced and there is double-spacing between paragraphs. (Ch. 11)

**Blog** Personal journal published on the World Wide Web. (Ch. 8)

**Book proposal** A document, outlining your idea and the market potential for your book, that you prepare and send to a literary agent or publisher. (Ch. 10)

**Bookings editor** The person who is responsible for securing models and hair and makeup artists and finding locations for photo shoots for a magazine. (Ch. 4)

**Boutique** A small, individually owned store that carries unique inventory items that other types of stores consider too risky to try to sell. (Ch. 1)

**Broadcasting** The airborne transmission of electromagnetic signals—audio signals for radio and audiovisual signals for television—that are available to a vast audience through widely available receivers. (Ch. 5)

**Broadsheet** The newspaper style, which measures 13 inches by 21.5 inches, used in the United States. (Ch. 3)

**Buffer statement** A neutral, noncontroversial declaration that both sender and receiver can agree on; the sender would include such text when delivering bad news. (Ch. 11)

**Business presentation** Opportunities—such as sales presentations, informational and motivational presentations, briefings, status reports, training sessions, and interviews—where you are commanding the attention of the audience through your public speaking skills. (App. E)

**Business-to-business magazine** Periodical published for a specific business, industry, or occupation. (Ch. 4)

**Byline** A line of text identifying the author of the story. (Ch. 8)

**Career** A profession for which one trains and that one undertakes as a permanent calling. (Ch. 12)

**Career ladder** The upward progression of jobs, each job building on the experience, responsibilities, and financial compensation of the previous job. (Ch. 12)

**Catalog retailing** Type of nonstore retailing that uses the mail as a distribution vehicle; provides toll-free phone numbers for customers to call to place their order, and uses credit card payments to close the sale. (Ch. 1)

**Category killer** Form of retailing in which superstores carry one type of good that is offered at great depth at low prices because of volume buying. (Ch. 1)

**Center-justified** Text is centered at the midpoint of a typed line. (Also referred to simply as *centered* text.) (App. C)

**Central idea** *See* Purpose statement. (Ch. 2)

**Chain organization** A group of four or more centrally owned stores. (Ch. 1)

**Channel** Method by which a message is translated in the communication model. (Ch. 1)

**Chronological order** The story starts at the beginning and runs through the end; especially useful when a series of events takes place. (Ch. 3)

**Chronological résumé** A traditional organization format for résumés, focusing on work history and education. (Ch. 12)

**Chunk** Information structured in a information units for Web-based writing. (Ch. 8)

**Citation** A method of giving credit to the original author or expert in written works. (Ch. 10)

**Claim** A request for an adjustment such as a refund, a replacement product, or a correction to a billing statement. (Ch. 11)

**Collaboration** Working with a ghostwriter, a partner, or a group of writers.

**Communication** The transmission or exchange of information and/or messages. (Ch. 1)

**Complex sentence** A sentence that includes one independent clause and one or more dependent clauses. (Ch. 2)

**Compound sentence** A sentence that contains two or more independent clauses connected by conjunctions (*and*, *but*, *because*, *since*, *until*, and others). (Ch. 2)

**Compound subject** Two or more nouns or pronouns linked by a conjunction, such as *and*, *but*, *or*, or *nor*. (Ch. 2)

**Compound–complex sentence** A sentence that contains at least two independent clauses and at least one dependent clause. (Ch. 2)

**Concept board** A collection of photos, sketches, and swatches that expresses trends, themes, and the design direction for a grouping, including color, silhouette, and fabric. (Ch. 1)

**Conclusion** A logical interpretation of the facts arrived at from collected research. (Ch. 11)

**Consumer magazine** Periodical that is targeted to the general public or to specialized groups that have specific interests in common—such as fashion, beauty, shelter, shopping, or some other, more narrowly defined niche. (Ch. 4)

**Consumer publication** Publication written with consumers as the intended audience. (Ch. 1)

**Contributing editor**  Freelance writer who contributes to the magazine frequently. (Ch. 4)

**Contributor**  Freelance writer who contributes to a magazine frequently. (Ch. 4)

**Convergence**  Alliances among print media (newspapers or magazines), broadcast media (broadcast or cable television and radio), and other forms of electronic media (the Internet and wireless communication devices). (Ch. 8)

**Converter**  Textile business that transforms greige goods into finished fabric through mechanical or chemical means. (Ch. 1)

**Copy editor**  Working on a tight deadline, the person who reviews the text of a manuscript for spelling, content, style, word usage, and grammar, and also resolves queries on proofs. (Ch. 4)

**Copyediting**  Checking for grammar, spelling, consistencies, and facts. (Ch. 10)

**Copyright**  A legal authorization that allows the author or artist to publish or sell a literary or artistic piece with protection from unauthorized use or duplication by others. (Ch. 10)

**Corporate culture**  The mixture of values, traditions, and habits that gives a company its atmosphere or personality. (Ch. 12)

**Cost sheet**  Record of cost of labor and materials for each style manufactured for a line. (Ch. 1)

**Cover letter**  Letter used to identify the purpose and content of a media kit. (Ch. 7). *See* Application letter. (Ch. 12).

**Creative director**  Title invented by Alex Liberman, editorial director of Condé Nast, for Anna Wintour in 1983 before she was promoted to editor-in-chief of *Vogue* (Ch. 4)

**Credibility**  A writer's ability to be believed because he or she is reliable and worthy of confidence. (Ch. 11)

**Cross-promotion**  An integrated promotional message that is presented across multiple media. (Ch. 6)

**Cross-sectional study**  Study in which data are gathered at one point in time, from a cross-section of the population, to find out an issue or a problem. (Ch. 9)

**Cue**  In broadcasting, you give your audience a hint of what is coming next, hoping that they will stay tuned for the piece. (Ch. 5)

**Daily newspaper**  This newspaper prints at least one edition each day, in either the morning or the evening. (Ch. 3)

**Dateline**  Text may begin with the location of the story, traditionally written with the name of the city followed by a dash, such as "SAN FRANCISCO—". The date of the story may also be included; for example, "SAN FRANCISCO, Sept. 24—". (Ch. 7)

**Decoding**  The interpretation or transforming of a message back to thought by the receiver after it has passed through a communication channel. (Ch. 1)

**Demographic information**  Data such as age, gender, race, income, and education level of the target audience. (Ch. 6)

**Department store**  Store that carries general lines of merchandise, including apparel, home fashions, and housewares. (Ch. 1)

**Dependent clause**  Within a sentence, a thought that must rely on another part of the sentence for its meaning. (Ch. 2)

**Descriptive statistics**  Statistics that describe what the data look like. (Ch. 9)

**Developmental editor**  The employee at the publishing company who reads the work and offers suggestions as well as professional criticism regarding the content and form of the book as the manuscript is created. (Ch. 10)

**Dialogue**  The discussion or interchange of ideas that takes place between two or more of the characters in a book. (Ch. 10)

**Digital Subscriber Line (DSL)**  A type of Internet access that provides much quicker response times than dial-up access can. (Ch. 8)

**Direct pattern**  Presents the main topic in the first sentence of a paragraph, followed by supporting detail presented in later sentences. (Ch. 2)

**Direct selling**  Type of nonstore retailing that allows independent sales associates to buy inventory and sell it directly to customers in their territory. (Ch. 1)

**Direct writing strategy**  The main idea of the message is delivered first, followed by explanation and details. (Ch. 11)

**Discount store**  A retail operation that sells goods for less than the suggested retail price. (Ch. 1)

**Discovery research**  Consulting general references that give a broad overview of a topic. (Ch. 9)

**Dissertation**  A written document representing and reporting original research. One requirement for earning a doctorate degree. (Ch. 9)

**Documentaries**  Films or television shows that tell nonfiction stories, analyze news, and explore social conditions through an in-depth yet dramatic or theatrical format. (Ch. 5)

**Double-spacing**  One blank line appears between lines of type. (App. C)

**Draft**  A preliminary version of a document. (Ch. 2)

**E-book**  A book that is published through electronic media. (Ch. 8)

**E-commerce**  Use of the Internet as way to transact business, providing products or services to customers via the Web. (Ch. 8)

**Editorial calendar**  The list of the editorial focus for each issue of a magazine during the year, in addition to any special reports or surveys, products, or events. (Ch. 4)

**Editor-in-chief**  The title that some magazines give to the person doing the managing editor's job. (Ch. 4)

**Education**  School details on a résumé. (Ch. 12)

**Electronic résumé**  Résumé sent in the body of an e-mail message, completely devoid of formatting so that undesired characters and formatting do not creep in. (Ch. 12)

**Electronic rights**  A term, with various on-line implications, used in book publishing contracts; addresses who—the author or the publisher—has the rights to publish the author's work in electronic media. (Ch. 8)

**Embedded résumé**  *See* Electronic résumé. (Ch.12)

**Emotional appeal**  A plea that uses human feeling to make the argument. (Ch. 11)

**Encoding**  A combination of words or symbols presented in written, oral, and/or visual form by the sender to be passed through a communication channel. (Ch. 1)

**Equal partner collaboration**  A writing partnership that involves two authors with equivalent responsibilities. (Ch. 10)

**Euphemism**  Considerate word used to present a negatively connoted word in a better light. (Ch. 11)

**Executive summary**  A brief statement, typically 1 to 2 pages long, that contains the key elements of a report. (Ch. 6)

**Experimental design**  Study to determine the cause-and-effect relationship between two or more variables. (Ch. 9)

**Exposition**  A type of journalistic story structure; allows the writer to stand between the reader and the information by ordering the facts. (Ch. 3)

**External message**  Business communication sent to recipients outside an organization. (Ch. 11)

**External proposal**  Proposal submitted from outside an organization. (Ch. 11)

**E-zine**  Magazine that is published exclusively in cyberspace. (Ch. 8)

**Fact sheet**  A stripped-down presentation of the Who, What, Where, and When outline of the news release—presented in a list with only the essential data. (Ch. 7)

**Factory outlet store**  Discount retail operations run by the designer or manufacturer. (Ch. 1)

**Fair use**  Doctrine through which other persons are permitted to quote sections (of a limited length) of an author's work without the author's permission. (Ch. 10)

**Fashion**   The prevailing style of expression popular at any given time. (Ch. 1)

**Fashion assistant**   The person who supports the fashion department of a periodical; this person has a balance of administrative and creative responsibilities, such as managing the editor's office as well as contributing to concept development for fashion pages. (Ch. 4)

**Fashion business**   Firms that design, manufacture, distribute, and/or promote fashion-related apparel and accessories for men, women, and children, and home fashions. (Ch. 1)

**Fashion count**   An organized plan for counting and classifying apparel components; used to forecast fashion trends. (Ch. 9)

**Fashion editor**   The person who works for a periodical to produce tight, fresh, modern features for the fashion pages. (Ch. 4)

**Fashion journalist**   Writer who uses his or her training in news-gathering and reporting to write about fashion trends, fashion shows, and fashion collections, and to cover newsmakers in the field. (Ch. 3)

**Fashion service**   Organization within the auxiliary level that provides fashion reporting, forecasting, and consulting—available as a fee service or through subscription—to help primary, secondary, and retail fashion businesses keep track of fashion information. (Ch. 1)

**Feature story**   Journalistic article that is original and descriptive. Some feature stories have entertainment as a focus, while other feature stories have the primary purpose of providing information. (Ch. 3)

**Features editor**   The person who works for a periodical to generate, edit, and package stories; recruit writers; and participate in all facets of editorial planning and production. (Ch. 4)

**Feedback**   Response from receiver to sender to indicate whether a message has been understood. (Ch. 1)

**Fiber**   Basic unit for making textile fabrics. (Ch. 1)

**Fiction**   Stories the author creates from her imagination with the intention of entertaining the reader. (Ch. 10)

**Figure**   A graphical or other pictorial representation of data; can include pie charts, bar charts, flow charts, illustrations, maps, and photographs. (Ch. 9)

**Filament length**   Long fibers measured in yards or meters. (Ch. 1)

**Filament yarn**   Yarns produced by throwsters from filament length fibers. (Ch. 1)

**Flashback**   A writing style that is a departure from the chronological events; allows the writer to take the reader back to earlier times or to another physical space. (Ch. 3)

**Flow chart**   Figure that displays a process or a procedure. (Ch. 11)

**Focus group**   Planned discussion with 6 to 12 participants to learn people's perceptions about a topic in a nonthreatening environment. (Ch. 9)

**Focus structure**   A type of journalistic story structure that is an alternative to the traditional inverted pyramid; allows writers to add humanity and creativity to a story while still providing information. (Ch. 3)

**Focused research**   A way of conducting research in which the researcher consults scholarly writings, specialized reference works, and books that relate to a topic. (Ch. 9)

**Follow-up letter**   *See* Appreciation letter. (Ch. 12)

**Font**   A complete range of capital letters, small capitals, lowercase letters, numerals, and punctuation marks for a particular typeface and type size. (App. C)

**Foreshadowing**   The writing technique that gives hints about what is coming next. (Ch. 3)

**Formal report format**   Format for a formal report containing specific elements before the text (prefatory parts) and after the text (supplementary parts). (Ch. 11)

**Formal report or proposal** Report or proposal organized into three major sections: prefatory parts, body, and supplemental parts. (Ch. 11)

**Formal writing** A strict writing tone. (Ch. 2)

**Formula** The list of topics that editors, writers, and readers can expect to see in each issue of a magazine. (Ch. 4)

**Footer** Book title, part title, chapter title, or section title that, along with the page number, is typed usually one-half inch from the bottom of the page within margin guidelines; serves as a guidepost to help the reader know where she is in a long document. (App. C)

**Frame of reference** How a message is understood based on the receiver's past experiences, attitudes, values, perceptions of fashion, and cultural background. (Ch. 1)

**Freelance writer** Individual who writes independently and is paid a fee for her or his contributions. (Ch. 4)

**Full-justified** Aligning the text at both margins. (Ch. 11, App. C)

**Functional résumé** Alternate organization format for résumés, focusing on skills rather than work history. (Ch. 12)

**Fund-raising letter** Unsolicited business letter sent to current or potential donors to raise money, identify new donors, increase organization visibility, boost public relations, identify potential volunteers, or publicize new programs. (Ch. 7)

**General application letter** Application letter used to apply for an unsolicited position. (Ch. 12)

**Generic promo** Broadcast announcement that is designed to air at any time, reminding the audience of when and where to find their favorite programs, rather than focusing on a specific episode. (Ch. 6)

**Ghostwriter** An experienced writer who is hired to help an individual put ideas into publication format. (Ch. 10)

**Gift bag** Small token of appreciation for attending events or presenting awards. This practice has evolved into "swag suites" full of long tables of gifts. (Also known as *goodie bag*.) (Ch. 7)

**Goodie bag** *See* Gift bag. (Ch. 7)

**Goodwill** The favor or prestige that a business has acquired beyond the mere value of what it sells. (Ch. 11)

**Goodwill message** Message that presents pleasing news to the reader. (Ch. 11)

**Grading** Increasing or decreasing the production pattern of a clothing item to reflect the firm's size range. (Ch. 1)

**Grammar** System of rules to define the structure of a language. (Ch. 2)

**Grant** A cash payment that directly supports the author and does not have to be repaid from future royalties. (Ch. 10)

**Grant of rights** The section of a book contract in which an author grants the publisher the rights to publish the author's work. (Ch. 10)

**Greige goods** Unfinished, manufactured fabrics that have not been washed, bleached, dyed, or subjected to other treatments. (Ch. 1)

**Header** Book title, part title, chapter title, or section title that, along with the page number, is typed usually one-half inch from the top of the page within margin guidelines; serves as a guidepost to help the reader know where she is in a long document. (App. C)

**Heading** Division of a topic or theme, arranged hierarchically. (App. C)

**Headline** Title of a newspaper article. (Ch. 3); A statement, written in present tense or recent past tense, to summarize the story's main point and thus generate interest in the story. (Ch. 7)

**Historical research** Study that concentrates on the meanings of events based on a reference period. (Ch. 9)

**Hyperlink**   Web connection to places where the reader can learn more about the topics in the story. (Ch. 8)

**Hypothesis**   A logical supposition or reasonable guess that provides a tentative explanation for a phenomenon under investigation. (Ch. 9)

**Identification**   Contact information on a résumé. (Ch. 12)

**Indentation**   Indenting the text at the beginning of a new paragraph; used as a visual transition to alert readers that they are about to start reading about a new idea. (App. C)

**Independent clause**   A complete sentence and a complete thought that can stand by itself. (Ch. 2)

**In-depth interview**   Lengthy interview with a participant to learn about a topic in detail. (Ch. 9)

**Indirect pattern**   Presents supporting detail in the first sentences of a paragraph and ends the paragraph with the main topic. (Ch. 2)

**Indirect writing strategy**   Explanation and details are presented before the main idea. (Ch. 11)

**Inferential statistics**   Statistics that allow the researcher to make inferences about larger populations by collecting data on smaller samples. (Ch. 9)

**Informal writing**   A conversational writing tone. (Ch. 2)

**Information reports**   Documents that present data and facts without analyses or recommendations. (Ch. 11)

**Informed consent**   A respondent has been told the nature of the study and has been given the choice to participate or not participate. (Ch. 9)

**In-house promotion division**   In a large retailing or manufacturing company, the department that is responsible for creating promotional strategies and activities. (Ch. 6)

**Institutional advertising**   Promotion that is geared toward building the reputation of the sponsor, enhancing civic sponsorship and community involvement, and developing long-term relationships between customers and the sponsor. (Ch. 6)

**Internal message**   Business communication sent to recipients within an organization. (Ch. 11)

**Internal proposal**   Proposal submitted within one's own firm. (Ch. 11)

**Internal Review Board (IRB)**   At a college, university, or research institution, when a proposed project would involve collecting data from human subjects, the IRB is a panel that evaluates the proposed project to make sure no unnecessary harm would be inflicted on potential participants. (Ch. 9)

**Internet**   A computer-based global information system; emerged from a U.S. military communication network that was created in the late 1960s. (Ch. 8)

**Internet Service Provider (ISP)**   A commercial service that has made the Internet available to a greater variety of users. (Ch. 8)

**Internet shopping**   Type of nonstore retailing that allows shoppers to visit a virtual version of the department store, specialty store, or catalog retailer; this virtual version contains editorial content and visual effects to enhance the experience of shopping on the Web. (Ch. 1)

**Interview**   A person-to-person interaction for the specific purpose of collecting data. (Ch. 9)

**In-text citation**   Within the body of a document, a reference that briefly tells the reader where the information originally came from. (Ch. 2)

**Inverted pyramid**   A type of journalistic story structure that puts the most important information first, arranges the paragraphs in descending order of importance, and requires the writer to rank the importance of information. (Ch. 3)

**Invoice price**   The amount of money that a book publisher is paid by bookstores and wholesalers. (Ch. 10)

**Job search log** A document used to track contacts during the job search. (Ch. 12)

**Journal article** A research report submitted to a scholarly journal. (Ch. 9)

**Justification** Aligning text at the margin. (Ch. 11, App. C)

**Knit fabric** Fabric made using one yarn interconnected through a series of loops. (Ch. 1)

**Knitters** Businesses that create knitted fabrics using knitting machines. (Ch. 1)

**Knitting machine** Machine used to make knitted fabrics. (Ch. 1)

**Lead** (a) In the first paragraph or two of a journalistic story, a simple, clear statement that contains the Who, What, Where, When, How, and Why. (Ch. 3); (b) The first few sentences or the first paragraph of a magazine article. (Ch. 4)

**Lead-in** An introduction to a prerecorded excerpt from another broadcast source or from a remote location. (Ch. 5)

**Left-justified** Text aligned along the left margin only, with a "ragged" right edge. (App. C)

**Letter** Formal message written to individual(s) outside of an organization. (Ch. 11)

**Letter format** Report written as a letter. (Ch. 11)

**Libel** False written or spoken statements that damage a person's reputation; subject the person to hatred, contempt, or ridicule; or injure the person's business or occupational pursuits. (Ch. 2)

**Line** The overall collection of garments for a particular season. (Ch. 1)

**Line chart** Figure that demonstrates changes in quantitative data over time. (Ch. 11)

**Line drawing** Figure that shows how an item might be used. (Ch. 11)

**Line spacing** The amount of space between lines of text. (App. C)

**Literary agent** The person who represents the author of a book while negotiating the terms of a book contract with a potential publisher. (Ch. 10)

**Logical appeal** A plea that uses human reason to make the argument. (Ch. 11)

**Logo** Visual image that serves as a visual identifier, such as the Nike swoosh or Target's red and white circles. (Ch. 6)

**Longitudinal study** Study in which data are gathered at several points in time and used to determine a pattern of change in relation to time. (Ch. 9)

**Loom** Machine used to make woven fabrics. (Ch. 1)

**Magazine** Print or electronic publication (periodical) that contains advertising and editorial content; available on a regular basis, published weekly, monthly, bi-monthly, or quarterly. (Ch. 4)

**Managing editor** The senior-level editor, with extensive management experience, who oversees the day-to-day management of the office; supervises staff, editorial, and photography budgets; produces actual pages of the magazine; and controls the editing process and closings. (Ch. 4)

**Manufactured fiber** Fiber that is produced and supplied by chemical producers. (Ch. 1)

**Manuscript report format** *See* Formal report format. (Ch. 11)

**Margin** Frame of space around a page to keep it from looking overcrowded. (App. C)

**Marker** Layout of pattern pieces on the fabric for cutting. (Ch. 1)

**Market research** Information provided to retailers and manufacturers about the buying habits and preferences of their clients' target markets. (Ch. 1)

**Masthead** A list of the people who create a magazine: from the publisher at the top, to the editors (managing editor or editor-in-chief) and creative editors (fashion, features, beauty, or art), to the editorial assistants and contributors and, on some magazine mastheads, even the interns. (Ch. 4)

**Media kit** Public relations communication techniques used to generate news stories about a company or group through its newsworthy initiatives; the kits are prepared to provide important news, background information, facts, perspectives, research, historical information, and biographies of people involved, among other items. (Ch. 7)

**Memo report format** Report written as a memo. (Ch. 11)

**Memorandum** A written interoffice communication. (Ch. 11)

**Merchandising function** Within an apparel manufacturing firm, area responsible for planning, development, and presentation of the product line; decisions on product; styling approval; establishment of pricing; and timing and scheduling deliveries. (Ch. 1)

**Microsite** Special Web site with unique address to catch the attention of a post-event audience. (Ch. 8)

**Mind-mapping** A visual representation of collected information before it is organized into an outline. (Ch. 2)

**Modified block letter format** Letter format in which the dateline, complementary close, and signature block begin at the horizontal center of the page. Paragraphs are single-spaced both within and between paragraphs, and the first line of each paragraph is indented five spaces. (Ch. 11)

**Multimedia communication** Communication that uses several methods of communication simultaneously to exchange information, often using information technology to assist in transmitting the message. (Ch. 1)

**Narration** A type of journalistic story structure that involves telling a story that arouses emotion, makes the reader laugh or cry, and is more easily recalled. (Ch. 3)

**Natural fiber** Fiber that is grown on a plant or an animal and supplied by a farmer or rancher. (Ch. 1)

**News anchor** Broadcaster who sits behind a desk, serving as a master of ceremonies and introducing stories and fellow newscasters. (Ch. 5)

**News release** A document that conveys newsworthy information about your organization to the news media. (Ch. 7)

**News story** Journalistic report that involves the day-to-day events and activities of people in the target audience. (Ch. 3)

**Newscaster** Reporter who works in specialized types of news, such as sports or weather, for large television stations; other newscasters work on any topic assigned by the news director. (Ch. 5)

**Newsletter** Niche publication that is prepared for members of an organization, members of a profession, or people with a common interest. (Ch. 7)

**Newspaper** Publication whose main function is to report the news as well as to provide special information to its readers. (Ch. 3)

**Newsprint** A grainy, lightweight paper used for newspapers. (Ch. 3)

**Noise** Outside factors that interfere with or distort the reception of the communication message. (Ch. 1)

**Nonfiction** The broadest category of written works; includes histories, biographies, and how-to books, as well as any narrative that offers opinions based upon facts and reality. (Ch. 10)

**Nonprobability sample** Sampling method in which not every person or item has the same chance of being selected. (Ch. 9)

**Nonstore retailing** Selling merchandising through means other than retail stores; includes direct selling, catalog retailing, TV home shopping, and Internet shopping. (Ch. 1)

**Nonverbal communication** Exchanging information without speaking, relying instead on actions or gestures to convey meaning. (Ch. 1)

**Nut (nut graph)** The transitional paragraph in a journalistic story, where the writer lets the reader know what the story is about and why she should read it. (Ch. 3)

**Objective** Statement on a résumé specifying the job the applicant is seeking. (Ch. 12)

**Observation** A systematic, selective way of watching or listening to an interaction. (Ch. 9)

**Off-price retailer** Type of retailer that sells brand-name and designer merchandise at "lower-than-normal" retail prices. (Ch. 1)

**Organization chart** Figure that defines a hierarchy of elements or a set of relationships. (Ch. 11)

**Outline** A plan for structuring a written message. (Ch. 2)

**Page numbering** The consecutive numbering of pages throughout a document. (App. C)

**Paper presentation** Research findings presented at regional, national, or international conferences sponsored by organizations within academic disciplines. (Ch. 9)

**Parallelism** Words or groups of words used similarly within a sentence, expressed in the same format. (Ch. 2)

**Passive voice** Sentences that emphasize the action itself rather than the person or thing performing the action. (Ch. 2)

**Peer-reviewed** Members of a review board who are experts in the field examine a manuscript before the article is accepted for publication. (Ch. 9)

**Personal Digital Assistant (PDA)** A wireless communication device, used by an individual. (Ch. 8)

**Persuasive message** Messages written to attempt to change someone's attitudes, beliefs, or actions. (Ch. 11)

**Phenomena** Observable facts or events. (Ch. 9)

**Photo opportunity sheet** Document designed to attract photographers to an event you are publicizing, especially when there is a visual component that will help publicize the occasion. (Ch. 7)

**Phrase** A part of a sentence that does not contain a subject or a verb and must always relate to or modify another part of a sentence. (Ch. 2)

**Pie chart** Figure used to visualize a whole unit, with its proportional parts represented as wedges in the pie. (Ch. 11)

**Pilot study** A practice study to test a procedure to discover problems before the actual study begins. (Ch. 9)

**Pitch letter** A document that pitches or promotes a story idea, prepared to attract the interest of a specific journalist. (Ch. 7)

**Plagiarism** The act of taking the idea, the writing, or the creative thought of another and using it as one's own. (Ch. 2)

**Plain-text résumé** *See* Electronic résumé. (Ch.12)

**Plot** An outline or plan of action that essentially details how a story begins, notes the story's major events, and describes how the story concludes. (Ch. 10)

**Portable Document Format (PDF)** A word processing program from Adobe Acrobat that allows a document to be converted into a printable format. (Ch. 8)

**Postscript (P.S.)** An emphasis statement appearing *after* the signature in a letter. (Ch. 7)

**Prefatory part** The part of a report that appears before the body of the report; includes the title page, the Table of Contents, and the Executive Summary or abstract. (Ch. 11)

**Pre-printed form** Fill-in-the-blank report. (Ch. 11)

**Press conference** A staged forum where journalists are invited to view a new product or hear an important announcement firsthand. (Ch. 7)

**Primary data**  Information that the researcher collects for purposes of the current study. (Ch. 9)

**Primary level**  First level of the fashion industry; consists of raw material (textile) producers who grow or develop fibers and spin them into fabric. (Ch. 1)

**Printed letterhead stationery**  Paper preprinted with the company's official name, street address, Web address, e-mail address, telephone and fax numbers, and the company logo. (Ch. 11)

**Printing-on-demand**  A computer-based system for distribution of books. (Ch. 8)

**Probability sample**  Sampling method in which every person or every item has the same likelihood of being chosen. (Ch. 9)

**Problem statement**  Declaration that tells the reader what the researcher intended to research. (Ch. 9)

**Product advertising**  Promotion of specific goods or services. (Ch. 6)

**Production function**  Area within an apparel manufacturing that is responsible for approving the technical design, developing specifications, costing the product, developing production patterns, grading, marker making, cutting, sewing, finishing, and arranging for distribution of the sewn products. (Ch. 1)

**Production script**  Written words provided to broadcasters. (Ch. 6)

**Promo**  Broadcast announcement that is designed to build and maintain a target audience for a particular program, to nurture the relationship between the audience and the station, or to demonstrate that the station operates in the public interest according to government licensing demands. (Ch. 6)

**Proofreading**  Rereading every word carefully to make sure a document is error-free. (Ch. 2)

**Proofs**  Typeset pages sent to author for final corrections. (Ch. 10)

**Proposal**  Special type of analytical report, persuasive in nature, that presents offers to others to solve problems, provide services, or sell equipment. (Ch. 11)

**Protagonist**  The main character of a story, often the hero. (Ch. 10)

**Psychographic information**  Attitudinal information, such as religious, political, and social beliefs. (Ch. 6)

**Publicity**  Communication by the initiating party seeking to tell others about a product, service, idea, or event, and is delivered to the public at the discretion of the media. (Ch. 7)

**Public relations (PR)**  The management function that establishes and maintains mutually beneficial relationships between an organization and the public on whom its success or failure depends (Ch. 7)

**Public service announcement (PSA)**  Persuasive message carried without charge by radio and television outlets to promote social causes sponsored by nonprofit and charitable organizations. (Ch. 7)

**Publisher**  The person who manages a periodical and is responsible for such issues as advertising revenue and circulation; market share; multi-media initiatives on the Internet, television, and in film; and brand extension launches. Also refers to a *company* that produces periodicals and books. (Chs. 4, 10)

**Publishing-on-demand**  *See* Printing-on-demand. (Ch. 8)

**Punctuation**  Standardized marks (commas, periods, etc.) used in writing to clarify meaning and to separate structural units such as phrases within a sentence and sentences within a paragraph. (Ch. 2)

**Purpose statement**  One or two sentences that direct a writing project by stating why a message is being written and what the message will accomplish. (Ch. 2)

**Qualifier**  Extra word, such as *very, pretty,* or *really,* that does not add to the topic but is used before the point of the sentence is made. (Ch. 2)

**Qualitative research** A research methodology that focuses on phenomena—observable facts or events—that occur in natural settings. (Ch. 9)

**Quality assurance** The commitment that a business makes to create and deliver high-quality products and service. (Ch. 1)

**Quantitative research** A research methodology that provides numerical descriptions of trends, attitudes, or opinions of a population; obtained by studying a sample of that population. (Ch. 9)

**Quasi-experimental** An experimental design studied in a natural setting. (Ch. 9)

**Query letter** (a) A proposal asking if the editor of a magazine is interested in your topic; in it, you assess and promote your ability to write and to create interest in your subject. (Ch. 4); (b) A document similar to a cover letter that brings all the elements of a book proposal package together. (Ch. 10)

**Questionnaire** Written lists of questions on which respondents record their answers. (Ch. 9)

**Radio news release script** A document created for radio broadcast with the same purpose as print news releases: to generate publicity for organizations. (Ch. 7)

**Radio reader** A script prepared by a public relations specialist for an announcer to read. (Ch. 7)

**Ragged edge** While the left margin is justified, the right margin is unjustified—leaving a ragged edge in which each line ends at the end of a word. (Ch. 11)

**Recommendation** Suggestion for actions. (Ch. 11)

**Redundancy** Phrases in which one word or idea is repeated unnecessarily. (Ch. 2)

**Refereed** *See* Peer-reviewed. (Ch. 9)

**Reference** An individual who can discuss your qualifications. (Ch. 12)

**Reference book** Publication that contains general information about a wide variety of subjects

and is a resource for quick answers to common questions. (Ch. 10)

**Reference list** At the end of a written document, an alphabetical listing of all resources used in the document. (Ch. 2)

**Reference page** Listing of actual works cited in a document, formatted according to APA writing style. (Ch. 11)

**Reliability** An instrument is consistent in what it measures. (Ch. 9)

**Report** Business document that systematically attempt to answer questions or solve problems. (Ch. 11)

**Request for Proposal (RFP)** A solicited bid for a contract. (Ch. 11)

**Research** The systematic investigation of a subject, aimed at uncovering new information and/or interpreting relations among a subject's parts. (Ch. 9)

**Research design** The planning of procedures for conducting a research study. (Ch. 9)

**Research objective** Goal the researcher sets out to achieve in a research study. (Ch. 9)

**Research proposal** The conceptualization of the total research process that the researcher plans to undertake. (Ch. 9)

**Research question** The problem to be investigated in a study, stated in question format. (Ch. 9)

**Résumé** A structured, written summary of your education, employment background, and job qualifications. (Ch. 12)

**Retail level** Third level of the fashion industry; sells consumers the goods purchased from the secondary level. (Ch. 1)

**Review of literature** A discussion of other studies, research reports, and scholarly writings that have direct relevance to the current study. (Ch. 9)

**Right-justified**  Text that is aligned along the right margin with a ragged left edge. (App. C)

**Roadmap paragraph**  A brief paragraph telling the reader how information in a report or proposal is organized. (Ch. 11)

**Routine message**  Message with a neutral tone that does not generate an emotional response from the reader. (Ch. 11)

**Royalties**  The share of the book sales that is paid to the author. (Ch. 10)

**Running foot**  *See* Footer. (App. C)

**Running head**  *See* Header. (App. C).

**Run-on sentence**  An improper sentence with two independent clauses that are not joined by a conjunction (*and*, *but*, *or*, *nor*, and so on) or by a semicolon (;). (Ch. 2)

**Sales promotion**  Activities that provide extra value or incentives for consumers; for example, contests, coupons, gift-with-purchase, purchase-with-purchase, point-of-sale displays, refunds, rebates, sweepstakes, and sampling. (Ch. 6)

**Salutation**  Courtesy greeting in an e-mail message. (Ch. 11)

**Sampling**  The process of selecting a few (a sample) from a larger population to become the estimate for predication of an unknown piece of information. (Ch. 9)

**Sans serif type**  Type characterized by bold, clean strokes without serifs. (App. C)

**Scannable résumé**  Computer-friendly résumé that a potential employer can scan (search) electronically. *See also* Electronic résumé. (Ch. 12)

**Scholarly writing**  Writing a research report to detail the findings and implications of a research study. (Ch. 9)

**Search engine**  Software program that allows an Internet user to look for information by topic; examples of search engines are Google, MSN, Yahoo!, and Ask.com. (App. D)

**Search strategy**  The process used to locate and evaluate source material. (Ch. 9)

**Searchable database**  A collection of citations that are linked to publishers, academic libraries, or other scholarly resources. (App. D)

**Secondary data**  Information that others have collected for research purposes. (Ch. 9)

**Secondary level**  Middle level of the fashion industry; consists of manufacturers who purchase fabrics, materials, and findings from primary-level members and produce apparel and accessories to sell to the retail level. (Ch. 1)

**Selling point**  Features and characteristics of the merchandise that make it desirable. (Ch. 11)

**Serif type**  Type distinguished by small lines or tails that finish the ends of letters. (App. C)

**Sexist language**  Language that does not apply the same terminology to men and women, used in a belittling manner considered offensive to the reader. (Ch. 2)

**Shell**  In a media kit, folder with internal pockets for documents and other support materials. (Ch. 7)

**Shovelware**  Publications that simply "shovel" the content of their print source to an online source. (Ch. 8)

**Signature file**  Contact information at the closing of an e-mail message; includes name, mailing address, e-mail address, phone and fax numbers, Web address, and other useful information. (Ch. 11)

**Signing bonus**  *See* grant. (Ch. 10)

**Simple sentence**  A sentence that consists of one independent clause that expresses only one complete thought. (Ch. 2)

**Simple subject**  A single noun or pronoun. (Ch. 2)

**Single-spacing**  No blank lines appear between rows of type. (App. C)

**Situation analysis** The research that helps the creative team fully understand the product or service, its benefits and values, and the consumers to whom the message will be directed. (Ch. 6)

**Slate** A screen used by video writers that identifies or introduces images that follow. (Ch. 7)

**Slogan** Phrase that states the promotional theme for the firm. (Ch. 6)

**Slug** (a) In broadcast media, a word (typically assigned by the producer) that identifies the story as it is processed. (Ch. 5); (b) In a news release, a condensed version of the headline, placed in the upper-left corner on the second page. (Ch. 7)

**Solicited proposal** A type of analytical report prepared at the request of a party who needs a service or product. (Ch. 11)

**Sound bite** A broadcast news release that contains taped comments from an organization representative, presented much like a quote in a print story. (Ch. 7)

**Special event** A one-time occurrence with planned activities focused on a specific purpose—to bring attention to a brand, manufacturer, retailer, or organization, or to influence the sale of merchandise. (Ch. 7)

**Special interest newspaper** Newspaper that is targeted to particular audiences, such as ethnic communities, large universities, unions and trade organizations, and arts groups. (Ch. 3)

**Specialty store** Type of retailer that offers limited lines of related merchandise targeted to a specific customer defined by age, size, or shared tastes. (Ch. 1)

**Speech** A scripted oration to be delivered by an individual in front of an audience. (Ch. 7, App. E)

**Spinner** Business that makes spun yarns. (Ch. 1)

**Spoken communication** Communication that uses the voice to exchange information. (Ch. 1)

**Spreading** Laying multiple layers of cloth on a table for cutting. (Ch. 1)

**Spun yarn** Yarns made from short, staple-length fibers. (Ch. 1)

**Stakeholder** Person who may be affected by the actions of an organization: manager, supervisor, employee, customer, client, vendor, media, stockholder, government, the public at large, or other important groups. (Ch. 11)

**Staple length** Short fibers measured in inches. (Ch. 1)

**Stereotype** Oversimplified perception of a characteristic or behavior of a group. (Ch. 11)

**Storyboard** Visual presentation of how words and pictures will be combined into a single persuasive message. (Ch. 6)

**Study design** The basic structure of a research study. Commonly classified by the number of contacts with the study population, the reference of the study, or the nature of the investigation. (Ch. 9)

**Stylebook** Publication that communicates specific rules of style. (Ch. 2)

**Subject** A noun or pronoun that interacts with a verb within a sentence. (Ch. 2)

**Summary** Brief restatement of the main ideas from collected research. (Ch. 11)

**Summary of qualifications** On a résumé, a rundown of a job candidate's strongest points, presented in three to eight bullet points to allow recruiters to immediately review the candidate's credentials. (Ch. 12)

**Supermarket tabloid** National weekly publication, printed on newsprint in the dimensions of a tabloid newspaper, which specializes in celebrity news, celebrity fashion, gossip, astrology, and peculiar stories about ordinary people. (Ch. 3)

**Supplementary part** Additional pages after the body of a report. (Ch. 11)

**SWOT analysis** In a situation analysis report, a discussion of the Strengths, Weaknesses, Opportunities, and Threats of the client and its products or services. (Ch. 6)

**Synopsis**  A brief narrative description of a book. (Ch. 10)

**Table**  Graphical presentation of data in columns and rows. (Ch. 9)

**Tabloid**  The newspaper style, which measures 10 inches by 14.5 inches, used in the United States. (Ch. 3)

**Tagline**  *See* Slogan. (Ch. 6)

**Target audience**  The viewers and listeners who are intended to use the product or service. (Ch. 6)

**Targeted application letter**  Application letter written in response to a specific position that has been advertised. (Ch. 12)

**Tease**  A method used by announcers to create audience interest for reports yet to come in a broadcast. (Ch. 5)

**Tee-up**  A method used by announcers to identify an unfamiliar name in the lead for a broadcast story. (Ch. 5)

**TelePrompTer**  Brand name for a computer into which a speech is typed so that it is delivered to a transparent screen that a person giving a speech can read while appearing to look directly at the audience. (Ch. 5, App. E)

**Terms of agreement**  The fundamental deal points—including such things as authorship credit, rights, distribution, author compensation, delivery of the manuscript, publication details, and plans for future editions—that the people making the book contract consider essential. (Ch. 10)

**Thank-you letter**  *See* Appreciation letter. (Ch. 12)

**Theoretical framework**  The main theme or theory that current research will be built on. (Ch. 9)

**Theory**  A statement or group of statements about how some part of the world works, often explaining relationships among phenomena. (Ch. 9)

**Thesis**  A written document representing and reporting original research. One requirement for earning a master's degree. (Ch. 9)

**Throwster**  Business that makes filament yarns. (Ch. 1)

**Tone**  The way a message sounds to the audience. (Ch. 2)

**Topic sentence**  Identifies the central idea of a paragraph. (Ch. 2)

**Topical promos**  Broadcast announcements that provide information about a specific program that will air at a definite time. (Ch. 6)

**Toss**  *See* Lead-in. (Ch. 5)

**Trade association**  Member of the auxiliary level that supports particular segments of the fashion industry. (Ch. 1)

**Trade magazine**  *See* Business-to-business magazine. (Ch. 4)

**Trade newspaper**  Periodical that provides information to specific businesses, industries, or occupations—but in newspaper format. (Ch. 3)

**Trade publication**  Publication with fashion industry members as the intended audience. (Ch. 1)

**Transmittal letter or memo**  Memo or letter that introduces a report or proposal to the recipient. (Ch. 11)

**Triple-spacing**  Two blank lines occurring between lines of text, used very specifically in letter format between the complementary close and the typed signature. (App. C)

**TV home shopping**  Type of nonstore retailing that demonstrates the merchandise to television viewers. (Ch. 1)

**Type size**  The size of a typeface. (App. C)

**Typeface**  A specifically designed set of letters, numbers, and punctuation marks; for example, Times New Roman. (App. C)

**Uniform Resource Locator (URL)**  The address for a Web site. (Ch. 8)

**Unsolicited proposal** Proposal written by a firm or an individual to obtain business or funding; written without a prior invitation to submit a proposal. (Ch. 11)

**Validity** An instrument measures what it is supposed to measure. (Ch. 9)

**Verb** The word in a sentence that shows action or describes a condition. (Ch. 2)

**Verb phrase** Within a sentence, a phrase that includes more than one verb where the last verb in the phrase is considered the main verb. (Ch. 2)

**Video news release (VNR)** The video version of a printed news release. (Ch. 7)

**Videoprompter** *See* TelePrompTer. (Ch. 5)

**Visual communication** Communication that uses sight to exchange information. (Ch. 1)

**Weaver** Business that makes woven fabrics. (Ch. 1)

**Web log** *See* blog. (Ch. 8)

**Webmaster** An individual who authors, designs, develops, markets, and/or maintains a Web site. (Ch. 8)

**Weekly newspaper** Newspaper that publishes once a week with news of interest to people in smaller geographic regions, such as a small city, a town, or a neighborhood. (Ch. 3)

**White space** The area that is intentionally left blank on a page to eliminate clutter and allow the reader's eyes to rest. Margins, indentations, and space around charts, graphs, and photographs create white space. (App. C)

**Wi-Fi** Wireless access to the Internet. (Ch. 8)

**Wordiness** Using more words to make a point when fewer words would be adequate. (Ch. 2)

**Work Experience** Listing of employment history on a résumé. (Ch. 12)

**World Wide Web (WWW or Web)** An Internet environment originally used by scientists to share information; now a medium in which text, graphics, audio, animation, and video can be shared around the world. (Ch. 8)

**Woven fabric** Fabrics made with two or more sets of yarns interlaced at right angles using a loom. (Ch. 1)

**Wrap-up** In television and radio broadcasts, a way of presenting material that helps the audience understand that a story is over before the broadcast goes on to the next story. (Ch. 5)

**Written communication** The exchange of information by forming symbols (words) on a surface (paper or computer monitor) with an instrument (pen or keyboard and word-processing software), providing a permanent record of the communication. (Ch. 1)

**Yarn producer** Business that combines fibers into usable yarn structures. (Ch. 1)

# INDEX

# PHOTO AND TEXT CREDITS

## PHOTO CREDITS

### Chapter 1
**1.3:** Courtesy of IBM.

### Chapter 3
**3.1:** Courtesy of Library of Congress.
**3.2a:** Courtesy of Fairchild Publications, Inc./Reprinted by permission of the New York Sun.
**3.2b:** Courtesy of Fairchild Publications, Inc./Reprinted by permission of the New York Sun.
**3.3:** Courtesy of Fairchild Publications, Inc.

### Chapter 4
**4.1:** Courtesy of Fairchild Publications, Inc.
**4.2:** Courtesy of Fairchild Publications, Inc./Condé Nast Publications, Inc.
**4.3:** Courtesy of Condé Nast Publications, Inc.
**4.4:** Courtesy of *Stores Magazine.*
**4.5:** Courtesy of Fairchild Publications, Inc.
**4.6:** Courtesy of ST Media Group International.

### Chapter 5
**5.1:** Courtesy Bravo/NBC Universal.

### Chapter 6
**6.1:** PRNewsFoto/Chanel.
**6.3:** Visa Inc./TBWA Chiat Day.
**6.4:** Obtained from Amanda Hobbs via authors, K. K. Swanson & J. C. Everett.
**6.7:** Obtained from Amanda Hobbs via authors, K. K. Swanson & J. C. Everett.

### Chapter 7
**7.1:** Courtesy of Fairchild Publications, Inc.
**7.2:** Courtesy of Condé Nast Publications, Inc.
**7.9:** Courtesy of K. K. Swanson & J. C. Everett.
**7.13:** Photo courtesy of Lucky Brand Jeans.
**7.15:** Courtesy of Fashion Group International.

**Chapter 8**
**8.1:** Courtesy of Glam.com.
**8.2:** Courtesy of Prada.
**8.3:** Courtesy of thebudgetfashionista.com.
**8.4:** Courtesy of Fairchild Publications, Inc.
**8.5:** Courtesy of Condé Nast Publications, Inc.
**8.6:** Courtesy of Zappos.com.
**8.7:** Courtesy of Glam.com.

**Chapter 11**
**11.6e:** Figure 1 courtesy of *InStyle Magazine.*
**11.7g:** Courtesy of Fairchild Publications, Inc.

**Appendix B**
**B.1:** Courtesy of *Women's Wear Daily.*

## TEXT CREDITS

**Figure 1.1**
Swanson, K. K., & Everett, J. C. (2007). *Promotion in the merchandising environment* (2nd ed.). New York: Fairchild Books.

**Table 1.1**
Adapted from Pfeiffer, W. (2004). *Pocket guide to technical writing* (3rd ed.). Upper Saddle River, NJ: Pearson Prentice Hall.
**Figure 2.1**
Adapted from Kirszner, L. G., & Mandell, S. R. (2005). *The Wadsworth handbook* [Instructor's Edition]. Boston: Thomson Wadsworth.

**Figure 2.8**
Adapted from the University of Chicago Press. (2003). *Chicago manual of style: The essential guide for writers, editors, and publishers.* (15th ed.). Chicago: University of Chicago Press.

**Figure 5.2**
Adapted from Diggs-Brown, B. (2007). *The PR styleguide: Formats for public relations practice* (2nd ed.). Belmont, CA: Thomson Wadsworth.

Marsh, C., Guth, D. W., & Short, B. P. (2005). *Strategic writing: Multimedia writing for public relations, advertising, sales and marketing, and business communication.* Boston: Pearson Education.

**Figure 5.5**
Dempsey, M. (2005). *Fashion mis-statements*. Retrieved July 22, 2005, from http://
lifestyle.msn.com/BeautyandFashion/PersonalStyle/ArticleMC.aspx?cp-
documentid=1203054.

**Figure 6.2**
Adapted from Marsh, C., Guth, D. W., & Short, B. P. (2005). *Strategic writing:
Multimedia writing for public relations, advertising, sales and marketing, and
business communications*. Boston: Pearson Education.

**Figure 6.5**
Obtained from Amanda Hobbs via authors, K. K. Swanson & J. C. Everett.

**Figure 6.6**
Obtained from Amanda Hobbs via authors, K. K. Swanson & J. C. Everett.

**Figure 6.8**
Obtained from Amanda Hobbs via authors, K. K. Swanson & J. C. Everett.

**Table 8.1**
Adapted from Hall, C. (2007, April 5). The WWD list: Brand power. *Women's Wear
Daily*, p. 12.

**Figure 9.2**
Adapted from Kumar, R. (2005). *Research methodology* (2nd ed.). London: Sage
Publications.

**Figure 9.3**
Adapted from Kirszner, L. G., & Mandell, S. R. (2005). *The Wadsworth handbook*
[Instructor's Edition]. Boston: Thomson Wadsworth.

**Figure 9.4**
Adapted from Leedy, P. D., & Ormrod, J. E. (2005). *Practical research* (8th ed.). Upper
Saddle River, NJ: Merrill Prentice Hall.

**Figure 9.5**
Adapted from Leedy, P. D., & Ormrod, J. E. (2005). *Practical research* (8th ed.). Upper
Saddle River, NJ: Merrill Prentice Hall.

**Figure 9.6**
Beaudoin, P., Lachance, M. J., & Robitaille, J. (2003). Fashion innovativeness, fashion
diffusion and brand sensitivity among adolescents. *Journal of Fashion Marketing
and Management*, 7, 23–30.

**Figure 10.5**
Courtesy of Fairchild Publications, Inc.

**Figure 11.7h**
Courtesy of Fairchild Publications, Inc.

**Figure 12.1**
Adapted from Guffey, M. E. (2007). *Essentials of business communication.* (7th ed.). Mason, OH: Thomson South-Western.

**Figure B.2**
Courtesy of *Women's Wear Daily.*

**Figure B.3**
Courtesy of the *Journal of Retailing.*

**Figure B.4**
Courtesy of the *Journal of Retailing.*

**Figure B.5**
Courtesy of the *New York Times.*

**Figure C.2**
American Psychological Association. (2001). *Publication manual of the American Psychological Association.* (5th ed.). Washington, DC: American Psychological Association.